Advances in African Economic, Social and Political Development

Africa is emerging as a rapidly growing region, still facing major challenges, but with a potential for significant progress – a transformation that necessitates vigorous efforts in research and policy thinking. This book series focuses on three intricately related key aspects of modern-day Africa: economic, social and political development. Making use of recent theoretical and empirical advances, the series aims to provide fresh answers to Africa's development challenges. All the socio-political dimensions of today's Africa are incorporated as they unfold and new policy options are presented. The series aims to provide a broad and interactive forum of science at work for policymaking and to bring together African and international researchers and experts. The series welcomes monographs and contributed volumes for an academic and professional audience, as well as tightly edited conference proceedings. Relevant topics include, but are not limited to, economic policy and trade, regional integration, labor market policies, demographic development, social issues, political economy and political systems, and environmental and energy issues.

All titles in the series are peer-reviewed. The book series is indexed in SCOPUS.

David Mhlanga • Emmanuel Ndhlovu
Editors

Economic Inclusion in Post-Independence Africa

An Inclusive Approach to Economic Development

Springer

Editors

David Mhlanga
College of Business and Economics
University of Johannesburg
Auckland Park, South Africa

Emmanuel Ndhlovu
Vaal University of Technology
Vanderbijlpark, South Africa

ISSN 2198-7262 ISSN 2198-7270 (electronic)
Advances in African Economic, Social and Political Development
ISBN 978-3-031-31430-8 ISBN 978-3-031-31431-5 (eBook)
https://doi.org/10.1007/978-3-031-31431-5

This Springer imprint is published by the registered company Springer Nature Switzerland AG
The registered company address is: Gewerbestrasse 11, 6330 Cham, Switzerland

Acknowledgements

This book is the product of the combined efforts of the editors and authors. The editors would like to take this opportunity to thank all the contributors to this volume for their hard work and commitment. The editors would also like to offer their deepest appreciation to the Springer editors, Lorraine Klimowich, Ruth Milewski, and Project Coordinator Kirthika Selvaraju for their support throughout the writing, production, and publication process.

About the Book

Africa is currently gaining a lot of attention from people all over the world due to both its significant problems, particularly post-independence, and its many accomplishments and degree of vibrancy. Human development indices are rising, there are a decreasing number of people living in poverty, and there are more active social movements that are bringing stigmatized issues and groups of individuals to public attention. However, despite all its successes, the continent continues to lag in several crucial areas. As a result, discussions about the importance of economic and social inclusion are increasingly gaining traction throughout the continent. The extension of technical innovation into previously inaccessible places because of the implementation of new laws and programs, on the other hand, has made it feasible for economic and social inclusion to become a reality. This is a direct outcome of technology progress spreading to previously unreachable areas. Throughout its history, various African states have led the march toward progress. Twenty chapters, each examining a different facet of economic and social inclusion, such as financial inclusion, digital financial inclusion, and gender, among other concerns, make up the book *Economic Inclusion in Post-Independence Africa: An Inclusive Approach to Economic Development*. Governments, development agencies, non-governmental organizations with a bias toward development, students, and university lecturers will all find this book interesting.

Contents

1 **Introduction: Theorising Economic and Social Inclusion in Post-Independence Africa** 1
David Mhlanga and Emmanuel Ndhlovu

Part I Economic Inclusion Implications for Livelihoods and Incomes

2 **Economic Inclusion: Transforming the Lives of the Poor and How to Make Economic Inclusion Work in Africa** 21
David Mhlanga and Emmanuel Ndhlovu

3 **Information Communication Technology (ICT) and Its Effects on Social and Political Inclusion in Africa** 45
Abisola Akinola and Olaniyi Evans

4 **Social Inclusion Interventions for Africa Towards Sustainable Development and Shared Prosperity** 59
David Mhlanga and Emmanuel Ndhlovu

5 **The Impact of Digital Financial Service Taxes and Mobile Money Taxes on Financial Inclusion and Inclusive Development in Africa** 81
David Mhlanga and Favourate Y. Mpofu

6 **The Political Economy of Financial Inclusion for Smallholder Farmers in Sub-Saharan Africa** 103
Miriam Hofisi

7 **Digital Financial Inclusion and Digital Financial Literacy in Africa: The Challenges Connected with Digital Financial Inclusion in Africa** 123
Favourate Y. Mpofu

8 Post-Independence Development and Financial Inclusion in Africa: Case Studies and the Way Forward to Support Further Financial Inclusion 149
David Mhlanga and Mufaro Dzingirai

9 The Future of Financial Inclusion 167
Peterson K. Ozili

10 On the Determinants of Foreign Direct Investment to West African Countries: Does Political Risk Matter? 179
Adewale Samuel Hassan

11 Comparative Analysis of Socioeconomic Change and Inclusion in Ghana: A Gendered Empirical Analysis Using Ghana Living Standards 1988 and Ghana Socioeconomic Panel Survey 2019 197
Tawonga Rushambwa

Part II Financial Inclusion in Agriculture

12 Rethinking Financial Inclusion for Post-Colonial Land Reform Beneficiaries in South Africa 221
Belese N. Majova

13 Peasant Financial Inclusion for Inclusive Development in Zimbabwe 237
Emmanuel Ndhlovu and David Mhlanga

Part III The Gendered Implications of Economic Inclusion and the Policy Proposals Towards Economic Inclusion

14 Artificial Intelligence (AI) Solutions for Financial Inclusion of the Excluded: What Are the Challenges? 257
David Mhlanga

15 Women Empowerment in the South African Agribusiness: Opportunities and Constraints in the Gauteng Province 273
Emmanuel Ndhlovu and Belese N. Majova

16 Gender-Inclusive Education in Science, Technology, Engineering, and Mathematics (STEM) Fields in Postindependence Zimbabwe 295
Gay Tapiwa Gweshe and Mervis Chiware

17 Policy Alternatives for Strengthening Women's Representation in African Local Authorities: Insights from Zimbabwe 311
Fortunate Jena, Joseph Tinarwo, Innocent Dingani, and Banele Mazhelo

18 The Digital Economy, Digital Financial Inclusion, and Digital Taxation in the Industry 4.0: A South African Perspective 329
David Mhlanga and Miriam Hofisi

19 Digital Transformation in the Healthcare Sector: The Role of Artificial Intelligence for Inclusive Long-Term Care Around the World, Lessons for Africa 347
David Mhlanga

Part IV Conclusions Economic Inclusion in Post-Independence Africa: An Inclusive Approach to Economic Development

20 *Economic and Social Inclusion in Post-independence Africa*: A Conclusion 365
David Mhlanga and Emmanuel Ndhlovu

Index 379

About the Editors

David Mhlanga is a Postdoctoral Researcher at the University of Johannesburg, South Africa. His research includes financial inclusion, poverty studies, and industry 4.0. Subject areas include Development economics, Economics of Artificial Intelligence, Health, and Education Economics.

Emmanuel Ndhlovu is a Postdoctoral Researcher at the Vaal University of Technology, South Africa. He holds a PhD in Development Studies from the University of South Africa. He conducts research on land and agrarian change in Africa, peasant livelihoods, food security, migration, and political economy of development.

About the Contributors

Abisola Akinola is a professional accountant with excellent analytical skills. Abisola teaches taxation, cost accounting, and auditing at Pan-Atlantic University. Abisola holds a PhD degree in Chartered Accounting from Bowen University.

Mervis Chiware holds a PhD in Public Management and Governance from the University of Johannesburg, South Africa and is a serving Lecturer in the Department of Public Management and Governance at the University of Zimbabwe. She is a lead researcher who in the past contributed to public management studies and often deals with gender and development issues. She has contributed to several book projects, therefore, impacting governance and public policy issues in Zimbabwe and the world at large.

Innocent Dingani (Masters in Development Studies) is a Board Member of the Chiredzi town council supporting the attainment of vision 2030 in Zimbabwe towards the development of the District. His research interests are public policy, corruption, and community development. He has contributed several articles in peer-reviewed journals.

Mufaro Dzingirai is a Lecturer in the Department of Business Management, at Midlands State University and a PhD candidate in Business Management at Midlands State University. He is also currently a Senior Fellow at the Nexus Think Tank (Zarawi Trust). He received his Master of Commerce in Strategic Management and Corporate Governance degree from Midlands State University in 2016. He was hired as a teacher by the Ministry of Education from 2014 to 2016. In 2013, he received the MSU Book Prize as the best graduating student. His research interests include Higher Education, Strategy, Management, Finance, Entrepreneurship, and Development.

Olaniyi Evans is a Nigerian economist, a public policy analyst, and a university lecturer teaching at Pan Atlantic University, Lagos, Nigeria. He is a recipient of the 2009 University of Lagos Certificate of Excellence and the 2019 Emerald Literati

Award for the Highly Commended Article. Evans is known in academia for his work on public policy, digital economy, financial inclusion, tourism, and DSGE. He earned his BSc first class, MSc distinctions, and went on to pursue a PhD all in economics from the University of Lagos. Evans is the author of best-selling textbooks and a substantial number of increasingly cited scholarly articles in top-rated academic journals. He is the Managing Editor of *BizEcons Quarterly* and the CEO of Hevanz International.

Gay Tapiwa Gweshe MSc, BSc (Department of Governance and Public Management, University of Zimbabwe), Dip HRM (Institute of People Management Zimbabwe). Currently a lecturer in the Faculty of Social and Behavioral Sciences, University of Zimbabwe; DPhil Student at North-West University, South Africa.

Adewale Samuel Hassan is a Postdoctoral Research Fellow in the School of Public Management, Governance and Public Policy at the University of Johannesburg, South Africa. He holds a PhD in Economics and has published many articles in international peer-reviewed journals. He has also presented papers at several international conferences. He regularly facilitates training and workshop sessions in econometric research methods. His research interests include environmental sustainability, energy economics, macroeconomic policy analysis, public policy and governance.

Miriam Hofisi is a Postdoctoral Research Fellow at the North West University, South Africa. Miriam research interests are in the fields of development in agriculture and smallholder farming. Gender and Financial inclusion, Smallholder agriculture and financial inclusion (FinTech), Food Security, Tenure Security and Sustainability, and others are some of the projects undertaken.

Fortunate Jena is a PhD Student (Public Management and Governance at North-West University (South Africa) and a Lecturer in the Department of Rural and Urban Development at Great Zimbabwe University, Zimbabwe. Her research interests are local authority systems and practices, public health administration, and public policy. She has contributed several articles in peer-reviewed journals.

Belese N. Majova is a doctoral student at the University of Johannesburg South Africa. Her research interests are on land and agrarian change, smallholder farming, women empowerment, and informal sector livelihoods. She is the Executive Chairman of the Zeleb Group and has also served on various boards in South Africa.

Banele Mazhelo is a former student at Great Zimbabwe University from the Department of Rural and Urban Development. Her research interests are local authorities, women empowerment, and public policy.

Favourate Y. Mpofu holds a PhD in Taxation and is currently a Post-Doctoral Researcher at the University of Johannesburg, South Africa. She holds a Master of Science in Finance and Investment, a Master of Commerce in Taxation, and CIMA Advanced Diploma. Her current publications and research interests are on tax policy in developing countries, focusing on the informal economy, digital economy, and transfer pricing.

Peterson K. Ozili is an Economist in the Economic Policy Office of the Central Bank of Nigeria. He works extensively in policymaking and is actively involved in academic research. He has experience in economic policy, financial inclusion, financial stability, financial innovation, banking regulation, and supervision. His areas of specialization are financial economics, international development, accounting, development finance, the economics of financial markets, banking and financial reporting. He has published extensively in many accounting and finance journals.

Tawonga Rushambwa is currently a PhD student at the KwaZulu-Natal University, South Africa. His research interests are in economics, political economy, finance, and digital technologies.

Joseph Tinarwo holds a PhD from the University of Johannesburg, South Africa. His research interests are in food systems, economic partnerships, and sustainable development. He is currently a Lecturer at the Great Zimbabwe University, Zimbabwe.

Chapter 1
Introduction: Theorising Economic and Social Inclusion in Post-Independence Africa

David Mhlanga and Emmanuel Ndhlovu

Abstract This chapter introduces the book Economic and Social Inclusion in Post-Independence Africa: An Inclusive Approach to Economic Development. It provides a general description of the line of argument pursued by the chapters in the book. This chapter historicises and theorises the key concepts of the book. Using a variety of case studies underpinned by multidisciplinary research approaches, the contributors in the book explore a wide range of economic or financial inclusion issues from its benefits and challenges to the steps that need to be taken to improve the level of economic inclusion on the continent. The central argument sustained by the chapters of the book is that economic and social inclusion remains at the forefront of development discussions across the continent. This has been facilitated by recent technological and innovation development, which reaches previously inaccessible regions. This chapter, therefore, flags these key issues as part of the introduction to the book. The chapter also provides a brief synopsis of the chapters in the book.

Keywords Africa · Economic inclusion · Development · Post-independence · Welfare

1.1 Introduction

Africa is currently receiving a lot of attention around the world not just because of its many accomplishments and its dynamism but also because of its significant problems. The number of people living in poverty has gone down, human

D. Mhlanga (✉)
College of Business and Economics, University of Johannesburg, Johannesburg, South Africa

E. Ndhlovu
Vaal University of Technology, Vanderbijlpark, South Africa

D. Mhlanga, E. Ndhlovu (eds.), *Economic Inclusion in Post-Independence Africa*, Advances in African Economic, Social and Political Development,
https://doi.org/10.1007/978-3-031-31431-5_1

development indicators have gone up, and vibrant social movements are assisting in the transformation of communities and drawing attention to stigmatised issues and groups of people (Das & Espinoza, 2020). The necessity of economic and social inclusion is being brought to the forefront of discussion across the continent through the implementation of new laws and programs, which has led to the expansion of technological innovation to previously inaccessible regions. Several African governments have been at the forefront of the movement towards progress. For example, during the last 10 years, more gender equality reforms have been implemented in Africa than in any other region on the planet (Das & Espinoza, 2020).

However, beneficial gains have been unequal in Africa, as they have been in other parts of the world, with many areas and groups being left behind (Söderbaum & Taylor, 2018; Anwar, 2019). This is the case for several reasons. People who do not have access to mobile phones or the Internet, for instance, may fall further behind because of the rise of digital technology. In a similar vein, enhanced infrastructure has resulted in better lives, but it also contains hazards, such as the possibility of the weakest people having their lands taken from them unfairly or of damage being done to the environment or people's means of subsistence. Certain regions can see a concentration of improvements in education and health, whereas some groups and regions that are afflicted with state and societal instability tend to lag in a spectrum of development outcomes. Over the past few years, there has been a growing worldwide movement toward strengthening and scaling up economic inclusion for the world's poorest people. Consideration is being given to the Sustainable Development Goals (SDGs), which aim to "end poverty in all its manifestations everywhere by 2030" and to "address inclusive and sustainable growth" (SDG 8). Key activities are now being implemented (Andrews et al., 2021).

A sustainable and inclusive economy that "leaves no one behind" is more vital than it has ever been, especially on the African continent. As economic inclusion programs for the poorest continue to develop, a story of high hopes and enormous scepticism is emerging. Even while transformative economic growth will ultimately be the primary factor in reducing poverty, this type of growth is not inevitably inclusive and does not always reach the people with the lowest incomes. When working to improve economic inclusion for the poorest, it is essential to acknowledge the existence of "poverty traps" and to acknowledge the fact that releasing the productive potential of people who are currently living in poverty requires the removal of multiple barriers through the application of a multidimensional response (Andrews et al., 2021). In actuality, the limits imposed by households, communities, economies, and institutions may have a disproportionately negative effect on certain subgroups of the population, such as women, young people, persons with impairments, and those who have been uprooted from their homes.

At its core, social and economic exclusion is about power connections, in which cultures create complex mechanisms to maintain existing social structures and preserve the status quo (Heleta, 2018; Thombs, 2019). One of how communities place some groups in a subservient position and others in a dominating status is through the processes of assigning status based on attitudes, beliefs, perceptions, and behaviours. These practices can include superstitions, stigmas, and rituals. In this sense, families, communities, legal systems, labour markets, land markets, and knowledge systems are all included under the umbrella term "structures and systems". It is also crucial to highlight that structures and processes support one another and are solidified by official and informal institutions, as stated by Das and Espinoza (2020). Belief systems, superstitions, social stigmas, and other practices prevent certain groups from being included in many contexts around the world (World Bank, 2017; Gumede, 2018). Fear is instilled by acts of intimidation and harassment, which prevents some groups from attaining their full potential and puts them in their place. In addition, social norms may assign males and females to jobs or may deem certain habits or body functions filthy.

Other practices, such as stigma and shunning, may also contribute to the invisibility of certain groups, such as people who have disabilities or people who have albinism. In a related vein, some cultures may hide people who have disabilities. This lack of visibility can have several repercussions, one of which is that these organisations might not be counted in official statistics. On the level of the family as well as the level of the nation, this means that they continue to be concealed and ignored. Most of the time, these discriminatory customs are sanctioned by religion or by individuals who interpret the scriptures of various religions (World Bank, 2017; Andrews et al., 2021). People who have a sexual identity that does not conform are frequently criminalised and expelled from society in many different cultures, and this exclusion and criminalisation are frequently justified by quoting religious texts. Beliefs about cleanliness and pollution usually exclude populations, either at certain times or during certain times of the month; taboos around menstruation women are ubiquitous in many regions of the world. In general, these activities are examples of techniques that are used to maintain social control and order (Das & Espinoza, 2020). In addition to providing an overall summary of the content of the book, this chapter will introduce the ideas of economic and social inclusion in the context of Africa

1.2 Economic Inclusion Explained?

As we will see in Chap. 2, an inclusive market economy ensures that all people, regardless of their gender, nationality, family history, age, or other situational factors over which they have no control, have full and equal access to employment, financial services, enterprise development, and, more generally, economic opportunity. To ensure a smooth and productive transition to a market economy, it is essential to promote economic inclusion, or the expansion of economic opportunities for underprivileged social groups (Lagarde, 2014; Lawal et al., 2021). Instead of being a matter of social policy preference, advocating for a market-based system boils down to questions of efficient (human) resource allocation. Consequently, openness is a must for a sustainable economic model. Therefore, economic inclusion is an important feature of a transition, because it encourages people to participate in economic growth-promoting activities like work, education, and other endeavours, if they are given the chance to do so (Lawal et al., 2021). The report, titled "The State of Economic Inclusion in 2021", defines economic inclusion as "the continuous integration of people and households into larger overall social and economic development practices, by tackling numerous limitations or institutional impediments encountered by the poor at various levels, including the household, such as human and physical capacity, the community, such as social norms, the local economy, such as direct connections to markets and services, and institutions". For structuralists, economic inclusion is about more than just taking part in global economic systems; it also means benefiting from them. They further argue that participation in the global economy may boost employment rather than destroy it. Contrary to common belief, participation in the global economy through employment is the path to reducing poverty or developing civilisation; but, for a sizable portion of the global labour population, the conditions of this inclusion can cause and perpetuate poverty. Rather than asking if there are ties to the global economy, the key question should be on the societal and political power dynamics that arise because of these relationships.

1.3 Social Inclusion Explained

The concept of social inclusion, or simply inclusion, has been gaining more and more popularity in discussions about development and wider policy issues. The process of making it easier for individuals and groups to participate in society is what's known as social inclusion, and it's described as such (World Bank, 2013; Das & Espinoza, 2020). Most conversations about social inclusion in Africa have taken place within the context of reducing poverty and responding to humanitarian crises. These conversations are driven by the fact that, despite significant progress being made in reducing poverty, it is estimated that more than 400 million people are still living in poverty. The result of social exclusion is poverty, although social exclusion can be both a process and a result. The processes of exclusion can have long-term repercussions on the mindsets, psyches, and dignity of subordinate or excluded groups, and this exclusion, in turn, impacts the ability of these groups to access the opportunities that have been made available to them (Beegle & Christiaensen, 2019). Slavery, apartheid, and the practice of untouchability were three of the most heinous forms of social segregation in human history (Das & Espinoza, 2020). Figure 1.1 is outlining the social inclusion framework.

Access to services, locations, and markets are all part of what is meant by social inclusion. This is illustrated in Fig. 1.1. Social inclusion incorporates the abilities, opportunities, and dignity of individuals.

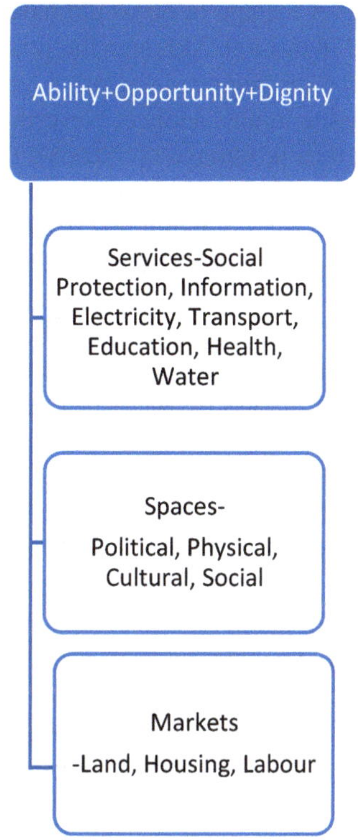

Fig. 1.1 Social inclusion framework. (Source: Authors)

1.4 Economic and Social Inclusion in Africa: Who's Left Behind?

Social, economic, and political transformations are sweeping the African continent. We discuss transitions under some broad categories: demographic changes and their relationship to the accumulation of human capital.

1.4.1 Demographic Trends and the Accumulation of Human Capital

The World Bank (2020) reports that Africa has the highest rate of demographic growth in the world, even though fertility rates are down in virtually every country. It is estimated that by the year 2050, there would be 362 million young people on the continent who are between the ages of 15 and 24. Currently, less than half of the region's population is under the age of 25. According to the UN DESA Population Division (2017), simultaneously, the population of many African countries will be becoming older: by the year 2050, it is predicted that Africa's population of people over the age of 60 would have more than tripled, going from 69 million in 2017 to 226 million. Although integrating older generations of Africans is not now a priority for the region, integrating younger generations of Africans is the most pressing issue it must address. Nevertheless, if the appropriate policies and opportunities are taken advantage of, Africa's rapidly expanding young population has the potential to significantly propel development and further lower levels of poverty in the continent (Das & Espinoza, 2020).

As was the case with fertility, Africa has witnessed advances in health and longevity; nonetheless, the mortality rate among children under the age of five remains high. The proportion of children who live to the age of five is a fundamental metric of welfare, but it also has other repercussions. For instance, high levels of infant and child mortality relate to greater rates of fertility. In addition, nations that struggle with high rates of child mortality are hampered in their ability to invest in human capital, because they are preoccupied with the most fundamental requirement of keeping children alive. According to estimates provided by the United Nations (UN), as well as those provided by the Our World in Data project and AfricaInData.org, there has been a significant drop in the rate of child mortality between the years 1980 and 2015. As compared to the other regions, Africa has experienced the most rapid population decrease between the years 1990 and 2016. Despite these advancements, Africa continues to have the highest under-five mortality rate in the world in 2016, with 78 fatalities for every 1000 live births. To put it another way, nearly one child in every thirteen does not make it to their fifth birthday (Suzuki & Kashiwase, 2017; Das & Espinoza, 2020). There is a significant amount of diversity between countries, with unstable regimes having the greatest rates of mortality among children under the age of five.

1.4.2 Education in Africa

Also, in the field of education, Africa has made considerable strides forward; nevertheless, like other regions of the world, there are substantial gaps in educational attainment based on a variety of identification markers (Pesando, 2021; Andrews et al., 2021). The gross enrolment ratio in primary schools across the region went from 68% in the year 1990 to 98% in the year 2015, while the number of kids who were enrolled increased from 63 million to 152 million (Andrews et al., 2021). Nevertheless, despite the rise in primary school enrolment rates, there are still an estimated 52.3 million children of primary and lower secondary school age who are not in school. These children range in age from 6 to 14 and 7 to 15, and they make up 45% of the total population of children who are not in school around the world (Bashir et al., 2018; Andrews et al., 2021). Even though literacy is the most fundamental educational outcome, there are still some people who are excluded. There is a sizable gender literacy gap between men and women in the United States. The gender difference in Western Africa is the largest, while the gender gap in Southern Africa is the smallest (Das & Espinoza, 2020).

The combination of gender with other markers of an identity confers an additional disadvantage in schooling, as it does in other areas of life as well. Demonstrate, with the help of census data, that female members of ethnic minorities in Senegal and Sierra Leone have a compounded disadvantage in terms of literacy, completion of primary school, and completion of high school. According to Taş et al. (2014), the likelihood of a woman in Senegal finishing primary school is reduced by 10 percentage points simply because she is a woman, 1.6 percentage points because she is an ethnic minority, and an additional 3.8 percentage points because she is an ethnic minority woman. Because of this, the likelihood that women who belong to ethnic minority groups in Senegal will complete primary school is around 15.4 percentage points lower than the likelihood that men who belong to ethnic majority groups will do so. Despite the enormous progress that has been made in South Africa since the end of apartheid, educational achievements for black and coloured South Africans continue to be dismal. Although the white population achieved the nearly full accomplishment of 12 years of schooling in 1920, the black population has yet to achieve that level today, 100 years later. This continues to perpetuate the legacy of racial tensions in education in South Africa, which remains a key cause of inequality and poverty (Donohue & Bornman, 2014; World Bank, 2018). The Systematic Country Diagnostic (SCD) for Benin reaches a similar conclusion, stating that the absence of instruction in mother languages in elementary schools places indigenous children at a disadvantage and causes them to drop out of school at an earlier age (World Bank, 2017; Das & Espinoza, 2020).

1.4.3 Economic Transitions, Poverty, and Employment

Since the 1990s, there has been a remarkable decline in the number of people living in poverty (Das & Espinoza, 2020). On the other hand, throughout the same period, the total number of people living in poverty has grown considerably. Even though the percentage of the African population that is living in poverty has steadily decreased from 57% in 1990 to 41% in 20,153, the total number of people who are living in poverty has increased from approximately 278 million to over 413 million (Das & Espinoza, 2020). There is a substantial gap in performance between the countries of Africa, which can be attributed to several different reasons, the most prominent of which being fragility, conflict, and the endowment of natural resources (Beegle et al., 2016; Das & Espinoza, 2020).

1.4.4 Technology Can Boost Social Inclusion but Leave Some Behind

According to Calderon et al. (2019), the technological age has officially arrived on a worldwide scale, and we are currently living in it. Nevertheless, the positive effects that technology has on countries, regions, communities, and families are conditional on whether these entities have access to relevant information and resources (Ndhlovu, 2022a). However, there is a substantial lot of variation between nations, even though it looks like Africa has jumped the queue when it comes to the digital economy in many areas. For instance, even though fragile countries have seen a somewhat faster increase in the number of mobile cellular subscriptions, the number of mobile cellular subscriptions is still significantly higher in nonfragile countries. This is because nonfragile countries have been able to better invest in their infrastructure (Mhlanga, 2022a, b; Mpofu & Mhlanga, 2022). In a manner parallel to this, the field of financial technology, sometimes known as FinTech, has seen substantial expansion across Africa. Now, 21% of people living in Africa have accounted for mobile money, and the number of these accounts has doubled since 2014.

This constitutes the highest proportion of any region in the entire world (Mhlanga, 2020, 2022b). The M-PESA mobile money transfer system is both one of Africa's most well-known and one of its most established examples of the application of financial technology (Mhlanga, 2022c). Recent research on the future of work in Africa that was published by the World Bank suggests that digital technology also has the potential to stimulate employment growth in the continent (Mhlanga, 2022c). This is the only country in Africa where approximately 60% of the population has access to the Internet, and there is a strong correlation between this statistic and the income level of the country. The percentage of the population in each African nation that can use the Internet is, in a manner that is highly associated with the amount of affluence in that nation, as one might anticipate (Das & Espinoza, 2020). The Pew Research Center Spring 2017 Global Attitudes Survey was carried out in six different countries, and the results showed that individuals with higher levels of education and income were more likely to use cell phones. This is according to Das and Espinoza (2020), who state that the findings of the survey showed that individuals with a higher likelihood of using cell phones. People who don't have cell phones have a far more limited range of options available to them for accessing various sorts of markets, services, and environments (Mhlanga, 2022c).

1.5 Participation in Politics and the Growth of Social Movements in Africa

It is common for progress to be made towards social inclusion when individuals or groups that feel excluded show their agency through social and political involvement. The form of such participation has evolved in many African countries, and this trend can be seen across the continent (Ake, 2019; Mhlanga, 2022d; Ndhlovu, 2022b). The probability of casting a vote is lower among African youth than it is among their seniors, and data from the Afrobarometer questionnaire suggest that the political involvement of young people has declined over the past decade and a half. According to Das and Espinoza (2020), recent surveys draw attention to decreasing involvement in formal political and civic processes, particularly among youth and women in Africa. However, the picture is complex with the likelihood of voting being lower among African youth than it is among their elders. Lekalake and Gyimah-Boadi (2016) found evidence that African youth are less likely to participate in civic activities than their elders and that young African women are even less likely to be involved in public affairs than their male counterparts. In addition, Lekalake and Gyimah-Boadi (2016) found that female respondents reported much lower interest in current affairs and the discussions that surrounded them compared to their male counterparts.

This trend of declining engagement in formal political processes may be an indication of several different factors, including disillusionment or a loss of faith in the procedures themselves. Additionally, it may imply that young people express their preferences through a variety of outlets, with the significance of social media deserving special note in this context. Because it is possible to remain anonymous online, the Internet gives a platform to groups who would not otherwise be able to express themselves through traditional forms of digital media. The younger generation in Africa is much more engaged on social media and other digital platforms than their elders are the same age. The proliferation of social movements demonstrates, among other things, that young people may use various civic channels to act on the issues that are important to them. Despite this, the potential dissatisfaction with political procedures can be an indicator of a wider dissatisfaction with the state. Despite what appears to be a falling level of engagement in official political processes, social movements across Africa continue to increase awareness about the importance of social inclusion. It is common knowledge that Africa has a long and illustrious history of social and political movements. Movements such as this include the illustrious ones for independence and decolonisation, the important ones in academia against Eurocentrism, movements for peace and civil liberties, and movements against various economic practices. Students in South Africa spearheaded the "Fees Must Fall" movement in 2015/2016, which highlights the reality that young people, even though they may not participate in official political processes, are nevertheless politically active (Cini, 2019; Griffiths, 2019).

1.6 How Can Africa Achieve Its Goal of Full Economic Participation?

According to Dörffel and Schuhmann (2022), the UN concept of Sustainable Development Goals is maybe the most well-known global policy framework for thinking about the issue of inclusive development, as will be highlighted in Chap. 2. (SDGs). These goals are intended to provide a thorough set of ideas, goals, and metrics to spark global action in support of development that yields more equal and long-lasting outcomes. While specific policy alternatives are still mostly specified, Dörffel and Schuhmann (2022) believe that they cover a wide range, from

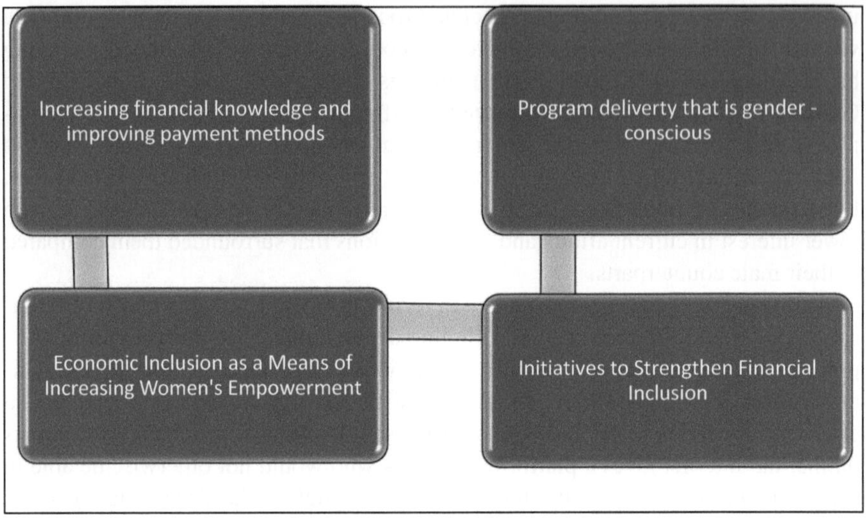

Fig. 1.2 How to make economic inclusion work in Africa. (Source: Authors)

environmental sustainability to poverty alleviation. One benefit of the SDGs is that they elevated several development objectives to the political agenda that had not previously received this attention. In this study, some tactics that can improve economic inclusion in Africa are shown in Fig. 1.2.

In Fig. 1.2, the initiatives that can help to improve economic inclusion in Africa are specified. These initiatives include "the promotion of more and better jobs and livelihoods, increasing financial knowledge and improving payment methods, Economic Inclusion as a Means of Increasing Women's Empowerment, Initiatives to Strengthen Financial Inclusion, and Program Delivery that is Gender Conscious".

1.7 Outline of the Chapters in the Book

The book is comprised of 20 chapters. After the introduction, the remaining 19 chapters are divided into four sections: namely, *Economic Inclusion Implications for Livelihoods and Incomes; Financial Inclusion in Agriculture; the Gendered Implications of Economic Inclusion and the Policy Proposals Towards Economic Inclusion;* and, finally, *Conclusions Economic Inclusion in Post-Independence Africa: An Inclusive Approach to Economic Development.*

Part 1 is comprised of ten chapters, which generally focus on the impact of economic inclusion on livelihoods, incomes, and reproduction. In Chapter 2, David Mhlanga and Emmanuel Ndhlovu explore the economic inclusion development and trajectory in Africa. The chapter found several major patterns as the sources of exclusion which include extreme poverty, informality, shock sensitivity, demographic dynamics, and the building of human capital. Once more, the chapter outlined initiatives that can aid in enhancing economic inclusion in Africa, such as promoting more and better jobs and livelihoods, enhancing financial literacy and payment options, using economic inclusion to boost women's empowerment, and bolstering financial inclusion initiatives, and gender-conscious program delivery. It also underlined the importance of women's empowerment as the foundation for all economic inclusion measures in Africa, in addition to the other ideas covered in the preceding paragraphs.

In Chap. 3, Abisola Akinola and Olaniyi Evans investigate the effects of ICT on social and political inclusion, using a system generalised method of moments for the case of Africa for the period 1995–2018. They found that ICT has a positive statistically significant effect on social and political inclusion, indicating that the higher the levels of ICT, the higher the levels of social and political inclusion. They recommend that the government of individual countries in Africa should increase efforts in fostering robust economies and sound institutions needed for the absolute implementation of ICT, to take advantage of all the benefits required for social and political inclusion.

David Mhlanga and Emmanuel Ndhlovu in Chap. 4 explore the background of social inclusion, reveal the causes of social exclusion in Africa, and suggest social inclusion strategies for the continent that can aid in sustainable development. The chapter also posits that a social justice perspective provides a more inclusive definition of social inclusion.

This is followed by Chap. 5 in which David Mhlanga and Favourate Mpofu investigated the digital economy, digital service taxes, and mobile money taxes in Africa to examine the effects of these taxes on tax administration in Africa, the effects of these taxes on financial inclusion in Africa, and the effects of these taxes on inclusive development in Africa. The chapter emphasises the detrimental effects that digital service taxes will have on inclusive development, because they may cause resources to be diverted from sectors that benefit low-income earners, such as digital financial services, in favour of those that may not directly benefit them.

In Chap. 6, Miriam Hofisi examines grey and academic literature to explore financial inclusion policies promulgated by governments in Africa. The study found that most governments in SSA have outdated financial regulatory frameworks that guide financial inclusion. In addition, countries with road and railway infrastructure had a high level of financial inclusion and the soft infrastructure, such as the regulatory framework is not updated to support financial technology lenders. In the era of mobile money accounts, the regulatory frameworks in SSA are not responsive to matters of secure identity that protect the client and the financial provider. Other barriers to financial inclusion include a lack of mobile phones, identity documents, and money. In light of the findings above, it is critical to know that the post-colonial government in the SSA has at its helm the potential ability to leverage the upsurge of mobile money for the economic benefit of smallholder farmers.

Chapter 7 by Favourate Mpofu explores digital financial inclusion and digital literacy in Africa. The chapter shows that digital financial inclusion is important for the empowerment of the population, their financial management, spending and investment decisions as well as the growth of the economy. The chapter also argues that digital financial inclusion is far from being attained in Africa due to challenges that include digital exclusion, digital financial literacy, redundancy barriers, lack of connectivity, and high Internet data costs and digital taxes.

In Chap. 8, David Mhlanga and Mufaro Dzingirai documented financial inclusion progress in Rwanda, Kenya, Uganda, and Ghana. They found financial inclusion was low and made some recommendations to increase financial inclusion in Africa which include the following: women, young people, and people with disabilities should be helped by financial institutions to increase their ability to make fundamentally sound financial decisions to encourage wider financial inclusion in Africa.

Peterson Ozili, in Chap. 9, provides insights into the trends to expect in the future of financial inclusion. The author identifies the past and recent changes occurring in the financial inclusion space and based on these changes make predictions about what to expect in the future of financial inclusion. The author predicts that, in the future, financial inclusion will witness increased digitalisation and increased personalisation of formal financial services, the provision of a wide range of formal financial services from a single platform, a shift from account numbers to a mobile number to drive financial inclusion; more women who will become financially empowered and financially independent, the government which will become more directly involved in delivering basic financial services to the poor, and the emergence of new financial innovations that continuously reduce transaction cost. These future trends will have implications for financial inclusion in Asia, Europe, and particularly in Africa, where the level of financial inclusion is relatively low.

This is followed by Adewale Samuel Hassan in Chap. 10 who investigates whether political risk matters for FDI inflows to the West African countries from 1986 to 2020. Panel regressions were conducted based on the dynamic common correlated effects (DCCE) and dynamic seemingly unrelated regression (DSUR). The estimates establish that improvement in the political rating scores of the West African countries enhances FDI inflows to the countries. Market potential, trade openness, and natural resources exploitation are also identified as important drivers of FDI. Furthermore, the Dumitrescu-Hurlin panel causality test results reveal that GDP has a bidirectional causal relationship with FDI, natural resources, and infrastructure, while natural resources Granger causes FDI, political risk, trade openness, and infrastructure. The study posits that the countries should improve political risk rating through the existing political and economic unions and embed their natural resource exploitation in a sound institutional framework.

Lastly, in Chap. 11, Tawonga Rushambwa uses the Ghana Living Standards Survey (GLSS) of 1987 and the 2019 Ghana Socioeconomic Panel Survey (GSPS) datasets for building a comparative descriptive socioeconomic profile of individuals across gender and the influence of other demographic variables. The study found the persistence of socioeconomic disparities across gender, regional location, and social marginalisation, which were more pronounced in the 2019 dataset. The study also observed a strong influence of the physical divide measured by socioeconomic performance, social marginalisation, and education attainment as influencing access to digital technologies using the 2019 panel dataset. It was concluded that the limiting socioeconomic development of post-independence Ghana is important in shaping the trajectory of future change and living standards for Ghanaians, given the importance of the physical divide in adaptation to external changes affecting welfare.

Part II consists of two chapters, which explore financial inclusion and exclusion in the context of peasant agriculture. Chapter 12 by Belese Majova problematises the existing conceptualisation of the concept of financial inclusion. They argue that the concept of financial inclusion is poorly understood and, therefore, vaguely implemented. The chapter shows that the current conceptualisation of financial inclusion does not allow for the creation of a mature scholarly debate in the context of land reform beneficiaries as the emphasis is placed on access to financial services instead of focusing on access to the finance itself. The chapter concludes that the starting point towards the realisation of financial inclusion for land recipients in South Africa should be the reconceptualisation of the concept itself, so that it can capture the context of the needs of the people and situations.

This is followed by Chap. 13 by Emmanuel Ndhlovu and David Mhlanga which takes issue with the conventional conceptualisation of financial inclusion as the delivery of financial services to the poor at an affordable cost. The chapter posits that finance itself and not simply financial services should be the basis of financial inclusion for inclusive development. The chapter analyses various epochs within the country's history to demonstrate what financial inclusion should constitute. It concludes that it is only when the concept is reconceptualised to relate to the context of circumstances and needs of people that it will be able to allow for a deeper understanding of how inclusive and sustainable development does not leave the peasantry outside the tide of development can be realised.

Part III consists of six chapters, which focus on economic inclusion and gender. Chapter 14 by David Mhlanga investigates the challenges associated with the adoption of AI solutions in the financial inclusion of the excluded. Using unobtrusive research techniques like conceptual and documentary analysis the study found out that employing AI in improving financial inclusion through digital tools is associated with many challenges apart from the various opportunities it presents. The study discovered, despite the benefits, the adoption of AI in the inclusion of the excluded households is associated with several challenges, which include consumer protection challenges, data protection, and cyberattacks. Other challenges include risks related to the reduction of competition, irresponsible deployment of AI, and the risk of fuelling the digital divide, exclusion, and displacements. Therefore, the study concludes that it is important that policymakers, in partnership with the private sector, prioritise the development of digital infrastructure as one of the foundations of their economic and social development plans, which will make it easy for those excluded to be able to participate fully. The development of digital infrastructure should be one of the foundations of the economic and social development plans, which will make it easy for those excluded to be able to participate fully. And this will go a long way in addressing many challenges related to the lack of adequate infrastructure.

Chapter 15 by Emmanuel Ndhlovu and Belese Majova explores the opportunities for and constraints of women empowerment in the South African Gauteng Province. The article posits that although the number of women involved in agribusiness has increased in South Africa and the Gauteng Province, women empowerment in terms of resource control and participation in decision-making in the agribusiness is still a real problem. Predicated interviews, secondary sources, and observations and also guided by the Longwe Frameworks, the article reveals that lack of funds, education and training, criminality, technological challenges, research and innovation, and lack of transformation are some of the key barriers to women empowerment within the agribusiness. In dealing with these challenges, the article recommends the deployment of its sustainable livelihoods framework-based interventions as part of the collective and continued effort to realise women's empowerment in the agribusiness in the province.

In Chap. 16, Tapiwa Gweshe and Mervis Chiware provide an evidence-based historical analysis of the implementation of a gender-inclusive approach in the Science, Technology, Engineering, and Mathematics (STEM) disciplines in Zimbabwe. The chapter studies the policy measures that have been undertaken by the government and higher and tertiary learning/research institutions to strengthen gender balance in STEM fields. They found that girls have remained marginalised, especially in the STEM fields. The lower-level practical subjects that qualify as STEM have perennially been gender-stereotyped. The system made them focus more on fashion and fabrics, food, and nutrition subjects, yet the global trajectory has migrated towards hard sciences. It is recommended that gender affirmative action be strengthened to increase the representation of women and girls in the STEM field.

This is followed by Chap. 17 by Fortunate Jena, Joseph Tinarwo, Innocent Dingani, and Banele Mazhelo. The chapter draws lessons from the case study of Zimbabwe on how to strengthen women's representation in African local authorities. The study revealed that there are several reasons for the poor participation of women in local government institutions and proffered cocktail of strategies is needed to support women's representation in local authorities, and these include strong legal and institutional frameworks, vibrant advocacy efforts, and multi-stakeholder partnerships. The study also proffered recommendations to address the causes of poor women's representation in councils, including awareness campaigns to promote women's involvement in council issues and fair and practical person specifications for the desired posts in the council to encourage women to apply for posts, among other factors. Therefore, the study concluded that indeed there is poor women representation in local authorities in Zimbabwe, hence the need of strengthening women's capacities in local government institutions in Africa.

Lastly, Chap. 18 by David Mhlanga and Miriam Hofisi discusses trust in digital financial services as well as the usage of digital financial services in the digital economy and the taxing of the digital economy. The chapter shows that taxing the digital economy could have detrimental, significant effects on digital financial inclusion, since the disadvantaged people who utilise these services might lose faith in them.

Chapter 19 by David Mhlanga was focusing on digital transformation in the healthcare sector with a focus on the role of artificial intelligence for inclusive long-term care around the world and the lessons for Africa. The results of the systematic literature review technique showed that, in the post-pandemic environment, digital transformation is advantageous for the provision of long-term care, because telemedicine programs can facilitate the provision of care at home. When there is a digital transformation, among other key components that can help with long-term care, issues like elder abuse and age discrimination in access to long-term services may be recorded. Therefore, it can assist long-term patient care programs around the world more; greater focus should be given to the digital transformation of the healthcare industry. Lastly, Part IV comprises one chapter, which provides conclusions and policy recommendations.

1.8 Conclusion

Africa is currently garnering a lot of attention from people all over the world, not just because of the numerous accomplishments it has accomplished and the degree of vitality it possesses but also because of the significant challenges that it is currently confronted with. The number of people who are living in poverty has decreased, human development indices have improved, and active social movements are helping in the change of communities and attracting attention to stigmatised issues and groups of people. The necessity of economic and social inclusion is currently at the forefront of discussion across the continent, thanks to the implementation of new laws and programs, which has led to the expansion of technological innovation to previously inaccessible regions. This is because new laws and programs have led to the expansion of technological innovation to previously inaccessible regions. This is happening as a direct result of the spread of technical innovation to previously unreachable locations, which has brought about the current situation. Throughout Africa's history, a few of its countries have been at the forefront of the push towards increased levels of development. This chapter's objectives are to (1) introduce the book Economic and Social Inclusion in Post-Independence Africa and (2) describe the course that the book will follow. Both objectives will be accomplished by reading this chapter. Following the completion of this chapter, a brief synopsis of the subsequent chapters in the book will be offered for your review.

References

Ake, C. (2019). The new world order: A view from Africa. In *Whose world order?* (pp. 19–42). Routledge.

Andrews, C., de Montesquiou, A., Sánchez, I. A., Dutta, P. V., Samaranayake, S., Heisey, J., et al. (2021). *The state of economic inclusion report 2021: The potential to scale*. World Bank Publications.

Anwar, M. A. (2019). Connecting South Africa: ICTs, uneven development, and poverty debates. In *The geography of South Africa* (pp. 261–267). Springer.

Beegle, K., Christiaensen, L., Dabalen, A., & Gaddis, I. (2016). Poverty in a rising Africa. World Bank Publications.

Beegle, K., & Christiaensen, L. (Eds.). (2019). *Accelerating poverty reduction in Africa*. World Bank Publications.

Bashir, S., Rizwan, M. S., Salam, A., Fu, Q., Zhu, J., Shaaban, M., & Hu, H. (2018). Cadmium immobilization potential of rice straw-derived biochar, zeolite and rock phosphate: extraction techniques and adsorption mechanism. *Bulletin of Environmental Contamination and Toxicology, 100*, 727–732.

Calderon, C., Kambou, G., Korman, V., Kubota, M., & Canales, C. C. (2019). Africa's pulse, No. 19, April 2019: An analysis of issues shaping Africa's economic future. World Bank Publications.

Cini, L. (2019). Disrupting the neoliberal university in South Africa: The# FeesMustFall movement in 2015. *Current Sociology, 67*(7), 942–959.

Das, M. B., & Espinoza, S. A. (2020). Inclusion matters in Africa. Available online: https://openknowledge.worldbank.org/bitstream/handle/10986/32528/IM-Africa.pdf

Donohue, D., & Bornman, J. (2014). The challenges of realising inclusive education in South Africa. *South African Journal of Education, 34*(2), 1.

Dörffel, C., & Schuhmann, S. (2022). What is inclusive development? Introducing the multidimensional inclusiveness index. *Social Indicators Research, 162*(3), 1117–1148.

Griffiths, D. (2019). # FeesMustFall and the decolonised university in South Africa: Tensions and opportunities in a globalising world. *International Journal of Educational Research, 94*, 143–149.

Gumede, V. (2018). Social policy for inclusive development in Africa. *Third World Quarterly, 39*(1), 122–139.

Heleta, S. (2018). Decolonizing knowledge in South Africa: Dismantling the 'pedagogy of big lies'. *Ufahamu: A Journal of African Studies, 40*(2), 47–65.

Lagarde, C. (2014, May). Economic inclusion and financial integrity—An address to the conference on inclusive capitalism. In speech presented at the Conference on Inclusive Capitalism (Vol. 27).

Lawal, A. A., Hassan, M. A., Zakaria, M. R., Yusoff, M. Z. M., Norrahim, M. N. F., Mokhtar, M. N., & Shirai, Y. (2021). Effect of oil palm biomass cellulosic content on nanopore structure and adsorption capacity of biochar. *Bioresource Technology, 332*, 125070.

Lekalake, R., & Gyimah-Boadi, E. (2016). Does less engaged mean less empowered? Political participation lags among African youth, especially women.

Mhlanga, D. (2020). Industry 4.0 in finance: The impact of artificial intelligence (ai) on digital financial inclusion. *International Journal of Financial Studies, 8*(3), 45.

Mhlanga, D. (2022a). Prospects and challenges of digital financial inclusion/Fintech innovation in the fourth industrial revolution. In *Digital financial inclusion* (pp. 163–182). Palgrave Macmillan.

Mhlanga, D. (2022b). Financial inclusion and the fourth industrial revolution. In *Digital financial inclusion* (pp. 39–57). Palgrave Macmillan.

Mhlanga, D. (2022c). Selected digital financial inclusion success stories across developing economies. In *Digital financial inclusion. Palgrave studies in impact finance*. Palgrave Macmillan. https://doi.org/10.1007/978-3-031-16687-7_17

Mhlanga, D. (2022d). Digital financial inclusion, and the way forward for emerging markets: Towards sustainable development. In *Digital financial inclusion. Palgrave studies in impact finance*. Palgrave Macmillan. https://doi.org/10.1007/978-3-031-16687-7_18

Mpofu, F. Y., & Mhlanga, D. (2022). Digital financial inclusion, digital financial services tax and financial inclusion in the fourth industrial revolution era in Africa. *Economies, 10*(8), 184.

Ndhlovu, E. (2022a). Contract farming and climate change adaptation in rural Zimbabwe. *Preprints*. https://doi.org/10.20944/preprints202209.0224.v1

Ndhlovu, E. (2022b). Socio-economic characterisation of resettled smallholder farmers in rural Zimbabwe. *Journal of Asian and African Studies, 57*(8), 1495–1510.

Pesando, L. M. (2021). Educational assortative mating in sub-Saharan Africa: Compositional changes and implications for household wealth inequality. *Demography, 58*(2), 571–602.

Söderbaum, F., & Taylor, I. (2018). *Regionalism and uneven development in Southern Africa: The case of the Maputo Development Corridor*. Routledge.

Suzuki, E., & Kashiwase, H. (2017, October 19). New child mortality estimates show that 15,000 children died every day in 2016. *World Bank Data Blog*. https://s.worldbank.org/opendata/new-child-mortality-estimates-show-15000-childrendied-every-day-2016

Taş, E. O., Reimão, M. E., & Orlando, M. B. (2014). Gender, ethnicity, and cumulative disadvantage in education outcomes. *World Development, 64*, 538–553.

Thombs, R. P. (2019). When democracy meets energy transitions: A typology of social power and energy system scale. *Energy Research & Social Science, 52*, 159–168.

UN DESA (United Nations Department of Economic and Social Affairs) Population Division. (2017). *World family planning 2017: Highlights*. United Nations. http://www.un.org/en/development/desa/population/publications/pdf/family/WFP2017_Highlights.pdf

World Bank. (2013). *Inclusion matters: The foundation for shared prosperity*. World Bank. Available online: https://openknowledge.worldbank.org/handle/10986/16195

World Bank. (2017). Social inclusion in Africa. Available online: https://www.worldbank.org/en/region/afr/brief/social-inclusion-in-africa.

World Bank. (2018). Global economic prospects, January 2018: Broad-Based Upturn, but for How Long?. The World Bank.

World Bank. (2020). *The COVID-19 pandemic: Shocks to education and policy responses*. World Bank. Available online: https://cdn.theewf.org/uploads/pdf/World-Bank-The-COVID-19-Pandemic-Shocks-to-Education-and-Policy-Responses.pdf

Part I
Economic Inclusion Implications for Livelihoods and Incomes

Chapter 2
Economic Inclusion: Transforming the Lives of the Poor and How to Make Economic Inclusion Work in Africa

David Mhlanga and Emmanuel Ndhlovu

Abstract In recent years, notably in Africa, a significant worldwide movement to improve and increase economic involvement for the poorest people has evolved. To show the forces of change that will influence Africa's economic inclusion and several methods that can help to improve economic inclusion in Africa, the chapter used document analysis. The chapter found several major patterns as the sources of exclusion, which include extreme poverty, informality, shock sensitivity, demographic dynamics, and the building of human capital. Once more, the chapter outlined initiatives that can aid in enhancing economic inclusion in Africa, such as promoting more and better jobs and livelihoods, enhancing financial literacy and payment options, using economic inclusion to boost women's empowerment, and bolstering financial inclusion initiatives, and gender-conscious program delivery. The chapter underlined the importance of women's empowerment as the foundation for all economic inclusion measures in Africa, in addition to the other ideas covered in the preceding paragraphs. Women's empowerment programs should make greater investments in the welfare and empowerment of women, empowering them to reject gender stereotypes and step outside of their customary positions.

Keywords Africa · Economic Inclusion · Transformation · Lives · Poor

2.1 Introduction

In light of the 2030 Agenda for sustainable development, there's been an increasing global drive to improve and expand the economic inclusion of the poor in

D. Mhlanga (✉)
The University of Johannesburg, College of Business and Economics, Johannesburg, South Africa

E. Ndhlovu
Vaal University of Technology, Vanderbijlpark, South Africa

D. Mhlanga, E. Ndhlovu (eds.), *Economic Inclusion in Post-Independence Africa*, Advances in African Economic, Social and Political Development,
https://doi.org/10.1007/978-3-031-31431-5_2

recent years (SDGs). Major initiatives are being taken to address equitable and sustainable development and "eradicate poverty in all its manifestations everywhere by 2030" (SDG 8) (Andrews et al., 2021). According to Andrews et al. (2021), the push for this change is the scaling up of government-led efforts that focus on social protection, lifestyle and jobs, and financial inclusion investments. Strong empirical support and a groundswell of knowledge, notably from graduating programs in the nonprofit sector, are further factors driving this transformation. Initiatives for economic inclusion employ a "great push" of coordinated actions to help the poorest individuals and families build up their assets and income.

These interventions frequently involve transfers of money or goods, mentoring or training opportunities, financial access, and market assistance. There is increasing international movement to support inclusive socioeconomic development to make sure that nobody is left behind. The State of Economic Inclusion 2021 Report states that initiatives promoting economic inclusion are expanding globally, reaching more than 20 million households, and providing benefits to close to 92 million people. According to the report, the size of state initiatives that focus on enhancing investments in social security, people's lives and talents, and access to financial services is what is causing the remarkable increase in economic inclusion programs. Particularly in areas threatened by conflict, climate change, and shocks, this tendency is anticipated to last. With over 90% of the programs focusing on women, economic empowerment for women is a primary driver of economic inclusion programming.

Initiatives to promote economic inclusion, which frequently includes financial or in-kind assistance, skill development or counselling, access to credit, and connections to the private sector, are swiftly emerging as a key component of many governments' comprehensive anti-poverty strategies (Asongu et al., 2021a, b). They are probably going to be around because of the COVID-19 outbreak, especially in areas that are susceptible to armed conflict, environmental destruction, and shocks. The State of Economic Inclusion Report of 2021 states that as part of coordinated government initiatives aimed at controlling the pandemic, preserving food and nutrition security, and fostering medium-term recovery, economic inclusion initiatives for the underprivileged have a high likelihood of improving lives. Social aid programs can be supplemented by economic inclusion initiatives rather than being replaced by them, as shown by instances from Egypt, Ethiopia, Ghana, Zambia, and other countries.

The State of Economic Inclusion Report 2021 provides insight into some of the most challenging problems facing practitioners and policymakers in the field of development: improving the socioeconomic conditions of the poorest and most vulnerable people on the planet. Economic inclusion programs, according to Meagher et al. (2016), are a collection of integrated, interdisciplinary activities that help individuals, families, and communities enhance their income and assets. A boom in research on "adverse incorporation," or "inclusion on less favorable terms," has been driven by an increased focus on the conditions of international inclusion for rural and urban employees in developing countries.

From 2000 to 2018, Asongu et al. (2021a, b) investigated whether female economic inclusion improves tax performance in a sample of 48 sub-Saharan African nations. Three tax performance variables are used by Asongu et al. (2021a, b): total tax revenues omitting social contributions, reporting tax revenue coming from environmental resource sources, and total non-resource tax revenue. The generalized method of moments was used to address endogeneity issues. Utilizing three indices of female inclusion female employment, labor force participation, and industry employment, Asongu et al. (2021a, b) found that increasing the number of women working in the sector had a net negative impact on total tax collection but a net good impact on non-resource taxes. In contrast to the importance of financial access in moderating the effect of the Gini coefficient on female unemployment, Asongu et al. (2020) research revealed a negative net effect from the role of financial access in moderating the influence of the Palma ratio on female labor force participation. Asongu et al. (2020) also found that the Gini coefficient and the Palma ratio for female employment are modulated by financial access, with net adverse effects.

According to Asongu and Odhiambo (2020a, b, c), the post-2015 development agenda's main policy problems for sub-Saharan Africa are inequality and gender economic exclusion. When it comes to inequality, Asongu and Odhiambo (2020a, b, c) established "thresholds" that should not be crossed if the government wants to encourage gender economic participation. Using the generalized method of moments, Asongu and Odhiambo (2020a, b, c) discovered that inequality levels of 0.708 for political stability, 0.601 for voice and accountability, 0.588 for government effectiveness, 0.631 for regulatory quality, 0.612 for the rule of law, and 0.550 for corruption control completely negate the beneficial effects of governance on female labor force participation. According to Asongu and Odhiambo (2020a, b, c), the thresholds for political stability and the rule of law at which female unemployment can no longer be reduced via governance channels are 0.561 and 0.465, respectively. Again, Asongu and Odhiambo (2020a, b, c) discovered that inequality levels of 0.608 for political stability, 0.580 for voice and accountability, 0.581 for government effectiveness, and 0.557 for the rule of law fully diminish the beneficial effects of governance on female employment.

Ofori et al. (2021) also made the case that the discussion over whether sub-Saharan African nations should enhance female engagement in the economy has been more heated as the African Continental Free Trade Area has come into effect and as good governance has become more prevalent. The combined effects of political, economic, and institutional governance, as well as economic integration, on female economic participation in sub-Saharan Africa, were examined by Ofori et al. in (2021). They concluded that a single effect of economic integration on female economic participation is necessary but insufficient. As a result, increasing female economic involvement in sub-Saharan Africa by combining economic integration with excellent governance. According to Ofori et al. (2021), policymakers should be concerned about the combined effects of economic integration and good governance to promote female economic inclusion. With this history and background in mind, the current chapter aims to define economic inclusion and evaluate how programs for it are impacting the poor in post-independence Africa.

2.2 What Is Economic Inclusion?

An inclusive market economy ensures that everyone has full and equitable access to employment opportunities, financial services, enterprise development, and, more commonly, economic opportunity, regardless of their gender, country of birth, family background, age, or other circumstances over which they have no control. Economic inclusion, or providing greater opportunities to poorly served socioeconomic groups, is vital to guarantee an economically efficient market economy transition (Lagarde, 2014; Lawal et al., 2021). The promotion of an equitable market-based system is therefore about effective (human) resource allocation instead of being a social policy choice. As a result, inclusiveness is a crucial element of a long-term market system. Economic inclusion is therefore a vital transition characteristic because it encourages people to engage in activities that promote economic growth, such as employment, education, and other pursuits if they are given the opportunities to improve (Lawal et al., 2021).

The State of Economic Inclusion 2021 report defines economic inclusion as the continuous integration of people and households into larger overall social and economic development practices, through tackling numerous limitations or institutional impediments encountered by the poor at various levels in the household, such as human and physical capacity; the community, such as social norms; the local economy, such as direct connections to markets and services; and institutional frameworks. According to structuralist viewpoints, economic inclusion involves more than simply participating in global economic systems; it also refers to sharing the advantages of the global economy.

They also make the argument that involvement in the global economy might increase employment rather than contribute to a decrease in it. Contrary to the popular assumption, involvement in the global economy through employment is the road to reducing poverty or advancing society, but the conditions of this inclusion can cause and perpetuate poverty for a substantial fraction of the labor force worldwide. The crucial query concerns the socioeconomic and power dynamics that those connections entail, not whether there are ties to the global economy.

2.2.1 Economic Inclusion Literature

Literature on economic inclusion in Africa has been gradually increasing over the years. Various scholars attempted to investigate economic inclusion from various perspectives producing various conclusions in the process. The impact of ICT on gender economic inclusion through channels for gender parity in education was examined by Asongu et al. in 2021a, b, using information from 49 sub-Saharan African countries for the years 2004 to 2018, broken down into 42 countries for the years 2004 to 2014 and 49 countries for the years 2008 to 2018. According to Asongu et al. (2021a, b), the secondary education channel should aim for ICT penetration levels of 165 mobile phones per 100 people, 21.471 Internet subscriptions per 100 people, and 3.475 fixed broadband subscriptions per 100 people to increase female labor force participation.

Again, Asongu et al. (2021a, b) found that the mechanism of higher education requires a 31.966 Internet penetration per 100 people thresholds for the same consequence of inducing a positive effect on female labor force participation. For the second sample, Asongu et al. (2021a, b) said that a mobile phone penetration threshold of 122.20 per 100 individuals is required for the higher education channel to have a positive impact on female labor force participation. The impact of environmental degradation on female economic inclusion was studied by Langnel et al. in 2021. A panel of 22 sub-Saharan African nations was analyzed using generalized least squares (GLS) and the instrumental variable approach in two-stage least squares. According to Langnel et al. (2021), environmental degradation disproportionately affects women's involvement in the labor market. Langnel et al. (2021) also argued that policies intended to reduce environmental pollution should also include steps to address gender exclusion, because doing so will not only lessen environmental vulnerability but will also open doors for women's empowerment in precarious circumstances. This emphasis has the potential to help sub-Saharan Africa achieve sustainable development goal number five of the SDGs.

For gender-inclusive education to increase gender-inclusive formal economic participation in sub-Saharan Africa, Asongu and Odhiambo (2020a, b, c) outlined the thresholds of inequality that should not be exceeded. Asongu and Odhiambo (2020a, b, c) discovered that while an inclusive tertiary education improves female economic inclusion, its relationship with inequality has the opposite effect. In addition, Asongu and Odhiambo (2020a, b, c) found that a Gini coefficient of 0.562 cancels out the positive incidence of inclusive tertiary education on female labor force participation and that a Gini coefficient and Palma ratio of 0.547 and 6.118, respectively, crowd out the unavoidable negative effects of inclusive tertiary education on female unemployment.

Again, Asongu and Odhiambo (2020a, b, c) found that a 6.557 Palma ratio, a 0.680 Atkinson index, and a 0.578 Gini coefficient are critical masses that negate the favorable, unconditional impacts of inclusive tertiary education on female employment. Meagher et al. (2016) examined the shift in global demand for African workers from formal to increasingly informalized labor arrangements, mediated by social enterprises, labor brokers, and graduate entrepreneurs, to refute recent claims that African workers have become functionally irrelevant to the global economy. Again, Meagher et al. (2016) examined why global labor linkages tend to increase rather than reduce problems of vulnerable and unstable working conditions within African countries and the economic and political conditions necessary for African workers to benefit from inclusion in the global economy. They focused on global employment connections initiated from above and from below.

In another study, from 2000 to 2018, Asongu et al. (2021a, b) investigated whether female economic inclusion improves tax performance in a sample of 48 sub-Saharan African nations. Three tax performance metrics were employed total taxes excluding social contributions reported taxes generated from natural resources, and total non-resource taxes as well as three measures of female inclusion female employment, female labor force participation, and female employment employed. According to Asongu et al. (2021a, b), the increase in female employment in the sector had a net negative impact on the total tax income but a net positive impact on non-resource taxes. Policymakers should supplement female economic inclusion with other economic measures aimed at enhancing tax performance in sub-Saharan Africa, according to the research by Asongu et al. (2021a, b). Through a strategy that ensures an equal potential for income creation, Reindl and Tyran (2021) conducted an experimental study to examine how income redistribution affects support for economic inclusion. Once more, Reindl and Tyran (2021) investigated a situation in which individuals with low endowments are barred from investment possibilities, unless people who have big endowments transfer funds to those individuals.

According to Reindl and Tyran's research (2021), support for economic inclusion is higher among respondents with significant endowments when income redistribution is expected to occur in the future as opposed to when it is purposefully prohibited. Again, Reindl and Tyran (2021) found that income redistribution spreads investment risks and rewards across the community, leading to a higher percentage of profitable investments. This possibility tends to encourage support for economic inclusion. Thus, income redistribution promotes public support for economic inclusion, leading to more equitable and effective outcomes. Additionally, Andrews et al. (2021) discovered that 219 economic inclusion initiatives targeted at extremely poor and vulnerable populations had been put into practice in at least 75 nations.

Economic inclusion programs, according to Andrews et al. (2021), are a collection of coordinated, multifaceted initiatives that aid people, households, and communities in their efforts to enhance their incomes and assets. Governments drive program scale-up, covering 93% of program users, according to Andrews et al. (2021), which has significant implications for design and implementation. According to Andrews et al. (2021), approximately 90% of the programs surveyed had a gender focus, demonstrating that women's economic empowerment remains a fundamental component of program design. According to Andrews et al. (2021), improving integrated responses linking the individual and household components of economic inclusion programs to larger community and local economy processes is necessary to unlock the productive potential of the extremely poor and vulnerable. Adapting to shifting poverty contexts and megatrends is also becoming increasingly important.

The COVID-19 pandemic, according to Berdibekov et al. (2021), has a considerable impact on the unemployment rate in the United States, and not every household experiences the same economic impact across states. To comprehend the evolving relationship between the coronavirus pandemic, rates of economic inclusion, and local economic well-being, Berdibekov et al. (2021) aimed to summarize the relationships between pandemic incidence, economic inclusion, unemployment, and bank branch closures. The predictive value of coronavirus incidence and mortality rates, county-level unemployment, and bank branch closure rates on rates of economic inclusion was also assessed by Berdibekov et al. (2021) using machine learning algorithms. Additionally, the textual data from the COVID-19 unemployment survey is analyzed using a natural language processing method. In response to the COVID-19 pandemic, Berdibekov et al. (2021) showed that economic inclusion programs for the poorest people exhibit significant promise as a component of integrated policy responses aimed at stopping the epidemic, ensuring food security, and fostering medium-term recovery.

According to Berdibekov et al. (2021), full-time workers experienced unemployment or underemployment, which exacerbated existing gender disparities and further marginalized people with disabilities. The negative effects on employment, particularly in the informal sector, were far-reaching and unprecedented. According to Berdibekov et al. (2021), those who are poor and vulnerable frequently face higher health risks, which are exacerbated by their inability to adhere to social distance norms in densely populated informal settlements and their lack of financial means to get testing and treatment.

In addition, Asongu and Odhiambo (2020a, b, c) examined how ICT modifies the impact of inequality on female economic participation in 42 sub-Saharan African nations between 2004 and 2014. The three inequality metrics employed by Asongu and Odhiambo (2020a, b, c) are the Gini coefficient, the Atkinson index, and the Palma ratio. The study by Asongu and Odhiambo (2020a, b, c) employed mobile phone penetration, Internet penetration, and fixed broadband subscriptions as their ICT indicators. Additionally, three variables of gender economic inclusion female labor force participation, female unemployment, and female employment were employed in the analysis. The study found that for female labor force participation, a minimum threshold of 165.714 mobile phone penetration per 100 people is required for the Palma ratio. This finding was made using the generalized method of moments. The study concluded that ICT must be improved beyond certain thresholds for it to mitigate inequality and improve gender economic participation. According to McHenry et al. (2017), financial technology, such as peer-to-peer lending, mobile insurance, and mobile money services, is promised to help the underbanked and unbanked achieve economic inclusion. Online financial services do, however, need an Internet connection, adoption, and digital literacy, according to McHenry et al.'s (2017) research. McHenry et al. (2017) found that fintech adoption, Internet access, and training in digital literacy may all be necessary to successfully increase financial inclusion and economic inclusion in the United States.

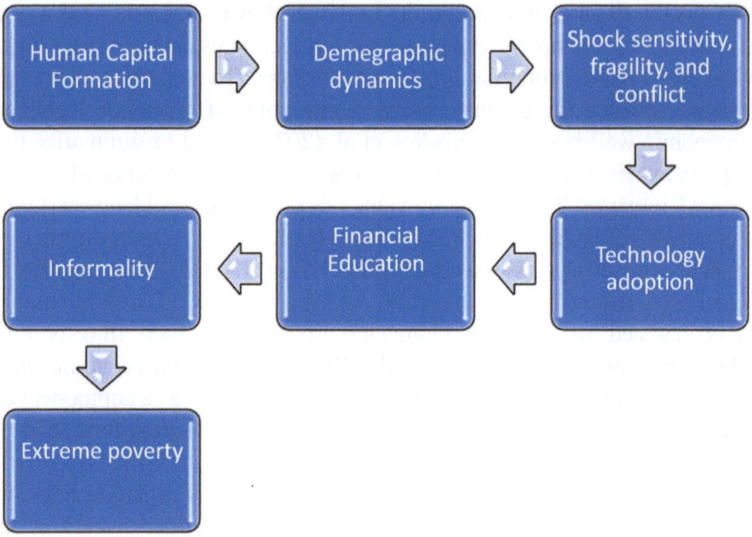

Fig. 2.1 Megatrends driving the future direction of economic inclusion at the country level. (*Source*: Authors)

2.2.2 The Drivers of Change That Will Shape Africa's Economic Inclusion

The structural alterations that are long term in character and have far-reaching effects on economies and societies at large are referred to as megatrends. The design and implementation of national plans for economic inclusion, particularly in Africa and other places where economies are developing, are greatly impacted by these megatrends. These major themes are depicted in Fig. 2.1 as extreme poverty, informality, shock sensitivity, demographic dynamics, and human capital formation.

In Fig. 2.1, the megatrends are outlined which include the following: human capital formation, demographic dynamics, shock sensitivity, technology adoption, Informality, and extreme poverty.

2.2.3 Human Capital Formation

From an economic perspective, capital is defined as "factors of production used to create commodities or services that are not themselves largely consumed in the production process" (Boldizzoni, 2008). In general, the term "human capital" refers to a combination of the words "human" and "capital". The person in charge of all economic activities, including production, consumption, and transactions, is referred to as a "human" in this context. Human capital can be inferred from the concept clarification that came before it, since it is one of the production elements that can produce added values by input. Inadequacies in children's health and education now have a significant impact on national economies and the productivity of the following generation of employees, according to Andrews et al. (2021).

According to Gatti et al. (2018), a child who is born in a nation with education and health levels that are at the 25th percentile globally will be just 43% as productive as a child who has access to both by the time they are adults. Evidence demonstrates the tight relationship between economic inclusion and human capital, which has significant effects across generations (Andrews et al., 2021). Because beneficiaries are then more capable of exercising agency, accessing, and processing information and taking risks with productive investments, it is thought that improved human capital can amplify the impact of economic inclusion initiatives on salaries and productivity (Robles, 2014). Once again, economic inclusion involvement can increase a beneficiary's skills, agency, and networks, while profits can be used to invest in both their own and their family's human capital (Andrews et al., 2021). Accumulated money might also help prevent unhealthy coping strategies during times of crisis by, for example, enabling children to stay in school and meet household health and nutrition needs (Andrews et al., 2021).

The effect of entrepreneurial human capital on youth economic inclusion through agripreneurship was studied by Lawal et al. (2021). The findings showed that agripreneurship has a considerable favorable impact on young people's economic inclusion, through both entrepreneurial administration and accounting abilities. A people-centered approach to economic development, according to Crawford-Lee and Hunter (2009), is crucial to opening development paths, because it acknowledges that ideas, information, and knowledge are what fuel success in a global economy. According to Crawford-Lee and Hunter (2009), local communities with a strong, adequately skilled human capital base are best positioned to use knowledge and convert it into cutting-edge manufacturing methods for goods and services. In a networked, knowledge-driven, global economy, investing in people's knowledge and skills is therefore essential to attaining continuous economic growth.

2.2.4 Population Dynamics

We are currently experiencing an unprecedented period of population increase, as evidenced by the fact that the world's population has more than quadrupled since the middle of the twentieth century and will reach approximately 8 billion by 2022. (Wilmoth et al., 2022). Although the rate of global expansion has slowed significantly since roughly 1970 and is predicted to stabilize by the end of the century, the UN forecasts indicate that the number of the world's population might increase to almost 11 billion by around 2050. (Wilmoth et al., 2022). It is thought that two trends, on the one hand, the gradual rise in average human longevity because of widespread advancements in "public health, nutrition, personal hygiene, and medicine, and on the other hand, the persistence of high fertility levels" in many countries, are the causes of the unprecedented growth of the global population that has taken place since 1950.

According to Andrews et al. (2021), the world's population will nearly double by 2050 in sub-Saharan Africa due to its higher fertility rate, while Eastern and Southeastern Asia would have a modest 3 percent growth. This compares to the world's population in 2019 of about 7.7 billion. The difficulty of guaranteeing inclusive and sustainable development in the future may be made more difficult by rapid population growth. Investments in education and health can greatly improve the favorable but transient economic impact of a favorable age distribution produced by a persistent reduction in fertility in nations with currently high birth rates. The disproportionate number of women, children, and rural residents who live in extreme poverty, as well as the ageing of the world's population, provides issues, according to Andrews et al. (2021). By the year 2050, it is predicted that there will be more than 1.5 billion individuals over the age of 65, with the least-developed countries experiencing the highest growth (United Nations, 2020). Given all of this, Wilmoth et al. (2022) stated that persistent, rapid population growth makes it more difficult to achieve social and economic progress and increases the amount of money and work needed to make sure that no one is left behind.

Once more, the population growth is making it more difficult for low-income and lower-middle-income countries to afford the increase in public spending per person that is required to end poverty, end hunger and malnutrition, and guarantee everyone has access to health care, education, and other essential services (Bowlus et al., 2022). Due to resource constraints, the eventual effect will be the widespread marginalization of disadvantaged populations. According to Wilmoth et al. (2022), millions of people around the world, primarily in low- and lower-middle-income countries, do not have access to the knowledge and resources required to decide whether to have children. In comparison to women without education living in the same country, it is thought that women with higher levels of education tend to have greater liberty to make these decisions (Labrague et al., 2019; Wulandari & Laksono, 2020). Additionally, academics asserted that allowing people, particularly women, to choose when and how many children they will have can significantly increase well-being and assist to break intergenerational cycles of poverty that exclude many generations (Kennedy et al., 2018; Shlafer et al., 2019; Annan et al., 2021). More people having access to high-quality reproductive healthcare, including safe and effective family planning technologies, may assist to reduce fertility and hasten economic, social, and economic inclusion.

2.2.5 Conflict, Fragility, and Shock Sensitivity

Programming for economic inclusion cannot be separated from the whims of vulnerability and external shocks, claim Andrews et al. (2021). Different sorts of shocks, such as economic shocks as well as underlying fragility brought on by conflict or climate change, will also influence the direction and nature of economic inclusion programs. In 2015, 54% of people living in unstable and conflict-affected areas were in sub-Saharan Africa, according to the World Bank (2018). The World Bank (2018) continued to make the case that while the share of the world's poor who live in fragile and conflict-affected situations has steadily increased since 2010, making up 23.2 percent of the world's extreme poor, while extreme poverty in fragile and conflict-affected economies declined sharply between 2005 and 2011, the poverty rate has since stagnated.

According to Dempster et al. (2020), there will be more doubt about refugees' economic integration as refugee-hosting countries deal with an impending economic downturn, growing unemployment, and rising xenophobia. The other difficulty is that refugees in low- and middle-income nations are more susceptible to the effects on the economy. One clear result is the necessity of adapting program design in the context of dynamic, short- and medium-term needs, in addition to program adaptability and flexibility to absorb shocks. Dempster et al. (2020), for instance, noted that before COVID-19, we find that refugees are 60% more likely than host populations to be employed in highly impacted sectors, such as accommodation and food services, manufacturing, and retail, placing them at risk of widespread loss of livelihoods and an increase in poverty among refugee populations. The effects of shocks, fragility, and conflict on economic inclusion are being made clearer by this knowledge.

2.2.6 *Acceptance of Technology*

The quick acceptance of technogy and the rising use of mobile phones, which allow individuals in developing nations to become more connected, are proving to be a huge opportunity for economic inclusion. Over 50% of the world's population has access to broadband Internet, and there are more mobile phone subscribers than people, according to the International Telecommunication Union (2018). According to the Global System for Mobile Communications Association (GSMA) (2019), there are currently more than 1 billion active mobile money accounts worldwide, which is promoting economic and financial inclusion. The International Telecommunication Union (2019) emphasized that while such quick technological advancement can lead to beneficial change, it can also worsen already-existing inequities and introduce new vulnerabilities, which can exclude many individuals from the mainstream economy. According to Andrews et al. (2021), it is also critical to remember that there is still a digital divide, because most of the world's population who make up half lives in underdeveloped nations and is increasingly made up of women. However, it is crucial to remember that embracing technology can truly ensure that economic inclusion is achieved.

2.2.7 *Using Safety Net Initiatives in the Social Sector*

According to Andrews et al. (2021), the continual supply of social safety nets and the inclusion of recipients into a social protection system has the potential to completely alter how economic inclusion initiatives are developed. Once more, the ongoing provision of social safety nets denotes a change from one-time and time-limited interventions to a more regularized system of assistance with the possibility of follow-up interventions. Additionally, this may alter perceptions of the viability and long-term effects of such programs (Andrews et al., 2021; Rice et al., 2020). The terminology "safety nets plus" or "cash-plus" is becoming more popular as governments broaden the scope and funding of social safety net programs, particularly cash transfers when cash is supplemented with extra inputs, service components, or ties to outside services. The social safety nets plus the agenda's primary driver are economic inclusion, which holds great promise to maximizing effects on incomes and productivity (Beegle et al., 2018; Christian et al., 2019; Andrews et al., 2021).

2.2.8 *Financial Literacy*

With financial services becoming the fastest-growing industry and significantly influencing economies in recent decades, governments and institutions have begun focusing on financial literacy and financial inclusion to target inclusive economic growth, which has resulted in a large body of research on the topic (Kaur & Verma, 2022). By providing adequate and formal access to financial products and services, Kazemikhasragh and Buoni Pineda (2022) noted that financial inclusion and education are strategies for creating programs that aim to close the gender gap in financial services. Financial inclusion also provides guidance and training to help people develop their financial skills and obtain financial independence. According to Mhlanga (2020), current financial, technological, demographic, and economic trends have led to an increased emphasis on the value of financial literacy and education. To improve people's financial situation, it is crucial in developing nations to raise financial literacy. This will help people become more aware of the financial services and products as well as the risks to which they are exposed. Financial decision-making requires a combination of financial behavior, knowledge, and attitude to attain financial well-being for individuals (Organisation for Economic Co-operation and Development, 2006; Lusardi, 2019).

Not only for investors but also for the normal family attempting to decide how to balance its budget, buy a home, pay for the children's education, and provide an income when the parents retire, financial literacy is becoming increasingly crucial. The pension issue is especially crucial because as life expectancy rises, people will be able to enjoy retirement for longer periods. If people lack financial literacy, they won't be able to select the best savings or investments for themselves and may be vulnerable to fraud. Financial literacy will encourage people to save more money and push financial service providers to create products that truly meet their needs, which should have a positive impact on investment levels, economic growth, and economic inclusion (Organisation for Economic Co-operation and Development, 2006; Lusardi, 2019).

According to Robles (2014), economic education is encouraged to improve the financial stability of families. Financial capabilities are denied as resilient behaviors that reflect making ends meet, planning for both the present and the future, and asset building connected to economic mobility aspirations short-run and long-run goal setting as well as entrepreneurial activities. Financial education that involves information gathering can take place in a variety of settings and is often most successful when the entire family is involved. It can even happen at cultural festivals and celebrations (Robles, 2014; Nurbekyan & Hovanessian, 2018).

2.2.9 *Informality*

According to the World Bank (2020), the informal sector accounts for 80.8 percent of jobs in Africa to become the main source of employment and the backbone of economic activity notably in metropolitan Africa. According to the World Bank, street sellers play a crucial role in providing food security, people working in the transportation industry keep the city and the economy moving, and the informal sector is vibrant and hard to miss in African cities. According to the World Bank (2020), the urban informal economy is a significant factor in reducing poverty and is especially prevalent among young people, accounting for 95.8 percent of those aged 15–24, and women, accounting for 92.1 percent. Economic inclusion programs, particularly for young people in metropolitan areas, should adapt to the reality of informality, according to Andrews et al. (2021). With some self-employment interventions having broad inclusion targets and others specifically looking for high-potential entrepreneurs, economic inclusion program approaches should differ.

The importance of urban market links is becoming more apparent, even though economic inclusion programs have a strong rural focus, because of the limited labor demand and rising informality in rural areas, as well as the rise in migration to urban centers, which presents both opportunities and challenges for the poorest. According to the World Bank (2020), while public sector primary consideration, initiatives seeking at formalizing micro- and small enterprises have never really proven successful, productivity gains will indeed assist informal businesses is gradually drawing closer to the formal economy while improving their workers' livelihoods.

The World Bank (2020) also stated that strategic partnerships with a financial inclusion focused on facilitating access to financing instruments tailored to the needs of the urban informal sector are one way to increase productivity. According to the International Monetary Fund (2019), the informal economy can give individuals in need money or a social safety net, but it is a complex issue, because poverty rates are often twice as high for those who work in the informal sector as they are for those who work in the official sector. Poor productivity, low salaries, and restricted access to government subsidies are the main causes. The International Monetary Fund (2019) reported that informality results in fewer tax revenues that impede the government's ability to invest in social programs and infrastructure, making it challenging for the people who need these services the most to access them.

2.2.10 Extreme Poverty and Economic Inclusion

Programs promoting economic inclusion are a crucial part of medium- and long-term recovery initiatives aimed at the poor and vulnerable (Dutta et al., 2020). However, Andrews et al. (2021) noted that a key claim of economic inclusion is that those who are poor and vulnerable and fall into poverty traps confront a variety of obstacles that call for a multifaceted response. While economic inclusion programs normally aim to address the various challenges that low-income households face, it is becoming more crucial for these initiatives to address challenges that go outside the home. These include basic variables including proximity to physical markets, regional market depth, accessibility to connective infrastructure, and production that limit chances for local economic growth. To reduce poverty that is dependent on geography and to give the extremely poor and vulnerable more opportunities to earn an income, it is crucial to develop connections to markets for inputs, labor, goods, and services.

The second significant issue is that there is an urgent interest in comprehending rural market dynamics and strategies to connect households to local, regional, and global markets, because many of the world's extremely poor reside in remote, rural areas with little access to markets. A thriving rural sector requires stakeholders to prioritize small rural producers, resilience development, and the improvement of the economic and productive ability of the rural poor in addition to supporting successful markets (FAO, 2018). According to Andrews et al. (2021), it is crucial to strengthen communication and negotiation with informal workers, producers, and entrepreneurs. It is also crucial to handle the opportunities and problems that migration and rural development present to build a vibrant rural sector. By improving and diversifying rural employment options, particularly for women and young people, assisting the poor in better risk management, and utilizing remittances for investments in the rural sector, rural households and communities may maximize the benefits of migration. The permanence of poverty and the poverty traps that the poor must overcome should be acknowledged in any effort to improve economic inclusion.

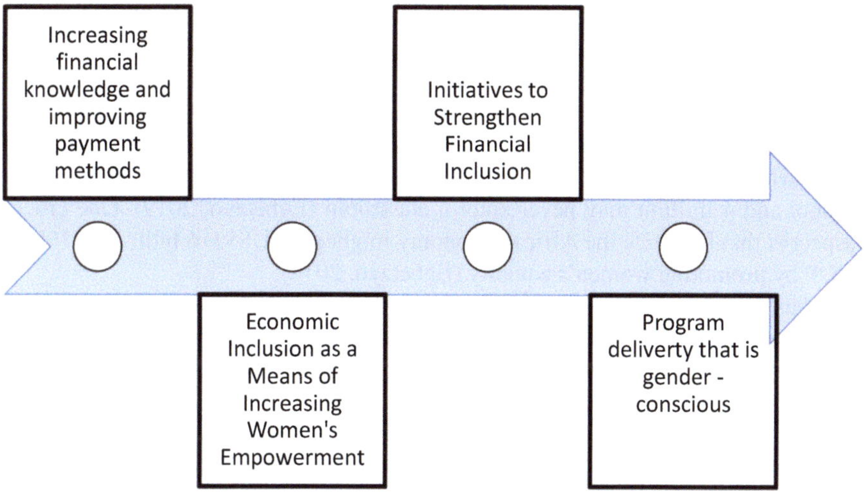

Fig. 2.2 How to Make Economic Inclusion Work in Africa. (*Source*: Authors)

2.3 How to Make Economic Inclusion Work in Africa?

The United Nations' notion of Sustainable Development Goals, according to Dörffel and Schuhmann (2022), is perhaps the most acknowledged global policy framework for considering the issue of inclusive development (SDGs). These objectives are thought to offer a comprehensive collection of concepts, objectives, and indicators for igniting international action in favor of development that produces more equitable and sustainable results. However, Dörffel and Schuhmann (2022) think that they cover a wide range, from environmental sustainability to poverty alleviation, while precise policy options are still largely undefined. One advantage of the SDGs is that they put several development goals that had not before received this focus on the political agenda. Several strategies that can aid in enhancing economic inclusion in Africa are presented in this study in Fig. 2.2.

In Fig. 2.2, the initiatives that can help to improve economic inclusion in Africa are specified; these include, "the promotion of more and better jobs and livelihoods, increasing financial knowledge and improving payment methods, Economic Inclusion as a Means of Increasing Women's Empowerment, Initiatives to Strengthen Financial Inclusion and Program delivery that is gender conscious".

2.4 Program Execution That Is Gender Sensitive

According to Egbetayo (2019), there is a US$42 billion funding gap between men and women in Africa, and 70% of women are financially excluded. The fact that women perform 60% of the work performed internationally yet only receive 10% of income and 1% of the property is another troubling development. Africa's gender parity is projected to be 0.58, with 1 being full parity, according to McKinsey's Power of Parity Report, Advancing Women's Equality in Africa. Without taking extreme measures, it might take the continent 140 years to achieve full parity, according to Egbetayo (2019). It is vital to close the gender gap for women and girls worldwide, but especially in Africa, where millions of girls are not currently in school and 4 million may never enter a classroom (Egbetayo, 2019). One crucial aspect is that by 2025, the African economy might gain US$316 billion by 10% in GDP by promoting women's equality (Egbetayo, 2019).

Many academics think it's critical to make it simpler for women to engage in programs by offering elements in a way that meets the unique challenges they encounter (Malhotra & Schuler, 2005; Nomaguchi & Milkie, 2020; Rosca et al., 2020). Fourth place went to Andrews et al. (2021), who included several recommendations for how to make this happen, including a major increase in staff capacity at all levels and the support of leadership, particularly when done through already-existing government structures. Making women's empowerment a primary goal of a program also adds another level of complexity and training to help staff better handle gender issues, teach local staff to identify their own biases, and better understand how gender barriers interact with numerous different forms of prejudice premised on race, ethnic background, sexual preference, religious doctrine, and other aspects of identity. In some situations, cultural norms can make it challenging for women to communicate with male program employees, according to Andrews et al. (2021). The Girls' Education and Women's Empowerment and Livelihoods (GEWEL) Project initiative in Zambia, for instance, is establishing a network of women volunteers in communities to provide life and business skills training and to coach recipients, eliminating the need for travel.

The methods for payments and delivery, which should be strengthened, are another crucial factor. Researchers think that e-coaching, access to digital financial services, and digitalization of transfers may make it simpler for women to access services and content from home, alleviating time, and mobility restrictions (Mariscal et al., 2018; Francis et al., 2019; Andrews et al., 2021). According to Andrews et al. (2021), program components must consider the fact that women are less likely to own and have access to important possessions like phones and bicycles. For instance, to better assist women, the GEWEL program in Zambia is modifying how program components are delivered. It has created a special payment system to distribute the grants, and women can select the one that works best for them.

Digital financial services, according to Wendy et al. (2019), can promote women's financial inclusion in settings where women have access to phones, but bank accounts are still frequently held by men. Digital transfers offer confidentiality, which may improve women's chances of controlling resources and reduce the chance that money will be misappropriated by other family members. The other component of economic inclusion is flexibility and childcare. For many women, childcare can limit their ability to participate in economic inclusion programs. Because of this, organizations working in Zambia, for example, modify how their programs are delivered to consider the needs of women by holding sessions close to beneficiaries' homes and allowing for flexible scheduling to maximize participation (Andrews et al., 2021).

2.5 Increasing Initiatives for Financial Inclusion

Financial inclusion, according to Andrews et al. (2021), can accelerate the expansion of economic inclusion. Direct access to financial services, such as credit, savings, insurance, and e-payments or mobile money, is a crucial starting point for increasing economic inclusion. The 1990s saw the emergence of microfinance organizations, which started providing small loans to individuals, families, and micro businesses as a means of escaping poverty. Since then, methods for promoting financial inclusion have seen significant evolution. A proliferation of financial services that show how goods other than loans may empower low-income individuals has adopted that strategy (Mhlanga, 2020, 2021; Pace et al., 2021; Anisa, 2021).

Recent advancements in technology and business models, such as pay-as-you-go asset finance and fintech, have reduced the cost of integrating excluded populations with the formal financial system (Mhlanga, 2020). Women can invest in the expansion and improvement of their enterprises as well as manage their income and savings when they have access to formal banking services and other financial institutions. Women might become less reliant on their husbands' income and less susceptible to their control when their wealth increases and they have the autonomy to decide where and how to spend their money (Holloway et al., 2017; Andrews et al., 2021). This independence can also include making decisions regarding marriage, leisure activities, and the use of contraceptives in addition to financial matters (Aker et al., 2016; Suri & Jack, 2016). As an illustration, consider the Boma Project in Kenya, which helps extremely impoverished women by forming business and savings groups and providing them with a digital financial product.

Participants had significant gains in their income and savings, which boosted their household's ability to make decisions and raised their spending on nutrition and education. However, Andrews et al. (2021) underlined that BOMA also found that impediments to the complete adoption of the digital product included illiteracy, innumeracy, and unfamiliarity with technology. The BOMA experience emphasizes the need for less complicated tools that are thoughtfully created for the target demographic, as well as for participants to have enough time to learn how to use them. Using the Child Grant model of the Social Cash Transfer program in Zambia, Pace et al. (2021) examined whether increasing exogenous income promoted economic inclusion among rural women. Economic inclusion was envisioned by Pace et al. (2021) as a process of transformation supported by four pillars: productive capability, financial inclusion, social power, and psychological assets.

Pace et al. (2021) discovered compelling evidence of the direct effects of the Child Grant on the productive ability, financial inclusion, and psychological assets of rural women. They did this using experimental data. Indicative evidence of indirect and mutually reinforcing links between changes in psychological assets brought about by the Child Grant and increases in beneficiaries' productive capacity and financial inclusion was also discovered by Pace et al. in 2021. According to Pace et al.'s (2021) findings, cash transfers may help women become more economically included, both directly through monetary effects and indirectly through the mediated effects of psychological assets. The expansion of government-to-person (G2P) payments also raises the key question of their ability to enhance financial services like microloans, savings, and local market information as well as the efficiency of fundamental cash transfer payments. It is thought that switching to electronic payments, for instance, can make it easier for those who were not previously banked to connect to the financial system.

Many nations, policymakers, and donors are looking into the possibility of utilizing social security payments as the "on-ramp" to get individuals into the formal banking system, especially when the payments are made to bank accounts or electronically, according to Andrews et al. (2021). For instance, the Better Than Cash Alliance advocates for the conversion of G2P payments from cash to electronic payments to promote ties between social protection and financial inclusion. For low-income individuals, electronic payment can open doors to a wider choice of financial services and is generally safer (particularly for women and girls) (Andrews et al., 2021).

2.6 Increasing Financial Literacy and Streamlining Payment Processes

Increasing financial literacy and improving payment systems are two crucial factors that can aid in enhancing economic inclusion in Africa, building on earlier ideas that financial inclusion can be used as a tool to increase economic inclusion. However, financial inclusion using savings groups, formal banking services, microcredit, government-to-person payments, and other methods has the potential to increase resilience and opportunities for the extremely poor and the vulnerable, particularly women. According to many scholars, numerous poor population sections tend to be excluded from financial services, including credit, savings, insurance, and e-payments or mobile money. As a result, nations are utilizing systems to send social protection transfers electronically or otherwise directly to bank accounts, providing a point of entry for people to enter the formal financial sector and a route to a wider range of financial products, including savings and credit.

Other academics contend that by utilizing cutting-edge technologies and business models like pay-as-you-go asset finance and fintech, digital services have reduced the cost of integrating disadvantaged groups into the formal financial system (Mhlanga, 2020, 2021; Mhlanga & Denhere, 2020). For digital G2P transfers to be successful, the literature suggests that several essential components must be in place, including "institutional arrangements and coordination between government agencies and the financial sector, a finance and banking regulatory framework to enable secure digital payments and mobile money options, mobile and broadband infrastructure, identification and robust know-your-customer criteria, and payment system interoperability" (Andrews et al., 2021; Ahn & Nam, 2022).

2.7 Fostering the Empowerment of Women

Women contribute significantly to the global economy, even in rural areas around the world, but they are subject to gender-specific barriers that reduce their productivity and ability to contribute to agricultural production, economic growth, and the welfare of their families and the community at large (Maunde et al., 2021). Most women, especially those living in rural areas, have less access to technical expertise and productive resources than men (Ndhlovu, 2020). As a result, increasing female empowerment has the potential to increase economic inclusion. Scholars argue that any progressive country should consider important concerns like gender equality and the economic empowerment of women to achieve sustainable development (Ndhlovu, 2022; Saeed, 2019). Higher female earnings are believed to have a significant positive impact on children's education and family health, which in turn affects a country's overall economic growth, according to academics and surveys. According to Saeed (2019), establishing women's economic empowerment is essential for addressing problems like gender inequality and poverty as well as promoting inclusive economic growth and participation. According to academics, women have a considerable impact on the economy through business, entrepreneurship, or unpaid labor (Ndhlovu, 2018, 2021).

While some women in developed nations play a significant role in making decisions and influencing others, gender discrimination persists as a crippling social problem throughout much of the world, particularly in Africa, where subordinate women are frequently alarmingly affected by poverty, discrimination, and other forms of vulnerable exploitation. Any developing country would agree that measures for gender inclusion are the key to social advancement and economic prosperity and that sustained economic growth is impossible without the empowerment of women (Cherayi & Jose, 2016; Panda, 2017; Siddik, 2017). Because working women significantly contribute to education, health, and wellness, they must work, and establishing gender equality is essential to the advancement of holistic development (Cherayi & Jose, 2016; Panda, 2017). Women need to have more job opportunities in Africa and be given leadership positions and decision-making responsibilities (Saeed, 2019; World Vision, 2022). All actions that can be taken to improve economic inclusion must prioritize the empowerment of women. Women's empowerment should be the cornerstone of all economic inclusion measures in Africa, in addition to the other ideas mentioned in the preceding sentences. Women's empowerment programs should make greater investments in the welfare and empowerment of women, empowering them to reject gender stereotypes and step outside of their customary positions.

2.8 Conclusion and Recommendations

A major global movement to enhance and expand economic participation for the poorest people has emerged in recent years, especially in Africa. The chapter employed document analysis to illustrate the drivers of change that will shape Africa's economic inclusion and several strategies that can aid in enhancing economic inclusion in Africa. The chapter discovered that megatrends are outlined, which include the following: human capital formation, demographic dynamics, shock sensitivity, technology adoption, informality, and extreme poverty. Again, the chapter identified initiatives that can help to improve economic inclusion in Africa, which include the promotion of more and better jobs and livelihoods, increasing financial knowledge and improving payment methods, economic inclusion as a means of increasing women's empowerment, initiatives to strengthen financial inclusion, and program delivery that is gender conscious. The chapter emphasized that all initiatives of economic inclusion in Africa should rest on women's empowerment among other proposals discussed in the earlier paragraphs. Women empowerment programmers should invest more in the welfare and empowerment of women, encouraging women to break free from their traditional roles and do away with gender stereotypes.

References

Ahn, S. Y., & Nam, Y. (2022). Does mobile payment use lead to overspending? The moderating role of financial knowledge. *Computers in Human Behavior, 134*, 107319.

Aker, J. C., Boumnijel, R., McClelland, A., & Tierney, N. (2016). Payment mechanisms and anti-poverty programs: Evidence from a Mobile money cash transfer experiment in Niger. *Economic Development and Cultural Change, 65*(1), 1–37.

Andrews, C., de Montesquiou, A., Sánchez, I. A., Dutta, P. V., Samaranayake, S., Heisey, J., et al. (2021). *The state of economic inclusion report 2021: The potential to scale*. World Bank Publications.

Anisa, N. (2021). *Fintech peer to peer lending as approach to encourage economic inclusion for rural communities in Indonesia*. ADB-IGF Special Working Paper Series "Fintech to Enable Development, Investment, Financial Inclusion, and Sustainability.

Annan, J., Donald, A., Goldstein, M., Martinez, P. G., & Koolwal, G. (2021). Taking power: women's empowerment and household well-being in Sub-Saharan Africa. *World Development, 140*, 105292.

Asongu, S. A., & Odhiambo, N. M. (2020a). Inequality and gender inclusion: Minimum ICT policy thresholds for promoting female employment in Sub-Saharan Africa. *Telecommunications Policy, 44*(4), 101900.

Asongu, S. A., & Odhiambo, N. M. (2020b). Inequality thresholds, governance and gender economic inclusion in sub-Saharan Africa. *International Review of Applied Economics, 34*(1), 94–114.

Asongu, S., & Odhiambo, N. (2020c). Thresholds of income inequality that mitigate the role of gender-inclusive education in promoting gender economic inclusion in Sub-Saharan Africa. *Social Responsibility Journal, 17*, 106.

Asongu, S. A., Nnanna, J., & Acha-Anyi, P. N. (2020). Inequality and gender economic inclusion: The moderating role of financial access in Sub-Saharan Africa. *Economic Analysis and Policy, 65*, 173–185.
Asongu, S. A., Adegboye, A., & Nnanna, J. (2021a). Promoting female economic inclusion for tax performance in Sub-Saharan Africa. *Economic Analysis and Policy, 69*, 159–170.
Asongu, S. A., Amankwah-Amoah, J., Nting, R. T., & Afrifa, G. A. (2021b). Information technology and gender economic inclusion in sub-Saharan Africa. *Journal of Global Information Technology Management, 24*(2), 120–133.
Beegle, K., Honorati, M., & Monsalve, E. (2018). Reaching the poor and vulnerable in Africa through social safety nets. In *Realizing the full potential of social safety nets in Africa* (pp. 49–86).
Berdibekov, T., Pasnoor, P. R., Annamaneni, A. R., & Ceesay, E. N. (2021, April). Economic inclusion in the United States: Predictive analysis of COVID-19 pandemic on county rates of unbanked households. In *2021 IEEE international IoT, electronics and mechatronics conference (IEMTRONICS)* (pp. 1–6). IEEE.
Boldizzoni, F. (2008). Means and ends. The idea of Capital in the West. New Your: Palgrave Macmillan, 8.
Bowlus, A., Park, Y., & Robinson, C. (2022). Contribution of human capital accumulation to Canadian economic growth (No. 2022-7).
Cherayi, S., & Jose, J. P. (2016). Empowerment and social inclusion of Muslim women: Towards a new conceptual model. *Journal of Rural Studies, 45*, 243–251.
Christian, P., Kandpal, E., Palaniswamy, N., & Rao, V. (2019). Safety nets and natural disaster mitigation: Evidence from cyclone Phailin in Odisha. *Climatic Change, 153*(1), 141–164.
Crawford-Lee, M., & Hunter, P. (2009). A people-centred approach to economic development (PCED): Brokering economic inclusion as a route way to improving competitiveness. *Local Economy, 24*(6–7), 473–486.
Dempster, H., Ginn, T., Graham, J., Ble, M. G., Jayasinghe, D., & Shorey, B. (2020). *Locked down and left behind: The impact of COVID-19 on refugees' economic inclusion*. Center for Global Development, Refugees International, and International Rescue Committee.
Dörffel, C., & Schuhmann, S. (2022). What is inclusive development? Introducing the multidimensional inclusiveness index. *Social Indicators Research, 162*, 1–32.
Dutta, J., Andrews, C., de Montesquiou, A., Clay, T., & Chaudhary, S. (2020). *Economic inclusion for the poorest and COVID-19: Adaptation and early priorities for medium-and longer-term recovery*. Partnership for Economic Inclusion World Bank.
Egbetayo, V. (2019). *One of the greatest threats to Africa's future: gender inequality*.
FAO (Food and Agriculture Organization of the United Nations). (2018). *FAO and Cash+: How to maximize the impacts of cash transfers*.
Francis, D. A., Brown, A., McAllister, J., Mosime, S. T., Thani, G. T., Reygan, F., et al. (2019). A five-country study of gender and sexuality diversity and schooling in Southern Africa. *Africa Education Review, 16*(1), 19–39.
Gatti, R. V., Kraay, A. C., Avitabile, C., Collin, M. E., Dsouza, R., & Dehnen, N. A. P. (2018). *The human capital project*. World Bank. http://documents.worldbank.org/curated/en/363661540826242921/The-Human-Capital-Project
GSMA. (2019). State of the industry report on mobile money. London: GSMA. Haushofer, Johannes, and Ernst Fehr. 2014. "On the psychology of poverty". *Science, 344*(6186), 862–867. https://doi.org/10.1126/science.1232491
Holloway, K., Niazi, Z., & Rouse, R. (2017). *Women's economic empowerment through Education https://www.oecd.org/finance/financial-education/37087833.pdf*
International Monetary Fund. (2019). The informal economy and inclusive growth. https://www.imf.org/en/News/Articles/2019/11/14/sp111419-the-informal-economy-and-inclusive-growth
International Telecommunication Union. (2018). *Measuring the information society report* (Vol. 1). ITU.
International Telecommunication Union. (2019). *Measuring digital development: Facts & figures* 2019. https://www.itu.int/hub/2020/05/measuring-digital-development-facts-figures-2019/

Kaur, A., & Verma, R. (2022). Financial literacy and financial inclusion: A systematic literature review. *ECS Transactions, 107*(1), 9893.

Kazemikhasragh, A., & Buoni Pineda, M. V. (2022). Financial inclusion and education: An empirical study of financial inclusion in the face of the pandemic emergency due to Covid-19 in Latin America and the Caribbean. *Review of Development Economics, 26*, 1785.

Kennedy, H. P., Cheyney, M., Dahlen, H. G., Downe, S., Foureur, M. J., Homer, C. S., et al. (2018). Asking different questions: A call to action for research to improve the quality of care for every woman, every child. *Birth, 45*(3), 222–231.

Labrague, L. J., McEnroe-Petitte, D. M., & Tsaras, K. (2019). Predictors and outcomes of nurse professional autonomy: A cross-sectional study. *International Journal of Nursing Practice, 25*(1), e12711.

Lagarde, C. (2014). Economic inclusion and financial integrity. In *Economic inclusion and financial integrity*. International Monetary Fund.

Langnel, Z., Amegavi, G. B., & Agomor, K. S. (2021). Environmental degradation and female economic inclusion in sub-Saharan Africa: Effort towards sustainable development goal 5. *Development Southern Africa, 38*(5), 717–730.

Lawal, N. A., Adebayo, J. O., Ojokuku, R. M., & Oladejo, K. S. (2021). *Impact of entrepreneurial human capital on youth economic inclusion through Agripreneurship in Osun state*.

Lusardi, A. (2019). Financial literacy and the need for financial education: Evidence and implications. *Swiss Journal of Economics and Statistics, 155*(1), 1–8.

Malhotra, A., & Schuler, S. R. (2005). Women's empowerment as a variable in international development. *Measuring Empowerment: Cross-disciplinary Perspectives, 1*(1), 71–88.

Mariscal, J., Mayne, G., Aneja, U., & Sorgner, A. (2018). *Bridging the gender digital gap. Economics Discussion* Papers, No 2018–60. Kiel Institute for the World Economy. http://www.economicsjournal.org/economics/discussion papers/2018-60

Maunde, R. M., Lyimo-Macha, J. G., & Jeckoniah, J. N. (2021). The contribution of improved chicken strains in promoting women empowerment in Bariadi and Muheza Districts, Tanzania. *Tanzania Journal of Agricultural Sciences, 20*(1), 94–100.

McHenry, G., Goldberg, R. M., Lewis, M., Carlson, E., & Mehta, I. (2017). *Digital and economic inclusion: How Internet adoption impacts banking status*. Available at SSRN 2944394.

Meagher, K., Mann, L., & Bolt, M. (2016). Introduction: Global economic inclusion and African workers. *The Journal of Development Studies, 52*(4), 471–482.

Mhlanga, D. (2020). Industry 4.0 in finance: The impact of artificial intelligence (ai) on digital financial inclusion. *International Journal of Financial Studies, 8*(3), 45.

Mhlanga, D. (2021). Financial inclusion in emerging economies: The application of machine learning and artificial intelligence in credit risk assessment. *International Journal of Financial Studies, 9*(3), 39.

Mhlanga, D., & Denhere, V. (2020). Determinants of financial inclusion in Southern Africa. *Studia Universitatis Babes-Bolyai, Oeconomica, 65*(3), 39.

Ndhlovu, E. (2018). Relevance of sustainable livelihood approach in Zimbabwe's land reform programme. *Africa Insight, 47*(4), 72–87.

Ndhlovu, E. (2020). Land acquisitions and relocations of the Shangane in Zimbabwe: Disintegratory or transformative? *Africa Insight, 49*(4), 55–71.

Ndhlovu, E. (2021). The land question in Africa: Sam's perspectives. In V. T. Gumede & T. Shonhe (Eds.), *Rethinking the land and agrarian questions in Africa*. Africa Century Editions Press.

Ndhlovu, E. (2022). Socio-economic characterisation of resettled smallholder farmers in rural Zimbabwe. *Journal of Asian and African Studies, 57*(8), 1495–1510.

Nomaguchi, K., & Milkie, M. A. (2020). Parenthood and well-being: A decade in review. *Journal of Marriage and Family, 82*(1), 198–223.

Nurbekyan, A., & Hovanessian, N. (2018). *Financial inclusion, regulation, financial literacy, and financial education in Armenia*.

Ofori, P. E., Asongu, S., & Tchamyou, V. (2021). *The synergy between governance and economic integration in promoting female economic inclusion in sub-Saharan Africa* (No. WP/21/071). AGDI Working Paper.

Organisation For Economic Co-Operation And Development. (2006). *The importance of financial.*

Pace, N., Silvio, D., Francesca, V., & Nicholas, S. (2021). *Cash transfers and women's economic inclusion.*

Panda, P. K. (2017). Inclusion and economic empowerment of rural-tribal women in lac value chain and market: A case study of Udyogini. *Journal of Social and Economic Development, 19*(1), 25–41.

Reindl, I., & Tyran, J. R. (2021). Equal opportunities for all? How income redistribution promotes support for economic inclusion. *Journal of Economic Behavior & Organization, 190*, 390–407.

Rice, S., O'Bree, B., Wilson, M., McEnery, C., Lim, M. H., Hamilton, M., et al. (2020). Leveraging the social network for the treatment of social anxiety: A pilot study of a youth-specific digital intervention with a focus on the engagement of young men. *Internet Interventions, 20*, 100323.

Robles, B. J. (2014). Economic inclusion and financial education in culturally diverse communities: Leveraging cultural capital and whole-family learning. *New Directions for Adult and Continuing Education, 141*(2014), 57–66.

Rosca, E., Agarwal, N., & Brem, A. (2020). Women entrepreneurs as agents of change: A comparative analysis of social entrepreneurship processes in emerging markets. *Technological Forecasting and Social Change, 157*, 120067.

Saeed, H. (2019). *5 ways we can empower women globally.* https://atlascorps.org/5-ways-we-can-empower-women-globally/

Shlafer, R. J., Hardeman, R. R., & Carlson, E. A. (2019). Reproductive justice for incarcerated mothers and advocacy for their infants and young children. *Infant Mental Health Journal, 40*(5), 725–741.

Siddik, M. N. A. (2017). The does financial inclusion promote women's empowerment? evidence from Bangladesh. *Applied Economics and Finance, 4*(4), 169–177.

Suri, T., & Jack, W. (2016). The long-run poverty and gender impacts of mobile money. *Science, 354*(6317), 1288–1292.

United Nations. (2020). *World population ageing 2019. ST/ESA/SER.A/444.* UNDESA. https://www.un.org/development/desa/pd/sites/www.un.org.development.desa.pd/files/files/documents/2020/Jan/un_2019_worldpopulationageing_report.pdf

Wendy, C., Kellison, L., Klugman, J., & Zimmerman, J. (2019). *Enhancing women's economic empowerment through digital cash transfers: Digitize/direct/design: The D3 criteria.* Bill and Melinda Gates Foundation. https://www.findevgateway.org/sites/default/files/publications/files/_bmgf_d3_criteria_june_1_2019.pdf

Wilmoth, M. J., Menozzi, M. C., & Bassarsky, M. L. (2022). Why population growth matters for sustainable development.

World Bank. (2018). *Poverty and shared prosperity 2018: Piecing together the poverty puzzle.* World Bank. https://openknowledge.worldbank.org/handle/10986/30418

World Bank. (2020). *Supporting Africa's urban informal sector: Coordinated policies with social protection at the core.* https://blogs.worldbank.org/africacan/supporting-africas-urban-informal-sector-coordinated-policies-social-protection-core

World Vision. (2022). *7 ways to empower women and girls.* https://www.worldvision.org/gender-equality-news-stories/seven-ways-empower-women-girls

Wulandari, R. D., & Laksono, A. D. (2020). Determinants of knowledge of pregnancy danger signs in Indonesia. *PLoS One, 15*(5), e0232550.

Chapter 3
Information Communication Technology (ICT) and Its Effects on Social and Political Inclusion in Africa

Abisola Akinola and Olaniyi Evans

Abstract Available statistics show that the overall social and political inclusion remains at startlingly low levels in many societies. However, it is believed that information communication technologies (ICT) can provide veritable tools for the promotion of social and political inclusion. This study, therefore, investigates the effects of ICT on social and political inclusion, using a system generalized method of moments for the case of Africa for the period 1995–2018. The empirical results show that ICT has a positive statistically significant effect on social and political inclusion, indicating that the higher the levels of ICT, the higher the levels of social and political inclusion. Whereas most of the studies in the literature have suggested a relationship between ICT and social inclusion, on one hand, and IC and political inclusion, on the other, this study has pushed the envelope and expanded the literature by confirming empirically the significant positive effect of ICT on social and political inclusion. Along these lines, the study shows that ICT plays an important role in social and political inclusion. ICT, therefore, holds much potential to foster social and political inclusion. It is recommended that the government of individual countries in Africa should increase efforts in fostering robust economies and sound institutions needed for the absolute implementation of ICT, to take advantage of all the benefits required for social and political inclusion.

Keywords ICT · Political inclusion · Social inclusion · System generalized method of moments estimator

---

A. Akinola (✉)
Pan-Atlantic University, Accounting Department, School of Management and Social Sciences, Lagos, Nigeria
e-mail: aakinola@pau.edu.ng

O. Evans
Pan-Atlantic University, Lagos, Nigeria

Victoria Island, Lagos, Nigeria
e-mail: oevans@pau.edu.ng

D. Mhlanga, E. Ndhlovu (eds.), *Economic Inclusion in Post-Independence Africa*, Advances in African Economic, Social and Political Development,
https://doi.org/10.1007/978-3-031-31431-5_3

3.1 Introduction

In every nation, certain strata of the population, whether young, old, educated, uneducated, rural jurisdiction, gender, race, and other minorities, encounter impediments that hinder them from absolutely participating in their country's social and political activity (Barnes, 2019; Bernard et al., 2019; Stanley et al., 2019; Pownall et al., 2020; Prattley et al., 2020). These groups are marginalized for various reasons, spanning from educational background, geographical location, religious beliefs, physical impediments, and gender bias, especially for political positions in Africa, which favour men folks. Thus, there is a need to curb these practices, because exclusion can affect the self-worth, safety, and freedom of such excluded groups. Considering that the disadvantages of exclusion outweigh the cost of inclusion, an inquiry is ethically and morally appropriate. The social or political exclusion of certain groups can affect the economic growth rate of a nation. The sense of social and political connectedness has been shown to play a crucial role in the attainment of social capital outcomes, horizon-broadening, emotional support, enhancement in offline participation, and networking benefits (Koroleva et al., 2011). For social and political inclusion, ICT has emerged as a key enabler considering its novel capabilities (AbuJarour et al., 2018).

The shift to mobile Internet has accelerated in recent years with the rise of feature-rich devices, super-fast Internet, a bevvy of applications, and social networks to drive exponential expansion in Internet traffic. The *Groupe Speciale* Mobile (GSMA) reports a 43% global penetration rate of mobile Internet in 2017. In sub-Saharan Africa, the adoption process is expanding more rapidly (see Fig. 3.1). At the end of 2017, 2G networks covered more than 90% of the population. In the first half of 2018, six new 4G networks were launched. According to GSMA

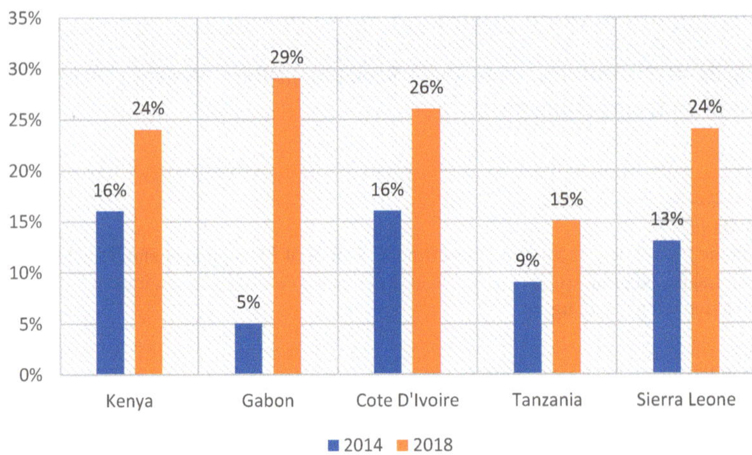

Fig. 3.1 Percentage of the population connected to mobile Internet (2014/2018). (Source: GSMA Intelligence (2020))

estimates, 120 such networks presently exist in the region, and these new networks, along with cheap smartphones, drive the change to mobile broadband in the region.

Based on the submission above, the central objective of this study is to investigate the role of ICT as a catalyst for the propagation of political and social inclusion initiatives. Inaddition the study was motivated by the fact that there is a paucity of empirical research in this area and the conclusion from extant studies are incongruent. Considering the above and the extant literature and theories, this study has two specific objectives:

(i) To investigate the effect of ICT on social inclusion
(ii) To determine the effect of ICT on political inclusion

Although researchers have explored the effect of ICT on social and political inclusion, surprisingly very little attention has been devoted to the lines of investigation in this study. This study uses the system generalized method of moments (GMM) over the period 1995–2018 for a sample of 46 African countries. Understanding the effect of ICT on social and political inclusion in Africa is important, as it will help policymakers in the design of Africa-specific plans to foster social and political inclusion. The remainder of the article is as follows. Section 3.2 provides the theory and a detailed review of the literature. Section 3.3 describes the data, models, and empirical methodology. Section 3.4 presents the empirical results and the related discussion. Section 3.5 concludes, with policy implications and directions for future research.

3.2 Theoretical Review

The social capital theory is a significant phenomenon, and its importance is based on explaining the effects of social networks and their features, such as universal trust, civic engagement, and norms of reciprocity on economic and social phenomena (Bhandari & Yasumobu, 2009). The theory of social capital is specifically grounded on the notion of beliefs, loyalty, standards, and unofficial networks that are perceived to be priceless resources that will yield future returns, and people can be rich or poor in social capital (Häuberer, 2011). Social capital is also a correlational phenomenon that can be owned by groups, local communities, and nations, and the role of the Internet in fostering social capital has been considered theoretically by many studies (Norris, 2003; Urquhart et al., 2008). Machalek and Martin (2015) also suggest that social assets are human resources that develop and accumulate over time.

Hence, the social capital theory is the basic theory underpinning this study, because it tends to validate the importance of social networks which is the bedrock of any inclusion programme. For instance, the concept of corporate social responsibility engaged in by corporate organizations is evolving from the traditional notion of improving the immediate communities, where their companies are situated to other remote communities to have wider coverage. Organizations can earn social capital through corporate social responsibility, which will eventually generate future returns. Urquhart et al.'s (2008) research on ICT and poverty reduction suggests that social capital is a major determinant of integrating ICT in developing countries. Similarly, Song et al. (2009) posit that social capital positively affects many realms of society, such as political participation, the health sector, and economic development.

3.3 Literature Review

3.3.1 ICT and Social Inclusion

Social inclusion is a fundamental aspect of any democratized and principled society and is the act of making all groups of people within a society feel valued (Abujarour & Krasnova, 2017). Social inclusion is interdimensional, and it also entails seeking ways of including the inhabitants of a community, which ranges from accommodating forcefully displaced people from other societies or countries to a marginalized or remote area of society. Therefore, the issue of social inclusion cannot be addressed separately without identifying what social exclusion or marginalization is. Social exclusion has evolved from the traditional definition of excluding an individual or a group of people from fundamental material possession or poor economic situations rather to a broader notion that entails capability deprivation of access to financial products, employment, education, family dynamics and geographical locations, quality of life, and good standard of living (Clayton & Mac Donald, 2013).

World Bank (2018) defined social inclusion in two ways: First, it entails the procedure of enhancing the items for individuals and groups to participate in society. Second, it also connotes making policies that will improve the capabilities and the dignity of disadvantaged groups to participate in society. Hence, ICT has been identified as one of the antidotes in solving social exclusion problems, and it has been proven over the years that ICT has contributed immensely to the social inclusion policies of many countries (Verdegem, 2011).

Social inclusion has been studied from different theoretical perspectives to date; these include the integration of migrants into the host community (Andrade & Doolin, 2016; AbuJarour et al., 2018) and the distance learning perspective featuring teacher-to-student relationships (O'Brien et al., 2009). Social inclusion can also be viewed from the perspective of entertainment, which binds people from various cultural backgrounds together (Sarkar et al., 2017; Rich & Tsitsos, 2016). In addition, earliest studies on social inclusion suggest that museums, sports, and associational memberships are antecedents of social inclusion (Sandell, 1998; Fleming et al., 2005; Carlsson et al., 2010).

The bulk of research on social inclusion focused on refugees and migrants' relationship with the host community, friends, and families. For instance, AbuJarour et al., (2018) did a qualitative study on the role of ICT in aiding social inclusion using refugees in Germany as a case study. The study used a semi-structured interview approach with several 15 correspondents. The analysis from the interview showed that the refugees were able to connect with society through effective telecommunication, mobile translation services, interface with the government, and ability to maintain a cultural identity, and these were made possible through the use of smartphones and basically via the apps on the smartphones.

A more specific study was done by Abujarour et al. (2021) on explaining how ICT enhanced the social inclusion of refugees in Germany. The study's result indicates that refugees from Syria were able to integrate well into society as a result of language translation on smartphones, and they were able to adapt to the new environment by being connected to the Internet.

Harb and Sidani (2021) examined the role of ICT in the inclusion of marginalized people in Lebanon using a qualitative approach based on a series of focused semi-structured interviews with 11 participants holding key positions in associations for disabled and marginalized people. The study suggests that ICT can greatly increase social inclusion through key determinants which entail the nature of an individual's impairment, including personal characteristics, the resources available to them, and government policies together with cultural practices.

Ramsten et al. (2019) investigated the impact of ICT as a catalyst in integrating young adults with mild to moderate disabilities in a social care context. The study used a qualitative research design in line with the social constructivist approach based on perceptions of staff working in these care homes. The results from the study indicate that young adults with disabilities were able to communicate effectively well with the help of cell phones and other ICT-enabled devices, thereby reducing the risk of social exclusion as a result of mild to moderate disabilities in young adults.

It is worthy of note that, in recent decades, mobile Internet is transforming African society in numerous ways (Evans 2019a, b; Vincent & Evans, 2019; Bosch et al., 2020; Emeana et al., 2020; Mwangama et al., 2020; Myovella et al., 2020). Traditionally, the Internet was accessed via fixed-line services on desktop computers and laptops. Thus, social inclusion through the use of ICT gave the refugees emotional support, and they were able to integrate with the rest of the populace by keeping track of new laws and translation services.

3.3.2 ICT and Political Inclusion

The literature has shown that ICT is a stimulus responsible for the dimensional transformation of political inclusion and participation from the conventional ways of joining a political party to an unconventional form of participating in politics (Lewis, 2013). Since the unconscious and conscious integration of ICT into the political sphere, there have been cases of Internet campaigns, political groups that receive instant messages on the same social media platform, and other forms of Internet-linked political stratification. Studies on political exclusion suggest that the following are the major causes of political exclusion, spanning from gender bias, candidate quotas, reserved parliamentary seats, geographical districts' preelection quotas, educational qualifications, and reserved ethnic seats (Stolle & Hooghe, 2011). Other studies, like Seifert et al., (2021), highlighted subsets of some of these identified causes of social exclusion, for example, gender bias regarding women folk has its sub-exclusion factors like the classification between educated women and the uneducated ones. This simply implies that highly educated women have better chances of participating fully in politics while the uneducated ones have slim chances of participation, except for grassroots politics and suburban political movements.

Most studies on political inclusion suggest that ICT has impacted the political process, and as a result, politicians can relate directly with their followers and populace and have larger coverage of supporters. For instance, Lindh and Miles (2007) conducted a study on 80 parliamentarians using the interview approach; the analysis connotes that ICT has been able to increase the popularity of political candidates and political parties via blogs, online discussions, online campaigns, and party websites. Another study done by Lewis (2013) on the impact of ICT on politics in China implies that the advent of the Internet increased people's access to information because, in China, the formalized media, like television stations, newspapers, and radio stations, normally suppress information regarding politics and the government to avoid sanctions. Furthermore, the results from the study found that there is a correlation between Internet use and online opinion expression, and this has greatly influenced China's voting system and governance structure.

Summarily, an empirical investigation of the effect of ICT on social and political inclusion has so far been mostly ignored, especially in Africa. The existing studies have focused largely on explaining the conceptual discussions of the effect of ICT on social and political inclusion, especially in developed country contexts, with scant attention to the case of Africa. Further, in the literature, an empirical investigation of the effect of ICT on social and political inclusion using a GMM model is practically nonexistent. This study, thus, determines the effect of ICT on social and political inclusion using a dynamic panel model. The findings of this study will contribute to the extant literature in this regard and will be of crucial significance in providing useful guidelines, especially for African governments and policymakers, in implementing appropriate policy frameworks for enlarged benefits of ICT for social and political inclusion.

3.4 Research Methodology

3.4.1 Model

Consistent with theory and the literature deliberated above, the econometric model for the study is:

$$I_{i,t} = \rho_1 \mathrm{ICT}_{i,t} + \rho_2 C_{i,t} + \xi_{i,t} \tag{3.1}$$

where $I_{i,t}$ represents either social or political inclusion, $ICT_{i,t}$ is information communication technologies, $C_{i,t}$ is a vector of control variables (capital formation, GDP per capita, government spending, natural resources, and government effectiveness), and $\xi_{i,t}$ is the error term.

Identification and proxies of the variables are grounded on the extant literature (Evans, 2019a, b; Nwaogwugwu & Evans, 2019; Adeola & Evans, 2020). In line with the literature, the proxy for political inclusion is *voice and accountability* and for social inclusion is the primary school enrolment rate. Most importantly, ICT is a multidimensional concept that no single variable can capture. In this study, therefore, the ICT index (*ICT*) is constructed from the two commonly used ICT proxies in the literature: mobile penetration and Internet usage. Theoretically, this index of ICT captures most of the information in the original dataset, which consists of two ICT indicators.

3.4.2 Econometric Technique

The system GMM estimator is used in this study for the empirical analysis of the effect of ICT on social and political inclusion, and complimented with this are the random and fixed effect models. The GMM estimation has the advantage of tackling potential problems of endogeneity of regressors and measurement errors common to dynamic panel models (Racicot, 2015). Compared to different GMMs, system GMM includes more instruments and increases the efficiency of the estimates (Roodman, 2009). Unlike the random effects (RE) and fixed effects (FE) estimation, system GMM neither requires normality nor accommodates heteroscedasticity. Two tests of robustness in GMM estimation are applied: the Sargan test (for overidentifying restrictions) and Arellano–Bond test (for autocorrelation).

3.4.3 Data Presentation

The study uses a panel data set of 46 African countries (see "Appendix" for the sample) for the years 1995–2018. The choice of the sample is based on data availability. The data is sourced from the World Development Indicators and Worldwide Governance Indicators provided by the World Bank (2020). The descriptive statistics of the variables are reported in Table 3.1. The most up-to-date and comprehensive global development database available, WDI, is widely used in the modern economic literature on account of its high quality and universal comparability (see Ram & Ural, 2014; Pinkovskiy & Sala-i-Martin, 2016; Uddin et al., 2017; Javed et al., 2018).

Table 3.1 Descriptive statistics of variables

	Mean	Median	Maximum	Minimum	Std. Dev.
Gross capital formation (% of GDP)	23.256	22.248	125.498	5.459	9.203
GDP per capita	2609.284	1232.720	20333.940	223.404	3192.917
Government effectiveness	0.251	0.250	0.750	0.000	0.181
Government spending (% of GDP)	15.741	14.813	39.451	2.736	5.714
Internet usage (% of the population)	9.233	4.000	57.080	0.000	12.292
Mobile penetration (% of the population)	48.279	39.855	167.298	0.000	40.317
Natural resources rents (% of GDP)	12.610	8.016	89.166	0.001	13.312
Voice and accountability	0.380	0.366	0.797	0.000	0.175
Primary enrolment rate	103.344	105.075	149.952	58.376	18.779

Table 3.2 Results of the correlation analysis

	Social inclusion	Political inclusion
ICT	0.174***	0.423***

Notes: ***, **, and *denote statistical significance at the 1%***, 5%**, and 10%* levels, respectively

3.4.4 *Empirical Analysis*

Descriptive statistics are descriptive coefficients that summarize a given data set (Evans, 2020). Table 3.1 reports the descriptive statistics of the data set: the mean, the minimum, the maximum, and the dispersion statistics. The results of the correlation analysis in Table 3.2 show the correlation between the variables. ICT is positively and significantly related to both social and political inclusion. By implication, ICT has a significant positive relationship with both social and political inclusion.

To account for the potential endogeneity of regressors and loss of dynamic information in the random and fixed effect models, this study estimates a system GMM model with results shown in column 4 of Table 3.3. The estimated model passes the diagnostic tests related to Sargan–Hansen tests of overidentifying restriction and the Arellano–Bond test for autocorrelation of the first-differenced residuals. To provide a better feel for the data and to show robustness to different specifications of the evidence, the analysis compares RE and FE models with GMM results. Table 3.4 presents the results of the regressions, where the dependent variable is the political inclusion in Panel A, but social inclusion in Panel B. The coefficient estimates obtained via GMM are shown in the fourth column. The estimated coefficients in the GMM somewhat validate those in the correlation analysis, the RE and FE models. The evidence shows that ICT plays an important role in social and political inclusion. ICT is a robust determinant of social and political inclusion regardless of the estimation technique used.

Concerning the control variables, capital formation, GDP per capita, government spending, natural resources, and government effectiveness prove to be robust

Table 3.3 The estimation results

Panel A. ICT and its effects on political inclusion			
	Dependent variable: Political inclusion		
	FE	RE	GMM
Lagged political inclusion	–	–	0.657*** (0.008)
ICT	1.275*** (0.338)	2.281*** (0.286)	−0.229*** (0.071)
Capital formation	0.074** (0.033)	0.032 (0.032)	−0.092*** (0.023)
GDP per capita	0.139*** (0.024)	0.032** (0.012)	0.136*** (0.007)
Government spending	−0.235** (0.106)	−0.120 (0.099)	−0.162*** (0.052)
Natural resources rents	0.032 (0.051)	−0.082* (0.046)	0.087*** (0.010)
Government effectiveness	0.179*** (0.041)	0.257*** (0.038)	−1.648* (0.918)
Panel B. ICT and its effects on social inclusion			
	Dependent variable: Social inclusion		
	RE	FE	GMM
Lagged social inclusion	–	–	0.763*** (0.013)
ICT	1.200*** (0.372)	0.199 (0.449)	0.209*** (0.064)
Capital formation	0.155*** (0.059)	0.172*** (0.060)	0.054*** (0.006)
GDP per capita	5.562*** (2.049)	16.291*** (3.392)	−0.759 (0.610)
Government spending	0.499*** (0.144)	0.556*** (0.151)	0.330*** (0.019)
Natural resources rents	0.225*** (0.069)	0.294*** (0.075)	0.086*** (0.014)
Government effectiveness	−7.246 (4.689)	−7.784 (4.863)	−1.568 (3.185)

Note: ***, **, and * represent 1%, 5%, and 10%, respectively. White period instrument weighting matrix. White period standard errors and covariance (d.f. corrected)

Table 3.4 Results of the pairwise Granger causality analysis

Lags	1	2	3
Panel A H_0: ICT does not Granger-cause political inclusion			
F-stat	2.548*	2.466*	2.163
Panel B H_0: ICT does not Granger-cause social inclusion			
F-stat	7.83***	4.365**	2.161*

Notes: ***, **, and *denote statistical significance at the 1%, 5%, and 10% levels, respectively determinants of social and political inclusion. There is evidence to justify their inclusion in both theories and empirical studies (e.g., You, 2016; Bebbington & Huber, 2017; Baker et al., 2018; Evans, 2018; Martelli et al., 2019; Stubbs & Zrinščak, 2020). Higher levels of capital formation, GDP per capita, government spending, and natural resources are important underlying factors for the promotion of social and political inclusion. High levels of government effectiveness promote social and political inclusion by eliminating institutional bottlenecks and operationalizing sound economic policies and regulations to permit and boost inclusion (You, 2016; Martelli et al., 2019). Thus, this study provides evidence that policies for increased levels of capital formation, GDP per capita, government spending, natural resources management, and government effectiveness are most likely to enhance social and political inclusion in Africa.

To appreciate the relationship between ICT and inclusion further, the Granger causality analysis is used to explore statistically whether ICT causes social and political inclusion, with the lag orders varying from 1 to 3. Evidently, from Table 3.4, ICT Granger-cause social and political inclusion, across all lag orders from one to three for social inclusion while only order one and two for political inclusion. This indicates that ICT promotes social and political inclusion.

Overall, the empirical evidence from this study suggests that ICT is highly interrelated to social and political inclusion. Some possible reasons why ICT has a significant relationship with social and political inclusion are as follows. ICT is a catalyst responsible for the dimensional transformation of political inclusion and participation from the conventional ways of joining a political party to an unconventional form of participating in politics (Evans, 2019a, b). Since the unconscious and conscious integration of ICT into the political sphere, there have been cases of Internet campaigns, political WhatsApp groups, and other forms of Internet-linked political participation in Africa. ICT has impacted the political process, and as a result, politicians can relate directly with their followers and populace and have larger coverage of supporters. This evidence is in line with Lindh and Miles (2007) who showed that ICT has been able to increase the popularity of political candidates and political party via blogs, online discussion, online campaigns, and party websites.

3.5 Conclusions

The empirical results have shown that ICT has a positive statistically significant effect on social and political inclusion, indicating that the higher the levels of ICT in Africa, the higher the levels of social and political inclusion. Whereas most of the studies in the literature have suggested a relationship between ICT and social inclusion, on one hand, and ICT and political inclusion, on the other (Taylor & Packham, 2016; Kania-Lundholm & Torres, 2018; Kivikuru, 2019; Lucattini et al., 2019), this study has pushed the envelope and expanded the literature by confirming empirically the significant positive effect of ICT on social and political inclusion. Along these lines, the study shows that ICT plays important roles in social and political inclusion. ICT, therefore, holds much potential to foster social and political inclusion.

The key implications for policymakers from this empirical analysis are as follows. The study has demonstrated that ICT has a positive and significant relationship with social and political inclusion. The results suggest that African governments and policymakers should boost the tourism sector through mobile telephony, the Internet, and ICT infrastructure that contemporaneously support social and political inclusion. By implication, as African countries begin to reinforce social and political inclusion, mobile telephony and the Internet infrastructure should be reconsidered as an open door for laying the foundations of social and political inclusion. Therefore, there is a need for the African continent to collaborate and consider creating basic ICT initiative schemes to reach out to the disenfranchised regions of individual countries, which is a key driver and tool needed for any inclusion program, whether political or social.

In addition, the study has shown that economic factors, such as capital formation, GDP per capita, government spending, natural resources management, and government effectiveness, have a positive and significant relationships with social and political inclusion. By implication, the use of ICT infrastructure alone is not adequate; ICT infrastructure cannot produce the desired benefits for social and political inclusion without complementary economics and institutions in place in various countries. Therefore, to consolidate the full gains of ICT infrastructure for social and political inclusion, a general policy recommendation from this finding is that African countries need to improve their economies – encourage capital formation, foster GDP per capita, increase government spending, deliver natural resources management, and raise government effectiveness. In line with Agenda 2063, emphasis must be on "an Africa of *good governance*" (African Union, 2020), highlighting the role of government effectiveness, particularly in the design of the economic and institutional structures required to support social and political inclusion. The governments of individual countries, therefore, need to increase efforts in fostering robust economies and sound institutions, thus creating a conducive environment for social and political inclusion.

Appendix: Sample of 46 African Countries

Algeria, Angola, Benin, Botswana, Burkina Faso, Cameroon, Cape Verde, Central African Republic, Congo-Brazzaville, Congo-Kinshasa, Cote d'Ivoire, Egypt, Equatorial Guinea, Ethiopia, Gabon, Gambia, Ghana, Guinea, Guinea Bissau, Kenya, Lesotho, Liberia, Libya, Madagascar, Malawi, Mali, Mauritania, Mauritius, Morocco, Mozambique, Namibia, Niger, Nigeria, Rwanda, Senegal, Seychelles, Sierra Leone, South Africa, Sudan, Swaziland, Tanzania, Togo, Tunisia, Uganda, Zambia, Zimbabwe.

References

Abujarour, S. A., Köster, A., Krasnova, H., & Wiesche, M. (2021, January). Technology as a source of power: Exploring how ICT use contributes to the social inclusion of refugees in Germany. In *Proceedings of the 54th Hawaii international conference on system sciences* (p. 2637).

AbuJarour, S., & Krasnova, H. (2017). Understanding the role of ICTS in promoting social inclusion: The case of Syrian refugees in Germany. In *Proceedings of the 25th European conference on information systems (ECIS)* (pp. 1792–1806).

AbuJarour, S., Krasnova, H., & Hoffmeier, F. (2018). ICT as an enabler: Understanding the role of online communication in the social inclusion of Syrian refugees in Germany. *Research Papers*. 27. https://aisel.aisnet.org/ecis2018_rp/27

Adeola, O., & Evans, O. (2020). ICT, infrastructure, and tourism development in Africa. *Tourism Economics, 26*(1), 97–114.

African Union. (2020). *Agenda 2063: Africa we want*. | African Union. [ONLINE] Available at: https://au.int/en/agenda2063/overview. Accessed 27 Feb 2020.

Andrade, A. D., & Doolin, B. (2016). Information and communication technology and the social inclusion of refugees. *MIS Quarterly, 40*(2), 405–416.

Baker, P., Friel, S., Kay, A., Baum, F., Strazdins, L., & Mackean, T. (2018). What enables and constrains the inclusion of the social determinants of health inequities in government policy agendas? A narrative review. *International Journal of Health Policy and Management, 7*(2), 101.

Barnes, M. (2019). *Social exclusion in Great Britain: An empirical investigation and comparison with the EU*. Routledge.

Bebbington, D. H., & Huber, D. G. (2017). Political settlements, natural resource extraction, and inclusion in Bolivia. *Effective States and Inclusive Development Working Paper*, (77).

Bernard, J., Contzen, S., Decker, A., & Shucksmith, M. (2019). Poverty and social exclusion in diversified rural contexts. *Sociologia Ruralis, 59*(3), 353–368.

Bhandari, H., & Yasunobu, K. (2009). What is social capital? A comprehensive review of the concept. *Asian Journal of Social Science, 37*(3), 480–510.

Bosch, T. E., Admire, M., & Ncube, M. (2020). Facebook and politics in Africa: Zimbabwe and Kenya. *Media, Culture & Society, 42*(3), 349–364.

Carlsson, B., Hjelseth, A., & Osborn, G. (2010). Erasmus Mundus and education: The leisure, entertainment and governance initiative. *ESLJ, 8*, xxxv.

Clayton, J., & Macdonald, S. J. (2013). The limits of technology: Social class, occupation and digital inclusion in the city of Sunderland, England. *Information, Communication & Society, 16*(6), 945–966.

Emeana, E. M., Trenchard, L., & Dehnen-Schmutz, K. (2020). The revolution of mobile phone-enabled services for agricultural development (m-Agri Services) in Africa: The challenges for sustainability. *Sustainability, 12*(2), 485.

Evans, O. (2018). Connecting the poor: The internet, mobile phones and financial inclusion in Africa. *Digital Policy, Regulation and Governance, 20*(6), 568–581.

Evans, O. (2019a). Digital politics: Internet and democracy in Africa. *Journal of Economic Studies, 46*(1), 169–191.

Evans, O. (2019b). Information and communication technologies and economic development in Africa in the short and long run. *International Journal of Technology Management & Sustainable Development, 18*(2), 127–146.

Evans, P. (2020). Techno-nationalism in China–US relations: Implications for universities. *East Asian Policy, 12*(02), 80–92.

Fleming, K., Thorson, E., & Peng, Z. (2005). Associational membership as a source of social capital: Its links to the use of local newspapers, interpersonal communication, entertainment media, and volunteering. *Mass Communication & Society, 8*(3), 219–240.

GSMA Intelligence (2020). The mobile economy 2020 https://www.gsma.com/mobileeconomy/wpcontent/uploads/2020/03/GSMA_MobileEconomy2020_Global.pdf

Harb, B., & Sidani, D. (2021). Smart technologies challenges and issues in social inclusion–case of disabled youth in a developing country. *Journal of Asia Business Studies, 16*(2), 308–323.
Häuberer, J. (2011). *Social capital theory*. Springer Fachmedien.
Javed, Z., Waseem, L., Shabbir, M., & Mushtaq, A. (2018). Political stability in absence of violence and economic growth in Pakistan. *Journal of History Culture and Art Research, 7*(5), 367–377. https://doi.org/10.7596/taksad.v7i5.1697
Kania-Lundholm, M., & Torres, S. (2018). Ideology, power and inclusion: Using the critical perspective to study how older ICT users make sense of digitisation. *Media, Culture & Society, 40*(8), 1167–1185.
Kivikuru, U. (2019). From community to assemblage? ICT provides a site for inclusion and exclusion in the global south. *The Journal of International Communication, 25*(1), 49–68.
Koroleva, K., Krasnova, H., Veltri, N. F., & Günther, O. (2011). *It's all about networking! An empirical investigation of social capital formation on social network sites*. International conference on information systems (ICIS 2011).
Lewis, O. A. (2013). Net inclusion: New media's impact on deliberative politics in China. *Journal of Contemporary Asia, 43*(4), 678–708.
Lindh, M., & Miles, L. (2007). Becoming electronic parliamentarians? ICT usage in the Swedish Riksdag. *The Journal of Legislative Studies, 13*(3), 422–440.
Lucattini, P., Jayousi, S., Martinelli, A., Mucchi, L., & Lombardi, G. (2019). Social inclusion for children with disabilities: The role of ICT in play and entertainment activities. In *EAI international conference on body area networks* (pp. 281–300). Springer.
Martelli, C. G., Almeida, C., & Lüchmann, L. (2019). The meanings of representation and political inclusion in the conferences of public policies in Brazil. *Brazilian Political Science Review, 13*(1), e0003. https://doi.org/10.1590/1981-3821201900010003.
Machalek, R., & Martin, M. W. (2015). Neo-darwinian evolutionary theory and sociology: throwing new light on an old path. In Handbook on Evolution and Society (pp. 2–30). Routledge.
Martelli, C. G., Almeida, C., & Lüchmann, L. (2019). The Meanings of Representation and Political Inclusion in the Conferences of Public Policies in Brazil. *Brazilian Political Science Review, 13*(1), e0003. https://doi.org/10.1590/1981-3821201900010003
Mwangama, J., Malila, B., Douglas, T., & Rangaka, M. (2020). What can 5G do for healthcare in Africa? *Nature Electronics, 3*(1), 7–9.
Myovella, G., Karacuka, M., & Haucap, J. (2020). Digitalization and economic growth: A comparative analysis of Sub-Saharan Africa and OECD economies. *Telecommunications Policy, 44*(2), 101856.
Norris, P. (2003). Digital divide: Civic engagement, information poverty, and the Internet worldwide.
Nwaogwugwu, C., & Evans, O. (2019). What are the short-run and long-run drivers of human capital development in Nigeria? In *A Festschrift in honour of professor Folayan Ojo, Lawanson O. I & Nwakeze N. M (Eds.)* (pp. 263–284). University of Lagos Press.
O'Brien, M., Atkinson, A., Burton, D., Campbell, A., Qualter, A., & Varga-Atkins, T. (2009). Social inclusion and learning networks: A 'wider notion of learning'or taking things in a different direction? *Research Papers in Education, 24*(1), 57–75.
Pinkovskiy, M., & Sala-i-Martin, X. (2016). *Newer need not be better: Evaluating the Penn world tables and the world development indicators using nighttime lights (No. w22216).* National Bureau of Economic Research.
Pownall, J., Wilson, S., & Jahoda, A. (2020). Health knowledge and the impact of social exclusion on young people with intellectual disabilities. *Journal of Applied Research in Intellectual Disabilities, 33*(1), 29–38.
Prattley, J., Buffel, T., Marshall, A., & Nazroo, J. (2020). Area effects on the level and development of social exclusion in later life. *Social Science & Medicine, 246*, 112722.
Racicot, F. É. (2015). Engineering robust instruments for GMM estimation of panel data regression models with errors in variables: A note. *Applied Economics, 47*(10), 981–989.

Ram, R., & Ural, S. (2014). Comparison of GDP per capita data in Penn world table and world development indicators. *Social Indicators Research, 116*(2), 639–646.
Ramsten, C., Martin, L., Dag, M., & Marmstål Hammar, L. (2019). A balance of social inclusion and risks: Staff perceptions of information and communication technology in the daily life of young adults with mild to moderate intellectual disability in a social care context. *Journal of Policy and Practice in Intellectual Disabilities, 16*(3), 171–179.
Rich, M. A., & Tsitsos, W. (2016). Avoiding the 'SoHo Effect'in Baltimore: Neighborhood revitalization and arts and entertainment districts. *International Journal of Urban and Regional Research, 40*(4), 736–756.
Roodman, D. (2009). A note on the theme of too many instruments. *Oxford Bulletin of Economics and Statistics, 71*(1), 135–158.
Sandell, R. (1998). Museums as agents of social inclusion. *Museum Management and Curatorship, 17*(4), 401–418.
Sarkar, A., Pick, J. B., & Rosales, J. (2017). *ICT-enabled E-entertainment services in United States counties: Socio-economic determinants and geographic patterns.*
Seifert, A., Cotten, S. R., & Xie, B. (2021). A double burden of exclusion? Digital and social exclusion of older adults in times of COVID-19. *The Journals of Gerontology: Series B, 76*(3), e99–e103.
Stanley, J., Stanley, J., Balbontin, C., & Hensher, D. (2019). Social exclusion: The roles of mobility and bridging social capital in regional Australia. *Transportation Research Part A: Policy and Practice, 125*, 223–233.
Song, J. O., Ha, J. S., & Seong, T. Y. (2009). Ohmic-contact technology for GaN-based light-emitting diodes: Role of p-type contact. *IEEE Transactions on Electron Devices, 57*(1), 42–59.
Stolle, D., & Hooghe, M. (2011). Shifting inequalities: Patterns of exclusion and inclusion in emerging forms of political participation. *European Societies, 13*(1), 119–142.
Stubbs, P., & Zrinščak, S. (2020). Social protection and social inclusion from Lisbon to Europe 2020. *From the Lisbon strategy to Europe 2020.*
Taylor, D., & Packham, G. (2016). Social inclusion through ICT: Identifying and overcoming barriers to ICT use. *Strategic Change, 25*(1), 45–60.
Uddin, M. A., Ali, M. H., & Masih, M. (2017). Political stability and growth: An application of dynamic GMM and quantile regression. *Economic Modelling, 64*, 610–625.
Urquhart, C., Liyanage, S., & Kah, M. M. (2008). ICTs and poverty reduction: a social capital and knowledge perspective. *Journal of Information Technology, 23*(3), 203–213.
Verdegem, P. (2011). Social media for digital and social inclusion: Challenges for information society 2.0 research & policies tripleC: Communication, capitalism & critique. *Open Access Journal for a Global Sustainable Information Society, 9*(1), 28–38.
Vincent, O., & Evans, O. (2019). Can cryptocurrency, mobile phones, and internet herald sustainable financial sector development in emerging markets? *Journal of Transnational Management, 24*(3), 259–279.
World Bank. (2018). *Kenya - social and economic inclusion project (English).* World Bank Group. http://documents.worldbank.org/curated/en/442271543719657009/Kenya-Social-and-Economic-Inclusion-Project
World Bank. (2020). Global economic prospects, June 2020. The World Bank. https://elibrary.worldbank.org/doi/abs/10.1596/978-1-4648-1553-9
You, K. (2016). The roles of political inclusion and democracy in economic development: Insights from Singapore and Botswana. *The Journal of Developing Areas, 50*(5), 327–334.

Chapter 4
Social Inclusion Interventions for Africa Towards Sustainable Development and Shared Prosperity

David Mhlanga and Emmanuel Ndhlovu

Abstract Social inclusion is the process of making it easier for people and groups to participate in society. African nations have taken the lead in several fields. For instance, of all the continents, Africa has implemented the most changes in favour of gender equality over the past 10 years. Positive developments have, like elsewhere in the world, not been equally distributed throughout Africa, with many areas and organizations have been forgotten. The goal of the chapter was to clarify what social inclusion is, reveal the causes of social exclusion in Africa, and come up with social inclusion strategies for the continent that can aid in sustainable development. It was emphasized that the neoliberal agenda of access views social inclusion as the first step towards a more inclusive understanding of social justice and human potential initiatives. The chapter also made clear that a social justice perspective provides a more inclusive definition of social inclusion. From the standpoint of social justice beliefs, it was emphasized that improving human rights, equality of opportunity, human dignity, and fairness for everyone is one way to improve social inclusion. The chapter's conclusion emphasized the significance of social inclusion interventions from human potential empowerment interventions for advancing social justice concerns in Africa by ensuring that no one is left behind.

Keywords Africa · Social Inclusion · Sustainable Development

D. Mhlanga (✉)
The University of Johannesburg, School of Business and Economics,
Johannesburg, South Africa

E. Ndhlovu
Vaal University of Technology, Vanderbijlpark, South Africa

D. Mhlanga, E. Ndhlovu (eds.), *Economic Inclusion in Post-Independence Africa*, Advances in African Economic, Social and Political Development,
https://doi.org/10.1007/978-3-031-31431-5_4

4.1 Introduction

Africa has drawn attention from throughout the world because of its unique accomplishments and competitiveness. Despite these successes, the area has drawn attention from around the world due to important problems like social isolation, food insecurity, poverty, inequalities, and joblessness, to name a few (Khalid Anser et al., 2021; Mhlanga et al., 2021). Challenges related to malnutrition and poverty have significantly diminished, and the progress that has followed has been excellent (Khalid Anser et al., 2021). The need for social inclusion has been highlighted by many organisations, as well as by current programs and policies across the continent, according to Khalid Anser et al. (2021) who claim that the socially constructed push is aiding in the transformation of societies and increasing awareness of previously ignored issues. A surge in the rate of population growth has been suggested as one explanation for the continent of Africa's increasing food insecurity and sluggish economic development (Das & Espinoza, 2020; Mhlanga & Denhere, 2020; Mhlanga & Ndhlovu, 2021; Andrews et al., 2021).

By 2050, Africa's population is expected to more than double, from 1.2 billion to more than 2 billion people, according to Khalid Anser et al. (2021). Africa is losing a chance to become self-sufficient and even export food, because its current methods of food production are unsustainable. Furthermore, Africa is disproportionately affected by climate change, which increases the need for transformation. If Africa wants to overcome these obstacles, agriculture needs to be revolutionized via the contributions of numerous inventions (Ndhlovu, 2022a). According to Das and Espinoza (2020), recent advancements in women's empowerment, public education, healthcare, and nutrition have been made in African nations and in several categories, Africa has advanced more than any other continent. Innovation is rife throughout Africa, and it manifests itself in many different ways. The expansion of digital technology, the development of new platforms that provide services to isolated and disadvantaged communities, and advocacy campaigns that increase public acceptance of once-marginalized people are just a few examples.

Das and Espinoza (2020) claim that despite positive developments, Africa still faces significant challenges, including reducing poverty, dealing with instability, and managing the growing effects of climate change. Additionally, Das and Espinoza (2020) raised a different issue, social exclusion as a major factor in why some groups of people have not profited from development advancements. According to Andrews et al. (2021), one strategy for Africa to promote social inclusion is to place a focus on developing human capital, empowering women, growing the digital economy, combating climate change, and addressing the root causes of fragility. Das and Espinoza (2020) also highlighted that social inclusion and peace and security are intrinsically linked. Furthermore, while concentrating on reducing poverty is important, doing so by itself won't halt the exclusion of specific people and groups.

According to academics, the process of fostering a more inclusive society is costly just as exclusion is. As a result, improving inclusion requires careful consideration of both the advantages and disadvantages. In other words, any nation must consciously choose its social inclusion strategy. According to Das and Espinoza (2020), social inclusion in Africa is well within reach, as numerous initiatives across the continent show, with a strong social contract and increased accountability of the state and service providers to inhabitants. With the adoption of the Sustainable Development Goals and the "leave no one behind" agenda, there is still a worldwide potential to make sure that marginalized people, not least disabled people, are included and accounted for in mainstream development efforts, according to Jolley et al.'s (2018) argument in the social inclusion literature. It is estimated that 1 billion people worldwide live with some form of disability. Jolley et al. (2018) further claimed that there is a lack of knowledge about disabilities and the policies and programs in place to better the lives of individuals affected in many low-income countries.

Further research by Jolley et al. (2018) led them to the conclusion that "standardized tools for ensuring the progress of programs and policies for including disability people at the state level must be enhanced; significantly increased stakeholder cooperative relationships; advancement and implementation of synchronized strategies to trying to measure disability and social exclusion; rigorous assessments of the efficiency of disability programs; and disaggregation of routine data by disability". Igonya et al. (2022) asserted that advocacy actors have a special responsibility to advance changes in sub-Saharan African society that would benefit sexual and gender minorities. Igonya et al. (2022) also argued that there is a significant gap between what researchers concentrate on and what evidence users need, which could hinder advocacy actors' efforts.

In addition, Russell and Carter (2019) stated that South Africa and Rwanda's present-day educational systems continue to be impacted by the legacy of a racial and ethnocentric past. Further, Russell and Carter (2019) claimed that despite the governments in both societies having adopted colour-blind or nonracial/ethnic policies that support national unity and reconciliation to address their oppressive and violent histories, these very same policies unintentionally serve to exacerbate existing tensions. According to Russell and Carter (2019), the implementation of colour-blind or nonracial/ethnic policies stifles open discourse regarding previous and present intergroup tensions, creating a paradox of social inclusion. The two techniques, non-racialization and non-ethnicization, respectively, aim to quiet explicit discourse and language regarding racial and ethnic differences through the propagation of "colour-blind" beliefs, Russell and Carter (2019) also found support for.

However, everyday actions and attitudes of individuals, including students and teachers, who have been imbued with past racial/ethnic ideologies continue to be rigid, have an impact on micro-level and school-level interactions, undermine the veracity of either colour-mute or colour-blind ideologies, and help to maintain boundaries. Information and communication technologies (ICTs) are becoming acknowledged as essential tools for the social inclusion of women, according to another study by Abubakar and Kah (2021). Abubakar and Kah (2021) looked at how mobile phone use affected women's social inclusion in Nigeria. The study's findings suggested that the usage of mobile phones by these women has made it possible for them to develop certain skills related to generating cash, being financially included, maintaining social contacts, and seeking pertinent information.

Even though these abilities depend on individual, societal, and environmental factors, Abubakar and Kah (2021) also mentioned this. We provide examples of how women use their agency to make appropriate use of mobile phones that improve their overall wellness and social participation in this new society. With this background, the chapter will attempt to respond to the questions below. What precisely is social inclusion? The study will also aim to identify the causes of social exclusion in Africa and develop social inclusion strategies for the continent that can support sustainable development.

4.2 The Significance of Social Inclusion in Africa

According to the World Bank (2019), Africa has drawn attention from around the world due to its tremendous accomplishments and vitality. Human development results have improved, poverty has decreased, and vibrant social movements are transforming communities and drawing attention to formerly taboo topics and groups of people. New policies and programs across the continent have highlighted the significance of social inclusion as technology has expanded to many isolated locations (World Bank, 2019). The World Bank (2019) went on to state that African nations have driven advancement in some areas. For example, in the last 10 years, more reforms supporting gender equality have been undertaken in Africa than in any other region of the world. Das and Espinoza (2020) reaffirmed the idea that Africa is currently in the spotlight due to both its significant difficulties and great accomplishments.

According to Das and Espinoza (2020), social movements are transforming communities and drawing attention to marginalized groups and issues, while poverty has decreased and human development results have improved. With the introduction of new laws and programs across the continent, technological innovation has reached numerous isolated regions and emphasized the value of social participation. Some African nations have taken the initiative to advance; for example, among all regions worldwide, Africa has undertaken the most changes supporting gender equality in the last 10 years. Positive developments have not been uniform across Africa; even though Africa has received attention for its significant problems in other areas of the world, many regions and demographics have been overlooked. Digital technology, for instance, can further marginalize those without access to mobile phones or the Internet.

Similar to how greater infrastructure has made lives better, it also entails hazards, such as the risk of the environment being harmed or of livelihoods being unfairly threatened (Ndhlovu, 2018). There may be a concentration of improvements in education and health for particular populations and demographic groups. A range of development outcomes is also behind in places, where there is state and societal fragility (Ndhlovu, 2020; Söderbaum & Taylor, 2018; Asongu & Odhiambo, 2019;

World Bank, 2019). People with impairments, members of underrepresented groups in society, young people, and former combatants are just a few of the many populations who require our explicit attention as African countries urbanize and go through several transitions (Valensisi, 2020; Grover et al., 2022).

Improved infrastructure has made lives better for many people, but it also brings hazards such as the environment being harmed or livelihoods being damaged. For example, digital technology can further isolate those without access to cell phones or Internet connections (World Bank, 2019). Areas that face state and societal fragility also lag in many development outcomes. Improvements in education and health can be concentrated in some places and benefit some groups more than others (World Bank, 2019). However, according to the World Bank (2019), social inclusion in Africa is eminently achievable with a robust social contract, creative finance, and public participation. The Sustainable Development Goals' (SGDs) catchphrase, "leave no one behind", has sparked a surge of demands and initiatives at many levels, according to Das and Espinoza (2020), who also made this argument. The movement for social inclusion has received a lot of support during the past several years.

In addition to being based on the principles of social inclusion, the World Bank Group (WBG) recently unveiled its new regional strategy for Africa. The World Bank Group and a variety of its partners have participated in various structured engagements as a result of the rise in thought and action, both within the WBG and globally. The World Bank Group has regularly undertaken Systematic Country Diagnostics (SCDs) for each of its partner nations, which have demonstrated that social inclusion issues are integral to poverty reduction but distinct from it (World Bank, 2019). One of the reasons social inclusion is crucial in Africa is that the majority of debates about it have been in the context of eradicating poverty and responding to humanitarian disasters. However, despite significant progress in reducing poverty, it is estimated that more than 400 million people still live in poverty (World Bank, 2019; Beegle & Christiaensen, 2019).

According to the "Inclusion Matters in Africa" report, social exclusion is both a process and a consequence while poverty is an outcome. The research further underlined how exclusionary practices can have a lasting impact on the minds, psyches, and dignity of oppressed or excluded populations. The report also referred to how this exclusion impacts these groups' capacity to take advantage of the opportunities that are made available to them. Slavery, apartheid, and untouchability in South Asia are a few instances of behaviours that had devastating effects on exclusion. The Inclusion Matters in Africa study also made a passing reference to less obvious behaviours that can still have disastrous impacts on inferior groups. Consider bullying as an illustration of an ingrained exclusionary process. Throughout the world, certain groups are bullied into submission. Bisexual people, people whose accents differ from the dominant group's, people who eat different foods, and people with other distinctive traits are some of the groups.

Worryingly, bullying can have a negative impact on a person's ability to pursue an education, lead to severe mental health issues and other life-altering consequences, and ultimately compel victims to leave a system that they believe to be supportive of bullying. In other words, even while poverty may not be a factor, discriminatory behaviours that keep bullied individuals from realizing their full potential do (Das & Espinoza, 2020; Khalid Anser et al., 2021). A person with mobility issues who lives in a wealthy household is not affected by poverty, but they may be prevented from engaging in activities outside the home due to inaccessible infrastructure and services, according to another example provided by Inclusion Matters in Africa. Das and Espinoza (2020) assert that it's critical to recognize that social exclusion occasionally has no connection to poverty, even though it frequently does. The conversation about inequality and poverty takes on a new dimension because of social inclusion.

The question of gender and poverty is another crucial justification for the need for social inclusion. A case in point is the connection between gender and poverty, which has a long history of investigation, according to the "Inclusion Matters in Africa" report. The study emphasized that households headed by men are not always better off than those headed by women or that women are often poorer than men. Milazzo and Van de Walle (2017) claim that households headed by women have reduced poverty more quickly than households headed by men in numerous African nations. Milazzo and Van de Walle (2017) continued by arguing that when we consider gender in conjunction with age and marital status, more complex findings become apparent: young married women, but more so those who are young and widowed, are especially vulnerable. The World Bank also noted that a study done in Kenya revealed that, as compared to men, women who are bereaved, separated, or divorced have greater rates of poverty. In addition to gender, the "Inclusion Matters in Africa" study found that race, ethnicity, and the presence of disabilities are important indicators of poverty.

The idea of social inclusion is significant, according to Das et al. (2017), because it has become more prominent on the global policy agenda as a result of four fundamental changes. First, the Sustainable Development Goals (SDGs) "leave no one behind" agenda calls for social inclusion; second, despite significant progress towards the Millennium Development Goals (MDGs), many countries have yet to meet the targets; and third, there is growing concern about inequality and the fact that some groups routinely lag in progress.

4.3 Evidence from a Theoretical Perspective

Max Weber, a sociologist in the nineteenth century, was a proponent of social cohesiveness and is credited with developing the idea of social inclusion (Hayes et al., 2008; Gidley et al., 2010). In terms of more recent history, the phrase is more easily identified through its counterpart, social exclusion, and this may be related to the French concept of less exclusive individuals excluded from the social insurance system in the 1970s, according to Hayes et al. (2008). The concept, according to Gidley et al. (2010), spread throughout Europe and the UK in the 1980s and 1990s. Das and Espinoza (2020) described social inclusion as the process of making it easier for people and groups to participate in society. They claim that this concept has acquired unstoppable traction in development and more general policy debates. Social identity is considered to be one of the factors that worsen social exclusion.

Various factors, including gender, age, disability, sexual orientation, gender identity, geography, occupation, race, ethnicity, religion, or citizenship status, are thought to represent social identity markers (World Bank, 2013). This was also consistent with the claims made by Das et al. (2017), who claimed that some of the most frequent identities that result in exclusion include gender, race, caste, ethnicity, religion, sexual orientation, disability, mental health condition, and addiction. Based on these group characteristics, social isolation can lead to lower social status as well as worse outcomes in terms of income, human capital, occupation, and involvement in local and national decision-making. The World Bank (2013) stated that inclusion should occur in markets, services, and spaces, where markets include land, housing, labour, and credit. The question that remains is under what conditions inclusion will occur. Services include, among other things, information, communication, technology, social protection, transportation, health, and education. According to Das and Espinoza (2020), the concept of space comprises both actual space and space in a more general sense. Das and Espinoza contend that social, political, and cultural environments, all either entrench exclusion or promote inclusion. Social inclusion, according to academics, improves people's chances, opportunities, and sense of worth in society. A breakdown of the areas where social inclusion ought to occur is shown in Fig. 4.1.

As shown in Fig. 4.1, inclusion should occur in markets, services, and locations where markets exist. Along with other factors, inclusion should occur in housing markets, regions, and gender. There are many levels of inclusion in inclusion.

4.3.1 Social Inclusion Levels

According to Gidley et al. (2010), social inclusion can be conceptualized as a tier-scheme of degrees of inclusion. The simplest explanation considers social inclusion from a neoliberal viewpoint as access; a more comprehensive explanation considers social justice from a participating perspective, and the most comprehensive explanation considers human potential from an empowering perspective.

The levels of social inclusion are represented in Fig. 4.2 as access under neoliberalism, involvement in social justice problems, and, ultimately, empowering human potential.

4.3.2 Access in a Neoliberal World

The most restrictive definition of social inclusion, according to Gidley et al. (2010), is connected to the neoliberal ideology that first gained traction in the 1980s. Gidley et al. (2010) further argue that from the viewpoint of neoliberal ideologies,

Fig. 4.1 Areas of social inclusion. (Source: Authors)

Fig. 4.2 Social inclusion levels. (Source: Authors)

improving skill shortages and investing in human capital are necessary for economic growth as part of a nationalist agenda to develop the country's economy so that it can compete more successfully in the global market (Gidley et al., 2010; Archangelo, 2014; Mant, 2017). The core principles of neoliberalism include the importance of economic growth, the necessity of free trade to promote growth, the unfettered free market, individual freedom, the elimination of unnecessary regulations, and the promotion of an evolutionary model of social development (Frodeman et al., 2012; Worth, 2014). According to Gidley et al. (2010), the neoclassical economic conception of humans as independent rational decision-makers free from social power imbalances allows access to be seen as an adequate manifestation of social inclusion from a neoliberal perspective. According to Hayes et al. (2008), one instance of social exclusion is the restriction of access to opportunities and the constraints of the capabilities needed to take advantage of these changes.

4.3.3 Engagement with Social Justice Issues

One way to increase social inclusion from the standpoint of social justice ideologies is through increasing human rights, equality of opportunity, human dignity, and fairness for all, according to scholars who believe that social justice ideology identifies a more inclusive interpretation of social inclusion (Farrington & Farrington, 2005; Gidley et al., 2010). The other significant issue is that, while social justice activism may or may not be related to economic concerns, its main goal is to enable everyone to participate fully in society while upholding their dignity. Therefore, any issues with community engagement and participation are highlighted. This can also be contextualized within paradigmatic definitions of involvement and connection to ideas of community sustainability (Eisler, 1987; Langworthy, 2008). The idea that social inclusion has to do with having the capacity to take part in the crucial activities in the society in which they live, according to Saunders et al. (2008), is an example of the participatory perspective. Gidley et al. (2010) noted that through university-community partnerships, universities and all institutions of higher learning can play a significant role in participatory social inclusion.

4.3.4 Human Potential Empowerment

The focus of human potential ideologies is on the interpretation of social inclusion as empowerment and sees it as a phenomenon that goes beyond just justice and human rights to maximize each person's potential through the use of models of possibility rather than models of deficiency (Bennett, 2002; Stewart et al., 2013; Balisi et al., 2019). Olsson (2008) asserts that empowerment places emphasis on the idea that all people, whether mainstream or marginalized, are multidimensional beings with needs and interests that go far beyond their role in the political economy of a nation. It also involves the moral imperative of working with the complexity of humanity, a form of complex integration. In this approach, social inclusion highlights collective individualism while valuing variety and diversity (Gidley et al., 2010). Nicholson (2012) asserted that education can be seen as transformative since it helps people achieve "a life of shared dignity via empowerment".

4.3.5 Social Inclusion Literature

In many nations around the world, the idea of social inclusion has now permeated both the official and development policy debate. After inclusion was acknowledged by development partners as one of the four pillars of poverty reduction, inclusion as an official policy started to make its way into government policy. A comprehensive process called social inclusion aims to ensure that all nations and people are freed from hunger and poverty while enhancing their access to better living conditions. The impact of innovation and social inclusion on food security in West Africa was studied by Khalid Answer et al. in 2021. Food security is fuelled by innovation and social inclusion, according to Khalid Anser et al.'s (2021) research. The result of this is that West Africa may experience an increase in food security of around 41.5 percent and 13.6 percent, respectively, due to increasing social participation and innovation.

Khalid Anser et al. (2021) concluded that social inclusion needs to be strengthened to lessen risk, susceptibility, and socioeconomic shocks experienced by agricultural households to feed the expanding African population. Additionally, agricultural innovation needs to be strengthened to boost production and provide sustainable food security (Ndhlovu, 2022b). In addition, Rawal (2008) suggested that in many cases, the notion of social exclusion or inclusion took the place of the concept of poverty in the policy discourse in France in the middle of the 1970s and was later accepted as a major concept by the European Union in the late 1980s. As a response to the welfare state dilemma, the idea of social inclusion initially surfaced in Europe, according to Rawal (2008), and it has since gained significant traction in Nepal's official and development discourses.

According to Napal Rawal (2008), the 2003 Poverty Reduction Strategy Paper (PRSP), which is also known as Nepal's Tenth Plan, included inclusion as one of its four pillars, giving the idea of social inclusion significant political clout. The debates over inclusion and exclusion have assumed a prominent role in Nepal's current political transition, according to Rawal (2008). Several groups, including Dalits, women, ethnic communities, donor communities, Madhesi communities, and regions, have made demands for an inclusive state, and as a result, the issue is now a part of the general public discourse. Rawal (2008) noted that it is important to keep in mind that the term is not universal in the way it has been used and defined. According to Rawal (2008), while some contend that social exclusion is more illuminating and holds the potential to improve our understanding of disadvantaged groups, others contend that this concept is so evocative, ambiguous, multidimensional, and elastic that it can be defined in a variety of ways and, as a result, may mean different things to different people.

The tribal people in central India are, according to Panda (2017), in many ways excluded from accessing and reaping the benefits of mainstream development. Despite playing many duties in the home, women are more neglected and ignored within tribal organizations than men, according to Panda's (2017) argument. Panda (2017) asserts once more that women's isolation from mainstream knowledge systems, and the market, and their restricted access to and control over resources have an impact on the general development of tribal groups. Panda (2017) argued that the promotion of women's physical and economic rights and equal participation is essential for the economic growth of tribal communities. As a result, purposeful planning of activities and institutional mechanisms are required for both socially inclusive economic empowerment and environmentally sustainable growth.

To address the geographical, social, technological, and economic inclusion of tribal women in the Lac supply chain and downstream market integration to improve their incomes in the Gumla district of Jharkhand state, Panda (2017) analysed and documented the findings of an inclusive Lac livelihood model implemented by Udyogini, a national-level NGO established by the World Bank in 1992. The study's findings showed that socially excluded women could be successfully organized, engaged, and integrated by utilizing a tried-and-true Lac-based livelihood model in value chains and markets for raising their incomes. This was accomplished by utilizing inclusive strategies, scientific technologies, and participatory approaches. Panda (2017) also discovered that women have entrepreneurial skills to manage markets and economic empowerment over the profits earned for family needs, primarily for health and education, though in some cases for asset creation.

Gidley et al. (2010) provided an overview of the state of university/community involvement in Australia and examined the literature on social inclusion there. According to Gidley et al. (2010), there is a spectrum of ideological viewpoints that underlie theory, policy, and practice, and the phrase "social inclusion"is debated in academic and policy literature and subject to a variety of interpretations. Gidley et al. (2010) have outlined the general theoretical framework for social inclusion in connection to the question of who should be included and the levels of inclusion ideology.

Once more, Gidley et al. (2010) placed fourth when considering the following possible inclusion criteria: socioeconomic status; culture, including indigenous cultures; linguistic group; religion; geography, which includes rural and remote/island areas; gender; sexual orientation; age, including youth and old age; physical and mental health/ability; and status concerning unemployment, homelessness, and incarceration. According to Gidley et al. (2010), the degree of inclusion is determined by a nested threefold schema that incorporates a spectrum of ideologies, from the most restricted to the most inclusive: the neoliberal focus on access and economic factors, the social justice focus on community involvement, and the human potential focus on individual and group empowerment derived from positive psychology and critical/transformative pedagogies. According to Coombs et al. (2013) and the Fourth National Mental Health Plan for Australia, social inclusion is important for mental health and well-being.

A measure of social inclusion might be a useful addition to the set of outcome measures already employed in public-sector mental healthcare, according to Coombs et al.'s (2013) argument. The rise of interest in socioeconomic determinants of health around the world, according to Rispel et al. (2009), offers a chance to take decisive action against countries' unacceptable and unjustifiable health disparities. In six chosen countries, Botswana, Mozambique, South Africa, Ethiopia, Nigeria, and Zimbabwe, Rispel et al. (2009) assessed three categories of social inclusion policies, cash transfers, free social services, and particular institutional structures for program integration. Rispel et al.'s (2009) key recommendations for sub-Saharan African governments include the following: health inequalities must be measured; social policies must be carefully crafted and successfully implemented to address the challenges identified; monitoring and evaluation systems require improvement, and community participation must be promoted through supportive and enabling environments.

To address health disparities and hold governments responsible for better health and reduced health inequalities, there has to be a robust civil society movement. To fill this gap, Muñoz Arce and Pantazis (2019) examined discourses of social exclusion and underlying assumptions held by social workers in charge of carrying out social policy interventions in Chile. They argued that social workers' perspectives are rarely heard and taken into account in policy debates in Chile. The research conducted by Muñoz Arce and Pantazis (2019) involved interviews with senior social workers from two significant nongovernmental organizations (NGOs) that work to combat social exclusion. According to Muñoz Arce and Pantazis (2019), the implementation of Chilean social policy is dominated by individual-based narratives and neoliberal logic; however, some social workers also engaged in anti-hegemonic tactics. The study by Huegler and Kersh (2021) concentrated on contexts where socioeconomic perspectives have dominated public discourses about the education of young adults, with a focus on the role of employment-related learning, skills, and opportunities and with active participation in the labour market as a top concern for policymakers.

Huegler and Kersh (2021) claim that a singular focus on "employability" has been associated with limited conceptions of participation, inclusion, and citizenship that emerged in the context of discourse shifts brought about by neoliberalism and that prioritize workfare over welfare and obligations over rights. A major criticism of these contexts, according to Huegler and Kersh (2021), is that rather than addressing participation constraints, the emphasis shifts to conceptualizing social inclusion primarily in terms of expectations of "activation" and occasionally assimilation. Young people who are not in school, the workforce, or training are among the main target demographics for discourses of activation, according to Huegler and Kersh (2021), while the exclusion of young migrants and members of ethnic minorities is frequently framed within the nuanced and contradictory interplay between discourses of assimilation and experiences of discrimination. Huegler and Kersh (2021) claim that these advancements have an impact on the area of adult education geared towards young people who are at risk of social exclusion. The promotion of young people's skills and talents that enable them to participate in forms of civic activism and challenge institutional barriers that result in exclusion is an alternative language to "activation", as Huegler and Kersh (2021) also noted.

4.4 Social Inclusion Interventions for Africa Towards Sustainable Development

According to Das and Espinoza (2020), the social inclusion ideas, strategies, and initiatives in Africa can serve as lessons for other African nations and for other regions that are struggling with social exclusion. It is crucial to emphasize that although change is occasionally unavoidable, it can also be difficult and painful. The focus on female secondary education in many countries meant that boys at the secondary level were left behind, and where refugees have settled in large numbers and have come with higher human capital endowments than their host communities, the hosts have felt afraid and anxious about jobs, services, and voice. Das and Espinoza (2020) argued that change is always complex and political and may create new excluded groups in some circumstances. Because of this, social inclusion is not a linear process, and societies and governments must actively choose to invest in it. Governments must start with a thorough knowledge of the benefits and drawbacks.

As was previously mentioned, investing in an inclusive society is not free and requires coordinated action to turn it into a victory for everyone. Social programs, for example, can be costly and influence fiscal sustainability, as stated by the World Bank (2013). As a result, governments are forced to make trade-offs by either raising taxes or lowering spending for other initiatives. The political costs of projects that focus on previously excluded populations can upend power relations, were some of the drawbacks that were emphasized. The World Bank (2013) emphasized that to ensure support for social inclusion, governments and politicians must create unambiguous social contracts with citizens. There are instances of people eager to pay for a more inclusive society all across the world. The most effective kind of support can sometimes be found in the financial sphere, when citizens pay taxes they are aware that will go towards programs and policies that promote greater social inclusion.

Initiatives for social inclusion, according to Gidley et al. (2010), can be identified by their apparent disciplinary focus and philosophy. Interventions that concentrate on the financial value of social inclusion are typically based on neoliberal economic theory, those that concentrate on social justice are typically based on social science and/or social theory, and interventions that concentrate on human potential are frequently based on positive thinking or social transformation instructional practices that emphasize spiritual and psychological values, according to Gidley et al. (2010).

4.5 Interventions for Social Inclusion from the Neoliberal Access

Figure 4.3 is an illustration of how social inclusion relates to the neoliberal agenda of access, and this may be seen as the first step towards interventions that are more inclusive in their understanding of social justice and human potential. The project depicted in Fig. 4.3 sheds light on neoliberal social inclusion innovations that, when implemented in Africa, can aid in the attainment of sustainable development.

Figure 4.3 clearly highlights some of the programs that, from a neoliberal access perspective, might hasten social inclusion in Africa and subsequently sustainable development. These programs are regarded as the initial steps towards more extensive social inclusion. These initiatives include better income support for low-income households; enhanced regional infrastructure, such as enhanced public transportation and improved rural access to technology; enhanced support for people with

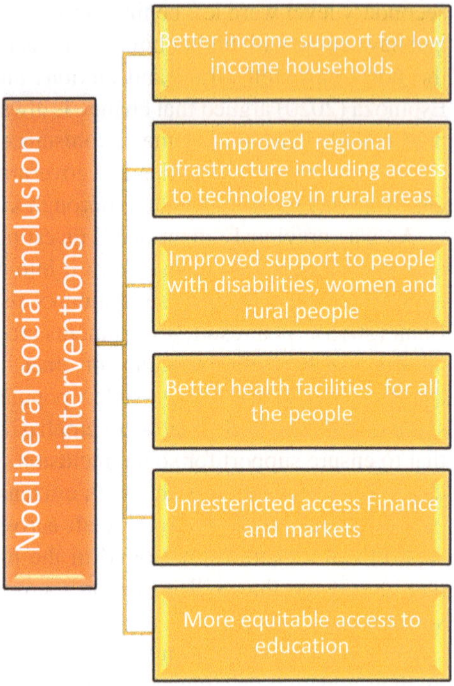

Fig. 4.3 Social inclusion interventions from the neoliberal access. (Source: Authors)

psychiatric challenges, such as people with disabilities; and enhanced support for women, young people, and rural residents. This covers issues with modifying the built environment to accommodate people with disabilities. According to Lloyd et al. (2006), people with mental disorders are marginalized and socially excluded from many facets of community life to the point where they frequently struggle to find employment, take part in activities, find affordable and sustainable housing, deal with financial and legal issues, find transportation, and have little access to or knowledge of the options that are available to them. The other program entails a significant upgrade of all people's healthcare facilities.

For instance, Das et al. (2017) extended the principles of social inclusion to health policy and practice, contending that it will be impossible to achieve the objective of universal healthcare without taking social and economic inclusion into account. According to Das et al. (2017), the concept of social inclusion in the attainment of universal health coverage is a broad one that tackles the policy environment, social behaviours, and institutions rather than just being focused on local-level initiatives. Further arguing that social exclusion occurs through the practices, procedures, and actions of elites, service providers, and those who are most likely to be excluded, Das et al. (2017) suggested that these practices may permeate the design and operation of both formal and informal institutions. Belle-Isle et al. (2014) asserted that the unequal allocation of economic and social resources, including power and reputation, can occasionally lead to health disparities between groups. According to Belle-Isle et al. (2014), social processes that result in unequal power relationships cause individuals or groups to be socially excluded. As a result, community organizations can improve the inclusion of marginalized community members by involving them in decision-making processes that have an impact on their lives. Other social inclusion measures for Africa include more egalitarian access to education as well as unrestricted access to markets and financing. The argument made in this chapter is that if these measures are carried out, social inclusion can be accomplished, helping to ensure that no one is left behind.

4.6 Social Justice Participation Interventions for Social Inclusion

As was previously mentioned, social justice ideology identifies a more inclusive understanding of social inclusion, and from the standpoint of social justice ideologies, increasing human rights, equality of opportunity, human dignity, and fairness for all is one strategy to increase social inclusion. The initiatives that African countries can take to achieve social inclusion from the perspective of social justice are outlined in Fig. 4.4. These initiatives can ultimately result in the achievement of sustainable development.

From a social justice and participation standpoint, some of the activities that can hasten social inclusion in Africa and subsequently sustainable development are clearly emphasized in Fig. 4.4. Collaboration and partnerships, social enterprise and social entrepreneurship mentoring, and increasing financial participation are a few of the approaches. Tett (2005) made the case that the concepts of cooperation and partnership are at the core of the vision of several projects created to combat social exclusion in nations like the United Kingdom. Tett (2005) argued that partnerships are characterized by processes of inclusion and exclusion, dominance, and subordination, that attention must be paid to the structures and processes involved, and that new ways of thinking about representation are necessary, with priority given to including those with the least power who are nonetheless the most expert in identifying the needs of their communities.

Carlisle (2010) further claimed that community involvement and multisectoral partnership projects are increasingly seen as effective strategies for addressing health and social inequality in the current UK policy framework. These programs are frequently implemented in areas that are experiencing an industrial and economic downturn, fractured neighbourhoods, strained public services, and persistent underinvestment in organizations in the nonprofit and community sectors. The concept of social enterprise and social entrepreneurship, according to academics, is one strategy to address deeply ingrained problems of social exclusion in the fields of regeneration, community empowerment, long-term unemployment, and enhancing public service delivery (Robbie, 2008; Gidley et al., 2010). Mervyn et al. (2014) published the findings of a recent study that focuses on the impact of mobile technologies on social exclusion in the Journal of Financial Participation.

Fig. 4.4 Social inclusion interventions from the social justice participation. (Source: Authors)

According to Mervyn et al. (2014), the direct access model for this segment of the community is fundamentally undermined by problems with literacy, technology proficiency, and, in some cases, the socioemotional state of some of the socially excluded people combined with the complexity of their information needs. To give targeted groups and individuals the best opportunity for success and benefit, Mervyn et al. (2014) found that it is crucial to comprehend and solve current information demands and hurdles, such as literacy and information technology literacy, as well as social-emotional difficulties. The use of mobile phones, the Internet, and varied interpretations of these information and communication technologies (ICTs) by homeless persons in central Scotland has been explored, according to Buré (2006). Buré (2006) showed that while homeless people frequently use ICTs in ways that reinforce the patterns and practices of their subculture, there is no standard way of using technology. As a result, digital inclusion does not always result in social inclusion in mainstream society.

As a result, Buré (2006) discovered that even if many homeless individuals use ICTs on a reasonably regular basis, mobile adoption can be more inclusive than Internet adoption. Digital finance, according to Kofman and Payne (2021), offers excellent prospects for the financial inclusion of women. More women may participate in the global economy and profit from financial services and markets, just like generations of people before them. Because it might help to socially include people from the perspective of social justice participation, it is crucial to encourage financial participation. One of the programs that can aid in the social inclusion of those who are excluded is mentoring. The usefulness of mentoring for fostering a feeling of community among young people in rural places, according to Gidley et al. (2010), can go a long way in including these people. Providing new career paths and job opportunities; giving communities a creative outlet to explore problems and aspirations; fostering participants' self-assurance, pride, and sense of belonging; as well as producing new and diverse artistic work and cultural experiences should be the main goals of mentoring programs that aim to engage socially excluded populations (Gidley et al., 2010).

4.7 Interventions for Social Inclusion from the Human Potential Empowerment

The human potential empowerment interventions' social inclusion interventions emphasize empowerment and the encouragement of individual potential to enhance social justice interests. From the perspective of maximizing human potential, Fig. 4.5 illustrates some of the efforts that might be implemented in Africa to increase social inclusion.

The social inclusion interventions from the human potential empowerment interventions shown in Fig. 4.5 attempt to strengthen social justice interests by putting a focus on empowerment and encouraging individual potential. The promotion of minority groups' voices (getting them heard); long-term planning and investment in social inclusion programs; the provision of high-quality, reasonably priced education to excluded groups; and cultural understanding are just a few of the initiatives. To ensure that minority groups are represented, it is possible to advance the opinions of minority groups and make them heard through reorganizing the political

Fig. 4.5 Social inclusion interventions from the human potential empowerment. (Source: Authors)

system of partner institutions, such as colleges, the creation of community networks, and the establishment of forums for discussion, enabling members of underrepresented groups to openly engage in conversations about inclusion.

For instance, Lane (2017) claimed that stakeholders in higher education must comprehend and be aware of the lived realities of students with disabilities. According to Lane (2017), knowing the challenges that these impaired students encounter may help to support inclusive and efficient teaching methods. This also applies to other excluded groups of people; to address their issues, it is crucial that relevant stakeholders, such as politicians, are aware of their situation. According to Lane (2017), hearing the perspectives of disabled students may be a useful strategy for involving students and encouraging inclusive participation in efforts to remove barriers and address issues, which would be advantageous for both students with disabilities and higher education institutions in terms of long-term planning and financial support for social inclusion initiatives. According to Gidley et al. (2010), it is preferable to engage in some sort of long-term future planning and/or imagining preferred future scenarios concerning certain underrepresented groups for social inclusion interventions to be effective as strategies to produce long-term gains.

Future researchers have emphasized the need for planning for the long term for decades, and different studies have highlighted the psychological and thus pedagogical worth of interventions that help young people envision a bright future (Gidley et al., 2010). Regarding the provision of education to socially marginalized groups, Thomas (2016), education has a significant impact on young refugees' futures and has the power to change lives for those who have access to it. According to Thomas (2016), schools are crucial in assisting refugee children in realizing their full potential as learners and in helping them feel a feeling of safety. Thomas (2016) continued by stating that to maximize the human rights and social inclusion approach, the community, government, school administration, mainstream teachers, social workers, students and their parents, and refugee students and their parents must work together to foster an environment conducive to active learning and socialization for a productive citizenry.

According to Thomas (2016), social work is in a unique position to promote a larger push for social inclusion, which is essential to the well-being of refugee children and enables them to become fully integrated members of society. Education is important because it fosters empowerment and hope. Festivals and cultural knowledge are also crucial for promoting social inclusion. People's ability to express their cultural values in ways that properly honour them, according to researchers, is one of the best ways to support the deeper feelings of social inclusion that align with engagement and empowerment, as opposed to having access but yet feeling disempowered. Access to education can help minority groups, such as the indigenous people of many African nations, become more socially integrated. However, involvement in higher education is not just about student participation and employment; it also involves what is considered knowledge in the academy. The focus of education should be on the people's culture. Indigenous students and staff, according to Bradley et al. (2008), have special knowledge and understandings that need to be incorporated into the curriculum for all students as well as used to guide research and scholarship. Gidley et al. (2010) went on to argue that any group that experiences social exclusion, including indigenous people, women, young people, physically or mentally ill people, or the elderly, should incorporate their culture into the educational system, as it is one of the best ways to include the people on a social level. It is unquestionably a step forward to expand not only access but also participation, engagement, and human potential to include voices from culturally varied backgrounds in the broadest interpretation of educational curricula and procedures.

4.8 Conclusion and Policy Suggestions

Social inclusion is the process of making it easier for people and groups to participate in society. African nations have taken the lead in several fields. For instance, of all the continents, Africa has implemented the most changes in favour of gender equality over the past 10 years. Positive developments have, like elsewhere in the world, not been equally distributed throughout Africa. The goal of the chapter was to clarify what social inclusion is, reveal the causes of social exclusion in Africa, and develop social inclusion strategies for the continent that can aid in sustainable development. The chapter emphasized that the neoliberal agenda of access views social inclusion as the first step towards a more inclusive understanding of social justice and human potential initiatives. The chapter also made clear that a social justice perspective provides a more inclusive definition of social inclusion. From the standpoint of social justice beliefs, it was emphasized that improving human rights, equality of opportunity, human dignity, and fairness for everyone is one way to improve social inclusion. The chapter's conclusion emphasized the significance of social inclusion interventions from the human potential empowerment interventions for advancing social justice concerns in Africa by highlighting individual potential and empowerment.

References

Abubakar, N. H., & Kah, M. M. (2021). Mobile phones and social inclusion of women in Africa: A Nigerian perspective. *The African Journal of Information Systems, 13*(2), 6.

Andrews, C., de Montesquiou, A., Sánchez, I. A., Dutta, P. V., Samaranayake, S., Heisey, J., et al. (2021). *The state of economic inclusion report 2021: The potential to scale.* World Bank Publications.

Archangelo, A. (2014). A psychosocial approach to neoliberalism, social exclusion and education. *Psychoanalysis, Culture & Society, 19*(1), 29–38.

Asongu, S. A., & Odhiambo, N. M. (2019). How enhancing information and communication technology has affected inequality in Africa for sustainable development: An empirical investigation. *Sustainable Development, 27*(4), 647–656.

Balisi, S., Moses, B., Madisa, M., & Molosiwa, P. P. (2019). *A multi-sectorial approach in education for equity, social inclusion and empowerment in Botswana.*

Beegle, K., & Christiaensen, L. (Eds.). (2019). *Accelerating poverty reduction in Africa*. World Bank Publications.

Belle-Isle, L., Benoit, C., & Pauly, B. (2014). Addressing health inequities through social inclusion: The role of community organizations. *Action Research, 12*(2), 177–193.

Bennett, L. (2002). *Using empowerment and social inclusion for pro-poor growth: a theory of social change*. Working draft of background paper for the social development strategy paper. Washington, DC: World Bank.

Bradley, M. M., Miccoli, L., Escrig, M. A., & Lang, P. J. (2008). The pupil as a measure of emotional arousal and autonomic activation. *Psychophysiology, 45*(4), 602–607.

Buré, C. E. (2006). Digital inclusion without social inclusion: The consumption of information and communication technologies (ICTs) in homeless subculture in Central Scotland. *The Journal of Community Informatics, 2*(2).

Carlisle, S. (2010). Tackling health inequalities and social exclusion through partnership and community engagement? A reality check for policy and practice aspirations from a Social Inclusion Partnership in Scotland. *Critical Public Health, 20*(1), 117–127.

Coombs, T., Nicholas, A., & Pirkis, J. (2013). A review of social inclusion measures. *Australian & New Zealand Journal of Psychiatry, 47*(10), 906–919.

Das, M. B., & Espinoza, S. A. (2020). *Inclusion matters in Africa*. https://openknowledge.worldbank.org/handle/10986/32528

Das, M. B., Evans, T. G., Palu, T., & Wilson, D. (2017). *Social Inclusion: What does it mean for health policy and practice. Health, Nutrition and Population Discussion Paper*. Washington DC: World Bank.

Eisler, R. (1987). *Polycyclic aromatic hydrocarbon hazards to fish, wildlife, and invertebrates: a synoptic review (No. 11)*. Fish and Wildlife Service, US Department of the Interior.

Farrington, J., & Farrington, C. (2005). Rural accessibility, social inclusion and social justice: Towards conceptualisation. *Journal of Transport Geography, 13*(1), 1–12.

Frodeman, R., Briggle, A., & Holbrook, J. B. (2012). Philosophy in the age of neoliberalism. *Social Epistemology, 26*(3–4), 311–330.

Gidley, J., Hampson, G., Wheeler, L., & Bereded-Samuel, E. (2010). Social inclusion: Context, theory and practice. *The Australasian Journal of University Community Engagement, 5*(1), 6–36.

Grover, A., Lall, S., & Maloney, W. (2022). *Place, productivity, and prosperity: Revisiting spatially targeted policies for regional development*. World Bank Publications.

Hayes, A., Gray, M., & Edwards, B. (2008). *Social inclusion: Origins, concepts and key themes*. Social Inclusion Unit, Department of the Prime Minister and Cabinet.

https://www.worldbank.org/en/region/afr/publication/social-inclusion-matters-africa

Huegler, N., & Kersh, N. (2021). Social inclusion, participation and citizenship in contexts of neoliberalism: Examples of adult education policy and practice with young people in the UK, The Netherlands and Ireland. In *Young adults and active citizenship* (pp. 57–78). Springer.

Igonya, E. K., Ajayi, A. I., Otukpa, E., Juma, K., Ouedraogo, R., Kibunja, G., et al. (2022). Co-created research agenda to support advocacy toward social inclusion for sexual and gender minorities in sub-Saharan Africa. *Journal of Gay & Lesbian Social Services, 34*, 1–9.

Jolley, E., Lynch, P., Virendrakumar, B., Rowe, S., & Schmidt, E. (2018). Education and social inclusion of people with disabilities in five countries in West Africa: A literature review. *Disability and Rehabilitation, 40*(22), 2704–2712.

Khalid Anser, M., Iqbal Godil, D., Aderounmu, B., Onabote, A., Osabohien, R., Ashraf, J., & Yao-Ping Peng, M. (2021). Social inclusion, innovation and food security in West Africa. *Sustainability, 13*(5), 2619.

Kofman, P., & Payne, C. (2021). Digital financial inclusion of women: An ethical appraisal. In *Handbook on ethics in finance* (pp. 133–157).

Lane, L. (2017). *'Am I being heard?'The 'voice of' students with disability in higher education: A literature review*.

Langworthy, A. (2008). Skills and knowledge for the future: Why universities must engage with their communities. *The Australasian Journal of Community Engagement, 2*(2), 57–72.

Lloyd, C., Tse, S., & Deane, F. P. (2006). Community participation and social inclusion: How practitioners can make a difference. *Australian e-Journal for the Advancement of Mental Health, 5*(3), 185–194.
Mant, J. (2017). Neoliberalism, family law and the cost of access to justice. *Journal of Social Welfare and Family Law, 39*(2), 246–258.
Mervyn, K., Simon, A., & Allen, D. K. (2014). Digital inclusion and social inclusion: A tale of two cities. *Information, Communication & Society, 17*(9), 1086–1104.
Mhlanga, D., & Denhere, V. (2020). Determinants of financial inclusion in Southern Africa. *Studia Universitatis Babes-Bolyai, Oeconomica, 65*(3), 39.
Mhlanga, D., & Ndhlovu, E. (2021). Socio-economic and political challenges in Zimbabwe and the development implications for Southern Africa. *Journal of African Foreign Affairs, 8*(2), 75.
Mhlanga, D., Ndhlovu, E., & Hofisi, C. (2021). Assessment of the 4IR challenges of radical innovation in service delivery in Africa. *Journal of Public Administration, 56*(4.1), 1002–1017.
Milazzo, A., & Van de Walle, D. (2017). Women left behind? *Poverty and Headship in Africa. Demography, 54*(3), 1119–1145.
Muñoz Arce, G., & Pantazis, C. (2019). Social exclusion, neoliberalism and resistance: The role of social workers in implementing social policies in Chile. *Critical Social Policy, 39*(1), 127–146.
Ndhlovu, E. (2018). Relevance of sustainable livelihood approach in Zimbabwe's Land Reform Programme. *Africa Insight, 47*(4), 72–87.
Ndhlovu, E. (2020). Communal rangelands and livelihoods development in rural Zimbabwe. *Yonsei Journal of International Studies, 11*(2), 31–49.
Ndhlovu, E. (2022a). Changing Agrarian discourses and practices and the prospects for food sovereignty in Zimbabwe. In G. Mkodzongi (Ed.), *The future of Zimbabwe's agrarian sector: Land issues in a time of political transition* (pp. 34–53). Routledge.
Ndhlovu, E. (2022b). Political economy of Chisa livelihoods in rural Zimbabwe. In K. Helliker, J. Matanzima, & P. Chadambuka (Eds.), *Livelihoods of ethnic minorities in rural Zimbabwe* (pp. 123–139). Springer International Publishing.
Nicholson, N. R. (2012). A review of social isolation: an important but underassessed condition in older adults. *The journal of primary prevention, 33,* 137–152.
Olsson, K. (2008). Social inclusion: What would a truly inclusive society look like? *Red*, 4–9.
Panda, P. K. (2017). Inclusion and economic empowerment of rural-tribal women in lac value chain and market: A case study of Udyogini. *Journal of Social and Economic Development, 19*(1), 25–41.
Rawal, N. (2008). Social inclusion and exclusion: A review. *Dhaulagiri Journal of Sociology and Anthropology, 2*, 161–180.
Rispel, L. C., de Sousa, C. A. P., & Molomo, B. G. (2009). Can social inclusion policies reduce health inequalities in sub-Saharan Africa?—A rapid policy appraisal. *Journal of Health, Population, and Nutrition, 27*(4), 492.
Robbie, K. (2008, Oct 15–16). *Working collaboratively with social enterprises: Lessons learned from the United Kingdom*. Paper presented at the Partnerships for Social Inclusion Conference, Centre for Public Policy, Melbourne.
Russell, S. G., & Carter, P. L. (2019). When the past is in the present: The paradox of educational opportunity and social inclusion in South Africa and Rwanda. *Sociology of Race and Ethnicity, 5*(4), 547–561.
Saunders, P., Naidoo, Y., & Griffiths, M. (2008). Towards new indicators of disadvantage: Deprivation and social exclusion in Australia. *Australian Journal of Social Issues, 43*(2), 175–194.
Söderbaum, F., & Taylor, I. (2018). *Regionalism and uneven development in Southern Africa: The case of the Maputo Development Corridor*. Routledge.
Stewart, J., Bleumers, L., Van Looy, J., Mariën, I., All, A., Schurmans, D., et al. (2013). *The potential of digital games for empowerment and social inclusion of groups at risk of social and economic exclusion: Evidence and opportunity for policy*. Joint Research Centre, European Commission.

Tett, L. (2005). Partnerships, community groups and social inclusion. *Studies in Continuing Education, 27*(1), 1–15.

The World Bank. (2019). *Inclusion Matters in Africa*.

Thomas, R. L. (2016). The right to quality education for refugee children through social inclusion. *Journal of Human Rights and Social Work, 1*(4), 193–201.

Valensisi, G. (2020). COVID-19 and global poverty: Are LDCs being left behind? *The European Journal of Development Research, 32*(5), 1535–1557.

World Bank. (2013). *Inclusion matters: The foundation for shared prosperity*. The World Bank. https://openknowledge.worldbank.org/handle/10986/16195

Worth, O. (2014). The far-right and neoliberalism: Willing partner or hegemonic opponent? In *The longue Durée of the far-right* (pp. 165–184). Routledge.

Chapter 5
The Impact of Digital Financial Service Taxes and Mobile Money Taxes on Financial Inclusion and Inclusive Development in Africa

David Mhlanga and Favourate Y. Mpofu

Abstract Globally, the digital economy is expanding rapidly. The Fourth Industrial Revolution (4IR) and ongoing technological advances are responsible for this enormous increase. The Covid-19 epidemic, which increased dependency on digital services, served as an additional catalyst for the growth of the digital economy. The chapter aimed to conduct a thorough investigation of the digital economy, digital service taxes, and mobile money taxes in Africa to examine the effects of these taxes on tax administration in Africa, the effects of these taxes on financial inclusion in Africa, and the effects of these taxes on inclusive development in Africa. The impact of digital financial services (DFS) taxes on financial inclusion can be examined from four key perspectives, including the increase in the tax burden, changes to how DFS are utilized, alterations in the market's structure or development, morale, and faith in the tax system. The chapter repeatedly emphasized the detrimental effects that digital service taxes will have on inclusive development, because they may cause resources to be diverted from sectors that benefit low-income earners, such as digital financial services, in favour of those that may not directly benefit them.

Keywords Africa · Digital financial service tax · Development · Financial inclusion · Mobile money taxes

5.1 Introduction

The digital economy is growing exponentially the world over. This unprecedented growth is attributed to the Fourth Industrial Revolution (4IR) and continuous

D. Mhlanga · F. Y. Mpofu (✉)
The University of Johannesburg, College of Business and Economics, Johannesburg, South Africa
e-mail: dmhlanga@uj.ac.za; fmpofu@uj.ac.za

D. Mhlanga, E. Ndhlovu (eds.), *Economic Inclusion in Post-Independence Africa*, Advances in African Economic, Social and Political Development,
https://doi.org/10.1007/978-3-031-31431-5_5

technological developments. The expansion of the digital economy was further driven by the Covid-19 pandemic, which led to a high reliance on digital services (Mhlanga & Denhere, 2020; Bunn et al., 2020; Mpofu, 2022). The African continent also experienced a rise in the digital economy, with considerable usage of digital financial services such as e-banking and mobile money services as well as online purchases. According to Shapshack (2021), the volume and value of mobile money transactions widened during the Covid-19 pandemic period with an estimated US 500 billion of transactions happening through mobile money. Several advantages are linked to the growth of the digital economy such as facilitating the affordability of and accessibility to financial and other services as well as broadening digital financial inclusion. The digital economy has led to the emergence of new business models and multisided businesses. This has ultimately given rise to new possibilities to derive value from externalities from free services and products such as contributions and data (Irimia et al., 2021). The value of intangible assets is progressively being recognized in the embodiment of digitalized assets. These intangible or digitalized assets come in various forms, such as intellectual property, copyrights, software, trademarks, and other various digitalized products. The digital economy facilitates economic growth and drives international trade. Despite the numerous advantages of the digital economy, the digitalization of the economy has put significant pressure on international tax laws. This has negatively affected tax revenue generation in both developed and developing countries. African countries have not been spared, and the situation is even more pressing for these countries owing to their weak taxation administration capacity, minimal financial resources, and fragile technical capacities (Sebele-Mpofu et al., 2021b). This is worsened by a huge informal economy (Mpofu, 2022; Rogan, 2019). The digitalization of the economy has put significant pressure on international tax laws as countries have been losing considerable revenues through inadequate taxation of the digital economy (de Mooij et al., 2020). The African continent is no exception (Ahmed et al., 2021; Megersa, 2020).

The digital economy has led to the growth of new business models and multisided businesses, which has ultimately given rise to new possibilities to derive value from externalities from new free products such as contributions and user data (Irimia et al., 2021). The value of intangible assets is progressively being recognized in the embodiment of digitalized assets. The value of these digitalized assets comes in various forms, such as intellectual property, copyrights, software, trademarks, and other digitalized services and products. The growth of the digital economy compromises tax revenue mobilization, through increased tax avoidance and evasion, especially by multinational enterprises (MNEs) (Bunn et al., 2020; Rukundo, 2020; Ahmed et al., 2021). The heightened potential of digital companies to minimize their tax obligations through tax planning and complex structures is further fuelled by the invisible nature of digital transactions and the ease of concealing them from tax authorities. This makes it difficult for governments to mobilize tax revenue from this rapidly growing economy (Gianni, 2018). The expansion of the digital economy challenges conventional tax rules based on brick-and-mortar activities.

Recognizing the inadequacy of traditional international tax rules when applied to tapping revenue from the digital economy, global development bodies, tax bodies, and individual governments are looking at new avenues to tax this economy. This has led to the promulgation of multilateral tax rules and discussion on taxing the digital economy through the OECD, African Continental discussion through ATAF, and national tax policy measures from both developed and developing countries. This has culminated in what has been described as digital services taxes (DSTs) and digital financial services taxes (DFSTs). There is a dearth of studies that have focused on DSTs and DFSs taxes in the African continent, especially concerning financial inclusion and inclusive development. This chapter explores the impact of DSTs and DFSs on financial inclusion and inclusive development in Africa. It builds on the few studies on the relationship of these taxes with financial inclusion, revenue generation, and the attainment of the 2030 Sustainable development Goals in Africa, such as Mpofu and Moloi (2022), Mpofu (2022), Munoz et al. (2022), and Santoro et al. (2022). While DFSTs such as mobile money taxes were introduced earlier than DSTs, which were formulated between the years 2019–2022, both taxes are in their early stages of evaluation and research. They are generally an under-researched area that is progressively gaining attention due to the importance of the digital economy to financial inclusion economic development and addressing the SDGs. The purpose of this chapter is to conduct an in-depth study of the digital economy, digital service taxes, and mobile money taxes in Africa. More specifically, the chapter will investigate the implications of digital service taxes and mobile money taxes on tax administration in Africa; the chapter will also investigate the implications of digital service taxes and mobile money taxes for financial inclusion in Africa, and the chapter will also investigate the implications of digital service tax for inclusive development in Africa. The rest of the document is organized as follows: the digital economy and the introduction of digital services taxes in Africa will be discussed first; the second section will focus on digital financial services, digital financial services taxes, and mobile money taxes in Africa; the document will also comment on the implications of digital financial service taxes on financial and will conclude on the implications of digital service taxes on inclusive development.

5.2 The Digital Economy and the Introduction of Digital Services Taxes in Africa

There is no agreement on the definition of the digital economy among researchers, but the consensus is on its dependence on information technology and communication (ICT), technological advancements, and the Internet as well as its virtual or invisible nature. The classification of the digital economy is challenging (Harpaz, 2021; Hathorne & Breunig, 2020). The digital economy is considered the Internet or virtual economy. The OECD (2018) characterizing the digital economy alludes to three critical features. These include (1) its ability to trade significantly without physical presence, "scale without mass"; (2) high dependence on intangible assets, such as intellectual property; and (3) the dependence on the synergies between data, user participation, and the use of intangibles and digital platforms. Therefore, the growth of the digital economy is linked to the usage and growth of information technology and technological advancements. This has pointed to the need to tax value created in the market jurisdictions. This economy occupies a sizeable portion of the global economy, estimated to be contributing 25% of global gross domestic product (GDP) (Low, 2020) and 75% of global economic activity. Its contribution is also huge in developing countries. In Indonesia, the digital economy was approximated at US$40 billion in 2019 and is expected to tremendously increase to reach US$130 billion by 2025 (Cahyadini et al., 2021). In Nigeria, the digital economy is expected to generate a revenue of approximately US$75 billion by 2025. Taxes generated from the digital economy do not correspond to the magnitude of the digital economy. The tax-to-GDP ratio for Nigeria ranges between 5% and 6%, way below the continent's average of 15% (Adebanjo, 2021). Therefore, according to Adebanjo (2021), taxing the digital economy would avail buffer financial resources for African countries working towards economic recovery from the Covid-19 pandemic.

While the digital economy signals new opportunities and significant prosperity, the growth of the digital economy compounds the challenges in revenue mobilization faced by developing countries, especially African countries (Ahmed et al., 2021; Becker, 2021; Rukundo, 2020). Researchers, such as Bunn et al. (2020), Munoz et al. (2022), and Silue (2021), point to the challenges of taxing the digital economy in Africa. The constraints include lack of financial and technical resources, the elusive nature of the digital economy and fragility of developing countries' revenue authorities. While focusing on MNEs operating in Africa, Sebele-Mpofu et al. (2021a) argue that MNEs exploited their complicated structures and intangibles to engage in aggressive tax planning, tax avoidance, and tax evasion. This ultimately led to the erosion of the tax base in African countries such as Zimbabwe. The invisibility and virtual nature of digital transactions compound the difficulties in taxing them in African countries. They can easily escape taxes such as value-added tax (VAT) and customs duty, as their delivery and consumption are virtual or online. As the digital economy expands, new business models such as app stores and electronic commerce are offered by digital or technological giants such as Google, Amazon, Facebook, Alibaba, Netflix, and PayPal. In the financial services sector, novel business models have also emerged to enable the delivery and consumption of DFSs, such transfer of information and funds, deposits and withdrawals, online purchases, and other financial services.

The growth in innovation has disrupted the status quo of all sectors of economies, including the fiscal or taxation landscape. Yahaya (2021) alludes to the increased demand for online services, and Odiase (2021) explains the challenges of taking the digital economy in an African context such as Nigeria. Aduloju (2022) alludes to the difficulty in taxing the digital economy in Nigeria while acknowledging that all other African countries are struggling to effectively tax this economy. The digitalized nature of the economy allows businesses to deliver in certain tax jurisdictions without necessarily having a physical presence in the jurisdiction (Irimia et al., 2021; Skaar, 2020). Digitalization enables companies to trade without permanent establishments and without paying taxes in those jurisdictions, where they operate virtually or have virtual establishments. This challenges traditional international tax laws that are founded on the principle of physical presence (Irimia et al., 2021). Conventional tax policy is becoming inadequate to mobilize revenue from the digital economy owing to the emergence of virtual establishments as opposed to physical branches or presence. Digital services include cloud services, video and movie streaming services, the sale of digital electronics, and other activities on digital platforms (Olbert & Spengel, 2017). Realizing that the taxation of profits based on the physical policy presence deprives countries of the right to tax income from digital transactions, countries (both developed and developing countries) have resorted to the construction of DSTs. The actual definition and categorization of taxable digital financial services and goods vary with the difference in tax policy in different countries. For example, in Kenya, the definition encompasses digital advertising, digital marketing, branding, and other electronic commerce activities.

5.2.1 Digital Services Taxes in Africa

The unprecedented expansion of the digital economy has propelled discussions on the amendment of current international tax rules and VAT legislation in various countries to adequately capture income generated from the digital economy into tax policy. DSTs aim to capture tax from revenue generated within a particular jurisdiction (Grondona et al., 2020; Kelbesa, 2020; Sánchez Rojas, 2020). According to Kelbesa (2020), "the digital economy offers a potentially unexploited source of tax revenue". Investors capitalize on the growth of the digital economy by investing in online platforms, such as social media platforms, online games, cryptocurrencies, and online shopping services. The need to mobilize more tax revenues to fund the post-Covid-19 pandemic economic recovery endeavours and the decline in commodity prices in Africa during the Covid-19 pandemic made the need to capture the digital economy eminent in African countries. The OECD through the G20/OECD inclusive framework sought to design a multilateral DST framework to be adopted internationally by member countries to tax the digital economy as well as to curb tax evasion and avoidance by MNEs. DSTs are defined as taxes levied on specific revenue streams of high-tech international companies or digital MNEs (Low, 2020). These revenue streams include intermediation, digital marketplaces, advertising, and data transmission. The argument is that there is value addition occurring in market jurisdiction; hence, this value creation must be subject to tax. According to Bunn et al. (2020), the recognition of digital value creation must take into cognizance the value contribution by users of digital platforms or services as their usage consequently translates to customer services and customer-oriented advertisements. Therefore, the taxation of digital services targets this value creation. The issue of value creation is contested among researchers (Olbert & Spengel, 2019). Kennedy (2019) argues that market users add no value; hence, the concept of value creation is invalid and hence DSTs are not justified.

The OECD inclusive framework on taxing the digital economy and reducing BEPS is constructed upon two pillars (OECD, 2021): Pillar 1 targets and addresses the allocation of tax between tax jurisdictions through the allocation of residual profits. Pillar 2 aims to reduce the aggressiveness of tax competition and introduce a global ant-BEPS mechanism. The pillar will deal with the problem of the non-taxation of the digital economy by implementing a 15% minimum tax (Irimia et al., 2021). Consequential to the delay and lack of consensus on the OECD global taxation measures, both developed and developing countries have implemented unilateral or country-specific DSTs to mobilize financial resources (both direct and indirect taxes). The taxes applied are applied to broad and heterogeneous groups of digital services and goods. Direct DST rates range between 1.5% and 7.5% for both developed and developing countries. There is no consensus on the definition of direct DSTs, with Lowry (2019) and Kennedy (2019) describing them as expansions of various types of taxation frameworks (tax heads), such as corporate taxes and excise taxes. The contention surrounds the nature of the DSTs, especially the fact that their tax base is the revenue and not the profits. Their criticism also coalesces on the thresholds set for the revenue bases in different counties and even the OECED of 20 million. Kennedy (2019) argues that the thresholds are discriminatory and merely target the big United States technology companies or large digital MNEs, such as Amazon, Google, and Facebook. Lowry (2019) adduces that DSTs are targeting incomes and profits that would ordinarily not have been subject to taxation under conventional international tax legislation. Tables 5.1 and 5.2 presents a summary of direct DSTs in selected developed and developing countries (African countries).

Developing countries, such as Malaysia, Indonesia, Kenya, Argentina, and Chile, have also introduced DSTs to mobilize revenue from the digital economy. In Africa, only a few countries have enacted the direct DSTs as shown in Table 5.2. Most African countries, such as Zimbabwe, South Africa, Malawi, Uganda, Kenya, and

Table 5.1 Digital services taxes in selected developed countries

Country	Rate (%) (revenue being the base)	Effective date
France	3	July 2019
Italy	3	January 2020
Poland	1.5	July 2020
Spain	3	January 2021
United Kingdom	2	April 2020
Turkey	7.5	March 2020

Compiled by Bunn et al. (2020) and Lowry (2019)

Table 5.2 Digital services taxes in selected African nations

Country	Effective implementation date	Tax rate (%)	Provisions/base	Threshold
Tunisia	1 January 2020	3	Gross income from the sale of digital services and computer applications	n/a
Kenya	1 January 2021	1.5	Income accruing through a digital marketplace. A digital marketplace is considered a place which enables buyers and sellers of goods to directly interact through electronic means	n/a
Zimbabwe	1 January 2019	5	Gross income received or accrued from satellite broadcasting services in relation to the delivery or provision of television or radio programs. In addition, income received by or accruing to e-commerce operators delivering or proving goods and/or services to persons resident in Zimbabwe	Revenue exceeding US$500,000 in any year of assessment.
Kenya	1 January 2021	1.5	Income accruing through a digital marketplace. A digital marketplace is considered a place which enables buyers and sellers of goods to directly interact through electronic means	n/a

Source: Authors' compilation

Zambia, among others, have expanded their VAT regulations to capture digital services into tax policies (Simbarashe, 2020). This chapter focuses mainly on both direct and indirect DSTs and DFSTs.

5.3 Digital Financial Services, Digital Financial Services Taxes, and Mobile Money Taxes in Africa

Due to the widening of the digital economy, digital transformation in the financial services sector, and the growth of fintech, the provision and usage of DFS have increased across the globe. DFSs provide countries globally with a room for facilitating sustainable economic development and economic growth, promoting digital financial inclusion, and improving communication between financial institutions and their customers. DFSs such as mobile money allow peer-to-peer remittances, business-to-business remittances and government-to-person remittances, as well as international remittances (Mpofu, 2022). Through mobile money, the previously excluded segments of the population are enabled to transact, transfer, and withdraw money and make purchases, thus facilitating financial inclusion, especially in Africa (Clifford, 2020; Muthiora, 2015). While citing Inner Circle (2019), Pushkareva (2021) states that nearly 370 million adults in Africa are unbanked or financially excluded. Financial exclusion refers to a lack of access to affordable and reliable financial services, such as banking, credit cards, savings account, and credit. The World Bank expostulates that financial inclusion is fundamental to poverty reduction and facilitating economic growth (Munoz et al., 2022). Therefore, financial inclusion and digital financial inclusion are a necessity for the African continent, which has 70% of the least developed economies (33 out of the 47 least developed countries). In these countries, women and girls are largely financially excluded, and this has a significant influence on economic growth and sustainable development. Mobile money provides an accessible, affordable, and convenient platform to boost the financial inclusion of these vulnerable and underserved groups. In affirmation, Pazarbasioglu et al. (2020) state that access to cheaper financial services is fundamental for economic growth and poverty eradication, "Digital financial services powered by fintech have the potential to lower the costs by maximizing economies of scale, to increase speed, security and transparency of transactions and to allow for more tailored financial services that serve the poor".

In Africa, mobile money penetration has increased tremendously over the years and more so during the Covid-19 pandemic (Clifford, 2020; Pushkareva, 2021; Mpofu, 2022 Shapshack, 2021). Rota-Graziosi and Sawadogo (2022) point out a market penetration rate of mobile network operators of 45% in Africa in comparison with 60% in other developing countries. GSMA (2020) approximated mobile network subscriber penetration to 44% and with projections that it could reach 50% in 2025 in Africa. Sixty-six percent of the sub-Saharan Africa (SSA) population was financially excluded. Africa is observed as the continent that has made significant growth in the use of mobile money services when compared to other contents. Pushkareva (2021) adduces that the 37 African countries studied had more registered mobile money and registered agents than bank branches. The researcher further asserts that "The number of customers of MNOs is also significantly larger than traditional banks: MTN Africa's largest mobile operator, has 171 million customers, while the biggest pan-African banks such as Ecobank, Standard Bank and Barclays Bank only have between 11 and 15 million customers" (Pushkareva, 2021). This difference is attributed to, firstly, the magnitude of mobile money penetration as compared to traditional banking, estimated at 80% and 40%, respectively, and to, secondly, the concentration of mobile money. Pushkareva (2021) adduces that while the top African banks arguably served approximately 22% of African clients, the top five African mobile operators served 60% of the telecommunications clients in the continent. If these projections are taken into the sector, they could contribute significantly to revenue generation through mobile money taxes, but at the same time, heavy taxing could be an impediment to economic growth, digital financial inclusion, and the achievement of Sustainable Development Goals (SDGs).

African countries have looked to the growth of the digital economy as an opportunity to mobilize more tax revenues that can be channelled to address economic challenges faced by these countries and to finance government objectives (Munoz et al., 2022; Ndung'u, 2019; Santoro et al., 2022). Countries, such as Zimbabwe, Uganda, Cote d'Ivoire, Chad, Cameroon, Zambia, and Gabon, among others, have introduced mobile money taxes (Clifford, 2020; Mpofu, 2022). Mobile money taxes come in various forms, such as VAT, corporate tax, excise duty, and telecommunications levies (GSMA, 2020; Pushkareva, 2021). The revenue mobilized could be used to achieve the 2030 SDGs such as reducing poverty (SDG 1), improving food security and reducing hunger (SDG 2), and improving public service delivery in areas such as education, health, sanitation, and the provision of clean energy (SDGs 3, 4, 5, 6, and 7). Despite the potential advantages of taxing the DFS through mobile money taxes, concerns have been raised on the fairness of these DFSTs and their impact on financial inclusion, the usage, and affordability of DFSs as well as on economic growth. Munoz et al. (2022) point to the discriminatory nature of DFSTs as they tend to be levied only on DFSs and not on traditional financial services. While focusing on DFSs, Mpofu (2022) found that Zimbabwe was the only African country levying tax on mobile money networks and traditional banking through its 2% intermediate monetary tax on transfers on local currency transactions and 4% on foreign currency transactions. All other African countries levied taxes on mobile money transactions only, excluding other DFSs. Some researchers contend that mobile money taxes disproportionately and overly burden the telecommunication sector and mobile money users (Muthiora & Raithatha, 2018). This could potentially cripple the attainment of the SDGs, financial inclusion, and sustainable economic development and revenue mobilization in Africa (Clifford, 2020; Mpofu, 2022; Shinyekwa, 2018; Silue, 2021). According to Koomson et al. (2022) while focusing on "*Mobile money and entrepreneurship in East Africa: The mediating roles of digital savings and access to digital credit*" submit that mobile money taxes discourage the usage of mobile money activities. Mobile money taxes could cripple entrepreneurial activities thereby increasing poverty, inequality, and unemployment.

Pushkareva (2021) and Clifford (2020) raise concerns about the multiplicity of mobile money taxes and the possible negative impact on the economy. The taxes are levied on both corporates (telecommunications providers) and users. For example, Pushkareva (2021) submits examples of different corporate tax rates applied to telecommunication companies in a few selected African countries. The tax rates are as follows: for the Democratic Republic of Congo (DRC), Gabon, Cameroon, Congo, Burkina Faso, and Cote d'Ivoire (30%), Zimbabwe (24.74%), Zambia (40%), and Tanzania (25%). For countries like Zambia and Cote d'Ivoire, the corporate tax regime is considered discriminatory with telecom providers paying more. The standard tax rate is 35% in Zambia and 25% in Cote d'Ivoire, compared to telecom companies' corporate taxes rates of 40% and 30%, respectively (Pushkareva, 2021). Table 5.3 presents a summary of the total usage taxes in selected African countries.

Given the various usage taxes, corporate taxes, and other levies charged on the telecommunication sector, Rota-Graziosi and Sawadogo (2022) contend that the telecom companies are taxed more heavily than the mining sector in Africa. This could affect the digital dynamism, market efficiency and economic development associated with mobile money operators and other telecommunications companies.

Table 5.3 Telecommunication services usage taxes

Country	DRC (%)	Gabon (%)	Cameroon (%)	Chad (%)	Zambia (%)	Guinea (%)
Sector-specific taxes	10	18	2	10	15	7
VAT on usage	16	18	19	18	16	20
Total usage taxes	26	36	21	28	31	27
Country	**Cote d'Ivoire (%)**	**Tanzania (%)**	**Uganda (%)**	**Kenya (%)**	**Ghana (%)**	**Malawi (%)**
Sector-specific taxes	3	17	12	10	6	10
VAT on usage	18	18	18	16	17.5	17
Total usage taxes	21	35	30	26	23.5	27

Source: Pushkareva (2021)

5.4 The Implications of Digital Service Taxes and DFSTs Tax Administration in Africa

The discussions on the role of the digital economy and DFSs, such as mobile money, give a comprehensive understanding of their importance in economic growth, digital financial inclusion, sustainable and inclusive economic growth, and the fulfilment of the SDGs. To highlight the implications of DSTs, Irimia et al. (2021) portend: "We conclude that DSTs: (i) is a very 'rough instrument', (ii) is not considered an income tax, so tax treaties often don't apply (iii) leads to double taxation, (iii) in addition since it is a tax on revenue, not income or profits, it can end up being a very effective tax rate; (iv) tax people generally really don't like DSTs and are hoping that an agreement on something like the OECD blueprint can truly result in the repeal of these taxes".

The implications of DSTs and DFSTs in Africa are contested and conflicting (Mpofu, 2022). While researchers such as Becker (2021), Bunn et al. (2020), and Onuoha and Gillwald (2022) advocate for DSTs based on sustainable revenue mobilization and equity grounds, Mpofu and Moloi (2022) raise concerns and encourage African countries to design the DSTs with the principles of an ideal tax policy in mind as a well as the role of tax policy in the economy. Mpofu and Moloi (2022) argue that in pursuit of the revenue mobilization policy, tax policy should not overlook other roles of taxation, such as facilitating economic growth, redistribution, reducing market externalities, governance, and encouraging or discouraging the consumption of some products or services. If not properly designed, DSTs' policy could result in negative implications, such as reduced consumption of digital services, distortions in the market structure, and overly burdensome taxes that could negatively affect the supply, access, and usage of digital services. According to Bunn et al. (2020) and Mpofu and Moloi (2022), DSTs should conform to the principles of taxation, such as economy, transparency, simplicity, administrative economy, efficiency, as well as fairness. Similarly, concerns on affordability, access, and usage were raised by Munoz et al. (2022), Pushkareva (2021), Clifford (2020), and Mpofu (2022) regarding DFSTs, especially mobile money taxes in Africa. The researchers point to areas where mobile money policies violate taxation principles, such as the economy and equity (tax rates and one-size-fit-all rates), fairness (double taxation of the same income, multiple taxes for telecoms operators and users), and certainty (the lack of stability and consistency). The violation of the canons of taxation affects the delivery and usage as well as making the investment climate uncertain and hostile.

In addition to the likelihood of negative externalities emanating from both DSTs and DFSs taxes. DSTs could lead to the emergence of trade wars linked to the sentiments that the taxes target US tech giants operating in international jurisdictions. This could affect African countries unfavourably owing to the weak political and economic power (ATAF, 2020). Aslam and Shah (2021) dispute the discriminatory argument, arguing that digitalization has enabled the so-called tech giants that were exploiting the first mover gains and network externalities to enhance profitability, capture a larger market, and structure themselves into the world's highly valued and prestigious companies. These companies were enjoying market presence and high profits and not paying tax in market jurisdictions, and it is only fair that tax authorities and governments are paying attention to them to mobilize their fair share of taxes from incomes generated within their borders. The possible effects of these taxes are complex in Africa owing to the possibilities of enhanced digital transformation, revenue mobilization, digital financial inclusion, and economic growth, yet the likelihood of impeding these three variables is equally persuasive. Non-taxation of DSTs that are offered virtually by these high-tech giants deprives African governments of tax revenues, enables MNEs to engage in base erosion and profit-shifting behaviour, and erodes the tax bases of African economies. In terms of competitiveness, these foreign companies get an advantage over domestic companies that pay corporate tax and VAT, because, under traditional tax laws, they supply goods and services without fulfilling any of the OECD's physical presence tests to justify taxation. From the revenue mobilization angle and equity grounds, DSTs are justifiable. From the possibility of crippling industrialization, digitalization, and digitization efforts, arguing for their cogency is difficult.

5.4.1 Implications of Digital Service Taxes for Financial Inclusion in Africa

The primary goal of imposing taxes on digital financial services in Africa is to increase income production across the continent and to capitalize on growing revenue streams (Mhlanga, 2020; Mpofu & Mhlanga, 2022). The requirement for fairness is still another secondary reason. This is done to guarantee that all enterprises operating within the financial industry contribute to the overall tax basket. The

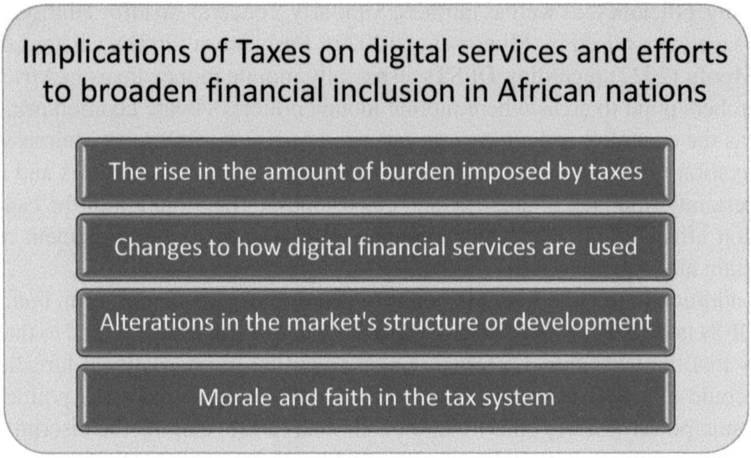

Fig. 5.1 Implications of taxes on digital services and efforts to broaden financial inclusion in African nations. (*Source*: Authors)

source rule or the physical presence that was the anchor of earlier international tax legislation has not been able to apply to digital transactions. As a result, digital transactions have avoided paying taxes. This resulted in businesses, such as Facebook, Amazon, Netflix, and Google, being exempt from paying taxes due to the digital nature of their operations, even though they were making extremely profitable sales. According to Munoz et al.'s (2022) findings, taxing the digital economy will result in the equitable distribution of resources being maintained. Contrarily, Tan (2022) posits that mobile money taxes will push the poor out of the digital economy. As summarised in Fig. 5.1, DFSTs can have unfavourable impacts on the cost and usage of DFSs.

The impact of DFS taxes and financial inclusion can be explored from four main dimensions, namely: the rise in the amount of burden imposed by taxes, changes to how digital financial services are used, alterations in the market's structure or development, morale, and faith in the tax system.

5.4.2 *The Rise in the Amount of Burden Imposed by Taxes*

The effects of implications of taxation on price decisions influence the economic and social well-being of consumers of DFS as well as the businesses that provide them. The effect of DFS taxes on pricing is rather convoluted and controversial, because it depends on how the tax-driven rise in price is allocated between customers and providers of DFS. This means that there is no clear answer to the question of what the effect of DFS taxes on prices will be. One of the outcomes that are least likely to occur because of DFS taxes is for the tax burden to be borne by the provider of financial services, which would result in a decrease in earnings. The second most likely outcome is that the burden of the tax will be passed on to the customers in the form of increased pricing (Munoz et al., 2022; Mhlanga, 2021, 2022). The degree of competitiveness in the market for financial services will have a significant impact on how the tax burden is distributed, which in turn will have a significant impact on how the tax liability is shared.

If the rivalry is based on pricing and there are alternative options for the service (or services), then the providers are probably more willing to share or absorb the tax liability to some level. For instance, in Cote d'Ivoire, providers of DFS were required to shoulder the costs of DFS taxes to encourage the utilization of DFS, which were thought to be as low as 20%. This was done to boost the usage of DFS. The viability of such an endeavour is not yet obvious, since it is conceivable for suppliers to find other less direct means to pass the cost on to customers.

On the other hand, when the impact of the tax is modest or the provider is not concerned about the price, they are likely to pass the cost of the tax on to customers by increasing prices. If the burden of the tax is passed on to the customers, there is a possibility that welfare will be reduced. Vulnerable groups, such as those with low incomes, those employed in the informal sector, and women, are likely to feel the effects of this loss more than others (Munoz et al., 2022; Mpofu & Mhlanga, 2022). Carboni and Bester (2020) point out that consumers in Rwanda could conveniently switch to cash, which implies that customers in the nation were substantially responsive to a rise in the fees, which led to an increase in the utilization of DFSs as providers continued to increase their prices as a means of forcing buyers to absorb the tax cost. As a result, a rise in the charges and taxes would most likely result in a reversal of the progress that has been gained in terms of financial inclusion. Whenever the cost of DFS is absorbed by providers of DFS in the form of fewer profits, this would consequently result in a reduction in investments in DFS. Both potential futures that have been considered may have unfavourable effects on financial inclusion. Customers of financial services may choose to switch to other services or reduce their usage, or businesses may choose to reduce the amount of digital financial services they offer. In comparison to other arguments, this one has received relatively little empirical investigation.

5.4.3 Changes to How Digital Financial Services Are Used

In addition to the expenses associated with welfare, taxes on DFS could also result in changes to the consumption patterns of financial services. Even if the shift in usage might not have much of an effect on welfare in certain instances, the shift in consumption might have a significant impact on welfare in other cases. This is dependent on the availability of alternative services to the one in question, as well as the significance of the service in question to potential short-, medium-, and long-term development. Opponents of implementing DFS taxes argue that these taxes would result in significant reductions in the use of DFS (Munoz et al., 2022), which would have a negative impact on economic development and growth, including the reversal of advancement made on financial inclusion in overall and digital financial inclusion on the African continent. This goes against the United Nations' recommendation for countries to work towards the goal of universal financial inclusion.

The term "financial inclusion" refers to having access to and making use of adequate, cost-effective, and appropriate financial services. According to Mungai and van der Linden (2021), there was a rise in the adoption and use of DFS in Rwanda when the National Bank of Rwanda removed fees on digital person-to-person and merchant payments. Mungai and van der Linden cite this as the reason for the increase. There has been little effort put into analysing the evidence around DFS taxes and usage effects, as well as their connection to financial inclusion. There may be a requirement to provide a contextualization of such consequences to poor groups, such as the informal economy, the poorer people, the poor, and women, because they may vary based on the group that is investigated. The implications can also be different, depending on the tax systems that are in placed in a country.

Because they may have a detrimental effect on people's access to financial services, opponents of DFS taxes push for their elimination. These adversaries have additionally advocated for the necessity of increasing the usage of DFS, by advocating for the implementation of tax incentives to encourage enterprises to increase their provision of DFS. This has the potential to broaden the extent of financial inclusion in nations that are still developing. There has been insufficient research conducted on these claims. There are still many unanswered questions regarding the best method to organize tax policy to encourage investments and growth in the service of expanding financial inclusion. Regarding the topic of digital transformation in economies, Mungai and van der Linden (2021) pose the following question: Can countries sustain the developmental impact of taxing digital payments without reversing the digitalization accomplishments made during the pandemic? It is also not sufficient to investigate financial inclusion and exclusion from the perspective of taxes because the condition of the infrastructure, the regulatory requirements, and Internet connectivity all have an impact on the demand and supply chain of financial services and financial inclusion. Consequently, this line of inquiry is also insufficient. The submission of tax incentives and other incentive schemes and their potential effect on the utilization of financial services and financial inclusion need further exploration. This is especially important when taking into consideration the ineffectiveness of tax incentives in developing countries as well as their potential for abuse. According to Oguttu (2018), multinational corporations have been abusing the tax incentives that African nations have provided them with to engage in base erosion and profit-shifting behaviour.

The tax policy would be regarded as discriminatory and as going against the ideals of justice and fairness, if taxes were only collected on DFS suppliers and not on traditional service providers. As a result of consumers switching to traditional financial services, digital financial inclusion will suffer. Traditional financial services are more affordable and are not subject to taxation. The playing ground for competition would be similarly uneven as a result of the financial impact of taxing, which would result in DFS being pricey. The profitability of DFS companies would suffer as a result of the unfair competition posed by traditional financial services. As a result of decreased profitability, the continuation and survival of certain digital operations could be jeopardized, which would have a detrimental impact on financial inclusion. African policymakers should think about how to design DFS fiscal policies in a way that encourages developmental-level beneficial changes in the market structure, particularly interoperability between various works. This should be done to maximize the potential benefits of these changes to the continent.

5.4.4 Alterations in the Market's Structure or Development

Taxes on DFS could have a substantial influence on shifts in the market for particular DFS or the DFS industry in general over the medium and long term. If taxes are levied on some financial products but not on others, the economy can become distorted as a result of consumers choosing less expensive alternatives. Pricing decisions typically take into account taxes as a cost of doing business. New taxes on digital financial services (DFS) or an expansion of existing taxes on financial services, in general, could stifle the expansion of the digital economy's financial sector (Munoz et al., 2022). Whether a change in market structure is seen as beneficial or detrimental to financial inclusion depends on the impact it has on economic fundamentals, long-term growth and development investment decisions, and the rise or drop in the usage of DFS. How governments strike a balance between the goal of maximizing revenue from a sector that had been undertaxed in the past and the long-term development of banking services and the access to financial services of vulnerable groups will determine how the effect of digital taxes on the economic system is interpreted.

There are two different ways to understand this. First, there is the appropriate taxation of a rapidly expanding but currently undertaxed industry. Second, there is the possibility of choking an up-and-coming industry that is still in its baby stages of development. Concerning the first point, it has been estimated that the ratio of taxes paid to GDP in Africa, particularly in SSA, is very low, coming in at roughly 15.6%, whereas the same ratio in Europe and North America is projected to be 24.2% and 24.2%, respectively. When compared to domestic revenue, governmental expenditure is typically higher in African countries, making DFS a potential source of revenue for those nations. The impact of Covid-19, which has had a detrimental effect on the economic growth and development trajectories of most countries, has contributed to a further increase in the budget deficits of most countries (Mungai & van der Linden, 2021). The taxation of DFS is an effective method for the mobilization of domestic money, yet there is a risk that it will have negative long-term effects on developmental outcomes. Consumers may be discouraged from using direct financial services (DFS), such as mobile money, which would result in a reduction in the benefits of financial inclusion. This is the case despite the possibility of benefits associated with the allocation of resources pooled together through taxes and inclusive public expenditure. Regarding the second point of view, tax policy would be regarded as discriminatory and against the principles of justice and fairness, if taxes were only assessed on DFS suppliers, and not on traditional service providers, if taxes were levied on traditional service providers.

As a result of consumers switching to traditional financial services, digital financial inclusion will suffer. Traditional financial services are more affordable and are not subject to taxation. The playing ground for competition would be similarly uneven as a result of the financial impact of taxing, which would result in DFS being pricey. The unequal competition posed by traditional financial services has the potential to cut into the profitability of DFS enterprises (Munoz et al., 2022; Mpofu & Mhlanga, 2022). As a result of decreased profitability, the continuation and survival of certain digital operations could be jeopardized, which would have a detrimental impact on financial inclusion. African policymakers must consider how to develop DFS tax policies in a way that encourages developmental-level beneficial changes in the market structure, particularly by creating connections between various projects. This should be done to maximize the potential benefits of these changes to the continent.

5.4.5 Morale and Faith in the Tax System

If the information on these taxes is not communicated openly and honestly and is not adequately understood by users, the taxation of digital transactions, particularly payments, can erode users' trust in the DFS. Strong mistrust and suspicion towards the government have resulted because of the ambiguity of tax policy, the lack of consistency in policymaking processes, and inadequate stakeholder engagement on DFS taxes in most African countries. This has in some cases rendered the use of digital financial services completely ineffective (Mpofu & Mhlanga, 2022). Consumers and businesses in Zimbabwe, for instance, voiced their disapproval of the imposition of a 2% IMTT. According to Mungai and van der Linden (2021), users of DFS in Uganda were effectively subjected to a tax rate that was four times higher than the standard rate. They were subject to taxation at every stage of the financial transaction, including when they deposited money, sent money, received money, and withdrew money. Customers felt as though they were being overtaxed because of this, and they responded by using digital financial services less frequently.

The number of transactions conducted person to person fell by more than half. The government of Uganda responded to the outrage from the public and the potentially negative ramifications for financial inclusion by lowering the DFS tax rates and only applying them to withdrawals. This meant that the tax was no longer applied to deposits, transfers, or purchases. The effects of decreased trust could be twofold: decreased utilization and diminished tax morale, both of which could lead to less taxation if trust levels continue to decline. To earn citizens' confidence and support, governments need to impose tax rates that are consistent with the economic tax principle of the economy. The idea behind this notion is that citizens should not be put in a worse financial position or forced into poverty because of taxation. In addition to this, governments are obligated to conduct stakeholder consultations with market participants, consumer advocacy groups, and DFS providers. It is argued that this is one of the obstacles that prevent an accurate evaluation of the influence of taxation on a variety of economic concerns, including financial inclusion. In this approach, the government will have the ability to gain access to data on digital transactions. African nations must work together, coordinate their efforts, and cooperate to go forward with major tax changes, improve DFS structures, and enhance administrative capabilities. There is an ongoing requirement to draw from and learn from one another's experiences.

5.5 Implications of Digital Service Tax for Inclusive Development in Africa

The effects of mobile money and digital service taxes on inclusive development primarily revolve around their impact on efficiency, which in some ways might influence the allocation of resources investment. The distribution of resources determines the mix of products as well as the pattern of output in an economy. Taxes tend to reallocate resources among various economic sectors and geographic areas. When higher taxes are levied on certain sectors of the economy, the resources that were previously allocated to those sectors will instead be allocated to sectors that are subject to lower taxes. In a similar vein, the provision of a tax rebate will encourage the allocation of resources in favour of the development of newborn industries. In this sense, the worst possible outcome is occurring, which is that these taxes can lead to a reallocation of resources away from digital financial services, which are advantageous for low-income earners, and toward other sectors, which may not have tangible benefits to low-income earners.

One definition of economic efficiency describes it as the state of a market or economy in which resources are created and dispersed in the most effective manner possible (Mpofu & Moloi, 2022). Because they influence economic decisions based on the tax's effect on pricing, taxes typically infringe on the optimal allocation of resources and/or skew the distribution in an unfavourable direction. It is essential to determine who bears the incidence of or the economic burden of DSTs to have complete knowledge of the ramifications of the distortions. The economic burden that must be borne by the suppliers of digital services or the customers, or how it must be split among these groups, is the topic at hand. Because suppliers are ultimately responsible for paying the tax that is collected by the government, the statutory incidence is irrelevant. Where there is full and healthy competition in the market for the delivery of digital services, the tax burden is passed on to customers by way of an increase in the cost of the services they purchase. According to Lowry (2019), "in a seamlessly profitable industry, companies supplying digital advertisements receive zero economic gain because they could achieve a greater return via alternative investment". This is because these businesses can earn a higher return from other investments. The digital service providers have the choice to either exit the market entirely and participate in other industries or sectors that are not subject to the tax or they can shift their investments to locations that are more accommodating to DST. These are the two options that are available to them.

Second, digital corporations can shift the tax burden onto the businesses and individuals who make use of their services. The first choice results in fewer investments being made in the economy, which slows economic expansion and lowers the amount of taxable money that can be collected through DSTs. The second choice might result in greater prices being charged, which would then lead to a reduction in the quantity of the good or service that is demanded. Consumption and the generation of new money are intimately related. When corporations suffer a loss of business, it results in lesser profits and less money collected in taxes. A reduction in the consumption of digital services results in a reduction in consumption taxes such as value-added tax (VAT). This is in addition to other external costs, such as a reduction in possibilities for technological and technological financial education, digital literacy, and access to financial services as well as communication. These externalities are very crucial to the success of African countries in achieving Sustainable Development Goals.

It is essential to keep in mind that the extent of the shifts in demand and utilization is a function of the elasticity or sensitivity of the market (individuals and enterprises) to shifts in price. It is for this reason that it is crucial to notice this relationship. The paradox of digital sales tax is that the implementation of digital taxes in most African nations was followed by a subsequent reduction in the number of people accessing and utilizing the Internet and other digitally linked services, which signalled a decrease in revenues mobilized. The restriction placed on the utilization of financial transactions would, in the end, have an impact on businesses, such as agricultural and financial services. Taxes make it even more difficult for people in African countries to purchase the Internet and other forms of digital service. Access to the Internet and its affordability are already issues in these nations because of high data charges and inadequate connectivity. The findings of Covid-19 have made it abundantly clear that connection and access to the Internet at more affordable prices are critical components of not just communication but also commercial transactions and economic activities.

According to what Lirri (2021) has stated, taxes that unfairly burden the poor, who are already reeling from issues related to their inability to afford necessities, or taxes that discourage investment in a particular industry are contrary to the principles of fair taxation. Mpofu and Moloi (2022) suggested that Uganda imposed a tax on social media in 2018 to widen the scope of the tax and generate a greater amount of tax revenue. Users turned to virtual private networks (VPN) as well as Wi-Fi networks available in places like restaurants and offices, while revenue mobilization suffered a dramatic fall. After extensive consultation with various stakeholders, the nation finally gave up on the tax in 2021 and instead imposed a tax of 12% on Internet data. For Africa to be able to provide effective delivery on e-services, which include fintech, health, education, and communication, the continent needs to bridge the accessibility and cost divide. The cost of e-services goes up because of DSTs, which also discourage investment. Mobile money has the potential to completely revolutionize financial inclusion through digital technology. Taxes based on DST will likely influence financial inclusion, exacerbate inequality, and make poverty more persistent in Africa.

According to the statement made by AAs, "Poverty is more than just the absence of money." It entails an absence of access to the tools and means by which those with lower incomes could improve their quality of life. One of the obstacles to achieving a world free of poverty is people's lack of access to formal financial systems, which is becoming an increasingly recognized issue. The rippling effects of digital taxes on other forms of revenue should be reexamined by African nations, with a particular emphasis placed on usage, affordability of access, and the effect on the market (Donovan, 2012; Mpofu & Moloi, 2022). In contrast, when there is monopoly power among providers of digital services, such as Facebook, Amazon, and Google, or when there are few players in that industry, the tax may be partially absorbed by these businesses in the form of reduced prices. This is the case when there are few players in that industry. The market power of service providers can be impacted when there is little competition or when there are no available alternatives. Because digital MNEs are operating in an oligopoly or almost monopoly conditions, they can earn abnormally high profits, because they can price their services at a higher level than the marginal cost of production. This is possible because "the cost of production of scalability production of their business is fairly low, if not costless". As an illustration, the marginal cost to Facebook of displaying an advertisement to a user is virtually nothing (Lowry, 2019; Mpofu & Moloi, 2022). Although the validity of these claims cannot be established with absolute certainty, they do suggest that MNEs may be able to realize exceptionally significant profits. If a company like Google allows its search engine to be accessed for free by individuals while at the same time it sells advertising space to corporations, then this argument may be invalid. As a result, the problem of rivalry with companies like Facebook and other non-digital means like television and radio is a reality, and it could lead to prices that are higher than the marginal cost of production. The fairness, justice, and economic productivity of DSTs are all called into doubt because of these arguments.

5.6 Conclusion

The expansion of the digital economy in every region of the world is phenomenal. This enormous rise can be linked to the Fourth Industrial Revolution (4IR) as well as ongoing advancements in technology. The Covid-19 epidemic, which caused a significant increase in people's dependency on digital services, was another factor that contributed to the rise of the digital economy. The purpose of this chapter was to conduct an in-depth investigation of the digital economy, digital service taxes, and mobile money taxes in Africa. The investigation's ultimate objective was to determine the implications of digital service taxes and mobile money taxes on tax administration in Africa, the implications of digital service taxes and mobile money taxes for financial inclusion in Africa, and the implications of digital service taxes for inclusive development in Africa. The influence of digital financial services taxes on financial inclusion can be examined from the perspectives of four primary dimensions, namely, the rise in the amount of burden imposed by taxes, changes to how digital financial services are used, changes in the structure or development of the market, and changes in morale and faith in the tax system. Again, the chapter emphasized the fact that taxes on digital services will have a negative impact on inclusive development. This is because these taxes can lead to a reallocation of resources away from digital financial services, which are advantageous for low-income earners, and towards other sectors, which may not have tangible benefits to low-income earners. In addition, the chapter emphasized that these taxes would have negative implications on inclusive development.

References

Adebanjo, A. (2021). Taxing Nigeria's emerging digital economy: A vital buffer to an ailing economy. *Journal of Business Diversity, 21*(3).

Aduloju, O. I. (2022). *Taxation of the Nigerian digital economy in view of the 2019 and 2020 Finance Act*. Available at SSRN 4002469.

African Tax Administration Forum (ATAF). (2020). Domestic resource mobilisation-digital services taxation. Available online: https://events.ataftax.org/index.php?page=documents&folder=18

Ahmed, S., Chinembiri, T., & Govan-Vassen, N. (2021). COVID-19 exposes the contradictions of social media taxes in Africa. Available online: https://www.africaportal.org/documents/21197/COVID-19-social_media_taxes_in_Africa.pdf

Aslam, A., & Shah, A. (2021). Taxing the digital economy. In *Corporate income taxes under pressure. Why reform is needed and how it could be designed* (pp. 189–226). International Monetary Fund.

Becker, C. (2021). Taxing the digital economy in Sub Saharan Africa. Available online: https://www.ibanet.org/Taxing-the-digital-economy-sub-Saharan-Africa

Bunn, D., Asen, E., & Enache, C. (2020). *Digital taxation around the world*. Tax Foundation, 20.

Cahyadini, A., Dewi, S., Sugiharti, D. K., & Muttaqin, Z. (2021). Direct tax for digital platform during the COVID-19 pandemic: Study in Indonesia. *Journal of Southwest Jiaotong University, 56*(2), 271.

Carboni, I., & Bester, H. (2020, May 19). *When digital payment goes viral: Lessons from COVID-19's impact on mobile money in Rwanda*. Cenfri.

Clifford, K. (2020). The causes and consequences of mobile money taxation an examination of mobile money transaction taxes in Sub-Saharan Africa. Available online: https://www.ictd.ac/event/mobile-money-taxation-africa-causes-consequences/

De Mooij, R. A., Prihardini, D., Pflugbeil, A., & Stavrev, E. (2020). *International taxation and Luxembourg's economy*. Available at SSRN 3772468.

Donovan, K. (2012). Mobile money for financial inclusion. *Information and Communications for Development, 61*(1), 61–73.

Gianni, M. (2018, January). OECD BEPS (In)Action 1. In *Proceedings. Annual conference on taxation and minutes of the annual meeting of the National Tax Association* (Vol. 111, pp. 255–298). National Tax Association.

GSMA. (2020). The causes and consequences of mobile money taxation. An examination of mobile money taxation in Sub Saharan Africa. Available online: https://www.gsma.com/mobilefordevelopment/resources/the-causes-and-consequences-of-mobile-money-taxation-anexamination-of-mobile-money-transaction-taxes-in-sub-saharan-africa/

Grondona, V., Chowdhary, A. M., & Uribe, D. (2020). *National measures on taxing the digital economy*. Research Paper No. 111.

Harpaz, A. (2021). Taxation of the digital economy: Adapting a twentieth-century tax system to a twenty-first-century economy. *The Yale Journal of International Law, 46*, 57.

Hathorne, C., & Breunig, R. (2020). *Digital service taxation: An introduction and policy options for Australia*. Australian National University.

InnerCircle (2019). Overview of Financial Inclusion in Africa–Startup Perspective/ InnerCircle, 2019. Available at https://gomedici.com/overview-financial-inclusion-africa-startups-perspective

Irimia, A., Tamas-Szora, A., & Dobra, I. B. (2021). On taxation of the digital economy. Where are we now and where are we going? *Finance: Challenges of the Future, 21*(23), 95–108.

Kelbesa, M. (2020). *Digital service taxes and their application*. Helpdesk Report

Kennedy, J. (2019). *Digital services taxes: A bad idea whose time should never come*. Information Technology and Innovation Foundation.

Koomson, I., Martey, E., & Etwire, P. M. (2022). Mobile money and entrepreneurship in East Africa: The mediating roles of digital savings and access to digital credit. *Information Technology & People, 36*, 996–1019.

Lirri, E. (2021). *Digital taxation doing more harm than good for access and rights in Africa*. Promoting Effectiveness and Inclusive ICT Policy in Africa. CIPESA. Available online: https://cipesa.org/2021/07/digital-taxation-doing-more-harm-than-good-for-access-and-rights-in-africa. Accessed on 16 June 2022.

Low, P. (2020). *Digital services taxes, trade and development*. Working Paper No. 2020-07.

Lowry, S. (2019). *Digital services taxes (DSTs): Policy and economic analysis*. Congressional Research Service Report, 45532.

Megersa, K. (2020). Tax reforms after COVID-19 and financial crises. Available online: https://opendocs.ids.ac.uk/opendocs/bitstream/handle/20.500.12413/15531/809%20_Tax_Reforms_After_COVID19_and_Financial_Crises.pdf?sequence=1

Mhlanga, D. (2020). Industry 4.0 in finance: The impact of artificial intelligence (AI) on digital financial inclusion. *International Journal of Financial Studies, 8*(3), 45.

Mhlanga, D. (2021). Financial inclusion in emerging economies: The application of machine learning and artificial intelligence in credit risk assessment. *International Journal of Financial Studies, 9*(3), 39.

Mhlanga, D. (2022). COVID-19 and digital financial inclusion: Policies and innovation that can accelerate financial inclusion in a post-COVID world through fintech. *African Journal of Development Studies (formerly AFFRIKA Journal of Politics, Economics and Society), 2022*(si2), 79–100.

Mhlanga, D., & Denhere, V. (2020). Determinants of financial inclusion in Southern Africa. *Studia Universitatis Babes-Bolyai, Oeconomica, 65*(3), 39–52.

Mpofu, F. Y. (2022). Industry 4.0 in financial services: Mobile money taxes, revenue mobilisation, financial inclusion, and the realisation of sustainable development goals (SDGs) in Africa. *Sustainability, 14*(14), 8667.

Mpofu, F. Y., & Mhlanga, D. (2022). Digital financial inclusion, digital financial services tax and financial inclusion in the fourth industrial revolution era in Africa. *Economies, 10*(8), 184. https://doi.org/10.3390/economies10080184

Mpofu, F. Y., & Moloi, T. (2022). Direct digital services taxes in Africa and the canons of taxation. *Laws, 11*(4), 57.

Mungai, K., & van der Linden, A. (2021). *The unpopular choice: Taxing digital payments in the era of digitalisation*. Available online: https://cenfri.org/articles/taxing-digital-payments-in-the-era-of-digitalisation/

Munoz, L., Mascagni, G., Prichard, W., & Santoro, F. (2022). *Should governments tax digital financial services? A research agenda to understand sector-specific taxes on DFS*. Working Paper 136.

Muthiora, B. (2015). *Enabling mobile money policies in Kenya. Fostering the digital revolution*. Mobile Money for the Ubanked. GSMA.

Muthiora, B., & Raithatha, R. (2018). *Rethinking mobile money taxation*. GSMA.

Ndung'u, N. S. (2019). *Taxing mobile phone transactions in Africa: Lessons from Kenya* (Policy Brief). Africa Growth Initiative.

Odiase, P. O. (2021). Taxing the digital economy: Nigeria's Financial Act 2019 and significant economic presence order 2020. *African Journal of Legal Studies, 14*(2), 269–275.

Organisation for Economic Co-operation and Development (OECD). (2018). Tax Challenges Arising from Digitalisation. Interim Report 2018: Inclusive Framework on BEPS, OECD/G20 Base Erosion and Profit Shifting Project. Paris: OECD Publishing.

OECD. (2021). *OCED/G20 base erosion and profit shifting project, two pillar solution to address the tax challenges arising from the digitalisation of the economy.*

Oguttu, A. W. (2018). International tax competition, harmful tax practices and the "race to the bottom": A special focus on unstrategic tax incentives in Africa. *Comparative and International Law Journal of Southern Africa, 51*(3), 293–319.

Olbert, M., & Spengel, C. (2017). International taxation in the digital economy: Challenge accepted. *World Tax Journal, 9*(1), 3–46.

Olbert, M., & Spengel, C. (2019). *Taxation in the digital economy – Recent policy developments and the question of value creation*. ZEW – Centre for European Economic Research Discussion Paper No. 19-010.

Onuoha, R., & Gillwald, A. (2022). *Digital taxation: Can it contribute to more just resource mobilisation in post-pandemic reconstruction?* Research ICT Africa.

Pazarbasioglu, C., Mora, A. G., Uttamchandani, M., Natarajan, H., Feyen, E., & Saal, M. (2020). *Digital financial services* (54p). World Bank Group.

Pushkareva, N. (2021). Taxing times for development: Tax and digital financial services in Sub-Saharan Africa. *Financing for Development, 1*(3), 33–64.

Rogan, M. (2019). Tax justice and the informal economy: A review of the debates. WIEGO. Available at www.wiego.org/publications/taxjusticeand-informal-economy-review-debates

Rota-Graziosi, G., & Sawadogo, F. (2022). The tax burden on mobile network operators in Africa. *Telecommunications Policy, 46*(5), 102293.

Rukundo, S. (2020). *Addressing the challenges of taxation of the digital economy: Lessons for African countries*. Working Paper 105. Brighton: Institute of Development Studies. Available online: https://opendocs.ids.ac.uk/opendocs/bitstream/handle/20.500.12413/14990/ICTD_WP105.pdf?sequence=1

Sánchez Rojas, A. A. (2020). *Deconstruct to reconstruct: Is it possible to tax big data, e-commerce, and the digital economy?* Ediciones Uniandes.

Santoro, F., Munoz, L., Prichard, W., & Mascagni, G. (2022). *Digital financial services and digital IDs: What potential do they have for better taxation in Africa?* Working Paper 137.

Sebele-Mpofu, F., Mashiri, E., & Schwartz, S. C. (2021a). An exposition of transfer pricing motives, strategies and their implementation in tax avoidance by MNEs in developing countries. *Cogent Business & Management, 8*(1), 1944007.

Sebele-Mpofu, F. Y., Mashiri, E., & Korera, P. (2021b). Transfer pricing audit challenges and dispute resolution effectiveness in developing countries with specific focus on Zimbabwe. *Accounting, Economics, and Law: A Convivium*. https://doi.org/10.1515/ael-2021-0026

Simbarashe, H. (2020). Digitalisation and the challenges for african administrations. *Financing for Development, 1*, 177–203.

Shapshack, T. (2021). *Mobile money in Africa reaches $500billion during the pandemic*. Available online: https://www.forbes.com/sites/tobyshapshak/2021/05/19/mobile-money-in-africa-reaches-nearly-500bn-during-pandemic/. Accessed on 16 March 2022.

Shinyekwa, I. (2018). *How will recent taxes on mobile money affect East Africans*. EPRC.

Silue, T. (2021). *E-money, financial inclusion and mobile money tax in Sub-Saharan African mobile networks*. Études et Documents No. 22. CERDI.

Skaar, A. A. (2020). *Permanent establishment: Erosion of a tax treaty principle*. Kluwer Law International BV.

Tan, K. W. (2022). *Africa's mobile money taxes risk driving the poor out of the digital economy.*

Yahaya, M. (2021). *Taxation of the digital economy in Nigeria: The post-covid world.* Cambridge Open Engage.

Chapter 6
The Political Economy of Financial Inclusion for Smallholder Farmers in Sub-Saharan Africa

Miriam Hofisi

Abstract The availability of financial capital amongst smallholder farmers immensely helps them to achieve sustainable livelihoods in sub-Saharan Africa (SSA). Conversely, smallholder farmers in SSA are pestered by income inequality since the postcolonial era. This is one of the leading factors for exclusive economic growth in the region. Although extant studies stress the key role played by financial inclusion, and digitization, in general, and amongst smallholder farmers, there is a dearth of literature when it comes to accounting for the role played by the postcolonial governments in the region. Using document analysis, this study examines grey and academic literature to analyse financial inclusion policies promulgated by governments. The study found that most governments in SSA have outdated financial regulatory frameworks that guide financial inclusion. In addition, countries with road and railway infrastructure had a high level of financial inclusion and the soft infrastructure, such as the regulatory framework is not updated to support financial technology lenders. In the era of mobile money accounts, the regulatory frameworks in SSA are not responsive to matters of secure identity that protect the client and the financial provider. Other barriers to financial inclusion include a lack of mobile phones, identity documents, and money. In light of the findings above, it is critical to know that the postcolonial government in the SSA has at its helm the potential ability to leverage the upsurge of mobile money for the economic benefit of smallholder farmers.

Keywords Economic growth · Financial inclusion · Mobile money · Smallholder farmers

M. Hofisi (✉)
North-West University, Potchefstroom, South Africa

D. Mhlanga, E. Ndhlovu (eds.), *Economic Inclusion in Post-Independence Africa*, Advances in African Economic, Social and Political Development,
https://doi.org/10.1007/978-3-031-31431-5_6

6.1 Introduction

Sub-Saharan Africa has been pestered by income inequality since the postcolonial era, and it has been one of the leading factors for exclusive economic growth in the region (Adedokun & Ağa, 2021; Jonathan Gimba et al., 2021; Menyelim et al., 2021; Odusola, 2017). Contemporary literature on development demonstrates that the postcolonial governments failed to account for the continued economic exclusion (Menyelim et al., 2021). Commonly reported factors have spawned inequality to include social upheavals (*weak institutions, credit market asymmetry, rising population, decline in human capital investment, high premium on technological skills, and financial globalization*) (Menyelim et al., 2021:1780). Given that purposive government action through policy can reconfigure the trajectory of poverty, this study seeks to investigate government policies in sub-Saharan Africa on financial inclusion. Although extant studies stress the key role played by financial inclusion in general and amongst smallholder farmers, there is a dearth of literature when it comes to accounting for the role played by governments in sub-Saharan Africa (Mhlanga & Dunga, 2020).

Smallholder farmers have existed on the periphery of the formal economy since the postcolonial period in the majority of sub-Saharan Africa (Chinaka, 2016). One of their major challenges is financial exclusion, which spurs cyclical poverty for generations (Mhlanga et al., 2020). Although their state has been on the backburner where development issues were tabled, they remain as untapped role players that can turn around economic growth in sub-Saharan Africa because of their numbers. While the Organization for Economic Co-operation and Development (OECD) countries have leveraged innovation, and digitization for economic growth, negligible results can be gleaned from Africa because, to some extent, of the unexplored potential of smallholder farmers (Riley & Kulathunga, 2017).

Poverty reduction in SSA can only be tackled if fundamental issues, such as income inequality, are addressed. The United Nations Development Programme (UNDP) also reiterates the same, arguing that sustainable poverty reduction in Africa will spur sustainable development and is one of the avenues that can propel the attainment of Sustainable Development Goals (Asongu & Odhiambo, 2019; Demirguc-Kunt et al., 2018). Menyelim et al. (2021) add that there is a synergistic relationship between reduced income inequality and economic development that is extant in contemporary literature (Senou et al., 2019; Kpodar & Andrianaivo, 2011; Sarma & Pais, 2011; Ozili, 2021; Van et al., 2021). Similarly, smallholder farmers have endured financial exclusion from the postcolonial period, with a few exceptions like Kenya (Bernards, 2021). In agriculture, studies that have been undertaken demonstrate that the inclusion of smallholder farmers plays a significant role in helping them (Adedokun & Ağa, 2021; Chinaka, 2016; Fowowe, 2020; Mhlanga, 2020; Menyelim et al., 2021). It is especially relevant in sub-Saharan Africa where more than 60% of the sub-Saharan African population derives their livelihoods from agricultural activities and 23% of the region's GDP comes from agriculture (Goedde et al., 2019:2). Three-quarters of those living in poverty are rural based farmers, trapped in cyclical poverty as they subsist from their agricultural activities (WDR, 2018). The majority of these farmers do not have access to formal credit (Madden, 2020). In countries like Ethiopia, Ghana, Kenya, Madagascar, Rwanda, and Uganda, smallholder farmers rely on informal credit, family, and friends and are vulnerable to exorbitant interest fees (Menyelim et al., 2021). It is therefore imperative for governments to make a substantial commitment to building the savings of farmers given that the majority rely on agricultural activities for livelihoods. Financial inclusion in an agrarian society is especially relevant, given that it has the potential to help attain the seven goals of the SDGs. These are as follows: no poverty, zero hunger, attaining food security, achieving nutrition and health, and promoting sustainable agriculture (Mhlanga & Dunga, 2020).

Extant literature reiterates that financial inclusion translates to economic growth for those who were excluded from the mainstream economy (Güngen, 2018). Although credit is perceived as the sine qua non of economic growth, by giving financial access to the poor, it should also be borne in mind that it is rooted within capitalist social relations of production (Güngen, 2018). It would be foolhardy to assume that market forces can help ameliorate the state of smallholder farmers. Therefore, a policy is key in ensuring that smallholder farmers participate in the market economy in a supportive manner (ACET, 2020). Financial inclusion seldom eradicates poverty without the involvement of the state to harness financial inclusion for the benefit of the poor. Therefore, state intervention plays a critical role in leveraging its benefits while guarding against the lender's power from extracting unnecessary profits at the expense of borrowers (Senou et al., 2019). The Oxford Policy Management (2021) also highlighted the increased recognition of the state in providing an enabling environment for a prosperous market environment. It stands to reason that efforts to create equitable access to affordable credit are deeply rooted in systems that are fraught with contradictions of the colonial political economy (Bernards, 2021; Rankin, 2013). In addition to that, financial credit institutions are steeped in capitalist fundamentals and cannot help eradicate financial poverty amongst smallholder farmers if the government cannot intervene through regulations. Rankin (2013) expresses concern about financial inclusion strategies, cautioning against passing on financial burdens of debt to the poor, where they can be subjugated through indebtedness. Financial lenders also wield a reasonable level of power through government-enabled regulations that give them the power to charge interests. More often than not, this enables them to continue operating unchecked, much to the exploitation of vulnerable people. The policies regulating credit extended to the poor, therefore, need to reflect the government's commitment to ensure that the poor are protected from indebtedness. Creating a conducive environment for economic growth remains an inalienable responsibility of the state and cannot be left to the private sector. To this end, some developing countries, like Ethiopia, Rwanda, Uganda, and Zambia, sought to achieve this by introducing caps on the interests charged to microcredit borrowers (Oxford Policy Management, 2020).

In addition, infrastructure is the key enabler of financial access to the poor, since it has been the major hindering factor in the lack of formal financial institutions in poor and remote communities. Banks have always deemed it unprofitable to build banking infrastructure in rural areas given their small clientele and poverty. The Reserve Bank of India also concluded that it is abortive to install banks in rural areas. In sub-Saharan Africa, many countries only have banks in the urban centres, except for Botswana, Mauritius, and South Africa (Business Financial Times, 2020).

With the popularized digitization of microfinance in sub-Saharan Africa, it is critical to get the involvement of the state in infrastructure building too. It should be borne in mind that total inclusion relies on the installation of sound telecommunications infrastructure in rural areas so that clients can access mobile money. Mobile interaction between clients and money lenders is critical. Studies undertaken show a positive correlation between infrastructure and the acceleration of financial services (Ravi and Gakhar in Senou). Mobile technology is especially plausible in bridging the financial divide. In 2013, M-PESA in Kenya managed to increase financial services by 66.7% in Kenya. According to Business Financial Times (2020), the proportion of mobile bank account holders was 11% in sub-Saharan Africa, the highest in the world. Moreover, the region hosts 27 of the 28 poorest countries in the world, making financial inclusion a critical avenue in eradicating poverty (Business Financial Times, 2020). This makes the investment into this sector even more convincing given the uptake and the potential to reconfigure the majority of economies in the region.

The focus of this study is directed at policies that protect smallholder farmers when borrowing, supportive initiatives in the digitization drive, and infrastructure that enable the digitization of remote areas. The structure of this chapter begins with the introduction. This is followed by a discussion on financial inclusion challenges in sub-Saharan Africa. Lastly is the review of policies and supportive initiatives of selected governments in sub-Saharan Africa and the conclusion.

6.2 Defining Financial Inclusion

According to the World Bank (2022:1), financial inclusion is "the degree that households and small enterprises could gain an access to financial services, such as deposits, loans, payments, remittances, and insurance". Daneshvar, Garry, López, Santamaría, and Villarreal (2017:12) state that financial inclusion is "access by the currently excluded population (including poor inhabitants) to a broad range of financial services tailored to its needs and supplied by a variety of regulated financial service providers, is a tool that fosters opportunities that enhance the capacity to achieve". Although results from South Africa show that a sizeable number of farmers have access to funding, similar to the Zimbabwean case of contract farmers who get funding, it should be borne in mind that they are a negligible number of smallholder farmers (Chisasa & Makina, 2012; Mazwi et al., 2019). Results show that these are capitalist farmers who are served by formal banks and contractors, who are driven by capitalist interests. IFC (2014:2) corroborates this fact by stating that only 1% of funding goes to agriculture, with only 4.7% of adults in rural areas (where smallholder farmers are concentrated) having loans from formal financial institutions. Research on access to credit has been critiqued for directing focus on commercial smallholder farmers who represent a narrow picture of the market, which tends to give a blindsided review of smallholder farmers. IFC in this regard cautioned against regarding the mode of access for agriculture as fair, given the observation above.

Following the realization that smallholder farmers have constrained access to borrow from the formal banks and the plight thereof, the author notes that financial inclusion should be a deliberate intervention to engage farmers at their level by meeting their needs. Financial inclusion is the existence of a varied ecosystem of service providers and distribution channels. Financial inclusion not only touches on the supply dimension where access and availability of services are regarded as critical. Recent literature notes that it should also entail product awareness, literacy of the availability of these financial services, and the ability to make informed choices (Morgan & Long, 2020). This conceptualization resonates with the Alliance for Financial Inclusion which touches on three key elements, which are articulated below: access, usage, and quality.

Different authors reiterate the importance of financial inclusion, but little attention in contemporary literature touches on the role of the state in ensuring that inclusion reaches the underserved (Chinaka, 2016; Mhlanga, 2020; Oji, 2015). Given the inalienable role that the government plays in resource distribution, it is critical to have policies that guide inclusion. As such, Menyelim et al. (2021) add that inclusion should especially be conceptualized as inclusive when it serves the underserved by mitigating equality and poverty-boosting capital for the poor. Therefore, financial inclusion in the sub-Saharan context should be understood within the political economy, where the provision of financial services is guided by the creation of an equitable financial system that caters to the excluded, with the support of the government (Table 6.1).

6.3 Financial Inclusion for Small-Scale Farmers: Challenges and Opportunities

The availability of financial capital amongst small-scale farmers immensely helps small-scale farmers achieve sustainable livelihoods (World Development Report, 2008). Financial capital entails cash, credit, debt, savings, as well as other economic assets. Financial assets can be in the form of a regular flow of cash like wages, remittances, pensions, social grants, and clubs (Bebbington, 1999). Stocks like

Table 6.1 Facets of financial inclusion

1	Access	Availability of formal, regulated financial services: physical proximity, affordability
2	Usage	Actual usage of financial services and products: regularity, frequency, duration of time used
3	Quality	Products are well tailored to client needs. Appropriate segmentation to develop prooducts for all income levels

Source: Triki & Faye (2013:31)

jewellery, livestock, and savings also help financially to farmers' lives (Ashley & Carney, 1999; Bebbington, 1999; Farrington et al., 1999; Krantz, 2001; Scoones, 1998). In addition, financial services, such as savings accounts, credit, and insurance, are a cornerstone of development. As reiterated, ownership of accounts with government-regulated institutions, such as credit union, microfinance institution, or mobile money service provider, enable farmers to safely make savings, send and receive money, plan for emergencies, invest in farming and education, and health (Global Findex, 2021). On the contrary, the excluded, those that are excluded from these financial services, are vulnerable to poverty since they cannot access these services. Therefore, access to affordable credit is critical, because it makes farmers proficient in savings and investments. Mobile money accounts are especially plausible, since they enable account holders to undertake transactions online, which cuts down on travelling time to remote, rural dwellers.

Below is evidence of the reported growth of mobile money accounts across sub-Saharan Africa.

In Sub-Saharan Africa, a gender gap barely exists for young adults who have only a mobile money account

Adults with an account (%), 2021

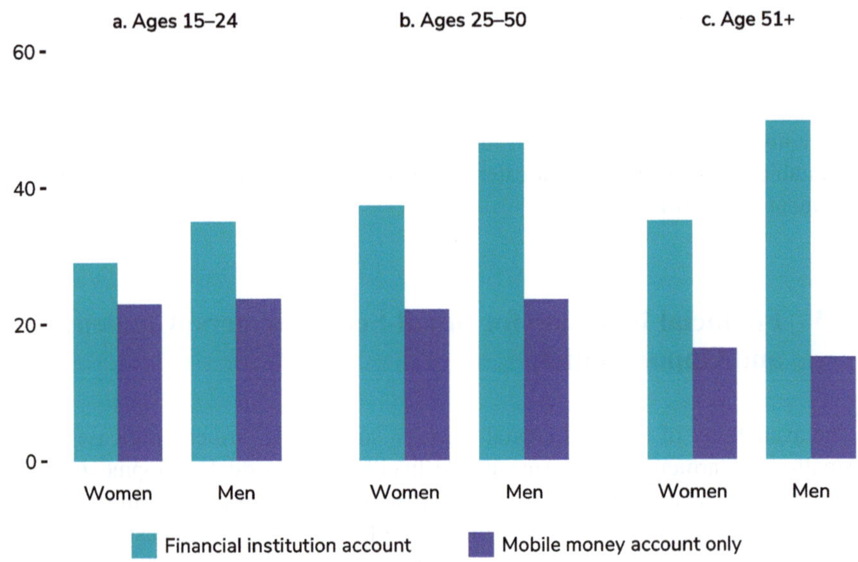

Source: Global Findex Database 2021.
Note: Data are shown for economies in Sub-Saharan Africa in which the share of adults with a mobile money account is greater than 20 percent.

Source: Demirguc-Kunt, Klapper, Singer & Ansar (2022)

The view that mobile money accounts are considered plausible to spearhead financial inclusion amongst the excluded has been corroborated in literature (Oji, 2015; Allen et al., 2016; Ozili, 2021). Global trends also show a 50% growth of account ownership by adults, which rose from 63% in the year 2011 to 76% in 2021 (Global Findex, 2021:1). A fair share of these accounts is tied to the mobile money accounts opened in developing countries. Sub-Saharan Africa hosts all 11 economies, where most adults have mobile money accounts. Fifteen percent of adults managed to make savings using mobile money accounts (Global Findex, 2021:3). Prospects of improved access to finance amongst smallholder farmers in developing countries are optimistic given the results stated above. However, it is still critical to underline the ineradicable role that governments need to play to ensure that equitable access is sustained.

Despite the upsurge in mobile money accounts in developing countries, some problems persist. Amongst the problems noted, lack of money, insufficient documentation, and lack of mobile phones continue to be cited as leading factors of exclusion (Global Findex, 2021). According to the Sustainable Livelihoods Approach (SLA), financial capital is one of the cornerstones of sustainable livelihoods (Scoones, 1998). Farmers are often plagued by a lack of financial resources (Ndhlovu, 2018). Smallholder farmers are locked in a state of perpetual poverty due to financial circumstances inhibiting them (World Development Report, 2018). The nature of the challenges that were commonly reported amongst the excluded warrants supportive efforts from the government as well as telecommunication companies to help smallholder farmers. Ellis in Kostov and Lingard (2002) note that smallholder farmers derive their livelihoods mainly from family agriculture, utilize mainly family labour in farm production, and are characterized by partial engagement input and output markets, which are often imperfect and incomplete. Schultz (1964) believes that low returns on small farms are a result of the lack of access to affordable credit (Huffman & Curtiss, 2006). It follows that necessary elements, like money, documentation, and mobile phones, subject them to the vagaries of the market forces, where they are made to compete with commercial farmers who can purchase high-yield inputs through cheaper credit. As a result, a condition (Schultz, 1964) termed "states of equilibrium" exists, whereby agricultural growth is stagnant and characterized by a lack of savings and investments.

6.3.1 Lack of Money

The lack of capital amongst some smallholder farmers in sub-Saharan Africa is closely tied to their lack of collateral like land (de Soto, 2000; Tooling, 2009). Farmers do not have the reasonable collateral required by lenders to do business. This is largely attributable to land policies in sub-Saharan Africa, where land held under customary tenure has not been allocated any bankable value. In cases where agrarian revolutions have reconfigured the agrarian sector amongst smallholder farmers like in China, the land was privatized, amongst other changes that were affected by the incumbent government. On the contrary, such changes have not taken place in sub-Saharan Africa since the postcolonial period (Binswanger & Rosenzweig, 1986). Therefore, it is critical to envisage the impact of financial inclusion amongst smallholder farmers in light of the existing challenges that farmers have experienced. The longstanding economic differentials that rural-based farmers have gone through since the colonial era are most notable in the women, the youth, child-headed households, and others. This is prevalent even in places where the land carries the highest collateral value and it has been allocated its economic value.

With constrained access to credit, smallholder farmers are often vulnerable to other operational challenges such as insurance. Given that agriculture is often vulnerable to weather-related catastrophes, like drought, floods, cyclones, and others, insurance plays a critical role in cushioning farmers from shocks like these. In addition to the investment, the financial inclusion of farmers fosters efficiency. When farmers can build infrastructure like storage, post-harvest management becomes efficient in that it offsets losses that come with a lack of storage.

IFC (2014) also reiterates that the availability of capital to farmers helps with investment, post-harvest management, lubricating household cash flow, mitigating setbacks, and access to markets. However, it takes a financial market with tailor-made products to spawn financial inclusivity. Kalunda (2014) and Singh (2017) added that financial markets should establish a wide range of products, like loans, deposits, and other services, that can help increase productivity and investment. Farmers are forced to live in subsistence statuses with a lack of capital. Therefore, a lack of capital is counterproductive. In Tanzanian rural households, little income came from agriculture, although they are agro-based. Of the 344 households interviewed, 46.6% of their income came from non-farm activities while remittances followed suit (IFC, 2014:14). Lamentably, developing countries in Africa grapple with establishing financial markets that afford credit to smallholder scale farmers. In Ethiopia, access to formal credit was only available in urban centres, where collateral was available (Salami et al., 2010). Despite the involvement of various financial interventions in Africa, results show a negligible impact of the inclusion of smallholder farmers (Meyer, 2015). It has been apparent that postcolonial governments have not had financial inclusion policies that offer a safe operational environment for borrowers.

6.3.2 *Insufficient Documentation*

For one to get a bank account, it is required of the client to produce a government-issued identity document and proof of residence in a traditional bank. For mobile money institutions, one must have a SIM card as well as a government-issued identity document. In sub-Saharan Africa, 105 million adults do not have identity documents, and 16% of adults in the region are unbanked (Global Findex, 2021:36). Countries with more than 40% of undocumented adults are Liberia, Mozambique, South Sudan, and Tanzania. Women formed the majority of those who do not have an identity in the region. As reiterated earlier, lack of credit is inimical to the growth of smallholder farmers and counterintuitive to the SDGs on ending hunger and poverty, as well as gender differentials in developing countries. India was also plagued by the same challenge of identity documents, as well as proof of residence. These are dynamic challenges, especially for hard-to-reach people. While credible identity is critical in finance, there is a dire need to bring the underserved people on board. To circumvent this challenge, the Indian government came up with a digital identifier called the Aadhar number, and it contributed to 80% inclusion of the previously excluded population in India (Global Findex, 2021:36). It is therefore incumbent upon the government and telecommunication companies as well as financial institutions to create enabling infrastructure that can make it safe to transact.

6.3.3 *Financial Illiteracy*

The process of extending finance has been slower in sub-Saharan Africa. One of the factors is financial illiteracy. In sub-Saharan Africa, 1/3 of the mobile money account holders needed assistance in using their accounts, and women were 5% more likely to require assistance (Global Findex, 2021:4). The major setback with financial illiteracy is that poor, subsistence farmers tend to choose bad financial products, such as loans due to lack of knowledge, and are most likely to end up poorer (Bire et al., 2019; Meyer, 2015; Ozili, 2021). Bad financial products are inherently risky, with high-interest rates, and smallholder farmers usually default on repayment (Bernards, 2021; Ephrem et al., 2021; Kahan, 2008). Due to illiteracy, one in five adults were vulnerable to fraud as results observed that some were charged unexpected transactional fees and did not question it. When interest rates are too high, they push away viable customers and maintain a pool of risky customers who are willing to incur the costs (Oji, 2015). This challenge is endemic amongst smallholder farmers, who are forced to incur these costs due to the inaccessibility of formal lending. For a prolonged period in Africa, the challenge of financial capital amongst smallholder farmers has been corroborated by authors and development practitioners alike (Bernards, 2021). Most common to this challenge is the fact that farmers borrow from unregulated, informal institutions which are predatory. Studies across Africa, from Malawi, Zimbabwe, Nigeria, Uganda, and many other sub-Saharan African, show that smallholder farmers still borrow from informal lenders (Ozili, 2021; Bernards, 2021; Morgan & Long, 2020). Research in sub-Saharan Africa corroborates the fact that poor, smallholder farmers are often burdened with debt repayment (Bernards, 2021). Resultantly, farmers perpetually spent their earnings on repayment of debt and subsist on the remainder. This phenomenon tends to affect women more than men in Africa (Ozili, 2021). The gender differentials narrative is pervasive in systems where competition for resources is stiff (Bernards, 2021). Financial education plays a key role in the lives of smallholder farmers.

6.3.4 *Gender Gaps in Financial Inclusion*

In the same vein, when access to critical resources is scant in an economy, the vulnerable are usually alienated. Women have been amongst the majority of the underserved in sub-Saharan Africa (Bernards, 2021; Ozili, 2021). Even though they are more than 50% of the labour force in sub-Saharan Africa, they have often been excluded from the formal lending environment (WDR, 2018:3). Although development practitioners anticipate changes in gender differentials through financial digitization, sub-Saharan Africa shows little change in account ownership. Of the unbanked people, 56% were women in the year 2017 (WDR, 2018:3). Zins and Weill (2016) also observed that in Africa, being female significantly diminished the probability of being excluded. Although the Global Findex Data of 2021 reports a reduced gender gap from 9% in

2018 to 6% in 2021, in sub-Saharan Africa, some developed countries have managed to close this gap (Global Findex, 2021:36). This is an indicator of the persistence of barriers embedded in financial systems that women continue to face.

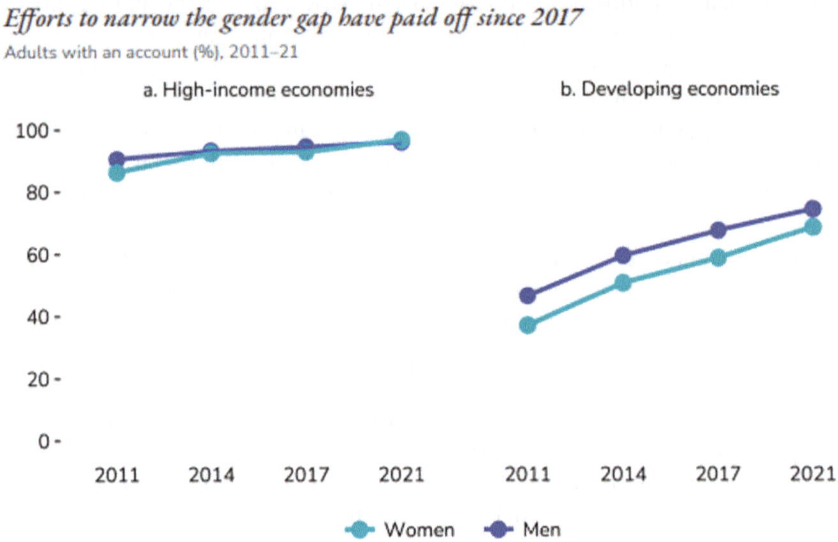

Source: Global Findex Database (2017)

6.4 Financial Inclusion and Economic Growth in Sub-Saharan Africa

Financial inclusion is the bedrock of economic empowerment in rural areas, where the majority have been excluded from the mainstream economy (Oji, 2015; Asuming et al., 2019). In general, it translates to equitable economic growth that is sustainable, especially for the excluded as their untapped latent potential is unleashed, reduces income inequality, and encourages entrepreneurial endeavours for the poor (Morgan & Long, 2020). Outside of the economic benefits that come with financial inclusion, mobile money eases the customer's cost of transactions in comparison to brick-and-mortar banking. It cuts travel time and encourages savings, and receiving remittances across borders has been made easier as well. In Nepal, women managed to spend 15% more on food and 20% on education, whereas in Malawi, farmers used 13% more on farm equipment, and it spurred an increase of their crop value by 15% when earnings were deposited into their mobile money accounts (WDR, 2018:2). For governments, digital payments help reduce corruption as mobile money transactions leave a digital footprint and increase transparency. In India, the loss of pension funds dropped by 47%, and in Niger, the cost of distribution of social benefit grants fell by 20% when transactions went digital (WDR, 2018).

Despite the rising figures of the financially included across the globe, sub-Saharan Africa has remained stuck with a significant proportion of adults excluded. Ownership of bank accounts in Kenya, Nigeria, Egypt, and the Democratic Republic of the Congo (DRC) was 42%, 30%, 10%, and 4% correspondingly, while South Africa has an outstanding percentage of 54% (Oji, 2015:5). This is despite the backdrop that at least $157 billion could be generated if the excluded were to be incorporated into the mainstream. In addition, the Maya Declaration, the World Bank 2020 Vision, and the G20 Financial Inclusion Plan all compel governments to demonstrate their commitment to the financial inclusion agenda (Asuming et al., 2019). Concurrently, people with lower access to formal financial institutions immensely rely on informal institutions, where they are often vulnerable to financial mishaps.

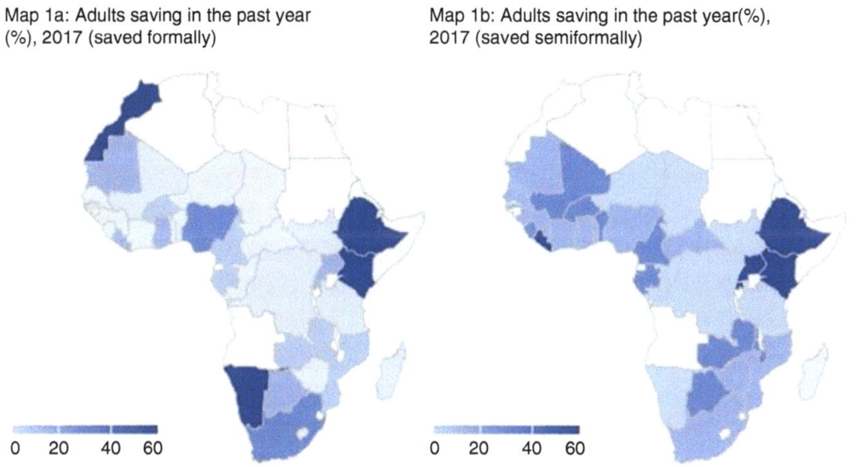

Source: WDR (2018)

Financial inclusion is a precursor for building household savings and contributes toward financial stability, and it mitigates inequality as well.

However, for one to make financially savvy decisions, literacy of financial products is key. It has been widely observed in the literature that financial literacy is of key importance to poverty, since it activates the latent ability of any individual to participate financially and make savings that can generate interest (Oji, 2015). There is a profound linkage between literacy and increased savings in both formal and informal financial institutions, which subsequently contribute to sustainable savings for the poor.

Financial literacy can be defined as "a set of skills and knowledge that enable individuals to make informed and effective decisions regarding money matters" (Ephrem et al., 2021:6). It is an aggregate of awareness, knowledge, financial responsiveness, skills, attitude, and behaviour that are critical for an individual to make a financial related decision, which in the end lead to sustainable financial well-being for consumers (OECD, 2012; Ephrem et al., 2021; Bire et al., 2019). The generally observable trend amongst smallholder farmers in sub-Saharan Africa is that farmers lack the plausible skills and knowledge to make financially savvy decisions (Bire et al., 2019). More often, these problems are seldom theirs, they often borrow semi-formally as they battle challenges like lack of identity documentation, collateral, and many other challenges (WDR, 2018; FDIP Report, 2017). However, these challenges are deeply embedded in the wider regulatory framework that drives financial inclusion in given countries. FDIP (2017) observed that in countries where the regulatory framework was supportive of the entities that drive inclusion, uptake synergistically followed. Below is a snapshot of different sub-Saharan countries and their reported levels of commitment to digitization, which is enable financial inclusion in the region.

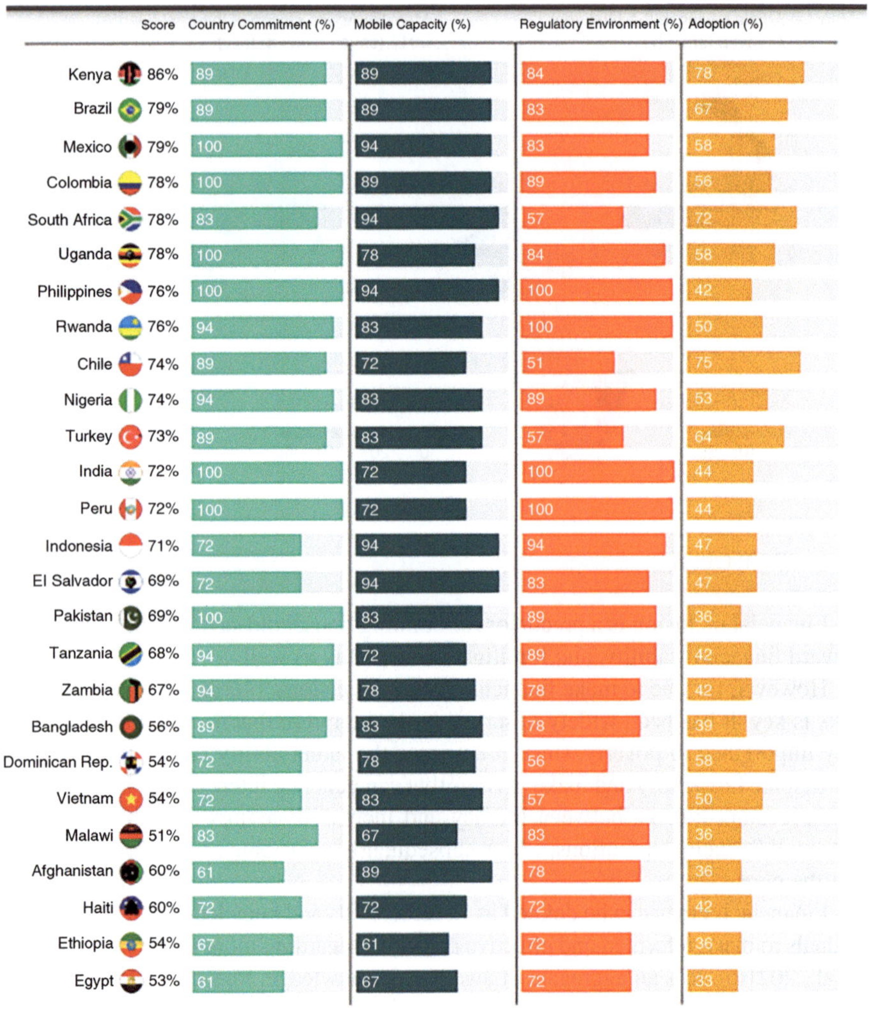

Source: Lewis, Villasenor, & West (2017:6)

Sub-Saharan Africa is dotted with risky informal microfinance institutions that serve the unbankable. Nigeria has *esusu*, a credit issuing club, where members are anonymous. Benin, Cameroon, Ghana, and Uganda call them tontine, *dajanggi*, *susu*, and *chilemba*, respectively (Oji, 2015). As reiterated in the literature, rural people gravitate towards informal institutions because of their proximity to lenders, they find them cheaper, and they do not have to fret about compliance that is required by formal lenders (Meyer, 2015). Despite their preferences for informal institutions, it is commonly noted that members of these groups remain vulnerable to defaulting payments, cannot get emergency loans, and are often vulnerable to exorbitant interest rates. Be that as it may, these people find themselves in a precarious situation, where they are patronized by the very system that they use and they do not have a choice. Below is the depiction of how adults still rely on informal means.

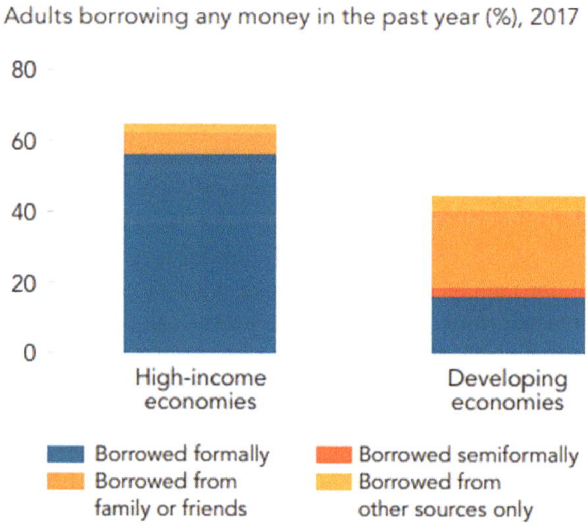

Source: WDR (2018:9)

There has been a heightened need for financial institutions to design financial products that are tailored to the rural populace. For the excluded to be catered for, there are key elements that need to be established. These are technology, appropriate regulations, policy, and infrastructure (Oji, 2015). In terms of policies and regulations that are supportive, it is key for financial institutions and the government to come together and devise innovative and supportive guidelines that nurture the evolution of financial institutions. In Nigeria, South Africa, Uganda, and Ghana, mobile money was introduced as Moneybox, Wizzit, mCash, and Paymenx correspondingly. Unfortunately, these did not have the same results as MPesa in Kenya, owing to regulatory models that are not similar to the successful MPesa. In terms of policy, the Central Bank of Kenya has been flexible and accommodating mobile money regulations as they evolved (Oji, 2015). MPesa has been innovative from the period of its inception to date by adding transactions that its clients can do, in particular payment of bills. Further to that, it has partnered with formal banks and has a product M-Shwari, where clients have access to loans and savings. These financial products have been necessitated by the regulatory framework that was responsive to the needs of the previously excluded.

Moreover, MPesa, like the Grameen Bank of Bangladesh and Fonkoze from Haiti, bypassed the rigidity of compliance needed by banks as a means to include the vulnerable in the financial system. While MPesa harnessed the presence of airtime sellers across the country, it managed to reach out to remote areas where people are naturally excluded. Similarly, the Grameen Bank and Fonkoze targeted poor women who cannot borrow from formal banks by offering loans without requiring loans. Fonkoze intentionally gave borrowers more time to pay back loans, as a means to allow them to recover in the process. As a result, these institutions are popular in rural areas, with Fonkoze having 96% of its branches in rural areas, while MPesa 11, 5 million of the population in Kenya got financial services from mobile money transfers and only 5.4 million used banks (Oji, 2015:5).

It stands to reason that one of the fundamental factors that necessitated the flourishing of MPesa is infrastructure. Infrastructure has been identified as one of the factors that determine the depth of inclusion in an economy (Sarma & Pais, 2011). The presence of cellular networks in remote areas of Kenya was leveraged by supportive infrastructure. Therefore, the government must consider working with the private sector in ensuring that remote areas are covered. Similar to the MPesa in Kenya where the government, through its central bank, designed a supportive regulatory framework for microfinance institutions, the government can also actively participate in infrastructure. According to the political economy imperatives, it is incumbent upon the government to ensure that the distribution of resources is equally disbursed.

6.5 Policies That Encourage Financial Inclusion

WDR (2021) reports that government agents and public institutions across Europe have committed to guarantor credit for small businesses in a post-Covid recovery. Credit guarantee schemes have been used as a tool for economic recovery in developed as well as emerging economies. In particular, Spain uses credit guarantees for medium and small businesses to increase financial access. According to WDR (2021), research in the OEDC countries revealed that banks showed reluctance in engaging in risky business while the government-supported credit agencies received overwhelming volumes of applications. When economies are still stabilizing or recovering from shocks, it is critical to have guarantors that support lenders in an economic environment where lending is risky (WDR, 2021). Credit guarantors are a critical part of financial inclusion for they balance the equation for lenders, and despite being important in stabilizing lenders, they can also be used on a long-term basis when reaching out to the underserved like smallholder farmers in rural areas.

6.6 Policies That Address Access and Risk in Sub-Saharan Africa

Studies carried out by OECD as well as in Africa corroborate the fact that infrastructure is a prerequisite for financial inclusion and resilience. Results from Kenya, South Africa, and various OECD countries demonstrate a strong correlation between infrastructural development and access to financial products.

Digital finance providers need to be regulated to guard against lending that is counterproductive. Although new digital financial lenders have emerged as key players in providing short-term loans to the poor and underserved, their activities still need to be regulated. This serves to guard against irresponsible and predatory lending. One example is Kenya, whose digital lenders provided short-term loans to borrowers between 2016 and 2019. They managed to attract a clientele, and usage of their products rose from 0.6% to 8.3% (WDR, 2021). However, instances of irresponsible lending also occurred, because they were not regulated. It stands to reason that while financial capital is undoubtedly critical, the provision of credit should also be imbued with integrity, consumer protection, and equity.

While financial inclusion has been synonymous with digital lenders like MPesa of Kenya, it should be borne in mind that there is also potential for these app-based lenders to be disruptive. Therefore, to leverage their uncontested benefits to the underserved in sub-Saharan Africa, there is a need for regulatory oversight. The introduction of a regulatory framework serves to protect consumers and also allows innovation to take place within a conducive financial environment. Different countries have endeavoured to encourage innovation, given the potential that digital lenders possess. Although results about financial inclusion reported by the WDR focused on post-Covid recovery, their experiences can be matched to the Sub-Sahara African economies, given that they bear similarities to the economic buildup of the weak.

Digital financial channels have become key in building the economy by opening up alternative lending solutions to the previously excluded across the globe. Governments in developing countries are therefore compelled to leverage their potential by catalysing their visibility to remote areas, where smallholder farmers live. It is commonly reported that smallholder farmers in rural areas are remotely located from the major connecting transport communication and travelling channels since colonial times (Oji, 2015). One way of helping smallholder farmers is to build infrastructure that facilitates the participation of farmers and service providers (WDR, 2021). In addition, policymakers across the globe need to revisit their legal financial regulatory frameworks as well as supervisory frameworks to create an enabling environment. Sub-Saharan Africa, therefore, needs to take financial inclusion by effecting regulatory frameworks that are up to date to encourage the uptake of digital financial products.

Financial infrastructure is made up of legal and regulatory structures as well as public and private sector institutions and practices that provide an enabling environment for the functioning of financial systems. These are further divided into three major elements that are critical when it comes to governing the financial sector in a given state. Digital identity, payment systems, and credit infrastructure are the three main pillars of financial inclusion. In building resilient financial infrastructure, it is key for the government to ensure that financial institutions are built on integrity. Digital identity is one of these key elements, and it entails establishing mutual trust between clients and financial service providers. Digital identities empower citizens to engage in digital transactions. The Indian government introduced the Aadhar number as a credible identity system that has contributed immensely to the inclusion of those without government-issued identity documents.

Following that are the payment systems, which include both physical and soft infrastructure for the smooth running of digitization. Physical infrastructure includes hardware that is needed for the transactions to happen. Soft infrastructures are rules and practices that encourage the participation of fintech in serving the underserved as well as digital transformation. Credit infrastructure includes asset registry systems and laws that regulate credit work to minimize lending costs to customers to encourage participation in fintech. To guarantee safety, systems must be updated as well to allow participation of fintech which were previously not part of the formal lenders. The People's Bank of China in tandem also gave access to fintech to the credit registry.

6.7 Innovative Collateral Amongst Smallholder Farmers

One of the major factors that kept smallholder farmers at the periphery of the mainstream market is access to formal credit. Despite the consensus that smallholder farmers are not indolent, access to credit has remained remote due to a lack of collateral. Movable property, as an innovative avenue, can be accepted as collateral from smallholder farmers to increase financial access. It is therefore critical for policies to speak to the innovative imperatives. Pakistan in particular launched a registry in 2020 that granted financial institutions to register rights to movable property, like furniture, machinery, inventory, accounts, receivables, and digital assets, to be accepted as collateral. Likewise, Mexico's Nafinet also accepts collateral in form of invoices and warehouse receipts as collateral (WDR, 2021). These measures have served as critical elements in providing capital to those who could easily be missed by traditional lenders.

6.8 Collaboration Across Borders and Sectors

One of the key defining features of fintech is that its operations cut across sectors that traditionally do not intersect. To increase financial access, it is critical to collaborate between these sectors and jurisdictions. Therefore, cross-sector collaboration is important. WDR (2021) reported that cross boarder financial providers have also been involved in providing finances to domestic customers usually falling under more than one jurisdiction. For instance, one fintech may fall under telecommunication information data, consumer protection competition, and other regulators. Under these auspices, a multi-stakeholder consultative committee needs to be established.

Collaborations ease access for smallholder farmers as observed with MPesa customers, who can pay utility bills and send mobile money under the same app. In addition, MPesa collaborates with several foreign providers like Visa and Bitcoin. The addition of fintech into the financial sector has been beneficial in easing access to money for remotely located people. Moreover, it has also introduced competition. Therefore, competition in a regulated market is beneficial to clients as service providers compete to please them.

6.9 Conclusion

From the deliberations above, it can be noted that financial inclusion is critical for smallholder farmers, and it holds the potential to lift them out of poverty. There are glaring challenges that have been widely reported in literature and reports. These include low levels of literacy rates that lead to bad financial decisions. In addition to that, smallholder farmers have been traditionally excluded due to a lack of money and collateral. The result is that they resort to informal lending, where they are exorbitant fees. It can be noted that farmers are largely patronized by the system that they resort to for borrowing, and they do not have an alternative. However, there are fundamental factors that determine inclusion in developing countries. Reports note that the regulatory framework that governs financial technology needs to speak to the contemporary imperative of mobile technology to encourage the uptake of these mobile money accounts at the domestic level. As reiterated by the political economy, it is incumbent upon each government to ensure that resources are distributed equitably. Given that smallholder farmers form the majority of the poor, it is fundamental to invest in endeavours that can reconfigure their state.

References

Adedokun, M. W., & Ağa, M. (2021). Financial inclusion: A pathway to economic growth in sub-Saharan African economies. *International Journal of Finance & Economics*. https://doi.org/10.1002/ijfe.2559

Africa Centre for Economic Transformation (2020). Transformation in a Generation – 2020 End of Year Report. Available at https://acetforafrica.org/annual-reports/transformation-in-a-generation-2020-end-of-year-report/

Allen, F., Demirguc-Kunt, A., Klapper, L., & Peria, M. S. M. (2016). The foundations of financial inclusion: Understanding ownership and use of formal accounts. *Journal of financial Intermediation, 27*, pp.1–30.

Ashley, C., & Carney, D. (1999). *Sustainable livelihoods: Lessons from early experience* (Vol. 7, No. 1). DFID.

Asongu, S. A., & Odhiambo, N. M. (2019). How enhancing information and communication technology has affected inequality in Africa for sustainable development: An empirical investigation. *Sustainable Development, 27*(4), 647–656.

Asuming, P. O., Osei-Agyei, L. G., & Mohammed, J. I. (2019). Financial inclusion in sub-Saharan Africa: Recent trends and determinants. *Journal of African Business, 20*(1), 112–134.

Bebbington, A. (1999). Capitals and capabilities: A framework for analyzing peasant viability, rural livelihoods, and poverty. *World Development, 27*(12), 2021–2044. https://pdfs.semanticscholar.org/f7e2/784ebbdeb70547af0ec6adfe0f87dcaac2f0.pdf

Bernards, N. (2021). Poverty finance and the durable contradictions of colonial capitalism: Placing 'financial inclusion'in the long run in Ghana. *Geoforum, 123*, 89–98.

Binswanger, H. P., & Rosenzweig, M. R. (1986). *Credit markets, wealth, and endowments in rural South India*. Research Unit, Agriculture and Rural Development, Operational Policy Staff, World Bank.

Bire, A. R., Sauw, H. M., & Maria, M. (2019). The effect of financial literacy towards financial inclusion through financial training. *International Journal of Social Sciences and Humanities, 3*(1), 186–192. https://doi.org/10.29332/ijssh.v3n1.280

Business and Financial Times. (2020). *The impact of digital finance on financial inclusion in Africa*.

Chisasa, J., & Makina, D. (2012). Trends in credit to smallholder farmers in South Africa. *International Business & Economics Research Journal (IBER), 11*(7), 771–784.

Chinaka, M. (2016). *Blockchain technology—Applications in improving financial inclusion in developing economies: A case study for small scale agriculture in Africa* (Doctoral dissertation, Massachusetts Institute of Technology).

Daneshvar, C., Garry, S., López, J., Santamaría, J., & Villarreal, F. G. (2017). Financial inclusion of small-scale rural producers: Trends and challenges. In F. G. Villarreal (Ed.), *Financial inclusion of small rural producers* (pp. 15–28). United Nations.

de Soto, H. (2000). *The mystery of capital: Why capitalism triumphs in the west and fails everywhere else*. Bantam Press.

Demirguc-Kunt, A., Klapper, L., Singer, D., & Ansar, S. (2018). *The Global Findex database 2017: Measuring financial inclusion and the fintech revolution*. World Bank Publications.

Demirgüç-Kunt, A., Klapper, L., Singer, D., Ansar, S., & Hess, J. (2018). Opportunities for expanding financial inclusion through digital technology.

Demirguc-Kunt, A., Klapper, L., Singer, D., & Ansar, S. (2022). The Global Findex Database 2021.

Ephrem, N., Wamatu, J., Alemayehu, F., & Anebo, D. (2021). *Financial literacy for smallholder sheep fattening farmers – Training manual*. International Center for Agricultural Research in the Dry Areas (ICARDA).

Farrington, J., Carney, D., Ashley, C., & Turton, C. (1999). Sustainable livelihhods in practice: early applications of concepts in rural areas (Vol. 42, pp. 1–2). London: ODI.

FDIP Report (2017). The 2017 Brookings Financial and Digital Inclusion Project ReportAvailable at https://www.brookings.edu/research/the-2017-brookings-financial-and-digital-inclusion-project-report/

Fowowe, B. (2020). The effects of financial inclusion on agricultural productivity in Nigeria. *Journal of Economics and Development, 22*(1), 61–79.

Goedde, L., Ooko-Ombaka, A., & Pais, G. (2019). *Winning in Africa's agricultural market*. McKinsey & Company.

Güngen, A. R. (2018). Financial inclusion and policy-making: Strategy, campaigns, and microcredit a la Turca. *New Political Economy, 23*(3), 331–347.

Huffman, W. E., & Curtiss, C. F. (2006). Discussion: AAEA session in honor of T.W Schultz in Oxford Journal, Economics, and Social Sciences. *Applied Economic Perspectives and Policy, 28*(3), 351–353.

IFC (International Finance Corporation). (2014). *Access to finance for smallholder farmers learning from the experiences of microfinance institutions in Latin America*. World Bank Group. www.ifc.org/wps/wcm/connect/07

Jonathan Gimba, O., Seraj, M., & Ozdeser, H. (2021). What drives income inequality in sub-Saharan Africa and its sub-regions? An examination of long-run and short-run effects. *African Development Review, 33*(4), 729–741.

Kahan, D. (2008). *Managing risk in farming*. Food and Agriculture Organization of the United Nations.

Kalunda, E. (2014). Financial inclusion impact on small-scale tea farmers in Nyeri County, Kenya. *World Journal of Social Sciences, 4*(1), 130–139. http://www.wjsspapers.com/static/documents/March/2014/10.%20Elizabeth.pdf

Kostov, P., & Lingard, J. (2002). Subsistence farming in transitional economies: Lessons from Bulgaria. *Journal of Rural Studies, 18*(1), 83–94. https://doi.org/10.1016/S0743-0167(01)00026-2

Kpodar, M. K., & Andrianaivo, M. (2011). *ICT, financial inclusion, and growth: Evidence from African countries*. International Monetary Fund.

Krantz, L. (2001). *The sustainable livelihood approach to poverty reduction*. Sida (Swedish International Development Cooperation Agency). Division for Policy and Socio-Economic Analysis. http://citeseerx.ist.psu.edu/viewdoc/download?doi=10.1.1.469.7818&rep=rep1&type=pdf

Lewis, R. J., Villasenor, J. D., & West, D. M. (2017). The 2017 Brookings financial and digital inclusion project report. Building a Secure and Inclusive Global Financial Ecosystem. Disponível em:< https://www.brookings.edu/wpcontent/uploads/2017/08/fdip_20170831_project_report.pdf.

Madden, P (2020). Figures of the Week. Financial Inlcusion of farmersin Africa. 30 September. Available at https://www.brookings.edu/blog/africa-in-focus/2020/09/30/figures-of-the-week-financial-inclusion-of-farmers-inafrica/

Mazwi, F., Chemura, A., Mudimu, G. T., & Chambati, W. (2019). Political economy of command agriculture in Zimbabwe: A state-led contract farming model. *Agrarian South: Journal of Political Economy, 8*(1–2), 232–257.

Menyelim, C. M., Babajide, A. A., Omankhanlen, A. E., & Ehikioya, B. I. (2021). Financial inclusion, income inequality, and sustainable economic growth in sub-Saharan African countries. *Sustainability, 13*(4), 1780.

Meyer, R. L. (2015). *Financing agriculture and rural areas in sub-Saharan Africa: Progress, challenges and the way forward*. IIED.

Mhlanga, D. (2020). *Financial inclusion and poverty reduction: Evidence from small scale agricultural sector in Manicaland province of Zimbabwe* (Doctoral dissertation, North-West University, South Africa).

Mhlanga, D., & Dunga, S. H. (2020). Measuring financial inclusion and its determinants among the smallholder farmers in Zimbabwe: An empirical study. *Eurasian Journal of Business and Management, 8*(3), 266–281.

Mhlanga, D., Dunga, S. H., & Moloi, T. (2020). Financial inclusion and poverty alleviation among smallholder farmers in Zimbabwe. *Eurasian Journal of Economics and Finance, 8*(3), 168–182.

Morgan, P. J., & Long, T. Q. (2020). Financial literacy, financial inclusion, and savings behavior in Laos. *Journal of Asian Economics, 68*, 101197.

Ndhlovu, E. (2018). Relevance of sustainable livelihood approach in Zimbabwe's land reform programme. *Africa Insight, 47*(4), 72–87.

Odusola, A. (2017). Agriculture, rural poverty and income inequality in sub-Saharan Africa. In *Income inequality trends in sub-Saharan Africa: Divergence, determinants, and consequences*. UNDP.

OECD (2012). PISA 2012 Financial Literacy Assessment Framework. From http://www.oecd.org/pisa/pisaproducts/46962580.pdf

Oji, C. K. (2015). *Promoting financial inclusion for inclusive growth in Africa*. https://www.africa-portal.org/publications/promoting-financial-inclusion-for-inclusive-growth-in-africa/
Ozili, P. K. (2021). Financial inclusion research around the world: A review. *Forum for Social Economics, 50*(4), 457–479.
Rankin, K. (2013). 'A Critical Geography of Poverty Finance'. *Third World Quarterly 34*(4), 547– 68.
Riley, T. A., & Kulathunga, A. (2017). *Bringing E-money to the poor: Successes and failures*. World Bank Publications.
Salami, A., Kamara, A. B., & Brixiova, Z. (2010). *Smallholder agriculture in East Africa: Trends, constraints, and opportunities* (Working Paper No. 105). African Development Bank. https://pdfs.semanticscholar.org/cfa3/09d7c77c5922291155296df2f4721d442829.pdf
Sarma, M., & Pais, J. (2011). Financial inclusion and development. *Journal of International Development, 23*(5), 613–628.
Schultz, T. W. (1964). *Transforming traditional agriculture*. Yale University Press.
Scoones, I. (1998). *Sustainable rural livelihoods: A framework for analysis* (Working Paper 72). IDS (Institute of Development Studies). http://opendocs.ids.ac.uk/opendocs/handle/123456789/3390
Senou, M. M., Ouattara, W., & Acclassato Houensou, D. (2019). Financial inclusion dynamics in WAEMU: Was digital technology the missing piece? *Cogent Economics & Finance, 7*(1), 1665432.
Singh, N. (2017). *Financial inclusion: Concepts, issues, and policies for India* (Working Paper No. 43). International Growth Centre synthesis paper.
The Global Findex Database (2017). Global Financial Inclusion (Global Findex) Database 2017 Available online https://microdata.worldbank.org/index.php/catalog/3246
The Global Findex Database (2021). lobal Findex Database 2021: Financial Inclusion, Digital Payments, and Resilience in the Age of COVID-19 Available online at https://www.worldbank.org/en/publication/globalfindex
The World Development Report (WDR). (2018). LEARNING to Realize Education's Promise Available online at https://www.worldbank.org/en/publication/wdr2018
The World Development Report (WDR). (2021). DATA FOR BETTER LIVES Available online https://www.worldbank.org/en/publication/wdr2021
Triki, T., & Faye, I. (2013). Financial inclusion in Africa. African Development Bank, p.146. https://www.afdb.org
Tooling, C. (2009). Securing land and property rights in sub-Saharan Africa: The role of local institutions. *Land Use Policy, 26*(1), 10–19.
Van, L. T. H., Vo, A. T., Nguyen, N. T., & Vo, D. H. (2021). Financial inclusion and economic growth: An international evidence. *Emerging Markets Finance and Trade, 57*(1), 239–263.
World Bank. (2022). *Financial inclusion overview*. World Bank. www.worldbank.org/en/topic/financialinclusion/overview
World Development Report. (2008). *Agriculture for development*. The World Bank.
Zins, A., & Weill, L. (2016). The determinants of financial inclusion in Africa. *Review of Development Finance, 6*(1), 46–57.

Chapter 7
Digital Financial Inclusion and Digital Financial Literacy in Africa: The Challenges Connected with Digital Financial Inclusion in Africa

Favourate Y. Mpofu

Abstract The Covid-19 pandemic disrupted the general status quo globally and affected all sectors of the economy. Governments responded to the pandemic with lockdown measures and social distancing requirements as well as encouraged reduced human interaction. Most companies encouraged remote working. The demand and access to cash were reduced and replaced by digital banking, digital transactions, and payments. Digital financial inclusion has thus become a topical global phenomenon as the demand for digital financial services heightened significantly. This increased demand for digital financial inclusion signalled the need for convenient and economical financial products to achieve inclusive and fair economic recovery in the aftereffects of the Covid-19 pandemic. While digital transformation and the Fourth Industrial Revolution are at an advanced stage in developed countries, the African continent is lagging. Much of the population is observed to be digitally and financially excluded. This chapter focuses on digital financial inclusion and digital literacy in Africa. This is because digital inclusion is vital for digital financial inclusion to be achieved, yet digital inclusion is affected by digital literacy. Through a comprehensive literature review, the chapter establishes that digital financial inclusion is important for the empowerment of the population, their financial management, spending, and investment decisions as well as the growth of the economy. It was also evident that digital financial inclusion is far from being attained in Africa due to challenges that include digital exclusion, digital financial literacy, redundancy barriers, lack of connectivity, high Internet data costs, and digital taxes.

Keywords Africa · Digital financial inclusion · Digital financial literacy · Economic growth · Digital literacy

F. Y. Mpofu (✉)
University of Johannesburg, Johannesburg, South Africa

D. Mhlanga, E. Ndhlovu (eds.), *Economic Inclusion in Post-Independence Africa*, Advances in African Economic, Social and Political Development,
https://doi.org/10.1007/978-3-031-31431-5_7

7.1 Introduction

Financial inclusion is a matter of concern the world over and more so in the African continent, where most of the population is argued to be financially excluded (Shipalana, 2019). The growth of the digital economy globally and in Africa, coupled with the Fourth Industrial Revolution as well as Covid-19 pandemic, has led to the expansion of fintech and the use of digital financial services (DFSs) (Mpofu, 2022; Mpofu & Moloi, 2022). The usage of mobile money services and other DFSs is on the rise in the African continent (Mpofu, 2022; Shapshack, 2021). Pushkareva (2021) tables that the increase in the usage of DFSs in the African continent could lead to a considerable improvement in financial inclusion and digital financial inclusion. This chapter centres on the challenges of digital financial inclusion in Africa. The concept has considerable significance and impact, especially concerning emerging economies. Understanding the challenges would help address the possible African opportunities to increase digital financial inclusion, thus providing insight into the critical roles of government, policymakers, and the financial services sector in building a conducive environment for beneficial and effective financial inclusion. Through a comprehensive literature review, the chapter seeks to give an overview of digital financial inclusion in Africa, identifying the challenges (practical and policy), with the hope of providing recommendations that could inform broader (continental) and narrower contextual (national) policy initiatives to broaden digital financial inclusion.

This chapter mainly employed a critical literature review approach, complemented by a document analysis of secondary data sources. These encompassed several peer-reviewed journal articles, book chapters, and reports on the global finance index from the McKinsey Institute, the African portal publications and policy papers and reviews from the Institute of Development Studies. The focus was on recently published journals and policy reports from national, continental, and international organisations on digital financial inclusion, constraints affecting effective usage of DFS and how digital financial literacy affects African countries on national, regional, and continental levels. Fifty-three articles were reviewed and referenced in the paper, while several others were just reviewed but not necessarily referenced as no specific ideas were extracted from these, but they generally aided in the development of the chapter.

7.2 Background

Financial inclusion is the process in which all segments of the population find it easy to access or use affordable financial services and products in the mainstream financial markets (Ozili, 2018). Approximately 3.5 billion people are financially excluded (the unbanked and underbanked), 2 billion adults are unbanked, and 300 million people are digitally excluded globally (not having access to mobile connectivity and the Internet) (Shipalana, 2019). This is despite the calls by the United Nations (UN) for countries to ensure financial inclusion for everyone especially the vulnerable segments through the Sustainable Development Goals 2030 (SDGs) (Munoz et al., 2022). SDG10 encourages countries to focus on reducing inequalities among the population, SDG5 deals with the need to address gender equality, SDG1 speaks to the need for increased poverty alleviation efforts to eradicate poverty, and SDG8 relates to the creation of decent work and enhance economic growth. Addressing these SDGs is inextricably connected to enhancing or increasing financial inclusion. As such, understanding financial inclusion and especially digital financial inclusion in this digital era are critical in the African context (where technology is lagging, and digital financial literacy remains problematic) (Cude, 2021).

The Fourth Industrial Revolution (4IR) is altering the activities of all economic sectors in society including the financial services sector. The adoption of 4IR technologies has changed banking services drastically. The way businesses perform their activities as well as the way humans interact has changed (Mhlanga, 2020; Ojo, 2022). The Covid-19 pandemic and the preventative measures, taken by countries to minimise the spread and impact of the pandemic on human lives and economic activity, have accelerated digital transformation in the financial services sector (Machasio, 2020), heightening the application of the 4IR tools by financial and non-financial institutions (Ojo, 2022). These 4IR technologies include blockchain technology, artificial intelligence (AI), big data, cloud computing, and machine learning. In addition to these, Paul (2019) points out some of the AI tools that can be used in the financial services sector to expand digital financial inclusion to encompass deep learning, natural language processing, robotics, audio processing, and expert systems. This digitalisation of the processes in the financial services sector has led to the term “fintech”. Fintech refers to the various digital activities and business models that can greatly transform the functions and services offered by the financial services sector (Mhlanga, 2020; Munoz et al., 2022). Digital financial inclusion is progressively becoming the core in the discussions on how to bring the disadvantaged, vulnerable, and conventionally underserved segments of the groups such as low-income earners into formal financial institutions.

Folwarski (2021) adduces that nonconventional institutions, such as microfinance institutions, have gradually been participating in financial markets, productively challenging the common financial institutions, and employing their significant databases and financial capabilities. Fintech has emerged to cover the void in financial inclusion created by traditional financial inclusion, hence the term digital financial inclusion. Fintech companies are employing AI technologies to enhance digital financial inclusion and to ensure that the poor, youth, women, small businesses, informal sector operators, and low-income earners are financially active. AI technologies can be employed in digital financial inclusion aspects, such as identifying, measuring and managing risks, providing customer helpdesk and support, minimising information asymmetry challenges, preventing and detecting errors and fraud, as well as increasing cybersecurity (Folwarski, 2021; Mhlanga, 2020) Even though the use of AI heralds a new dawn in financial activities of financial and non-financial institutions, digital literacy continues to be a hindrance (Alameda, 2020). AI and the growth in fintech provide great possibilities for ensuring digital financial inclusion of the financially inactive and vulnerable members of society with minimum hurdles and maximum advantages.

Financial inclusion avails complementary and incremental solutions to address poverty and foster development and economic growth and the achievement of the SDGs. Digital financial inclusion is a fundamental building block in development globally. Shipalana (2019) states that the core principles of financial inclusion include affordability, accessibility, appropriateness, quality of services, usage, simplicity, consumer financial knowledge and awareness, diversification, and innovation. Digital financial services (DFS) aided by the technological transformation in the financial sector have become a pivotal driver for digital financial inclusion in developing and emerging markets. Several studies have been conducted on financial inclusion with a national focus (Mhlanga, 2020), digital financial inclusion in national contexts (Shipalana, 2019), and digital financial services or the role of fintech on heightening financial inclusion with a regional orientation (Berkmen et al., 2019; Blancher et al., 2019; Mhlanga & Denhere, 2020; Mhlanga, 2020; Mhlanga, et al., 2021). Most studies focused on the drivers and challenges of traditional financial inclusion (Mhlanga, 2021a, b; Mhlanga et al., 2021; Mutsonziwa & Maposa, 2016; Evans, 2016), while few studies have centred on digital financial inclusion, which is driven by fintech with a continental focus, yet the Covid-19 pandemic accelerated digital transformation in the financial services industry (Ojo, 2022; Pushkareva, 2021).

7.3 Literature Review

This section reviews relevant literature to elaborate on the relationship between digital literacy, financial literacy, digital financial literacy, and digital financial inclusion in Africa.

7.3.1 Financial Inclusion

Financial inclusion is referred to as the sustainable provision of reachable, safe, and affordable financial services through an all-inclusive system that avails opportunities for receiving, sending, depositing, withdrawing, and banking funds in a way that allows risk reduction and capital growth (Shipalana, 2019). Financial inclusion is described as an all-encompassing approach to supplying financial services to the financially excluded constituent of the population, making sure the unbanked population is ushered into the mainstream financial sector (Ozili, 2018, 2020). Massa (2013) describes financial inclusion as a process in which financial institutions deliver affordable financial services to all members of society. These services include money exchange, money transfer, and safe keeping and investment, among other functions of financial institutions. Financial inclusion is key to achieving social cohesion and inclusion, promotion of sustainable economic growth, and poverty alleviation (Kelikume, 2021; Ozili, 2020; Salampasis & Mention, 2018).

7.3.2 Digital Finance and Digital Financial Services (DFS)

DFS describes financial services that are provided and accessed through digital means as well as mobile devices; these rely on digital tools for delivery and consumption. These services include those provided by banks such as *cell phone banking, credit, and debit cards (Munoz et al., 2022; Ojo, 2022). In addition, the services encompass those offered to asset management firms, insurance companies, pension funds, other financial institutions, capital markets, and money markets (Shipalana, 2019). The services also cover novel designs founded on cloud computing and digital platforms including mobile payments, and crypto assets among other services. DFS include mobile financial services, automated teller machine services, electronic or plastic money, and online banking. These services are encapsulated in the word "Fintech" (Agur et al., 2020; Makina, 2019). DFS was harnessed to reduce the accessibility to financial institution's problems, trading challenges, and the inequalities heightened by the Covid-19 pandemic. DFS is used to describe financial activities such as sending and receiving funds; making deposits, withdrawals, and savings; accessing credit and insurance services; making transfers; and accessing pensions and other social grants and benefits. Customers can also be able to access their data such as balances and previous transactions, make payments and purchases, and download the proof of payments for the transactions without going to the bank. The government can also use government-to-persons (G2P) platforms to pay salaries, pensions, and other social welfare funds. This brings convenience and flexibility in the management of finances by individuals and can contribute to the realisation of SDGs 1, 10, and 12.

7.3.3 Digital Financial Inclusion

Digital financial inclusion is a global phenomenon that is difficult to appropriately define. The World Bank (2020) asserts "Digital financial inclusion involves the deployment of the cost-saving digital means to reach currently financially excluded and underserved populations with a range of formal financial services suited to their needs that are responsibly delivered at a cost affordable to customers and sustainable for providers". Digital financial inclusion entails access to DFS and new and digitally transformative technologies (Pushkareva, 2021). Through digital financial inclusion, a larger segment of the traditionally underserved and financially excluded population is moving from mainly using cash-backed transactions to formal financial channels. The use of DFS enables access to services that a faster, more convenient, and affordable for vulnerable groups to conduct financial activities, such as payments, savings, payments, insurance, as well as credit employing mobile money or another novel digital technology (Ozili, 2018). The importance of digital financial inclusion in economies is irrefutable as it leads to access to reliable services for the poor, leading economic empowerment, and strengthening poverty alleviation efforts, thus assisting in financial growth, economic development, and growth. Digital financial inclusion leads to an increase in customers, thus fostering long-term improved profitability. Digital financial inclusion differs from traditional or ordinary financial inclusion in that while traditional financial inclusion has failed to capture the vulnerable and rural population due to access, costs, and affordability challenges, digital financial inclusion does so at a lower marginal cost. This argument albeit recognises that digital financial inclusion requires substantial investment in digital infrastructure in the first instance, and in the long run, the marginal cost of delivering DFS is significantly reduced (Shipalana, 2019).

7.3.4 Digital Literacy, Financial Literacy, and Digital Financial Literacy

There is no precise definition of digital literacy. It has been defined in variegated ways to reflect versatility, the quick and continuous technological changes associated with it, and its objective towards bridging the global digital divide. Despite their variations, most definitions centre on the ability to use technology (Radovanović et al., 2020). Digital literacy is connected to the educational and socioeconomic orientation of a person. Prete (2022) defines digital literacy as the capability to use digital platforms, services, and applications. Financial literacy on the other hand relates to the financial decision-making, response to monetary policy prescriptions and their outcomes, and choices of financial assets and liabilities. Hartanto (2022:1) defines financial literacy "as a combination of financial awareness, knowledge, skills, attitudes and behaviours necessary to make sound financial decisions and ultimately achieve individual financial wellbeing". Affirming the same line of thought, Prete (2022) posits that it is the capacity to comprehend the basics or foundational concepts of finance and economics in making financial choices and relationships such as savings, consumption, and investment decisions while recognising the associated risks. Evans (2016), while studying the determinants of financial inclusion in 15 African countries, found that the drivers of financial inclusion include literacy, Internet connectivity, domestic credit, and deposit interest rates. Digital literacy is a key driver for digital inclusion, and thus, digital inclusion is a necessity for digital financial inclusion. Digital financial literacy combines digital literacy and financial literacy.

Digital financial literacy is increasingly becoming topical in this digital era. The expansion of the digital economy requires consumers to know how to make use of fintech services and products effectively and avoid fraud and other costly mistakes

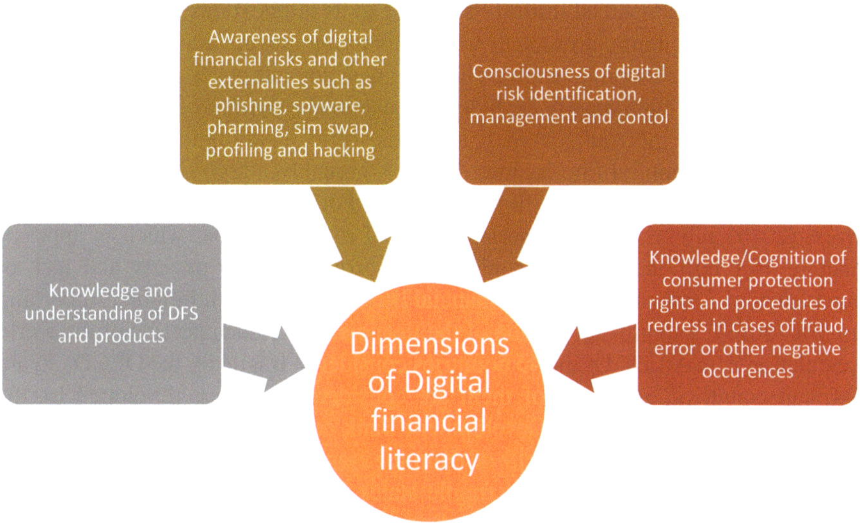

Fig. 7.1 Dimension of digital financial literacy. (*Source*: Own Compilation)

(Cude, 2021; Morgan et al., 2020; Panos & Wilson, 2020). Access to DFS is not enough. Access to DFS calls for consumers to have high levels of digital financial literacy to make productive use of them while mitigating the impact of fraud activities, such as phishing, hacking, mis-selling, and fraudulent use of data as well as discriminatory treatment and negative financial behaviour such as over-borrowing. Digital financial literacy is multifaceted. Morgan et al. (2019, 2020) point to four perspectives of digital financial literacy, and these are summarised in Fig. 7.1.

Digital financial literacy is thus pivotal for digital financial inclusion to be achieved and for the realisation of the SDGs. It is not enough to only know how to use digital platforms and access them (digital literacy) but also crucial to know how to use them, as they relate to DFS, and to have knowledge of these DFS, the institutions offering them, their benefits, and accompanying risks, so that digital financial inclusion can be achieved. Globally, countries need to come up with clear definitions of the digital financial literacy concept, put in place measures to assess it, and design programs and strategies to promote digital financial literacy, especially the greater focus on the vulnerable constituent of the population (the uneducated, the less educated, the elderly, owners of SMEs and startup businesses, informal sector operators, and women).

7.4 Digital Financial Inclusion in Africa

Digital financial inclusion is a topic of high interest in development, poverty alleviation, and financial inclusion discussions globally and in the African continent. It is a major topic that has piqued the interest of researchers, governments, policymakers, and financial institutions owing to its implications for poverty reduction, boosting economic growth, as well as its promising economic transformative power and the likelihood to heighten development advantages. Traditional financial service providers significantly excluded a considerable portion of the population in Africa, especially the youth, women, and girls, those operating in the informal sector and those earning a low income. There is arguably a high degree of financial exclusion in Africa, especially in fragile states. For example, Adetunji and David-West (2019) submit that in Nigeria, 41.6% of the population, which is approximately 40.1 million adults, are unbanked or excluded with poverty and lack of awareness of financial services or financial literacy being key inhibitors. According to Sile (2013), a significant portion of the financially excluded portion of the world population is in Africa. Of the 45 countries considered fragile by the OECD, 26 are African countries, and most of them are considered the least developed by the United Nations. The African Development Bank considers that of the 54 African countries that are its members, 19 of them are fragile states. Poverty is a big challenge in Africa, especially in the fragile states. Fragile states have low levels of development in the financial sector and accordingly low levels of financial inclusion. In the fragile African states, only 14% of the adults are banked, which is comparatively low with the banked in sub-Saharan Africa (SSA) and Africa, which are at rates of 24% and 23%, respectively (Sile, 2013). The vulnerability and instability in these countries compromise the infrastructural development and peace-building initiatives, which are fundamental conditions for creating an inclusive and even digitally driven financial sector.

Despite the high degrees of financial exclusion in Africa, mobile money usage has expanded consequentially to fill the financial inclusion gap, thus widening financial inclusion. Sixty-four percent of developing countries have mobile money services. Even though digital financial inclusion is a challenge in the African continent, the continent has made tremendous progress in the usage of mobile as a digital tool to broaden financial inclusion (commendable as articulated by Mhlanga, 2020). Mobile money is described as the leading driver in enhancing digital financial inclusion, "with Africa emerging as the world leader in mobile money" (Shipalana, 2019). The researcher alludes to the fact that those that own mobile phones in Africa greatly exceed those that have access to basic services such as clean water and electricity. Munoz et al. (2022) estimate that in sub-Saharan (SSA) in 2019 over 40% of the region's population made use of mobile money accounts, though the relevant percentages varied widely from one region to another and from one country to another. According to Shipalana (2019), citing the 2017 Global Finance Index SSA encouragingly demonstrates the power of digital financial technology to widen access and usage of mobile money accounts, with an approximated 45% account penetration rate. For example, countries like Namibia, Kenya, Uganda, Tanzania, Zimbabwe, and Ghana heavily depended on mobile money to financially transact both formally and informally (Kakungulu-Mayambala & Rukundo, 2018; Ndung'u, 2019; Simatele, 2021).

Various and widespread imbalances in financial inclusion and digital financial inclusion exist between regions, countries, and rural and urban populations. While some countries have well-developed and smoothly functioning financial systems and adequate digital infrastructure to support DFS and digital financial inclusion, some countries lack the requisite enablers for an effective digital financial system such as Internet connectivity and other digital infrastructure. For example, in the Central African Republic, Congo, Guinea, the Democratic Republic of Congo, Burundi, Sudan, and Chad, 90% of the adults are unbanked, with security threats, underdeveloped financial markets, and poor infrastructure as key impediments. This points to greater financial exclusion in the fragile African states as compared to the non-fragile ones. There are also variations in the usage of DFS across countries concerning demographic characteristics, such as age, education, and gender, including with other factors such as the type of business, employment, and income levels. For example, while in Tanzania many of the people were financially included using mobile money in rural areas as compared to those in urban areas (Munoz et al., 2022), in Lesotho many of the rural dwellers were financially excluded (Sekantsi & Motelle, 2018).

Digital financial inclusion is a key component of inclusive development and the poverty eradication agenda, as it can help the underserved segments of the population to have better lives. The improved access to digital finance at affordable costs avails better financial management opportunities to serve even those operating in the informal economy, thus helping financially empower the poor and low-income earners. Financial inclusion of those operating in the informal has become pivotal in alleviation efforts, addressing inequality and ensuring inclusive growth, especially in Africa, where the informal sector contributes significantly to GDP, employment, and household incomes. For example, while citing the International Labour Organisation (ILO) (2018), Rogan (2019) submits that 61% of the global workforce is employed in the informal economy, and in East Africa and SSA, the informal economy represents 92% and 89% of the labour force, respectively. In Africa, there are approximately 78% of nonagricultural jobs and 61% of employment in urban areas and 93% of new jobs in the informal sector (Mpofu, 2021; Rogan, 2019). Bhorat et al. (2017) adduce that the informal sector occupies a critical domain in developing countries, representing approximately 50–80% of GDP, 60–90% of employment, and 90% of new jobs. Conservatively in SSA, the informal sector contributes 40–60% of GDP (Dickerson, 2014), and Zimbabwe has the second largest informal sector in the world after Bolivia (contributing around 61% of GDP) (Medina & Schneider, 2018). The figure might even have grown significantly due to increased job losses, retrenchments, and business collapse induced by the Covid-19 pandemic.

Notwithstanding that these estimations are fraught with challenges owing to the hidden nature and scarcity of data in the informal sector, if the figures are anything to go by digital financial inclusion of those operating in the informal economy, is fundamental. It is not only critical for poverty reduction endeavours and economic growth but also for domestic revenue mobilisation (taxes). The informal economy is argued to contribute very minimal amounts to the national tax coffers in Africa (Sebele-Mpofu & Moyo, 2021; Rogan, 2019) around 3% of total tax revenue (Maina, 2017). Domestic revenue mobilisation is crucial for funding government expenditure, for reducing overdependence on donor funding, for government to enhance legitimacy and control over all sectors of the economy, and for fostering government-citizen stakeholder bargaining and engagement (implicit social contract) (Sebele-Mpofu, 2020, 2021).

In addition to these concerns, digital financial inclusion is important in Africa, because the digital economy has expanded tremendously, and Covid-19 fuelled this growth. The UNCTAD (2018) estimates Facebook to have in excess of 200 million users in Africa and that nearly 21 million people in the African continent constantly engage in online buying and selling. Contemporary tax debates and discussions on possible tax reforms and avenues to widen domestic revenue mobilisation have paid renewed focus to taxation of the digital economy (Bunn et al., 2020; Kelbesa, 2020; Mekgoe & Hassam, 2020; Santoro et al., 2022). The argument is that governments are losing a lot of untapped tax revenue from the digital economy, especially in African countries, where this is compounded by tax avoidance and evasion schemes conducted by multinational enterprises through aggressive transfer pricing strategies (Sebele-Mpofu et al., 2021). If individuals and small businesses are digitally financially included, it might be possible to widen the tax base by including them, and boost tax compliance as audit trail (digital footprints) can provide information for tax audits and tax return assets. This would boost revenue mobilisation and help stimulate under benefits of tax compliance.

7.5 Importance and Benefits of Digital Financial Inclusion in Africa

The growth in fintech is linked to the loss of confidence in conventional financial institutions (Folwarski, 2021). Digital finance and financial inclusion have numerous benefits to digital service providers, governments, users of financial services, the economy, and the public at large. Digital financial inclusion is a critical driver for financial development, economic growth, and poverty alleviation (Kelikume, 2021). There are several advantages of digital financial inclusion in Africa. Figure 7.2 presents a snapshot of some of the advantages to foreground an in-depth discussion of the possible gains.

7.5.1 Increased Access to Financial Services

Digital financial services are a critical component of digital financial inclusion. Digital services can enable banks to be able to service rural populations and those in remote areas through access to affordable financial services by low-income earners and those operating in the informal economy (Optix, 2015; Ozili, 2020; Peric, 2015).

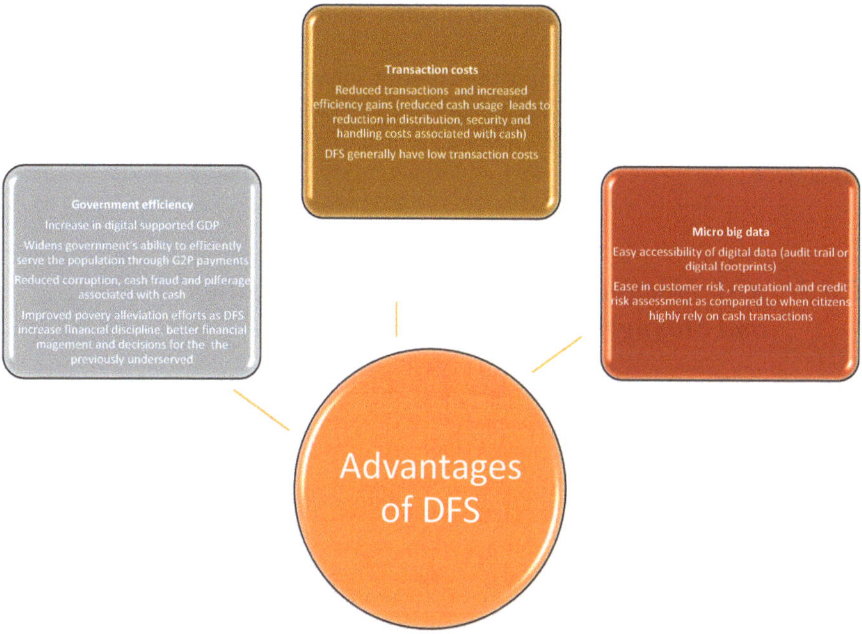

Fig. 7.2 Summary of selected advantages of digital financial inclusion. (*Source*: Own Compilation)

Mobile money usage, therefore, provides financial services in Africa to the generally unbanked portion of the population, thus ushering them into the conventional financial system. This promotes the possibility of savings mobilisation for the financially disadvantaged, the informal sector, the low-income earners, and the poor (Ouma et al., 2017). According to Pushkareva (2021), DFS provided SSA countries with a peculiar opportunity to enhance sustainable economic growth, as it avails additional revenue through taxation and "even improves gender balance". Online platforms, Robo-advisers, and digital banks lead to the digital transformation of financial intermediaries, as borrowers and lenders can be directly connected. This allows for easy access to saving and borrowing by low-income earners and those in remote areas while promoting entrepreneurial operations and their growth. The McKinsey Global Institute (2016) affirms that DFS gives greater access to financial services through the reduction of transaction costs. Digital technologies can reduce the cost of offering financial services by 80–90% in developing countries, expanding financial inclusion, and supporting poverty reduction efforts.

Demirgüç-Kunt et al. (2018) allude to the increase in peer-to-peer remittance transactions through banks and mobile money in 2017 in low-income countries. The sophistication of DFS has also advanced over the years to include payments for government services through digital means, government to individuals and individuals to individuals. The primary dependence on and the usage of cash was reduced by the Covid-19 pandemic in most African countries. Financial services stimulate development. They facilitate investment in businesses, education, security, and health in a country, in addition to assisting in poverty alleviation (Demirgüç-Kunt et al., 2018).

DFS leads to the digital transformation of international remittances and payments. Those outside their domestic countries can easily send remittances to their countries of origin. Therefore, DFS can spur both domestic and international commerce.

7.5.2 Risk Identification, Measurement, Mitigation, and Management

Digital banking services also mitigate the risks of such as theft, loss, fraud, bribery, and corruption due to cash transactions. Financial inclusion relies on the digitisation and digitalisation of financial services (Beck, 2020), as services can be tailor-made to address the needs of clients taking into consideration their financial context. Increased usage of digital finance leads to financial integration (Folwarski, 2021). Computer algorithms can be used to help make decisions on loan qualifications and creditworthiness; this reduces forms of discrimination such as bias or race-oriented discrimination. It is important to note that even though the algorithms can minimise bias, they can further reinforce prevailing bias, as the algorithms are constructed by humans depending on historical data. Additionally, for algorithms, digital literacy, financial literacy, and digital financial literacy remain important challenges to consider as failure to address them can lead to algorithm aversion. Algorithm aversion is the lack of trust in or fear of depending on an algorithm-generated outcomes.

7.5.3 Achievement of SDGs

Digital financial inclusion contributes to the achievement of SDGs (Ojo, 2022; Shipalana, 2019). Financial inclusion has been identified as pivotal in the attainment of nine SDGs. These include SDG 1 on eliminating poverty, SDG 2 on relating to attaining food security, SDG 3 on ensuring good health and well-being, SDG 5 focusing on ensuring gender equality, SDG 8 on the provision of decent work and fostering economic growth, SDG 9 centred on ensuring industry innovation, SDG 10 for reducing inequalities, and SDG 12 that encourages countries to promote responsible consumption and production. Lastly, SDG 17 calls for partnerships to deliver on the goals. When relating digital financial inclusion to SDGs, one could focus on, for example, SDG 8, which seeks to ensure economic growth that is both sustainable and inclusive as well as to ensure the provision of decent work. DFS provides governments, businesses, and consumers with efficiency, security, and convenience in conducting financial transactions. DFS foster significant financial inclusion by allowing those without access to formal banking services to have access to the services. Two critical issues are addressed, affordability and access. When those that were not able to transact, access credit, save invest, and spend in an affordable and productive manner can do so, this drives economic growth, and small enterprises can improve productivity and efficiency, thus increasing opportunities for decent work. With SDG 12, which encourages savings mobilisation and responsible consumption, DFS can be a key enabler. Fulfilment of these SDGs would drive financial inclusion and spur economic growth. Theoretical, anecdotal, and empirical supporting evidence has been submitted on financial inclusion (traditional and digital) on poverty alleviation efforts, economic growth, and fulfilment of the SDGs (Mhlanga & Dunga, 2020).

There is increasing empirical support for the argument that financial inclusion is vital for enabling broader economic growth and the attainment of wider development goals (Mhlanga, 2022; Osafo-Kwaako et al., 2018; Omar & Inaba, 2020 Cicchiello et al., 2021). Sarpong and Nketiah-Amponsah (2022) state that financial inclusion appears to complementary and incremental tool to attaining the UN millennium development goals. Digital financial inclusion could help in building effective financial economies and pooling of domestic resources through savings (responsible consumption, SDG 12) and contributing to enhanced government revenue mobilisation. By enabling DFS providers to extend savings, payments, and credit opportunities to the poor and low-income earners through digital means, digital financial inclusion is expanded, thus contributing considerably to sustainable economic development and growth. For example, when small to medium enterprises and sole traders benefit from these opportunities for financial inclusion, they can contribute to reducing inequalities, hunger, and poverty as well as to the creation of decent employment (SDGs 10, 2, 1, and 8). Osafo-Kwaako et al. (2018) point out that digital finance can drive inclusive growth by an additional US$3.7 trillion to the GDP of emerging economies in the next 10 years.

Ojo (2022), while focusing on *Digital Financial Inclusion for women in the Fourth Industrial Revolution* in Africa and the achievement of SDG 5 and snapping on Kenya, Lesotho, Namibia, and Ghana allude to the fact that women and girls are still disadvantaged and marginalised in the African continent. The researchers posit that the two groups remain traditionally, financially, and digitally excluded (owing to digital financial literacy challenges). The researcher concludes that even though women and girls are financing digital literacy and inclusion challenges in adopting the 4IR tools, the 4IR technologies can help close the gender gap in digitalisation and help in the realisation of SDG5 on gender equality. To achieve that, digital literacy is key; therefore, African countries must work tirelessly to bridge the digital literacy gap to foster digital financial inclusion of the underserved, including women and girls.

Digital financial inclusion tools, such as mobile money and online banking, are viewed as avenues to reduce inequality and foster an equitable and inclusive society. Affirming this argument, Salampasis and Mention (2018), focusing on *FinTech: Harnessing innovation for financial inclusion*, state that fintech is fundamental to the empowerment of the previously marginalised segments of the population through the following two ways. Firstly, it provides access to affordable financial services for the poor and informal economy, thus reducing inequality and overdependence by those without access to financial services on those that can easily access (overdependence opens room for exploitation, corruption, and abuse). Secondly, fintech provides diverse avenues and products to narrow the gap between the banked, the underbanked, and the underbanked; between the rural and urban populations; and between developing and developed economies. Therefore, fintech extends digital financial inclusion in Africa, which in turn is important for effective poverty alleviation efforts. Fintech technology alone is not sufficient for either digital financial inclusion or poverty alleviation; it must be supported by digital and financial literacy (digital financial literacy).

Dawei et al. (2018), in their study *Big data technology: application and cases*, explain that the 4IR tools, such as big data, are essential components to be employed in the rollout of DFS. These technologies help expand digital financial inclusion as well as the penetration of DFS platforms by those that were traditionally and financially excluded. The lower income earners and the poor can transact on small financial transactions that they were not able to transact on traditional financial platforms. According to Mhlanga (2020), most African countries, such as Kenya, South Africa, Zimbabwe, Tanzania, and Botswana, use mobile money as a tool for financial inclusion, economic development, and financial services expansion. Digital platforms are also used to send remittances regionally and internationally. All this points to ways that would lead to the SDGs coming to fruition.

Financial inclusion is arguably key to addressing vulnerability and poverty in Africa's fragile states as it ensures access and usage of financial services for the underserved and unserved segments of the population (Sile, 2013). A greater portion of the population in these states is financially excluded due to a lack of access to financial states. This is worsened by a weak institutional environment, poor infrastructure, conflicts, political instability, underdeveloped or weak financial systems, weak law enforcement, and a hostile investment climate.

Sile (2013) in the study, *Financial inclusion in fragile states*, portends that there is the increased usage of formal accounts to get international remittances in fragile African states, such as Zimbabwe and Somalia, the estimated usage being 55% and 66% of adults, respectively. This could reduce poverty and resource shortages, which are prominent features of fragile states. The increases in international remittance inflows present an opportunity for financial services providers to design other products and savings around these inflows, thus addressing SDG1, poverty reduction; SDG 16, peace, justice, and building strong institutions; SDG12, responsible consumption; and SDG 9, industry innovation and infrastructure.

Inoue and Hamori (2016), while focusing on "Financial access and economic growth: Evidence from sub-Saharan Africa", assessed 37 African countries and concluded that financial inclusion has a positive influence on economic growth. Increased demand for financial services improves the financial capacities of financial institutions to give loans to businesses and individuals and ultimately boosts profits and economic activity.

7.5.4 *Increased Market Share and Profitability of Financial Services Providers*

Events such as economic recessions, the Covid-19 pandemic, and many other factors have led to the loss of confidence in the banking sector, a reduction in bank competitiveness, and a negative impact on profitability. The failure to embrace digital transformation and the rollout of DFS have affected the financial and non-financial performance of financial service providers such as banks and insurance companies. Shipalana (2019) states that analysts forecast a possible 35% reduction in market share and a 35% decline in net profits for less innovative and digitally lagging financial service providers, such as banks and insurance companies, by 2020. By improving access to affordable, simple, dynamic, innovative, quality, diverse, and appropriate DFS, financial service providers can expand the usage of financial services, extend their market share, and improve company performance, such as profitability, goodwill, improved customer loyalty, brand name, and reputation.

7.5.5 *Risks Associated with DFS and Their Implications for Financial Inclusion*

Even though there are potential advantages to using DFS, these innovations come with significant risks. The risks associated with the use of DFS include fraud schemes, failure to transact owing to network challenges, not enough agent liquidity, complicated user interfaces, unclear or delayed customer recourse in case of losses due to fraud or system malfunction, invisible fees, insufficiencies in data security, privacy, confidentiality, and protection (Ozili, 2018). These risks compromise the digital financial inclusion efforts by financial institutions as they can lead to huge losses, DFS aversion by customers, and a lack of trust in digital finance. To mitigate these risks, digital literacy, financial literacy, and digital financial literacy promoting strategies are crucial. The various risks affecting various stakeholders to digital financial inclusion have been categorised in three broad categories as they rake to the key stakeholders (Fig. 7.3). These stakeholders include the government, DFS providers, and customers or consumers.

7.6 The Challenges of Digital Financial Inclusion in Africa

Even though consumers can benefit from fintech through the creation of novel models that result in a better assessment of products and the alignment of financial services to customer needs, there several challenges affecting digital financial inclusion in the African continent key among them digital literacy. One can only trust, use,

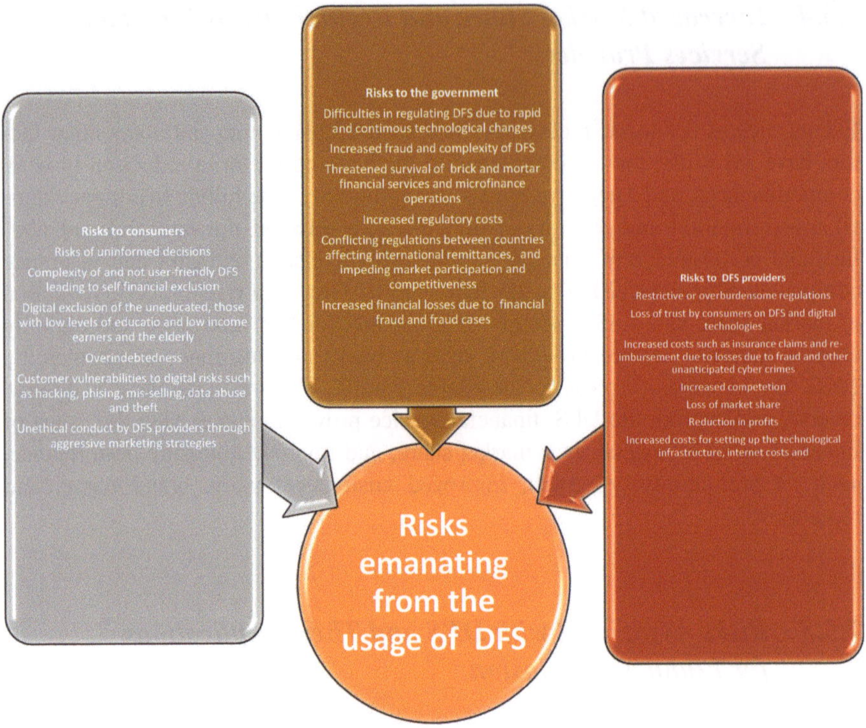

Fig. 7.3 Risks associated with digital financial inclusion. (*Source*: Author's Compilation)

and refer others to use what they know, understand, have confidence in, and are familiar with. The challenges to the effective deployment of DFS and technology-driven financial systems include stringent regulations, scarcity of qualified agents, Internet access and connectivity challenges, low levels of income and low levels of digital financial literacy, as well as limited interoperability (IMF, 2021; Massa, 2013). To foreground the discussion on the challenges affecting digital financial inclusion in Africa, Fig. 7.4 presents the fundamental principles of digital financial inclusion. These principles give an insight into what a productive digital financial inclusion framework should address. An understanding of the considerations of an effective digital financial system would help to illuminate the constraints as to why it is difficult to deliver on these key principles with Africa.

7.6.1 *Lack of Trust and Confidence in DFS*

Lack of trust is one of the fundamental challenges towards the uptake of DFS and the expansion of digital financial inclusion. Financial service providers face difficulties in convincing customers and building their trust in DFS. The stakeholder

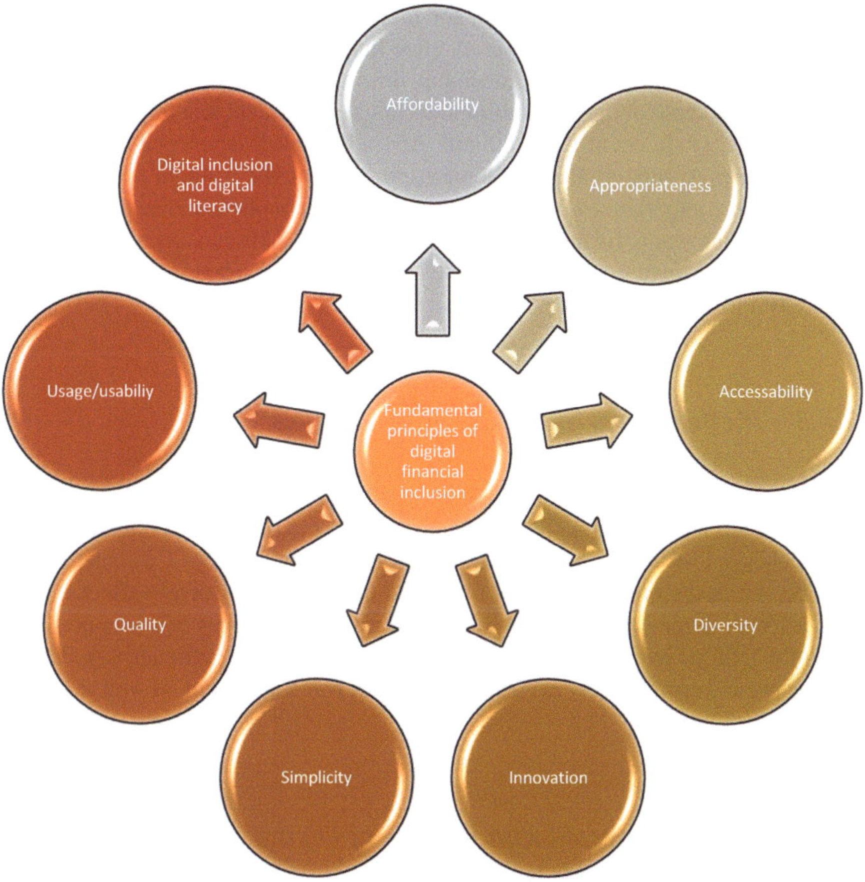

Fig. 7.4 Fundamental principles of digital financial inclusion. (*Source*: Own Compilation)

buy-in to the digital vision and strategies of financial service providers are generally low in some countries owing to digital financial illiteracy, DFS systems complexities, and the risks associated with digital services and platforms.

7.6.2 Access to Digital Equipment and Digital Infrastructure

The lack of access to digital equipment and digital infrastructure impedes digital financial inclusion, as it compromises one of the key dimensions that underpin the use of DFS to achieve financial inclusion. These are access, quality, usage, and choice. Researchers argue that the marginal costs for providing DFS are low and that labour costs required for face-to-face interaction are reduced (Mhlanga, 2020). Even though the argument is true, it is important to recognise that significant capital expenditure is needed. For example, for financial service providers to be able to deliver relevant, responsible, and productive financial services to all groups of the population, they need appropriate digital infrastructure. Setting up the requisite digital infrastructure requires a substantial capital investment that might be lacking. For example, while countries like South Africa have well-developed digital financial structures to support DFS, in some African countries, it might be lacking. To emphasise the importance of digital infrastructure as a fundamental enabler for digital financial inclusion, Evans (2016), while assessing 44 African countries, points to a significant positive connection between mobile money usage and Internet connectivity and financial inclusion.

7.6.3 Inefficiencies in Financial Institutions

Inefficiencies in financial institutions often discourage the adoption of DFS. The bureaucracies and lack of support to clients by banks in the cases of digital errors or fraud leads to loss of trust in DFS, hence discouraging their usage. Customer loyalty will be lost in the process, and the morale to use DFS is negatively affected. This also affects the reputation of banks and their image in the eyes of consumers. The usage of DFS heavily relies on the perception of reputation, efficiency in dealing with fraud and error, quality of customer support, risk assessment, as well as trust in financial institutions.

7.6.4 Risks Connected with the Use of Digital Financial Services

Several risks are linked to the use of DFS and discourage their usage even in cases where they are accessible. These risks include fraud risks, misleading advertisements, inexplicit costs, profiling, and many others (Morgan et al., 2019). Engels et al. (2020) affirm the loss of customer morale due to fraud and lack of trust in financial institutions. The researchers reiterate the importance of digital financial literacy contending that the more knowledgeable a person is, the greater the chances of detecting and preventing fraud, which is increasingly becoming sophisticated. In concurrence, Lyons and Kass-Hanna (2021), while assessing "Financial inclusion, financial literacy and economically vulnerable populations in the Middle East and North Africa", conclude that financial literacy is positively associated with financial inclusion. The researchers show that those with high degrees of financial literacy exhibit positive financial behaviour; they are more likely to display a positive saving culture and less likely to imprudently borrow especially from informal finance providers, and hence they are less prone to the risk of excessive borrowing.

7.6.5 Digital and Financial Literacy

Huston (2020) describes financial literacy as how well one comprehends and makes use of personal finance-oriented information. The complicatedness of some of the DFS and digital platforms used, make it challenging for consumers, especially the vulnerable groups to use DFS. This is further compounded by the lack of digital financial literacy. Consumers become risk-averse towards using DFS due to fear and knowledge inadequacies (Ozili, 2018, 2020). In concurrence, Shipalana (2019) points out that digital literacy is also a challenge even to financial institution employees as well who will often find it to assist customers with their queries and challenges, making the process long, cumbersome, time-consuming, and frustrating for the consumer. This not only leads to a loss of consumer morale but also to the loss of customer loyalty, goodwill, and brand reputation and ultimately hurts profitability.

7.6.6 Impact of Taxation

Tax is a cost to both businesses and individuals. In as much as it plays diverse and crucial roles in economies (such as revenue mobilisation, addressing market externalities, increasing citizen-government engagement through the "implicit social contract and being a fiscal policy too), it negatively affects businesses" profits and operations as well as disposable incomes of individuals. Revenue authorities globally and in African countries have introduced and, in some cases, expanded digital service taxes (DSTs) and DFS taxes (both direct and indirect) in response to the tremendous expansion of the digital economy owing to technological innovation, digital transformation, and increased usage of digital services driven by the Covid-19 pandemic. In Africa, countries such as Tunisia, Zimbabwe, Nigeria, and Kenya have introduced direct DSTs (Bunn et al., 2020; Kelbesa, 2020), and, for example, Zimbabwe, Kenya, Tanzania, Zambia, South Africa, and Nigeria have expanded their value-added tax regulation to cover digital services (Simbarashe, 2020). Countries such as Cote d'Ivoire, Zimbabwe, and Kenya have mobile money taxes, with Zimbabwe further having an intermediate tax on transfers (IMTT) of 2% on bank transfers and swipes and 4% on domestic foreign currency transfers (Mpofu, 2022; Pushkareva 2021). These taxes have led to a decline in the usage of DFS activities and other digital activities, thus further reducing profitability and digital financial inclusion (Munoz et al., 2022; Santoro et al., 2022).

7.6.7 Fragility, Political Instability, and Financial Instability

Financial instability, political instability, and fragility influence the sustainability or lack of sustainability of financial institutions. For example, this was the case in the DRC and Zimbabwe, where bank collapses, unstable monetary policies, weak currency, and inconsistent regulations led to a lack of trust in financial institutions, heightening preferences for saving and borrowing informally (Sile, 2013). Fragility influences the country's propensity to supply basic financial services through both formal and informal channels. Financial institutions in some African countries especially the fragile economies find it challenging to provide appropriate, affordable, and well-developed financial products when the macroeconomic environment is unfavourable and characterised by small economic growth, high rates of inflation and increased unemployment, as well as underdeveloped digital infrastructure. Cull et al. (2012) argue that there is a link between political instability and financial inclusion. The researchers posit that when income inequality is reduced through financial development as well as inclusion, this promotes social inclusion and political stability, which could ultimately drive the stability of the financial system.

7.7 Digital Financial Literacy, Digital Inclusion, and Digital Financial Inclusion in Africa

For the use of DFS or fintech to fully achieve digital financial inclusion, there is a need for digital and financial literacy at all levels of the population served or targeted by financial services providers (Prete, 2022). Informed decisions regarding personal finances require financial literacy, while the ability to use DFS to execute these informed choices calls for digital literacy, hence the topical interest in digital financial literacy among researchers, financial service providers, governments, and policymakers. For one to be digitally financially included, they must be digitally included first as well as being financially conversant. Radovanović et al. (2020), in their research *Digital literacy key performance indicators for sustainable development*, while focusing on Senegal, Burkina Faso, Mali, and Tanzania, point out that digital literacy is a challenge in African countries. Scholars table that constraints to effective digital literacy and inclusion include the absence of local language digital connection points or interfaces that have a local orientation. The researchers further adduce that there is generally a lack of training on the use of digital interfaces, especially considering that the use of audio and icons digitally excludes the illiterate as it does not address their local languages.

7.8 Conclusion, Recommendations, and Areas of Further Research

In this chapter, a critical literature review was conducted to understand digital financial inclusion in Africa (overview, benefits, risks, and challenges as well as how digital financial literacy affects digital financial inclusion in Africa). The review revealed that a larger portion of the African population is traditionally and digitally financially excluded. The findings were that the affordability, usage, quality, and accessibility of DFS were key to digital financial inclusion in Africa. Several benefits, risks, and challenges relating to digital financial inclusion were identified in the chapter. The benefits include accessibility of financial services, fulfilment of the SDGs, increased profitability and market share, improved productivity, and improved risk identification and reduction, while the risks identified were grouped with consumers, financial service providers, and the government. These risks include fraud risks, usage risks, and regulatory risks. The challenges to effective digital financial inclusion include demand and supply constraints, lack of credit, high levels of digital and financial illiteracy, limited capacity of financial institutions, poor digital infrastructure, poor levels of digital financial literacy, as well as the underdevelopment of financial systems. The chapter advocates for African countries to make formidable efforts to ensure the digital financial inclusion of their citizens, especially the vulnerable, the financially unserved, and the underserved. Digital financial inclusion is key to meeting the SDGs.

Digital financial inclusion alone is not enough to realise the SDGs or to encourage the utilisation of DFS and to stimulate digital financial inclusion; there is a need for appropriate digital education, knowledge sharing, and awareness initiatives accompanied by adequate digital infrastructure.

Considering the discussion above the chapter makes the following recommendations:

Regulatory Measures
Financial institutions, financial sector regulatory bodies, and governments must put in place measures to mitigate and/or address risks arising from the use of DFS and the application of the 4IR technologies, such as data bases, the complexity of digital interfaces and instructions, violation of ethical principles, and negative externalities.

Ways to Promote Digital Financial Literacy
As highlighted in the review, a combination of digital capabilities and financial know-how is fundamental to the effective use of DFS and the promotion of digital financial inclusion. African countries must work towards the development of digital financial literacy programs, as these are critical to promoting financial inclusion through digital means.

Clear Ways of Risk Identification, Management, Monitoring, and Control
Financial institutions must enhance risk management policies, because the sophistication of DFS implies a growing sophistication fraud scheme as well; therefore, risk management policies must be continuously evolving. There must also be clear channels of addressing clients' grievances, concerns, challenges, and losses to boost customer morale and trust.

Increased Research
There must be increased research on ways to expand digital financial inclusion in Africa and increase the usage of and access to DFS as well as how improve digital financial literacy.

Digital Knowledge Sharing and Collaboration

To help expand digital financial inclusion, there must be collaborative efforts and knowledge sharing on digital technologies, risk management, digital inclusion, digital financial literacy, and other key aspects of digital financial inclusion among African countries. The collaborative efforts can be at the national level, regional level, and continental level.

References

Adetunji, O. M., & David-West, O. (2019). The relative impact of income and financial literacy on financial inclusion in Nigeria. *Journal of International Development, 31*(4), 312–335.

Alameda, T. (2020). *Data, AI and financial inclusion: The future of global banking—Responsible finance forum, responsible finance forum BBVA 2020*. Accessed at https://responsiblefinance-forum.org/data-ai-financial-inclusion-future-global-banking

Agur, I., Martinez, P. S., & Rochon, C. (2020). Digital financial services and the pandemic: Opportunities and risks for emerging and developing economies. *International Monetary Fund Special Series on COVID-19 Transactions, 1*, 2.

Beck, T. (2020). Fintech and financial inclusion: Opportunities and pitfalls (No. 1165). ADBI working paper series.

Berkmen, P., Beaton, M. K., Gershenson, M. D., del Granado, M. J. A., Ishi, K., Kim, M., ... & Rousset, M. M. V. (2019). Fintech in Latin America and the Caribbean: Stocktaking. *International Monetary Fund.*

Bhorat, H., Naidoo, K., & Ewinyu, A. (2017). *Increasing employment opportunities: Navigating Africa's complex job market*. Brookings Institution.

Blancher, M. N. R., Appendino, M., Bibolov, A., Fouejieu, M. A., Li, M. J., Ndoye, A., ... & Sydorenko, T. (2019). Financial inclusion of small and medium-sized enterprises in the middle east and central Asia. *International Monetary Fund.*

Bunn, D., Asen, E., & Enache, C. (2020). Digital taxation around the world. *Tax Foundation.* Washington, DC. https://files.taxfoundation.org/20200527192056/Digital-Taxation-Around-the-World.pdf

Cicchiello, A. F., Kazemikhasragh, A., Monferrá, S., & Girón, A. (2021). Financial inclusion and development in the least developed countries in Asia and Africa. *Journal of Innovation and Entrepreneurship, 10*(1), 1–13.

Cude, B. J. (2021). Defining financial literacy. In *The Routledge handbook of financial literacy* (pp. 5–17). Routledge.

Cull, R., Demirgüç-Kunt, A., & Lyman, T. (2012). *Financial inclusion and stability: What does research show?* Available at https://openknowledge.worldbank.org/bitstream/handle/10986/9443/713050BRI0CGAP0f0FinancialInclusion.pdf?sequence=1

Dawei, L., Anzi, H., & Gen, L. (2018). Big data technology: Application and cases. In *Handbook of blockchain, digital finance, and inclusion* (Vol. 2, pp. 65–82). Academic Press.

Demirgüç-Kunt, A., Klapper, L., Singer, D., Ansar, S., & Hess, J. (2018). *Opportunities for expanding financial inclusion through digital technology*. Available at https://elibrary.worldbank.org/doi/abs/10.1596/978-1-4648-1259-0_ch6

Dickerson, C. M. (2014). Bringing formal business laws to Cameroon's informal sector: Lessons and cautions from the tax law example. *Washington University Global Studies Law Review, 13*, 265.

Engels, C., Kumar, K., & Philip, D. (2020). Financial literacy and fraud detection. *The European Journal of Finance, 26*(4–5), 420–442.

Evans, O. (2016). *Determinants of financial inclusion in Africa: A dynamic panel data approach.* https://mpra.ub.uni-muenchen.de/81326/1/mpra_paper_81326.pdf

Folwarski, M. (2021). The FinTech sector and aspects on the financial inclusion of the society in EU countries. *European Research Studies, 24*, 459–467.

Hartanto, R. (2022). Digital financial literacy and digital supervisory in financial services. In *Fourth social and humanities research symposium (SoRes 2021)* (pp. 534–538). Atlantis Press.

Huston, S. J. (2020). Measuring financial literacy. *Journal of Consumer Affairs, 44*(2), 296–316.

Inoue, T., & Hamori, S. (2016). Financial access and economic growth: Evidence from sub-Saharan Africa. *Emerging Markets Finance and Trade, 52*(3), 743–753.

ILO. (2018). Women and men in the informal economy: A statistical picture (3rd ed.). *International Labour Office*.

International Monetary Fund. (2021). Measuring digital financial inclusion in emerging market and developing economies: A new index. *Asian Economic Policy Review*. https://www.imf.org/-/media/Files/Publications/WP/2021/English/wpiea2021090-print-pdf.ashx

Kakungulu-Mayambala, R., & Rukundo, S. (2018). Implications of Uganda's new social media tax. *East African Journal of Peace & Human Rights, 24*, 2.

Kelbesa, M. (2020). *Digital service taxes and their application.* https://opendocs.ids.ac.uk/opendocs/bitstream/handle/20.500.12413/16968/914_Digital_Service_Tax.pdf?sequence=1 & isAllowed=y

Kelikume, I. (2021). Digital financial inclusion, informal economy and poverty reduction in Africa. *Journal of Enterprising Communities: People and Places in the Global Economy, 15*, 626.

Lyons, A. C., & Kass-Hanna, J. (2021). Financial inclusion, financial literacy and economically vulnerable populations in the Middle East and North Africa. *Emerging Markets Finance and Trade, 57*(9), 2699–2738.

Machasio, I. N. (2020). *Covid-19 and digital financial inclusion in Africa: How to leverage digital technologies during the pandemic.* https://openknowledge.worldbank.org/bitstream/handle/10986/34637/COVID-19-and-Digital-Financial-Inclusion-in-Africa-How-to-Leverage-Digital-Technologies-During-the-Pandemic.pdf?sequence=1

Makina, D. (2019). The potential of FinTech in enabling financial inclusion. In *Extending financial inclusion in Africa* (pp. 299–318). Academic Press.

Maina, A. W. (2017). Are presumptive taxes the answer to informal sector taxation? Kenya's Experience. African Tax Research Network, Working Paper 05.

Massa, I. (2013). DFIs support to financial inclusion in Africa. Triki, T. & Faye, I. (Eds.). *Financial Inclusion in Africa*, 116–129.

McKinsey Global Institute. (2016). *Digital finance for all: Powering inclusive growth in emerging economies*. McKinsey & Company.

Medina, L., & Schneider, M. F. (2018). *Shadow economies around the world: What did we learn over the last 20 years?* International Monetary Fund. Available at https://www.elibrary.imf.org/view/journals/001/2018/017/article-A001-en.xml

Mekgoe, N., & Hassam, M. (2020, August 6). *Digital services tax in Africa–The journey so far.* Deloitte.

Mhlanga, D. (2020). Industry 4.0 in finance: The impact of artificial intelligence (AI) on digital financial inclusion. *International Journal of Financial Studies, 8*(3), 45.

Mhlanga, D. (2021a). Financial inclusion in emerging economies: The application of machine learning and artificial intelligence in credit risk assessment. *International Journal of Financial Studies, 9*(3), 39.

Mhlanga, D. (2021b). Factors that matter for financial inclusion: Evidence from sub-Saharan Africa-The Zimbabwe case. *Academic Journal of Interdisciplinary Studies, 10*(6), 48–48.

Mhlanga, D. (2022). COVID-19 and digital financial inclusion: Policies and innovation that can accelerate financial inclusion in a post-COVID world through fintech. *African Journal of Development Studies, 2022*(si2), 79.

Mhlanga, D., & Denhere, V. (2020). Determinants of financial inclusion in Southern Africa. *Studia Universitatis Babes-Bolyai, Oeconomica, 65*(3), 39.

Mhlanga, D., & Dunga, S. H. (2020). Measuring financial inclusion and its determinants among the smallholder farmers in Zimbabwe: An empirical study. *Eurasian Journal of Business and Management, 8*(3), 266–281.

Mhlanga, D., Dunga, S. H., & Moloi, T. (2021). Understanding the drivers of financial inclusion in South Africa. *Journal of Economic and Financial Sciences, 14*(1), 8.

Morgan, P. J., Huang, B., & Trinh, L. Q. (2019). *The need to promote digital financial literacy for the digital age*. In the Digital Age.

Morgan, P. J., Huang, B., & Trinh, L. Q. (2020). *Minding the gaps in digital financial education strategies*. Available at https://www.g20-insights.org/wp-content/uploads/2020/11/minding-the-gaps-in-digital-financial-education-strategies-2-1606224578.pdf

Mpofu, F. Y. S. (2021). Informal sector taxation and enforcement in African countries: How plausible and achievable are the motives behind? A critical literature review. *Open Economics, 4*(1), 72–97.

Mpofu, F. Y. (2022). Industry 4.0 in financial services: Mobile money taxes, revenue mobilisation, financial inclusion, and the realisation of sustainable development goals (SDGs) in Africa. *Sustainability, 14*(14), 1–24.

Mpofu, F. Y., & Moloi, T. (2022). Direct digital services taxes in Africa and the canons of taxation. *Laws, 11*(4), 57.

Munoz, L., Mascagni, G., Prichard, W., & Santoro, F. (2022). *Should governments tax digital financial services? A research agenda to understand sector-specific taxes on DFS*. Institute of Development Studies. https://opendocs.ids.ac.uk/opendocs/bitstream/handle/20.500.12413/17171/ICTD_WP136.pdf?sequence=1

Mutsonziwa, K., & Maposa, O. K. (2016). Mobile money – A catalyst for financial inclusion in developing economies: A case study of Zimbabwe using FinScope survey data. *International Journal of Financial Management, 6*(3), 45–56.

Ndung'u, N. S. (2019). *Taxing mobile phone transactions in Africa: Lessons from Kenya. 2019*. Available online: https://www.africaportal.org/publications/taxing-mobile-phone-transactions-africa-lessons-kenya/

Ojo, T. A. (2022). Digital financial inclusion for women in the fourth industrial revolution: A key towards achieving sustainable development goal 5. *Africa Review, 1*(aop), 1–26.

Optix (2015). Low Income Households in the Developing World Face a Triple Threat when Managing their Financial Well Being. Optix Focus Note 1

Osafo-Kwaako, P., Singer, M., White, O., & Zouaoui, Y. (2018). Mobile money in emerging markets: The business case for financial inclusion. *McKinsey Global Institute*, March. https://www.mckinsey.com/~/media/McKinsey/Industries/Financial%20Services/Our%20Insights/Mobile, 20.

Omar, M. A., & Inaba, K. (2020). Does financial inclusion reduce poverty and income inequality in developing countries? A panel data analysis. *Journal of Economic Structures, 9*(1), 1–25.

Ouma, S. A., Odongo, T. M., & Were, M. (2017). "Mobile financial services and financial inclusion: Is it a boon for savings mobilization?". *Review of Development Finance, 7*(1), 29–35. https://doi.org/10.1016/j.rdf.2017.01.001

Ozili, P. K. (2018). Impact of digital finance on financial inclusion and stability. *Borsa Istanbul Review, 18*(4), 329–340.

Ozili, P. K. (2020). Social inclusion and financial inclusion: International evidence. *International Journal of Development Issues, 19*, 169.

Panos, G. A., & Wilson, J. O. (2020). Financial literacy and responsible finance in the FinTech era: Capabilities and challenges. *The European Journal of Finance, 26*(4–5), 297–301.

Paul, S. (2019). Use of block chain and artificial intelligence to promote financial inclusion in India. Smita Miglani Indian Council for Research on International Economic Relations. Available online: https://economictimes/

Peric, K. (2015). Digital financial inclusion. *Journal of Payments Strategy & Systems, 9*(3), 212–214.

Prete, A. L. (2022). Digital and financial literacy as determinants of digital payments and personal finance. *Economics Letters, 213*, 110378.

Pushkareva, N. (2021). Taxing times for development: Tax and digital financial services in sub-Saharan Africa. *Journal on Financing for Development, 1*(3), 33–64.
Radovanović, D., Holst, C., Belur, S. B., Srivastava, R., Houngbonon, G. V., Le Quentrec, E., et al. (2020). Digital literacy key performance indicators for sustainable development. *Social Inclusion, 8*(2), 151–167.
Rogan, M. (2019). *Tax justice and the informal economy*. Available at https://www.wiego.org/sites/default/files/publications/file/Rogan_Taxation_Debates_WIEGO_WorkingPaperNo41_2020.pdf
Salampasis, D., & Mention, A. L. (2018). FinTech: Harnessing innovation for financial inclusion. In *Handbook of blockchain, digital finance, and inclusion* (Vol. 2, pp. 451–461). Academic Press.
Santoro, F., Munoz, L., Prichard, W., & Mascagni, G. (2022). *Digital financial services and digital IDs: What potential do they have for better taxation in Africa?* Available at https://opendocs.ids.ac.uk/opendocs/bitstream/handle/20.500.12413/17113/ICTD_WP137.pdf?sequence=1
Sarpong, B., & Nketiah-Amponsah, E. (2022). Financial inclusion and inclusive growth in sub-Saharan Africa. *Cogent Economics & Finance, 10*(1), 2058734.
Sebele-Mpofu, F. Y. (2020). Governance quality and tax morale and compliance in Zimbabwe's informal sector. *Cogent Business & Management, 7*(1), 1794662.
Sebele-Mpofu, F. Y. (2021). The informal sector, the "implicit" social contract, the willingness to pay taxes and tax compliance in Zimbabwe. *Accounting, Economics, and Law: A Convivium.* https://doi.org/10.1515/ael-2020-0084
Sebele-Mpofu, F. Y., & Moyo, N. (2021). An evil to be extinguished or a resource to be harnessed-informal sector in developing countries: A case of Zimbabwe. *Journal of Economics and Behavioral Studies, 13*(3), 53–72.
Sebele-Mpofu, F. Y., Mashiri, E., & Korera, P. (2021). Transfer pricing audit challenges and dispute resolution effectiveness in developing countries with specific focus on Zimbabwe. *Accounting, Economics, and Law: A Convivium.* https://doi.org/10.1515/ael-2021-0026
Sekantsi, L. P., & Motelle, S. I. (2018). The role of mobile money in financial inclusion in Lesotho. *MEFMI Research and Policy Journal, 3*(2), 77–99.
Shapshack, T. (2021). Mobile money in Africa reaches $500billion during the pandemic. Available online: https://www.forbes.com/sites/tobyshapshak/2021/05/19/mobile-money-in-africa-reaches-nearly-500bn-duringpandemic/?sh=54c697db3493
Shipalana, P. (2019). *Digitising financial services: a tool for financial inclusion in South Africa?* Available at https://www.africaportal.org/documents/19566/Occasional-Paper-301-shipalana.pdf
Sile, E. (2013). Financial inclusion in fragile states. In *Financial inclusion in Africa* (pp. 94–104). African Development Bank (AfDB).
Simbarashe, H. (2020). Digitalisation and the challenges for African administrations. *Financing for Development 1*, 177–203.
Simatele, M. (2021). E-payment instruments and welfare: The case of Zimbabwe. *The Journal for Transdisciplinary Research in Southern Africa, 17*(1), 1–11.
UNCTAD (2018) UNCTAD B2C E-Commerce Index 2018: Focus on Africa, United Nation.
World Bank. (2020). Digital Financial Inclusion. Available online: https://www.worldbank.org/en/topic/financialinclusion/publication/digital-financial-inclusion

Chapter 8
Post-Independence Development and Financial Inclusion in Africa: Case Studies and the Way Forward to Support Further Financial Inclusion

David Mhlanga and Mufaro Dzingirai

Abstract The process of making sure that people, households, and enterprises in a community have sufficient access to formal financial services and products such as transactions, credit cards, payments, savings, and insurance, and that these are provided sustainably is known as financial inclusion. This study aims to establish the successful examples of financial inclusion and to come up with proposals that can help to further improve financial inclusion in Africa. Using document analysis, this chapter documented financial inclusion progress in Rwanda, Kenya, Uganda, and Ghana. This chapter concluded by outlining some recommendations to increase financial inclusion in Africa, which include the following: women, young people, and people with disabilities should be helped by financial institutions to increase their ability to make fundamentally sound financial decisions to encourage wider financial inclusion in Africa. A robust institutional framework is necessary to improve and expand financial inclusion. Collaboration and participation in this endeavor are possible between the private sector, civil society, government entities, and regulatory bodies. It is also essential to promote consumer confidence in the utilization of digital financial services, which calls for a robust focus on the protection of end users. It is the responsibility of regulators of financial services to ensure that customers are treated fairly by financial institutions, particularly those institutions that might utilize their information advantage at the expense of the customer.

Keywords Africa · Development · Financial inclusion · Post-independence development

---

D. Mhlanga
College of Business and Economics, University of Johannesburg, Johannesburg, South Africa

M. Dzingirai (✉)
Department of Business Management, Faculty of Commerce, Midlands State University, Gweru, Zimbabwe
e-mail: dzingiraim@staff.msu.ac.zw

D. Mhlanga, E. Ndhlovu (eds.), *Economic Inclusion in Post-Independence Africa*, Advances in African Economic, Social and Political Development,
https://doi.org/10.1007/978-3-031-31431-5_8

8.1 Introduction

The process of making sure that people, households, and enterprises in a community have sufficient access to formal financial services and products such as transactions, credit cards, payments, savings, and insurance, and that these are provided sustainably is known as financial inclusion (Mhlanga et al., 2020; Cicchiello et al., 2021). The need to provide an adequate level of financial inclusion in the least-developed countries has been highlighted at numerous international conferences, including the conference that the United Nations sponsored in 2019. Without adequate levels of financial inclusion, people and businesses would not be able to fully participate in the national economy, making financial inclusion one of the most important issues surrounding monetary policy in recent years. Growing evidence from the literature suggests that inclusive financial markets help people to access bank loans and insurance coverage, lower rates of poverty and to reduce inequality (Mhlanga & Denhere, 2020; Cicchiello et al., 2021; Mhlanga, 2021). Financial inclusion, in the opinion of Ajide (2020), is thought to encourage the emergence of fresh, inventive businesses and the growth of mature ones, resulting in the creation of jobs that boost national savings.

Finally, financial inclusion helps adolescents, women, and other formerly excluded groups become more economically independent and actively participate in the financial system. To better understand the impact of finance on economic development in Africa, several studies on the continent were conducted. The fourth-placed conclusions were from a variety of writers, but they were all in agreement that financial inclusion has a significant beneficial impact on economic growth and economic inclusion in Africa. For instance, a study by Cicchiello et al. (2021) used annual data from 42 countries from the years 2000–2019 to examine the relationship between the financial inclusion index and development indicators in the least-developed nations in Asia and Africa. According to Cicchiello et al. (2021), financial inclusion is influenced by unemployment and literacy rates and is a function of economic progress.

According to Cicchiello et al. (2021), women are more susceptible to issues with financial inclusion than men. Additionally, Cicchiello et al. (2021) discovered that citizens in less developed nations are less financially inclusive, especially those who reside in the rural areas. These nations' economies are primarily dependent on agriculture. Another finding by Cicchiello et al. (2021) was that pay disparity lowers financial inclusion rates, which has a detrimental effect on development, and that a low financial inclusion rate lowers the levels of development in these nations. Further, Cicchiello et al. (2021) said that policymakers should consider measures to raise literacy, remove gender discrimination, and increase pay equity to improve the environment for development. Matekenya et al. (2021) also asserted that most African countries continue to have significant levels of inequality, poverty, and unemployment despite the tremendous economic growth seen during the 1990s. The impact of financial inclusion on human development in sub-Saharan Africa was studied by Matekenya et al. in 2021. Matekenya et al. (2021) concluded that having access to and using financial services might help people invest in their health and education, establish new businesses, manage risk, and be less affected by financial shocks, all of which would help advance human development.

The findings of Matekenya et al. (2021) showed that financial inclusion has a positive impact on human development, which necessitates that policymakers take steps to lower the costs of accessing and using financial services, such as making infrastructure investments and increasing awareness of the financial services that are offered. In addition, Léon and Zins (2020) asserted that regional foreign banks have rapidly increased in size over the past 10 years in emerging and developing nations and have an increasing impact on banking systems. Léon and Zins (2020) were tasked with determining if the growth of regional foreign banks in Africa, commonly known as Pan-African banks, affects the financial inclusion of businesses and households. According to Léon and Zins (2020), there is limited evidence that the presence of Pan-African banks favors middle-class financial access by reviving consumer confidence in banks.

In Kelikume (2021), the nexus between financial inclusion, the informal economy, mobile technology, and poverty eradication was investigated. According to a study by Kelikume (2021), there is a strong correlation between internet and mobile usage and the informal economy, and a developed informal economy is linked to greater financial inclusion. Kelikume (2021) also discovered that internet usage and cellphone penetration have a significant positive link with poverty reduction. These two factors play key roles in the interaction between the financial inclusion and the informal economy. Again, according to Kelikume (2021), the informal economy also has significant effects, indicating that the growth of the informal economy is related to poverty reduction, and financial inclusion also has significant effects, indicating that higher financial inclusion is associated with increased poverty reduction. Kebede et al. (2021) made the case that financial inclusion is a worldwide policy objective that should be prioritized since it gives individuals and businesses with a variety of needs access to financial services like savings, payments, risk management, and credit. Financial inclusion will be measured and its relationship to the market structure of banks in 17 African nations will be examined using panel data from 2004 to 2018 for these nations. According to Kebede et al. (2021), bank market power increases accessibility and availability while decreasing utilization. According to Kebede et al. (2021), a larger regime market power has a poorer influence on utilization than a lower regime market power. Again, Kebede et al. (2021) found that with a lower regime concentration, the effects of asset concentration on overall financial inclusion, availability, and usage are more obvious.

In a study to determine whether more financial inclusion in Africa is correlated with higher GDP per capita, Evans and Alenoghena (2017) placed fourth. The results show that GDP per capita has significant impacts on financial inclusion, indicating how increases in GDP per capita can be used to drive the necessary financial inclusion in Africa. The datasets used were the World Bank Development Indicators datasets for 15 African countries over the period from 2005 to 2014. Even though financial inclusion was deemed to be insignificant by Evans and Alenoghena (2017), it had a favorable effect on GDP per capita. Once more, Evans and

Alenoghena (2017) found evidence to support the idea that broad money, credit supply, literacy, internet users, and servers have beneficial and significant effects on financial inclusion. Additionally, Evans and Alenoghena (2017) discovered that the internet is emerging as an important determinant, suggesting that more focus is needed on expanding internet access in Africa for the advancement of financial inclusion. Even though various scholars' conclusions ranked fourth, they all agreed that financial inclusion has a significant positive impact on economic growth and economic inclusion in Africa. As a result, this chapter aims to present successful examples of financial inclusion and to come up with proposals that can help to further improve financial inclusion in Africa. The rest of this chapter is organized as follows.

8.2 Conceptualization of Financial Inclusion

The conceptualization of financial inclusion is of utmost importance since this concept has been defined from different perspectives by authors from various disciplines like economics, finance, management, and development. There is no doubt that financial inclusion is a complex and multidimensional concept as well as a relative concept because there is no standard definition in the financial inclusion literature. According to Chhabra (2015), financial inclusion refers to the provision of financial services and products like credit and debit cards to all members of society at an affordable price. Based on this definition, effective financial inclusion must address the problem of financial exclusion in a country. More interestingly, Rangarajan (2008) defined financial inclusion as the provision of financial services to previously excluded members of society at a low cost. On the other hand, financial inclusion can be described as easy access to financial products and services by the marginalized groups in society that were previously excluded by formal financial institutions (Ambarkhane et al., 2016; Mhlanga, 2022). This means that the main purpose of financial inclusion revolves around the accessibility, usage, availability, and affordability of financial services and products. Therefore, financial inclusion is linked to an increase in savings, poverty reduction, employment creation, increase in capital, and economic growth and development (Park & Mercado, 2018). The marginalized groups of the entire society must access financial services at a very low cost. It is well accepted in the financial inclusion discourse that mobile money is a game-changer in solving the financial exclusion of vulnerable people (Senyo & Osabutey, 2020).

8.3 Theoretical Frameworks

Two theoretical frameworks were applied to broaden our understanding of financial inclusion. These theories are vulnerable group theory and systems theory, which are explained in the following sections.

8.3.1 Vulnerable Group Theory

This theoretical perspective is linked to the fact that the main principle of financial inclusion is to address the financial needs and wants of the much-neglected groups of society like youths, women, and elderly people. As such, the initiatives and programs that are devised to deal with financial inclusion must be informed by the financial needs and wants of the weaker groups of people (Ozili, 2020). The vulnerable group theory argues that vulnerable and marginalized people are normally affected by economic recessions and financial crises. As such, it is logical and necessary to design and implement financial inclusion programs to incorporate these marginalized groups into the formal financial industry. The programs can be in form of social cash transfers and mobile money transfers with the understanding of the needs and wants of vulnerable groups. More interestingly, mobile operators are now implementing mobile money transfers, mobile savings, and mobile health payments as a strategic move to incorporate poor, young, and elderly people into the financial industry.

This theory is relevant as it aims to explain how to curb the financial exclusion of vulnerable groups in society. It is, therefore, necessary to deal with the financial needs and wants of vulnerable people in the quest to solve the problem of financial exclusion in a country (Ozili, 2020). Moreover, with an understanding of the tenets of the vulnerable group theory, it is easy to identify people who are financially excluded in each society which then becomes very easy to address their financial needs and wants. Notably, the marginalized members of society can be identified according to the extent of vulnerability concerning gender, income level, age, and other demographic features. Given the relevance of financial inclusion, multilateral organizations like United Nations (UN) and the World Bank are now advocating for the expansion of the use of mobile money to reduce poverty and stimulate economic growth and development (Senyo & Osabutey, 2020).

8.3.2 Systems Theory

The major argument of the systems theory of financial inclusion is that outcomes of financial inclusion can be attained through sub-systems like technological, social, and financial systems (Ozili, 2020). This means that a considerable change in a subsystem can affect the expected outcomes of financial inclusion, for instance, the imposition of favorable regulations on the financial industry can help financial institutions in accelerating the achievement of the outcomes of financial inclusion since they can provide quality and affordable financial products and services to the potential clients. The systems theory suggests that the effectiveness and efficiency of the available sub-systems accelerate the attainment of the national agenda of financial inclusion. The economic, technological, social, and financial systems in a country must be evaluated to ascertain the extent to which the outcomes of financial inclusion can be attained. The systems theory is relevant as it acknowledges the essence of technological, social, economic, and financial systems in promoting the achievement of the financial inclusion outcomes of a specific country. More interestingly, it offers a macro perspective to financial inclusion as it captures the essence of macro-factors or structures when addressing financial exclusion in a specific country. Notably, the systems theory provides an understanding of the interrelationships among various sub-systems of the country.

8.4 Importance of Financial Inclusion in Africa

Although financial inclusion is a global phenomenon, there is a dire need to intensify financial inclusion programs in African countries. The essence of financial inclusion in promoting economic growth in Africa has been widely accepted (Triki & Faye, 2013). This is supported by the notion of inclusive growth where all segments of the population must participate in the economic growth agenda (Triki & Faye, 2013). With effective financial inclusion programs, all segments can access and afford financial services and products which then ensure sustainable economic growth in African countries. A well-functioning financial sector allows companies and individuals as well as governments to actively engage in economic activities. This is also supported by Sarpong and Nketiah-Amponsah (2022) who provided evidence that the usage of financial services and products enhances inclusive growth in sub-Saharan Africa. Going forward, the financial inclusion initiatives have promoted the establishment and growth of Small and Medium Enterprises (SMEs) in Africa. The financial institutions in African countries have transformed the operations of SMEs. It is widely accepted that SMEs operating in African countries are facing financial challenges due to a lack of collateral security (Dzingirai, 2021a; Dzingirai & Baporikar, 2021; Triki & Faye, 2013). It is within this context that Oshora et al. (2021) stressed that African countries are coming up with financial inclusion programs to assist SMEs. Therefore, the expansion of financial inclusion initiatives will mobilize household savings, promote the growth of SMEs, marshal large capital for investment, and increase disposable income.

Financial inclusion plays a crucial role in poverty reduction when it comes to African countries. In this regard, Popescu (2019) concluded that financial inclusion produces considerable benefits to the marginalized and poor members of society. In the same vein, Swamy (2010) documented that financial inclusion is of paramount importance in the poverty reduction process. Notably, Dzingirai (2021b) indicated that marginalized agricultural communities in Zimbabwe are associated with high levels of poverty. It means that there is a need for financial initiatives targeting marginalized agricultural communities in Zimbabwe to reduce poverty. This is the reason why international institutions like World Bank are coming up with financial packages aimed at reducing poverty in Africa (Dzingirai & Ndava, 2022; Senyo & Osabutey, 2020). After capturing the importance of financial inclusion in Africa, the following section presents some of the success stories linked to financial inclusion in Africa.

8.5 Empirical Literature

It is worth noting that Bekele (2022) carried out a comparative study between Kenya and Ethiopia on the determinants of financial inclusion. He applied a generalized linear model using data extracted from the 2017 Global Findex Database. The results revealed that Kenya has a higher level of financial inclusion as compared to Ethiopia. The variation in macro-factors was linked to mobile money service expansion, financial liberation policy, and the percentage of rural people. In terms of micro-factors, differences were attributed to means of mobile money transfers, government transfers, and literacy rates. More interestingly, the variables like age, gender, owning a mobile phone, and employment status had positive effects on financial inclusion.

Furthermore, Eustache and Claude (2021) conducted a study in Rwanda on the impact of financial inclusion on the performance of SACCOs by applying descriptive and correlation design with a sample of 178 people. The findings revealed a positive relationship between financial advice and Umurenge's financial performance, a positive effect of affordable credits on performance, and also a positive effect of saving service provided on performance. The study concluded that Umurenge SACCOs improved saving service quality and enhanced the quality of affordable credits and insurance in the Rusizi District. In the case of Uganda, Hamdan et al., (2022) conducted a study on mobile money and financial inclusion. They adopted an experimental design in trying to understand the challenges associated with mobile money in promoting financial inclusion. As such, the experiment revealed that high fees were a barrier to the effectiveness of mobile money usage. Furthermore, poor infrastructure and lack of financial education were also identified as challenges. They recommended policy measures that address the negative impact of these barriers to effective financial inclusion.

Going forward, Takyi, Sorkpor, & Asante (2022) explored the impact of mobile money on saving practices in Ghana. The study employed an Instrumental Variable (IV) to estimate using the data extracted from Financial Inclusion Insight (FII). The results revealed that mobile money increased savings in Ghana. More interestingly, they found that mobile money was mostly used in rural areas than counterparts in urban areas. The research recommended that policymakers should scale up the programs targeting mobile money to enhance financial inclusion in Ghana. In the context of Tanzania, Magali (2013) investigated the effect of the SACCOs variables on loan default risks using 37 SACCOs. This study employed a purposive sampling strategy and then a multivariate regression model for data analysis. The results found that savings and deposits reduce the default risk of the rural SACCOs. On the other hand, the age of the SACCOs, the chairperson loans committee, education, and the age of the chairperson of the board were not significant factors to explain the loan default risks of the rural SACCOs. The study recommended the advancement of training for risk management and crop insurance coverage in Tanzania. More interestingly, Shilimi (2021) examined the challenges linked to the low integration of SACCOs in Zambia. The quantitative results revealed a positive relationship between the adoption of SACCOs and awareness education, financial literacy societal influence, and governance. Age was not a statistically significant factor. The study recommended that communities could be empowered by adopting SACCOs.

8.5.1 Case Studies of Financial Inclusion in Africa

Several nations in Africa have achieved a satisfactory level of financial inclusion; the countries in question are depicted in the figure that follows.

In Fig. 8.1, selected case studies of financial inclusion are shown which will be discussed in this study. Some of the countries include Kenya, Uganda, Rwanda, and Ghana.

Kenya

M-Pesa is a well-documented success story of financial inclusion using digital financial products and services in Kenya. According to Ndung'u (2017), it is in the public domain that M-Pesa as an electronic money transfer has transformed the lives of Kenyans since its launch in 2007. It allowed the citizens to store their wealth on mobile phones and consume some digital financial services. M-Pesa as an efficient and effective digital solution to financial exclusion offers a multiplicity of financial services like virtual savings and credit supply by microfinance institutions, commercial banks, and cooperatives (SACCOs) (Demirgüç-Kunt et al., 2018; Ndung'u, 2017; Tiwari et al., 2019). Marginalized people like women and young people managed to enjoy the benefits of M-Pesa whereby they can send and receive domestic financial services as well as international remittances via their mobile phones.

More interestingly, the coming of M-Pesa in Kenya led to a reduction in transaction costs, lowering barriers to entry when it comes to formal financial systems

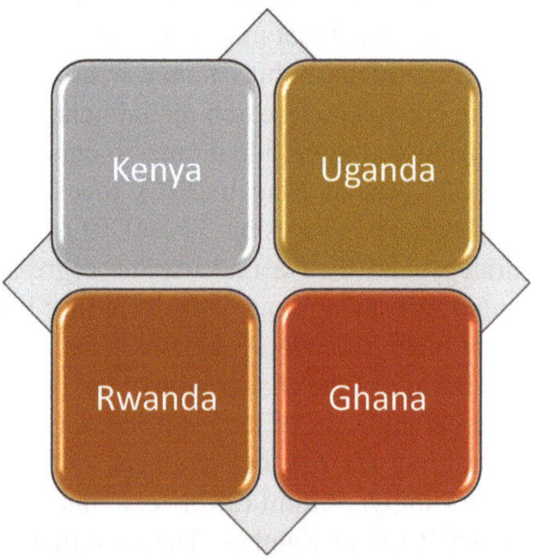

Fig. 8.1 Selected African cases of financial inclusion. (*Source*: Authors' Analysis)

(Bekele, 2022; Ndung'u, 2017). Notably, the national payments technology has significantly augmented in the sense that even the disadvantaged members of the community are now able to create micro-accounts, make deposits, and promote virtual customer networks just by using their mobile phones (Bekele, 2022). It must also be noted that before the M-Pesa was introduced in Kenya, the Kenyan government introduced the microfinance model in the early 2000s to strategically deal with financial exclusion, especially in the eyes of rural women (Ndung'u, 2017). Worryingly, 40% of Kenyans were excluded from financial products and services in 2006. This allowed the establishment of M-Pesa in 2007 to cater for the marginalized 40%. Currently, people in Kenya are now able to buy insurance, access bank accounts, and take credit as well as save money using their mobile phones. Therefore, M-Pesa is widely regarded as the major success story related to financial inclusion and poverty reduction in Africa (Omwansa & Sullivan, 2012; Suri & Jack, 2016; Tiwari et al., 2019). Nonetheless, Bekele (2022) found that there are some challenges that were faced in promoting financial inclusion in Kenya like lack of trust and lack of proper documentation.

8.5.2 *Financial Inclusion Trends in Kenya*

Bringing the underserved and financially excluded into the formal economy creates new chances for people and companies to fight poverty and increase shared prosperity. Additionally, more people must have access to and utilize formal financial services to create a future that is more secure, resilient, and inclusive. According to Deloitte, financial inclusion refers to the availability to both individuals and businesses of relevant financial services and products that are both inexpensive and suit their needs (2022). The following three factors—access to financial services, use of financial services, and the caliber of the goods and services—are typically used to gauge financial inclusion. The trends in Kenya's financial inclusion are shown in Fig. 8.2, which is based on data from Deloitte (2022).

Figure 8.2 illustrates the rise in financial inclusion in Kenya since 2009. From 40.4% in 2009 to 83.7% in 2021, financial inclusion increased. In addition, since 2009, the proportion of households without access to formal finance has decreased. Households having official access decreased from 26.8% to 4.7% in 2021, whereas the percentage of excluded households decreased from 32.7% in 2009 to 11.6% in 2021. These numbers demonstrate significant advancement in financial inclusion in Kenya over time. Ombane (2021) claims that M-Pesa has been a key tool in improving major financial inclusion, particularly for the unbanked and the underprivileged. Significant notable milestones have been reached from the time M-Pesa was introduced in March 2007 to the present. For instance, Ombane (2021) noted that Safaricom's chief executive estimated that every second of the day, M-Pesa processes a loan, and every minute, 3900 people buy airtime while 1500 people receive money from family and friends. This estimate was made during a presentation at the Central Bank of Kenya's 50th anniversary in 2016. While 240 people will deposit

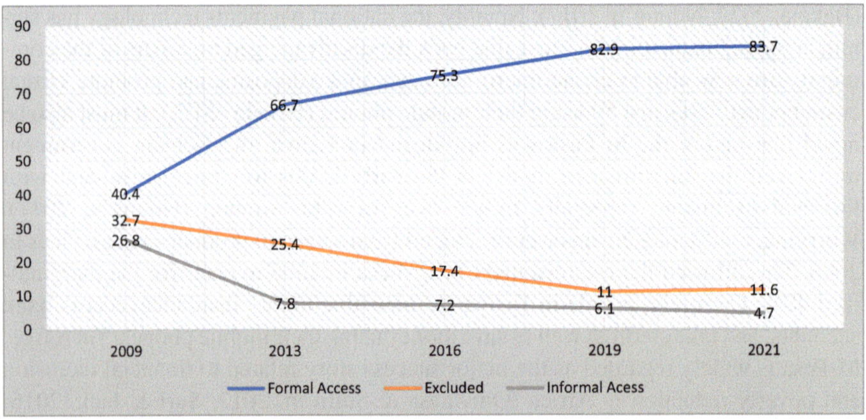

Fig. 8.2 Financial inclusion trends in Kenya. (*Source*: Authors' Analysis)

money into or withdraw money from their banks, another 1700 people will utilize it to pay for services and bills. More than 15 companies will pay other companies. This demonstrates how effective mobile technology is at promoting financial inclusion.

Rwanda

In the case of Rwanda, a financial inclusion success story is linked to the excellent performance of community savings and credit cooperatives widely known as Umurenge SACCOs (Harelimana, 2021). In a space of 3 years from the introduction of Umerenge SACCOs, an increase of 1.6 million new clients consuming digital financial services was registered in Rwanda. Interestingly, access to financial products and services increased from 21% to 42% as revealed in a 2012 FinScope survey (Alliance for Financial Inclusion, 2014). Given the success of the Umurenge SACCOs in Rwanda, the government of Rwanda came up with the Vision 2020 Umerenge Program as a strategic move to promote financial inclusion and economic growth in rural areas. It is suggested by Eustache and Claude (2021) that the Umurenge SACCOs helped the government to also eliminate rural poverty since the poor people in rural communities have access to financial products and services which is in line with the Sustainable Development Goals (SDGs). Notably, SACCOs are widely known as member-based cooperatives that aim to eliminate the financial exclusion of marginalized people and entrepreneurial people in Rwanda (Eustache & Claude, 2021; Harelimana, 2021). It is interesting to note that SACCOs are regulated in the context of Rwanda as they are monitored under the Microfinance Law of 2008. Going forward, the contributions of Umurenge SACCOs are in the public domain. In this regard, 79% of people in Rwanda under 18 years were unbanked. Notably, Umurenge SACCOs are experiencing an exponential increase in adoption as they are used as a source of funding for state social programs. Moreover, farmers are also using SACCOs to settle their accounts and to pay for fertilizers. The health sector is not an exception since SACCOs are adopted to fund health insurance in

Rwanda. However, there are some challenges encountered when running SACCOs such as poor governance, poor internal control systems, low level of financial literacy among the SACCOs members, and lack of infrastructure (Alliance for Financial Inclusion, 2014).

Going forward, it is prudent to capture the changes in the level of financial inclusion in the past decade. In this context, the Government of Rwanda has implemented various programs to promote financial inclusion whereby people in the rural area who were previously excluded were incorporated into various financial inclusion initiatives. Apart from the government, the informal sector has also played a significant role in promoting financial inclusion in Rwanda. To reveal this positive development when it comes to changes in financial inclusion in Rwanda, the following figure depicts the comparisons between 2016 and 2020:

As illustrated in Fig. 8.3, the comparison of the financial inclusion in Rwanda between 2016 and 2020 indicates a notable shift stemming from a sharp increase in the uptake of informal and formal financial products. It has been observed that only 0.5% (38,786) of the adults in Rwanda depend exclusively on banking services down from approximately 1% (60,627) in 2016. Based on Fig. 8.3, it is clear that 63% of the people in Rwanda use a mixture of informal and formal financial mechanisms to cater for their financial needs and wants (up from 52% in 2016). This reveals that their financial needs and wants are not fully addressed by the formal financial institutions and also reveals that those who previously used informal financial mechanisms are now utilizing formal financial mechanisms to effectively meet their financial needs and wants. Notably, 1.1 million (16%) of the adult people in Rwanda depend only on informal financial mechanisms like village savings and loans dropping down from 21% in 2020. This positive trend related to the uptake of financial products in Rwanda is mainly attributed to the adoption of banking services, savings groups, and mobile money.

It is worth mentioning that mobile money platforms have contributed significantly when it comes to financial inclusion in Rwanda. According to FinScope

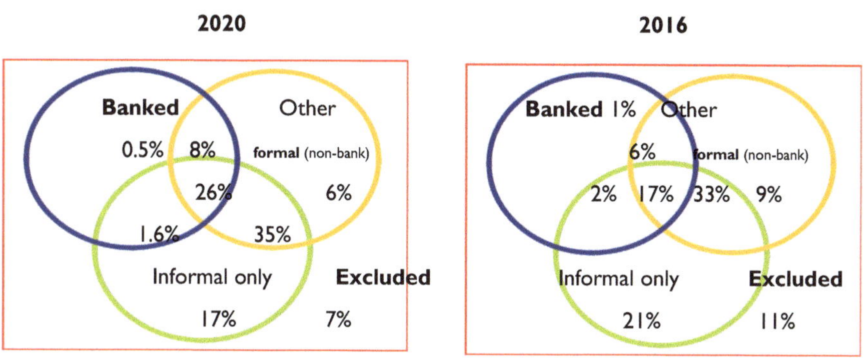

Fig. 8.3 Comparison of the level of financial inclusion between 2016 and 2022. (*Source*: Fin Scope Rwanda Consumer Survey Report (2020))

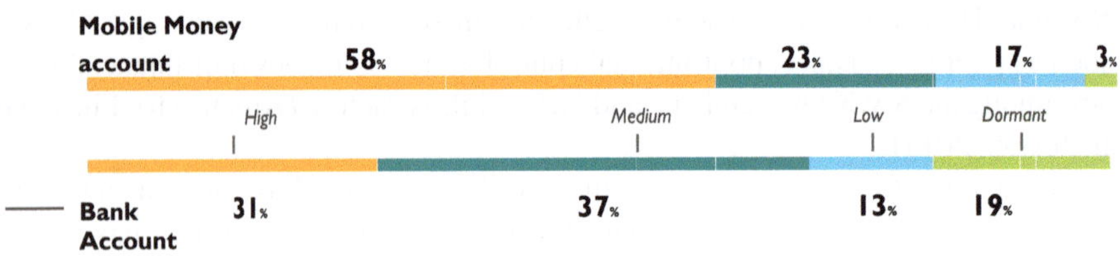

Fig. 8.4 Transactional account use. (*Source*: FinScope Rwanda Consumer Survey Report (2020))

Rwanda Consumer Survey Report (2020), appropriately 6.2 million adults (37%) in Rwanda have access to mobile phones whereby 90% (men) have access to a mobile phone while 84% (female) have access to a mobile phone. In this regard, about 3 in 5 (61%) adults in Rwanda use mobile money accounts, while more males (68%) in Rwanda have mobile money accounts. Going forward, the transactional account use in Rwanda is depicted below.

Figure 8.4 indicates that mobile money accounts are widely utilized regularly in Rwanda. In this respect, 58% of the mobile money accounts transact three or more times monthly and 23% more users use their mobile money account at least once or twice each month. Moreover, 1.7 million (68%) of the banked population in Rwanda use their bank accounts. Based on the above statistics, the high and medium adoption of transactional channels (mobile money platforms and banks) is a positive development when it comes financial in Rwanda which strengthened digital payments.

Uganda

In Uganda, many rural people were financially excluded before the introduction of digital financial products and services (FinScope, 2018; Hamdan et al., 2022). Given this challenge, USAID established the Rural SPEED in 2004 as a program to enhance rural savings and promote micro-enterprise development by expanding access to financial products and services with a special focus on disadvantaged rural people (USAID Rural SPEED Report, 2007). Rural SPEED is a success story of financial inclusion in Uganda as it managed to provide new financial products and services, training, and development as well as widening awareness campaigns related to financial inclusion. For example, it opened 300,000 new savings accounts and borrowed billions to financially assist farmers and owners of Small and Medium Enterprises (SMEs) in Uganda (USAID Rural SPEED Report, 2007). The impact of Rural SPEED has been witnessed in terms of expanding mobilization of savings as supported by an increase of 321,000 new savers in rural communities of Uganda; expansion of agricultural finance where the value of new loans related to farming increased by UGX155 billion; supporting financial institutions as evidenced by training of 223 institutions on SACCOs' monitoring and evaluation; and stimulate the private sector investment through a partnership of the public and private sector, and expanding services delivery mechanisms. According to Aron (2018), mobile money plays a fundamental role in the achievement of financial inclusion through the provision of digital financial services across Uganda. However, it has been observed that there are skill shortages when it comes to mobile banking in Uganda (Kiconco et al., 2019).

Ghana

In the context of Ghana, MTN is a major success story when it comes to the promotion of financial inclusion. MTN as a mobile operator which is registered in Ghana has contributed immensely to financial inclusion through the provision of excellent digital financial services such as digital money transfers. In 2017, ten million customers of MTN were registered on MTN's mobile money transfer platform (Sackitey, 2018). In this regard, MTN mobile money platform plays a central role in promoting financial inclusion as it allows the customers to send and receive money, top-up airtime, settle utility charges, pay school fees and salaries of workers, pay insurance policies, online shopping, and pay airline tickets in Ghana. Going forward, it is worth noting that MTN mobile money platform has several financial packages and services to cater for the financial needs of the clients. Notably, it contributed a lot to financial inclusion in the eyes of youths and women in Ghana. As such, MTN offered OWIK Loan through its mobile money platform in collaboration with AFB Ghana and provide Yellow Save financial services in conjunction with Fidelity Bank Ghana aiming at creating mobile saving accounts for different clients (Aforkpah, 2017). More interestingly, MTN mobile money digital platform allows easy access to treasury bills which permitted clients to invest using mobile phones (Aforkpah, 2017; Sackitey, 2018). To this end, the illiterate, underprivileged, and poor rural people are frequently neglected by big financial players such as commercial banks and are now benefitting from the digital financial services mainly offered by FinTech companies such as mobile operators in Ghana. As such, MTN mobile money platform is a big player in the process of promoting financial inclusion in the context of Ghana.

It must be noted that there has been notable growth in financial inclusion in Ghana. As a developing country, Ghana has also experienced many challenges that hindered the effectiveness of the financial inclusion agenda. However, the National Financial Inclusion and Development Strategy (2018–2023) revealed an improvement in financial inclusion as indicated in Fig. 8.5.

The usage and the number of registered mobile money clients are in line with the increase in mobile phone penetration. The number of mobile subscribers increased by 44% from 25.6 million in 2012 to 36.7 million in 2017 as indicated in Fig. 8.5. Moreover, the registration of mobile money accounts grew 529% from 3.8 million in 2012 to 23.9 million in 2017. Consequently, mobile money transactions increased which translated into an improvement in financial inclusion in Ghana.

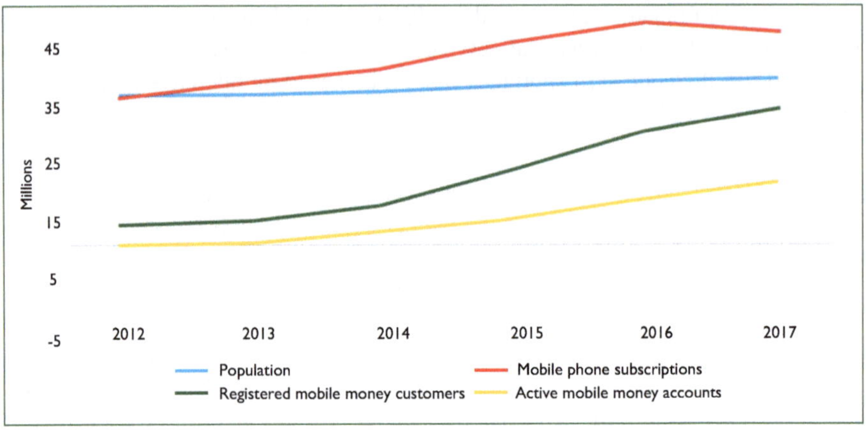

Fig. 8.5 Mobile phone penetration and mobile money usage (millions). (*Source*: National Financial Inclusion and Development Strategy (2018–2023))

8.6 To Support Further Financial Inclusion, the Following Needs to Be Done in Africa

Some of the proposals to further improve financial inclusion in Africa are clearly outlined in Fig. 8.6, including the fact that financial institutions should assist women, young people, and people with disabilities in increasing their ability to make fundamentally sound financial decisions to encourage wider financial inclusion in Africa. A robust institutional framework is required to improve and expand financial inclusion, and other initiatives.

As clearly outlined in Fig. 8.6, to support further financial inclusion in Africa, financial institutions should help women, young people, and persons with disabilities improve their capacity to make fundamentally sound financial decisions. Again, a strong institutional framework to enhance and broaden financial inclusion is necessary in promoting financial inclusion in many African countries. The commercial sector, civil society, government organizations, and regulators can collaborate and participate in this. It is also important to foster confidence in the use of digital financial services which requires a strong emphasis on consumer safety. Financial services regulators must make sure that clients are treated fairly by financial firms that might make use of their information advantage at the expense of the customer.

The other critical issue is having advanced financial literacy. This is because more financially literate consumers can manage risks and make better financial decisions, including decisions regarding spending, saving, and borrowing. They also understand their rights and obligations as financial product customers. For instance, customers who have better financial literacy are more inclined to value saving habits and increase savings. The establishment of a financially sound infrastructure that fosters accountability and transparency in financial transactions, such as a credit reporting system is critical as well. Access to finance is a crucial enabler

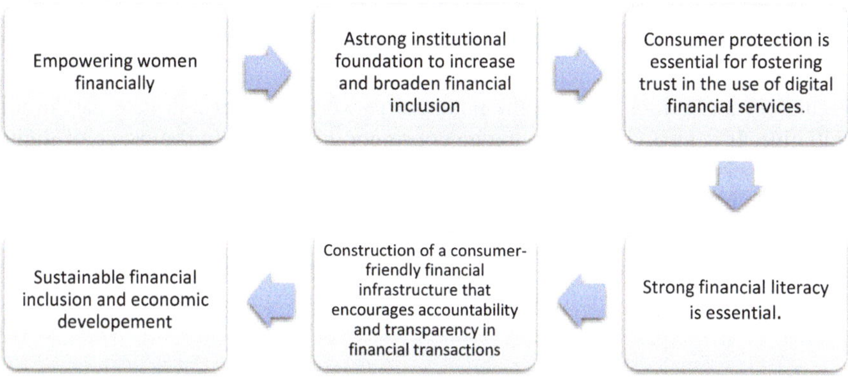

Fig. 8.6 Proposals to further improve financial inclusion in Africa. (*Source*: Authors)

for economic growth and sustainable development through starting and growing businesses, investing in education, controlling risk, absorbing financial shocks through insurance, raising employment, and boosting consumer power. The World Bank Group's Universal Financial Access 2020 effort, which came to an end at the end of 2020, was particularly interested in financial inclusion. Even if this campaign yielded many successes, the fact that more work needs to be done is a sign of how difficult the situation is. Daily life is made easier by having access to money, which also helps families and businesses prepare for everything from long-term objectives to unanticipated emergencies. Account holders are more likely to use additional financial services like credit and insurance to launch and grow enterprises, make investments in their children's or own health or education, manage risk, and recover from financial setbacks, all of which can enhance their overall quality of life. The need for greater digital financial inclusion has been furthered by the ongoing COVID-19 dilemma.

8.7 Conclusion

Financial inclusion refers to the process of ensuring that individuals, households, and businesses within a community have sufficient access to formal financial services and products like transactions, credit cards, payments, savings, and insurance and that these are provided sustainably. This can be accomplished by ensuring that these services and products are provided in a manner that meets the needs of the community. This chapter provided documentation of the progress made toward financial inclusion in Ghana, Kenya, Uganda, and Rwanda by using document analysis. This chapter came to a close by providing an outline of some recommendations to increase financial inclusion in Africa. Some of these recommendations include the following: women, young people, and people with disabilities should be helped by financial institutions to increase their ability to make fundamentally sound financial decisions to encourage wider financial inclusion in Africa. An institutional framework that is strong and well established is required to increase and grow financial inclusion. The commercial sector, civil society, government institutions, and regulatory authorities all have the potential to work together and take part in this initiative. It is also vital to encourage consumer confidence in the usage of digital financial services, which calls for a rigorous focus on the security of end users. This is because it is essential to develop consumer confidence in the utilization of digital financial services. The regulators of financial services must guarantee that consumers of financial institutions are treated fairly. This is especially the case for financial firms that may use their information advantage at the expense of the customer.

References

Aforkpah, E. (2017). *MTN launches 'MTN Yello Save' with Fidelity Bank*. Myjoyonline.com. Retrieved 20 May 2022, from https://www.myjoyonline.com/business/2017/February-6th/mtn-launches-mtn-yello-save-withfidelity-bank.php

Ajide, F. M. (2020). Financial inclusion in Africa: Does it promote entrepreneurship? *Journal of Financial Economic Policy, 12*, 687.

Alliance for Financial Inclusion. (2014). *RWANDA'S financial inclusion success story Umurenge SACCOS*. Retrieved 20 May 2022, from https://www.afi-global.org/wp-content/uploads/publications/afi_case_study_rwanda_finalweb.pdf

Ambarkhane, D., Singh, A. S., & Venkataramani, B. (2016). Measuring financial inclusion of Indian states. *International Journal of Rural Management, 12*(1), 72–100.

Aron, J. (2018). Mobile money and the economy: A review of the evidence. *The World Bank Research Observer, 33*(2), 135–188.

Bekele, W. D. (2022). Determinants of financial inclusion: A comparative study of Kenya and Ethiopia. *Journal of African Business*, 1–9. https://doi.org/10.1080/15228916.2022.2078938

Chhabra, N. (2015). *Financial inclusion in India*. Retrieved 22 June 2022, from http://hdl.handle.net/10603/36960

Cicchiello, A. F., Kazemikhasragh, A., Monferrá, S., & Girón, A. (2021). Financial inclusion and development in the least developed countries in Asia and Africa. *Journal of Innovation and Entrepreneurship, 10*(1), 1–13.

Deloitte. (2022). *Beyond financial inclusion: Redefining financial services for financial health in Kenya*. Available online: https://www2.deloitte.com/za/en/kenya/pages/financial-services/articles/beyond-financial-inclusion.html. Accessed 19 July 2022.

Demirgüç-Kunt, A., Klapper, L., Singer, D., Ansar, S., & Hess, J. (2018). *The Global Findex Database 2017: Measuring financial inclusion and the Fintech revolution*. World Bank.

Dzingirai, M. (2021a). Challenges to necessity-driven nascent entrepreneurship. In A. Carrizo Moreira & J. Dantas (Eds.), *Handbook of research on nascent entrepreneurship and creating new ventures* (pp. 194–210). IGI Global.

Dzingirai, M. (2021b). The role of entrepreneurship in reducing poverty in agricultural communities. *Journal of Enterprising Communities: People and Places in the Global Economy, 15*(5), 665–683.

Dzingirai, M., & Baporikar, N. (2021). Role of microfinance for entrepreneurial success. *International Journal of E-Entrepreneurship and Innovation, 11*(1), 1–16. https://doi.org/10.4018/IJEEI.2021010101

Dzingirai, M., & Ndava, R. (2022). Global institutional role to promote the achievement of the sustainable development goals in Zimbabwe. In N. Baporikar (Ed.), *Handbook of research on global institutional roles for inclusive development* (pp. 99–117). IGI Global.

Eustache, H., & Claude, R. (2021). Financial inclusion strategies and performance of SACCOs in Rwanda: A case study of Umurenge SACCOs in Rusizi District. *Journal of Economics and Finance, 12*(3), 61–68.

Evans, O. L. A. N. I. Y. I., & Alenoghena, O. R. (2017). Financial inclusion and GDP per capita in Africa: A Bayesian VAR model. *Journal of Economics & Sustainable Development, 8*(18), 44–57.

FinScope. (2018). FinScope Uganda 2018 survey report. Financial Sector Deepening Uganda (FSDU), Kampala, Uganda. Retrieved 1 June 2022, from http://fsduganda.or.ug/finscope-2018-survey-report/?download=1

FinScope Rwanda Consumer Survey Report. (2020). *FinScope financial inclusion*. Retrieved 20 July 2022, from https://www.bnr.rw/fileadmin/user_upload/2020_Rwanda_Finscope.pdf

Hamdan, J. S., Lehmann-Uschner, K., & Menkhoff, L. (2022). Mobile money, financial inclusion, and unmet opportunities: Evidence from Uganda. *The Journal of Development Studies, 58*(4), 671–691.

Harelimana, J. B. (2021). Impact Umurenge SACCO to financial inclusion in Rwanda. *Business and Economics Journal, 12*(2), 1–3.

Kebede, J., Naranpanawa, A., & Selvanathan, S. (2021). Financial inclusion: Measures and applications to Africa. *Economic Analysis and Policy, 70*, 365–379.

Kelikume, I. (2021). Digital financial inclusion, informal economy and poverty reduction in Africa. *Journal of Enterprising Communities: People and Places in the Global Economy, 15*, 626.

Kiconco, R. I., Rooks, G., Solano, G., & Matzat, U. (2019). A skills perspective on the adoption and use of mobile money services in Uganda. *Information Development, 35*(5), 724–738.

Léon, F., & Zins, A. (2020). Regional foreign banks and financial inclusion: Evidence from Africa. *Economic Modelling, 84*, 102–116.

Magali, J. J. (2013). The influence of rural savings and credits cooperatives societies (SACCOS') variables on loans default risks: The case study of Tanzania. *Research Journal of Finance and Accounting, 4*(19), 77–91.

Matekenya, W., Moyo, C., & Jeke, L. (2021). Financial inclusion and human development: Evidence from Sub-Saharan Africa. *Development Southern Africa, 38*(5), 683–700.

Mhlanga, D. (2021). Financial access and poverty reduction in agriculture: A case of households in Manicaland province, Zimbabwe. *African Journal of Business and Economic Research, 16*(2), 73.

Mhlanga, D. (2022). COVID-19 and digital financial inclusion: Policies and innovation that can accelerate financial inclusion in a post-COVID world through Fintech. *African Journal of Development Studies (Formerly AFFRIKA Journal of Politics, Economics and Society), 2022*(si2), 79–100.

Mhlanga, D., & Denhere, V. (2020). Determinants of financial Inclusion in Southern Africa. *Studia Universitatis Babes-Bolyai, Oeconomica, 65*(3), 39.

Mhlanga, D., Dunga, S. H., & Moloi, T. (2020). Financial inclusion and poverty alleviation among smallholder farmers in Zimbabwe. *Eurasian Journal of Economics and Finance, 8*(3), 168–182.

National Financial Inclusion and Development Strategy. (2018–2023). *Republic of Ghana national financial inclusion and development strategy (2018–2023)*. Retrieved 23 July 2022, from https://mofep.gov.gh/sites/default/files/acts/NFIDs_Report.pdf

Ndung'u, N. (2017). *M-Pesa: A success story of digital financial inclusion*. Retrieved 16 June 2022, from https://www.bsg.ox.ac.uk/sites/default/files/2018-06/2017-07-M-Pesa-Practitioners-Insight.pdf#:~:text=M-Pesa%20and%20similar%20digital%20financial%20services%20represent%20a,over%2075%25%20of%20the%20adult%20population%20in%20Kenya

Ombane, D. B. (2021). *Financial inclusion key to Kenya's growth*. Available online: https://www.businessdailyafrica.com/bd/opinion-analysis/letters/financial-inclusion-key-kenya-growth-3598304. Accessed 19 July 2022.

Omwansa, T. K., & Sullivan, N. P. (2012). *Money, real quick: Kenya's disruptive mobile money innovation*. Guardian/Balloonview.

Oshora, B., Desalegn, G., Gorgenyi-Hegyes, E., Fekete-Farkas, M., & Zeman, Z. (2021). Determinants of financial inclusion in small and medium enterprises: Evidence from Ethiopia. *Journal of Risk and Financial Management, 14*(7), 286.

Ozili, P. K. (2020). *Theories of financial inclusion. In uncertainty and challenges in contemporary economic behaviour*. Retrieved 22 June 2022, from https://mpra.ub.uni-muenchen.de/101810/1/MPRA_paper_101810.pdf

Park, C. Y., & Mercado, R. (2018). *Financial inclusion: New measurement and cross-country impact assessment*. Retrieved 22 June 2022, from https://www.adb.org/sites/default/files/publication/408621/ewp-539-financial-inclusion.pdf

Popescu, A. D. (2019). Empowering financial inclusion through financial literacy. *Journal of Business and Management, 6*, 198–215.

Rangarajan, C. (2008). *Report of the committee on financial inclusion*. Ministry of Finance, Government of India. Retrieved 23 June 2022, from https://www.findevgateway.org/sites/default/files/publications/files/mfg-en-paper-report-of-the-committee-on-financial-inclusion-jan-2008.pdf

Sackitey, D. T. (2018). Achieving financial inclusion in Ghana through mobile money. *Texila International Journal of Academic Research, 5*(1), 1–5.

Sarpong, B., & Nketiah-Amponsah, E. (2022). Financial inclusion and inclusive growth in sub-Saharan Africa. *Cogent Economics and Finance, 10*(1), 2058734.

Senyo, P., & Osabutey, E. L. C. (2020). Unearthing antecedents to financial inclusion through FinTech innovations. *Technovation, 98*, 102155.

Shilimi, M. C. (2021). Examining challenges leading to low integration of savings and credit co-operative societies (SACCOs) in national economies: A study of Zambia. *Open Journal of Business and Management, 9*(3), 1338–1366.

Suri, T., & Jack, W. (2016). The long-run poverty and gender impacts of mobile money. *Science, 354*(6317), 1288–1292.

Swamy, V. (2010). *Bank-based financial intermediation for financial inclusion and inclusive growth and inclusive growth*. Retrieved 22 June 2022, from https://papers.ssrn.com/sol3/papers.cfm?abstract_id=2126834

Takyi, P. O., Sorkpor, C., & Asante, G. N. (2022). Mobile money for financial inclusion and saving practices: Empirical evidence from Ghana. *Journal of Economic and Administrative Sciences*, (ahead-of-print).

Tiwari, J., Schaub, E., & Sultana, N. (2019). Barriers to "last mile" financial inclusion: Cases from northern Kenya. *Development in Practice, 29*(8), 988–1000.

Triki, T., & Faye, I. (2013). *Financial inclusion in Africa*. Retrieved 22 June 2022, from https://www.afdb.org/fileadmin/uploads/afdb/Documents/Project-and-Operations/Financial_Inclusion_in_Africa.pdf

USAID Rural SPEED Report. (2007). *Rural speed quarterly performance report*. Retrieved 16 June 2022, from https://pdf.usaid.gov/pdf_docs/pdack900.pdf

Chapter 9
The Future of Financial Inclusion

Peterson K. Ozili

Abstract This chapter provides insights into the trends to expect in the future of financial inclusion. The author identifies the past and recent changes occurring in the financial inclusion space, and based on these changes, makes predictions about what to expect in the future of financial inclusion. The author predicts that, in the future, financial inclusion will witness increased digitalization; increased personalization of formal financial services; the provision of a wide range of formal financial services from a single platform; a shift from account numbers to a mobile numbers to drive financial inclusion; more women will become financially empowered and financially independent; the government will become more directly involved in delivering basic financial services to the poor; and the emergence of new financial innovations that continuously reduce transaction cost. These future trends will have implications for financial inclusion in Asia, Europe, and particularly in Africa where the level of financial inclusion is relatively low.

Keywords Financial inclusion · Digital finance · Fintech · Access to finance · Central bank digital currency · Women

JEL Classification G21 · G28

9.1 Introduction

The purpose of this chapter is to offer some insights into the future of financial inclusion. I have been an avid observer of global research and development in financial inclusion for many years now. Financial inclusion started as a scheme to expand

P. K. Ozili (✉)
Central Bank of Nigeria, Abuja, Nigeria

D. Mhlanga, E. Ndhlovu (eds.), *Economic Inclusion in Post-Independence Africa*, Advances in African Economic, Social and Political Development,
https://doi.org/10.1007/978-3-031-31431-5_9

access to finance for poor people and the unbanked segments of the population. It has since become a recognized solution to reduce extreme poverty in developing and poor countries. Many financial inclusion enthusiasts see financial inclusion as a tool for development or a gateway to end poverty and increase shared prosperity, meaning that financial inclusion is widely acknowledged to be a means to an end. And they are right! The need to reduce poverty accelerated government and private sector efforts to increase the level of financial inclusion in poor and developing countries. Meanwhile, in developed countries, financial inclusion has gone beyond expanding access to finance for poor people and unbanked adults, it has now become a gateway to living a financially fulfilled life in developed societies.

Using critical discourse analysis, I have carefully and critically assessed the new developments in the financial inclusion space, such as the evolution of Fintech, mobile banking, agent banking, artificial intelligence, blockchain, and central bank digital currency for financial inclusion (Ozili, 2018, 2021b). These developments have changed the way financial inclusion is being achieved today, and more changes will emerge in the future. These developments increased my curiosity to understand what these innovations seek to achieve, and to gain more knowledge and insight into what the future holds for financial inclusion. The outcome of my knowledge finding, my interaction with industry experts, and my critical reflection of the changes occurring in the global financial inclusion space led me to make some predictions of financial inclusion.

Today, the global economy is becoming more digital, investment in technology is growing, the automation of financial services is increasing, the use of data is increasing, and the use of cash is declining. These developments will play a major role in driving inclusive growth and in reshaping the global financial sector. These developments will affect how people engage with formal finance, it will affect how access to finance is granted, and it will have implications for the future of financial inclusion.

The existing literature has explored the role of past and present innovations in increasing the level of financial inclusion (see, e.g., Lumsden, 2018; Kempson & Collard, 2012; Adams, 2018; Sawadogo & Semedo, 2021; Kumar & Pathak, 2022). The literature has also examined how microfinance institutions and digital financial innovations have helped to promote financial inclusion (see, e.g., Morduch, 1999; Schreiner, 2002; Chemin, 2008; Lacalle-Calderon et al., 2018; Ozili, 2022). But no studies have attempted to offer insights into what to expect from financial inclusion in the future. This chapter fills the gap in the financial inclusion literature, by offering some insights into what to expect from financial inclusion in the future.

The insights offered in this chapter contribute to the literature in the following ways. First, it contributes to the literature that examines the emerging changes that affect the level of financial inclusion in many countries. Second, the insights offered in this chapter contribute to the development literature that explores how innovations can change the face of development in the future. Finally, the insights offered in this chapter add to the debate about the changing role of banks and government in the pursuit of financial inclusion.

The rest of this chapter is structured as follows. The review of related literature is presented in Sect. 9.2. Section 9.3 presents a discussion of how financial inclusion has been achieved in the past. Section 9.4 presents a discussion on how financial inclusion is achieved today. A discussion about what to expect from financial inclusion in the future is presented in Sect. 9.5. The conclusion of this chapter is presented in Sect. 9.6.

9.2 Literature Review

Several studies acknowledge that the field of financial inclusion is changing rapidly. For instance, Sriram (2019) shows that financial inclusion which, in the past, was an agenda driven by the State with institutional, policy, and regulatory interventions, has now shifted to become an agenda driven by private sector agents with the aid of digital technology. Lumsden (2018) also show that digital technology is used to solve the poverty problem by helping poor people take advantage of the benefits of formal financial products and services in the financial system. Murthy, Vidal, Faz, and Barreto (2019) point out that donors and investors are supporting new Fintech innovations that maximize development impact for low-income and excluded customers. Barr, Harris, Menand, and Xu (2020) argue that central banks can take advantage of emerging digital technologies from virtual currencies to mobile payments and QR codes which provide opportunities for central banks to develop the payments infrastructure and support ongoing efforts to reduce poverty and inequality. Lumsden (2018) argued that implementing innovations, such as mobile financial systems, can speed up financial inclusion and spur economic growth, and countries that resist these innovations will miss many opportunities.

The opportunities for financial inclusion are enormous. For instance, Kempson and Collard (2012) envisioned financial inclusion to be about ensuring that everyone has access to an appropriate account into which income is paid and the account can be held securely, accessed easily, and used to make remote purchases by telephone and on the Internet. Adams (2018) argued that financial inclusion matters because it helps individuals to take advantage of economic opportunities, and it provides valuable services to the neglected segments of society. Lee, Wang, and Ho (2022) show evidence that foreign aid inflow increases financial inclusion in the recipient country. Sawadogo and Semedo (2021) show that financial inclusion reduces income inequality in countries with high institutional quality. Sakyi-Nyarko, Ahmad, and Green (2022) show that greater financial inclusion can potentially improve food consumption, medical treatment, cash income, and school attendance outcomes.

Other studies identify the enablers of financial inclusion. Kumar and Pathak (2022) show that more financial awareness through education increases the level of financial inclusion. Similarly, Sharif, Naghavi, Waheed, and Ehigiamusoe (2022) found that education reduces the gender gap and improves financial inclusion. Ozili (2018) argued that digital finance that is offered through Fintech providers has positive effects on financial inclusion, particularly because of the convenience that digital finance provides to individuals with low and variable incomes. Demirgüç-Kunt et al. (2018) also emphasize that digital technology offers benefits beyond expanding account ownership and increasing account use. They show that digital technology can also be used for digitizing payments which can improve payment efficiency by increasing the speed of payments and reducing the cost of disbursing and receiving payments, and it can also enhance the security of payments and thus lower the incidence of associated crime.

Other studies have called for caution in the way financial inclusion is being achieved due to hidden risks and institutional bias that exists. For instance, Ozili (2021a) draws attention to the economic bias that exists in banks. He argued that banks issue tailored products and services that exclude poor customers and favor wealthy bank customers. Ozili (2021a) warned that if such barriers are not removed, banked adults who are dissatisfied with such bias may end up leaving the formal financial sector and become unbanked again. Markose, Arun, and Ozili (2022) show that certain financial inclusion interventions delivered through public banks are not always economically viable as the government has to subsidize the cost of delivering and sustaining financial inclusion interventions.

Other studies show a relationship between financial inclusion outcomes and improvements in other areas of the economy and society. For instance, Dikshit and Pandey (2021) argue that financial inclusion can contribute to achieving the sustainable development goals because it addresses the challenges related to poverty, inequality, climate, environmental degradation, prosperity, peace, and justice. Ozili (2021b) argued that policymakers should understand the interaction between financial inclusion and poverty levels, financial innovation, financial stability, the state of the economy, financial literacy, and regulatory systems.

9.3 Financial Inclusion in the Past

In the past, financial inclusion was achieved mostly through the proliferation of microfinance institutions in remote communities. This strategy involves opening a microfinance bank or institution in remote communities and moving credit officers to the bank to serve customers in the communities. The marketing officers and credit officers go out to persuade members of the community to patronize the microloans offered by the microfinance bank or institution. Establishing microfinance institutions (MFIs) as a strategy to increase the level of financial inclusion became a popular idea in the late 1990 and early 2000s. It was also considered to be a strategic intervention for development due to its focus on small or microloans for poor people and people who cannot access formal loans from major financial institutions.

The microfinance movement allowed poor households to improve their lives either as customers or through membership (Morduch, 1999). Some of the many benefits of using microfinance institutions to promote financial inclusion include the following: improved welfare of the poor (Schreiner, 2002), increased access to finance (Chemin, 2008), the provision of microcredit to the poorest individuals (Lacalle-Calderon et al., 2018), employment benefits for members of the local community as they can work in the microfinance institutions in their local community (Mosley & Rock, 2004), and increased school enrolment for boys and girls in the community as parents can borrow money from microfinance institutions to pay the tuition of their children (Chemin, 2008). The desire to take advantage of these benefits led many developing countries to establish microfinance institutions. Soon after, hidden risks and issues began to emerge which include non-personalized financial products and services, high overhead costs, top management executives using MFI's funds to live a lavish lifestyle, discriminating against single women when issuing loans, gender discrimination, and favoritism, among others. Despite the presence of regulation, these issues have been difficult to eradicate in microfinance institutions. As a result, a new strategy for achieving financial inclusion has emerged which involves using digital technology to increase the level of financial inclusion.

9.4 Financial Inclusion in the Present

Today, financial inclusion is driven mainly by digital technology embedded in mobile phones, Fintech software, banking applications or digital devices, for example, the ATM, point-of-sale (POS), quick codes, or unstructured supplementary service data (USSD) codes. The use of digital technology as a strategy to achieve financial inclusion began just after the 2008 global financial crisis, and it soon became a popular approach to drive the financial inclusion agenda. This strategy ensures that a person who has a smartphone and owns a smartphone can remotely access basic formal financial services, such as deposit and savings products, without needing to visit a physical financial institution or microfinance institution. The use of digital technology to achieve financial inclusion is superior to the microfinance model because it brings formal finance into the hands of people through their mobile (smart) phones, and it avoids the high fixed cost incurred by microfinance institutions in expanding financial services to underserved communities. The digital technology revolution has also led to the emergence of InsurTech, RegTech, Proptech, and Fintech players, payment service banks (PSPs) and payment service providers (PSPs), who also play an important role in delivering payment services to underserved communities for greater financial inclusion. Some of the many benefits of using digital technology to promote financial inclusion include the following: it reduces the time to request a loan and the time to receive the loan, Fintech credit increases credit supply in the local community (Schreiner, 2002); low cost of financial services (Sahay et al., 2020; Ozili, 2018), fast and efficient financial services (Peric, 2015), convenience to users (Ozili, 2018), it saves time (Yahaya & Ahmad, 2018), low fixed cost incurred, etc. Due to these benefits, many financial institutions have partnered with technology firms to develop financial technology that can assist in expanding the reach of formal financial services to people in underserved communities. The use of digital technology to increase financial inclusion also presents some risks which include privacy issues, unauthorized use of customer data, cyber-security threats, high rates of fraud, high transaction costs, etc. These risks, and the efforts being made to counter these risks, will likely lead to a new strategy for achieving financial inclusion in the future.

9.5 The Future of Financial Inclusion: What to Expect

Financial inclusion has proven to be a game changer in the quest to uplift people from extreme poverty. Below are some developments to expect from financial inclusion in the future.

9.5.1 The Future of Financial Inclusion Is Digital

The future of financial inclusion will be digital. The digital finance revolution which started in the early 2000s has shown that the future of financial inclusion is digital. Digital technology has made it possible for unbanked adults to open a bank account using their mobile phone without visiting a bank branch (Ozili, 2018). In the future, more financial services will be embedded into digital devices, or mobile phones, to enable poor people to perform basic transactions such as buying and selling on e-commerce platforms. Also, in the future, Fintech players will increase their alliance with banks to find an easier way for unbanked adults to access digital payments and financial services, such as personal loans and mortgage finance, which can help them improve their welfare and livelihoods.

9.5.2 Increased Personalization of Formal Financial Services

In the future, there is likely to be heightened personalization of basic financial services, such as personalized savings products, personalized interest-bearing loans, and personalized account opening packages. The personalization of basic formal financial services will be the key ingredient to attract customers who want financial services that take into account their personal life situation and circumstance. The digitalization of financial services will play a role in personalizing basic financial services, and there will be increased coordination between interpersonal customer service and digital technology in delivering personalized finance to members of society.

9.5.3 A Wide Range of Financial Products and Services Will Be Offered in a Single Platform

Presently, many types of financial services are offered at different financial institutions and through multiple mobile banking applications. The implication is that it leads to an increase in transaction costs when using multiple banking applications to access different financial services. It also leads to an increase in transaction costs when moving from one financial institution to another financial institution to access multiple financial services. Future developments in financial inclusion, enabled by digital technology, will usher in an era where all types of basic financial services will be available to banked adults from a single source. This source can be a mobile app, a digital device, or a financial institution. This development in financial inclusion can encourage a large number of unbanked adults to join the formal financial sector to enjoy the numerous financial services that are available and offered from a single source. Unbanked adults, after joining the financial sector, will no longer need to visit different banks or use different mobile banking apps to access formal deposit, savings, investment, and mortgage finance products. Rather, they will be able to access multiple financial services from a single source, thereby reducing transaction costs and saving time.

9.5.4 A Shift from Account Number to a Mobile Number to Drive Financial Inclusion

Many scholars point out that achieving financial inclusion through bank account ownership requires providing documentation which may be burdensome to unbanked adults (Karpowicz, 2016; Ozili, 2021b). It is difficult to significantly reduce the account opening documentation requirements because providing account opening documentation fulfills the know-your-customer (KYC) requirement in existing anti-money laundry (AML) laws.

Financial technology companies that want to reach unbanked adults will find a way to help unbanked adults deal with the burdensome account opening problem. They will seek to bypass the bank "account number," and find another number that bears user identification information which can be used to drive financial inclusion for unbanked adults. As a result, there will be a shift away from bank "account number" – which presents some documentation difficulties for unbanked adults – to a shift to "mobile number" to drive financial inclusion. Since most people in rural areas already have a mobile number, the mobile number can be used as a gateway to access basic financial services because mobile numbers already carry some important user-identifying information. Fintech and other technology companies will push for the use of the mobile number to access basic financial services to bypass the cumbersome documentation requirement associated with the bank "account number" that discourage unbanked adults from joining the formal financial sector.

9.5.5 More Women Will Become Financially Empowered and Financially Independent

Existing international financial inclusion programs, led by the Bill and Melinda Gates Foundation, CGAP, and the Women's World Banking, are already providing unbanked women and poor women with the tools they need to improve their access to basic financial services. The goal of such programs is to ensure that more women become financially independent and economically empowered to improve their lives and the lives of their households. These programs are helping vulnerable women to protect their finances by opening savings, checking accounts, and formal loans without needing the validation or permission of a male head. As a result, in the future, more women will be able to utilize basic financial services such as loans, credit, and insurance. They will be able to invest and seek profitable investment opportunities and compete financially with men in society. In the future, technology such as AI and blockchain will play an important role in reducing the gender bias that hinders access to basic financial services for women. Such technologies can be modified (using AI and machine learning) to give women more access to basic financial services so that no woman is left behind. Full financial inclusion cannot be achieved in the future without carrying women along.

9.5.6 Government Will Become More Directly Involved in Delivering Basic Financial Services to the Poor

Presently, the government does not issue financial services directly to customers. The government usually license Fintech agents and financial institutions to offer financial services to users within a regulatory framework. This has been the status quo in the last three decades. Recently, many governments have begun to invent their innovative financial products, services, and payments infrastructure such as government-to-person (G2P) payment solutions and central bank digital currencies (CBDC). These government-led innovations can help to increase financial inclusion. The government or authorities will be able to use these innovations to drive financial inclusion without competing directly with Fintech and financial institutions. Consequently, in the future, we will witness many governments becoming directly involved in delivering basic financial services directly to unbanked adults. A government will be able to use its innovative financial products and services (e.g., CBDC) to reach unbanked adults in communities where Fintech agents and financial institutions are unwilling to serve. This means that, in the future, the financial inclusion ecosystem will no longer be dominated by financial institutions, Fintech agents, and technology companies alone. The government and its agents will become key players in the financial inclusion space.

9.5.7 *Emergence of New Financial Innovations That Continuously Reduce Transaction Cost*

In the future, innovations will emerge to significantly reduce the cost of financial transactions or the cost of delivering financial services. These cost-reducing innovations will focus on the cost structure of financial services. They will redesign the cost structure, and seek ways to eliminate some cost components to reduce the cost of financial transactions or the cost of delivering financial services. As a result, the future will witness intense competition among financial sector agents as each agent will seek new ways to reduce the cost involved in delivering financial services to banked and unbanked adults. The emergence of cost-reducing financial innovations will also lead to a race to lower transaction costs which is beneficial for financial inclusion but might be harmful to financial institutions and Fintech players who are unable to reduce their transaction costs below a threshold due to its effect on their fee income and profitability.

9.5.8 *Consumer Protection, Data Privacy, and Unethical Technology Will Remain a Major Issue*

Presently, the use of digital technology to promote financial inclusion has raised some debate about consumer protection, data privacy, and the presence of exploitative digital technology. There are also issues about the way consumer data will be used and the limit to which consumer data can be used by third parties including the government. Even though many countries have begun to take steps to address some of these issues, there is no immediate quick-fix solution to address these issues. As a result, these issues will persist for a long time. Therefore, consumer protection, data privacy, and the ethical nature of digital technology will remain major issues in the future of financial inclusion. There will be contention about who should grant access to consumer data, and whether the customer (i.e., data owner) and data aggregators should jointly provide consent before private consumer data can be shared with third parties for commercial purposes. There will be contention about government control over digital financial transactions due to fears that the government can easily manipulate digital financial systems and create a system of social control. Large corporations will also seek to exploit data from digital systems and use it for commercial purposes.

9.6 Conclusion

This chapter makes some predictions about what to expect from financial inclusion in the future. Three major forces will change financial inclusion in the future. They are (1) technological developments, (2) the growing demand for personalized financial services, and (3) the need to make a profit from consumer data. The selection of trends was done based on my experience as a senior scholar of financial inclusion. I predicted that the future of financial inclusion will witness increased digitalization, increased personalization of formal financial services, and the provision of all financial services from a single source which might be a location, platform, or device. I also predicted that there will be a shift from account numbers to mobile numbers to drive financial inclusion. In addition, more women will become financially empowered and financially independent. The government will become more directly involved in delivering basic financial services to the poor. There will be the emergence of new financial innovations that continuously reduce transaction costs. There will be challenges regarding consumer protection, data privacy, and unethical technology. These predictions highlight the trends to expect in the future of financial inclusion. These future trends will have implications for financial inclusion in Asia, Europe, and particularly in Africa where the level of financial inclusion is relatively low. African countries need to prepare for the future of financial inclusion beginning today if they do not want to be left behind. African countries need to introduce reforms in their payment system and financial system. Such reforms should help to achieve financial inclusion outcomes. Future studies can offer additional predictions of financial inclusion. Future studies can also develop models that assess the relationship between financial inclusion and individual welfare in the long run.

References

Adams, T. D. (2018). *Why financial inclusion matters*. Center for Financial Inclusion, Accion (CFI).

Barr, M. S., Harris, A., Menand, L., & Xu, W. M. (2020). *Building the payment system of the future: How central banks can improve payments to enhance financial inclusion*. University of Michigan Law & Econ Research Paper, No. 038.

Chemin, M. (2008). The benefits and costs of microfinance: Evidence from Bangladesh. *The Journal of Development Studies, 44*(4), 463–484.

Demirgüç-Kunt, A., Klapper, L., Singer, D., Ansar, S., & Hess, J. (2018). *Opportunities for expanding financial inclusion through digital technology*. World Bank Publications.

Dikshit, S., & Pandey, A. C. (2021). Role of financial inclusion in realising sustainable development goals (SDGs). *International Journal of Research in Finance and Management, 4*(2), 35–39.

Karpowicz, I. (2016). Financial inclusion, growth and inequality: A model application to Colombia. *Journal of Banking and Financial Economics, 6*(2), 68–89.

Kempson, E., & Collard, S. (2012). *Developing a vision for financial inclusion*. University of Bristol for Friends Provident Foundation.

Kumar, R., & Pathak, D. C. (2022). Financial awareness: A bridge to financial inclusion. *Development in Practice, 32*(7), 968–980.

Lacalle-Calderon, M., Perez-Trujillo, M., & Neira, I. (2018). Does microfinance reduce poverty among the poorest? A macro quantile regression approach. *The Developing Economies, 56*(1), 51–65.

Lee, C. C., Wang, C. W., & Ho, S. J. (2022). Financial aid and financial inclusion: Does risk uncertainty matter? *Pacific-Basin Finance Journal, 71*, 101700.

Lumsden, E. (2018). The future is mobil: Financial inclusion and technological innovation in the emerging world. *Stanford Journal of Law, Business & Finance, 23*, 1.

Markose, S., Arun, T., & Ozili, P. (2022). Financial inclusion, at what cost? Quantification of economic viability of a supply side roll out. *The European Journal of Finance, 28*(1), 3–29.

Morduch, J. (1999). The microfinance promise. *Journal of economic literature, 37*(4), 1569–1614.

Mosley, P., & Rock, J. (2004). Microfinance, labour markets and poverty in Africa: A study of six institutions. *Journal of International Development, 16*(3), 467–500.

Murthy, G., Vidal, M. F., Faz, X., & Barreto, R. (2019, May). *Fintechs and financial inclusion. Focus Note*. CGAP. https://www.cgap.org/research/publication/fintechs-and-financial-inclusion

Ozili, P. K. (2018). Impact of digital finance on financial inclusion and stability. *Borsa Istanbul Review, 18*(4), 329–340.

Ozili, P. K. (2021a). Financial inclusion-exclusion paradox: How banked adults become unbanked again. *Financial Internet Quarterly, 17*(2), 1–10.

Ozili, P. K. (2021b). Financial inclusion research around the world: A review. *Forum for Social Economics, 50*(4), 457–479.

Ozili, P. K. (2022). Digital financial inclusion. In Big Data: A game changer for insurance industry (pp. 229–238). Emerald Publishing Limited.

Peric, K. (2015). Digital financial inclusion. *Journal of Payments Strategy & Systems, 9*(3), 212–214.

Sahay, M. R., von Allmen, M. U. E., Lahreche, M. A., Khera, P., Ogawa, M. S., Bazarbash, M., & Beaton, M. K. (2020). *The promise of Fintech: Financial inclusion in the post COVID-19 era*. International Monetary Fund.

Sakyi-Nyarko, C., Ahmad, A. H., & Green, C. J. (2022). The role of financial inclusion in improving household well-being. *Journal of International Development, 34*, 1606.

Sawadogo, R., & Semedo, G. (2021). Financial inclusion, income inequality, and institutions in sub-Saharan Africa: Identifying cross-country inequality regimes. *International Economics, 167*, 15–28.

Schreiner, M. (2002). Aspects of outreach: A framework for discussion of the social benefits of microfinance. *Journal of International Development, 14*(5), 591–603.

Sharif, S. P., Naghavi, N., Waheed, H., & Ehigiamusoe, K. U. (2022). The role of education in filling the gender gap in financial inclusion in low-income economies. *International Journal of Emerging Markets*.

Sriram, M. S. (2019). Financial inclusion: Agenda for policy intervention. *Vikalpa, 44*(4), 163–166.

Yahaya, M. H., & Ahmad, K. (2018). Financial inclusion through efficient zakat distribution for poverty alleviation in Malaysia: Using Fintech & mobile banking. In *Proceeding of the 5th international conference on management and Muamalah* (pp. 15–31).

Chapter 10
On the Determinants of Foreign Direct Investment to West African Countries: Does Political Risk Matter?

Adewale Samuel Hassan

Abstract The drivers of FDI have been a subject of constant investigation in the literature over the years. However, the role of politics has not been adequately explored, especially in the context of West African countries. This study investigates whether political risk matters for FDI inflows to West African countries from 1986 to 2020. Panel regressions were conducted based on the dynamic common correlated effects (DCCE) and dynamic seemingly unrelated regression (DSUR). The estimates establish that improvement in the political rating scores of the West African countries enhances FDI inflows to the countries. Market potential, trade openness, and natural resources exploitation are also identified as important drivers of FDI. Furthermore, the Dumitrescu-Hurlin (D-H) panel causality test results reveal that GDP has a bidirectional causal relationship with FDI, natural resources, and infrastructure, while natural resources Granger causes FDI, political risk, trade openness, and infrastructure. The study posits that the countries should improve political risk rating through the existing political and economic unions and embed their natural resource exploitation in the sound institutional framework.

Keywords FDI · Political risk · DCCE · DSUR · Natural resources · Market size · GDP

10.1 Introduction

Achieving sustainable growth is a crucial objective of every economy, and an important means that many economies explore for the attainment of this objective is the attraction of foreign direct investment (FDI). This is because of due to the unique role that the FDI plays in driving industrialization, which has been identified as a

A. S. Hassan (✉)
College of Business and Economics, University of Johannesburg, Johannesburg, South Africa

D. Mhlanga, E. Ndhlovu (eds.), *Economic Inclusion in Post-Independence Africa*, Advances in African Economic, Social and Political Development,
https://doi.org/10.1007/978-3-031-31431-5_10

principal catalyst for economic growth and development (Akinlo, 2004). Previous studies have highlighted the key role of FDI in promoting productivity and galvanizing the general macroeconomic performance through the channels of technology transfer, managerial talent, and provision of financial capital (Akinlo, 2003; Khan, 2007; Ugwuegbe et al., 2014). Such roles of the FDI could "spill over" effect to the other sectors and subsequently propel growth (Rappaport, 2000).

Since the 1990s, most developing countries have formulated and implemented different FDI-oriented policy frameworks, aimed at increasing their stock of FDI inflows. Such frameworks have led to the signing of international investment agreements, the establishment of investment promotion agencies and facilities, and the setting up of special schemes such as export processing zones, to attract FDI. It is thus not surprising that since 1990, FDI has been on the increase in developing countries such that it rose to about $500 billion in 2007 and $720 billion in 2019 (UNCTAD, 2021). Even though the COVID-19 pandemic induced a global collapse in FDI in 2020, the developing countries still managed to achieve a record 72% share of FDI across the world (UNCTAD, 2021).

The key objective of this study is to examine the impact of political risk as a determinant of FDI inflows in West Africa. According to Robock and Simmonds (1973), political risk in the context of international investment refers to situations of disruption in the business environment, which are difficult to foresee, and are engendered by political change. Agmon (1985) is more exhaustive in defining political risk as unexpected changes in the political factors that influence the relative prices of traded production factors, as well as those of goods and services, such as are attributable to the governments/other political groups' actions and reactions. Intuitively, political risk should rate high among the most important determinants of FDI given the fact that how external bodies relate to a country is highly influenced by how stable its economic and political environments are.

This is because investors are generally averse to systematic risks which are mainly external and out of their control. Since all the components of political risk are systematic, foreign investors are bound to be wary of them, which could ultimately influence the flow of FDI. Root (1987) opined that any foreign investment project must be assessed from the perspective of its economic, social, political, and cultural environments. Therefore, it is not surprising that in making their offshore investment decisions, multinational companies are often more favorably disposed to countries where they may encounter low risk and generate high returns on their investment.

This study is important for the West African sub-region for these reasons. First, over the last few decades, West Africa has recorded increased growth and driven the regional cooperation cause (Marc et al., 2015). However, the escalation in the spate of violence, conflict, and military coups in the sub-region, especially, since the 2000s could stymie the hard-worn economic performance and prospects of FDI inflows. Particularly, West African countries have grappled with political crises which include interstate conflicts – Burkina Faso and Mali in April 1985, Mauritania and Senegal in April 1989 (Souaré, 2010), several civil wars and local unrests (M'Cormack, 2011), series of election-induced violence (Human Rights Watch,

2011; Souaré, 2010), drug trafficking (O'Regan & Thompson, 2013; UNODC, 2013), maritime piracy and criminality (Center for International Peace Operations, 2012; UNODC, 2013), terrorism and religious extremism (Dowd, 2013), and military intervention in politics, with five military coups in the past 2 years. Therefore, it is not surprising that some of the West African countries are ranked very poorly by the Fragile States Index (2021). For example, out of 179 countries assessed, Nigeria, Guinea, Niger, Guinea-Bissau, Cote d'Ivoire, Burkina Faso, and Togo are adjudged the 12th, 14th, 21st, 27th, 28th, 36th, and 38th most fragile states. The OECD (2018), which also considers the fragility of states as consisting of political, environmental, economic, social, and security dimensions, posits that the challenges of a fragile state constitute some form of deterrent to foreign investors.

Second, in addition to the fact that sub-Saharan Africa (SSA) falls behind other developing regions in terms of FDI inflows [e.g., Africa received 3.4%, 4.1%, and 4.4% of global FDI in 2018, 2019, and 2020, respectively, relative to those of Asia – 33.4%, 33.2%, and 55.4%, respectively, and Latin America and the Caribbean – 9.9%, 10.7%, and 11.8%, respectively (UNCTAD, 2021)], there are also marked differences in FDI inflows across the sub-regions that make up the SSA. For example, West Africa led the pack in 2019 with $11 billion out of the $32 billion for SSA (UNCTAD, 2021). These differences could have been engendered by various sub-regional characteristics like population, natural resources endowment, and political and macroeconomic stability, which may not be even across the region. According to Anyanwu and Erhijakpor (2004), the inflows of FDI to SSA are characterized by regional heterogeneity, considering the disposition of the West African sub-region to FDI inflows, relative to other sub-regions.

Despite this key attribute of FDI inflows in SSA, studies on the determinants of FDI in SSA, with a focus on the sub-regions, particularly, West Africa, are sparse. The few studies that focus on West Africa include Anyanwu (2012), Anyanwu and Erhijakpor (2004), Anyanwu and Yameogo (2015a, b), Emediegwu and Edo (2017), and Sane (2016). Notably, all these studies explored FDI determinants that are associated with the size/growth and the cost competitiveness attributes of the economy such as market size, domestic investment, natural resources, and trade openness. This study is therefore a departure from previous studies on the determinants of FDI in West Africa, as it explores whether the extra-economic attributes of West Africa in respect of the various components of political risk matter for FDI inflows in the sub-region.

10.2 Literature Review

FDI has been considered very crucial for bridging the savings-investment gap in the developing economies of the world (Sabir & Khan, 2018). This is owing to its ability to enhance the level of capital accumulation that the traditional neoclassical growth model considers crucial for the much-needed increase in the level of a nation's per capita income (Koopmans, 1965). Therefore, this section is devoted to a review of the empirical literature on the determinants of FDI inflows to the host countries, with a particular interest in political risk factors. Using the two-stage least-squares method, the effect of national risk on FDI in Iran is investigated by Rafat and Farahani (2019) for 1985–2016. Their results indicate that indicators of national risk that include religious and ethnic tensions, external conflicts, socioeconomic status, and military tension are major factors impacting the FDI in the economy.

Similarly, the impact of economic, political, and financial risk is investigated for 10 MENA countries between 2000 and 2017 by Salehnia et al. (2019). Empirical results from their estimation show that all three types of risk affect the FDI negatively, with the economic risk being the most influential of the three. This result is corroborated by a recent study of a MENA country, Egypt, for the period 2005–2015 by Salem and Younis (2021), who find both economic and political risks as determinants of FDI in the country with economic risk the more influential of the pair. It is, however, found that financial risk has no impact on the FDI. Meanwhile, in an earlier similar study for the MENA countries, Souria and Ghani (2018) identified political risk as the dominant determinant of FDI in the region.

An investigation of the impact of political and financial risks on FDI inflow to 90 countries from 1985 to 2007 is conducted by Hayakawa et al. (2013), using the generalized method of moments (GMM) estimator. Their results which concentrate mainly on the developing countries indicate that of all the components of political risk estimated, the following are closely associated with FDI flows: religious tension, democratic accountability, corruption, ethnic tension, socioeconomic condition, investment profile, and government stability. Regarding the components of financial risk, only exchange rate stability is found to positively impact the FDI, while the remaining components are either insignificant or negative. Also investigating the effect of political and financial risk on the FDI in Algeria from 1990 to 2012 is Sissani and Belkacem (2014). They conclude that political and financial risks are critical to FDI inflows, with financial risk as a strong determinant. In a related study, Krifa-Schneider and Matei (2010) examine the effect of political risk and business climate on the FDI in 33 developing and transition economies by using both the fixed-effect model and GMM estimator over the period 1996–2008. Estimates from their analysis reveal that the reduction of political risks leads to an increase in FDI inflows, while business climate constitutes a key driver of FDI flows.

The impact of political risk and economic growth on FDI in South Africa is investigated by Meyer and Habanabakize (2018) for the period 1995–2016. Findings from their analysis revealed that the impact of political risk on FDI is higher relative to that of GDP. In the same vein, the effect of political risk in Lebanon is investigated for the period 2008–2018 by Bitar et al. (2020), who reclassified ICRG political risk variables into three components: cohesion, institutional quality, and governance. Their results reveal that all three components are significantly associated with FDI inflows to Lebanon. They, therefore, conclude that political stability is a critical determinant of FDI. Furthermore, the impact of political risk on FDI in 146 economies is investigated by Goswami and Haider (2014), who employed factor analysis within a panel framework to determine the components of political risk that are more deleterious to FDI inflows. Their results point to government failure as being fundamentally responsible for abysmal FDI inflows. Moreover, cultural conflict and the attitude of partner countries toward the host country are high on the list of variables found as disincentives to FDI inflows.

In a related study by Almahmoud (2014), the link between political, economic, and financial components of Saudi Arabia's country risk rating and its stock market movements is examined using the ARDL method on monthly data between 2005 and 2012. Results from the analysis show that country risk ratings are closely associated with stock market movements in the country, with financial risk exhibiting the most robust sensitivity among the three components. The study concludes that prospective FDI investors in the country should seriously consider such financial risk indicators as external debt servicing, exchange rate stability, and current account balance before embarking on any strategic investment in Saudi Arabia. Similarly, Hammoudeh et al. (2011) examine the individual BRICS countries' country risk ratings related to their respective stock markets. Their findings specifically point to China as being sensitive to all components of country risk, while Russia and China are found to be highly sensitive to political risk relative to others.

10.3 Data and Methodology

10.3.1 Description of Data

This study explores the role of political risk as a determinant of FDI inflows in West African countries which comprise Burkina Faso, Cote d'Ivoire, Gambia, Ghana, Guinea, Guinea-Bissau, Liberia, Mali, Niger, Nigeria, Sierra Leone, Senegal, and Togo, using annual data over the period 1986–2020. The independent variable is the FDI inflows, which are measured by FDI inflows as a percentage of GDP and are drawn from the World Development Indicators (WDI). The main explanatory variable is political risk, which evaluates the level of political stability in a country. To capture political risk, this study utilizes the political risk rating system of the International Country Risk Guide (ICRG) provided by the Political Risk Services (PRS). The ICRG variables have been used by previous studies in measuring political risk (e.g., Bitar et al., 2020; Busse & Hefeker, 2007; Khan & Akbar, 2013; Nassour et al., 2020; Topal & Gul, 2016).

The ICRG system is based on the following 12 variables, with their corresponding risk point ranges in parentheses: government stability (0–12), socioeconomic conditions (0–12), investment profile (0–12), internal conflict (0–12), external conflict (0–12), corruption (0–6), military in politics (0–6), religious tensions (0–6), law and order (0–6), ethnic tensions (0–6), democratic accountability (0–6), and bureaucracy quality (0–4). Consequently, the ICRG political risk is allotted a total of 100 points, and the higher the computed rating of a country, the lower the political risk, and vice versa. Following extant studies on the drivers of FDI in West Africa (Anyanwu, 2012; Anyanwu & Erhijakpor, 2004; Anyanwu & Yameogo,

2015a, b; Emediegwu & Edo, 2017), other explanatory variables include the market size measured by real GDP, trade openness measured by the total trade (% of GDP), natural resources measured by total natural resource rent (% of GDP), and infrastructure measured by gross fixed capital formation – all obtained from WDI.

Table 10.1 presents a synopsis of the statistical attributes of the variables in the study. While the upper compartment of the table contains the descriptive statistics, the correlation matrix of the variables is in the lower compartment. The mean of FDI indicates that over the study period, FDI inflows to the West African countries amounted to only 2.22% of GDP. This implies that FDI inflows are still low in the sub-region. The average score of 53.12/100 for political risk is above average, but there is still a need for improvement considering the very low minimum score of the sub-region. Overall, the mean values of all the variables exceed their respective median values. This suggests that the data distribution of each of the variables in the study is skewed to the right. The highest FDI inflows/GDP ratio is 32.30 attained by Sierra Leone in 2011, while the lowest of −28.62 is recorded for the same country in 1986.

The best political risk score of 71/100 is achieved by Gambia in 1999, while the worst of 25/100 is recorded for Sierra Leone in 1993. Nigeria, reputed for being the largest economy in Africa, recorded the highest GDP of $502.94 billion in 2019, while the lowest GDP of $538.18 million was recorded by Guinea-Bissau in 1986. The kurtosis of POLRISK is approximately 3, indicating a mesokurtic data distribution shape. The implication of this is that POLRISK is relatively characterized by the normal distribution. The kurtosis values of all the other variables are greater than 3, which indicates that the shapes of their data distribution are leptokurtic. Furthermore, the skewness statistics show that all the variables (except POLRISK which is skewed to the left) are skewed to the right.

Moving to the lower compartment of Table 10.1, the correlation matrix of the variables in the study suggests that there is no evidence of multicollinearity. This is due to the very low values of the correlation coefficient among the variables, with the highest being 0.328 between FDI and TRADE, which is still very low and indicates no correlation. These correlation coefficient results imply that the analysis of the impact of political risk as a driver of FDI inflows to West Africa does not suffer from the issue of multicollinearity variations in FDI inflows in the sub-region.

10.4 Theoretical Framework and Model Specification

The theoretical framework for this study is predicated on the eclectic paradigm theory based on Dunning (1979) internalization theory, also known as the OLI model, which rests on a three-tiered framework, namely, ownership, location, and internalization (OLI). The OLI is an important framework for assessing whether prospective FDI projects are suitable and profitable. It suggests that for any FDI to benefit the investor, it must possess an ownership advantage, locational advantage, and internalization advantage. The concept of locational advantage is extended by

Table 10.1 Summary statistics of variables

Descriptive	FDI	POLRISK	GDP	TRADE	NATRES	INFRAST
Mean	2.215900	53.12134	31.66587	55.29884	9.616751	18.70078
Median	1.366025	52.95833	5.885419	53.28882	8.447161	18.08332
Maximum	32.30120	71.00000	502.9420	131.4854	31.79159	54.94827
Minimum	−28.62426	25.00000	0.538184	9.135846	1.294241	−2.424358
Std. Dev.	3.479597	8.161809	83.03795	18.55791	5.898394	8.442227
Skewness	1.132748	−0.218355	4.066666	1.013937	0.806040	1.358674
Kurtosis	34.06955	2.981659	19.84565	4.482902	3.264562	6.439865
Observations	428	428	428	428	428	428
Correlation						
FDI	1.000000					
POLRISK	0.240558	1.000000				
GDP	−0.040532	−0.228081	1.000000			
TRADE	0.328098	0.138082	−0.265863	1.000000		
NATRES	0.035761	−0.356392	0.179714	0.057224	1.000000	
INFRAST	0.253642	−0.11152	0.209801	0.068695	0.287508	1.000000

Note: *FDI* foreign direct investment inflows (% of GDP), *POLRISK* political risk score, *GDP* gross domestic product (constant 2015 US$), *TRADE* total trade (% of GDP), *NATRES* total natural resource rents (% of GDP), *INFR* investment in infrastructure (% of GDP)

Dunning (1998) with the addition of institutional factors to the existing economic factors. He argues that the higher the quality of institutions and economic facilities in an economy, the more attractive the economy to foreign investors because the investors consider their profitability to be positively related to institutional quality and sound macroeconomic indicators. His position is in line with North (1990) and Lucas (1993) that institutional factors, alongside purely economic factors, are crucial for an economy to attract FDI. Thus, the determinants of FDI inflow, based on Dunning (1998), Lucas (1993), and North (1990) propositions, comprise market size, other economic factors, and the quality of institutions of the investment destination. This can be expressed as follows:

$$\text{FDI} = f\left(\text{market size, macroeconomic stability, institutions}\right) \tag{10.1}$$

where FDI is foreign direct investment, market size is a key determinant of FDI and is measured by real GDP, macroeconomic stability is the country's economic situation and is proxied by economic variables which comprise trade openness, natural resources availability and investment in infrastructure, while institutions stand for political risk, as indicators of political risk as abovementioned have been used to measure the quality of institutions in the literature (Gazdar & Cherif, 2015; Hassan et al., 2019; Hassan, 2021; Law et al., 2018). Therefore, based on Eq. (10.1), the empirical model for this study is specified as follows:

$$\text{FDI}_{it} = \alpha_1 + \alpha_2\text{PR}_{it} + \alpha_3\text{GDP}_{it} + \alpha_4\text{TOP}_{it} + \alpha_5\text{NR}_{it} + \alpha_6\text{INF}_{it} + \epsilon_{it} \tag{10.2}$$

where FDI is FDI inflows, PR is political risk, GDP is real GDP, TOP is trade openness, NR is natural resources availability, ϵ is an error term, t and i are time index and cross-sectional index, respectively, while α_1, α_2, α_3, α_4, α_5, and α_6 are parameters to be estimated.

In estimating Eq. (10.2), all the variables are converted to their logarithm forms. This is to mitigate likely heteroscedasticity, handle possible outliers, and engender elasticity relationships (Ejemeyovwi et al., 2018).

10.5 Methods

10.5.1 Cross-Sectional Dependence and Panel Unit Root Tests

The implication of the presence of cross-sectional dependence (CD) in panel data has been explored increasingly in recent times as a way of avoiding misleading estimates in panel data analysis. According to Pesaran (2004), panel data often become cross-sectionally dependent due to idiosyncratic dependence, spatial dependence, and the error terms. Furthermore, De Hoyos and Sarafidis (2006) argue that increased interaction among countries, as well as financial integration, driven by globalization has increased the likelihood for CD, so much so, that CD is presently considered a basic feature, rather than an expectation in a panel (Turkay, 2017). In light of this, the econometric process begins with a CD test in the series, following the approach of Pesaran (2004).

A notable consequence of the presence of CD in panel data is that conventional unit root tests are predisposed to generating misleading results. This is because those tests are ineffectual in accommodating the size attributes of data and also could falsely reject the null when CD is present (Banerjee et al., 2001). To avoid such issues in this study, the Pesaran (2007) CADF and CIPS panel stationarity tests are conducted. The CADF test statistics are expressed thus:

$$\Delta Z_{it} = \beta_i + a_i z_{i,t-1} + \alpha_i \overline{z}_{t-1} + \sum_{j=0}^{k} b_{ij} \Delta \overline{z}_{t-j} + \sum_{j=1}^{k} \delta_{ij} \Delta z_{i,t-j} + \varepsilon_{it} \tag{10.3}$$

where $\overline{z}_{t-1}$ is the lagged level of cross-sectional averages, while $\Delta \overline{z}_{t-j}$ is first-order integration of every cross section.

Moreover, the CIPS test statistics are obtained from CADF as follows:

$$\text{CIPS} = N^{-1} \sum_{i=1}^{N} \text{CADF}_i \tag{10.4}$$

10.5.2 Panel Cointegration Test

Due to the inadequacy of the traditional panel unit root tests in handling key panel data issues of CD, serial correlation, and heteroscedasticity, the Westerlund (2007) test for cointegration is employed in this study. The ECM-based approach handles these issues effectively and is applicable in the case of the heterogeneous panels. It involves the computation of four test statistics. Two of them are based on group statistics (G_t and G_a), while the remaining two are predicated on panel statistics (P_t and P_a). It is estimated based on the following least-squares model:

$$\Delta Z_{it} = \rho_i' d_t + \delta_i \left(Z_{it-1} - \alpha_i' x_{it-1} \right) + \sum_{j=1}^{pi} \delta_{ij} \Delta z_{it-j} + \sum_{j=-p_i}^{pi} \theta_{ij} \Delta x_{i,t-j} + \varepsilon_{it} \tag{10.5}$$

For the group statistics (G_t and G_a), t-statistics are derived as follows:

$$G_t = \frac{1}{N} \sum_{i=1}^{N} \frac{\Psi_i}{SE(\Psi_i)} \tag{10.6}$$

$$G_a = \frac{1}{N} \sum_{i=1}^{N} \frac{TY}{\Psi_i'(1)} \tag{10.7}$$

Moreover, for the panel statistics (P_t and P_a), t-statistics are derived as thus:

$$P_t = \frac{\Psi_i}{SE(\Psi_i)} \tag{10.8}$$

$$P_a = T\Psi \tag{10.9}$$

where Ψ_i is the adjustment speed to long-run equilibrium.

10.5.3 Panel Regression

To compute long-run elasticities among the variables in Eq. (10.2), we employ the dynamic common correlated effects (DCCE) technique of estimation suggested by Chudik and Pesaran (2015). This approach is preferred to the traditional estimation methods because it accounts for several panel data estimation issues which are ignored by them. One such issue is CD which DCCE handles by including the logs and averages of the cross sections. Besides, it allows for heterogeneous slopes and through the recursive mean adjustment, can generate reliable outcomes in the face of a small sample (Chudik & Pesaran, 2015). It is also applicable to cases with unbalanced panels and structural breaks (Ditzen, 2016; Kapetanios et al., 2011).

The DCCE model for this study is specified in line with Chudik and Pesaran (2015) as follows:

$$\ln \text{FDI}_{it} = \alpha_i \ln \text{FDI}_{it-1} + \delta_i X_{it} + \sum_{p=0}^{P_T} \gamma_{\text{xip}} \overline{X}_{t-p} + \sum_{p=0}^{P_T} \gamma_{\text{yip}} \overline{X}_{t-p} + \mu_{it} \tag{10.10}$$

where ln FDI is the log of FDI and its lag is an independent variable, X_{it} is a set of the other independent variables, and P_T is the lag of cross-sectional averages.

Furthermore, to check the robustness of the DCCE estimates, the dynamic seemingly unrelated regression (DSUR) estimation procedure of Mark et al. (2005) is employed. This approach was developed by extending the single-equation DOLS, it is suited for panel data in which the time dimension is higher than the cross sections and it accounts for the problems of endogeneity, heterogeneity, and CD (Mark et al., 2005). Previous studies that have used the DSUR approach include Rua (2018) and Yang et al. (2021).

We also proceed to test for causality among the variables. The need for testing for this is motivated by Engle and Granger (1987), who argues that evidence of cointegration between variables implies the existence of at least one-way causality between them. Besides, information about causality among the variables can assist toward the right policy direction in driving FDI inflows. It could also guide policymakers on the role of political risk, market size, openness to international trade, natural resources exploitation, and infrastructure in galvanizing the economy through FDI. To this end, we apply the Dumitrescu and Hurlin (D-H) (2012) causality test, which overcomes the issues of heterogeneity and CD in panel data. The null assesses the non-homogeneous causality between the variables.

10.6 Results and Discussion

Table 10.2 presents the results of the Pesaran (2004) CD test conducted on the series, under the null that the series does not contain CD. As shown by the results, the null hypothesis is rejected for all the variables, indicating that all the variables are cross-sectionally dependent. Considering these results, conducting tests of stationarity based on conventional and first-generation unit root tests is not advised, as they may produce misleading results due to the presence of CD. Therefore, we employ Pesaran's (2007) second-generation CADF and CIPS panel unit root tests, which can handle CD issues. The results are presented in Table 10.3 and they show that all the variables are I (1) processes, as they become free from the unit root only after the first difference. In light of this, a test of cointegration needs to be carried out to determine whether the variables co-move in the long run (Table 10.3).

Table 10.4 presents the results of the cointegration test based on Westerlund (2007). The null hypothesis that the variables do not co-move in the long run is rejected by the two group statistics and one of the panel statistics, while only P_t

Table 10.2 Pesaran cross-sectional dependence test results

Variable	FDI	POLRISK	GDP	TRADE	NATRES	INFRAST
CD test	7.382***	15.293**	12.741***	10.635**	6.822**	8.357***
p-value	0.000	0.013	0.004	0.001	0.037	0.000

Note: *** and ** denote 1% and 5% significance levels, respectively
All variables are in logarithm forms
FDI foreign direct investment inflows (% of GDP), *POLRISK* political risk score, *GDP* gross domestic product (constant 2015 US$), *TRADE* total trade (% of GDP), *NATRES* total natural resource rents (% of GDP), *INFR* investment in infrastructure (% of GDP)

Table 10.3 Pesaran panel unit root tests

	CADF		CIPS	
	Level	1st difference	Level	1st difference
Foreign direct inv.	−0.934	−2.764***	−1.113	−4.381***
Political risk	−1.109	−3.293***	−2.331	−4.603***
GDP	−2.471	−4.616***	−2.070	−5.919***
Trade openness	−1.299	−3.528***	−1.504	−3.714***
Natural resources	−0.813	−2.196***	−1.914	−5.445***
Infrastructure	−1.822	−3.040***	−1.981	−3.201***

Note: *** denotes a 1% level of significance
All variables are in logarithm forms

accepts the null hypothesis. As 3 out of 4 statistics reject the null, it is concluded that cointegration exists among the variables.

Table 10.5 presents the outcomes of panel regressions based on DCCE and DSUR approaches. The DCCE estimates show that the lag of the dependent variable is positive and significant at the 1% level. This indicates that FDI inflows are persistent and path-dependent in the West African sub-region. As such, the previous trend of FDI inflows in the countries has a positive impact on the current level of the variable. The log of political risk is positive and significant at 5%, which implies that improvement in the political risk rating or score is associated with an increase in FDI inflows. Specifically, a 1% increase in political risk score (i.e., a decrease in political risk) leads to an increase in FDI inflows by 0.38%. This finding suggests that if other factors are held constant, reducing the political risk of the West African sub-region engenders increased inflows of FDI. It is also noteworthy that of all the variables in the model, the coefficient of political turn out to be the highest. This is indicative of the huge relative role that political risk plays in influencing the inflows of FDI. This research outcome agrees with extant studies such as Almahmoud (2014), Bitar et al. (2020), Brada et al. (2006), Hammoudeh et al. (2011), Salehnia et al. (2019), and Sissani and Balkacem (2014), which argue that political risk is a key influencer of FDI inflows.

The log of GDP is positive and significant at the 1% level, which implies that GDP exerts a direct impact on FDI inflows. Precisely, a 1% increase in GDP is associated with a 0.16% rise in FDI inflows, with other factors remaining the same. This result suggests that market size remains a crucial influencing factor regarding the

Table 10.4 Westerlund panel cointegration test

Test	Value	*Z*-value	*p*-value
G_t	−8.164***	−7.401	0.000
G_a	−13.532**	6.339	0.024
P_t	−16.307	−8.849	0.161
P_a	−10.612***	4.503	0.000

Note: *** and ** represent 1% and 5% levels of significance, respectively

Table 10.5 Panel regression results

	DCCE		DSUR	
	Coefficient	*p*-value	Coefficient	*p*-value
FDI (−1)	1.218***	0.000		
Political risk	0.381**	0.017	0.274***	0.000
GDP	0.161***	0.000	0.093***	0.000
Trade openness	0.127*	0.063	0.180**	0.049
Natural resources	0.292***	0.003	0.109**	0.014
Infrastructure	0.010	0.131	−0.002	0.155

Note: Dependent variable = FDI; ***, ** and * represent 1%, 5% and 1% levels of significance respectively
All variables are in logarithm forms

inflow of FDI in West Africa. This result is not surprising because market availability is usually considered a key factor in deciding investment destination by foreign investors, and this has been established by previous studies such as Khan and Akbar (2013), Meyer and Habanabakize (2018), Sabir and Khan (2018), and Salem and Younis (2021). Trade openness is positive and weakly significant, indicating that allowing more international trade in West Africa is associated with the increased influx of foreign investors. Precisely, the DCCE estimate implies that holding other factors constant, a 1% increase in total international trade increases FDI inflows by about 0.13%. This research outcome supports previous findings by Anyanwu (2012), Anyanwu and Yameogo (2015a), and Emediegwu and Edo (2017) on the impact of trade openness as a determinant of FDI in West Africa.

Natural resources are also found as a key determinant of FDI in the West African sub-region, considering the variable's positive and significant coefficient, which is only second in magnitude to political risk. Particularly, if we hold other variables constant, a 1% increase in natural resource availability would enhance the inflow of FDI by 0.29%. This result implies that the availability of natural resources is a crucial driver of FDI in the countries, and it corroborates previous studies that posit that natural resources promote the inflows of FDI (Anyanwu, 2012; Anyanwu & Yameogo, 2015a; Sane, 2016); however, the result is at variance with the finding of Asiedu (2013) that natural resource availability stymies FDI inflows in developing countries, which is deemed an FDI-natural resource curse situation. Finally, investment in infrastructure is not significant and this implies that infrastructure changes do not influence the level of FDI inflows in the countries.

Table 10.6 Dumitrescu-Hurlin panel causality test

Variable	FDI	POLRISK	GDP	TRADE	NATRES	INFRAST
FDI		2.139	1.838**	2.163	0.386	2.607*
		[0.135]	[0.039]	[0.120]	[1.473]	[0.053]
POLRISK	2.417***		2.607**	4.066*	3.134	1.316
	[0.000]		[0.018]	[0.062]	[0.531]	[0.224]
GDP	2.140***	1.360		0.937***	0.215**	1.283**
	[0.000]	[0.241]		[0.000]	[0.010]	[0.029]
TRADE	0.354	3.218	0.787		0.217	1.360
	[0.318]	[0.612]	[0.418]		[0.243]	[1.216]
NATRES	5.261***	1.449***	2.341***	1.384*		0.144**
	[0.003]	[0.000]	[0.006]	[0.066]		[0.037]
INFRAST	0.762	0.831	0.162*	1.631	0.617	
	[0.185]	[0.162]	[0.054]	[0.128]	[0.109]	

Note: ***, **, and * represent 1%, 5%, and 1% levels of significance, respectively; *p*-values are in brackets
All variables are in logarithm forms

Overall, the DSUR estimates are like those of the DCCE regression. Therefore, the same discussion and interpretation are applicable, and this affirms the robustness of the outcomes from the study.

Table 10.6 presents the results of the D-H panel causality test. This test is important because information about causality among the variables can assist toward the right policy direction in driving FDI inflows. The results could also guide policymakers on the role of political risk, market size, openness to international trade, natural resources exploitation, and infrastructure in galvanizing the economy through FDI. As displayed in the table, GDP has a bidirectional causal relationship with FDI, natural resources, and infrastructure. This suggests feedback exists between GPD and the variables, as well as the central role that market size plays in the mix. Furthermore, there is unidirectional causality from political risk to FDI, GDP, and trade openness. As this result indicates that political risk Granger causes FDI and its important determinants, it aligns with the DCCE and DSUR estimates that identified political risk as a crucial driver of FDI. Besides, natural resources availability Granger causes FDI, trade openness, infrastructure, and political risk. Finally, there is evidence of unidirectional causality from FDI and GDP to infrastructure and trade openness, respectively.

10.7 Conclusion

Investigation into the factors that drive FDI inflows has grown massively over the years, especially in the context of developing regions of the world, and this is due to the crucial role that FDI plays in the development process. Though several factors have been identified as important promoters of FDI, the debate remains unremitting because many research outcomes are mixed and inconclusive. Besides, most studies did not consider the peculiarities and heterogeneities of the countries in larger regional groupings. Therefore, this study focuses on the West African sub-region by examining the determinants of FDI inflows with a particular focus on the role of political risk over the period 1986–2020. Both DCCE and DSUR methods of panel data estimation were employed due to their ability to overcome many panels' econometric issues, especially CD. Furthermore, the D-H panel causality test was conducted to test for causality among the variables.

The research outcomes from both DCCE and DSUR establish that political risk matters for FDI inflows as improvement in political risk rating is associated with increased FDI inflows. Furthermore, the market potential in the countries is an important driver of FDI, as GDP is found to have a positive relationship with FDI. Natural resource availability is another variable with a huge impact on FDI inflows, while trade openness weakly determines the level of FDI inflows. Contrariwise, investment in infrastructure does not have any impact on FDI inflows as its coefficient is not significant. Meanwhile, the results from the D-H panel causality test reveal both GDP and natural resources to be quite influential in the mix of the variables. While GDP has a bidirectional causal relationship with FDI, natural resources and infrastructure, natural resources Granger almost all the other variables, namely, FDI, political risk, trade openness, and infrastructure.

These results underscore the need for West African countries to deliberately pursue greater political stability and achieve higher political risk scores. This can be achieved through a concerted effort by all the countries under the Economic Community of West African States (ECOWAS) and the West African Economic and Monetary Union (WAEMU), as evidenced in Anyanwu and Yameogo (2015a, b). The market potentials of the countries also need to be enhanced by ensuring the stability of macroeconomic and corporate structures in the countries. Furthermore, the exploitation of natural resources in the countries should be embedded in a sound institutional framework to enhance competitiveness in respect of FDI attraction.

References

Agmon, T. (1985). *Political economy and risk in world financial markets*. Lexington Books.

Akinlo, A. E. (2003). *Globalization, international investment and stock market growth in Sub-Saharan Africa. Institute of Developing Economies VRF Monograph Series* (Vol. 382). Jetro.

Akinlo, A. E. (2004). Foreign direct investment and growth in Nigeria: An empirical investigation. *Journal of Policy Modeling, 26*(2), 627–639.

Almahmoud, A. I. (2014). Country risk ratings and stock market movements: Evidence from emerging economy. *International Journal of Economics and Finance, 6*(10), 88–96.

Anyanwu, J. C. (2012). Why does foreign direct investment go where it goes? New evidence from African countries. *Annals of Economics and Finance, 13*(2), 425–462.

Anyanwu, J. C., & Erhijakpor, A. E. O. (2004). Trends and determinants of foreign direct investment in Africa. *West African Journal of Monetary and Economic Integration*, Second Half, 21–44.

Anyanwu, J. C., & Yameogo, N. D. (2015a). What drives foreign direct investments into West Africa? An empirical investigation. *African Development Review, 27*(3), 199–215.

Anyanwu, J. C., & Yameogo, N. D. (2015b). Regional comparison of foreign direct investment to Africa: An empirical analysis. *African Development Review, 27*(4), 345–363.
Asiedu, E. (2013). *Foreign direct investment, natural resources and institutions*. Working Paper, International Growth Centre.
Banerjee, A., Cockerell, L., & Russell, B. (2001). An I (2) analysis of inflation and the markup. *Journal of Applied Econometrics, 16*(3), 221–240.
Bitar, N., Hamadeh, M., & Khoueiri, R. (2020). Impact of political instability on foreign direct investment in Lebanon. *Asian Social Science, 16*(1), 41–48.
Brada, J. C., Kutan, A. M., & Yigit, T. M. (2006). The effects of transition and political instability on foreign direct investment inflows. *The Economics of Transition, 14*(4), 649–680. https://doi.org/10.1111/j.1468-0351.2006.00272.x
Busse, M., & Hefeker, C. (2007). Political risk, institutions and foreign direct investment. *European Journal of Political Economy, 23*(2), 397–415. https://doi.org/10.1016/j.ejpoleco.2006.02.003
Center for International Peace Operations (ZIF). (2012). *The West African region: Between peace dividends and the road to recovery*. ZIF.
Chudik, A., & Pesaran, M. H. (2015). Common correlated effects estimation of heterogeneous dynamic panel data models with weakly exogenous regressors. *Journal of Economics, 188*(2), 393–420.
De Hoyos, R. E., & Sarafidis, V. (2006). Testing for cross-sectional dependence in panel-data models. *Stata Journal, 6*(4), 482–496.
Ditzen, J. (2016). xtdcce: Estimating dynamic common correlated effects in Stata. SEEC discussion papers, 1601.
Dowd, C. (2013). Tracking Islamist militia and rebel groups. Research Brief 8, Climate Change and African Political Stability (CCAPS) and Armed Conflict Location and Event Data Project (ACLED), Austin, TX.
Dumitrescu, E. I., & Hurlin, C. (2012). Testing for Granger non-causality in heterogeneous panels. *Economic Modelling, 29*(4), 1450–1460.
Dunning, J. H. (1979). Explaining changing patterns of international production: In defence of the eclectic theory. *Oxford Bulletin of Economics and Statistics, 41*, 269–295.
Dunning, J. H. (1998). Location and the multinational enterprise: A neglected factor? *Journal of International Business Studies, 29*(1), 45–66.
Ejemeyovwi, J. O., Osabuohien, E. S., & Osabohien, R. (2018). ICT investments, human capital development and institutions in ECOWAS. *International Journal of Economic and Business Research, 5*(4), 463–474.
Emediegwu, L., & Edo, S. (2017). The effect of corruption on foreign direct investment in West African sub-region. *West African Financial and Economic Review, 17*(2), 119–140.
Engle, R. F., & Granger, C. W. J. (1987). Cointegration and error correction: Representation, estimation, and testing. *Econometrica, 55*(2), 251–276.
Fragile States Index. (2021). *United States fund for peace*. 20 May 2021.
Gazdar, K., & Cherif, M. (2015). Institutions and the finance-growth nexus: Empirical evidence from MENA countries. *Borsa Istanbul Review, 15*(3), 137–160.
Goswami, G. G., & Haider, S. (2014). Does political risk deter FDI inflow? An analytical approach using panel data and factor analysis. *Journal of Economic Studies, 41*(2), 233–252.
Hammoudeh, S., Sari, R., Liu, T., & Uzunkaya, M. (2011). The dynamics of BRICS's country risk ratings and stock markets, U.S. stock market and oil price.mn. https://doi.org/10.2139/ssrn.1894210
Hassan, A. S. (2021). Foreign aid and economic growth in Nigeria: The role of institutional quality. *Studies of Applied Economics, 39*(3), 1–16.
Hassan, A. S., Meyer, D. F., & Kot, S. (2019). Effect of institutional quality and wealth from oil revenue on economic growth in oil-exporting developing countries. *Sustainability, 11*, 3635.
Hayakawa, K., Kimura, F., & Lee, H. H. (2013). How does country risk matter for foreign direct investment? *The Developing Economies, 51*(1), 60–78.

Human Rights Watch. (2011, May 17). *Nigeria: Post-election violence killed 800*. http://www.hrw.org/news/2011/05/16/nigeria-post-election-violence-killed-800

Kapetanios, G., Pesaran, M. H., & Yamagata, T. (2011). Panels with nonstationary multifactor error structures. *Journal of Economics, 160*(2), 326–348.

Khan, A. (2007). *Foreign direct investment and economic growth: The role of domestic financial sector*. Pakistan Institute of Development Economics (PIDE) Working Paper.

Khan, M. M., & Akbar, M. I. (2013). The impact of political risk on foreign direct investment. *International Journal of Economics and Finance, 5*(8), 147–156. https://doi.org/10.5539/ijef.v5n8p147

Koopmans, T. C. (1965). On the concept of optimal economic growth. In *Study week on the econometric approach to development planning* (pp. 225–300). North-Holland Publishing Co..

Krifa-Schneider, H., & Matei, I. (2010). Business climate, political risk and FDI in developing countries: Evidence from panel data. *International Journal of Economics and Finance, 2*(5), 54–65.

Law, S. H., Kutan, A. M., & Naseem, N. A. M. (2018). The role of institutions in finance curse: Evidence from international data. *Journal of Comparative Economics, 46*(1), 174–191.

Lucas, R. E. (1993). On the determinants of direct foreign investment: Evidence from East and Southeast Asia. *World Development, 21*(3), 391–406.

M'Cormack, F. (2011). *Conflict dynamics in West Africa*. Helpdesk research report, October 17. Governance and Social Development Resource Centre, University of Birmingham.

Marc, A., Verjee, N., & Mogaka, S. (2015). *The challenge of stability and security in West Africa*. Africa Development Forum, a co-publication of Agence Française de Développement and the World Bank.

Mark, N. C., Ogaki, M., & Sul, D. (2005). Dynamic seemingly unrelated cointegrating regressions. *Review of Economic Studies, 72*, 797–820.

Meyer, D. F., & Habanabakize, T. (2018). An analysis of the relationship between foreign direct investment (FDI), political risk and economic growth in South Africa. *Business and Economic Horizons (BEH), 14*, 777–788.

Nassour, A., Meftah, S., & Mirani, S. H. (2020). Does political risk affect foreign direct investment inflows? Empirical evidence from selected MENA economies. *Studies of Applied Economics, 38*(3), 1–13.

North, D. (1990). *Institutions, institutional change and economic performance*. Cambridge University Press.

O'Regan, D., & Thompson, P. (2013). *Advancing stability and reconciliation in Guinea Bissau: Lessons from Africa's first Narco-state*. ACSS special report 2, Africa Center for Strategic Studies.

OECD. (2018, December 4–5). *FDI in fragile and conflict affected economies in the Middle East and North Africa: Trends and policies*. Background note, Islamic Bank, Jeddah, Kingdom of Saudi Arabia.

Pesaran, M. H. (2004). *General diagnostic tests for cross section dependence in panels, CESifo Working Papers No. 1233*, pp. 255–260.

Pesaran, M. H. (2007). A simple panel unit root test in the presence of cross-section dependence. *Journal of Applied Economics, 22*(2), 265–312.

Rafat, M., & Farahani, M. (2019). The country risks and foreign direct investment (FDI). *Iranian Economic Review, 23*(1), 235–260.

Rappaport, J. (2000). *How does openness to capital flows affect growth?* Federal Reserve Bank of Kansas City: Mimeo.

Robock, S. H., & Simmonds, K. (1973). *International business and multinational enterprise*. R. Irwin.

Root, F. R. (1987). Entry strategies for International markets, 2nd ed, Lexington Books, Josey-Bass: San Francisco, p 128–129.

Rua, A. (2018). Modelling currency demand in a small open economy within a monetary union. *Economic Modelling, 74*, 88–96.

Sabir, S., & Khan, A. (2018). Impact of political stability and human capital on foreign direct investment in East Asia & Pacific and South Asian countries. *Asian Journal of Economic Modelling, 6*(3), 245–256.
Salehnia, N., Alavijeh, N. K., & Shadmehri, M. T. A. (2019). The effect of economic, financial, and political risks on foreign direct investment in selected countries of the MENA region. In *3rd International conference on modern developments in management, economics and accounting*, Tehran, Iran.
Salem, R., & Younis, R. (2021). The effect of country risk on foreign direct investment: Evidence from Egypt. *Scientific Journal for Economic and Commerce, 51*(2), 276–243.
Sane, M. (2016). Determinants of foreign direct investment inflows to ECOWAS member countries: Panel data modelling and estimation. *Modern Economy, 7*, 1517–1542.
Sissani, M., & Belkacem, Z. (2014). The effect of political risk on foreign direct investment: The case of Algeria. *Hyperion Economic Journal, 2*(3), 29–35.
Souaré, I. K. (2010). *A critical assessment of security challenges in West Africa*. The Africa Portal: Centre for International Governance Innovation. https://www.africaportal.org/publications/a-critical-assessment-of-security-challenges-in-west-africa/
Souria, H., & Ghani, C. (2018). *The impact of country risk on FDI in the MENA region: Panel data analysis on OPEC and non-OPEC countries*. https://www.researchgate.net/publication/327069449_the_impact_of_country_risk_on_fdi_in_the_mena_region_panel_data_analysis__on_opec_and_non-opec_countries. Report, October 18. Institute of Security Studies.
Topal, M. H., & Gul, Ö. S. (2016). The effect of country risk on foreign direct investment: A dynamic panel data analysis for developing countries. *Journal of Economics Library, 3*(1), 141–155.
Turkay, M. (2017). Heterogeneity across emerging market central bank reaction functions. *Central Bank Review, 17*(3), 111–116.
Ugwuegbe, S. U., Modebe, N. J., & Onyeanu, E. (2014). The impact and foreign direct investment on capital formation in Nigeria: A cointegration approach. *International Journal of Economics, Finance and Management Science, 2*(2), 188–196.
UNCTAD. (2021). *Investment trends monitor. Issue 38, January 2021*. United Nations.
[UNODC] United Nations Office on Drugs and Crime. (2013). *Transnational organized crime in West Africa: A threat assessment*. UNODC.
Westerlund, J. (2007). Testing for error correction in panel data. *Oxford Bulletin of Economics and Statistics, 69*(6), 709–748.
Yang, B., Jahanger, A., & Ali, M. (2021). Remittance inflows affect the ecological footprint in BICS countries: Do technological innovation and financial development matter? *Environmental Science and Pollution Research, 28*, 2348–2350.

Chapter 11
Comparative Analysis of Socioeconomic Change and Inclusion in Ghana: A Gendered Empirical Analysis Using Ghana Living Standards 1988 and Ghana Socioeconomic Panel Survey 2019

Tawonga Rushambwa

Abstract The study uses the Ghana Living Standards Survey (GLSS) of 1987 and the 2019 Ghana Socioeconomic Panel Survey (GSPS) data sets for building a comparative descriptive socioeconomic profile of individuals across gender and the influence of other demographic variables. Dimension reduction methods are employed to reduce the number of variables in analysis while covering a larger set of aspects of socioeconomic analysis. The empirical analysis is directed toward contributing to socioeconomic modeling for decision-making with the findings of the analysis being the basis for contributions both to the research theory and practice. The study's results and contribution are important as existing socioeconomic dynamics among Ghanaians are important in mapping adaptation strategies in a dynamically changing environment. The study found the persistence of socioeconomic disparities across gender, regional location, and social marginalization which were more pronounced in the 2019 dataset. The study also observed a strong influence of the physical divide measured by socioeconomic performance, social marginalization, and education attainment as influencing access to digital technologies using the 2019 panel dataset. It was concluded that the limiting socioeconomic development of post-independence Ghana is important in shaping the trajectory of future change and living standards for Ghanaians given the importance of the physical divide in adaptation to external changes affecting welfare.

Keywords Africa · Development · Economic inclusion · Ghana · Gender

T. Rushambwa (✉)
University of KwaZulu-Natal, Durban, South Africa

D. Mhlanga, E. Ndhlovu (eds.), *Economic Inclusion in Post-Independence Africa*, Advances in African Economic, Social and Political Development,
https://doi.org/10.1007/978-3-031-31431-5_11

11.1 Introduction

The socioeconomic analysis of individuals and /or regions refers to a multidimensional approach incorporating social, economic, and cultural factors in seeking an understanding of influences shaping individuals' and communities' developmental trajectories and outcomes (Krishnan, 2010). Socioeconomic analyses have been conducted in various studies to model the effect of policies or interventions on the social and economic characteristics of individuals, households, and regions that act as proxies for changes in qualitative or material welfare. Studies have modeled the influence of socioeconomic status on health-seeking behavior (Uzochukwu & Onwujekwe, 2004; Ahmed et al., 2005; Li et al., 2020), and more recently, socioeconomic analysis has been used in modeling outcomes and effects of digital transformation processes (Afonasova et al., 2019; Strohmaier et al., 2019; Aly, 2022). Other studies have employed socioeconomic analysis to assess regional disparities in human development (Mohiuddin & Hashia, 2012; Shraim et al., 2017; Guilmoto & Dumont, 2019). The studies are varied as are the methods that have been used in the construction of socioeconomic indices and the choices in the variables that have been used as socioeconomic indicators.

Empirical evidence suggests that socioeconomic factors of individuals, communities, and regions are inversely related to developmental outcomes such as educational aptitude and performance, health, and so on (Mohiuddin & Hashia, 2012; Shraim et al., 2017; Zhou & Liu, 2019; Li et al., 2020). Socioeconomic analysis as such is a multidimensional approach to understanding individual and group welfare dynamics using socioeconomic factors such as income, education level, occupational composition, labor market participation, household characteristics, infrastructure, and other variables (Zagórski, 1985; Havard et al., 2008; Pampalon et al., 2009; Krishnan, 2010). The multiplicity of empirical studies that have used socioeconomic modeling and spanning several decades demonstrate the usefulness of the indicators in understanding changes in human development.

In this chapter, we implement socioeconomic analysis in an original research study to understand differences in socioeconomic performance in Ghana between the years 1988 and 2019. We focus on the distribution of three main constructs of the study: the socioeconomic index; the social inclusion and exclusion index; and the digital access index across gender, spatial location, and Age. In undertaking socioeconomic modeling, we implement the Zagórski (1985) modeling approach in the analysis of Ghana's socioeconomic data for 1988 and 2019 to model a comparative analysis of socioeconomic change over demographic variables and project the implications of observed socioeconomic differentiation on the future of Ghana society. In the study, we observed differences in socioeconomic performance between the two periods differentiated by gender, spatiality, and age. We also observed heterogeneity in the distribution of socioeconomic index, social inclusion and exclusion, and digital access in 2019, indicating spread among the greater population than in 1988. However, gender and age and regional disparities remain entrenched in 2019 as in 1988 with implications for future socioeconomic progress given the influence of digital transformation on existing socioeconomic patterns (Afonasova et al., 2019).

This chapter is divided as follows: Sect. 11.2 is a summarized review of Ghana's socioeconomic development, Sect. 11.3 and its sub-sections discuss the methods employed in the study, Sect. 11.4 is a presentation of the results, and Sect. 11.5 is a discussion of the results, literature integration, and conclusions of the study.

11.2 Socioeconomic Change in Ghana Since 1987

The 1997 Ghana Human Development Report (HDR) documented the country's difficult and equivocal development experience since the early 1960s, which showed a trajectory of consistent decline from middle-income status and promising socio-economic advance toward lower middle income and poor socioeconomic change (Tettey et al., 2003). In the early 1960s, the high middle-income status of Ghana was complemented by a highly competitive educational system in West Africa with the country reporting the largest number of university graduates (Tettey et al., 2003). By 1997, changes in health among Ghanaians had remained poor with high rates of infant and maternal morbidity, low access to modern healthcare and insurance, and declining per capita public health expenditure and while the education system had expanded covering a larger proportion of the population, quality had declined with evidence of functional illiteracy. By 1997, nearly 50% of Ghanaians were living in absolute poverty, with high levels of unemployment, poor levels of health, and illiteracy. The geography of poverty by the late 1990s was both a rural and an urban phenomenon, with over 20% of urban households being characterized as poor (Takyi & Addai, 2003).

Two decades after independence, the economy was on the precipice of imminent collapse, widespread hunger, and deprivation with attempts at economic recovery undertaken through the growth economic recovery program motivated by the World Bank and IMF's structural adjustment programs. The program was accompanied by sharp declines in standard of living and welfare losses, through the decline in formal wage employment and public sector spending cuts, per capita household income plummeted. The Program of Action to Mitigate the Social Costs of Adjustment (PAMSCAD) was a policy approach aimed at reversing widespread socioeconomic losses which had been experienced under the earlier program (Takyi & Addai, 2003). The 1990s were characterized by attempts at economic recovery to improve living conditions among Ghanaians, while marked political transformation toward democracy became marked with political contestation and governmental transition. The challenges of socioeconomic and human development decline continued through the twenty-first century with Ghana in the early decades being increasingly characterized by uneven economic performance creating challenges for development programs. The deteriorating material conditions of life for the majority of Ghanaians became marked as the century wore on (Tettey et al., 2003).

In the early post-independence years, Ghana adopted several poorly planned interventionist policies oriented toward an urban industry with import substitution directed at replacing manufactured imports with locally produced goods. Such policies were accompanied by political instability and violent power transitions from the mid-1960s to the early 1980s. Economic liberalization policies in the 1980s were a response to a rapidly deteriorating economic landscape with worsening local social and economic conditions. The key measures of human development, namely, per capita income, health (life expectancy, undernourishment, child mortality), and educational attainment (literacy and schooling) demonstrated marked deterioration (Todaro & Smith, 2012).

The 2010 HDR placed Ghana as a medium human development country, with an HDI of 0.526 when compared to its 1990 value of 0.360, showing slight progress in human development, and this has also been accompanied by institutional quality improvement. However, using the New Human Development Index (NHDI), for the same data, Ghana was ranked among countries with low human development (0.467), low average life expectancy (57.1), low mean years of schooling (7.1), and a non-income HDI value of 0.556 (Todaro & Smith, 2012). The Gini index reflecting income inequality in Ghana was 36.0 in 1987 and rose to 42.80 and 43.50 in 2005 and 2016, respectively, showing that between 1987 and 2016, uneven development in Ghana has resulted in income inequality among Ghanaians (World Bank, 2022). Thus, over the period, social (education and health) and economic (income) inequalities make countries vulnerable to external forces leading to an exacerbation of these existing inequalities (Aryeetey & Kanbur, 2017). Access to quality education, healthcare, and health insurance are indicators of both human development and, more importantly, are fundamental measures of social inequalities in society. The decline of access to these aspects of human development thus showed that the changes have resulted in growing marginalization and social exclusion among Ghanaians. Urban socioeconomic development has been counteracted by growing urban poverty (Aryeetey & Kanbur, 2017).

External influences can be seen to have shaped Ghana's post-independence society. From an economic perspective, depressed commodity prices, poor access to capital markets, and economic policies worsened socioeconomic outcomes. However, coupled with these were internal factors primarily, political instability following independence, public mismanagement, economic stagnation (over-reliance on primary products without diversifying), urban bias in development planning, and social inequities influenced by custom and traditions and population growth (Takyi & Addai, 2003). We argue in this study that external factors are exacerbated by internal factors such as socioeconomic processes and demographic changes. Post-independence governments in Ghana have made policy instruments to solve divided developmental challenges affecting mostly rural areas, and increasing rural-to-urban migration, such as health decay, worsening poverty, poor access to health care and education, poor public service provision (water, sanitation, and modern energy), and poor communication networks. Despite these efforts, the shape of divided development remains, with worsening economic performance having worsened rural socioeconomic conditions. The depth of poverty, poor health, and environmental conditions have continued to deepen (Adjei & Buor, 2012). Socioeconomic progress as measured by improvements in health, environment (housing infrastructure, access to water and sanitation), income, education levels, social networks, and access to developmental opportunities shape the level of human capital endowments of the individual and thus the shape of socioeconomic mobility.

11.3 Data and Methods

11.3.1 Design

In undertaking a comparative analysis, the study adopted a descriptive quantitative approach in which parameters measuring distribution such as mean, median, standard deviation, and percentiles are computed. In a descriptive comparative study, the investigation considers non-manipulated variables to consider the nature of the variables and the differences in their difference based on reference categories (Creswell & Creswell, 2017). In the design, the first stage of the descriptive design was a descriptive-analytical approach in which variables were described through further analysis to assess the areas where differences lay across gender and other variables, and in the second stage, such differences were contrasted across time while accounting for possible changes in the matrix of differences. In this study, while assessing the distributional properties of the variables, comparative descriptive analysis was carried out by comparing differences in gender and gender-weighted demographic variables to assess how socioeconomic status, social inclusion, and access to digital technology and skills have changed between 1988 and 2019.

11.3.2 Socioeconomic Analysis Approach

Various studies have employed various approaches to socioeconomic analysis influenced mostly by available data, the focus of the studies, and more important theoretical considerations between hypothesized values and an indicator of interest such as health, social mobility, and so forth of the target group (Betti & Lemmi, 2021). With data considerations, researchers have mostly considered measures of occupational status, educational attainment, access to health care, level of poverty, access to health care, assets and finance, nutrition and household income or expenditure, and household-level infrastructure (Vyas & Kumaranayake, 2006). Some studies have used these variables in bivariate and regression-based models in testing an eliminated target variable against the rest of the socioeconomic variables and assessing the distribution of variance using post hoc analysis (Ahmed et al., 2005; Adjei & Buor, 2012; Guilmoto & Dumont, 2019; Strohmaier et al., 2019). Other studies have used raw variables to assess the impact of policies, development trajectories, and exogenous factors on these socioeconomic variables (Popova & Bogacheva, 2017). These methods have proven to be effective and insightful where quality data have been available, particularly in upper-middle-income countries and the developed world.

Challenges with access to data on various socioeconomic indicators have contributed to innovation in socioeconomic analysis with recourse to the use of multiple variables to generate a composite proxy. Innovative studies have used subjective measures of well-being where objective data in target variables has not been available and made significant contributions (Posel & Rogan, 2016; Posel, 2021). However, the majority of studies have used variations of socioeconomic analysis employing proxy variables to measure the various aspects of socioeconomic indicators. Household-level assets and infrastructure have been used to estimate household income (Vyas & Kumaranayake, 2006; Havard et al., 2008; Krishnan, 2010). In this study, for data considerations, recourse is made to the implementation of the second approach where multiple proxy variables are used to an individual's economic, occupational, and educational profile to construct a composite index for socioeconomic status.

As discussed in the data, this study uses two-panel data sets, the 1988 and 2019 Ghana Panel surveys, to undertake a comparative socioeconomic analysis. Several challenges arise such as different measuring methods for the same variables between both waves, changes in metrics, social attitudes, and valuations which can present challenges in the methodological approach as such changes are factors for univariate and bivariate analysis. Composite indexes can eliminate differences in these and create comparable measures for an indicator or group performance. Three primary indices are constructed for comparative analysis, the socioeconomic index measuring a household's socioeconomic score, the social inclusion index measuring participation in institutions such as labor markets and access to services, and the digital index which assesses access to any form of digital asset or skills. In creating these indices, any demographic variables were eliminated to avoid correlations in group analysis, also cases with missing values above 20% were eliminated from the analysis. Principal components analysis,[1] a method of dimensional reduction was used in the construction of the indices and we will discuss its applications.

Principal components analysis is a multivariate technique to reduce the dimensionality of a multivariate data set while accounting for as much of the original variation in the variables as possible in the dataset. The new set of variables called components are linear combinations of the original variables that are uncorrelated and each accounts for variation in the original variables (Everitt & Hothorn, 2011). The components can be used to create new variables using component scores based on variables in each component with the highest loading and use these new variables in the analysis. The component scores can be used in creating a composite

[1] For an in-depth discussion of principal components analysis see: (Vehkalahti & Everitt, 2018), multivariate analysis for the behavioral sciences.

index using the summation of the weighted component scores proposed by Zagórski (1985) as follows:

$$\text{Composite Index} = \Sigma \frac{1}{2}\left(\left(\frac{(\%)\text{component}}{\%\text{Comulative var}}\right) * \text{Componet Score}\right)$$

The use of principal components analysis in this study is based on the assumption that the first few components account for a substantial proportion of the variation in the original variables ($x_1, x_2, \ldots, x_n$). This is useful to this study since the goal is to reduce the dimensional of multiple proxy variables to create a robust composite measure. Since most of the variables in the datasets used in this study were factor variables with multiple categories, they were reduced to binary (0–1) variables to fit in a Cartesian plane, and be used in principal components analysis as continuous variables, which strategy has been employed in other studies (Vyas & Kumaranayake, 2006; Odeku & Meyer, 2019). Two critical issues were also considered with the PCA methodology, choice of components and accounting for differences in measurement scales among variables. Theoretically, all components were retained whose eigenvalue (a measure of variance contribution for each component, the larger the eigenvalue the larger the variance) was at least equal to 1 (Krishnan, 2010). Since the variables were composed of different measurement scales, the theoretical premise of using the correlation matrix in deriving the principal components was implemented since it accounts for differences in metrics when deriving component loadings (Jolliffe, 2002). With these design premises, PCA was implemented on a two-stage basis, in which all the selected variables were used, with the elimination method retaining components with an eigenvalue of at least 1. Principal components analysis was then run on the same variables with the retained components, and subsequent elimination of all variables with loading values less than 0.35. Principal components analysis was then implemented with components meeting the threshold retained and factor score calculated on the principal components as new variables based on the variable with the highest loading for the component. Finally, summation was then used in creating composite indices used in the comparative analysis.

11.3.3 Data

In this study, we employed two datasets, the 1988 first round of the Ghana Living Standards Survey (GLSS) designed by the World Bank to monitor income, expenditure, and poverty trends and the Ghana Socioeconomic Panel Survey (GSPS) of 2018–2019. The GLSS 1988 was designed to provide the government with data to track and measure the living standards of the population and the trajectory of change in living standards. The dataset provides information on aspects of Ghanaian household economic and social activities and is collected at three levels: the individual, household, and community (Ghana Statistical Office, 2008). The GSPS uses individuals and households as units of analysis and collects data on household assets, economic activity, and health and social characteristics of these households and individuals. The dataset is nationally representative (Ghana Institute of Statistical and Economic Research, 2021).

11.3.4 Core Variables and Data Analysis

The analysis of the data in this study was conducted using the STATA 17.0 (Version 17.0, College Station, Texas) software for quantitative data analysis and the level of significance for all tests was set at $p < 0.5$. The comparative analysis focused on three indices, the socioeconomic index, the social inclusion index, and the education and skills index. For the 2019 dataset, a digital index was created which was then assessed on educational outcomes. From an array of variables measuring income, expenditure, household composition, housing characteristics, sanitation, and household infrastructures, for the 1988 and the 2019 data, household composition, housing characteristics, and household infrastructures were consistent in determining socioeconomic status. For both datasets, social inclusion was consistently measured through access to services, access to institutions, personal facilities, and networks, and these were consistent across all datasets. The educational index for both datasets compared educational attainment. The four indices were assessed in their distribution across gender and other demographic variables. Decomposed group analysis was then carried out to assess differences in the indices across gender and other demographic variables with the results presented in tables and bar charts. The analysis presented traces the mean of the indices as the parameter of interest.

11.4 Results: Ghana Living Standards Survey, 1988 Socioeconomic and Social Inclusion Index

11.4.1 General Distribution of Socioeconomic Performance, 1988 Versus 2019

Figure 11.1 shows the overall distribution of the socioeconomic index between 1988 and 2019. In 1988, the bulk of the population was concentrated on the lower end of the scale, while the 2019 data show that while the distribution remains positively skewed, more individuals had slightly higher values of the socioeconomic index. Persistent low socioeconomic status has been observed in other studies of Ghana, with adverse effects on human development (Doku et al., 2010; Krefis et al., 2010).

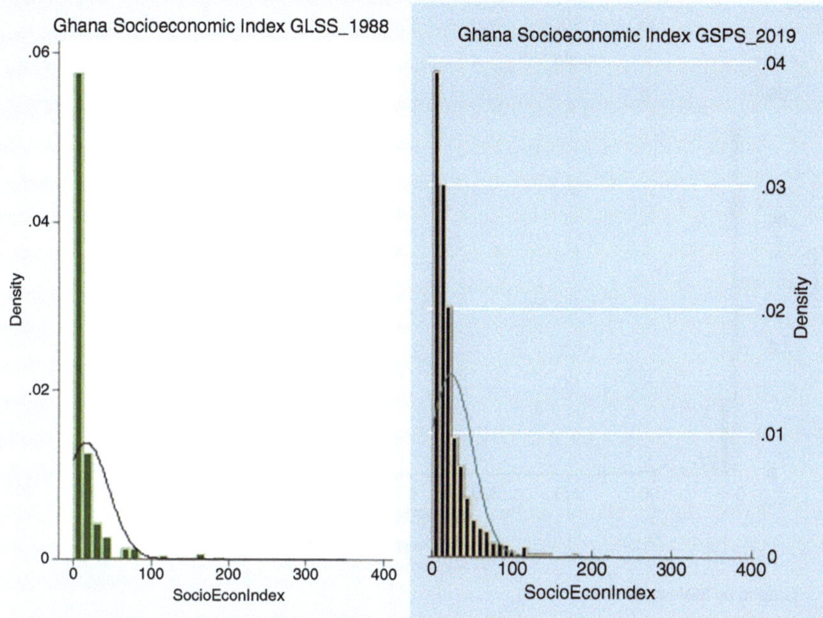

Fig. 11.1 Ghana household socioeconomic performance 1988 versus 2019. (*Source*: Own calculation using GLSS 1988 and GSPS 2019)

Figure 11.2 shows the socioeconomic index over gender and is complemented by a table which compares the grouped mean values and their standard deviations. Table 11.1 shows that there were more males than females, showing that males had more access to income, assets, and infrastructures which were components included in the computation of the index when compared to females.

While the mean index was lower in general as shown in Fig. 11.2 with a high concentration of low values for both groups, the mean socioeconomic index for males was higher than for females (18.66 vs. 10.39), with higher variability for males (33.35 vs. 12.92) for females.

To compare the significance of these differences in socioeconomic index across gender groups, a one-way ANOVA was conducted to determine if the differences were statistically significant. A statistically significant difference between groups was determined by the one-way ANOVA ($F\ (1{,}856) = 8.96,\ p = 0.0028$). A Tukey post hoc test further revealed that socioeconomic performance was significantly lower for females than for males for the GLSS 1988 data. Given our measure of socioeconomic performance, men had better opportunities for socioeconomic progress than females in 1988. The results of the post hoc analysis are presented in the appendix. Assessments were made for spatiality, age categories, and marital status using ANOVA. The ANOVA model was significant with model $F = 4.65$ *and a p-value of 0.0000,* showing that socioeconomic performance differences across spatial locations were significant at the 5% level while socioeconomic differences

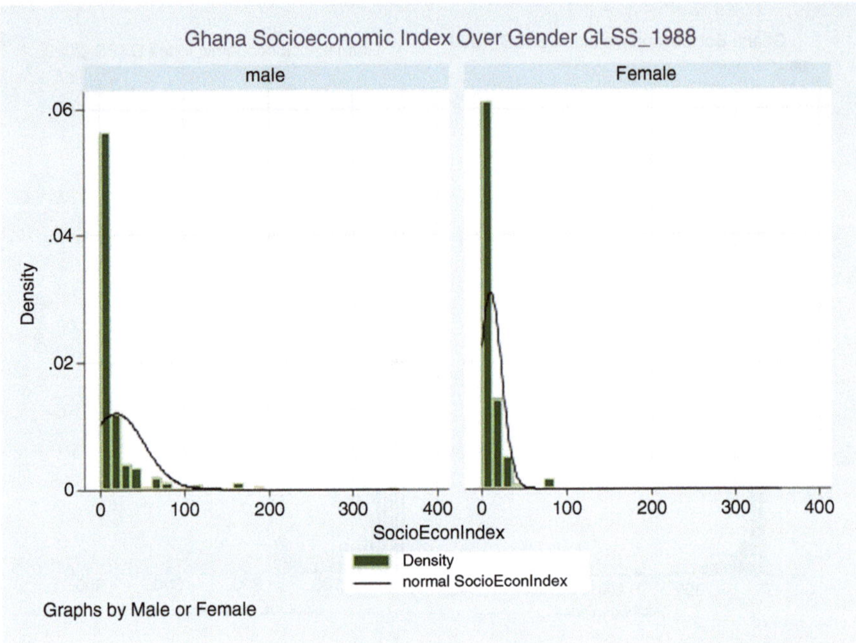

Fig. 11.2 Assessing socioeconomic differences across gender. (*Source*: Own calculations using GLSS_1988)

Table 11.1 Mean of socioeconomic index over gender groups, GLSS 1988

Gender Group	Mean	Standard	Frequency
Male	18.66	33.35	596
Female	10.39	12.92	262

Source: Own calculations using GLSS 1988 Data

across age groupings were statistically significant at the 10% level. Marital status was not an important determinant of socioeconomic performance, according to the ANOVA model (Table 11.2).

11.4.2 Social Inclusion

The composite index measuring social inclusion in the study assessed an individual's access to medical facilities for consultation (to assess general health and personal upkeep), access to financial institutions and markets, educational institutions, and social security. Figure 11.3. shows the distribution of the social inclusion and exclusion index across gender groups. Generally, individuals in the sample showed very small values of the index, indicating very low social inclusion, as shown by the

Table 11.2 ANOVA, socioeconomic differences over spatial location, age groups, and marital status, GLSS 1988

	Number of obs = 460 Root MSE = 35.4355		R-squared = 0.1025 Adj R-squared = 0.0805		
Source	Partial SS	df	MS	F	Prob > F
Model	64244.959	11	5840.4508	4.65	0.0000
SpatialLo~n	56504.586	8	7063.0733	5.62	0.0000
AgeCatego~s	6216.3389	2	3108.1695	2.48	0.0853
MaritalSt~s	2897.0238	1	2897.0238	2.31	0.1295
Residual	562542.63	448	1255.6755		
Total	626787.59	459	1365.5503		

Source: Own calculations using GLSS_1988

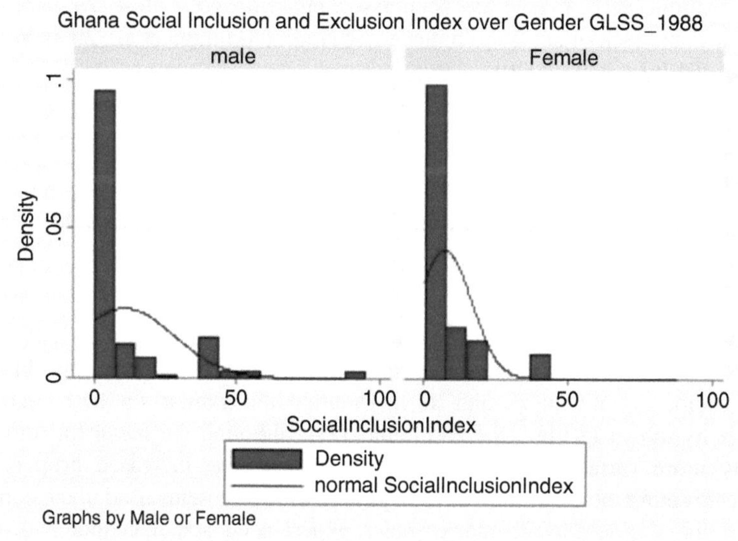

Fig. 11.3 Social inclusion index over gender, GLSS 1988. (*Source*: Own calculations using GLSS_1988)

positive skew in the distributions in Fig. 11.3. Individuals in the sample in both groups showed low access to healthcare facilities, financial and educational institutions, and social security.

Table 11.3, assessing the mean of social inclusion for males versus females, showed that the overall mean was higher for males than females. Thus, in 1988 women generally experienced low levels of social participation when compared with men. Examining the historical development of social participation in Ghana, women are more active in non-formal social institutions creating informal financial arrangements and market strategies for beneficial social participation (Tettey et al., 2003).

Table 11.3 Mean of social inclusion over gender, GLSS 1988

Gender Group	**Mean**	**Standard**	**Frequency**
Male	10.79	17.28	118
Female	6.93	9.28	32

Source: Own calculations using GLSS 1988 data

A one-way ANOVA (F (1,148) = 1.47, p = 0.2274) showed no statistically significant differences between the social inclusion of means for both males and females. This shows that while social inclusion was experienced equally for both groups, women seem to have taken strategies to ameliorate their social challenges and advance. Tracing the two indices, we have examined, socioeconomic performance and social exclusion, the majority of Ghanaians in the sample showed very low socioeconomic performance which seems to result in social exclusion. Low socioeconomic performance has been associated with poor lifestyles, poor health outcomes, and lack of access to finance and credit (Akudugu et al., 2009; Wrigley-Asante, 2012; Li et al., 2020).

11.4.3 Ghana Socioeconomic Panel Survey 2019: Socioeconomic Performance and Social Inclusion Among Ghanaians

Assessing gendered trends in socioeconomic performance using the 2019 dataset showed significant improvements for males and females as shown in Fig. 11.4. The mean socioeconomic index and its distribution are similar for both males and females as shown in Fig. 11.4 and Table 11.4, although the mean for females is slightly more variable when compared to males. The increased proportion of females meeting the criteria in terms of having access to items used in the computation of the socioeconomic index shows experienced social economic mobility among women with a tendency toward gendered equity. Thus, while the socioeconomic performance of males remained better than that of females shown by higher numbers of males when compared to females, the intervening years have shown great improvement in the performance of females in access to conditions for material social mobility and socioeconomic improvement.

A one-way ANOVA assessing differences in socioeconomic performance for gender groups with (F (1, 14,875) = 0.96, p = 0.3280) showed that the differences in the mean values of the socioeconomic index between males and females were not statistically significant. Thus, females in Ghana in 2019 showed more access to household infrastructure, productive assets, and greater income, enabling upward socioeconomic mobility. Other studies have shown that access to increased prospects for farming and capital has improved the socioeconomic outcomes for women in Ghana (Akudugu et al., 2009; Asomani-Boateng et al., 2015).

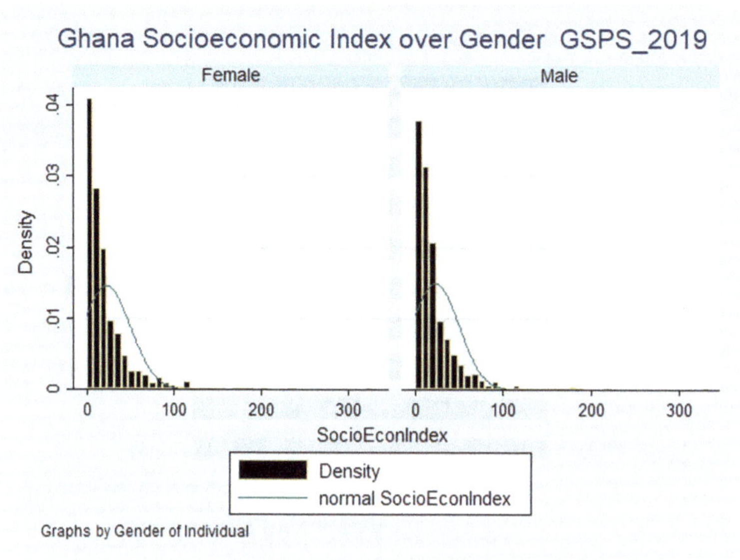

Fig. 11.4 Socioeconomic performance across gender groupings, GSPS 2019. (*Source*: Own calculations using GSPS_2019)

Table 11.4 Socioeconomic performance across gender, GSPS 2019 Data

Gender Group	Mean	Standard	Frequency
Male	22.39	26.77	8171
Female	22.83	27.43	6706

Source: Own calculations using GSPS, 2019 data

In Fig. 11.5, regional disparities in socioeconomic performance are shown. Regions that have experienced better investments in infrastructure and institutions have very high socioeconomic indices when compared with other regions. Population density was observed to be an important influence on regional socioeconomic differentiation. In Fig. 11.5, the Ashanti Region has a lower socioeconomic index than the Northern region which is viewed as less developed while comprising 31% of Ghana's land area and population concentration. Our analysis also observed that the socioeconomic index was greater for rural areas when compared to urban areas, which is partly explained by more participants in the 2019 panel being from rural areas. This may be indicative of increased access to infrastructure for socioeconomic progress in rural areas as demonstrated in another where increases in education in rural Ghana showed better health profiles among men (Addo et al., 2017).

Testing for statistical significance, an ANOVA test with F (10, 12,421) = 54 and p-value = 0.0000 showed that the regional and rural-urban dynamics were statistically significant. The Tukey post hoc analysis showed that on average regional urban differences were not statistically significant while regional urban-rural

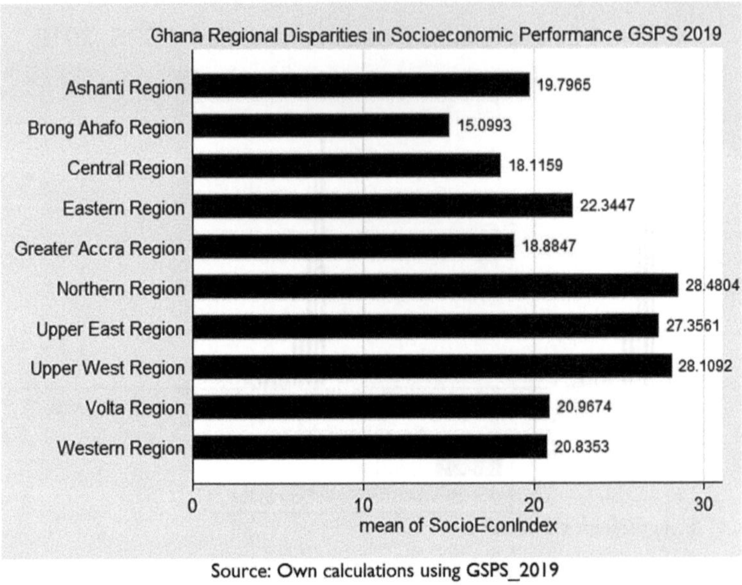

Fig. 11.5 Regional differences in mean socioeconomic performance, GSPS 2019. (*Source*: Own calculations using GSPS_2019)

Table 11.5 Socioeconomic distribution over gender and spatial location, GSPS_2019

Community Type	Female	Male	N
Urban	18.25 (21.15)	17.90 (20.12)	3072
Rural	24.78 (29.57)	23.40 (26.97)	9360

Source: Own calculations GSPS_2019

differences were statistically significant. Improved socioeconomic performance observed in the analysis aligns with a study which found that urbanization in Ghana has increased the share of rural households in the non-farm economy and increased farm innovation leading to better socioeconomic outcomes (Diao et al., 2019).

An analysis of the rural-urban distribution of socioeconomic status for males and females showed higher socioeconomic outcomes for women and males in rural areas than in urban areas as shown in Table 11.5. This may be explained by the over-representation of the rural population in the 2019 panel data since we generally expect higher socioeconomic performance to be associated with urban areas, particularly when accounting for infrastructure access, income, and productive capital in computing socioeconomic status (Vyas & Kumaranayake, 2006; Krishnan, 2010).

Social Inclusion Index

Figure 11.6 shows the positively skewed distribution of the social inclusion and exclusion index for males and females for 2019 panel data. The distributions show

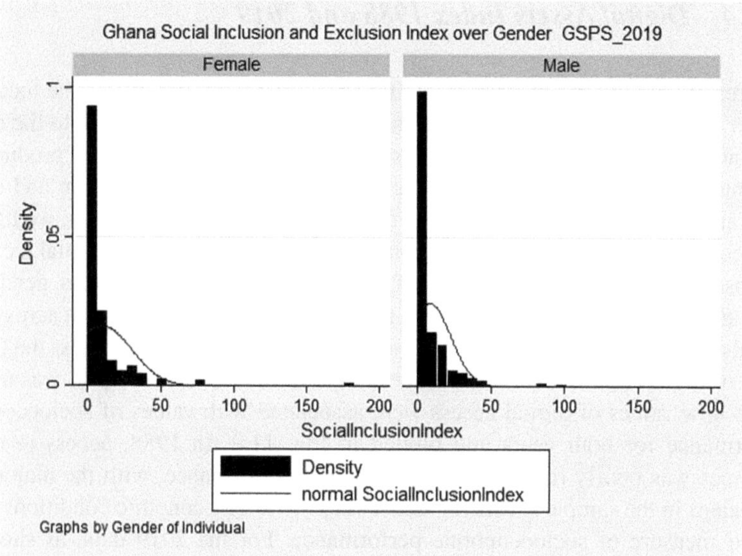

Fig. 11.6 Social inclusion index by gender, GSPS 2019 Data. (*Source*: Own calculations using GSPS_2019)

Table 11.6 Tabulating social inclusion over gender, GSPS 2019

Gender Group	Mean	Standard	Frequency
Male	8.18	14.34	361
Female	9.98	19.96	402

Source: Own calculations using GSPS 2019 Data

the persistence of low values for the social inclusion and exclusion index which was composed of access to networks, rural and urban agencies, education institution access, family support networks, and access to financial institutions. The distributions thus show that very few individuals have access to broader social institutions and facilities.

Table 11.6 shows the mean values of social inclusion for males and females. There were more females in the sample with the mean social inclusion index being slightly higher for females than males, with slightly higher variability as shown by the slightly higher standard deviation. Given the construction of the social inclusion index, women seem to be generally more connected than males. The small frequency of individuals in the sample, that is, those with complete cases over the range of variables explains the small total number of observations given the total sample size. A one-way ANOVA with F (1, 761) = 2.01 and $p = 0.1566$ showed no statistically significant differences in the mean distribution of social inclusion for females versus males. Low social inclusion is associated with student migration in Ghana (Kyei, 2021), and it disproportionately affects those with disabilities (Naami, 2019).

11.4.4 Digital Assets Index 1988 and 2019

We created two indices measuring digital access for 1988 and 2019. The focus was not on the similarity of composition in the two indices but on access to the digital innovations associated with the periods which improved general social productivity and interaction. For the 1988 data, we focused on access to television and digital news and access to telephone systems and postages. For the 2019 data, we focused on access to computers, smartphones and internet access, and other digital facilities.

Observing the two distributions of the digital access index across gender for 1988 and 2019 in Figs. 11.7 and 11.8, the importance of digital access across individuals was more pronounced in 2019 when compared to 1988. To assess the importance of digital access over socioeconomic performance, a scatterplot was used to assess how values of digital access were associated with values of socioeconomic performance for both years and plotted in Fig. 11.9. In 1988, access to digital resources was poorly related to socioeconomic performance, with the majority of Ghanaians in the sample subsisting under very low socioeconomic conditions based on our measure of socioeconomic performance. For the 2019 data, as shown in Fig. 11.9, digital access rises with socioeconomic performance over very low values, yet higher values of the digital access index are observed with low values of socioeconomic status and also higher values of the socioeconomic index are associated with very low values of the digital access index. This is explained by our prior observations, concerning the spatial distribution of socioeconomic status across spatial dimensions, particularly for the latter dataset.

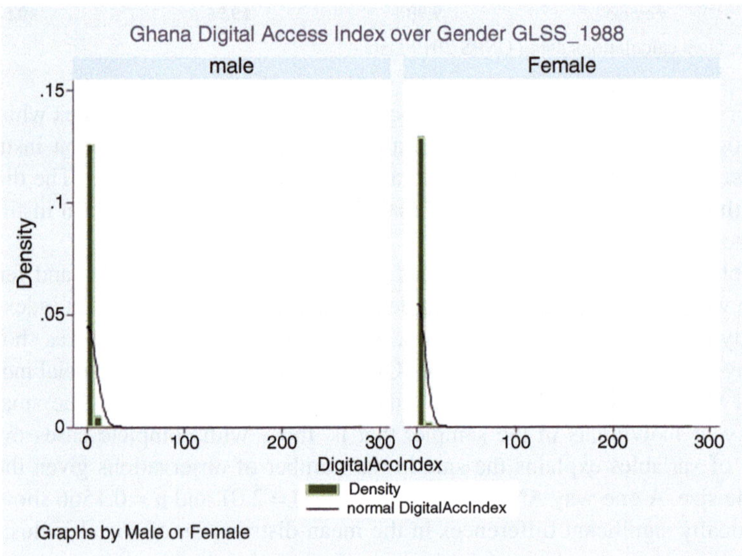

Fig. 11.7 Digital access index by gender, GLSS 1988 Data. (*Source*: Own calculations using GLSS_1988 Data)

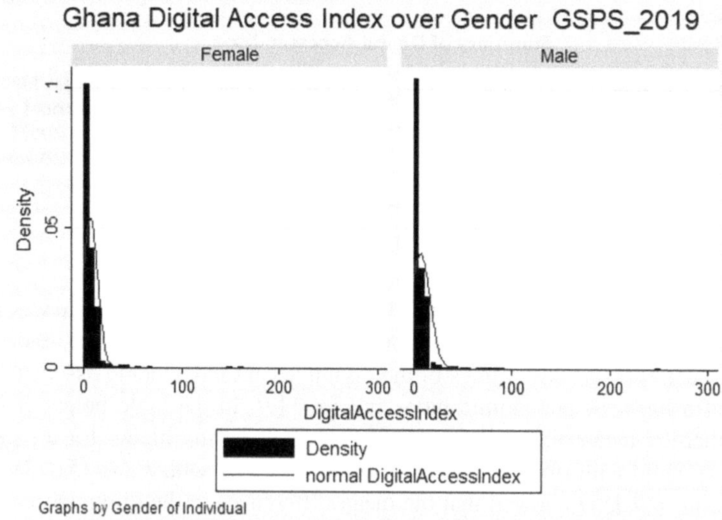

Fig. 11.8 Digital access index by gender, GSPS 2019 Data. (*Source*: Own calculations using GSPS_2019)

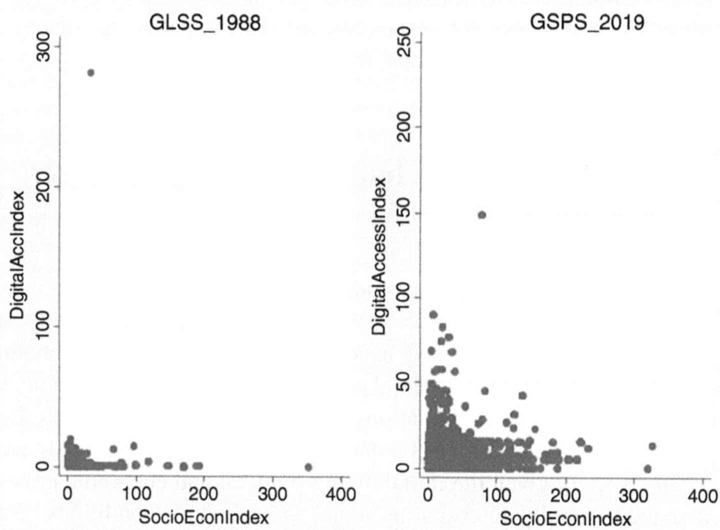

Fig. 11.9 Scatterplot of digital access and socioeconomic performance, GL 1998 and GSPS 2019. (*Source*: Own calculations using GLSS1988 & GSPS2019 data)

Table 11.7 Digital access index across rural-urban spatiality, GSPS_2019

Summary of Digital Access Index

Community Spatial Location	Mean	Standard Deviation	**Bartlett's Test for Equal Variances**
Urban	7.133 *(N = 5207)*	11.796	*Chi2(1) = 0.0025* *p-value = 0.0000*
Rural	6.995 *(N = 10107)*	6.620	

Source: Own calculations using GSPS_2019 Data

In the 2019 dataset, it was observed that socioeconomic performance was generally higher for people in rural when compared to those in urban areas, Table 11.5. Thus, we can see very low values of the digital access index being associated with values of a high socioeconomic index in Fig. 11.9. In the table below, it is also shown that the mean of the digital access index is slightly higher for urban areas when compared with rural areas. However, an ANOVA with $F\ (1,\ 15{,}312) = 0.86$ and $p\text{-}value = 0.3551$ showed that the mean differences in the digital access index across rural and urban groups were not statistically different for the sample. The Bartlett's test for equal variances reported in the table also attested to the absence of statistically significant differences in the mean of the two groups. While accounting for limitations in our constructs, the lack of statistically significant differences in the mean of digital access between rural and urban areas shows that digital infrastructural development and access in Ghana is not urban concentrated which may prevent rural-urban migration for example and its potential to distort future developmental potential for rural areas (Table 11.7).

11.5 Discussion, Literature Integration, and Conclusion of the Study

Our analysis shows that the early post-independence decades of Ghana were characterized by very low socioeconomic progress which disproportionately affected females. While Ghanaians were living in conditions of limiting socioeconomic conditions, with limited access to household assets, infrastructure, and income, women experienced more structural deprivation when social inclusion and exclusion is added to the analysis. These findings correlate with the historically reported conditions of Ghana society given the destabilizing political and economic policy landscape which led to rapidly deteriorating social and economic conditions (Todaro & Smith, 2012). Research studies also observed that these conditions of socioeconomic deprivation continued to be prevalent in the twenty-first century (Doku et al., 2010; Krefis et al., 2010). In these early decades of the post-independence period, regional differences were very significant in predicting socioeconomic performance, which may be the outcome of socioeconomic investments as the government took a very strong interventionist role in social and economic transformation. Analysis of the 2019 data showed improvement with more people having access to household assets, productive assets, and infrastructure and income, which are associated with non-farm and rural farm economic activity. While generally low socioeconomic conditions remained prevalent, socioeconomic inequality was observed by concentrations of a large class at the lower end of the scale and very few individuals with very high socioeconomic index values, Fig. 11.1.

The social inclusion and exclusion index was generally low in both the immediate post-independence period and in 2019, showing the persistence of structural inequities in access to social infrastructures and networks. Among the social infrastructures in the construct was educational access, indicating more Ghanaians were experiencing poor access to education, which was premised on national-level economic challenges (Nyarko, 2020). These were the outcomes of the economic and social crisis that were outcomes of the economic liberalization and social policies of the post-independence period (Todaro & Smith, 2012). The conditions of social exclusion persisted through the comparison period, with no differences in observed experiences of general social exclusion among males and females, with exacerbated social exclusion among those having aggravated limiting conditions such as disabilities (Ae-Ngibise et al., 2015; Jaha & Sika-Bright, 2015; Nyarko & Asante, 2015). This showed a preponderance of lower socioeconomic conditions which based on both datasets showed significant gendered differentiation, with the 2019 data showing demographic differentiation along with age and regional variables. We notice as a result that the pattern of low socioeconomic improvement and socioeconomic marginalization observed in other studies is demonstrated in the analysis presented in this study (Aryeetey & Kanbur, 2017).

We further argue in this study that socioeconomic performance, social inclusion, and education/skills resources are the physical divides that shape the response of individuals and households to the effect of policies and other external influences on their living conditions. Countries across the globe are undergoing structural change through a digital transformation which will undoubtedly affect the trajectory of Ghanaian development and countries in a similar developmental trend. Using a composite index of socioeconomic status which contained access to water and sanitation showed the persistence of low socioeconomic performance indicating similar poor access to these infrastructures. Gendered disparities in development in socioeconomic performance and regional disparities were also observed in another study which observed a similar pattern of low socioeconomic development among women, as demonstrated in regional disparities in contraceptive usage (Nyarko, 2020). Another study observed resilient patterns of social marginalization, brought about by political competition that results in poor regions remaining marginalized from the contours of economic mobility in Ghana (Abdulai & Hulme, 2015).

In 1988, access to digital services was not associated with social inclusion or exclusion with the relationship of digital services access being unrelated to socioeconomic performance. Thus, we concluded that digital assets were not important to the material welfare of Ghanaians with their contribution being of minimal influence on socioeconomic welfare maintenance. In the analysis for 2019, social inclusion and exclusion were weakly related to the digital access index, while socioeconomic performance was moderately related, due to the rural bias evidence in the 2019 data. Although consistent with other studies, we observed that higher average values of socioeconomic performance were associated with higher average values of digital services access for the urban population explained by urban bias in developmental planning (Todaro & Smith, 2012). However, the rural-urban differences were not significant.

11.6 Conclusion

This chapter's contribution has attempted to discuss and demonstrate the usefulness of socioeconomic analysis in understanding socioeconomic change in countries using Ghana as a case for analysis. Some key aspects of creating indices were discussed and implemented, and while consistent as demonstrated by observing similar conclusions in other studies, it was also observed that using multiple attributes in generating indices results in truncation and loss of observations delimiting analysis to a small number of complete cases. While this results in reducing the analytical space and representativeness of the findings, it helps with assessing the extent to which sample participants meet the threshold of what is being measured. When properly designed indices are consistent in reducing analysis toward using a single index to measure a comprehensive array of dimensions of socioeconomic performance, such constructs can be useful in assessing periodic changes in welfare.

The post-independence challenges of socioeconomic marginalization in Ghana continue to persist in the present era, with the socioeconomic fundamentals for economic and more importantly technological transformation not having solidified. The results of these adverse socioeconomic outcomes can be linked to social and economic policies, which have caused economic and social challenges and created structural socioeconomic problems and challenges. Similar experiences are evident in other African countries. Given the changing digital skills content of work and economic activity being reproduced by the digital transformation process, the state of socioeconomic and socio-structural conditions in Ghana might lead to welfare losses and exacerbated exclusion. In research on digital transformation and its socioeconomic impacts, economic marginalization has been argued to be the result of transformation-induced worsening of the existing socioeconomic conditions of deprivation.

References

Abdulai, A.-G., & Hulme, D. (2015). The politics of regional inequality in Ghana: State elites, donors and PRSPs. *Development Policy Review, 33*(5), 529–553. Available at: https://doi.org/10.1111/dpr.12124

Addo, J., et al. (2017). Association between socioeconomic position and the prevalence of type 2 diabetes in Ghanaians in different geographic locations: The RODAM study. *Journal of Epidemiology and Community Health, 71*(7), 633. Available at: https://doi.org/10.1136/jech-2016-208322

Adjei, P. O.-W., & Buor, D. (2012). From poverty to poor health: Analysis of socio-economic pathways influencing health status in rural households of Ghana. *Health Sociology Review, 21*(2), 232–241. Available at: https://doi.org/10.5172/hesr.2012.21.2.232

Ae-Ngibise, K. A., et al. (2015). The experience of caregivers of people living with serious mental disorders: A study from rural Ghana. *Global Health Action, 8*(1), 26957.

Afonasova, M. A., et al. (2019). Digitalization in economy and innovation: The effect on social and economic processes. *Polish Journal of Management Studies, 19*, 22.

Ahmed, S. M., et al. (2005). Socioeconomic status overrides age and gender in determining health-seeking behaviour in rural Bangladesh. *Bulletin of the World Health Organization, 83*, 109–117.

Akudugu, M. A., Egyir, I. S., & Mensah-Bonsu, A. (2009). Women farmers' access to credit from rural banks in Ghana. *Agricultural Finance Review, 69*(3), 284–299. Available at: https://doi.org/10.1108/00021460911002671

Aly, H. (2022). Digital transformation, development and productivity in developing countries: is artificial intelligence a curse or a blessing?. *Review of Economics and Political Science, 7*(4), 238–256.

Aryeetey, E., & Kanbur, S. M. R. (Eds.). (2017). *The economy of Ghana sixty years after independence* (1st ed.). Oxford University Press.

Asomani-Boateng, R., Fricano, R. J., & Adarkwa, F. (2015). Assessing the socio-economic impacts of rural road improvements in Ghana: A case study of Transport Sector Program Support (II). *Case Studies on Transport Policy, 3*(4), 355–366. Available at: https://doi.org/10.1016/j.cstp.2015.04.006

Betti, G., & Lemmi, A. (2021). *Analysis of socio-economic conditions: Insights from a fuzzy multi-dimensional approach*. Taylor & Francis. Available at: https://books.google.co.za/books?id=W7QgEAAAQBAJ

Creswell, J. W., & Creswell, J. D. (2017). *Research design: Qualitative, quantitative, and mixed methods approach*. Sage Publications.

Diao, X., et al. (2019). *Ghana's economic and agricultural transformation: Past performance and future prospects*. Oxford University Press.

Doku, D., et al. (2010). Do socioeconomic differences in tobacco use exist also in developing countries? A study of Ghanaian adolescents. *BMC Public Health, 10*(1), 758. Available at: https://doi.org/10.1186/1471-2458-10-758

Everitt, B., & Hothorn, T. (2011). *An introduction to applied multivariate analysis with R*. Springer Science & Business Media.

Ghana Institute of Statistical and Economic Research. (2021). *Ghana socioeconomic panel survey 2018–2019, Wave 3*. Institute of Statistical, Social and Economic Research. Available at: https://www.datafirst.uct.ac.za/dataportal/index.php/catalog/885/study-description

Ghana Statistical Office. (2008). *Ghana – Ghana living standards survey: 1987–1988, First round – Overview*. Available at: https://www2.statsghana.gov.gh/nada/index.php/catalog/7/study-description. Accessed: 5 Apr 2022.

Guilmoto, C. Z., & Dumont, A. (2019). Trends, regional variations, and socioeconomic disparities in cesarean births in India, 2010–2016. *JAMA Network Open, 2*(3), e190526.

Havard, S., et al. (2008). A small-area index of socioeconomic deprivation to capture health inequalities in France. *Social Science & Medicine, 67*(12), 2007–2016.

Jaha, I. R., & Sika-Bright, S. (2015). Challenges of the livelihood empowerment against poverty programme in the upper west region of Ghana: The institutional perspective. *UDS International Journal of Development, 2*(1), 188–205.

Jolliffe, I. T. (2002). *Principal component analysis for special types of data*. Springer.

Krefis, A. C., et al. (2010). Principal component analysis of socioeconomic factors and their association with malaria in children from the Ashanti Region, Ghana. *Malaria Journal, 9*(1), 201. Available at: https://doi.org/10.1186/1475-2875-9-201

Krishnan, V. (2010). *Constructing an area-based socioeconomic index: A principal components analysis approach*. Early Child Development Mapping Project [Preprint].
Kyei, J. R. K. O. (2021). "I have to further my studies abroad": Student migration in Ghana. *Social Inclusion, 9*(1), 299–307.
Li, X., et al. (2020). Effect of socioeconomic status on the healthcare-seeking behaviour of migrant workers in China. *PLoS One, 15*(8), e0237867.
Mohiuddin, S., & Hashia, H. (2012). Regional socio-economic disparities in the Kashmir Valley (India)–A geographical approach. *Bulletin of Geography. Socio-economic Series, 18*, 85–98.
Naami, A. (2019). Access barriers encountered by persons with mobility disabilities in Accra, Ghana. *Journal of Social Inclusion, 10*(2), 2019.
Nyarko, S. H. (2020). Spatial variations and socioeconomic determinants of modern contraceptive use in Ghana: A Bayesian multilevel analysis. *PLoS One, 15*(3), e0230139.
Nyarko, J., & Asante, K. O. (2015). Social exclusion of the deaf in corporate television advertising in Ghana: A pilot study. *Journal of Communication, 6*(2), 284–295.
Odeku, K. O., & Meyer, E. (2019). Socioeconomic implications of energy poverty in South African poor rural households. *Academy of Entrepreneurship Journal, 25*(3), 1–12.
Pampalon, R., Hamel, D., & Gamache, P. (2009). A comparison of individual and area-based socio-economic data for monitoring social inequalities in health. *Health Reports, 20*(4), 85.
Popova, O., & Bogacheva, E. (2017). Analysis of the methods for assessing socio-economic development level of urban areas. In *AIP conference proceedings* (p. 050015). AIP Publishing LLC.
Posel, D. (2021). Intra-household and inter-personal comparisons of subjective well-being: Dorrit Posel. *Applied Research in Quality of Life, 16*(6), 2527–2529.
Posel, D., & Rogan, M. (2016). Measured as poor versus feeling poor: Comparing money-metric and subjective poverty rates in South Africa. *Journal of Human Development and Capabilities, 17*(1), 55–73.
Shraim, M., et al. (2017). Regional socioeconomic disparities in outcomes for workers with low back pain in the United States. *American Journal of Industrial Medicine, 60*(5), 472–483.
Strohmaier, R., Schuetz, M., & Vannuccini, S. (2019). A systemic perspective on socioeconomic transformation in the digital age. *Journal of Industrial and Business Economics, 46*(3), 361–378.
Takyi, B. K., & Addai, I. (2003). Demographic processes, economic growth and socio-economic development in Ghana, 1960–2000. In *Critical perspectives on politics and socio-economic development in Ghana* (pp. 223–237). Brill.
Tettey, W., Puplampu, K. P., & Berman, B. (Eds.). (2003). *Critical perspectives in politics and socio-economic development in Ghana* (African social studies series) (Vol. 6). Brill.
Todaro, M. P., & Smith, S. C. (2012). *Economic development*. Addison-Wesley.
Uzochukwu, B. S., & Onwujekwe, O. E. (2004). Socio-economic differences and health seeking behaviour for the diagnosis and treatment of malaria: A case study of four local government areas operating the Bamako initiative programme in south-East Nigeria. *International Journal for Equity in Health, 3*(1), 1–10.
Vehkalahti, K., & Everitt, B. S. (2018). *Multivariate analysis for the behavioural sciences*. CRC Press.
Vyas, S., & Kumaranayake, L. (2006). Constructing socio-economic status indices: How to use principal components analysis. *Health Policy and Planning, 21*(6), 459–468. Available at: https://doi.org/10.1093/heapol/czl029
World Bank. (2022). Gini index (World Bank estimate) – Ghana | Data. Available at: https://data.worldbank.org/indicator/SI.POV.GINI?locations=GH. Accessed: 7 Apr 2022.
Wrigley-Asante, C. (2012). Out of the dark but not out of the cage: Women's empowerment and gender relations in the Dangme West district of Ghana. *Gender, Place & Culture, 19*(3), 344–363. Available at: https://doi.org/10.1080/0966369X.2011.572435
Zagórski, K. (1985). Composite measures of social, economic and demographic regional differentiation in Australia. *Social Indicators Research, 16*(2), 131–156.
Zhou, Y., & Liu, Y. (2019). The geography of poverty: Review and research prospects. *Journal of Rural Studies [Preprint]*. Available at: https://doi.org/10.1016/j.jrurstud.2019.01.008

Part II
Financial Inclusion in Agriculture

Chapter 12
Rethinking Financial Inclusion for Post-Colonial Land Reform Beneficiaries in South Africa

Belese N. Majova

Abstract The literature on financial inclusion has blind spots regarding how this development approach could improve the lives of the people, particularly would land reform beneficiaries in South Africa. Studies which can inform policy design and implementation on what financial inclusion means and how it can be implemented are, therefore, needed. Drawing from empirical evidence gathered through in-depth interviews with land reform recipients as well as government officials and private land experts, this chapter shows how the concept of financial inclusion is poorly understood and, therefore, vaguely implemented. The chapter shows that the current conceptualisation of "financial inclusion" does not allow for the creation of a mature scholarly debate in the context of land reform beneficiaries, as the emphasis is placed on access to financial services instead of focusing on access to the finance itself. The chapter concludes that the starting point towards the realisation of financial inclusion for land recipients in South Africa should be the reconceptualisation of the concept itself, so that it can capture the context of the needs of the people and situations.

Keywords Farmers · Financial inclusion · Land recipients · Land reform · South Africa

12.1 Introduction

The literature on financial inclusion has blind spots with how this development approach can be applied in the context of land reform recipients in South Africa. Despite financial inclusion increasingly being recognised and adopted as one of the

B. N. Majova (✉)
University of Johannesburg, Johannesburg, South Africa

D. Mhlanga, E. Ndhlovu (eds.), *Economic Inclusion in Post-Independence Africa*, Advances in African Economic, Social and Political Development,
https://doi.org/10.1007/978-3-031-31431-5_12

major solutions to unlocking the potential of the various sectors of national economies, in South Africa interrogations on what financial inclusion is to land reform beneficiaries are lacking. While the literature on the potential impacts of land reform on the broader economic abounds (Gumede, 2014; Masilela & Weiner, 1996; Maphoto, 2012; Hall, 2009), the literature on what financial inclusion constitutes and how it can be mobilised and practised are either embryonic or nonexistent. With many land reform beneficiaries in South Africa facing finance-related challenges, including inadequate access to productive assets, input shortages, inaccessible markets, and soaring transport costs and operating at subsistence levels due to a lack of resources (Mpandeli & Maponya, 2014), financial inclusion is one of the contemporary approaches to boost production by these farmers and also enable them to move from subsistence production to producing for the market. This would help not only eliminate poverty but also contribute to the broad-based rural economy.

South African farmers and Black land reform beneficiaries, however, continue to face operational challenges (Majova, 2016). Some of the reasons pointed out by scholars have been the failure of the government to provide post-resettlement support. While farmers are being encouraged to operate as businesses, they are not provided with adequate support, which could enable them to improve their operations. This has placed pressure on the land beneficiaries (Rusenga, 2019). To mobilise funding for farming, the government encouraged farmers to accept partnerships and joint ventures to boost production (Rusenga, 2019). However, this move is criticised by some scholars who viewed it not as financial inclusion, but rather as regrouping capital which could eventually utilise its opportunistic tendencies to displace farmers from their lands or redirect their profits (Ndhlovu, 2022a, b). In this view, for land recipients to accrue the benefits of land reform in terms of improved livelihoods and an improved rural economy, reconceptualised financial inclusion is needed. To the best of our knowledge, there are no studies that have sought the concrete reconceptualisation of "financial inclusion" from a mere focus on services to the accessibility and provision of the finance itself. This chapter could be the first to undertake this task in South Africa. The study has the potential to at least influence policy formulation even though implementation will require the political will of state officials.

In the next sections, the chapter outlines the research methods for the study. Next, it discusses the concept of financial inclusion to highlight how the concept could apply to land reform beneficiaries in South Africa. This is followed by a discussion on the land reform programmes in South Africa with a focus on the opportunities for and challenges of financial inclusion. Thereafter, a reconceptualisation of "financial inclusion" is made using empirical evidence drawn from fieldwork. Lastly, conclusions and implications for the study are made.

12.2 Research Methods

The study was conducted in the Gauteng Province, South Africa. Data was collected through in-depth interviews that were conducted face-to-face with farmers between January and July 2021. A total of 50 farmers, who were land reform beneficiaries, were selected through referrals by officials in the Gauteng Department of Agriculture, Land Reform, and Rural Development (DALRRD) located in Johannesburg. A total of 20 land and agrarian change experts including government officials in the DALRRD and other experts in the private sector were also interviewed virtually as key informants. Number codes were assigned to both farmers and key informants for ease of reference. In addition, secondary sources were also reviewed alongside empirical investigation. A detailed literature review on land reform was conducted, including an analysis of viewpoints, policy, and strategy documents. The search for germane documents was conducted in academic and grey literature databases using land reform, agrarian change, financial inclusion, and smallholder farmers as keywords. The aim was to explore the financial inclusion status of participants. The key variable was the participants' sources of capital used to fund operations on the farm. The study gathered information on farmers' sources of capital, and income, as well as other types of support, which allowed them to operate. Guided by reviewed literature, the study also examined how history, education levels, primary sources of income, age, race, gender, and marital status impacted the participants' potential to access financial support from various stakeholders. Thematic data analysis was used to present and structure the discussion.

12.3 Rethinking Financial Inclusion for Land Recipients in South Africa

The term "financial inclusion" is believed to have been first introduced in 1993 by some geographers who sought solutions to the lack of physical access to banking services due to the closure of bank branches (Mhlanga & Dunga, 2021). However, it is the European Commission which introduced the financial inclusion criteria, namely, savings, credit, insurance, and banking (Claessens, 2006). Financial inclusion is broadly understood as the delivery of financial services to the poor at an affordable cost (Chartier & Louis, 2017). It is the delivery of banking services to most disadvantaged and low-income groups at an affordable cost (Demirguc-kunt et al., 2018). The World Bank (2017) defines financial inclusion defined key goals of inclusive finance as access to a range of financial services, such as saving, credit, insurance, remittance, and other banking payment services, to all bankable households and enterprises at a reasonable cost.

What is clear in the literature is that financial inclusion is mainly described as the delivery of banking services to disadvantaged and low-income groups at an affordable cost. Emphasis is rarely placed on the delivery of "finance" itself. This chapter takes issue with this kind of conceptualisation and argues that financial inclusion should not be merely about the delivery of financial services but also the broadening of finance access by people, farmers, and other small businesses, for instance, to enable them to increase the level of their production activities. In South Africa, the political economy of separate development places the majority of prime land in the hands of the White minority, thereby, excluding Blacks, economically.

The South African land reform programme emerges from Section 25(5) of the Constitution which obligates the state to "…take reasonable legislative and other measures, within its available resources, to foster conditions which enable citizens to gain access to land on an equitable basis" (Republic of South Africa, 1996). Land reform was recognised as key to rural development, employment creation, increasing rural incomes, and dealing with overcrowding (Department of Land Affairs, 1997). This was consequently expected to translate into improved livelihoods and the emergence of a broad-based rural economy (DRDLR, 2013). Land reform was thus adopted with a rural development focus. However, even though land reform was implemented, the challenge remains on how to fundamentally change South Africa's distorted agrarian structure, including the racially prejudiced financial inclusion agenda as well as the institutions that influence access to components of the agricultural arrangement other than land including inputs, technology, expert knowledge, finance, water rights, and markets of diverse kinds. With Black farmers racially barred from accessing state support which their White counterparts easily obtained (Rusenga, 2019), the new government in South Africa introduced policies and practices meant to empower Black farmers.

From 1995 to 1999, the government provided a total of R16,000 per household under the Settlement and Land Acquisition Grants (SLAG) to enable poor households to purchase land on which they could put their labour to use in farming (Boudreax, 2009). Initially, land reform was essentially pro-poor. However, in the face of financial constraints for a government emerging from a century of colonialism as well as decades of apartheid, adjustments were made to funding. Thus, in 2001, the SLAG was replaced by the Land Redistribution for Agricultural Development (LRAD) programme, in which land applicants also needed to contribute to the land cost. The contribution was between R5000 and R400,000 and, "depending on the level of this contribution, would be eligible for a matching grant of between R20,000 and R100,000, on a sliding scale" (Hall, 2004: 216). Considerations were also made to allow the poor to contribute through labour provision instead of cash. The LRAD was later replaced by the Proactive Land Acquisition Strategy (PLAS), with the focus now drifting towards the creation of a class of Black commercial farmers with resources to finance their activities.

A huge body of empirical evidence depicts a lack of post-resettlement support in South African land reforms (Aliber & Cousins, 2013; Boudreax, 2009; Cousins, 2015; Rusenga, 2017). Kirsten and Van Zyl (1998) found that credit is available to most farmers. It was also found that small-scale producers in South Africa experienced challenges be able to attain access to water, purchasing equipment, and undertaking irrigation (Majova, 2016). Chisasa and Makina (2012) found that the performance of emerging farmers in South Africa lagged globally because of a lack of access to credit. On the other hand, large-scale farmers, most of whom are White, have greater access and enjoy far better credit support provided by various credit institutions (Gaanakgomo, 2015). Credit providers, such as commercial banks, prefer lending to commercial farmers and non-farm in the private sector which are able to demonstrate financial viability and offer collateral. Emerging farmers, particularly Blacks, generally lack these attributes and are deemed high risk (Chisasa & Makina, 2012).

Another challenge to accessing credit is the lack of clear land rights (Gaanakgomo, 2015). Many of the emerging farmers do not own their land but only have permission to occupy land, and therefore, they cannot use their land as collateral to access financing. Farmers would require a credit package, which covers production, investment and consumption credits, and credit for the redemption of prior debts. Such packages are not available to them in formal credit markets (Land Bank Research Report, 2012). Lack of adequate funding also constrains farmers on the types of new technologies to acquire and use. This ultimately negatively impacts farm output and reduces the chances of farmers accessing more funding from financial institutions, which might be requiring a certain level of productivity. Where this obtains, financial exclusion becomes the major source of financial inclusion, which spreads out to become a myriad form of exclusions. The next sections present the results gathered for the study.

12.4 Results and Discussion

The data gathered from land reform beneficiaries in the Gauteng Province indicated a vital need for a rethinking of what financial inclusion constitutes. Departing from the conventional factors of access to banking services (bank accounts, credit access, insurance, remittance, and other banking payment services) to the most disadvantaged and low-income groups at an affordable cost (Demirguc-kunt et al., 2018), participants posited that it was access to the capital which would allow them to put their labour to productive use in farming and not access to bank services.

12.4.1 Impact of Colonial History

Most participants linked their financial challenges to South Africa's colonial and apartheid past, where the exclusion of Blacks from finance, resources, and general development (defined as "the capacity of a state to achieve higher outcome of production for the satisfaction of citizens and empower them to make demands" (Brobbey, 2010: 1)) was a national policy. The colonial agrarian policy, beginning with the Natives Land Act of 1913, was built on the pursuit of racially steeped separate development, which favoured Whites while side-lining accumulation by Blacks. One participant stated that while "the government acquired land for the people, the same systems and policies that were being used by Whites to deny Africans access to resources are still in place, and thus, most farmers are as good as without land" (Farmer 7, 2021). This view was also confirmed by officials from the DRDLR who mentioned that while the government was making efforts to avail funds to Black farmers, the private sector, particularly financial institutions, continued to be reluctant just like in the colonial days when Blacks were considered inefficient, unproductive, ad risky, and therefore risky (Informant 3, 2021).

It was found that financial institutions were reluctant to extend support to land reform beneficiaries, most of whom had no experience and collateral and, therefore, are considered risky (Mutero et al., 2016). The age and educational and training level of the applicant farmer were considered very important with credit institutions preferring to lend to farmers within the economically active age group (Mutero et al., 2016). This financially excluded the elderly, most of whom acquired land under the land reform (Ngomane, 2016). Lending institutions also used education and training levels to predict the productive capacity of the farmer. Mutero et al. (2016) aver that credit providers and insurance firms in South Africa were not keen to deal with smallholder farmers, because they pose a covariant risk as a result of factors, such as inability to payback. Lending institutions were also reluctant to deal with these farmers, as they will have to conduct many small credit transactions, including checking credit worthiness, collateral verification, and monitoring loan repayments. These activities led to extra expenses, which cannot be justified by the sum total borrowed by these smallholders (Poulton et al., 2010). Van Schalkwyk et al. (2012) argue that although smallholder farmers in South Africa acquired land, no title deeds were issued to them. As a result, they face financial exclusion when they are denied loans by lending institutions due to a lack of collateral.

Participants mentioned that financial inclusion "should be when we are supported and to have access to finance so that we can do what needs to be done to be productive" (Farmer 12, 2021). They compared the department's tendency to provide farmers with inputs which farmers did not even request to colonialism, which controlled farmers by dictating to them what and how to produce. One participant mentioned that:

> Once in a while, we are invited to get some input from the department. They do not even do proper research. I once was invited to get tomato seeds and yet I am into chicken production. One farmer I know was listed for tomato-related training and yet she is into egg production. For me, this shows that, just like the apartheid government, the new government does not value farming by Blacks. Land reform was possibly a political statement with no intention to improve agriculture through bringing Blacks on board. (Farmer 9, 2021)

Officials from the department, however, defended the government's position arguing that it was doing all within reach to ensure that land reform beneficiaries access funds. It was positing that "…from the start, land reform has always been pro-poor unlike during the colonial era when rich whites were targeted" (Informant 15, 2021). Another official also averred that given the financial constraints for the first democratic government emerging from a century of colonialism as well as decades of apartheid, funding for broad-based financial inclusion for land recipients was not readily available (Informant 8). Officials also mentioned that the replacement of the SLAG by the LRAD programme in 2001 was meant to enable farmers to strengthen the government's financial inclusion agenda. The contribution was between R5000 and R400,000 and, "depending on the level of this contribution, would be eligible for a matching grant of between R20,000 and R100,000, on a sliding scale" (Hall, 2004: 216).

The views of farmers and officials on the impact of the country's colonial history were therefore divergent with officials defending the status quo, while the farmers themselves blamed the government for sustaining colonial tendencies, which thwarted broad-based financial inclusion, particularly for Blacks. The views of farmers are, however, widely supported by literature which posits that legislation, such as the Natives Land Act of 1913, served to dispossess Blacks of their lands so that Whites can occupy them (Ncapayi, 2013). The "separate development" project was first officially introduced by the National Party in 1948 and was sustained by various regimes over the years that appropriate resources for White businesses while Blacks had no such support. While this racial policy shattered the lives and livelihoods of Blacks, it deliberately empowered Whites to dominate all sectors of existence – socioeconomic and political. As a result, at independence in 1994, one of the approaches towards the realisation of development by the newly elected democratic government would be to implement a land reform programme which would, among other things, be meant to correct the Black exclusion.

Most of the farmers also indicated that they were unable to acquire loans and credit because of strict inspection and authentication by financial institutions, most of which are biased towards large-scale farming (Informant 2, 2021). Most of the verification requirements disqualified smallholder applicants who are required to demonstrate trustworthiness and potential for success (Informant 9). However, these land beneficiaries did not have the required resources to perform to the level expected by lenders, and thus, remain financially excluded.

With limited education and training due to colonial policies, information accessibility became another financial inclusion obstacle. There is a direct link between access to relevant and effective information and funding access. Masuki et al. (2010) posit that access to agricultural information can help smallholder farmers to access funding opportunities, improve production capacity, and improve their access to better remunerative markets. In South Africa, it was found that most land reform beneficiaries only "mostly possessed traditional and indigenous farming knowledge passed from generation to generation" (Informant 17, 2021). This information is no longer adequate in the contemporary world, and lending institutions do not consider it. This leaves many of these farmers excluded in terms of access to finical support. The International Fund for Agricultural Development (IFAD) (2012) also found that women, indigenous farmers, and young people were highly deprived of training and up-to-date information much to their exclusion when seeking funding opportunities. When compared to men, women had much less access to information through agricultural extension services (Quisumbing & Pandolfelli, 2010), and hence their chances of sources and processes of funding remain low. This same situation was reported by farmers across the province particularly women, most of whom grew limited amounts of vegetables due to a lack of funds to enlarge production.

12.4.2 Access to Productive Assets

Participants as well as reviewed secondary documents revealed a chronic lack of productive and infrastructure by land beneficiaries in South Africa (Chisasa & Makina, 2012). Participants mentioned that "while the government provided us with land, funds to acquire assets that are needed on the farm remains a challenge since farm assets are expensive for most of us" (Farmer 9, 2021). Most of the participants did not have basic farm equipment such as tractors and assets such as boreholes and water tanks. This, therefore, undermined their capacity to produce and attract investors. It was also mentioned that "financial institutions and other lenders also considered the value of productive assets which farmers have before they can offer loans" (Informant 4, 2021). However, since most farmers had limited assets, they remained outside the web of financial inclusion. Jari and Fraser (2009) also found that land recipients did not have access to on-farm infrastructures, such as storerooms and cold-rooms, to keep their products in condition after harvesting.

Lack of ownership and access to assets did not only diminish the chances of access to funding but also negatively impacted the quality of products, "especially those that need certain storage conditions" (Farmer 14, 2021). Where products are compromised by inadequate storage conditions, entry into formal markets gets also compromised, since the emphasis of buyers is more on quality. Poor storage facilities mostly affected farmers who produce fruits and vegetables. Some farmers who produced eggs revealed that lack of assets forced them to hire more unnecessary labour as they must clean, grade, and package the eggs manually. While the hire of labour creates job opportunities as one of the intended aims of the land reform programme, such employment is created at the expense of farmers who are eventually left with nothing to invest in the farm itself. This constrained their "capacity to save money for the purchase assets and sustain their livelihoods" (Farmer 34, 2021). In this view, employment is being created through the financially disposing of the farmers themselves. Poor access to and ownership of assets affect how farmers can benefit from opportunities in the agricultural markets, thereby further making them financially excluded. Most of the farmers were over the age of 50 and had no other sources of income except farming. This made them unattractive to potential investors and lending institutions, which prefer "young and educated farmers who can easily be couched into capitalist commercial farmers unlike the elderly" (Informant 13, 2021).

Inadequate access to inputs was mentioned alongside asset access and ownership challenges by farmers. Informants reported that funds also barred them from accessing inputs which were mostly sold in large quantities are often "packaged for the needs of large-scale commercial farmers who purchase in bulk" (Informant 17, 2021). Inadequate access to inputs coupled with weak infrastructure condemned most farmers to "producing low quantities of produce which is of poor quality" (Informant 4, 2021), which further complicated their chances to be considered for funding by investors.

12.4.3 Agribusiness Model Incongruity

The South Africa government, through its policy pronouncements and actions, emphasises the large-scale agribusiness model as opposed to its small-scale counterpart which land reform recipients can easily succeed in (Rusenga, 2019). This neoliberal proclivity has been the source of the marginalisation of land recipients. The government expects land beneficiaries to emerge as successful commercial farmers even though it does not provide the requisite support that was central to the development of White commercial farming historically. For this reason, Rusenga (2020) argues that the government is setting land beneficiaries up for failure. One key informant lamented that "the failure by the state to subdivide the land to give to each recipient only a suitable size is one of the major challenges. Farmers end up underperforming as they try to utilise the entire farm" (Informant 7, 2021). During the interviews, the authors also found that some farmers had 20 hectares of land and yet* were only afforded to raise about 10,000 chickens due to insufficient resources. The failure to subdivide the land in the presence of limited resources for farmers eventually translates into underutilisation of the land as most of it lies idle. The state does not subdivide the land with the belief that "the new farmers should be able to utilise it at the same levels with their previous white counterparts who were viewed as efficient and productive" (Informant 16, 2021). While the new farmers are encouraged to adopt large-scale business models, it is ironic that adequate resources are not being provided to these farmers.

Participants and informants agreed that commercial agriculture was expensive and therefore, needed financial support. It was found to be "impractical to operate on a large scale, especially for farmers who lacked financial support without financial assistance" (Farmer 4, 2021). Farmers, therefore, indicated that they were financially excluded, because they did not receive any form of support from the state besides the land. (Farmer 2, 2021). Some farmers reported that they "depended on their sources of funding, such as household off-farm income, informal loans, and assistance by family members, and therefore, could not afford expensive inputs" (Farmer 1, 2021).

Most of the participant farmers in this study were engaged in crop farming and poultry. They indicated that other slots in the value chain would be expensive for them due to a lack of adequate funding to finance operations. Farmers did not indicate any intention to even add value to their products arguing that adding value would not add much in terms of income.

The government exhorts land reform beneficiaries to approach financial institutions for funding or engage either in joint ventures or contract arrangements instead of funding them themselves (DRDLR, 2013). Financial institutions or the private actors with which farmers are encouraged to team up are expected to contribute expertise and finance while the farmers contributed land. This is viewed as part of the broader effort to empower previously disadvantaged groups, especially Blacks. What is not considered though is that leaving these resource-poor farmers at the mercy of financial institutions exposes them to land grabs by capital when they fail to payback the loans. Mazwi et al. (2018: 8) argue that:

> Markets offer many chances for opportunistic behaviour and tend to favour strong market actors, that is, those with the capital, know-how, and information to protect and expand their property rights, and to buffer themselves against risk. The local culmination of the process is a gradual transfer of land rights via the market to capital-rich actors, and a gradual concentration of land ownership in the hands of those who can invest to achieve optimal economies of scale in production and commercialization.

Where farmers are left at the mercy of private actors in joint ventures or contract farming arrangements, the result could be a loss of control of the farm with compromised sovereignty (Ndhlovu, 2022a). What is disturbing is that acceptance of a mentor or strategic partner has been made to be one of the conditions for the "financial inclusion" of farmers. Farmers with a mentor or strategic partner who will undertake business planning duties are eligible to receive funding under the Recapitalization and Development Programme (RADP). This neoliberal approach to financial inclusion is not likely to reap benefits for farmers but for the other members in the partnership.

Land experts have taken issue with the kind of strategic partners with which farmers are to team up with to qualify for funding. Hall and Kepe (2017) observed that these partners are mostly monopoly-finance capital in the form of agribusiness entities and White large-scale farmers. Using their financial influence, these entities exhibit their opportunistic nature to subvert land control to their favour. While the government committed itself to oust monopoly capital in the pursuit of equality and Black empowerment discourses, policy practices, such as the Proactive Land Acquisition Strategy (PLAS) contrarily, according to Rusenga (2019), sustain modernist and colonial conventions predicated on commercial viability criteria, and therefore, do not meaningfully empower land beneficiaries to transform their livelihoods and income profiles through farming. Functional land reform for societal transformation should be defined by the empowerment of land beneficiaries to lead in determining how they can successfully utilise their land, depending on their contexts of culture and context of situations (Ndhlovu, 2018, 2021). The failure to take this into account by the government prompted Kepe and Hall (2018) to conclude that the South African land reform enforces a colonial present instead of decolonisation.

12.4.4 Unethical Behaviour

The other financial inclusion challenge reported by farmers was corruption by the political elite, who practised the political economy of affection where resources were being distributed in a manner that enabled them to accrue political capital. Farmers reported that connections mattered a lot in the acquisition of support. One farmer mentioned that:

> I have been waiting for a polyethene plastic for tomatoes for three now. We had a fire accident here. Officials from the department came and assessed and promised to assist with another one, but nothing is yet up to now. Another farmer, well-connected to the structures got a polyethene plastic in a matter of days. Its connection does things here. (Farmer 17, 2021)

The political economy of affection also played out when particular farmers were reported to be selected time and again to receive training, inputs, funding, and assets. Some farmers were reported to have "multiple sources of funding as a result of their political connections" (Framer 19). While officials from the department denied corruption allegations positing that they used consistent criteria in the "selection of farmers who should be linked to certain sources of funding following the nature and types of their products" (Informant 6, 2021), farmers argued that these officials rarely visited farmers "but in their offices in Johannesburg where they cracked deals on behalf of their preferred farmers who give them kick-backs" (Farmer 32, 2021).

Some officials, however, acknowledged that, more often than not, the "department failed to follow its procedures in the distribution of state funds, land allocations, and providing support to land recipients" (Informant 4, 2021). This issue is also shared by Tom (2021: Online) who posits that in the Eastern Cape Province, "government funding allocated to 'bonafide' commercial and small-scale farmers" in the province never get to them. Instead, the money ended up in the pockets of people with no real ties to the agricultural industry. Bent McNamara, the CEO of Agri Eastern Cape also mentioned that:

> Even some of the farms that have been purchased by the state have gone to beneficiaries that, again, are not the correct beneficiaries. Some of them even got the farms because they are financially or politically connected to government officials. Those farms end up not getting used to farming productively. (Quoted by Tom, 2021: Online)

Participants mentioned that while the government's good intentions to financially empower farmers, such intentions had "actually not translated into implementation on the ground" (Farmer 14, 2021). It has also become common practice for agricultural land and finds to be distributed to people who are not farmers and for resources given to people connected with people in high places, influential positions, or to farmers who are already financially resourced, thereby excluding the financially excluded. South Africa has ranked the 73rd most corrupt country out of 180 countries in the world (Martin & Solomon, 2016). This corruption affects the poor more than anyone else.

Participants complained that the political elites across the country were known for looting public funds meant for the poor and financially excluded. These views are also confirmed by previous studies which found that, in some cases, those who were entitled to land reform support were not permitted to access it and that some government officials also inflated land prices to benefit themselves (Mubecua et al., 2020). de Jager (2019) found that corruption and nepotism among farmers and government officials are responsible for the failed land reform in South Africa. Corruption as an endemic challenge which faces land reform recipients was also reported in Zimbabwe, where state bureaucrats manipulated the mechanisation distribution programme to predominantly favour the political capital. The distribution of the Reserve Bank of Zimbabwe Farm Mechanisation was not only political, but it was also biased in favour of ruling Zimbabwe African National Union-Patriotic Front (ZANU-PF) elites (Magaisa, 2020; Gono, 2020). Where the corruptions obtain, the result is the further financial exclusion of the same people that the land reform programme was initially meant to financially include. Part of the efforts towards financial inclusion for land recipients, therefore, is the clamping down on corrupt activities across all economic sectors.

12.5 Toward Financial Inclusion for Land Beneficiaries

For the financial inclusion agenda to be pursued rigorously and be implemented sustainably, there is a need, first, to reconceptualise the concept of "financial inclusion" itself. Once the concept is conceptualised to emphasise finance access instead of access to banking services, policymakers will then be able to design policies that can yield results in terms of directing funds to the people (farmers). Ensuring the financial inclusion of land beneficiaries requires the government itself to set aside some funds specifically meant to funding the operation activities of the farmers. The South African government generally promotes the large-scale agriculture production model over the small-scale one (Hall & Kepe, 2017; Rusenga, 2019). To be able to grow up to a level where land beneficiaries can operate on a large scale, investments need to be made by the government by providing all the necessary resources. This support should start as soon as the people have been given land.

It is also important that a private body or entity be established to over the rolling out if support to farmers and to ensure that they operate as businesses rather than operating at a subsistence level. State officials have been widely documented as having failed to appropriately undertake their duties (Chisasa & Makina, 2012; Majova, 2016). This, therefore, justifies the need for the involvement of private actors. While partnerships and joint ventures cab inject the much-needed resources into a business, the government must put in place some principles and standards that can be used to guide partnerships and joint ventures, so that farmers will not end up being exploited by their resourced partners who will seem to dominate operations.

12.6 Conclusion

This chapter has argued for the need for a rethinking of the concept of financial inclusion, particularly intending to insert new categories of knowledge in the context of the land reform recipients in Africa. It argues that the current conceptualisation of "financial inclusion" does not allow for the creation of a mature scholarly debate in the context of land reform, as the emphasis is placed on access to financial services instead of focusing on access to the finance itself. This article argues that financial inclusion should not be simply all about the delivery of financial services to people. It should rather encompass the actual delivery of the finance itself to them at an affordable cost. This is particularly important where financial inclusion is anticipated to be the key to economic growth and development and to the realisation of national objectives, which are focused on the generation of market-driven, productive, and competitive economies. Through empirical evidence, the article that what land reform recipients in South Africa are mostly concerned about is not access to financial services but rather to the finance itself, which they could use to support their operations.

The article argues that the first challenge sustaining financial exclusion is how the whole discourse and practice is structured. Financial inclusion is merely viewed in terms of the intangibles (the services) offered by financial institutions and rarely viewed in terms of the tangibles (the cash) that people need to improve their situations. This could make the financial inclusion concept meaningful. Farmers need access to finance itself as the first sign of inclusion. It has also been found that the institutions in charge of financial support for the agricultural sector in South Africa are biased towards large-scale, capitalist farmers while land reform beneficiaries are marginalised. This has further sustained financial exclusion.

The article also revealed that the financial exclusion of land reform beneficiaries has been worsened by the government's inclination to encourage land recipients to adopt the large-scale and capital-intensive land use model despite their lack of background in large-scale production nor in the substantive resources required to sustain production (Aliber & Cousins, 2013). In the last 10 years, the government tried to solve the financial and production challenges in land reform projects through the implementation of mentorships and strategic partnerships. However, such arrangements are poorly packaged such that they benefitted the commercial mentors and agribusinesses while beneficiaries remained poor and financially excluded. As a result, land reform in South Africa has had minimal impact on social justice, poverty reduction, and financial inclusion. The article concludes that the starting point towards the realisation of financial inclusion for land recipients in South Africa should be the reconceptualisation of the concept itself so that it can capture the context of the needs of the people and situations.

References

Aliber, M., & Cousins, B. (2013). Livelihoods after land reform in South Africa. *Journal of Agrarian Change, 13*(1), 140–165.

Boudreax, C. (2009). Land reform as social justice: The case of South Africa. In S. G. Mazibuko, (2011). *Analysing contemporary development debates and issues: Reader for DVA4801.* Pretoria: South Africa.

Boudreax, K. (2009, October). Land reform as social justice: The case of South Africa. Working paper no. 09–37. The Mercatus Center at George Mason University.

Brobbey, P. (2010). *Theories of social development.* University of Ghana, Department of Sociology.

Chartier, F., & Louis, L. (2017). Financial inclusion in South Africa: An integrated framework for financial inclusion of vulnerable communities in South Africa's regulatory system reform. *Journal of Comparative Urban Law and Policy, 1*, 13.

Chisasa, J., & Makina, D. (2012). *Trends in credit to smallholder farmers in South Africa*. University of Pretoria.

Claessens, S. (2006). Access to financial services: A review of the issues and public policy objectives. *The World Bank Research Observer, 21*, 207–240.

Cousins, B. (2015). 'Through a glass, darkly': Towards agrarian reform in South Africa.' In B. Cousins & C. Walker (Eds.). *Land Divided, Land Restored. Land Reform in South Africa for the 21st Century*. Auckland Park: Jacana.

de Jager, T. (2019). It's not the willing seller, but the corrupt buyer sabotaging land reform. *News24*. Available at: https://www.news24.com/news24/columnists/guestcolumn/itsnot-the-willing-seller-but-the-corrupt-buyer-sabotaging-land-reform20190624. Accessed 23/10/2021.

Demirguc-kunt, A., Klapper, L., Singer, D., Ansar, S., & Hess, J. (2018). *The Global Findex Database 2017: Measuring financial inclusion and the Fintech revolution*. The World Bank.

Department of Land Affairs. (1997). *White paper on South African land policy*. Government Printers.

Department of Rural Development and Land Reform (DRDLR). (2013). *Policy for the recapitalisation and development programme of the Department of Rural Development and Land Reform*. Government Printers.

Farmer 01, 05/01/2021, Magalisburg.

Farmer 02, 12/01/2021, Magalisburg.

Farmer 04, 12/01/2021, Kempton Park.

Farmer 07, 11/01/2021. Magalisburg.

Farmer 09, 11/01/2021. Westonaria.

Farmer 12, 12/01/2021, Kempton Park.

Farmer 14, 22/01/2021, Germiston.

Farmer 17, 05/02/2021, Germiston.

Farmer 32, 09/04/2021, West Rand.

Farmer 34, 16/04/2021, Soutpan.

Gaanakgomo, T. (2015). *Challenges and opportunities facing emerging farmers in North West Province, South African case study: DR. Kenneth Kaunda District Municipality-Ventersdorp Local Municipality*. North West University-Mafikeng.

Gono, G. (2020). Gideon Gono: The truth about RBZ debt and farm mechanisation. *The Herald*. Harare. Available at https://www.zimlive.com/2020/07/19/gideon-gono-the-truth-about-rbz-debt-and-farm-mechanisation/downloaded

Gumede, V. (2014). Land reform in post-apartheid South Africa: Should South Africa follow Zimbabwe's footsteps? *International Journal of African Renaissance Studies, 9*(1), 50–68.

Hall, R. (2004). A political economy of land reform in South Africa. *Review of African Political Economy, 31*(100), 213–227.

Hall, R. (2009). *Another country? Policy options for land and agrarian reform in South Africa*. PLAAS.

Hall, R., & Kepe, T. (2017). Elite capture and state neglect: New evidence on South Africa's land reform. *Review of African Political Economy, 44*(151), 122–130.

Informant 02, 12/01/2021, Department of Agriculture.

Informant 03, 13/01/2021, Department of Agriculture.

Informant 04, 22/01/2021, Department of Agriculture.

Informant 06, 25/02/2021, Department of Agriculture.

Informant 07, 26/02/2021, Industrial Development Corporation (IDC).

Informant 13, 19/03/2021, Land Bank.

Informant 15, 26/03/2021, Department of Agriculture.

Informant 16, 21/05/2021, Industrial Development Corporation (IDC).

Informant 17, 28/05/2021, Land Bank.

International Fund for Agricultural Development. (2012). *Summary of the findings of the project implemented by MIJARC in collaboration with FAO and IFAD: Facilitating access of rural youth to agricultural activities*. FAO and IFAD.

Jari, B., & Fraser, G. (2009). *Influence of institutional and technical factors on market choice of smallholder farmers in the Kat River Valley*. South Africa.

Kepe, T., & Hall, R. (2018). Land redistribution in South Africa: Towards decolonisation or recolonisation? *Politikon, 45*(1), 128–137.

Kirsten, J. F., & Van Zyl, J. (1998). Defining small-scale farmers in the South African context. *Routledge Taylor & Francis, 37*(4), 551–562.

Land Bank Research Report. (2012). *Addressing challenges of financing emerging farmers South Africa*. Land Bank.

Magaisa, A. (2020). BSR EXCLUSIVE: Beneficiaries of the RBZ farm mechanisation scheme. *The Big Saturday Read Blog*. Available at https://www.bigsr.co.uk/single-post/2020/07/18/BSR-EXCLUSIVE-Beneficiaries-of-the-RBZ-Farm-Mechanisation-Scheme

Majova, N. B. (2016). *Women empowerment in the South African agri-business: Impact, policy and implementation in Gauteng province* (Unpublished MBA dissertation). Milpark Business School, South Africa.

Maphoto, T. A. (2012). *Land claims in South Africa: Progress report by Minister, from Parliamentary Monitoring Group*. Available at www.pmg.org.za

Martin, M. E., & Solomon, H. (2016). Understanding the phenomenon of —state capture in South Africa. *Southern African Peace and Security Studies, 5*(1), 21–35.

Masilela, C., & Weiner, D. (1996). *Resettlement planning in Zimbabwe and South Africa's rural land reform discourse*. TWPR.

Masuki, K. F., Kamugisha, R., Mowo, J. G., Tanui, J., Tukahirwa, J., Mogoi, J., & Adera, E. O. (2010). *Role of mobile phones in improving communication and information delivery for agricultural development: Lessons from South Western Uganda*. Workshop at Makerere University, Uganda (pp. 22–23). Available at: http://outputs.worldagroforestry.org/record/5546/files/PP10288.pdf.

Mazwi, F., Tekwa, N., Chambati, W., & Mudimu, G. T. (2018). *Locating the position of peasants under the 'new dispensation': A focus on land tenure issues*. Sam Moyo Africa Institute for Agrarian Studies.

Mhlanga, D., & Dunga, S. H. (2021). Financial inclusion in agriculture: Lessons from Zimbabwe. *Academy of Accounting and Financial Studies Journal, 25*(2), 1–12.

Mpandeli, S., & Maponya, P. (2014). Constraints and challenges facing the small scale farmers in Limpopo Province, South Africa. *Journal of Agricultural Science, 6*(4), 135–143.

Mubecua, M. A., Mbatha, M. W., Mpanza, S. E., & Tembe, S. K. (2020). Conflict and corruption: Land expropriation without compensation in South Africa. *African Journal of Peace and Conflict Studies, 9*(2), 61–76.

Mutero, J., Munapo, E., & Seaketso, P. (2016). Operational challenges faced by smallholder farmers: A case of Ethekwini Metropolitan in South Africa. *Environmental Economics, 7*(2), 40–52.

Ncapayi, F. (2013). *Land and changing social relations in South Africa's former reserves: the case of Luphaphasi in Sakhisizwe Local Municipality, Eastern Cape* (PhD thesis). University of Cape Town, South Africa.

Ndhlovu, E. (2018). Relevance of sustainable livelihood approach in Zimbabwe's land reform programme. *Africa Insight, 47*(4), 72–87.

Ndhlovu, E. (2021). The land question in Africa: Sam's perspectives. In V. T. Gumede & T. Shonhe (Eds.), *Rethinking the land and agrarian questions in Africa*. Africa Century Editions Press.

Ndhlovu, E. (2022a). Changing agrarian discourses and practices and the prospects for food sovereignty in Zimbabwe. In G. Mkodzongi (Ed.), *The future of Zimbabwe's agrarian sector: Land issues in a time of political transition* (pp. 34–53). Routledge.

Ndhlovu, E. (2022b). Political economy of Chisa livelihoods in rural Zimbabwe. In K. Helliker, J. Matanzima, & P. Chadambuka (Eds.), *Livelihoods of ethnic minorities in rural Zimbabwe* (pp. 123–139). Springer International Publishing.

Ngomane, T. S. (2016). Land as an economic empowerment tool: access, control and ownership of land by rural women in the Mpumalanga province, South Africa. PhD thesis. University of Limpopo, South Africa.

Poulton, C., Dorward, A., & Kydd, J. (2010). The future of small farms: New directions for services, institutions, and intermediation. *World Development, 38*(10). Available at: http://www.sciencedirect.com/science/article/pii/S0305750X10000987

Quisumbing, A. R., & Pandolfelli, L. (2010). Promising approaches to address the needs of poor female farmers: Resources, constraints, and interventions. *World Development, 38*(4). Available at: http://www.sciencedirect.com/science/article/pii/S0305750X09001806

Republic of South Africa 'Constitution of the Republic of South Africa'. (1996). Retrieved from http://www.justice.gov.za/legislation/constitution/SAConstitution-web-eng.pdf

Rusenga, C. (2017). *The socio-economic consequences of the agribusiness model on the land reform beneficiaries in the Greater Tzaneen Municipality, South Africa: The case of the Elangeni project* (Unpublished PhD thesis). University of Cape Town, Cape Town, South Africa.

Rusenga, C. (2019). The agribusiness model in South African land reform? Land use implications for the land reform beneficiaries. *Agrarian South: Journal of Political Economy, 8*(3), 440–461.

Rusenga, C. (2020). Setting them up to fail: Enforcement of the agribusiness model on land reform projects in South Africa. *Review of African Political Economy, 47*(165), 382–398.

Tom, S. (2021). *Corruption in EC cripples black farmers*. Foodformzansi. www.foodformzansi.co.za

Van Schalkwyk, H. D., Groenewald, J. A., Fraser, G. C. G., Obi, A., & van Tilburg, A. (2012). *Unlocking Markets for Smallholder in South Africa*. Wageningen Academic Publishers.

World Bank Group. (2017). *Achieving effective financial inclusion in South Africa: A payments perspective*. In M. O. Finance (Ed.). Government of South Africa.

Chapter 13
Peasant Financial Inclusion for Inclusive Development in Zimbabwe

Emmanuel Ndhlovu and David Mhlanga

Abstract The existing conceptualisation of financial inclusion has basic analytical challenges which do not allow for the framing of a mature scholarly debate on poverty alleviation and the attainment of inclusive development, especially for the peasantry. Using the Zimbabwe case study and drawing on secondary literature sources accessed in academic and grey literature databases using financial inclusion, farmer support, and credit and loan access as keywords, this chapter takes issue with the conventional conceptualisation of financial inclusion as delivery of financial services to the poor at an affordable cost. It posits that finance itself and not simply financial services should be the basis of financial inclusion for inclusive development. The chapter analyses various epochs within the country's history to demonstrate what financial inclusion should constitute. It concludes that it is only when the concept is reconceptualised to relate to the context of circumstances and needs of people that it will be able to allow for a deeper understanding of how inclusive and sustainable development does not leave the peasantry outside the tide of development can be realised.

Keywords Financial inclusion · Inclusive development · Peasants · Poverty · Zimbabwe

JEL G2 · G15 · G28 · G5

E. Ndhlovu (✉)
Vaal University of Technology, Vanderbijlpark, South Africa

D. Mhlanga
School of Business and Economics, The University of Johannesburg, Johannesburg, South Africa

D. Mhlanga, E. Ndhlovu (eds.), *Economic Inclusion in Post-Independence Africa*, Advances in African Economic, Social and Political Development,
https://doi.org/10.1007/978-3-031-31431-5_13

13.1 Introduction

The conceptualisation of financial inclusion has basic analytical challenges which do not allow for the framing of a mature scholarly debate on poverty alleviation and the attainment of inclusive development. While available literature is celebratory of this 'new' development concept, the literature is superficial on how this concept can be implemented and realised. This is despite the huge emphasis and widespread recognition of financial inclusion as one of the key solutions to unlocking the potential of the various sectors of the national economies (Amoah et al., 2020; Mhlanga & Denhere, 2021). Influential policy institutions such as the World Bank have even recommended countries develop National Financial Inclusion Strategies (defined as roadmaps of actions, agreed, upon and defined at the national or subnational level) as the basic path towards the realisation of financial inclusion (World Bank, 2018).

What emerges poignantly in the financial inclusion literature are some sweeping generalisations on what the concept entails and how it can be achieved. Both policy institutions and financial inclusion experts aver that financial inclusion is the viable provision of affordable financial services that bring the poor into the formal economy (United Nations, 2016) and or the usage of formal financial services by poor people (Ozili, 2018). For some, the concept refers to the process of ensuring the availability and ease of access to the formal financial sector (Mhlanga & Dunga, 2020). According to Eldomiaty et al. (2020), financial inclusion is the process of ensuring access to appropriate financial products and services required by all categories and sub-categories of society in general and vulnerable groups, such as weaker sections and low-income groups, at an affordable cost fairly and transparently by regulated mainstream institutional players. What is problematic about this conceptualisation is the silence on the 'finance' itself as the emphasis is placed on 'services'. The conceptualisation assumes that people already have money and that they only lack access to banking services. This is misplaced and dangerous, especially in an era where concerted efforts are needed for the realisation of inclusive development, that is, 'development that includes marginalized people, sectors and countries in social, political and economic processes for increased human wellbeing, social and environmental sustainability, and empowerment' (van Gent, 2017: 10). Financial inclusion, therefore, needs to be reconceptualised so that it speaks to the socio-economic realities that allow for inclusive and sustainable development.

This chapter problematises the current conceptualisation of financial inclusion and proposes a reconceptualisation that is pro-poor and that is pro-vulnerable economic or livelihoods sectors. Situated in Zimbabwe – a country that is currently experiencing a broad-based economic crisis – the chapter reconceptualises financial inclusion to speak to the peasant majority who make up 70% of the inhabitants of the country (Worldometers, 2019). The reconceptualisation places emphasis on the need for improved access to formal 'finance' as opposed to mere 'services' articulated in the literature. It argues that access to finance instead of services wields concrete potential towards the realisation of inclusive development as it could allow peasants to access the finance which they need for the purchase of inputs and equipment needed to enable them to put their labour to productive use in farming.

This chapter is based on a review of land and agrarian change discourses and policy practices in Zimbabwe since colonial times. A detailed literature review on farmer support was conducted, including an analysis of viewpoints, policy, and strategy documents. The peasantry (defined as 'small-scale family farmers who mainly depend on family labour and produce a significant share of their food and may use their labour for off-farm activities and wage labour' (Moyo, 2016: 1)) was chosen because it makes most of the Zimbabwe population (Worldometers, 2019). It is also the most vulnerable category given the unfolding broad-based economic crisis and regrouping neoliberalism as well as climate change (Mhlanga & Ndhlovu, 2021a). The search for germane documents was conducted in academic and grey literature databases using financial inclusion, farmer support, and credit and loan access as keywords.

The next section provides a historical background of financial inclusion. This is followed by its contextualisation in Zimbabwe using four distinct epochs. Thereafter, the chapter proposes how financial inclusion could be reconceptualised. Lastly, conclusions and implications of the findings are made.

13.2 The History of Financial Inclusion

The concept of financial inclusion is believed to have been first coined for the first time in the early 1990s by geographers who observed how certain population categories struggled to physically access banking services due to their geographical location which institutions seemed to avoid (Eldomiaty et al., 2020; Mhlanga & Denhere, 2021). These geographers coined the term financial inclusion to posit that population categories which inhabit geographically prohibitive areas are financially excluded and, therefore, are poor and vulnerable. Financial inclusion is defined as the delivery of financial services to the poor at an affordable cost (Ozili, 2018). It is the delivery of banking services to the vast majority of disadvantaged and low-income groups at an affordable cost (Eldomiaty et al., 2020). Amoah et al. (2020) aver that financial exclusion features as the major socio-economic challenge in contemporary economics.

What is disappointing about the existing definitions of financial inclusion is the deafening silence on the importance of finance access (and not services) as the major component of financial inclusion. The definitions emphasise the delivery of banking services to disadvantaged and low-income groups at an affordable cost. This is very problematic because human well-being and inclusive development is based on the tangibles (material things) and not merely the intangibles (services). It is worrisome to confine financial inclusion merely to the delivery of financial services without emphasizing how to broaden finance access by people to enable them to increase the level of their production activities. How financial inclusion is currently conceptualised does not, therefore, speak to the context of situations of the same poor and vulnerable categories of society for whom it is meant to find solutions.

Ozili (2020) informatively chronicles a series of critiques of financial inclusion. He argues that the current conceptualisation of financial inclusion is a mere invitation for the poor and the vulnerable to live by finance. This, according to him, is nothing other than the financialisation of poverty as well-being will not be measured in monetary terms. Ozili (2020) also notes that the mobilisation of people to get into the formal economy through the utilisation of bank services is cosmetic since the benefits of having a bank account or access to services usually disappear after a few years. Ozili (2020) also takes issue with how financial inclusion ignores how poverty affects financial decision-making by the poor and how it promotes digital money which most of the poor and vulnerable sections of society find difficult to understand. More apparently, financial inclusion efforts bear a semblance to a crusade against having cash-in-hand (Ozili, 2020). This series of critiques by Ozili is demonstrable in the analysis of how financial inclusion could imply vulnerable population categories, such as the peasantry located at the periphery of the global political economy. One of the countries in which Peterson Ozili's critiques are demonstrable, especially with a focus on the peasantry, is Zimbabwe.

13.3 Financial Inclusion in Zimbabwe

Zimbabwe's financial inclusion reality falls within four identifiable periods as discussed in the next subsections.

13.3.1 The Colonial Experience

It is ironic that in Zimbabwe where 70% of the population is peasantry (Worldometers, 2019) financial inclusion is also merely defined as: 'the effective use of a wide range of quality, affordable and accessible financial services, provided fairly and transparently through formal or regulated entities to all Zimbabweans' (Reserve Bank of Zimbabwe, 2016). With 84% of the population classified as poor at the end of 2019 (Quinn, 2019), it is problematic to assume that the delivery of financial services would translate into poverty reduction and inclusive development particularly since the material base is not supported adequately. The reason for the lack of financial inclusion for the Zimbabwe peasantry is their financial exclusion as a result of a race-biased political economy which deliberately promoted the financial inclusion of Whites only. As a result, financial inclusion and inclusive development challenges need to be understood in the country's historical context also bearing in mind that financial inclusion for inclusive development promotes and facilitates access to the finance itself and not simply services.

The exclusion of peasants from finance and wealth goes back to 1894 when the Pioneer Column – a group of British South African Company policemen and pioneers – defeated the Matabele (Moyana, 1984). With the defeat of the Matabele army, which was the most powerful in the country, Whites subsequently expropriated the entire country. Thus, land expropriation became the first instance of wealth exclusion which later, as land became commoditised by Europeans, became financial exclusion.

In addition to some fraudulently acquired documents, such as the Rudd and the Lippert concession, which transferred land from Blacks to Whites which Lobengula was duped to sign, the White government also instituted a myriad of prohibitive legislative frameworks to exclude Blacks from their national wealth. The Rudd and Lippert concession became the basis for all other pieces of legislation required by Whites to completely financially exclude the indigenous people from their wealth. In 1898, the Native Reserves Order in Council was adopted to create Native Reserves for Africans to ensure the availability of more land for Whites who continued to pour into the country. The reserves were not only planned hurriedly but were also meant to ensure that Africans were in low-potential areas where they were financially excluded to make them always available in the labour market (Ndhlovu, 2021). The Order-in-Council ruled that Africans could purchase, hold and trade land under the same conditions as those of the non-native (Pollak, 1975). However, few Africans had the resources to buy land at the time (Floyd, 1962). By 1921, European settlers had acquired 31 million acres of land versus the 40,000–47,000 purchased by African farmers (Arrighi, 1967).

To deter accumulation rivalry, the colonial regime did little to support commercial African agriculture (Chingozha & von Fintel, 2019). Instead, Africans continued to face displacement (Pollak, 1975). The Morris Carter Commission of 1925 was formed to cement the exclusion of Africans from wealth and development and to consolidate European's domination of land and wealth. The outcome of the commission was that racial tension in the colony emerged from the contact between the European and African races and that this could be resolved by complete separation (Floyd, 1962; Pollak, 1975). The recommendations of the Morris-Carter Commission were promulgated as the Land Apportionment Act (LAA) in 1930 (Pollak, 1975). The LAA cemented the financial exclusion of Blacks. Like the South African Native Land Act of 1913, the Act enabled Whites to completely wrench and alienate Africans from their ancestral lands and confine them to Purchase Areas (Pas) (Moyana, 1984). The LAA shared land as follows: 8.8 million hectares for Native Reserves, three million for Native Purchase Areas, 19.9 million hectares for White farming and urban areas, and 7.2 million hectares of unallocated land (Ndhlovu, 2021). The Act was further accompanied by restraints, such as the Cattle Levy Act which reduced the number of cattle owned by an individual through increased tax and the Maize Control Act which restricted blacks from accessing marketing outlets. By 1963 the native African population (approximately over 2.5 million) occupied only 50,000 square miles of land, while about a fifth of a million settlers occupied the other 75,000 square miles (Chingozha & von Fintel, 2019).

Increased land and pasture shortages and the concomitant soil erosion led to the institutionalisation of further Black financial exclusion arrangements such as the Land Husbandry Act of 1951 which imposed conservation measures, introduced private land ownership, and enforced destocking practices on lands owned by Africans (Utete, 2003). While the Act restricted land use by Africans, unlike Whites who received an extension and financial support from the government to deal with land degradation, Blacks, including Black commercial farmers, did not receive such support. As if that was not enough to completely stamp the financial exclusion of Blacks, the 1969 Land Tenure Act was instituted. The Act categorised lands into European, African, and National lands (Moyana, 1984). This enabled the Rhodesia Front government to concentrate financial support on European areas where farmers were regarded as more productive. The supposed productivity of White farmers over their Black counterparts was ironic in that it was premised on government support which was also not extended to Black farmers. All of the Acts adopted by colonial regimes were premised not on inclusive development but on separate development philosophies, whereby Whites were given all the necessary financial support. These Acts were meant to suppress the financial participation of Blacks in economic activities and, thus, were the basis of their financial exclusion which the government had to grapple with at independence.

The government in Rhodesia therefore pursued limited financial inclusion and inclusive development efforts. Whatever seeming inclusive efforts it made, such efforts were made to avoid violent resistance by natives. Such compromises included the so-called Native Purchase Areas (NPAs) which allowed Africans to buy land. This was introduced knowing that very few Africans would have the financial resources to acquire land. The rights of Africans to land were thus effectually suspended, except in the 81 NPAs (Floyd, 1962). Africans who did not afford to buy land in the NPAs were forcibly moved to Tribal Trust Areas (TTA) where communal land tenure existed.

In the 1950s, white farmers in Southern Rhodesia produced abundant tobacco more than in any other country in Africa (Haviland, 1953). By 1979–1980 the country even became a net agricultural exporter (Munslow, 1985). The productivity of the White farmers was based on which focus on improving the conditions of White farmers (Chingozha & von Fintel, 2019). On the other hand, the State made production for markets by Africans very difficult with transport, and communication infrastructure also planned to support the economic activities of White farmers who were mostly located in the Highveld of the eastern highlands (Machingaidze, 1991). Roads, railways, and communication networks were created to connect European farming areas to markets and urban centres (Chingozha & von Fintel, 2019), while TTAs and NPAs did not receive the same basic infrastructure, thereby further worsening their exclusion. Less than 25% of African farmers were located within 25 miles of a rail line as compared to over 75% of their European counterparts (Chingozha & von Fintel, 2019).

The promotion of racially biased development in Southern Rhodesia and the denial of adequate land for Blacks led to the emergence of continuous agriculture, which consequently resulted in soil erosion and reduced soil fertility (Arrighi,

1967). Inadequate land access and utilisation limited the extent to which Africans could actively participate in economic development (Moyana, 1975). Exclusion from economic activities resulted in many Blacks settling on European farms where they provided labour (Moyana, 1984).

The racially biased separate development strategy pursued by the colonial government ensured that the land to which Africans were pushed was dry and drought-prone to drive them into the labour market. In contrast, Whites acquired lands in areas that received good rainfall amounts and that were conducive to intensive crop and animal production (Ndhlovu, 2021). Whites held almost all areas suitable for dairy farming (Machingaidze, 1991), and more than three-quarters of land was suitable for intensive farming (Moyana, 1984). African agricultural returns were too meagre to allow reinvestment, and they could also not undersell the European farmers who, in most cases, sold produce on behalf of the Africans (Phimister, 1974). This cemented the exclusion agenda that the government had to contend with at independence.

13.3.2 Inclusion for Inclusive Development (1980–2000)

Zimbabwe gained independence from British colonial rule in 1980 through negotiations. This was after several years of the war for liberation. The negotiations culminated in the first democratic elections on 18 April 1980. The new government inherited a population that was highly financially excluded particularly in the countryside where agriculture activities were a key source of livelihood. Many Black households had been pushed to dry agro-ecological zones where participation in the only sector, agriculture, in which they had indigenous knowledge and skills, was constrained (Moyana, 1984). Faced with high poverty levels, the first step by the new government was to implement a land reform to promote wealth accessibility by Blacks. In a setting where the people had long been denied accessibility to assets that were the source of financial inclusion and inclusive development, such as land, capital, and skills by colonialism and minority domination, providing land became fundamental (Ndhlovu, 2021). According to Kinsey (2004: 1669), the government had to prioritise 'addressing unequal land distribution, rectifying land scarcity in CAs [Communal Areas], and providing economic opportunities for the total national economy'. In other words, the government prioritised financial inclusion for inclusive development.

The land reform programme, which started in September 1980, initially gave preference to those who had been displaced by the liberation struggle, returning refugees, and to the poorest families with no land in communal areas (Ndhlovu, 2017). A general target of resettling about 18,000 households over a five-year timeframe from the congested CAs was set (Ndhlovu, 2021). The government, however, still needed to operate within the iron cages of the Lancaster House Constitution compromises which had led to independence. Some of the clauses included in the Constitution were that the new government would not compulsorily acquire land

and that any redistribution of land would be in terms of 'willing buyer, willing seller' arrangements. Chapter 3, Section 16, of the Constitution required that the 'authority [requiring land] to pay promptly adequate compensation for acquisition' and that 'if the acquisition is contested, to apply to the General Division or some other court before or not later than thirty days after the acquisition for an order confirming the acquisition'. This meant that the state could not expropriate any lands for redistribution even though it had inherited a racially biased land ownership pattern. As a result, land for resettlement during this period could only be acquired on market-based principles of willing buyer – willing seller with the state paying for the land at the full market price as well as competing for land with prospective buyers on the open market (Moyo, 2011). This land redistribution approach frustrated the pace of financial and wealth inclusion. However, although criticised for not reaching targets, the government was able to resettle a total of 60,000 households between 1980 and 1985 and a total of 10,000 households between 1985 and 1990 (Masiiwa, 2004).

Loosed from the Lancaster House Constitution in 1990, the government revisited the property rights section of the Constitution. The Land Acquisition Act of 1992 which provided for compulsory land acquisition for redistribution was enacted to improve land access by Africans. However, the neoliberal inclinations of the government in the 1990s frustrated the land redistribution pace. The Centre for Housing Rights and Evictions (2001) reports that the government acquired less than one million hectares and was able to resettle not more than 20,000 households in the 1990s (Ndhlovu, 2021) such that, by 1999, a staggering 11 million hectares of the prime agricultural lands were still owned by only 4500 commercial farmers most of whom were Whites (Commercial Farmers Union, 2001). More so, it was mostly senior government officials rather than the landless poor who got the land. Increasing lobbying for attention and the means of survival by war veterans in the mid-1990s influenced the government to pursue radical policy proposals. This culminated in a 1998 Donor's Conference on Land which led to the Inception Phase of Framework Plan (1998–1999) of the Land Reform and Resettlement Programme 2 (LRRP2). Phase one of the land reform only resettled 43% of the targeted 162,000 families and also failed to acquire the required land size. This was not enough to alter land relations which favoured Whites and excluded the majority of Blacks. A Donor Conference was convened to source funds for more inclusive land reform.

The Donor Conference of 1998 was an attempt to raise a sum of US$1.9 billion to be used for Phase Two of land reform (GoZ, 2001). However, only 0.02% of the required amount was raised at the conference. According to Makunike (2014), the conference failed because the government did not clarify how the US$1.9 billion would be used by the donors who were in favour of a market-oriented approach. Thus, although there were inadequate funds raised at the Land Donor Conference of 1998, in recognition of the need to address the plight of the black majorities, Phase Two of the land reform was launched in 1999 to acquire five million hectares and resettle 150,000 families (GoZ, 2001). However, the fact that the government still needed to pay for land frustrated wealth redistribution. Most Blacks, therefore, remained excluded. This led to the pursuit of a radicalised fast-tracked land reform in the 2000s.

13.3.3 Inclusion for Inclusive Development (Post-2000)

In the year 2000, Zimbabwe launched a radicalised land reform famously known as the Fast Track Land Reform Programme (FTLRP). Its major intention was to accelerate both the acquisition and redistribution of land as part of wealth redistribution efforts. The programme was meant to be undertaken in a short-circuited manner relying on domestic resources (Dabale et al., 2014) to get over 3000 farms and redistribute them under the A1 small-sized model and A2 (commercial farming) fast-track models. The project which started as an illegal project was eventually launched on 15 July 2000. The legitimisation and implementation involved surveying and pegging the invaded farms and recognising them as settled farms. The programme had been targeted at derelict and underutilised land, land owned by those who had other farms, and land close to CAs (Ndhlovu, 2021, 2022a). By October 2001, the State had acquired about 1948 farms for redistribution, but the number of people requiring land had swollen to 104,000 instead of only 25,000 as had been projected in the previous year (CFU, 2001). By 2003, land ownership by the large-scale commercial sector had been reduced from 30% to 12%, and the small-scale agricultural sector had expanded from 54% to 71% (Moyo, 2004), and, by the year 2010, the land had been reallocated to over 150,000 urban dwellers, farm workers, peasants in the countryside, and civil servants under the A1 scheme, while an additional 20,000 recipients were allocated A2 farms (Moyo, 2013: 39). The programme resulted in a net transfer of wealth and reconfiguration of power from a racial minority to various classes of Black citizens particularly the rural landless whose livelihoods are dependent on agricultural activities. It slashed the number of large capitalist farms by 75%, while large foreign and domestically owned agro estates were trimmed by 16% (Moyo, 2011).

The programme also modified the bi-modal structure (comprising white commercial farmers and agro-industrial estates on one hand and small-scale Black commercial farmers and Black peasant households on the other) into a tri-modal agrarian structure made up of the peasants (communal areas, old resettlement, and A1 farms), medium-to-large-scale farms (A2 farms), and Agro estates and agro conservancies (state or private owned) (Moyo, 2011). The bi-modal agrarian structure represented unequal and discriminatory relations of land ownership, with large-scale farmers, mostly White, holding private property rights, while peasants held communal tenure rights. The emergent tri-modal structure was essential given the massive exclusion of Blacks (Moyo, 2011). The new agrarian structure ushered in by the programme is summarised in Table 13.1.

The FTLRP was therefore of a highly redistributive character which afforded land access to Blacks. It has, however, its challenges, such as the disregard for human and property rights as well as corruption which often saw the elite benefiting State resources ahead of the poor. For instance, Magaisa (2020) reports how political elites and other well-connected citizens benefited from the country's mechanisation programme ahead of the poor. Besides these instances of greed, the programme was the first major attempt at inclusion and inclusive development because it

Table 13.1. The new agrarian structure in Zimbabwe

		Farms/households		Areas		
Farm class	Land tenure	Numbers	% of total	Hectares (millions, ha)	% of total	Farm size (ha)
Smallholder	Communal	1.100.000	81.2	16.400	49.9	15
	Old	75.000	5.5	3.667	11.2	49
	resettlement	145.800	10.8	5.759	17.5	40
	A1	1.321.000	97.6	25.286	78.6	20
	Subtotal					
Small-to-medium-sized commercial	Old SSCF	8.500	0.6	1.400	4.3	165
	Small A2	22.700	1.7	3.000	9.1	133.9
	Subtotal	31.200	2.3	4.400	13.4	142
Large-scale commercial	Medium-large	217	0.07	0.509	1.6	2.345
	A2	956	0.03	0.531	1.6	555
	Black LSCF	198	0.01	0.117	0.4	593
	White LSCF	1.371	0.11	1.157	3.5	844
	Subtotal					
Corporate Estates	Corporates	20	0.001	0.806	2.5	40.320
	Conservancies	8	0.001	0.247	0.8	30.875
	Parastatals	106	0.01	0.296	0.9	27.88
	Institutions	113	0.01	0.146	0.4	1.289
	Subtotal	247	0.022	1.495	4.5	6.051
Total		**1.3554.00**	**100**	**32.878**	**100.0**	**24.3**

Source: Moyo (2011)

provided the people with the asset needed for development. With the extension of post-resettlement support, livelihoods are widely documented as greatly improved across the country because of the project (African Institute for Agrarian Studies, 2014; Ndhlovu, 2017, 2022b; Scoones et al., 2015).

What emerges clearly, therefore, is that financial inclusion for inclusive development, therefore, should be conceptualised in terms of access to 'finance' and not to 'financial services'. After providing land as well as support in form of its Special Maize Programme for Import Substitution, popularly known as Command Agriculture, for instance, Zimbabwe was able to record the highest maize output. The Command Agriculture facility, which was launched in 2016, assisted farmers who produced cereals for domestic consumption with inputs and a ready market (Ndhlovu, 2022a). It did not require farmers to provide collateral upfront and, therefore, was accessible unlike in the private sector where some farmers had to offer their properties in towns as collateral (Shonhe, 2019). As a result, significant food production increases were recorded across the country. Through the facility, Zimbabwe experienced a major maize production increase of 321% in the 2016/2017 season, while crops which were not covered under the facility dismally performed (Mhlanga & Ndhlovu, 2021a, b). Through this facility, the average household maize production in Mashonaland West was 739.2 kilograms, while the least was 174.5 kilogrammes in Matabeleland South. Masvingo was with an average of 356 kilograms (Zimbabwe Vulnerability Assessment Committee (ZimVAC), 2020). This was confirmed as the first major maize output in which 'yields were also high, surpassing the national maize requirements for the first time…' since the onset of the FTLRP (Mazwi et al., 2019: 15). The provision of inputs and other required forms of support, therefore, delivered tangible results than could the delivery of financial services.

Contract farmers and those in joint ventures also performed very well in sugarcane, tobacco, and cotton (Mazwi et al., 2017). Farmers who are contracted are supplied with agrochemicals to control crop diseases and insects and, thus, minimise the impact on yield (Svotwa & Mapfumo, 2015). Contracted farmers also receive inputs or advice on disease and insect-tolerant crop varieties that can help minimise losses, thereby reducing climate exposures. This has allowed farmers to accumulate more and faster and, thus, become concretely 'financially included' more than just being integrated with the formal economy ran by financial institutions. Private sector marketing agencies, such as the Cotton Company of Zimbabwe (Cottco), engage in contracts with farmers who grow cotton. They provide inputs, packaging, transportation, and, in some instances, technical support to farmers. The State, on the other hand, contracted farmers who grew grains through Command Agriculture. These dealings enable farmers to succeed in operating on the farms.

The Command Agriculture was funded through a public-private partnership between the government and its private partners. The role of the private partners was to provide capital (finance) and to coordinate (services) the marketing of produce, including exporting, sharing of best practices, and farming knowledge, and transfer of expertise through farmers training, while the role of the government was to provide an enabling environment and oversee the whole process (Odunze & Uwizeyimana, 2019). The Command Agriculture facility commenced in October 2016 and was rolled out for three consecutive planting seasons. With its expiration, some farmers were also contracted under the *Pfumvudza/Intwasa* which also focuses on the production of grains. While the participation of private agencies saw an increase in both tobacco and cotton production (Mazwi et al., 2018; Svotwa & Mapfumo, 2015), the Command Agriculture and the *Pfumvudza/Intwasa* also resulted in bountiful maize production (Mhlanga & Ndhlovu, 2021a, b; Odunze & Uwizeyimana, 2019). Contracting, therefore, provide both the finance and the services. For the first time since the FTLRP, Zimbabwe experienced a major decrease in grain imports following the bountiful harvest of the 2016/2017 season under the Command Agriculture. The import expenditure for maize dropped by 86% in 2017 (ZimVAC, 2020). Several qualitative studies across the country also found improved livelihoods and increased accumulation in resettled areas (Mazwi et al., 2017; Ndhlovu, 2017, 2018, 2022a; Shonhe, 2019).

If, therefore, the land is wealth (Ndhlovu, 2020a), then the FTLRP can be viewed as having redistributed wealth to the previously excluded. This justifies the need for a reconceptualisation of the concept of 'financial inclusion' so that it goes beyond focusing on the provision of services and bringing the poor into the formal economy to also out emphasis on the finance aspect. If the poor peasant majorities are support are provided he necessary funds and support needed to put their labour to productive use in successful farming and have finances, they will integrate themselves into the formal economy. Financial inclusion, therefore, should be more about strengthening the financial base of the poor. In fact, with the policy uncertainties that characterise Zimbabwe's financial system as well as the challenges of getting funding, especially by smallholder farmers (Kairiza, 2012), many people rarely approach banks. If they have some money to save, they prefer to keep it at home (Mhlanga & Ndhlovu, 2021a, b). Thus, mobilising these farmers to take their meagre savings to banks in a country characterised by hyperinflation instead of keeping their savings in the form of assets is not only irresponsible but also deceptive as it becomes 'a campaign against having cash-in-hand' and a mobilisation of the poor to live by finance thereby financialising their poverty (Ozili, 2020). Such a campaign is not useful for an inclusive development agenda in a developing country such as Zimbabwe and, thus, the important need to have the entire concept reconceptualised. The success of the FTLRP was premised on providing the people with a tangible good (land). The provision of inputs by the State as well as other private actors through contract farming and joint ventures also bolstered its success.

13.3.4 Financial Inclusion for Inclusive Development in the New Dispensation

The 'new dispensation' presided over by President Emmerson Mnangagwa has had several contradictions in terms of financial inclusion for inclusive development, especially for peasant categories. To revive the ailing economy, the government made huge compromises through its Transitional Stabilisation Programme Reforms Agenda (TSP) which, among other things, opened up the agriculture sector for local and foreign investment. The agriculture sector has been at the heart of Zimbabwe's turmoil into crisis, especially following the FTLRP which had transferred land from Whites to Blacks without compensation. This move triggered international isolation and sanctions which crippled the economy. Thus, in a bid to end isolation and sanctions, the new regime opened the country to foreign investment under its 'Zimbabwe is open for business' development approach. Paradoxically, this approach has been one of the most divisive and excludes the country's peasant majority from development. Under the approach, the government side-lines its smallholder producers in favour of large-scale producers as part of its pursuit of '…a private sector-led economic growth' (GoZ, 2018a: 21) and as part of an intention to 'transform agriculture in the next five years' and 'open the [agricultural] sector for global businesses' with a focus to promote large-scale farming (Zimbabwe African National Union-Patriotic Front (ZANU-PF), 2018: 23).

Instead of supporting local farmers who are the pillars of food security and development and yet who lack adequate resources to operate successfully (GoZ, 2018b), the regime requires land reform beneficiaries to demonstrate effectiveness and efficiency or face displacement (GoZ, 2018c). Instead of providing support to smallholders, the government is excluding them by requiring them to adopt the large-scale production model which it considers more effective and efficient to avoid having their land redistributed to capital-intensive users who can produce on a large scale (GoZ, 2020). The government also plans to '… revoke the offer letters of resettled farmers currently occupying [FTLRP acquired] … pieces of land and offer them alternative land elsewhere regardless of model' so that former White farmers can reapply for their farms and produce on a large scale (GoZ, 2020: 3).

In its Vision 2030 plans, the government states that: '18,000 A2 farmers are going to be transformed to agricultural entrepreneurs and the farms to become enviable businesses by 2025 [while] 360,000 A1 farmers to become viable and formal Small to Medium Enterprises by 2025' (GoZ, 2020: 1). The aim is to force peasants to adopt the expensive large-scale production model which they cannot afford. A deadline of 31 January 2021 was made for farmers to 'submit mandatory production returns' failure of which their farms would be classified as abandoned, derelict, or underutilised and, thus, requiring reallocation (GoZ, 2020: 2). These land practices further financially exclude the poor peasants most who were disadvantaged by the colonial regimes and who continue to lack resources and adequate support to produce on a large scale.

Ironically, White farmers who enjoyed State support during the colonial period have also been prioritised in the new dispensation. The government has '… decided to finalize compensation to all former farmers affected by the Land Reform Programme…' (GoZ, 2018c: 27). On 27 July 2020, the government signed a US$ 3.5 billion Global Compensation Deed meant to compensate former farmers who no longer require land. The financial plight of Blacks who were disempowered for a century by colonial administration is not prioritised. This serves to further financially exclude vulnerable categories such as the peasantry who lack resources and funds to operate. More, exhortations to adopt the large-scale model by the peasantry is misleading and misinformed because most of these farmers in the country do not have experience in large-scale farming due to the racialised character of the agricultural sector before 1980. Thus, the large-scale production model will not make them financially include but will instead impoverish them. Financial inclusion, therefore, is not realised by the change of the production model, but by the extension of support so that these farmers operate within a model in which they already have skills and experience.

Apart from a few farmers who get support through the *Pfumvudza/Intwasa* initiative – a crop production intensification model under which farmers ensure the efficient use of inputs and labour on a small area of land to optimise its management (Odunze & Uwizeyimana, 2019) – peasants are exhorted to team up with foreign capital in the form of contract farming and joint ventures with former White farmers or other investors to operate as businesses to access resources and funds (GoZ, 2018c). The government has commenced reducing the reliance of farmers '... on government support [with the aim] to enhance private sector support gather momentum, [to supposedly overcome] potential development of voids in capacitating production by the farmer' (GoZ, 2018c: 27). In other words, contrary to its inclusive development campaign, the government has relieved itself of the responsibility of financial inclusion has left farmers at the mercy of the private sector. The regime has discontinued the Command Agriculture facility which did not require farmers to provide collateral upfront and, therefore, was accessible by most peasants and, therefore, more financially inclusive and had the potential to result in the realisation of inclusive development.

Under the new regime, farmers are encouraged to seek financial support from financial institutions and other private actors since the government would no longer play any key role in financing agricultural activities but would limit its interventions to the provision of procedures through which financial institutions and enterprises can engage willing farmers on their terms on a commercial basis (GoZ, 2018a). The reduction of state support to farmers does not only bolster financial exclusion, but it also leaves farmers at the mercy of financial institutions which could dispossess them of their land when they fail to pay back the loans. Mazwi et al. (2018: 8) observed that:

> Markets offer many chances for opportunistic behaviour and tend to favour strong market actors, that is, those with the capital, know-how, and information to protect and expand their property rights, and to buffer themselves against risk. The local culmination of the process is a gradual transfer of land rights via the market to capital-rich actors, and a gradual concentration of land ownership in the hands of those who can invest to achieve optimal economies of scale in production and commercialisation.

Financial institutions can utilise their opportunistic behaviour and dispossess farmers of their lands, thereby aggravating the financial exclusion of Blacks farmers. Where this obtains, sources of peasant income and livelihoods are destroyed, thereby further plunging them into poverty. In addition, where peradventure manages to secure funding from private institutions and should they fail to raise funds to pay back, they can, on their own, dispose of farm equipment to repay loans. Where this obtains, it does not only become a financial inclusion issue, but it also becomes a livelihood threat matter.

The fear of losing land under the new regime is reported to have motivated the utilisation of private moneylenders by farmers seeking to improve productivity (Mhlanga, 2020) where the interest charged is so high, thereby complicating inclusive development prospects. In some areas, threats of land displacement have resulted in mass outmigration especially from FTLRP-acquired land back to previous communal areas, thereby negatively impacting production (Ndhlovu, 2018, 2020b). Both the decrease of State support and peasant land repossession threats in favour of capitalists not only compromise prospects for financial inclusion but also work against the country's inclusive development agenda.

13.4 Rethinking Financial Inclusion for Inclusive Development

Financial inclusion, as indicated above, wields much potential in reducing vulnerable categories of the world's population. However, financial inclusion only works when it is conceptualised and practised in a manner that speaks to the context of circumstances and needs of the people for whom it is meant. Conceptualising 'financial inclusion' simply as the delivery of banking services to disadvantaged and low-income groups at an affordable cost (Eldomiaty et al., 2020; World Bank, 2018) is not useful for the vulnerable populations such as the peasantry – a diverse, often less recognised population category – in Zimbabwe who needs access to funds to purchase inputs and equipment and not mere access to a bank account. It is when peasant farmers are provided with this form of support that they can view themselves as financially included. It is when these farmers are empowered to put their labour to productive use in farming that inclusive development, that is, 'development that includes marginalized people, sectors and countries in social, political and economic processes for increased human wellbeing, social and environmental sustainability, and empowerment' (van Gent, 2017: 10) can be achieved. Thus, financial inclusion needs to be reconceptualised in a manner that emphasises access to finance and not to services.

With the current broad-based socio-economic crisis and monetary policy inconsistencies in Zimbabwe, studies have shown that people prefer to keep their savings out of the banking system (Sikwila, 2013; Southall, 2017). Peasants also prefer investing in assets and livestock to bank deposits. Using thus form of saving, much accumulation in terms of farm equipment (tractors, harrows, lorries, ploughs, etc.), livestock, and properties such as houses have been recorded by various categories of peasants in the countryside (see African Institute for Agrarian Studies, 2014; Ndhlovu, 2017, 2022b; Shonhe, 2019). In its current form, financial inclusion would require farmers to keep their savings not in assets, but in bank accounts so that they can be recognised as financially included. This is not congruent with the needs of these farmers. More, such 'financial inclusion' would expose farmers to the ravages of hyperinflation and policy inconsistencies that characterise Zimbabwe now. Ozili (2020: 1), therefore, justifiably argues that financial inclusion is nothing other than 'an invitation to live by finance and leads to the financialisation of poverty…promotes the use of transaction accounts [and bears] a resemblance to a campaign against having cash-in-hand'. In its current form, financial inclusion is not useful for the realisation of inclusive development. A proper approach would be the provision of finance and assets to farmers. Farmers can then be educated on how they can save time needed for farm work when they use non-cash means of payment for goods and services, among others. Financial inclusion, therefore, needs to be reconceptualised to emphasise finance instead of financial services.

13.5 Conclusion

This chapter argues that the existing conceptualisation of financial inclusion has basic analytical challenges which do not allow for the framing of a mature scholarly debate on poverty alleviation and the attainment of inclusive development. It emphasises access to financial services instead of access to funds. This is problematic when peasant populations are studied. What peasants need, in a country like

Zimbabwe, are not mere financial services, bank accounts, for instance, but rather they need the finance itself to as to functionally operate. The article has demonstrated this through an analysis of what financial inclusion would constitute using the country's four major epochs. It posits that the concept, thus, needs to be reconceptualised to speak to the context of circumstances and needs that can lead to the realisation of inclusive development which does not leave the peasantry outside the tide of development. The findings imply that financial inclusion needs to be reconceptualised so that it emphasises the 'finance' aspects instead of the 'services' one. This will make it better placed to relate to the socio-economic realties of people, particularly the peasantry who need funding to obtain inputs and equipment to successfully produce. In its current form, financial inclusion's potential to reduce poverty is mere rhetoric.

References

African Institute for Agrarian Studies. (2014). *Land use, food security and agricultural production survey*. AIAS.

Amoah, A., Korle, K., & Asiama, R. K. (2020). Mobile money as a financial inclusion instrument: What are the determinants? *International Journal of Social Economics, 47*(10), 1283–1297.

Arrighi, G. (1967). *The political economy of Rhodesia* (Vol. Vol. 16). Mouton, The Hague.

Centre on Housing Rights and Evictions (2001). Land, Housing and Property Rights in Zimbabwe (Geneva: COHRE)

Chingozha, T., & von Fintel, D. (2019). *Property rights, market access and crop cultivation in southern Rhodesia: Evidence from historical satellite data*. Stellenbosch Economic Working Papers: WP03/2019. www.ekon.sun.ac.za/wpapers/2019/wp032019

Commercial Farmers Union. (2001). *The commercial farmer's union statement*. CFU.

Dabale, W. P., Jagero, N., & Chiringa, C. (2014). Empirical study on the fast-track land reform program (FTLRP) and household food security in Zimbabwe. *European Journal of Research and Reflection in Management Sciences, 2*(2).

Eldomiaty, T., Hammam, R., & El-bakry, R. (2020). Institutional determinants of financial inclusion: Evidence from world economies. *International Journal of Development Issues, 19*(2), 217–228.

Floyd, B. N. (1962). Land apportionment in southern Rhodesia. *Geographical Review, 52*(4), 566–582.

GoZ. (2018a). *Investment guidelines and opportunities in Zimbabwe*. Government of Zimbabwe.

GoZ. (2018b). *Transitional stabilisation programme reforms agenda*. Government of Zimbabwe.

GoZ. (2018c). *Amendments to Zimbabwe's indigenisation laws to open economy to foreign investment*. ENS Africa.

GoZ. (2020, December 18). *Press statement by the Minister of Lands, Agriculture, Water, and Rural Settlement, Hon. Dr A. J. Masuka on enhancing production, productivity and profitability on A2 and A1 farms*.

GoZ. (2001). *Zimbabwe's land reform programme*. Government Printers.

Haviland, W. (1953). Tobacco farm organization, costs and land-use in Southern Rhodesia. *South African Journal of Economics, 21*(4), 367–380.

Kairiza, T. (2012). *Unbundling Zimbabwe's journey to hyperinflation and official dollarization*. Discussion Paper 09-12. National Graduate Institute for Policy Studies (GRIPS), Tokyo.

Kinsey, B. H. (2004). Zimbabwe's land reform program: Underinvestment in post-conflict transformation. *World Development, 32*(10), 1669–1696.

Machingaidze, V. E. (1991). Agrarian change from above: The Southern Rhodesia Native Land Husbandry Act and African Response. *International Journal of African Historical Studies, 24*, 557–588.

Magaisa, A. (2020). *BSR EXCLUSIVE: Beneficiaries of the RBZ farm mechanisation scheme*. The Big Saturday Read Blog. Available at https://www.bigsr.co.uk/single-post/2020/07/18/BSR-EXCLUSIVE-Beneficiaries-of-the-RBZ-Farm-Mechanisation-Scheme

Makunike, B. (2014). *Land reform and poverty alleviation in Mashonaland east, Zimbabwe* (Unpublished PhD thesis). University of the Free State, Bloemfontein.

Masiiwa, M. (Ed.). (2004). *Post-independence land reform in Zimbabwe: Controversies and impact on the economy*. Friedrich Stiftung.

Mazwi, F., Muchetu, R. G., & Chibwana, M. (2017). Land, agrarian reform in Zimbabwe viewed from a transformative social policy perspective. *Africanus Journal of Development Studies, 47*(1), 1–17.

Mazwi, F., Tekwa, N., Chambati, W., & Mudimu, G. T. (2018). *Locating the position of peasants under the 'New Dispensation': A focus on land tenure issues*. Sam Moyo Africa Institute for Agrarian Studies.

Mazwi, F., Chemura, A., Mudimu, G., & Chambati, W. (2019). The political economy of command agriculture in Zimbabwe: A state-led contract farming model. *Agrarian South: Journal of Political Economy, 8*(1–2), 1–26.

Mhlanga, D. (2020). *Financial inclusion and poverty reduction: Evidence from small scale agricultural sector in Manicaland Province of Zimbabwe* (Unpublished PhD thesis). North-West University, South Africa.

Mhlanga, D., & Denhere, V. (2021). Determinants of financial inclusion in Southern Africa. *Studia Universitatis Babes-Bolyai Oeconomica, 65*(3), 39–52.

Mhlanga, D., & Dunga, S. H. (2020). Measuring financial inclusion and its determinants among the smallholder farmers in Zimbabwe: An empirical study. *Eurasian Journal of Business and Management, 8*(3), 266–281.

Mhlanga, D., & Ndhlovu, E. (2021a). Financialised agrarian primitive accumulation in Zimbabwe. *African Renaissance, 18*(3), 185–207.

Mhlanga, D., & Ndhlovu, E. (2021b). Surrogate currency and its impact on the livelihoods of smallholder farmers: A Zimbabwean case. *African Journal of Development Studies, 11*(4), 93–115.

Moyana, H. V. (1975). Land and race in Rhodesia. *African Review, 5*(1), 17–41.

Moyana, H. V. (1984). *The political economy of land in Zimbabwe*. Mambo Press.

Moyo, S. (2004). 'The Land and Agrarian Question in Zimbabwe': Paper presented on the Conference on 'The Agrarian Constraint and Poverty Reduction: Macro-economic Lessons for Africa', Addis Ababa, 17-18 December, 2004.

Moyo, S. (2011). Changing agrarian relations after redistributive land reform in Zimbabwe. *Journal of Peasant Studies, 38*(5), 907–934.

Moyo, S. (2013). Land reform and redistribution in Zimbabwe since 1980. In S. Moyo & W. Chambati (Eds.), *Land and agrarian reform in Zimbabwe: Beyond white-settler capitalism*. CODESRIA.

Moyo, S. (2016). *Family farming in sub-Saharan Africa: Its contribution to agriculture, food security and rural development*. Food and Agriculture Organization of the United Nations and the United Nations Development Programme. Working Paper Number 150.

Munslow, B (1985) Prospects for the socialist transition of agriculture in Zimbabwe. *World Development, 13*(1), 41–58.

Ndhlovu, E. (2017). *An analysis of household livelihoods under the fast track land reform programme in Chiredzi, Zimbabwe* (MA dissertation). University of South Africa.

Ndhlovu, E. (2018). Relevance of sustainable livelihood approach in Zimbabwe's land reform programme. *Africa Insight, 47*(4), 72–87.

Ndhlovu, E. (2020a). Decolonisation of development: Samir Amin and the struggle for an alternative development approach in Africa. *The Saharan Journal, 1*(1), 87–111.

Ndhlovu, E. (2020b). The migration-livelihoods nexus: Emerging opportunities, emerging challenges in rural Zimbabwe. *Yonsei Journal of International Studies, 12*(2), 24–40.

Ndhlovu, E. (2021). *Land, agrarian change discourse and practice in Zimbabwe: Examining the contribution of Sam Moyo* (PhD thesis). University of South Africa, Pretoria.

Ndhlovu, E. (2022a). Changing agrarian discourses and practices and the prospects for food sovereignty in Zimbabwe. In G. Mkodzongi (Ed.), *The future of Zimbabwe's agrarian sector: Land issues in a time of political transition* (pp. 34–53). Routledge.

Ndhlovu, E. (2022b). Political economy of Chisa livelihoods in rural Zimbabwe. In K. Helliker, J. Matanzima, & P. Chadambuka (Eds.), *Livelihoods of ethnic minorities in rural Zimbabwe* (pp. 123–139). Springer International Publishing.

Odunze, D. I., & Uwizeyimana, D. E. (2019). Zimbabwe's special maize programme for the import substitution (command agriculture) scheme: A hit-and-miss affair. *Journal of Reviews on Global Economics, 8*, 1329–1338.

Ozili, P. K. (2018). Impact of digital finance on financial inclusion and stability. *Borsa Istanbul Review, 18*(4), 329–340.

Ozili, P. K. (2020). *Financial inclusion: a strong critique*. Munich Personal RePEc Archive Paper No. 101813. Online at https://mpra.ub.uni-muenchen.de/101813/

Phimister, I. R. (1974). Rhodes, Rhodesia and the Rand. *Journal of Southern African Studies, 1*(1), 74–90.

Pollak, O. B. (1975). Black farmers and white politics in Rhodesia. *African Affairs, 74*(296), 263–277.

Quinn, L. A. (2019). *Causes of poverty in Zimbabwe*. The Borgen Project. borgenproject.org/causes-of-poverty-in-Zimbabwe/. Accessed 18/11/2019.

Reserve Bank of Zimbabwe. (2016). *Zimbabwe national financial inclusion strategy 2016–2020*. Reserve Bank of Zimbabwe.

Scoones, I., Morongwe, N., Mavedzenge, B., Murimbarimba, F., & Mahenehene, J. (2015). Zimbabwe's land reform: New political dynamics in the countryside. *Review of African Political Economy, 42*(144), 190–205.

Shonhe, T. (2019). *Tractors and agrarian transformation in Zimbabwe: Insights from Mvurwi*. APRA Working Paper 21, Future Agricultures Consortium.

Sikwila, M. N. (2013). Dollarization and the Zimbabwe's economy. *Journal of Economics and Behavioral Studies, 5*(6), 398–405.

Southall, J. R. (2017). Bond notes, borrowing, and heading for bust: Zimbabwe's persistent crisis. *Canadian Journal of African Studies, 51*(3), 89–405.

Svotwa, E., & Mapfumo, T. (2015). Cotton production under contract system in small holder farming sector of Zimbabwe. *International Journal of Innovative Science, Engineering and Technology, 2*(1), 631–639.

United Nations. (2016). *Digital financial inclusion. International telecommunication union (itu), issue brief series, inter-agency task force on financing for development, July*. United Nations. Available at: http://www.un.org/esa/ffd/wp-content/uploads/2016/01/Digital-Financial-Inclusion_ITU_IATFIssueBrief.pdf. Accessed 10/11/2021.

Utete, C. M. B. (2003). *Report of the presidential land review committee under the chairmanship of Dr. Charles MB Utete Vol. 1: Main report to his excellency, the president of the Republic of Zimbabwe*. Government Printers.

van Gent, S. (2017). *Beyond buzzwords: What is "inclusive development"?* INCLUDE.

World Bank. (2018). *Atlas of sustainable development goals from world development indicators*. World Bank.

Worldometers. (2019). *World population prospects: The 2019 revision*. Available at https://esa.un.org/unpd/wpp/. Accessed 29/08/2019.

ZANU-PF. (2018). The People's Manifesto 2018. ZANU PF.

ZimVAC. (2020). *2020 Rural livelihoods assessment*. https://www.bing.com/search?q=ZIMVAC+2017+UPTO+2020+MAIZE&qs=n&form=QBRE&sp=1&pq=zimvac+2017+upto+2020+m&sc=023&sk=&cvid=D9EF736D2E274BF0B0034DFEBA78515B. Accessed 04/08/2020.

Part III
The Gendered Implications of Economic Inclusion and the Policy Proposals Towards Economic Inclusion

Chapter 14
Artificial Intelligence (AI) Solutions for Financial Inclusion of the Excluded: What Are the Challenges?

David Mhlanga

Abstract The objective of this study is to critically investigate the challenges associated with the adoption of AI solutions in the financial inclusion of the excluded. Using unobtrusive research techniques like conceptual and documentary analysis, the study found out that employing AI in improving financial inclusion through digital tools is associated with many challenges apart from the various opportunities it presents. The study discovered, despite the benefits, the adoption of AI in the inclusion of the excluded households is associated with several challenges which include consumer protection challenges, data protection, and cyberattacks. Other challenges include risks related to the reduction of competition, irresponsible deployment of AI, and the risk of fueling the digital divide, exclusion, and displacements. Therefore, the study concludes that it is important that policymakers, in partnership with the private sector, prioritize the development of digital infrastructure as one of the foundations of their economic and social development plans which will make it easy for those excluded to be able to participate fully. The development of digital infrastructure should be one of the foundations of the economic and social development plans which will make it easy for those excluded to be able to participate fully. Also, this will go a long way in addressing many challenges related to the lack of adequate infrastructure.

Keywords Adoption · Artificial intelligence (AI) · Challenges · Excluded · Financial inclusion

D. Mhlanga (✉)
College of Business and Economics, The University of Johannesburg, Johannesburg, South Africa

D. Mhlanga, E. Ndhlovu (eds.), *Economic Inclusion in Post-Independence Africa*, Advances in African Economic, Social and Political Development,
https://doi.org/10.1007/978-3-031-31431-5_14

14.1 Introduction

Financial inclusion has been recognized as one of the important tools for achieving economic growth and poverty reduction (Izquierdo & Tuesta, 2015; Mhlanga et al., 2020). The objective of achieving universal financial access by 2020 buttressed the idea that financial inclusion can indeed help to achieve economic growth and poverty reduction. Issues around financial inclusion are becoming more critical, especially among international institutions, policymakers, central banks, financial institutions, and governments (Mhlanga, 2020a). It is generally believed that private financial institutions are major and critical agents of financial inclusion because of their role in the provision of financial products to the people. Many financial technology (fintech) companies are playing a critical role in making digital financial resources available to the people at the lower of the pyramid) (Mhlanga & Denhere, 2021).

These institutions are building on digital ways that were in use for years through the direct application of AI to improve access even to the people who were previously served by formal financial institutions (Peric, 2015; Alameda, 2020). AI is coming forth with massive changes in the traditional banking sector by transforming the paper and physical distribution of cash (Alameda, 2020; Mhlanga, 2020a). Biallas and O'neill (2020) stated that the application of AI is contributing more to addressing the obstacles to financial inclusion for low-income earners which include the high cost of saving rural customers, assessing creditworthiness, and establishing customer identity. Most of the obstacles that prevent rural people from accessing financial resources are dealt with when AI is productively applied in the financial sector. It is also taken as a fact that, to realize the benefits of financial inclusion through the application of AI, there must be a massive adoption of competitive market settings and continued investment in the appropriate infrastructure (Biallas & O'neill, 2020). Studies that are increasingly assessing the influence of AI in different sectors of the economy are on the rise in recent times, but this literature is still scant, especially the research that assesses the application of AI to reduce the problems of financial exclusion and the applications that exacerbates the vulnerability of customers. Theodoridis and Gkikas (2019) assessed the application of AI in digital marketing practices, particularly the challenges that businesses face when they try to integrate AI into the digital marketing of their financial services. Theodoridis and Gkikas (2019) also argued that the application of AI to digital marketing is not as simple as collecting big data; there is a need to have the necessary knowledge that will allow the technology to target their customers effectively.

Paschen et al. (2020) also came up with a study to investigate the interaction of humans and AI technology in value co-creation. Using service-dominant logic as a lens, the study successfully investigated the activities, roles, and resources that are being exchanged in the process of AI-enabled value co-creation. The study suggested that AI-based value co-creation is a complex interaction between human and nonhuman actors. Mhlanga (2020a) also investigated the impact of AI technologies on digital financial inclusion. The study discovered that AI has a strong influence on digital financial inclusion in areas related to risk detection and the management of information asymmetry. It was also highlighted that AI is critical in the provision of customer support through helpdesks and chatbots. The other important aspect as articulated by Mhlanga (2020a) was the fact that AI plays a critical function in risk detection and cybersecurity. All these studies are highlighting the critical importance of AI in this era. Therefore, this study intends to critically investigate the challenges associated with the adoption of AI solutions in the financial inclusion of the excluded. The rest of the chapter is organized as follows: the chapter will describe the artificial intelligence innovation in financial services and AI applications in the financial market with case studies. FarmDrive case study in Kenya will be described followed by an empirical literature review and the methodology. A discussion of the challenges associated with the adoption of artificial intelligence (AI) solutions in financial inclusion of the excluded was also given followed by the conclusion and recommendation.

14.2 Artificial Intelligence Innovation in Financial Services

Biallas and O'neill (2020) define AI as: "The science and engineering of making machines intelligent, especially intelligent computer programs. AI can therefore be characterized as a series of systems, methods, and technologies that display intelligent behaviour by analyzing their environments and taking actions with some degree of autonomy toward achieving prespecified outcomes."

AI is viewed as the constellation of technologies that allow machines to perform their duties with higher levels of intelligence. AI-powered machines can emulate human capabilities to be able to sense, comprehend, and act (Access Partnership, 2020). In some ways, it can be put as AI allows machines to sense the environment they operate from, in some cases to think, and learn while being able to act in a response to the environment and the available circumstances (Meunier, 2018). The growth in sophistication of AI applications is making many corporations to be able to apply it in their operations. According to Meunier (2018), there are three types of machine learning which are unsupervised learning, supervised learning, and reinforced learning.

Unsupervised learning is where statistical tools are used for data clustering to establish hidden patterns without external feedback, for instance, customer segmentation. Supervised learning is where the machine is trained for a specific classification task using labelled data and direct feedback, for example, analysis of creditworthiness for customers (Meunier, 2018). Reinforced learning on the other hand uses algorithms to learn and react to an environment through repeating strategies over and over to maximize rewards, for example, adjustment of a sale offer based on acceptance or rejection rates (Meunier, 2018). Biallas and O'neill (2020) argued that AI was established as a discipline around 70 years, but its application has risen in recent years. The evolution in machine learning and computing power improvements, data storage, as well as effective and efficient communication networks has allowed the application of AI to improve greatly. The general fall in the

Internet cost, the increase in mobile penetration, and the rise in computing power over the past revolution assisted digital consumers and operations to be able to generate a wealth of new and real-time data through mobile phones and other digital devices. The coming up of advanced ways of data storage capacities and the relatability in energy supply analyzed data to be cost-effective for firms which are now making financial service providers start the integration of AI technologies in their service offerings.

A survey conducted by the World Economic Forum and the Cambridge Centre for Alternative Finance of 151 firm's fintech firms and traditional banks agreed to the fact that AI is being integrated with their operations. Approximately, 85 percent of the respondents highlighted that they are currently using AI in their operations (Biallas & O'neill, 2020; Meunier, 2018). In many emerging markets, people find themselves being excluded from the mainstream formal financial market because many lack the traditional identification, collateral security, and credit history for them to be able to access financial services such as credit. However, AI is addressing these problems by creating alternative ways of analyzing the identity and creditworthiness of individuals and businesses premised on the data collected from mobile phones and satellites. The other major obstacle to financial inclusion in emerging markets is the fact that the cost of reaching and subsequently saving the customers is extremely high compared to their financial transactions as well as the revenue they represent. Meunier (2018) stated that AI is helping a lot in addressing this problem through the automation of different processes such as customer service and engagement to reduce costs. This in its way allows the low-value tractions to be offered in high volumes turning the previously underserved customers into profitable markets increasing financial inclusion. The speed, extent, as well as efficiency of the adoption of AI systems to realize the benefits of financial inclusion depends more on several factors which include the efforts by government, businesses, and investors to create and generate institutional and market settings that facilitate responsible and sustainable integration of AI into financial services. This marks the thrust of this study to critically investigate the institutional settings that may act as challenges in the application of AI solutions in the inclusion of the excluded individuals. Some of these conditions include generating trust by financial service providers through: "lending responsibly, addressing algorithmic bias and error, managing cyber risk, and striving for informed consent in the use of consumer data."

14.3 AI Applications in the Financial Market with Case Studies

Financial exclusion has been worse in emerging markets because of the way traditional data is used to generate credit scores. In the generation of credit scores, traditional data is used: "formal identification, bank transactions, credit history, income statements, and asset value." In developing nations, many households do not have access to the traditional forms of collateral or identification that creditors require for them to provide financial services (Mhlanga, 2020b; Mhlanga et al., 2020). With the use of alternative data sources such as public data, satellite images, company registries, and social media data like SMS and messenger services interaction data, AI can assist service providers to assess a consumer's behavior as well as assess their ability to repay the loan (Mhlanga, 2020c; Mhlanga & Dunga, 2020). The critical application of AI in emerging markets in the financial sector is to analyze alternative data points and real-time behavior, to "Improve credit decisions; identify threats to financial institutions and help meet compliance obligations, and address financing gaps faced by businesses in emerging markets. Improving credit decisions" (Biallas & O'neill, 2020). Lenders and credit rating agencies constantly use AI to analyze to establish the creditworthiness of potential borrowers.

14.3.1 FarmDrive Application in Kenya

FarmDrive is an agricultural data analytics company that delivers financial services to smallholder farmers who are unbanked or underserved while assisting financial institutions to increase their agricultural loan portfolios cost-effectively (Biallas & O'neill, 2020; Tinsley & Agapitova, 2018). The FarmDrive application uses simple mobile phone technology, alternative credit scoring, and machine learning techniques to try and reduce the data gaps that have been preventing smallholder farmers from accessing formal financial services that would permit them to expand their agribusinesses and increase the levels of their incomes (Biallas & O'neill, 2020; Bosire, 2017; Henze & Ulrichs, 2016). The application works in a way that it collects one farmer's data using questions and answers via text messaging. The questions asked are designed in such a way that the application should at the end be able to capture the following: the farmer's location, crops cultivated, farm size, assets such as tractors, and farming activities (Biallas & O'neill, 2020).

The captured data will now be combined with already existing data to develop a complete credit profile of the farmer. The application also makes use of testing to determine the probability of the farmer repaying the loan. The uniqueness of the FarmDrive is that the profile of the farmer that is created from the application will be shared with financial institutions for credit assessment and funding purposes. According to Biallas and O'neill (2020), the application is on the second stage; during the first stage which happened between December 2015 and December 2016 through the application of environmental data, economic data and social data were collected. The data is aggregated at fed into FarmDrive's algorithm to generate credit scores that can be used by lending institutions (Biallas & O'neill, 2020; Tinsley & Agapitova, 2018). In its development phases, it is believed that FarmDrive will expand the environmental arm of the algorithm by adding more data sets such as satellite imagery and remote sensing data. The environmental data set will also be used in combination with crop cycle data to improve the prediction ability of the application. Biallas and O'neill (2020) argued that once these data sets are combined the application can predict the seasonal yield and influence of agricultural insurance products. This application is assisting smallholder farmers to be able to access formal financial services like credit which will allow them to contribute more to economic development and improve their livelihoods (Biallas & O'neill, 2020).

14.4 Empirical Literature Review

The literature on the impact of AI on financial inclusion is increasing though it is still in its nascent stages. Scholars are increasingly giving credit to AI in addressing the exclusion of low-income earners, small businesses, women, and youth from assessing formal financial services such as credit, for instance, Mhlanga (2020a), Duan et al. (2019), Feng et al. (2020), and Ellahham et al. (2020). Feng et al. (2020) in a study of AI in marketing, a bibliographic perspective, revealed that AI as a concept was born in the mid-twentieth century to give a full description of computer science which was focusing on the simulation of human learning. Feng et al. (2020) went on to state that the advancement in computing power, data collection, and storage enabled AI to become one of the critical aspects for researchers and practitioners in various disciplines of business and social sciences. Duan et al. (2019) research AI for decision-making, in the era of big data, evolution, challenges, and research agenda. Supported the work of Feng et al. (2020), by arguing that AI has been in existence for some time, however, the existence of Bid Data technologies has empowered AI which made it an attractive topic across disciplines and for researchers. Duan et al. (2019) assessed the challenges associated with the application and impact of revitalized AI base systems decision-making and for information systems researchers. The research came out with twelve propositions for information systems researchers where AI can assist in research.

The research by Ellahham et al. (2020) also agreed with the research by Duan et al. (2019), where Ellahham et al. (2020) articulated the application of AI in the healthcare safety context. Ellahham et al. (2020) pointed out that, though there are opportunities for the application of AI in the health sector through providing diagnosis and treatment processes, there are still challenges related to safety. The review of literature perfumed by Ellahham et al. (2020) revealed that safe design, safety reserves, safe fail, and procedural safeguards are key strategies that can help to reduce the challenges associated with the use of AI in the health sector. The study by Ellahham et al. (2020) also discovered that cost, risk, and uncertainty associated with the use of AI should be identified. The other important point discovered by Ellahham et al. (2020) was that there must be clear guidance that should be shared with all the stakeholders in the development and adoption of safe AI applications in the health sector.

Mhlanga (2020a) also supported Ellahham et al. (2020) though the study was directly focused on the financial sector. Mhlanga (2020a) investigated the impact that AI brings on the digital financial inclusion of the excluded groups. The study by Mhlanga (2020a) found that fintech companies are increasingly using AI applications to make sure that the goals of financial inclusion are realized. Mhlanga (2020a) also pointed out that AI is being used to allow the excluded groups, the poor, the women, and the youth, to be able to access formal financial services. It was highlighted that AI has a strong impact on financial inclusion in areas related to the detection, measurement, and management of risk; it is also important in addressing the challenge of information asymmetry, fraud detection, and availing customer support.

Ozili (2018) also investigated the issues around digital finance. Ozili (2018) just like Mhlanga (2020a) found out that digital finance and financial inclusion have many benefits to financial users and financial service providers, the governments, and the economy. Ozili (2018) also discovered that several issues are persisting which when addressed can allow digital finance to work better for businesses, households, and governments. One issue that was highlighted is the issue of the existing gap between the availability of finance and its accessibility. There is also the issue of bias in the provision of digital finance among other many issues. Saon et al. (2019) also assessed the use of AI and blockchain in the promotion of financial inclusion in India. Saon et al. (2019) discovered that the use of AI in finance can help to spur efficiency gains in the financial sector; it can also help the financial service providers to offer a variety of better products and services which can help to deepen financial inclusion in the developing world. Saon et al. (2019) also found that the application of AI can pose risks if application of AI undermines competition, trust, and monetary policy. Saon et al. (2019) went on to highlight that the financial sector has five broad functions which are to make and receive payments, to save, to borrow, to manage risks, and to get advice on all other services.

This was supported by Radcliffe et al. (2012) who investigated the digital pathway to financial inclusion. Radcliffe et al. (2012) discovered that the payments provided by the financial sector are the connective tissue of all the economic systems. Just like the arguments by Saon et al. (2019), Radcliffe et al. (2012) stated that financial services help people to buy goods, electricity, and water and even send money to friends and relatives. It was also highlighted that digital financial services help governments in the collection of taxes and the disbursements of social payments and even assist suppliers to collect payments from buyers. Radcliffe et al. (2012) believe that digital finance helps transaction costs to be cheaper and more convenient. The argument put forward was that when transaction costs are costly and inconvenient, economic activity is highly affected. Wang and He (2020) in a study on digital financial inclusion and farmers' vulnerability to poverty, evidence from China, stated that access to finance is one of the critical factors important in poverty alleviation, but the expansion of access to the poor remains one of the hurdles that need to be dealt with by financial institutions. Wang and He (2020) stated that digital financial inclusion remains one of the options that can easily be taken advantage of in addressing the problem of financial exclusion and poverty. The study by Wang and He (2020) found that the use of digital finance by farmers, in China, helped in the reduction of farmer's vulnerability. One of the critical findings by Wang and He (2020) was that digital finance from information technology companies had a greater impact on farmers' vulnerability compared to finance from traditional banks.

How et al. (2020) also argued that financial service providers should acknowledge that the application of AI on legacy data can assist in influencing how prospective customers can respond when they are approached. How et al. (2020) also indicated that it remains a challenge, especially for financial service providers who cannot do computer programming to implement AI projects. Again, How et al. (2020) in the study came up with a noncoding human-centric AI-based approach to simulate the possible dynamics between the financial profiles of prospective customers. The purpose of the study was to predict the intentions toward the financial products being offered and to illustrate how AI for social good can be accessible to people who are not well-versed in computer science. Kandpal and Khalaf (2020) also argued that it is very difficult for banks to reach all the people with financial products through a brick-and-mortar model. However, technology like AI is allowing banks to reach a lot of people through branchless banking. Kandpal and Khalaf (2020) stated that AI in banking provides a cost-effective efficient solution for the provision of services to financially excluded individuals. Digital technology makes it cheaper for financially excluded households to be able to access financial products. Ozili (2021) also discussed the benefits and issues associated with the use of big data and AI for financial inclusion. Ozili (2021) discovered that the benefits of big data and artificial intelligence include improved efficiency and risk management for financial services providers and the provision of smart financial products and services to unbanked individuals. AI can simplify the account opening process for financially excluded households as well as the creation of credit scores using alternative information.

14.5 Methodology

The purpose of the study is to study intently and to critically investigate the challenges associated with the adoption of AI solutions in the financial inclusion of the excluded. Unobtrusive research techniques like conceptual and documentary analysis were used in this study. Documentary analysis is a form of qualitative methodology where research where documents are reviewed to investigate various themes in a study. The process of dissecting documents involves the process of coding content into various subjects such as focus groups.

14.6 Discussion of the Challenges Associated with the Adoption of Artificial Intelligence (AI) Solutions in Financial Inclusion of the Excluded

The discussion on the challenges associated with the adoption of AI solutions in financial inclusion of the excluded followed unobtrusive research techniques like conceptual and documentary analysis. Many scholars like Wang and He (2020),

Radcliffe et al. (2012), Saon et al. (2019), Mhlanga (2020a), and Ozili (2018) having digital finance is a critical component in the development of the economy and improvement in the welfare of the people. However, scholars like Mhlanga (2020a), Ellahham et al. (2020), and Feng et al. (2020) among others believe that AI is critical in improving financial inclusion; however, in their studies, Ellahham et al. (2020), and Feng et al. (2020) attest to the fact that there are some challenges associated with the adoption of AI application in addressing the issue of financial exclusion. This part of the study will show some of the challenges associated with the adoption of AI applications in addressing financial exclusion.

14.6.1 Consumer Protection Challenges: Data Protection and Cyberattacks

The integration of AI in the financial sector comes with several challenges especially challenges to the financial consumer. Biallas and O'neill (2020) stated that the provision of digital finance and the application of AI is associated with agent risks since the new providers of financial services are in most cases not subject to consumer protection provisions that are sometimes applied to traditional financial institutions. Again, Biallas and O'neill (2020) highlighted that digital technology has some risks that can cause loss of data and, in some instances, loss of payment instructions due to dropped messages. In other instances, the use of AI can result in problems related to the risk of privacy or security breach which result from digital transmittal as well as the storage of data (Biallas & O'neill, 2020). As if not enough, Biallas and O'neill (2020) also highlighted that the integration of AI in financial services presents challenges related to privacy and algorithmic bias. This was supported by several organizations including the International Committee on Credit Reporting (ICCR). The ICCR discovered different risks that are related to credit scoring models when AI is in use. Some of the risks include inaccuracies in data, using data without full and informed consumer consent, and the potential for bias as well as discrimination in the design and decisions of algorithms (Biallas & O'neill, 2020; International Committee on Credit Reporting, 2019).

The other critical component that was highlighted is the heightened exposure of consumers to cyber risks. These risks as articulated by Biallas and O'neill (2020) are enhanced in AI models where data is fed back into systems to refine the process of decision-making. Some technologies like biometric technology have been hailed in the process of identifying data subjects which made them widely applied in the identification of users. However, Kaspersky (2019) argued that there were several data leaks and many attempts in using the leaked biometric data. This poses a lot of risk to the consumers especially when there is a leaking of data. Apart from the use of biometric technology, Bouveret (2018) uses distributed ledger technology. The most common use of distributed ledger technology is blockchain, and this has been popular due to its high levels of security. However, there were numerous cyberattacks on crypto exchanges that exposed the vulnerability of the technology (Biallas

& O'neill, 2020; International Committee on Credit Reporting, 2019; Bouveret 2018). Bouveret (2018) stated that more than 10 online exchanges were subjected to cyber fraud which accumulated to approximately US$1.45 billion since 2013.

The other critical technology that was used in the financial sector is cloud computing, which made data, services, and various applications to be moved to the cloud. This motivated many credit reporting service providers to embrace cloud computing services and their various applications. The main challenge that credited reporting service providers to face is that they tend to outsource the security function of certain infrastructures to third parties. The problem which arises is that some of the third parties are small companies that are not regulated (International Committee on Credit Reporting, 2019; Newman, 2017). Any attack on these small service providers will affect the credit reporting service provider. This information stands as a testimony that, though AI application there numerous benefits in the provision of financial services, however, there are still some challenges that need to be addressed to ensure that those who were previously excluded from accessing formal financial services. As if not enough, many providers of digital finance make use of mobile applications in the provision of services to low-income earners, women, the youth, and small businesses. Some credit bureaus came up with innovative ways of development of consumer-driven data-sharing platforms that have the intention to provide portability credit for credit data (Newman, 2017). However, the expansion of services through mobile applications comes with problems of cyberattacks which can derail the progress of the provision of financial services.

14.6.2 Risks Related to the Reduction in Competition and Irresponsible Deployment of AI

The challenge related to the integration of AI in the financial inclusion of the excluded is the issue of competition. In situations where early adopters of AI in financial services enjoy the first-mover advantage, can actually allow them to consolidate market power which can prevent other participants to enter the market creating a winner-take-all scenario (International Committee on Credit Reporting, 2019; Biallas & O'Neill, 2020). When this happens, competition will be reduced which can make consumers lose their choice and lose the benefits associated with price competition in the long run (Biallas & O'neill, 2020).

On the other hand, AI applications can create new business models that can enhance cost-competitiveness among the technology suppliers which can help with the pricing of products making their services affordable to low-income consumers (Biallas & O'neill, 2020; International Committee on Credit Reporting, 2019). The most notable way to ensure that there is competition and that the winner-take-all scenario is addressed is through government regulation. The government can do monitoring to weed out any anticompetitive business practices so that consumers enjoy the benefits of AI in financial services (Oliver & Marsh, 2019). The other critical component in the adoption of AI in the financial sector is the responsible deployment of AI. Financial service providers should make it a priority they attract staff with the proper skills in the understating of AI applications such as credit scoring algorithms (Oliver & Marsh, 2019). A critical understanding of these applications is important because any lending should be done in a responsible way to avoid AI applications doing more harm to poor customers than the good it has been intended. If the AI applications are not deployed responsibly by experienced people, there are risks of increasing the indebtedness of vulnerable consumers. The other danger is the losing of trust by these consumers in the industry, and when that happens the objective of using AI to improve the financial inclusion of the excluded will not be realized (Biallas & O'neill, 2020; Oliver & Marsh, 2019). Adding to the above challenges, systemic risk is one risk that should be guarded against when deploying AI applications, especially credit scoring. Once the vulnerable customers are affected, they can lose trust in the system which has the potential to affect the whole financial system. The adoption of responsible lending and effective risk management practices can help in preventing the overindebtedness of vulnerable consumers (Biallas & O'neill, 2020). Also, these risks come because the adoption of AI demands financial service providers to actively govern their operations concerning data ownership, privacy, security, and biases (Newman, 2017).

Biallas and O'neill (2020) highlighted that the proper management of data ownership, privacy and security biases, cybersecurity, as well as supervisory regulations or processes demands the coordination between financial service providers, international organizations, industry, and the government to facilitate AI adoption across the sector. In situation where the prerequisites for the successful adoption of AI are not in place, effort is required by governments and investors in the development of these settings to avoid the various risks associated with the adoption of AI (Tinsley & Agapitova, 2018). One example that was given by Biallas and O'neill (2020) was the consultative Group to Assist the Poor which discovered that the requirements for successful digital financial innovation are the massive investment in open digital platforms, share market infrastructure and data, as well as support for public goods like foundational identity cards (IDs) (Emeana et al., 2020). Without these prerequisites, it has been found that the adoption of AI will not have any considerable and significant contribution to reducing financial exclusion.

There are various examples where the World Bank through the International Finance Organization (IFC)'s digital financial services and fintech practice offered advice to 150 financial services providers since 2007 to ensure that AI is adopted responsibly to achieve the World Bank Group's twin goals of ending extreme poverty and boosting shared prosperity (Biallas & O'neill, 2020). In Myanmar, the Yoma Bank, one of the IFC clients, managed to develop a scoring algorithm to offer loans to suppliers and distributors. Through this algorithm, the bank manages to leverage the payment of suppliers and order data to come up with a loan book that provided funds for micro, small, and medium enterprises (MSMEs). The nonperforming loan ratio for Yoma bank is below one percent as of 2020 (Biallas & O'neill, 2020; Tinsley & Agapitova, 2018).

The other example that shows the responsible adoption of AI is Ant Financial, one of the subsidiaries of Alibaba Group. This organization applied machine learning that can leverage online transaction data to do assessments of the creditworthiness of loan applicants including those without collateral security (Biallas & O'neill, 2020; Mhlanga, 2020b). Collateral security has been one of the variables that provide comfort to lenders, but overreliance on it has caused a lot of small businesses to be excluded from enjoying formal financial services, even some businesses with the potential. Taking advantage of over 560 million people connected to the Internet and small firms increasingly operating online, Ant Financial was able to apply AI to big data and use actual payment history to assess the creditworthiness of small businesses to an extent that it managed to bring high-performing small businesses into the customer base at a rapid pace and lower cost which would be hard for traditional banks. Ant Financial was able to increase its loan portfolio from US$0.5 billion to US$4 billion over 4 years (Biallas & O'neill, 2020).

IFC is also engaging in partnerships with Mastercard Foundation in the year 2017 to publish a handbook on how data analytics are applied to digital financial services including how practitioners can use data in the development of algorithm-based credit scoring models for financial inclusion. The World bank through the ICCR came up with guidelines on credit scoring approaches that include some guidelines on how AI can be used in credit scoring (International Committee on Credit Reporting, 2019; Oliver & Marsh, 2019). The IFC also come together with private investors to develop guidelines for responsible investing in digital finance. This initiative has been endorsed by over 100 investors and financial service providers. All these efforts were put in place to ensure that AI applications are deployed responsibly and that financial institutions maintain consumer trust in digital financial services as well as reduce the risk of harmful lending practices (Biallas & O'neill, 2020; Oliver & Marsh, 2019).

14.6.3 The Risk Fueling Digital Divide, Exclusion, and Displacements

The success of the digital economy particularly the application of AI in the finance sector requires solid infrastructure. The private sector investors and the government must invest heavily in telecommunication and energy infrastructure to improve the enabling environment for the digital economy. Without this proper and sustainable support, there is a huge risk that financial services despite using AI applications will continue to be commercially and practically infeasible which will lead to the deepening of the digital divide and financial exclusion. One other critical risk is the issue of job displacements in emerging economies. The automation and the integration of AI in the financial system come with job displacements. Biallas and O'neill (2020) argued that natural language processing can replace outsourced customer care services which is an industry that employs quite a several workers in the financial sector and the telecommunication sectors in countries like South Africa, Vietnam, and Morocco.

Cuevas (2020) argued that even though AI has a lot of applications and the potential for financial inclusion, there are still some inherent risks that could aggravate the exclusion problem from the system and sometimes unintentionally. The first aspect that was highlighted by Cuevas (2020) was that the moment financial ecosystems become a hundred percent digital can be a huddle for elderly people and people with disabilities which can act as a barrier toward access to financial resources which could not be given full consideration in the initial stages of implementation. The other aspect was that AI model on their own is developed from algorithms and datasets which could include unconscious bias which include the inability to represent the diversity of the needs of the unbanked population concerning ethnicity, gender, and even socioeconomic condition (Cuevas, 2020; Oliver & Marsh, 2019). The other challenges emanate from novelty risks on the services that involve AI in their applications. Some vulnerable financially excluded groups may not be well equipped to understand the products, services, and providers of the products which can open the vulnerability of these people to exploitation and abuse (Cuevas, 2020; Xie, 2019). The other layer of challenges rests in the financial illiteracy of underserved individuals. Financial illiteracy with little or no experience with digital tools, whether mobile or online, can result to a huge problem for policymakers and service providers as they try to expand financial services to the previously excluded and underserved groups (Newman, 2017; Cuevas, 2020). All these are real challenges that should be taken into consideration when AI is implemented to eliminate the impact of financial exclusion of vulnerable groups (Cuevas, 2020).

There are numerous AI applications that are assisting to automate the various aspects of digital financial which include customer engagement, customer service, and reduction in cost to financial service providers when offering tailor support to a wider range of customers. The research conducted by Juniper Research revealed that, by 2023, banks will save US$7.3 billion in operating costs due to the use of chatbot applications (Biallas & O'neill, 2020). One of the examples where the chatbot is being used is Bank BCP in Peru. Bank BCP partnered with IBM Watson in the development of a personalized chatbot called Arturito. This chatbot helps customers to convert currencies, meet credit card repayments, and access 24-hour customer support through Facebook. Also, in Brazil, Banco Bradesco partnered with IBM Watson in the development of a chatbot that can answer 283,000 questions in a month of about 62 products with an accuracy of 95 percent (Biallas & O'neill, 2020; Oliver & Marsh, 2019). Automation and tailoring have a big potential to improve financial inclusion if financial services reach the individuals and businesses who were previously excluded and those who were unable to transact in their language or to physically access a branch or banking agent. Another example is MTN Cote d'Ivoire, one client of IFC who is working with Juntos, a tech company to incorporate AI in its digital wallet MoMo to enable customers to understand their financial products and obligations. This has allowed almost 95 percent of MTN's digital dialogue conversations to be automated. However, Biallas and O'neill (2020) highlighted that the use of chatbots and language processing to assist in addressing the issue of trust and financial literacy barriers for consumers in accessing financial services is still an area that needs to be explored in emerging markets. Despite all the uses of AI, the issue that still needs to be explored is the use of AI to ensure that the problems of trust and financial literacy barriers are addressed to ensure that AI application reaches their full potential in addressing financial exclusion (Biallas & O'neill, 2020; Oliver & Marsh, 2019).

14.7 Conclusion and Policy Recommendation

The objective of this study is to critically investigate the challenges associated with the adoption of AI solutions in the financial inclusion of the excluded. Using unobtrusive research techniques like conceptual and documentary analysis, the study found out that employing AI in improving financial inclusion through digital tools is associated with many challenges apart from the various opportunities it presents. The study discovered that AI presents opportunities for financial inclusion. For instance, financial exclusion has been worse in emerging markets because of the way traditional data is used to generate credit scores. In the generation of credit scores, traditional data is used: "formal identification, bank transactions, credit history, income statements, and asset value" which many households do not have access. With the use of alternative data sources such as public data, satellite images, and company registries and social media data like SMS and messenger services interaction data, AI has assisted service providers to assess a consumer's behavior as well as to assess their ability to repay the loan. This has improved financial access by many households. However, the study found that the adoption of AI in the inclusion of the excluded households is associated with several challenges which include consumer protection challenges, data protection and cyberattacks. Other challenges include risks related to the reduction of competition, irresponsible deployment of AI, and the risk of fueling the digital divide, exclusion, and displacements. Therefore, the study concludes that it is important that policymakers, in partnership with the private sector, prioritize the development of digital infrastructure as one of the foundations of their economic and social development plans which will make it easy for those excluded to be able to participate fully. The development of digital infrastructure should be one of the foundations of the economic and social development plans which will make it easy for those excluded to be able to participate fully. Also, this will go a long way in addressing many challenges related to the lack of adequate infrastructure.

References

Access Partnership. (2020). *Artificial intelligence for Africa: An opportunity for growth, development, and democratization.*

Alameda, T. (2020). Data, AI and financial inclusion: The future of global banking—Responsible finance forum, responsible finance forum BBVA 2020. Available online: https://responsiblefinanceforum.org/data-ai-financial-inclusion-future-global-banking/. Accessed on 12 May 2020.

Biallas, M., & O'neill, F. (2020). *Artificial Intelligence Innovation in Financial Services.* www.ifc.org/thoughtleadership

Bosire, P. (2017). *Peris Bosire-founder, FarmDrive.*

Bouveret, A. (2018). *Cyber risk for the financial sector: A framework for quantitative assessment.* Working paper WP/18/143. International Monetary Fund, Washington, DC.

Cuevas, L. (2020). *AI for financial inclusion: Banking the unbanked.* https://blog.strands.com/ai-for-financial-inclusion-banking-the-unbanked

Duan, Y., Edwards, J. S., & Dwivedi, Y. K. (2019). Artificial intelligence for decision making in the era of Big Data – Evolution, challenges, and research agenda. *International Journal of Information Management, 48*, 63–71. https://doi.org/10.1016/j.ijinfomgt.2019.01.021

Ellahham, S., Ellahham, N., & Simsekler, M. C. E. (2020). Application of artificial intelligence in the health care safety context: Opportunities and challenges. *American Journal of Medical Quality, 35*(4), 341–348. https://doi.org/10.1177/1062860619878515

Emeana, E. M., Trenchard, L., & Dehnen-Schmutz, K. (2020). The revolution of mobile phone-enabled services for agricultural development (m-Agri services) in Africa: The challenges for sustainability. *Sustainability (Switzerland), 12*(2), MDPI AG. https://doi.org/10.3390/su12020485

Feng, C. M., Park, A., Pitt, L., Kietzmann, J., & Northey, G. (2020). Artificial intelligence in marketing: A bibliographic perspective. *Australasian Marketing Journal, 29*, 252. https://doi.org/10.1016/j.ausmj.2020.07.006

Henze, J., & Ulrichs, C. (2016). *The potential and limitations of mobile-learning and other services in the agriculture sector of Kenya using phone applications.*

How, M. L., Cheah, S. M., Khor, A. C., & Chan, Y. J. (2020). Artificial intelligence-enhanced predictive insights for advancing financial inclusion: A human-centric AI-thinking approach. *Big Data and Cognitive Computing, 4*(2), 8.

International Committee on Credit Reporting. (2019). *Cybersecurity in credit reporting guidelines.*

Izquierdo, N. C., & Tuesta, D. (2015). Factors that matter for financial inclusion: Evidence from Peru. *Aestimatio: The IEB International Journal of Finance*, 10–31.

Kandpal, V., & Khalaf, O. I. (2020). Artificial intelligence and SHGs: Enabling financial inclusion in India. In *Deep learning strategies for security enhancement in wireless sensor networks* (pp. 291–303). IGI Global.

Kaspersky Lab. (2019). *Cyberthreats to financial institutions 2019: Overview and predictions.* Kaspersky Lab, Moscow. https://media.kasperskycontenthub.com/wp-content/uploads/sites/43/2018/11/27083106/Financial-cyber-threat predictions-for-2019.pdf

Meunier, S. (2018). *The impacts and challenges of artificial intelligence in finance.* https://internationalbanker.com/finance/the-impacts-and-challenges-of-artificial-intelligence-in-finance/

Mhlanga, D. (2020a). Industry 4.0 in finance: The impact of artificial intelligence (AI) on digital financial inclusion. *International Journal of Financial Studies, 8*(3), 1–14. https://doi.org/10.3390/ijfs8030045

Mhlanga, D. (2020b). *Artificial intelligence (AI) and poverty reduction in the fourth industrial revolution (4IR).* https://doi.org/10.20944/preprints202009.0362.v1

Mhlanga, D. (2020c). *Financial inclusion and poverty reduction: Evidence from small scale agricultural sector in Manicaland Province of Zimbabwe* (Doctoral dissertation). North-West University, South Africa.

Mhlanga, D., & Denhere, V. (2021). Determinants of financial inclusion in Southern Africa. *Studia Universitatis Babes-Bolyai Oeconomica, 65*(3), 39–52. https://doi.org/10.2478/subboec-2020-0014

Mhlanga, D., & Dunga, S. H. (2020). Measuring financial inclusion and its determinants among the smallholder farmers in Zimbabwe: An empirical study. *Eurasian Journal of Business and Management, 8*(3), 266–281. https://doi.org/10.15604/ejbm.2020.08.03.008

Mhlanga, D., Dunga, S. H., & Moloi, T. (2020). Financial inclusion and poverty alleviation among smallholder farmers in Zimbabwe. *Eurasian Journal of Economics and Finance, 8*(3), 168–182. https://doi.org/10.15604/ejef.2020.08.03.004

Newman, L. H. (2017). Equifax officially has no excuse. *Wired*, September 14. https://www.wired.com/story/equifax-breach-no-excuse/

Oliver, W., & Marsh, H. (2019). *Artificial intelligence applications in financial services.*

Ozili, P. K. (2018). Impact of digital finance on financial inclusion and stability. *Borsa Istanbul Review, 18*(4), 329–340. https://doi.org/10.1016/j.bir.2017.12.003

Ozili, P. K. (2021). *Big data and artificial intelligence for financial inclusion: Benefits and issues.* Available at SSRN 3766097.

Paschen, J., Paschen, U., Pala, E., & Kietzmann, J. (2020). Artificial intelligence (AI) and value co-creation in B2B sales: Activities, actors and resources. *Australasian Marketing Journal, 29*, 243. https://doi.org/10.1016/j.ausmj.2020.06.004

Peric, K. (2015). Digital financial inclusion. *Journal of Payments Strategy & Systems* [Internet], *9*(3):212–214. Available from: https://www.ingentaconnect.com/content/hsp/jpss/2015/00000009/00000003/art00001. [Cited January 2021].

Radcliffe, D., Voorhies, R., & Gates Foundation, M. (2012). *A digital pathway to financial inclusion.* http://ssrn.com/abstract=2186926

Saon, R., Sadeep, P., & Smita, M. (2019). *Use of Blockchain and artificial intelligence to promote financial inclusion in India.* https://economictimes

Theodoridis, P. K., & Gkikas, D. C. (2019). *How artificial intelligence affects digital marketing* (pp. 1319–1327). https://doi.org/10.1007/978-3-030-12453-3_151

Tinsley, E., & Agapitova, N. (2018). *Private sector solutions to helping smallholders succeed social enterprise business models in the agriculture sector.*

Wang, X., & He, G. (2020). Digital financial inclusion and farmers' vulnerability to poverty: Evidence from rural China. *Sustainability (Switzerland), 12*(4). https://doi.org/10.3390/su12041668

Xie, M. (2019). Development of artificial intelligence and effects on financial system. *Journal of Physics: Conference Series, 1187*(3). https://doi.org/10.1088/1742-6596/1187/3/032084

Chapter 15
Women Empowerment in the South African Agribusiness: Opportunities and Constraints in the Gauteng Province

Emmanuel Ndhlovu and Belese N. Majova

Abstract This article explores the opportunities for and constraints of women empowerment in the South African Gauteng Province. This article posits that, although the number of women involved in agribusiness has increased in South Africa and the Gauteng Province, women empowerment in terms of resource control and participation in decision-making in the agribusiness is still a real problem. The article is guided by the Longwe framework. Utilising interviews, secondary sources, and observations, the article reveals that lack of funds, education and training, criminality, technological challenges, research and innovation, and lack of transformation are some of the key barriers to women's empowerment within agribusiness. In dealing with these challenges, this article recommends the deployment of sustainable livelihoods framework-based interventions as part of the collective and continued effort to realize women's empowerment in the agribusiness in the province.

Keywords Agribusiness · Agriculture · Farmers · South Africa · Women empowerment

15.1 Introduction

The postapartheid democracy of nonracial and nonsexist society in South Africa ushered in the beginning of a long and continuous process of employment equity and empowerment. The Employment Equity Act, No. 55 of 1998, also initiated a national policy framework for female emancipation and gender equality in the agribusiness. However, engagement in the agribusiness remains a huge challenge,

E. Ndhlovu (✉)
Vaal University of Technology, Vanderbijlpark, South Africa

B. N. Majova
The University of Johannesburg, Johannesburg, South Africa

D. Mhlanga, E. Ndhlovu (eds.), *Economic Inclusion in Post-Independence Africa*, Advances in African Economic, Social and Political Development,
https://doi.org/10.1007/978-3-031-31431-5_15

particularly for women (Rusenga, 2019). South African women have not made a significant impact in agribusiness as they continue to lack access to and control of land (Kepe & Hall, 2018; Ncapayi, 2013). This is despite widespread recommendations that women have the potential to contribute significantly not only to the much-neglected rural economy but also to the broader economy of the country (Aliber et al., 2013; Cousins, 2015; Hall & Kepe, 2017; Nkwinti, 2010). Gender and gender dynamics inherent in agribusiness continue to marginalize women seeking engagement in the sector. South African women are confronted with a range of challenging socioeconomic, cultural, and political factors which limit their opportunities and ability to lobby for and gain access to agribusiness. Those who managed to enter the agribusiness sector also face challenges such as access to markets, access to finance and affordable business premises, the acquisition of skills and managerial expertise and access to appropriate technology, funding, information, and government support. Various government initiatives including the country's land reform program have tried releasing land to women and also coming up with agribusiness-related projects that are deliberately biased toward women. However, empirical evidence shows that these initiatives have not succeeded in addressing the funding and support challenges faced by women in agribusiness (Beinart et al., 2020; Mubecua & Nojiyeza, 2019; Ndhlovu, 2021).

Targeting women as mere recipients of projects has not provided them with the support that they need to engage, build, and sustain viable agribusinesses. Empowering women in agribusiness should entail empowering them to have control over material and nonmaterial assets that can allow them to put their labor to productive use. This argument speaks to Malhotra et al. (2002: 5–6) who view the term "empowerment" as a process that "operates from below and [which] involves agency as exercised by individuals and groups" and as the "enhancement of assets and capabilities of diverse individuals and groups to engage, influence and hold accountable the institutions that affect them."

Some of the legal frameworks introduced to promote women's empowerment in agribusiness in South Africa include the Reconstruction and Development Programme, the *Constitution*, the White Paper on South African Land Policy (WPSALP) (1997) and its related programs, the Broad-Based Black Economic Empowerment (BBBEE), and the Agricultural Black Economic Empowerment (AgriBEE) (Republic of South Africa, 1996). These were developed and introduced to support the Land-Reform Policy initiatives in which women could access agricultural assets. Developing legislation that supports women's access to agricultural assets was premised on the faith that efficient and equitable access to land by women would create jobs and therefore make a marked impact on the total economy of the country. The RDP in particular was built on the view that the national Land-Reform Policy and its programs were central and driving forces of rural development. This article (i) explores the opportunities for and constraints of women in agribusiness and (ii) proposes the sustainable livelihoods framework (SLF) as the model through which women's empowerment in agribusiness can be remolded.

After the current introduction, this article reviews the literature that is related to the study with a focus on international and national frameworks supporting the concept of women empowerment. A historical background discussion on inequality in South Africa is also presented. Thereafter, the Longwe framework is presented as the framework guiding data analysis. This is followed by a discussion of the research methods used in the article, a discussion of the findings, SLF as the proposed model, and a conclusion.

15.2 Women Empowerment: A Conceptual Framework

Women empowerment has been a buzzword concept in recent years particularly as societies increasingly adopt more democratic systems of governance (Kepe & Hall, 2018; Mubecua & Nojiyeza, 2019; Ncapayi, 2013; Ndhlovu, 2022a). The concept has received different yet interrelated definitions from scholars. Fernando (1997: 156) defines it as an institutional change through which women can: "Take control over material assets, intellectual resources, and ideology. The material assets over which control can be exercised may be physical, human, or financial, such as land water, forests, people's bodies and labour, money and access to money. Intellectual resources include knowledge information, and ideas." Malhotra et al. (2002: 5–6) define "empowerment" as the "enhancement of assets and capabilities of diverse individuals and groups to engage, influence and hold accountable the institutions that affect them." The authors add that the empowerment process "operates from below and involves agency as exercised by individuals and groups." According to Malhotra et al. (2002: 06), the empowerment of women involves altering relations of power which constrain their options and independence and adversely affect their potential. This definition focuses on women's ability to make choices to enhance their empowerment and well-being.

For Doss et al. (2008), the empowerment of women includes cognitive and psychological elements involving their understanding of the conditions of subordination and the causes of such conditions at both micro and macro levels of society. It also involves understanding the need to make choices that are considered inconsistent with prevailing cultural and social expectations. According to Hart and Aliber (2012), women empowerment is a process through which women can organize themselves to intensify their self-reliance, assert their autonomous right to make choices, and control resources which can assist them in challenging and eliminating their subordination. Peters and Peters (1998) consider women's empowerment to be a developmental rather than a gender issue. Makombe (2006) perceives women's empowerment as a process that leads women to the realization that they are able and are entitled to decide what they want with their own lives. They can decide their own choices in life and to be involved in choosing the direction of change through the ability to gain control over critical material and nonmaterial resources.

Kabeer (1999: 437) views women's empowerment as comprising three components: resources, agency, and achievements. Malhotra et al. (2002: 9) aver that the main components of empowerment are resources, perceptions, relationships, and power.

Women's empowerment, as a process, takes place in three main areas: household, community, and further afield. It has the following dimensions: economic, sociocultural, interpersonal, legal, political, and psychological (Malhotra et al., 2002: 14). These dimensions have, in their turn, a range of sub-domains. A development intervention may promote women's empowerment in a certain aspect without automatically having any impact in other dimensions. This study focused on the individual/household arena. The dimensions of interest were economic, sociocultural, and psychological. The choice of the individual/household arena as one of the arenas of focus was justified on two grounds. First, the household is a central locus of women's disempowerment. Second, it supports patriarchal structures requiring systemic transformation. The focus was also placed on land access, ownership, and utilization as important for women's empowerment in agribusiness.

Land access, ownership, and utilization are very important if women should be successful in agribusiness. In patriarchal societies, land continues to be owned by males (Moeng, 2011). Land asset is the most important item in the agricultural sector. One reason why land ownership is important for women's empowerment is the growing evidence between asset accumulation and declining levels of poverty (Carter, 2003). There is a negative relationship between the risk of rural poverty and land access. This is because the land has both direct benefits (from growing crops, fodder, or trees) and indirect benefits (land can serve as collateral for credit or can be sold during the crisis). As a result, there have been both international and national efforts toward the realization of women's empowerment through equality, including in land ownership.

15.2.1 Frameworks of Women's Empowerment

South Africa makes use of both internationally and nationally crafted frameworks for women empowerment as detailed in the next subsections.

15.2.2 International Frameworks Supporting Women's Empowerment

The need to incorporate women into mainstream development is roughly linked to the first United Nations International Conference on Women held in Mexico in 1975 and the declaration of the International Decade for Women. These two developments had their themes revolving around equality, development, and peace, thus opening new discourses on gender equality. Subsequent meetings have since been held as follow-up conferences on women. These included the Nairobi Conference in

1985 and the Beijing Conference held in 1995. Additional efforts, through relevant international conventions, including the Convention on the Elimination of all Forms of Discrimination against Women (CEDAW) were undertaken. Some of the international declarations agreed upon about women's empowerment are the Millennium Development Goals (MDGs), Agenda 21, and World Summit on Sustainable Development.

In the MDGs, the need for women's empowerment was covered in Goal 3 which sought to achieve equality between men and women to reduce poverty and ensure that all people can fully participate in development initiatives within their communities. The goal supported that both women and men should hold positions as leaders in their communities, should equally be able to participate in all levels of education, and can equally undertake paid employment. It also supported equal access to the property, such as land by women.

Another important development effort benefiting women is Agenda 21, a move in over 18 government leaders endorsed as an action plan for sustainable development at a United Nations Conference. The Agenda 21 framework was aimed at development with a considerable bias toward the development of women. It aimed at strengthening the role of major groups, such as women, children and youth, and indigenous people. It emphasized the development of marginalized groups, such as women, and people with disabilities through access to finance; improved technology transfer and science; education, skills training, and capacity-building; and international institutions, in terms of partnerships and legal measures with information management. Agenda 21 also advocates for the need to permit women to play meaningful roles in communities to contribute to developmental initiatives. South Africa is a signatory to the Agenda 21 agreement and also hosted the World Conference on Sustainable Development and the National Land Summit in 2002. The Conference emphasized environmental conservation in all developmental projects. The National Land Summit, aimed at creating a platform in which South Africans would be able to find practical solutions to accelerate land delivery for sustainable development, was also held in 2005 at NASREC in Johannesburg by the then Minister of Agriculture and Land Affairs. The participants at the National Land Summit (comprising of governments, commercial agriculture, and social movements) agreed on several issues including a promise to redistribute at least 30% of white-owned agricultural land by the year 2014. The government committed itself to slashing poverty and unemployment by half over the next decade, beginning in 2005. It was realized that land reform was not only required to undo the injustices of the past but also that it should be central to economic transformation. However, at the time of writing this article, 16 years after the National Land Summit and resolutions, land issues and the need for women's empowerment have been largely shelved. It is against this backdrop that the need to take a new look at women, as beneficiaries of land reform, becomes imperative.

15.2.3 Domestic Frameworks and Initiatives

South Africa introduced land-related policies, such as the RDP (1994), the Constitution (1996), the WPSALP (1997) and its related programs, the BBBEE (2003), and the AgriBEE in which women could access agricultural assets. The WPSALP raised concerns about the lack of any effective and integrated environmental management because of landlessness and overcrowding, especially in the former homelands, and incorrect farming practices on commercial farms. It posited that the land management system in the country was fragmented and not well coordinated. It also bemoaned the slow pace, in terms of land delivery to women. It acknowledged that gender disparities persisted in democratic South Africa when the access to agricultural assets are analyzed.

The BBBEE emanates from the Act that supports it; Act, 2003 (Act 53 of 2003). According to the BBBEE, support for Human Development Induces must be prioritised, especially towards women, youths and people with disabilities. In the RDP (1994: 21), women were identified as having specific challenges that required them to be prioritized. According to Section 2 of the BBBEE Act, 2003, the objectives of this Act, among many, included increasing the extent to which black women, in particular, own and manage existing and new enterprises and improving their access to economic activities and infrastructure; promoting investment programs that lead to broad-based and meaningful participation in the economy by black people—to achieve sustainable development and general prosperity; empowering rural and local communities by facilitating access to economic activities, land, infrastructure, ownership, and skills; and promoting access to finance for black economic empowerment. Section 3 of the Act mandates that this Act must be interpreted toward realizing the *Constitution* (1996). The limited access to resources, including agricultural resources such as land, as well as lack of skills, was emphasized by the BBBEE (2003). This confirmed the call for equitable redistribution and allocation of land, especially for women. Prosperity, economic development, and sustainable development have been identified as the main goals of the BBBEE (2003), the RDP (1994: 78), the WPSALP (1997: 5), and Section 195 (1) (b) and (c) of the *Constitution* (1996).

National policies designed for ensuring the achievement of broad-based black economic empowerment had to be established—such as the AgriBEE. The former Department of Agriculture launched the AgriBEE framework as part of the BBBEE to guide black economic empowerment within the agricultural sector in 2004. The AgriBEE is intended for the promotion of equity in agriculture-related initiatives. The charter for the AgriBEE noted that empowerment starts with improved access to land and tenure security. The charter put in place a distinction between land and enterprise ownership, with voluntary sales of land from the current landowners. Preference is to be given to land sale transactions that benefit the employees within that enterprise. The charter confirmed the target, as stated by the WPSALP (1997), that 30% of the agricultural land had to be targeted and viable and sustainable enterprises were to be established.

The South African government has also mobilized a variety of stakeholders to partner with the state to ensure the empowerment of women. The South African Women Entrepreneurs' Network (SAWEN) is an institution that was established for the development and coordination of women in business in the country. SAWEN works as a useful conduit to the government for businesswomen, including those in agribusiness. Although there have been concerns raised about the long-term sustainability of SAWEN, the institution is proving to be a viable one as it continues to offer women a platform on which they continue to lobby for business support.

The other important institution which is at the forefront of promoting the empowerment of businesswomen in South Africa is Small Enterprise Development Agency (SEDA). This institution is aimed at empowering businesswomen in all sectors, including agribusiness. SEDA programs are designed to provide support specifically for women. The National Youth Development Agency (NYDA) is also another mainstream which propagates the empowerment of women in its programs and services.

The Women on Farms Project (WFP) is another nongovernmental organization working with women, particularly those living on farms. This platform assists women by providing them with socioeconomic rights and gender education as well as support for the building of social groups. This platform is also used by women to lobby for funding of cooperatives as a group. Uthando South Africa is also another platform which assists women in agriculture and gardening with training, education, and advice.

15.2.4 Inequality in the Agriculture Sector in South Africa

In the former homelands which comprise the 13% of the land reserved for African occupation by colonial and apartheid policies, access and use land rights are still largely confined to male heads of households (Mubecua & Nojiyeza, 2019; Ndhlovu, 2022b). Women's land access, control, and utilization continue to be largely (although not exclusively) mediated through their relationship with a male household head, whether a husband, brother, son, or another male relative (Akinola, 2018; Antwi & Chagwiza, 2018). The principal male right to direct land allocation coincides with and defines a wider set of primary rights within the household and community at large. Women's secondary rights to highly valued property, such as land, similarly match secondary rights in respect of other household activities, depicting them as subjects, or minors, both within their households and within the wider community.

Women themselves came to a point they accepted their position in the community as second-class citizens. According to Cross and Hornby (2002), women's assertion of right over land in the 1980s was large part of the struggle against apartheid and the institutions of the former homelands created by that system and not specifically the outright need to use it. With independence, the land struggles by women have subsided. However, this might be largely due to the lack of a robust political will by the state or the reluctance of men to accept the legislative changes which have provided the space for the allocation of land rights to women (Cross & Hornby, 2002).

Since its independence in 1994, the government of South Africa shows its continued commitment to making its agricultural sector stronger and more robust. Crucial to this strategy, at first, was to increase the equity among those in the agribusiness in terms of racial and gender representation and access to land, modern technologies, and other inputs. However, Hart and Aliber (2012) lament the fact that the intention to give support to the poor and most vulnerable farmers, especially female farmers, has been subordinated to an overwhelming focus on the better-resourced and more commercially oriented black farmers while most women, who are resource-poor, are left out in the tide of development. According to Hart and Aliber (2012), the existing support provided by the government to farmers, particularly to smallholders, promotes the implementation of new technologies but does not pay consideration to the variety of farmers in a range of circumstances. According to them, for new technologies to be utilized, those in the agribusiness need access not only to land but also to education, technologies appropriate to the farming needs, and appropriate agricultural extension support. In this view of the above, it is argued that for the majority of women in South Africa, the current socio-economic rights, as assured in the Constitution, remain inaccessible resulting in the continuation and increase as well as the feminization of poverty (Moeng, 2011). In addition, for rural women and those women on farms, the Constitution's guarantees of equality and nondiscrimination remain merely theoretical rights that lack practical implementation.

Stimulating growth in agriculture in South Africa would be key to poverty alleviation because of the effects that agriculture has on overall economic growth and because many poor people in rural areas derive their incomes from agriculture. An indirect effect is that agricultural growth drives reductions in the price of food, with benefits for the poor. As a result, the argument holds that agricultural growth has superior impacts on poverty reduction, nutrition, and/or food security, compared to growth in other sectors (Ndhlovu, 2021, 2022c). This viewpoint embeds some strong and internally consistent arguments, but they still need to be dealt with carefully, especially because there is no gender-disaggregated data to precisely estimate the actual position of women who make up the majority of those in poverty.

15.2.5 The Women's Empowerment Framework

The Women's Empowerment Framework s developed by Sara Hlupekile Longwe guided data analysis for this study. The Longwe framework was designed to assist development planners to question what women's empowerment and equality mean and what it entails in practice and, from this point, to assess critically to what extent a development intervention is supporting women's empowerment (Longwe, 1999). Longwe requires that women empowerment enables women to take an equal place with men and engage on an equal basis in the development process to achieve control over the factors of production. The Longwe framework hinges on the concept of five "levels of equality" which show the degree to which women are equal with men and have therefore achieved empowerment. These five levels of equality can be used to investigate and assess the likelihood of particular development interventions promoting equality and women's empowerment. These levels are summarized below:

Control	↑	↑
Participation	Increased equality	Increased empowerment
Conscientization		
Access		
Welfare		

Source: Longwe (1999)

The above levels of equality are said to be hierarchical. If a development intervention focuses on the higher levels, the probability is high that the empowerment of women will be realized than if the project focuses on the lower levels. If intervention focuses on welfare, chances are high that women will be empowered. According to the framework, equal participation in the making of decisions about resources is more essential for achieving women's empowerment than equal access to resources. Even participation and access are not as important as equal control (Ndhlovu, 2018).

In the event that the levels of equality are employed in the analysis of the impact of development interventions on women's equality and empowerment, it is indispensable to understand that an ideal intervention does not necessarily reveal activities on every level. According to Longwe, an intervention which is empowering for women will have numerous components which fit into the higher categories, but none in the lower ones. The "welfare" level focuses on access to material resources. Thus, an intervention which addresses control over resources can be classified at a higher level under "Control."

In this study, the Longwe framework reveals how women's equal participation in the designing of policies and programs that relate to agribusiness could lead to their empowerment. The participation of South African women is crucial if it leads to equal control of agriculture resources by women and not simply increasing their access to assets.

15.3 Research Methods

This chapter is based on a qualitative study that was conducted in fulfillment of a master's degree. Data was collected between December 2015 and January 2016. The study gathered in-depth interviews from a total of 25 women in agribusiness and a total of 5 officials in the Department of Agriculture in the Gauteng Province who were chosen purposefully and who consented to participation. Farm observations and secondary documents were also used as sources of data. This multi-method approach was part of the general approach to improving the quality and validity of case data through triangulation (Creswell, 2018). The methods were used in tandem to give an in-depth understanding of gender relations on access to agricultural assistance and control over agricultural property by men and women. Thematic data analysis—a process where themes are allowed to emerge from the collected data—was used. Each interview with agribusiness proprietors as well as with officials was allocated a number by which it could be identified. The numbers for proprietors ranged from 1 to 25, while for officials, the numbers ranged from 1 to 5. The numbering does not identify the participants but rather identifies the interview.

15.4 Results Interpretation and Discussion

The results of the study are placed into two broad categories of themes, namely, constraints of and opportunities for women empowerment in the agribusiness in the Gauteng Province.

15.4.1 Constraints of Women's Empowerment

South African women in agribusiness, as in other developing countries, faced several challenges ranging from lack of finance, adequate infrastructure, limited training and education, and criminality to stunted innovation and power and water cuts.

15.4.1.1 Funding Constraints

Finance is the most important requirement for any business. Without enough funding, a business cannot thrive. No business can be established in the absence of funding, whether acquired through a loan or any other source. Money is needed for starting up a business. Funding was found to be the major challenge for most women in agribusiness. It was revealed that: "money is needed for the purchase of goods and services to be used in the business, payment of labour when we have to pay for it."[1] Money was also needed "for paying the rentals where the infrastructure used does not belong to us, as well as paying for any other necessary business needs."[2] Due to a lack of adequate funds, "black farmers, the majority of who were women, were unable to access the needed resources and infrastructure to enable them to

[1] Interview 4, 04/12/2012, Soutpan.

[2] Interview 3, 04/12/2015, Soutpan.

perform at their best."[3] The problem was rampant, especially among smallholder black women.

Participants indicated that they relied on personal savings both in starting up enterprises and for maintaining them. They indicated that they avoided engaging the private for funding due to its exorbitant interest rates. Financial institutions also required collateral before they could provide funding. Most of those in the agribusiness, particularly women, indicated that they did not have some properties which they could present as collateral during loan applications and, thus, were often disqualified.[4] Some institutions also needed business licenses in which most small agribusinesses did not have such certificates. Thus, they were unable to access funding. The challenge of collateral was especially heavy on black women. Due to the patriarchal nature in which South Africa is steeped, most women did not own physical property, particularly land and infrastructure. This then presented a huge challenge for female proprietors as they could not claim equality of voice and decision-making with men who already possessed property as espoused by Longwe. While institutions such as SAWEN, SEDA, and NYDA exist to assist women with funding and other business resources, such intervention lingers around the lower categories of empowerment, namely, access and welfare, and, therefore, does not lead to structural transformation which can result in full-fledged empowerment in the agribusiness.

15.4.1.2 Rigorous Screening for Resource Applications

When women in agribusiness approached institutions for funding, their applications were often subjected to strict inspection and authentication.[5] This "was stricter when the applicant was a black woman."[6] This was viewed as a common procedure because lenders wanted to make sure that they will be able to get their money back.[7] Participants also agreed that: "If lending institutions do not investigate the backgrounds of applicants, they will run the risk of losing out to borrowers who fail to pay back the money."[8] It was for these reasons that "lenders have put in place strict measures by which they can disregard inauspicious applicants."[9] Empirical evidence shows that over 70% of small businesses in South Africa, for instance, failed within the first 10 years of inception (Bhorat et al., 2018); therefore, banks needed to take precautionary measures to ensure that they will not loss out. The verification and vetting can sometimes take longer. When this happens, some applicants may be

[3] Informant 2, 15/01/2016, Department of Agriculture.

[4] Interview 15, 11/12/2015, Kempton Park.

[5] Informant 2, 15/01/2016, Department of Agriculture.

[6] Informant 4, 15/01/2016, Department of Agriculture.

[7] Informant 5, 16/01/2016, Department of Agriculture.

[8] Interview 21, 27/12/2015, Kempton Park.

[9] Interview 17, 19/12/2015, Soshanguve.

frustrated. Some of the requirements in the entire process disqualify applicants as they might be required to demonstrate trustworthiness. Where this obtains, proprietors focus on access and welfare components of empowerment as their ability to lobby for high-level components (participation and control) is hampered by a lack of collateral and rigorous application processes which do not consider the historically disadvantaged background of black women as encapsulated in the AgriBEE and BBBEE frameworks.

15.4.1.3 Cultural and Infrastructural Constraints

The problem of infrastructure inadequacy has been majoring particularly in Africa (Kessey, 2014). Agribusiness proprietors lacked well-equipped infrastructure from which to operate. Personal observations revealed that most women proprietors operated from very old buildings while others operated from shacks. One participant mentioned that women's marginalization in terms of employment opportunities, both colonial and postcolonial South Africa, has resulted in a severe lack of economic opportunities, limited infrastructure, and a serious breakdown of social capital.[10] Due to infrastructural challenges, "women in the agribusiness continued to operate under extremely poor conditions."[11] Although the Gauteng Province cannot be considered a rural province, discussions with key informants revealed that infrastructural challenges were pervasive as most women were located in the primary sector of the agribusiness with most of them engaging in land cultivation, which is normally a rural activity. Women also suffered a double burden of culture which denies them assets. Due to their prescribed low status, women encountered several challenges which rendered them incapable of owning productive assets, such as land, blocking them from participating in politics, and the general economy, including land access and utilization.[12] Unless women are regarded as equals to men, they will never have full access, ownership, and control of the land. Since the land has an economic value, it is crucial that women also access and utilize it for inclusive development and for women empowerment to be realized.

Participants recommended that to enable them to increase productivity and realize their empowerment, the "government needed to provide us with as much affordable and basic infrastructure as possible, such as electrical power supplies networks or buildings from which to operate."[13] This would enable women to take an equal place with men and engage on an equal basis in the development process to achieve control over the factors of production as espoused in the Longwe framework. Empowering women through the provision of infrastructure would enable them to function better in agribusiness and contribute to employment creation and to the

[10] Interview 10, 10/12/2015, Soshanguve.

[11] Informant 5, 16/01/2016, Department of Agriculture.

[12] Informant 4, 16/01/2016, Department of Agriculture.

[13] Interview 19, 19/12/2015, Soshanguve.

broader economy and the general livelihood development of those who own or who work in these businesses. This would be in line with the government's BBBEE framework which prioritizes human development, especially toward women, youths, and people with disabilities. This would also be in line with the RDP framework which identifies women as having specific challenges that required them to be prioritized.

15.4.1.4 Education and Training

Most of the participant proprietors in the agribusiness did not have professional training. Some did not even have any background in agriculture. Education and training empower individuals to be able to weigh their own decisions and apply their training, as well as the information acquired to business situations. Education aids an individual to look for information that may be useful to their business. Education empowers business owners with the skills and tactics to research what is needed in the market as well as the quality of the products which are under demand (Ghina, 2014).

One informant mentioned that "in the modern world where people and businesses are now closely knit by the fast and evolving technological communications, people can acquire the type of information they want in a very short space of time… Education and training ensure that businesses have the necessary information and skills which are needed in operating a business."[14] Some participants revealed that their lack of education and training emanated from South Africa's history of colonialism and apartheid which denied black equal opportunities to education and training. While the challenge also affected black men, women were reported to be the most affected due to several factors including patriarchy and colonial history.[15] Women also lacked proper education qualifications that could be used to convince the private sector to assist their agribusinesses.

The challenge of lack of skills and adequate education levels in developing countries, particularly Africa, is confirmed as linked to colonial tendencies that denied the colonized to acquire skills to ensure that they would always be servants and never employers or skilled personnel (Bhorat et al., 2018). In the case of South Africa, apartheid policies ensured that the education that was accessible to Africans was always inferior (Nomvete & Mashayamombe, 2019). With limited education and without adequate skills to engage in business, "many agribusiness proprietors are not able to draft business proposals that can be shown to lenders or to the relevant government departments for support."[16] As a result of this challenge, most of the women farmers were unable to benefit from the various opportunities that

[14] Informant 4, 16/01/2016, Department of Agriculture.

[15] Informant 1, 10/01/2016, Department of Agriculture.

[16] Informant 2, 10/01/2016, Department of Agriculture.

existed in terms of input support and further training.[17] This condemned them to pursue the lower components of empowerment (access and awareness), while the high-level components (control and participation) are left to men. Participants confirmed that they faced challenges in accounting and sales capabilities and that "agriculture education and training would allow them to improve their businesses and perform better."[18] For women farmers to realize empowerment, they need access not only to land but also to education, training, and appropriate agricultural extension support.

Key informants posited that gender and gender dynamics inherent in agricultural production needed to be considered if women farmers were not to continue being marginalized members within the agribusiness. Empowering women in line with the Longwe framework requires transcending considering women simply as recipients of projects and inputs as this will not provide them with the support that they need to build and sustain viable agribusinesses that can lead to control and participation needs.

15.4.1.5 Research and Innovation

Every business has a greater chance of doing well when research is conducted continuously to establish what is required in the market. Research also enables the business to determine whether they can transform their ideas into practicality (Haselip et al., 2014). The study found that lack of education and training, as detailed above, hampered the chances of proprietors in the Gauteng agribusiness to thrive. Investing in research would allow proprietors to obtain innovative solutions through discovery (Kessey, 2014). Businesses that innovate have a higher chance of growing than those that do not innovate. Key informants revealed that South African smallholder farmers, in particular, were less innovative when compared to those in other countries.[19] In South Africa, innovation is frustrated by the failure of agribusiness proprietors to form strong associations with larger and well-established businesses which could assist them with more business information and financial support.[20] It was argued that the inability to create linkages, particularly by women farmers in the country, denied them "chances for technology diffusion."[21] In this view, it is suggested that the South African government needs to promote women's empowerment in agribusiness through the provision of incentives for research and development initiatives. The aim would be to encourage innovation and reinforce lasting linkages among domestic and foreign knowledge-intensive businesses.

[17] Informant 4, 16/01/2016, Department of Agriculture.

[18] Interview 24, 28/12/2015, Winterveldt.

[19] Informant 4, 16/01/2016, Department of Agriculture.

[20] Informant 2, 10/01/2016, Department of Agriculture.

[21] Informant 2, 10/01/2016, Department of Agriculture.

15.4.1.6 Criminality

Participant agribusiness proprietors also reported criminal tendencies that undermined the realization of women's empowerment through successful business operations. This situation is supported by reviewed literature which notes increasing criminality in South Africa (Muchiri, 2016). Incidences such as farm robberies, theft, and murder have continued to frustrate the operations of farmers. The OECD (2015) reported that crime in South Africa was forcing many businesses to either close or step up security spending way above what they can afford. In agribusiness, farmers have to increase their security details. One participant mentioned: "Living on the farm is now very risky. You have to put in place several things to be safe. We find it to be very expensive due to the general lack of funds."[22] The security details needed on the farms were more on farms run by women. One women participant mentioned that "as a woman, I have to increase security. Men are not as vulnerable as we are. So, we generally spend more. This does not mean that I afford it. It is a matter of can't help."[23] This makes women underperform in terms of production as they use more on security details and not on operations.[24] Where this obtains, women continue to linger in the lower components of Longwe's components of women empowerment. Criminality on South African farms can only be realized when the South African security agents step up their presence on farms.

There have also been increased reports of rampant corruption and nepotism. Some participants mentioned that men were always ahead in the queue in acquiring state support in terms of farm inputs and assets.[25] Some participants reported that assistance intended for them was often diverted elsewhere by politicians who focused on their supporters and relatives, thereby leaving farmers stranded.[26] Coupled with this was official incompetence by extension officers who rarely make visits to farms to see how farmers can be assisted to deal with official corruption and nepotism. Structural transformation at various levels of government is therefore needed to deal with criminal tendencies that frustrate women's empowerment in agribusiness.

15.4.1.7 Technological Challenges

Agribusiness proprietors in the Gauteng Province also face the challenge of technology use.[27] This challenge was found to be worse in agribusinesses owned by black women. These businesses seemed to struggle to acquire and make use of appropriate

---

[22] Interview 22, 22/12/2015, Mamelodi.

[23] Interview 21, 22/12/2015, Mamelodi.

[24] Informant 2, 10/01/2016, Department of Agriculture.

[25] Interview 16, 17/12/2015, Winterveldt.

[26] Interview 21, 22/12/2015, Mamelodi.

[27] Informant 2, 10/01/2016, Department of Agriculture.

technologies. Key informants revealed that small-scale agribusinesses in the Gauteng Province "are known for their low productivity as a result of little technology use."[28] This makes them uncompetitive with larger enterprises. Agribusinesses owned by women did also not maximize their machinery utility and also "displayed a very limited interest of improving the use of modern technologies."[29] Most women farmers, particularly those that were in crop production, largely made use of technology with no attempts to adapt these technologies to suit their own specific needs. The farmers justified this tendency by arguing that they "showed no technology innovation due to financial restraints."[30] Some farmers revealed that they "lacked adequate knowledge and ability to choose the right technology for their business needs,"[31] while some simply had "limited knowhow on the importance of making use of technology."[32] This compromises these women's chance to empowerment especially through the realization of the higher components of women empowerment by Longwe (1999).

In dealing with the technological challenge, the World Bank (2014) recommends that African entrepreneurs commence investing in relevant technology to increase capacity, quality, and productivity. Increasing technology use has the potential to increase competitiveness in the long run. South African agribusinesses could engage the government so that they can get support regarding technology initiatives and networks.

South Africa's approach to assisting women in the agricultural sector is criticized by Hart and Aliber (2012) who argue that the country adopts a delivery approach based on the top-down transfer of technology models. This approach is not participatory and therefore promotes the delivery and adoption of universally designed modern technologies to improve productivity and increase output. It does not consider the significance of local situations, such as local knowledge, resource endowments, and aspirations (Hart & Aliber, 2012). The most common technologies transferred are "spillover technologies" which, more, were targeted at established and well-resourced commercial farmers and not the poor or women. The primary focus has been to support the black farmers in South Africa, but with an implementation biased toward more commercially oriented black farmers who are better able to use spillover technologies. Hart and Aliber (2012) criticize this approach for not sufficiently acknowledging women farmers and their circumstances. Understanding the variety within the agribusiness sector is imperative, and technology needs to be developed and adjusted to the differences in the skills, resources, motivation, and objectives of agribusiness proprietors.

---

[28] Informant 4, 16/01/2016, Department of Agriculture.

[29] Informant 3, 15/01/2016, Department of Agriculture.

[30] Interview 21, 22/12/2015, Mamelodi.

[31] Interview 16, 17/12/2015, Winterveldt.

[32] Informant 3, 15/01/2016, Department of Agriculture.

15.4.2 Opportunities for Women's Empowerment

There were also some opportunities for women empowerment in agribusiness that were reported both by proprietors and by key informants in the Department of Agriculture. These opportunities are presented here in a summary format.

Transformation

Participants also reported the existence of some opportunities that would see their businesses grow. The transformation was one of these opportunities.[33] "Change could be done by speeding up cash flows and inflows by targeting bigger clients in a step-change arrangement."[34] This is when businesses change their activities and operations in line with their real growth changes, as well as in line with the pressures exerted by other businesses within the same field. Women proprietors could know their funders and, thus, position their businesses in a way that can convince the funders to offer support. Participants revealed that they were already transforming their businesses and therefore "expected to see the fruits of this kicking in."[35]

Digital technology was also now being embraced to cater for clients who buy online. This is part of an effort to have a positive attitude in the business environment.

15.4.2.1 Collaboration and Cooperation

Women participants also engaged in some entrepreneurial communities in which they "purchased inputs in bulk to obtain better discounts."[36] The presence of networks may also go beyond the "production" and "protection" aspects. Networks may be steeped in prospects for social cohesion which may be more important for women than is often realized. Social cohesion and collaboration may lead to women's empowerment as women could use their large number to lobby for opportunities to take part in decision-making and control of productive resources. The promotion of collaborations and social cohesion can be exploited to boost production. This networking can be targeted by development practitioners to mobilize for popular participation in the sector.

---

[33] Ibid.

[34] Informant 3, 15/01/2016, Department of Agriculture.

[35] Interview 10, 10/12/2015, Soshanguve.

[36] Interview 21, 22/12/2015, Mamelodi.

15.4.2.2 Employment and Income-Generating Opportunities

Women farmers reported that their businesses not only generate employment but also provided some decent incomes which they now used to expand their operations. Some farmers now combined crop production with poultry.[37] These were seen as opportunities that could attract government attention and make it renew its initial commitment to the empowerment of women through land reform programs.

15.4.2.3 Establishment of Socioeconomic and Political Networks

For some farmers, engagement in agribusiness created opportunities to establish important socioeconomic contacts with those who came from other areas and to establish contacts with senior government officials. Some participants had managed to forge connections with the ruling party and reported that they now managed to access inputs and preferential treatment with input purchase and tillage.

15.5 A Proposed Framework for Empowering Women in the Agribusiness

To realize the empowerment of women in the agribusiness in the Gauteng Province, it is important that both local and national governments, as well as donor actors who support women, deploy interventions that are based on the five capitals of the SLF, namely, natural, physical, financial, human, and social capitals.

- *Natural capital*: This relates to natural goods such as land, quality soils, and sufficient water bodies. Since most women in agribusiness engage in primary activities, including crop production and poultry, land with secure tenure must be provided as part of empowerment efforts. Land and water are productive resources, and thus, providing women with these goods could boost their confidence and increase their empowerment through the attainment of high-level components of empowerment.
- *Physical capital*: This relates to the assets that sit on the natural capital. Availability of tangible assets and infrastructure (farms equipment, livestock for draught power, transport, and communication networks, among others) should be central to both the discourse on women's empowerment. The government needs to invest in infrastructure as part of its commitment to empowering women by linking their businesses with markets. The government should also work with women and assist them with basic assets and inputs to meet them halfway in terms of costs.

[37] Interview 10, 10/12/2015, Soshanguve.

- *Human capital*: This includes human labor, the knowledge possessed by members on local production, education (formal and informal), and the health of household members to contribute to labor and so forth. Both the government should invest in the education and training of its women farmers. Women proprietors in agribusiness should also go a step further to get training and train their workers so that they keep abreast with changing times. This will increase the rate of women's empowerment in the sector.
- *Financial capital*: This includes savings, credit and loan acquisition opportunities, remittances, and pensions, among others, which women can use to support their activities. The government should support women's businesses financially so that they do not get broke. The aim should be to enable these women to be financially independent in the long term.
- *Social capital*: This refers to social resources (social, political, and religious networks; local cooperatives; access to agriculture and research institutions, among others) that enable women to sustain their activities. These need to be supported and increased to assist women to ascend from low-level to high-level components of empowerment.

15.6 Conclusion

The women empowerment discourse is rife in South Africa. Several domestic frameworks have been introduced, while some international ones have been accepted to guide the commitment and implementation of local efforts. However, when viewed from the Longwe framework, women empowerment in the agribusiness sector in South Africa remains mere rhetoric. These women face a myriad of challenges ranging from lack of funds, education and training, criminality, and technological issues to research and innovation. The opportunities that exist for women are far outweighed by the challenges faced. In dealing with these challenges, it would help that SLF-based interventions be used as part of the collective and continued effort to realize women's empowerment in the agribusiness in the province.

References

Akinola, A. O. (2018). Land reform in South Africa: An appraisal land reform in South Africa: An appraisal. *Taylor & Francis, 1*, 1–16.

Aliber, M., Maluleke, T., Manenzhe, T., Paradza, G., & Cousins, B. (2013). *Land reform and livelihoods: Trajectories of change in Northern Limpopo Province, South Africa*. HSRC Press.

Antwi, M., & Chagwiza, C. (2018). Factors influencing savings among land reform beneficiaries in South Africa. *International Journal of Social Economics, 46*(1), 474–484.

Beinart, W., Mnwana, S., & Wotshela, L. (2020). Land reform, rural inequality, and agrarian change: The case of Isidenge, Stutterheim, Eastern Cape. *Transformation: Critical Perspectives on Southern Africa, 102*, 27–48.

Bhorat, H., Asmal, Z., Lilenstein, K., & Van der Zee, K. (2018). *SMMES in South Africa: Understanding the constraint*. Working Papers. DPRU, University of Cape Town.

Carter, M. R. (2003). *Designing land and property rights reform for poverty alleviation and food security*. Paper presented at 29th session of the Committee on World Food Security, Rome, 12–16 May. http://www.fao.org/docrep/006/j0415t/j0415t06.htm. Accessed on 15 Feb 2016.

Cousins, B. (2015). Through a glass darkly': Towards agrarian reform in South Africa. In B. Cousins & C. Walker (Eds.), *Land divided, land restored: Land reform in South Africa for the 21st century* (pp. 250–269). Jacana.

Creswell, J. W. (2018). *Qualitative inquiry and research design: Choosing among five traditions* (4th ed.). Sage.

Cross, C., & Hornby, D. (2002). *Opportunities and obstacles to women's land access in South Africa. A research report for the promoting women's access to land programme*. Centre for Rural Legal Studies.

Doss, C. R., Grown, C., & Deere, C. D. (2008). *Gender and asset ownership: A guide to collecting individual-level data*. Policy Research Working Paper, WPS4704. World Bank, Washington, DC. http://elibrary.worldbank.org/docserver/download/4704.pdf?expires=1338036651&id=id. Accessed on 26 May 2016.

Fernando, J. L. (1997). Non-government organisations, micro credit and empowerment of women. *Annals of the American Academy of Political and Social Science, 554*, 150.

Ghina, A. (2014). Effectiveness of entrepreneurship education in higher education institutions. *Procedia – Social and Behavioral Sciences, 115*, 332–345.

Hall, R., & Kepe, T. (2017). Elite capture and state neglect: New evidence on South Africa's land reform. *Review of African Political Economy, 44*, 122–130.

Hart, T., & Aliber, M. (2012). *Inequalities in agricultural support for women in South Africa*. PLAAS, University of the Western Cape.

Haselip, J., Desgain, D., & Mackenzie, G. (2014). Financing energy SMEs in Ghana and Senegal: Outcomes, barriers and prospects. *Energy Policy, 65*, 369–376.

Kabeer, N. (1999). Resources, agency, achievements: Reflections on the measurement of women's empowerment. *Development and Change, 30*, 435.

Kepe, T., & Hall, R. (2018). Land redistribution in South Africa: Towards decolonisation or recolonisation? *Politikon, 45*(1), 128–137.

Kessey, K. D. (2014). Micro credit and promotion of small and medium enterprises in informal sector of Ghana: Lessons from experience. *Asian Economic and Financial Review, 4*(6), 768.

Longwe, Z. S. (1999). "Women's empowerment" (framework). In *A guide to gender-analysis*. Oxfam.

Makombe, I. A. M. (2006). *Women entrepreneurship development and empowerment in Tanzania: The case of SIDO/UNIDO-supported women micro entrepreneurs in the food processing sector* (Unpublished PhD thesis). University of South Africa.

Malhotra, A., Schuler, S. R., & Boender, C. (2002). *Measuring women's empowerment as a variable in international development*. Final version of a paper commissioned by the Gender and Development Group of the World Bank. www.worldbank.org/po9verty/empowerment/events/feb03/pdf/malhotra

Moeng, J. K. (2011). *Land reform policies to promote women's sustainable development in South Africa* (Unpublished PhD thesis). University of Pretoria.

Mubecua, A. M., & Nojiyeza, S. (2019). Land expropriation without compensation: The challenges of black South African women in land ownership. *Journal of Gender, Information and Development in Africa, 8*(3), 7–19.

Muchiri, G. R. (2016). *Xenophobia: A critical study of the phenomenon and pragmatic solutions to South Africa* (LL.D thesis), University of South Africa, Pretoria.

Ncapayi, F. (2013). *Land and changing social relations in South Africa's former reserves: The case of Luphaphasi in Sakhisizwe Local Municipality, Eastern Cape* (PhD thesis). University of Cape Town, South Africa.

Ndhlovu, E. (2018). Relevance of sustainable livelihood approach in Zimbabwe's land reform programme. *Africa Insight, 47*(4), 72–87.
Ndhlovu, E. (2021). The land question in Africa: Sam's perspectives. In V. T. Gumede & T. Shonhe (Eds.), *Rethinking the land and agrarian questions in Africa*. Africa Century Editions Press.
Ndhlovu, E. (2022a). Socio-economic characterisation of resettled smallholder farmers in rural Zimbabwe. *Journal of Asian and African Studies, 57*(8), 1495–1510.
Ndhlovu, E. (2022b). Changing agrarian discourses and practices and the prospects for food sovereignty in Zimbabwe. In G. Mkodzongi (Ed.), *The future of Zimbabwe's agrarian sector: Land issues in a time of political transition* (pp. 34–53). Routledge.
Ndhlovu, E. (2022c). Political economy of Chisa livelihoods in rural Zimbabwe. In K. Helliker, J. Matanzima, & P. Chadambuka (Eds.), *Livelihoods of ethnic minorities in rural Zimbabwe* (pp. 123–139). Springer International Publishing.
Nkwinti, G. (2010). *Address at the AgriSA commodity congress*. AgriSA Commodity Congress.
Nomvete, S., & Mashayamombe, J. (2019). South Africa's fees must fall: The case of UPrising. *South African Review of Sociology*. https://doi.org/10.1080/21528586.2019.1699441
OECD. (2015). *OECD economic surveys: South Africa*. Organisation for Economic Co-operation and Development.
Peters, B. L., & Peters, J. E. (1998). Women and land tenure dynamics in pre-colonial, colonial and post-colonial Zimbabwe. *Journal of Public and International Affairs, 9*, 184–203.
Republic of South Africa. (1996). *Constitution of the Republic of South Africa*. Republic of South Africa.
Rusenga, C. (2019). The agribusiness model in South African land reform? Land use implications for the land reform beneficiaries. *Agrarian South: Journal of Political Economy, 8*(3), 440–461.
South Africa. (1997). *White paper on South African land policy*. Department of Land Affairs.
World Bank. (2014). *World Bank's entrepreneurship survey and database*. World Bank. http://econ.worldbank.org/research/entrepreneurship. Accessed 17/10/2016.

Ndhlovu, E. (2018). Relevance of sustainable livelihood approach in Zimbabwe's land reform programme. [illegible], 72–87.

Ndhlovu, E. (2021). The land question in Africa: South's perspectives. In V. [illegible] & T. [illegible] (Eds.), Reimagining land and agrarian questions in Africa. Africa Century Editions Press.

Ndhlovu, E. (2022). Socioeconomic characteristic of resettled smallholder farmers in rural [illegible]

[illegible]

Chapter 16
Gender-Inclusive Education in Science, Technology, Engineering, and Mathematics (STEM) Fields in Postindependence Zimbabwe

Gay Tapiwa Gweshe and Mervis Chiware

Abstract The challenge of embracing a gender-inclusive approach to science education in postindependence African education institutions continues to hamper the attainment of various national development initiatives. This chapter seeks to give an evidence-based historical analysis of the implementation of a gender-inclusive approach in the science, technology, engineering, and mathematics (STEM) disciplines in Zimbabwe. It studies the policy measures that have been undertaken by the government and higher and tertiary learning/research institutions to strengthen gender balance in STEM fields. The research results are drawn from an extensive documentary search. Findings reveal that on the attainment of independence in 1980, Zimbabwe adopted a myriad of educational reforms many of which had a policy thrust of leaving no one behind. For decades now, it has been a concern of the education fraternity that women remain underrepresented in STEM subjects. It was found that girls have remained marginalized, especially in the STEM fields. The lower-level practical subjects that qualify as STEM have perennially been gender-stereotyped. The system made them focus more on fashion and fabrics, food, and nutrition subjects, yet the global trajectory has migrated toward hard sciences. It is recommended that gender affirmative action be strengthened to increase the representation of women and girls in the STEM field.

Keywords Gender · Inclusion · STEM · Postindependence · Education

16.1 Introduction

Research suggests that globally, STEM programs can be traced back to the United Nations initiatives of 2008 that advocated for the adoption of technical programs in

G. T. Gweshe (✉) · M. Chiware
University of Zimbabwe, Harare, Zimbabwe

D. Mhlanga, E. Ndhlovu (eds.), *Economic Inclusion in Post-Independence Africa*, Advances in African Economic, Social and Political Development,
https://doi.org/10.1007/978-3-031-31431-5_16

education (Tsvara et al., 2018: 6). Within the Zimbabwean context, it is a widely held view that this STEM initiative was birthed earlier in the 1990s when the government launched the Nziramasanga Commission economic blueprint. Tsvara et al. (2018: 9) hold the view that the Commission recommended a wide range of educational reforms with a primary focus on teacher education, the sciences, technology, and skills, thus giving way to the establishment of the Scientific and Industrial Research Development Centre (SIRDC). It is against this background that in 2012, the government of Zimbabwe pronounced the "Second Science, Technology, and Innovation Policy" framework which was geared to empower students with cutting-edge skills that would see them participate actively in both local and global economies (Dube, 2018: 3329; Tsvara et al., 2018: 6). The government of Zimbabwe then implemented the STEM program in 2016 in which free education to all advanced level (A level) students registered for STEM subjects was provided (Zimbabwe Gender Profile, 2020: 46).

The chapter advances that the general conception of STEM programs is that the reforms contribute toward economic development, industrialization, critical thinking, and problem-solving, providing individuals with occupational skills for employment in specific jobs or a cluster of jobs (Tsvara et al., 2018: 3). Considering these views, the study seeks to analyze the policy measures that have been undertaken by the government to strengthen gender balance specifically in the STEM fields. This objective led to the following research question: How many girls have been enrolled on the stem program since its inception in Zimbabwe? What has the government done to enhance the enrolment of STEM women in Zimbabwe? Lastly, the chapter recommends that Zimbabwe needs to reimagine education systems where gender-responsive STEM learning happens in every classroom (UNICEF, ITU, 2020: 3). The study adopts a qualitative approach and is informed by a feminist epistemology. The primary research tool used to collect data is documentary search. The documents were purposively selected based on the qualities of authenticity and credibility. Data is analyzed using content analysis.

16.2 Background and Orientation of the Study

STEM subjects are critical in supplementing national economic development. In Zimbabwe, the ultimate objective of the STEM revolution has been to position Zimbabwe as a global leader in scientific discoveries and technological breakthroughs and effective exploitation of economic prospects from the commercialization of research results enhancing her competitiveness (Ministry of Higher and Tertiary Education, Science and Technology Development, 2016: 5). By the time it was launched in 2015, Kutsvaa et al. (2018: 2) argued that the achievement of the Zimbabwe Agenda for Sustainable Socio-Economic Transformation (ZimAsset 2015–2020) was heavily dependent on the country's ability to embrace and unpack the intrinsic value of a STEM-driven system of education. According to the Ministry of Higher and Tertiary Education, Science and Technology Development, the STEM project aims to

1. Increase the number of STEM students who will enroll on STEM degree programs at the country's universities, in 2018 [and beyond].
2. Promote STEM careers, in response to ZimAsset's human capital objectives.
3. Develop STEM skills that are critically needed for the country's new industrialization thrust.
4. Address the problem of unemployment.
5. Empower young people through the promotion of science and innovation (Mberi & Phambili, 2016: 12).

Previous studies of Marume (2017: 20) clearly show the role that gender stereotyping as well as the colonial legacy still plays even in the so-called liberal education system of Zimbabwe. The underrepresentation of girls and women in STEM is prevalent in Zimbabwe. This predicament is deeply rooted in unequal gender norms that tell us that girls are not cut out for subjects that require problem-solving and an inquisitive mind (Rosser, 2017: 5). Mutekwe and Modiba (2012) discovered that generally, both male and female teachers preferred to teach boys citing that they are more active, outspoken, and willing to exchange ideas and information than girls. Rosser (2017: 5) laments this death of women in science citing that even the roles of women in science labs are gendered as women perform the experimental work involved in pipetting, centrifuging, and sequencing, while men analyze data, conceive the experiments, contribute resources, or write up the study (Rosser, 2017: 3). The chapter acknowledges that there is a learning crisis in which education systems have allowed gender divides to be perpetuated and to disproportionally affect the most marginalized girls (UNICEF, ITU, 2020: 3). Even among the students themselves, male scholars habitually overrate the knowledge of their male peers and underestimate the knowledge of their female peers (Rosser, 2017: 3).

Meanwhile, the NDS1 (2020: 189) outlined the following gender mainstreaming strategies that will be implemented during the NDS1 period (2020–2025):

- Youth and women affirmative action
- Equal opportunity for all program
- Promoting women into positions of influence
- Promoting equality at all levels of society
- Advancing women's political representation
- Youth and women advocacy initiatives
- Enhancing access to financing for women in business

Women continue to be underrepresented in STEM programs. Although the national pass rates in the science subjects at the Ordinary Level in Zimbabwe are high, what is worrisome is that the number of candidates who attempt these subjects at the "A" level is very low. Over the years, a very small percentage of candidates take up science subjects at the "A" level, and in 2014, these students constituted less than 10% of the "A" level candidates (Gadzirayi et al., 2016: 24). In a study by Marume (2017: 39), one of the students noted that:

> I observed that girls are more like passengers when it came to maths, biology, physics, and chemistry in our class. Not many of them participate especially when it comes to voluntary presentations. They have always seemed to be outwitted by boys. I also see that even though they lag, they are not staying for some extra-time lessons as we, their male counterparts do.

More specifically, while the NDS1 has a gender mainstreaming component, it seems the strategy is not specific on the measures that the government of Zimbabwe will adopt in the STEM field.

Throughout this chapter, the main argument of the study is that after all has been said and done, the number of women and girls attaining degrees in STEM subjects compared to their male counterparts remains low. The study is premised on the argument that the implementation of STEM programs and even the STEM subjects themselves has been gendered. In 2018, the government of Zimbabwe launched Vision 2030 to chart Zimbabwe's new development trajectory to achieve an upper middle-income society by 2030. As Zimbabwe adopts this fourth industrial revolution agenda, there is an urgent need to create authentic STEM education. Girls deserve to access an education that prepares them for the jobs of the future and to be ready and equipped to participate in the Fourth Industrial Revolution (UNICEF, ITU, 2020: 3). Trends disturbingly show that specifically subjects like food and nutrition, fashion, and fabrics continue to be reserved for women whereas the global development trajectory is rooted in the hard sciences (Rosser, 2017: 5). According to the National Development Strategy 1 (2020: 186), women in Zimbabwe still face hurdles in respect of opportunities to ascend to commanding heights in the national economy.

16.3 Literature Review

16.3.1 Defining Gender Equality

Gender equality refers to equal rights, opportunities, and outcomes for girls and boys and women and men. It does not mean that women and men are the same, but their rights, responsibilities, and opportunities do not depend on whether they are born female or male (OSAGI 2001, Cited in Dugarova, 2018: 10). Gender equity in this chapter means fairness of treatment for women and men, according to their respective needs. This may include equal treatment and/or treatment that is different but is considered equivalent in terms of rights, benefits, obligations, and opportunities (Chabaya & Gudhlanga, 2013: 125). Gender equality is not about transferring opportunities from men to women but about creating conditions where each person regardless of his or her gender has the right and ability to realize their human potential (Dugarova, 2018: 10).

16.3.2 Conceptualizing STEM

The acronym STEM stands for science, technology, engineering, and mathematics. Previously STEM was known as science, mathematics, engineering, and technology (SMET) (Tsvara et al., 2018: 2). Many countries in the world have introduced STEM education as part of the formal school system. Globally, only 35% of higher education students pursuing studies in STEM fields are women (UNESCO, 2018: 4). The low participation of girls in the field of STEM is not unique to Zimbabwe. It is a phenomenon that is affecting all developing countries, especially in Africa. In line with this, one should also note that even the developed world is facing a decline in the number of girls taking up sciences, especially at advanced levels. The study defines the acronym STEM as an integrated approach to marrying science subjects such as science, technology, engineering, and mathematics and other technology-related subjects to develop human skills and impart knowledge to better the manufacturing industry and the economy at large (Zhou, 2016: 5).

16.3.3 Other Country Experiences

Since the incarnation of STEM, governments across the globe have designed policies that do support STEM-related fields in their education systems' curricula (Zhou, 2016: 3). However, research points out that the low participation of women in sciences is a global threat to the development of so many nations (Marume, 2017: 43). In countries like Malaysia, the government is widely taken as the forerunner of STEM education with a gender-biased perspective (IBE-UNESCO, 2017, Cited in Zhou, 2016: 3). There are still more men in STEM than women. Gender inequalities carry on. Zhou (2016: 3) further cites that on the contrary, the USA has emerged and developed as a global leader through the genius and hard work of its scientists, engineers, and its innovators and it has been gender-sensitive in the implementation of the STEM program. The USA has wholeheartedly embraced and inculcated the philosophy as they attempt to prepare students for an uncertain and shifting work landscape.

Within the developing countries' context, according to (Musiimenta et al., 2019: 31), to encourage girls' participation in STEM subjects, Uganda made all science subjects compulsory at the ordinary level of education in 2004. Although the program has been effective, they were addressing the symptoms. Research suggested that these efforts could have been more impactful if combined with a thorough understanding of the factors that constrain girls' involvement in STEM, as well as putting strategies to address these barriers (Musiimenta et al., 2019: 31). In countries like Rwanda, the STEM program is not inclusive. In outstanding research, Masanja (2010: 6) argues that although Rwanda has registered great achievement in gender parity on the political front, girls are still underrepresented in government schools and are instead in more expensive private universities, of lower quality and with few or no science and technology programs. There are significant gender gaps in STEM fields in higher education in Africa, particularly in ICT and engineering, manufacturing, and construction. In most countries with data, women represent less than one in four students in these fields (UNESCO, 2018: 4). Further to that, Masanja (2010: 6) outlined that in Rwanda, girls' participation in public higher education institutions ranges between 25% and 27%. Participation in SMT subjects at the secondary school level ranges from 5% in technical subjects to 40% in biological and chemistry subjects, while in overall SMT subjects, girls account for 35%. Even in planning and projections, the targets to increase the number of women in SMT are generally very modest.

In other countries like Vietnam, the Ministry of Education and Training, with the assistance of UNICEF, the Global Partnership for Education, and other education stakeholders, is putting in place a raft of measures to make the education system address inequalities and champion gender inclusion. These reforms include the following:

- Integrating comprehensive sexuality education into STEM, starting from preschool to secondary, and including substantial content on gender, power dynamics, and human rights in teacher guidelines.
- Developing gender-responsive career counseling to encourage girls to become interested in STEM jobs and providing ethnic minority girls with STEM mentors.
- Focusing teaching and learning materials for 3–6-year-olds on "unstereotyping" so that teachers promote progressive and positive portrayals of girls, women, boys, and men in the learning environment.
- Building gender-sensitive budgeting and a digital literacy framework into the new Education Sector Plan, to close gaps in STEM learning outcomes for girls and address the digital divide.
- Introducing augmented and virtual reality (AVR) education solutions in Vietnam's remote mountainous provinces where teachers have difficult access to STEM training. AVR will empower marginalized girls to learn by doing by directly engaging with their STEM subject matter through gamification and immersive interactive experiences (UNICEF, ITR, 2020: 21).

16.4 Conceptualizing Development

The term development is a variegated word. In the African context, Gumede (2016: 16) argues that development is a term that is associated with advancement in people's lives. A deeper perspective by the International Development Strategy for the Second Development Decade, development is comprehensively defined as:

> ...to bring about sustained improvement in the well-being of the individual and to bestow benefits on all. Women comprise more than half of the human resources and are central to the economic as well as the social well-being of societies, hence development goals cannot be fully reached without their participation. Women and development are thus a holistic

concept wherein the goal of one cannot be achieved without the success of the other. Women, therefore, must have both the legal right and access to existing means for the improvement of oneself and society.

Drawing from the definitions, it can be argued that progress is an indispensable element of development. The discussion on development in the contemporary African context must include progress toward the inclusion of women as strategic partners in discussions of development. When it comes to the implantation of STEM initiatives, the chapter espouses that the state should play a leading and facilitating role in the programs. However, in this increasingly pluralized environment, the STEM program is now seen as the responsibility of both the state and the private companies and, increasingly, private nongovernmental organizations (NGOs) (Reddock, 2000: 22). In addition, the market is seen as the main arbiter of decision-making. Whereas most of the discussions on sustainable development have taken place within the context of mainstream development economics, feminist activists have for the most part seen sustainable development as part of a larger alternative model of development or societal transformation (Reddock, 2000: 22). Gender-responsive STEM education is an approach to teaching and learning with the transformative potential to deliver on the promise of the girls' education and empowerment agenda in the twenty-first century (UNICEF, 2020: 4). This gender-inclusive approach to learning is considered a sustainable development exertion.

16.5 Theoretical Framework

The chapter is informed by the gender and development (GAD) approach. The GAD approach emerged in the 1980s as an alternative to the earlier women in development focus (Rathgeber, 1989: 11). The GAD approach analyzes the nature of women's contribution within the context of work done both inside and outside the household, including non-commodity production, and rejects the public/private dichotomy which commonly has been used as a mechanism to undervalue family and household maintenance work performed by women (Rathgeber, 1989: 12). It is an approach to development that focuses on global and gender inequalities (Connelly et al., 2000: 89). These are unequal power relations (rich vs. poor; women vs. men), which prevents equitable development and women's full participation. GAD also puts greater emphasis on the participation of the state in promoting women's emancipation, seeing it as the duty of the state to provide some of the social services which women in many countries have provided on a private and individual basis (Rathgeber, 1989: 13). The state should promote equitable, sustainable development, with women and men as decision-makers, as well as empowering the disadvantaged and women and transforming unequal relations (Connelly et al., 2000: 89). A GAD perspective leads not only to the design of the intervention and affirmative action strategies which will ensure that women are better integrated into ongoing development efforts. It leads, inevitably, to a fundamental reexamination of social structures and institutions and, ultimately, to the loss of power of entrenched elites, which inevitably will affect some women as well as men (Rathgeber, 1989: 13). It seeks to reconceptualize the development process, taking gender and global inequalities into account through identifying and addressing practical needs, as determined by women and men, to improve their condition, and, at the same time, addressing the strategic interests of women (Connelly et al., 2000: 89).

16.6 Synopsis of the Education Reforms in Zimbabwe from Independence

16.6.1 The Postindependence Zimbabwe Inherited a Gender-Biased Curriculum

This section discusses the education reforms in Zimbabwe since 1980. Immediately after attaining independence in 1980, Zimbabwe, like most developing countries, alluded to the eradication of all forms of inequalities in its society, including gender inequalities in education (Chabaya & Gudhlanga, 2013: 123). The postindependence Zimbabwe inherited a gender-biased curriculum. Prominent research by Marume (2017: 27) strongly emphasized that the school curriculum inherited by postindependence Zimbabwe was modeled on the English system, with Zimbabwean girls being educated for domesticity while boys were educated for employment and the role of family head and breadwinners. On the same note, Marume (2017) further argued:

> that boys and girls were taught different practical and vocational subjects, with boys having to study technical subjects such as metal work, agriculture, technical graphics and building, and being encouraged to pursue science subjects like mathematics, chemistry, biology and physics, while girls were offered domestic science subjects, typing and shorthand, being encouraged to pursue arts subjects.

16.6.2 Education Reforms

The government of Zimbabwe adopted a series of reforms to redress the challenges that bedeviled the education sector since the pre-independence era. The first decade of political independence saw the government directing its efforts toward the mass improvement of educational access and equity (Chitate, 2016: 27). According to Kutsvaa et al. (2017: 3), the reforms in the first decade focused on addressing quantities, and significant increases in the number of schools and colleges were registered. In 1980, there were five teachers' colleges, two polytechnic colleges, and one university. By 1990, teachers' colleges had increased to 14, technical colleges to 8, 2 vocational training centers (VTCs) established, and still 1 university. Since the dawn of independence, the government has prioritized the education of its populace, something that has meant that citizens are treasured both within and outside the confines of its borders (Tshuma, 2021: 1). The educational reforms from 1990 were more focused on the relevance and quality of education. New approaches to content, technologies, teaching methodologies, skills provision, and decentralization of technical and teachers' colleges were used to effect these reforms, including the establishment of college advisory boards. According to Dube (2018: 3329), the Atlas of Global Development (2009) and the evaluation of the Industrial Development Policy (2012–2016) compiled by the Ministry of Industry and Commerce in Zimbabwe discovered the mismatch between education policy and employment opportunities.

This was followed by the rollout of the Nziramasanga Commission which investigated the state of education in Zimbabwe. According to Saiden (2017: 148), the findings of the commission were that the education system did not extol the virtues of self-reliance and entrepreneurship and did not aggressively promote the teaching of science, mathematics, technology, vocational and technical subjects, and local languages. Hence, it recommended the upholding of STEM and entrepreneurship. It is from that moment that the education system migrated toward a computer-based higher education system as well as promoting computer use and technology at all levels of education (Kutsvaa, 2017) Howsoever, in March 2012, the government presented, to the nation, the "Second Science, Technology, and Innovation Policy," which recognized the criticality of science and technology, in the industrialization of the country. This marked the birthing of the STEM program (Chitate, 2016: 30).

16.6.3 The Gender Gap in the STEM Program in Zimbabwe

Research revealed that the greatest challenge for the government of Zimbabwe is closing the gender gap in the STEM fields. The government and state of Zimbabwe have tirelessly made efforts to solve gender disparities in the system to afford equal opportunities economically and politically to both men and women (Zhou, 2016: 14). In a study by Chabaya and Gudhlanga (2013: 123), it was revealed that:

> ...since 1980, several policies and strategies were put in place to promote gender equity in education and they included the introduction of education for all, free primary education and attracting international agencies that support education in the country. A significant increase in the education of girls and women in terms of numbers was noted in all levels of education although equity is yet still to be achieved.

For example, the Gender Profile (2020: 47) outlined that the STEM initiative was enrolled to ensure equal enrolment opportunities for females and males; STEM, therefore, provided free education to all female and male students at the advanced level across Zimbabwe. The Ministry of Women's Affairs is of the view that the STEM initiative is a strategy that has been introduced to redress the existing gender gap in science subjects in schools. In a survey by Tshuma (2021: 1), findings indicated that the STEM initiative is gendered. The survey outlined that:

> …there is an underrepresentation of women and girls, and it is a serious barrier to the empowerment and the contributions they can make to strengthening tertiary education and science and innovation systems in ways that are necessary to achieve economic and societal transformation.

Contrary to the government goal, Marume (2017: 42) highlighted:

> the STEM Initiative is not directly gender-sensitive. This is so because it does not have any mechanism or any special provisions that are only in support of the girl child.

As a result, there is an ironic situation in which more girls are going to school than before, but numbers fall disturbingly when women enter tertiary education and careers in STEM (Tshuma, 2021: 1). Findings reveal that there is parity in school attendance and completion at primary school level up to lower secondary schools (Form 1–4); the situation changes in upper secondary school level (Form 5–6) and tertiary level where the gap widens in favor of boys (Zimbabwe Gender Profile, 2020: 9). The trend is influenced by child marriage, poverty, socialization, gender-based violence, and early pregnancies (Zimbabwe Gender Profile, 2020: 9). The focus on expanding science and technology without reorientation of these subjects to focus on both boys' and girls' education does nothing to promote gender equality in education and turn the employment opportunities for both boys and girls (Kutsvaa et al., 2017: 6). The gap lies in adopting mechanisms that mainstream gender in education. The low enrolment of females in science-related disciplines could be attributed to the fact that fewer females opt for science subjects at secondary school due to various reasons (Kutsvaa et al., 2017: 6).

To ensure the elimination of gender disparities and equal access to education, attention must be paid to the roles that influence the expectations of girls, boys, women, and men at home, in the community, at school, in the workplace, and in society (UNESCO, 2018: 6). According to Marume (2017: 47), the idea of gender sensitivity has not yet sunk into the minds of most teachers in schools who keep on perpetuating gender stereotyping by allocating subjects and roles as well as treating boys and girls according to their sexes instead of their abilities and capabilities. Eliminating these persistent gender disparities requires a concerted effort between governments, private sector, researchers, communities, and girls and young women themselves (UNICEF, ITF, 2020: 5). Therefore, this warrants for the pre and post teacher training with great emphasis on gender issues so that they will be equipped with as much knowledge that will help them to shun gender-based discrimination in classes and the subject and role allocation at schools (Marume, 2017: 47).

16.7 Strategies That Have Been Adopted to Promote a Gender-Inclusive STEM Program in Zimbabwe

16.7.1 Legal and Policy Framework

Various legal and policy instruments continue to shape the gender landscape in the STEM program in Zimbabwe. From post-2000 onward, the government of Zimbabwe has tried to instill gender balance in STEM programs through legislation of gender policies that are directed toward the education sector, and the policies have a direct bearing on STEM. One of the policies adopted has been the Zimbabwe National Gender Policy 2017. A gender policy is viewed as an instrument for tackling gender deficiencies in an organized manner (Chabaya & Gudhlanga, 2013: 124). As highlighted in the Zimbabwe Gender Profile (2020: 47), the Zimbabwe National Gender Policy has an unparalleled call for gender justice, equality, amalgamation, inclusivity, and collective responsibility for sustainable development in Zimbabwe. Regards to education is premised on the need to ensure equal access to education and training opportunities for men and women.

Findings indicated that historically, before the introduction of the Zimbabwe Gender Policy 2017, Zimbabwe, as one of the developing countries, has adopted other policies that set the benchmarks for Zimbabwean commitment toward gender equality (Zimbabwe Gender Profile, 2020: 19). These gender-centric policies are STEM neutral, but they set a positive tone for a gender-sensitive environment in which the STEM program is being bred. Since 1980, the government of Zimbabwe has ratified several international treaties, conventions, and protocols linked to gender equality and women's empowerment including the Convention on the Elimination of all Forms of Discrimination Against Women (CEDAW), Beijing Declaration and Platform for Action, Protocol to the African Charter on Human and People's Rights on The Rights of Women in Africa, and the South African Development Community Protocol on Gender and Development. Zimbabwe is also committed to the Sustainable Development Goals with SDG5 on gender equality being one of the priority goals for the country. It is through these policies that the government has been able to adopt a gender-inclusive STEM program and other education sector policies that promote gender equality in education.

Another strategy that promotes a gender-inclusive STEM program is the adoption of a Pro-Gender Constitution in 2013. Section 17(1) of the Constitution of Zimbabwe Amendment No. 20 states that

1. The state must promote full gender balance in Zimbabwean society. In particular
    (a) The state must promote the full participation of women in all spheres of Zimbabwean society based on equality with men.
    (b) The state must take all measures needed, including legislative measures, to ensure that

(i) Both genders are equally represented in all institutions and agencies of government at every level.
(ii) Women constitute at least half the membership of all commissions and other elective and appointed governmental bodies established by or under the Constitution or any Act of Parliament.

(c) The state and all institutions and agencies of government at every level must take practical measures to ensure that women have access to resources, including land, based on equality with men.

2. The state must take positive measures to rectify gender discrimination and imbalances resulting from past practices and policies.

This constitutional provision infiltrates all other legal frameworks that contribute to gender equality in Zimbabwe. The STEM program is guided by this provision. The government of Zimbabwe seeks to promote 50/50 participation of men and women in STEM programs at all levels of education in Zimbabwe. Despite this supreme provision, the gender gap is still prevalent in STEM. According to the World Bank (2021: 1), a gender gap resembles an inefficient allocation of labor and talent and a missed opportunity for economics.

16.7.2 Institutional Framework

The creation of and dedicated Ministry of Women Affairs, Gender and Community Development, the existence of gender focal points in all government ministries, and the fact that the country is a signatory to international conventions on gender demonstrate the country's firm commitment to addressing gender disparity (Garwe & Chikwiri, 2021: 579). Further to that, Zimbabwe instituted the Gender Commission to monitor gender equality issues and carry out investigations of possible violations of gender rights (Gender Profile, 2020: 47). These policy interventions had a positive impact on increasing female participation at different levels of the education system (Garwe & Chikwiri, 2021: 579).

16.8 Gender Mainstreaming Reforms in Tertiary Education

The government of Zimbabwe has adopted reforms that aim at affording equal opportunity to boys and girls in tertiary education. One of the deliberate policies that have been put in place to advance gender-inclusive education is the Affirmative Action Policy of 1992. The crux of the initiative is to increase the number of women who participate in education at the highest level (Zimbabwe Gender Profile, 2020: 46). The Affirmative Action Policy of 1992 states that the cutoff points for prospective female university students be two points lower than those for their male counterparts. This policy has promoted the number of girls that have enrolled in tertiary institutions. This policy works hand and glove with the New Education Act of 2020 in which the government of Zimbabwe adopted a policy which allows for the continuation and completion of school attendance by female students who would have fallen pregnant and taken a break to deliver babies (Zimbabwe Gender Profile, 2020: 46). The challenge with these policies is that the policies are not STEM specifically. Existing STEM initiatives have limited reach and sustainability, mostly benefitting girls who are in well-resourced urban schools. The rural/urban divide is impacting exposure to STEM learning. STEM education may be more available in cities because of better schooling infrastructure or more readily available private sector-supported initiatives (UNICEF, ITU, 2020: 19).

There has been an increase in girls and women enrolling in tertiary education. But the implications resonate with what Rosser (2017) noted:

> Results have been that in social sciences and the life sciences, women have reached parity in the percentages of degrees received yet in other areas, such as the geosciences as well as mathematics and physical sciences, the percentages of women continue to increase, although they have not approached parity (Rosser, 2017: 5).

Overall, at the bachelor's level, women earn most of the degrees in the nonscience and engineering fields, such as humanities, education, and fine arts, and in the science fields of psychology, the social sciences, and biological sciences. Men earn most of the degrees in the physical, earth, atmospheric, and ocean sciences, mathematics, and statistics, especially in computer sciences and engineering (Rosser, 2017: 3). According to UNICEF, ITU (2020: 3), for these reforms to be successful, the government should therefore provide adequate budgetary allocations to the education sector and prioritize allocations within the sector to provide equal access to and quality of education. When adequate resources are availed for policy and program implementation, follow-up should be made on whether the programs are appropriate and well-targeted.

16.9 The Government Has Been Investing in Gender-Inclusive STEM Learning Methods

Gender-responsive pedagogies have been introduced in a deliberate attempt to transform existing paradigms that favor men over females in the education sector, thus challenging gender stereotypes, for example, the Belvedere Technical Teachers College is implementing gender-responsive pedagogy (gender-sensitive teaching and learning) from African Women Educationalist Zimbabwe (FAWEZI) (Zimbabwe Gender Profile, 2020: 46). Such programs have been effective in enhancing the numbers of women in STEM. However, gender-inclusive pedagogies must be adopted at an early stage in education:

> It is vital to nurture children in their early childhood education, primary, secondary, and tertiary education and boost girls' learning and confidence to solve real-world problems

using technology and building skills among primary teachers and secondary STEM teachers helping them to understand and address unconscious bias in the teaching practice and assessments and to engage all learners equally. (UNICEF, ITU, 2020: 23)

16.10 Conclusions and Recommendations

Since the attainment of independence in 1980, the government of Zimbabwe has been embracing a gender-inclusive approach to science education. This chapter provided a historical analysis of the implementation of a gender-inclusive approach in the science, technology, engineering, and mathematics (STEM) disciplines in Zimbabwe. It managed to analyze the policy measures that have been undertaken by the government and higher and tertiary learning institutions to strengthen gender balance in STEM fields. Findings revealed that on the attainment of independence in 1980, Zimbabwe adopted a myriad of educational reforms many of which had a policy thrust of leaving no one behind. For decades now, it has been a concern of the education fraternity that women remain underrepresented in STEM subjects. Women and girls have remained marginalized in the STEM fields. STEM programs have perennially been gender-stereotyped.

This chapter recommends that the government should move to promote and develop STEM-specific career guidance platforms in schools from the primary level up to the secondary level to equip all the students on the importance of STEM programs. The guidance counselors must be gender-sensitive and promote girls venturing into careers that they otherwise would not because of tradition and sociocultural norms (Kapungu, 2007: 6). According to Saiden (2017: 148), in countries like Japan and China, entrepreneurship education begins at elementary school. In Namibia, entrepreneurship education has also begun in elementary school and spans the entire education.

This chapter recommends that the gender-inclusive pedagogy in Zimbabwe must be reformed to consider gender in lesson planning, teaching, and learning materials (UNESCO, 2018: 9). The government must consider the implementation of a phased approach in curriculum and textbook reform to promote girls' participation in STEM courses and enhance parity in enrolment in technical and vocational education and training (Zimbabwe Gender Profile, 2020: 49). The government must extend the gender-inclusive STEM initiatives to provide community-based digital skills training for out-of-school girls using existing community groups or forming new STEM clubs for girls, with the use of devices that they already have access to and use regularly (UNICEF, ITU, 2020: 23). This training is in line with the Zimbabwean Education 5.0 curriculum which emphasizes community outreach programs. These techniques can be used to cultivate girls' interest in STEM. The reforms include the use of online resources and resources available locally, including in the natural world, as well as students' exposure to extracurricular activities, clubs, camps, and role models to better understand STEM studies and careers (UNESCO, 2018: 11). Furthermore, the government should work toward increasing access to STEM education through increased digital connectivity for all children, especially for girls in hard-to-reach areas with limited capacity. Every girl should be able to take advantage of the increased access to world-class digital learning solutions and have the tools and motivations to engage with digital technologies, as users and creators (UNICEF, ITU, 2020: 23).

This chapter also recommends that the STEM initiative should have a clear provision or mechanism that gives a certain proportion to be occupied by girls (Marume, 2017: 47). The proportional representation will enable girls to feel encouraged by knowing that there is a place waiting to be filled in by them; hence, they work toward occupying that reserved space. The proportional representative model must be institutionalized in Zimbabwean higher and tertiary institutions. The government should also invest in women teachers and women teacher educators, so that they develop STEM knowledge and skills that enable them to inspire girls and facilitate their learning, thereby developing a female teacher pipeline for STEM subjects (UNICEF, ITU, 2020: 23). The government must work toward creating more female role models to inspire women to engage in STEM programs.

References

Atlas of Global Development (2009), Available at Atlas of Global Development, 4th Edition : A Visual Guide to the World's Greatest Challenges (worldbank.org)

Chabaya, S., & Gudhlanga, E. S. (2013). Striving to achieve gender equity in education: A Zimbabwean experience – Successes and challenges. Zimbabwe Journal of Educational Research, 25(1), 123–148.

Chitate, H. (2016). Science, technology, engineering and mathematics (STEM): A case study of Zimbabwe's educational approach to industrialisation. *World Journal of Education, 6*(5), 25–35.

Connelly, P., Li, T. M., MacDonald, M., & Parpart, J. L. (2000). *Feminism and development: Theoretical perspectives*. Online: https://www.idrc.ca/sites/default/files/openebooks/272-4/index.html#page_xiii. Accessed on 28 May 2022.

Dube, S. P. (2018). An investigation of the science technology engineering and mathematics (STEM) initiative in the Zimbabwean education system. *International Journal for Cross-Disciplinary Subjects in Education (IJCDSE), 9*(1), 3329–3334.

Dugarova, E. (2018). *Gender equality as an accelerator for achieving the sustainable development goals*. United Nations Development Program.

Gadzirayi, C. T., Bongo, P. P., Ruyimbe, B., Bhukuvhani, C., & Mucheri, T. (2016). *Diagnostic study on status of STEM in Zimbabwe*. BUSE.

Garwe, E., & Chikwiri, E. (2021). De-gendering stem: Best practices from a case study of a Women's University in Africa. *Global Scientific Journals, 9*(1), 576–593.

Gumede, V. (2016). Post-apartheid South Africa: Economic and social inclusion. Cambria Press.

Kapungu, R. S. (2007). *The pursuit of higher education in Zimbabwe: A futile effort?* http://archive.kubatana.net/docs/chiyou/kapungu_cipe_essay_higher_education_071002.pdf. Accessed on 28 May 2022.

Marume, W. (2017). *An assessment of the girl child participation in science subjects at advanced level with the introduction of the stem initiative: A case study of Glen View suburb schools* (MSU undergraduate dissertation). Gweru.

Masanja, V. G. (2010). *Increasing women's participation in science, mathematics and technology education and employment in Africa Paris, France 28 September – 1 October 2010*. United Nations Division for the Advancement of Women (DAW, part of UN Women) United Nations Educational, Scientific and Cultural Organization (UNESCO).

Mberi, N., & Phambili, M. (2016). Science, technology, engineering and mathematics craze hits Zimbabwe. *The Sunday News: STEM Supplement*, 28 February–5 March, 12.

Ministry of Higher and Tertiary Education, Science and Technology Development. (2016). *Concept Note (revised 13 January 2016)*. Paper presented at the 1st national conference on Science, Technology, Engineering and Mathematics (STEM) at Harare International Conference Centre from 28–28 January. Harare, Zimbabwe.

Ministry of Women Affairs Community, Small and Medium Enterprises Development. (2020). *Zimbabwe gender profile*. Government Printers.

Mutekwe, E., & Modiba, M. (2012). Girls career choices as a product of a gendered school. *South African Journal of Education, 32*(3), 279–292.

Musiimenta, A., Tumuhimbise, W., Bangumya, E., Mugaba, A. T., Mugonza, R., Kobutungi, P., & Nankunda, M. J. (2019). Exploring the gender gap in science, technology, engineering, and mathematics (STEM), and soft skills, and knowledge of role of models among students in rural Uganda. *Journal of Education and Development, 3*(3), 31–38.

National Development Strategy 1 (NDS1) (2020), Available at www.mic.gov.zw/wpcontent/uploads/2023/05/National-Development-Strategy-1-NDS.pdf

Rathgeber, E. M. (1989). *WID, WAD, GAD: Trends in research and practice*. International Development Research Centre.

Reddock, R. (2000). *Why gender? Why development?* Online: https://www.idrc.ca/sites/default/files/openebooks/272-4/index.html#page_xiii. Accessed on 28 May 2022.

Rosser, S. V. (2017). *Academic women in stem faculty: Views beyond a decade after POWRE*. Palgrave Macmillan.

Saiden, T. (2017). Towards an entrepreneurship and stem education primary school curriculum in Zimbabwe: A case study of Bumburwi of Gweru District. *Advances in Social Sciences Research Journal, 4*(18), 148–159.

The World Bank. (2021). *Infographic: the equality equation: advancing the participation of women and girls in Science, Technology, Engineering and Mathematics (STEM)*. Online: https://www.worldbank.org/en/news/infographic/2021/04/19/the-equality-equation-advancing-the-participation-of-women-and-girls-in-science-technology-engineering-and-mathematics-s. Accessed on 29 Apr 2022.

Tshuma, A. (2021). *Open up spaces for women, girls in STEM*. Online: https://www.chronicle.co.zw/open-up-spaces-for-women-girls-in-stem/. Accessed on 29 May 2022.

Tsvara, P., Chitate, T., & Johan, J. B. (2018). Examining the impact of Science, Technology, Engineering and Mathematics (STEM) in Zimbabwe's high schools. In *Raising the impact of education research in Africa* (pp. 1–25). https://doi.org/10.4102/aosis.2018.BK53.06

UNESCO. (2018). *Report of the regional training for Francophone Africa ©UNESCO cracking the code: Quality, gender-responsive STEM education*. United Nations Educational Scientific and Cultural Organisation.

UNICEF Annual Report (2020). Online: https://www.unicef.org/reports/unicef-annual-report-2020. Accessed 29 May 2022.

United Nations Children's Fund, ITU. (2020). *Towards an equal future: Reimagining girls' education through STEM*. UNICEF.

Zhou, T. (2016). *STEM dysfunctionally applied in Zimbabwe? Zim also lacking in blended learning*. Online: https://www.sundaymail.co.zw/stem-dysfunctionally-applied-in-zimbabwe-zim-also-lacking-in-blended-learning. Accessed on 29 May 2022.

Chapter 17
Policy Alternatives for Strengthening Women's Representation in African Local Authorities: Insights from Zimbabwe

Fortunate Jena, Joseph Tinarwo, Innocent Dingani, and Banele Mazhelo

Abstract Local authorities in Africa are male-dominated. Women are, thus, not adequately represented, and their role is neglected in decision- and policy-making. The underrepresentation of women in influential decision-making bodies threatens the achievement of sound service delivery by local authorities in Africa. Yet literature is scant on the policies for improving women's participation in African local authorities. The purpose of this study is to draw lessons from the case study of Zimbabwe on how to strengthen women's representation in African local authorities. A mixed research approach was adopted for this study. The study revealed that there are several reasons for the poor participation of women in local government institutions and proffered cocktail of strategies is needed to support women's representation in local authorities and these include strong legal and institutional frameworks, vibrant advocacy efforts, and multi-stakeholder partnerships. The study also proffered recommendations to address the causes of poor women's representation in councils, including awareness campaigns to promote women's involvement in council issues and fair and practical person specifications for the desired posts in the council to encourage women to apply for posts among other factors. Therefore, the study concluded that indeed there is poor women representation in local authorities in Zimbabwe, hence the need of strengthening women's capacities in local government institutions in Africa.

Keywords Local authorities · Women's representation

F. Jena (✉) · J. Tinarwo · B. Mazhelo
Great Zimbabwe University, Masvingo, Zimbabwe
e-mail: fjena@gzu.ac.zw; jtinarwo@gzu.ac.zw

I. Dingani
Chiredzi Town Council, Chiredzi, Zimbabwe

D. Mhlanga, E. Ndhlovu (eds.), *Economic Inclusion in Post-Independence Africa*, Advances in African Economic, Social and Political Development,
https://doi.org/10.1007/978-3-031-31431-5_17

17.1 Introduction

This chapter sought to establish factors contributing to poor women's representation in local authorities in Africa and proffer alternatives for strengthening women's participation in local government institutions in Zimbabwe. Feminism in broad terms can be said to be a conviction that women should have equal social, political, and economic chances as men in society. This chapter shall be premised on the theory of liberal feminism by Patricia McFadden (1997), which focuses on the challenges and prospects for the African women's movement in the twenty-first century. The theory asserts that gender is an important element that shapes societies. Feminists hold the perspective that women are found unequal in the social arrangement, frequently cheapened, abused, and mistreated. Chapman (2004) opines that there is a need for political and legal reforms aimed at achieving equity between men and women; hence, there are political, economic, and social variables that need to be examined, and these variables significantly influence the support and involvement of women in governance.

Probably the most popular model for addressing any form of inequality would be the Marxist theory. This is a social worldview based on the ideas of the German philosopher Karl Marx and his associate Friedrich Angels which advocate for a classless society (Ebenstein, 1973). On a similar note, the above model can be used to view class as men on one hand and women on the other. Marxists also assert that those in power oppress the less privileged through the knowledge that they possess, knowledge that the oppressed are in want of. This knowledge is found in established institutions which for the greater part lack women representation. Therefore, it all boils down to power, which men possess and abuse to achieve dominance over women in local government institutions.

This study utilized a mixed approach research design, combining both qualitative and quantitative research methods to gain different perspectives on the topic and enhance the validity and reliability of the study. Qualitative research provides insight and understanding of the problem setting, while quantitative research generates knowledge and creates understanding about the social world using scientific inquiry and relies on data that are observed or measured to examine questions about the sample (Mays & Pope, 2020; Patton, 2002; Ravitch & Carl 2019). The target population was 50 employees from the Plumtree Town Council who constitute the decision-making from 2015 to 2019. In this study, the researcher adopted a purposive sampling technique as known as selective or subjective sampling. For data collection, in-depth interviews and questionnaires were used as the main research instruments. Content analysis and thematic and descriptive analysis were used to analyze the data collected during the fieldwork.

17.2 Background

The women of Africa make a sizeable contribution to the continent's development, yet they are underrepresented in local government institutions. There are even fewer women in management positions in local authorities. Women's voice in Zimbabwe has grown in strength due to a significant increase in the number of women's organizations (Kurebwa, 2014). Good local governance must address gender equality and social inclusion. Local government institutions have increasingly become arenas offering opportunities to women to influence the development agenda. In a largely patriarchal world order, women have always played a subordinate role in society. They are treated more as second-class citizens relative to their male counterparts (McDowell & Pringle, 1992). Across Africa, patriarchy and social, cultural, and religious influences have resulted in women being rendered second-class citizens. The Convention on the Elimination of all forms of Discrimination Against Women (CEDAW), often referred to as Women's Bill of Rights which was adopted by the United Nations General Assembly on December 19, 1979, and came to force on December 3, 1981, provides for equal treatment of both men and women in all spheres of life. Despite the existence of the above cited legal frameworks that have been put in place and the work of women advocacy groups to ensure that the cause of women is championed and promoted, it is sad that the global share of women in parliament continues to rise slowly.

It should be noted that Zimbabwe is a signatory to several regional and international instruments that call for gender equality in various spheres of life. The 2013 Zimbabwean Constitution section 17 stipulates that women should have equal opportunities as those men in all spheres. However, local government institutions have been hailed as a training ground for women in politics, and women constitute a mere 21% of councilors in 19 countries for which complete data would be obtained (Africa Barometer Women's Political Participation, 2021).

With the deficit in women's participation in leadership positions in local authorities obtaining both in the local and global sphere, there is a need to ascertain the factors that are leading to this lethargic development to find lasting solutions that will bring about the gender equity and mainstreaming in the local governance front and ultimately lead to the development of societies, especially in sub-Saharan Africa where this phenomenon is still largely pronounced. It is against this background that this chapter seeks to address the following research objectives: the rationale of women representation in local authorities in Africa, formal and informal factors contributing to poor women's representation in local authorities, ways in which governments are strengthening women's capacities in local authorities, and lastly proffered recommendations for improved women participation in local government institution's public space.

17.2.1 Arguments for Women's Representation in Local Authorities in Africa

Santiago (2015) states that women's participation in decision-making is highly beneficial and their role in designing and applying public policies has a positive impact on women's lives. The underrepresentation of women at any level of governance and decision-making results in a democratic deficit. Sundell and Wangnerud (2012) argue that women's local legislative representation can lead to greater gender equity and equality in terms of income and employment status. It has been proven time and again that diverse groups make better decisions. This is particularly true when it comes to a task as challenging as representing the interest of citizens at the local level. The local government often makes important policy decisions that affect the lives of women and men with housing and security, among other things.

Women's equal representation in local decision-making processes is critical for prioritizing women's practical needs and issues in local governments' agendas and for localizing Sustainable Development Goals. According to Meier and Funk (2017), women at the local level can represent women's substantive interests, and increasing women's presence as elected officials and public administrators in councils leads to the adoption of more women-friendly policies and public services for women. This is the case in other jurisdictions. For example, in the USA, women councilors and mayors influence city expenditure decisions in ways that benefit women (Holman & Smith, 2014), and in India, women-elected leaders invest in infrastructure projects related to women's issues Duflo and Chattopadhyay (2004).

An increase in women's representation in local governments can change the structure and practices of local institutions (Smith, 2015). Research has found that women may increase their employment representation in municipal bureaucracies, especially in traditionally male dominant sectors like Finance (Kerr et al., 1998). Also, it is having been argued that women are less likely to engage in corruption and patronage policies (Brollo & Troiano, 2016). Women's representation in local authorities may also help improve transparency, accountability, and information asymmetries as was found in the case of the Spanish local government (Araujo & Tejedo-Romero, 2016).

Panday (2008) asserts that women's representation at the government local level is a key driver for their empowerment. Global evidence about women's actual presence in rural local governments and their potential impact is still very scarce (Irwin, 2009). Opare (2005) argues that the ability of any group of people or their chosen representatives to participate in decisions affecting their lives not only puts them in a position to contribute ideas but also provides them with the tools and options for reshaping the course, direction, and outcome of specific programs and activities which will determine their future. It is therefore critical to engage women in decision-making processes within the communities where they reside and obtain their livelihoods.

17.2.2 Women in Local Council Offices

In as much as other cultural traits compounded with religious practices are also held to shape the cultural acceptability of women in politics, with countries dominated by Catholicism and Islam least supportive of women in public office (Reynolds, 1999), one feature to which close attention must be paid is the relative strength and importance of kinship groups in the political culture, in other terms, the extent to which family is more significant than gender in determining an individual's access to power. One study that attempts to capture this variable is a cross-national review of determinants of the numbers of women in office by McDonagh, the only such study to focus on political systems that privilege kinship group capture of high office or symbolic positions (McDonagh, 2002).

Women in local politics and education quotas and reservations for women in national-level politics are generally enjoyed by women who have long been active in politics, have good contacts, have elite family backgrounds, and differ little from elite male politicians in being highly educated and financially secure (Hamandishe, 2018). It is in efforts to increase the numbers of women participating in local politics that we see an influx of women to politics with significantly lower endowments than men in human and social capital and material assets. Uganda's 1997 Local Government Act, which included provisions to ensure that 30% of local councils should be composed of women, initially stipulated that a minimum educational achievement of a secondary school completion certificate would be required of any candidate for local government office (Paper commissioned for the EFA Global Monitoring Report 2003/4, The Leap to Equality). Protests from the women's movement because this would exclude most rural women from running for local office produced an amendment reducing the educational requirement to primary school completion.

On the other hand, African countries such as Uganda, Rwanda, and Mozambique, which are among the poorest countries in the world with female adult literacy levels of just 41, 60.2, and 28.7%, respectively, have parliaments in which between 25 and 30% of legislators are women (Paper commissioned for the EFA Global Monitoring Report 2003/4, The Leap to Equality). In Zimbabwe, which is the case study in this chapter, about a third of the women's population have at least one tertiary education qualification. Some women have held positions of power. For example are the community services officer for Chiredzi town council Mrs. Prettymore Chikerema and the Director of Housing at Chiredzi town council Mrs. Paradza.

The educational achievements of the large numbers of new female entrants to local government do tend to be significantly lower than that of their male colleagues (Ahikire, 2003), and indeed in India significant numbers of women local government councilors and chairpersons are not even literate. A sample of 1019 local councilors in 3 Indian states (843 of the sample were women) in a study by Nirmala Buch found that 51.9% of the women were illiterate compared to 18.7% of the men, with a further 18.6% of women claiming that they were literate but lacking even a primary qualification, compared to 13.1% of the men.

After the adoption of the new constitution in 2013 in Zimbabwe, the proportion of women in the National Assembly more than doubled, rising from 14% to 32% in 5 years from 2008 to 2013. In 2018, however, this fell back to 29% (Mhlophe, 2021). This fall was probably because women were subjected to more unfair scrutiny from the media and public scrutiny than male politicians (Zimbabwe Gender Commission, 2021). The Southern African Development Community (SADC) Protocol on Gender and Development prioritizes the achievement of 50% of women's representation in all spheres of decision-making by 2030.

In Zimbabwe, there is no educational requirement to become a councilor. The Councillors' Handbook (2009: 42) states: "It does not matter if you are male or female, old or young, educated or unschooled, left or right wing, you should aim to be the best councillor you can be." In 2018 in Zimbabwe, 1156 females participated in local government elections. In theory, this provided grassroots women with role models that they could emulate. Holding public offices is a symbol of attaining a voice in the Zimbabwean male-dominated society and political field. For Pauline Ada Uwakweh, political voicing is self-defining, liberating, and cathartic (1995). Therefore, only women representing themselves can be regarded as a reliable source of grievances as the rendering of the concerns and their commentaries affords the public an opportunity to accept it as an authoritative account.

17.3 Findings and Analysis

17.3.1 The Importance of Women's Representation in Local Authorities

Respondents were asked to respond to whether they perceived women's representation in decision-making as of any importance in local authorities. A majority of 90% of the respondents responded in the affirmative. This shows that most respondents perceive women's representation in decision-making in local authorities as important and, as such, a move that should be fostered and supported. This is in concurrence with the submissions of Reynolds (2017) who asserts that if societies are to excel in their quest to achieve the millennium development goals, women must be made an integral part of this trajectory and indeed will be vital cogs to this realization. This finding is also in sharp contrast to the foreboding tradition that has always held women in subordinating capacities and as rather secondary antecedents in matters of development, while their male counterparts take the driver's seat.

Asked whether they perceived the current levels of representation of women in key decision-making bodies in local authorities as fair, 87% of the respondents responded in the negative. This statistic reveals that local authorities are still far from ensuring gender parity in matters of local authority development as stemming from their participation in decision-making. This is compounded by the fact that the data shown in the table reveal that in the period under review, only one female councilor served the local authority under review, an indeed alarming figure. The findings validate the concerns raised by Harold (2010) that it is very confounding to notice that there are some in the present millennial who still support the traditional status quo that see nothing wrong with women held in the fringes of decision-making in local authorities, hence the 13% that responded in the affirmative of the motion.

In a quest to uncover the main rationale behind women's representation in local authorities, the researcher asked respondents to rank file their perceptions on which of the key drivers contributed the most to women's participation in decision-making. The factors were mainly those suggested by previous research (Bradley, 2013) as the key drivers that justify the need for women to participate actively in the affairs of local authorities as far as decision-making is concerned. These factors were economic emancipation, social recognition, the quest for political mileage, and finally permissive legislation obtaining. Table 17.1 presents the results obtained from this survey:

The results above show that respondents perceived permissive legislation as the key and most important driver of women's participation in decision-making, followed by economic reasons, then the motivation to gain political mileage, and finally the need for social recognition. It is therefore clear that there is a need for government to enact enabling legislation to promote equal treatment of women and men in social, economic, and political spheres of life to contribute to the development of their local authorities. This represents a trajectory from the tradition view where laws were rather repressive against women. In this light, a need arises for local authorities to enact policies to promote the cause of the formerly marginalized women. Economic reasons were cited as second in importance among the factors in question. This is in sync with the opinion expressed by Tejedo-Romero who advances that the increased participation of women in politics is much more likely to contribute toward the improvement of the gross domestic product. The results also reveal that there is a general lethargy among women to engage in active politics as they view such as a risky endeavor and hence the preserve of their male counterparts who have the thick skin to face such rough terrain. Lastly, women's participation in decision-making in local authorities was revealed by this study as less motivated by the need for social recognition than it is for improving the

Table 17.1 Factors motivating women to participate in local government

Factor	Average respondents' rating of factor
Economic reasons	2
Need for social recognition	4
Motivation to gain political mileage	3
Permissive legislation	1

Key

1—most important contributing factor to women's participation in decision-making
2—second most contributing factor to women's participation in decision-making
3—third most contributing factor to women's participation in decision-making
4—least contributor to women's participation in decision-making

functionality of institutions of government. As such, it can be concluded that the results of this study in this realm well corroborate past findings.

Respondents were asked if they viewed the participation of women in decision-making in local authorities as of any importance at all as 39 of 48 (81.25%) respondents affirmed that women's participation in decision-making in local authorities is very important while 9 of 48 (18.75%) responded that it is not important. This result shows that most people are adopting a more progressive mindset that opines that women are equal and thus their participation is of equal importance. It should thus on the other hand be a point of worry that certain individuals still perceive women's participation in local governance as a rather peripheral and useless agenda that should not be championed.

Asked to outline in what ways they thought women's participation in decision-making would add value to the decision-making process, most respondents revealed that, women, as compared to their male counterparts, are more calculative and thus are more risk averse; hence, the decisions that are likely to be taken tend to be more rational and moderate than adverse. This thus would minimize the myriad risks that most local authorities find themselves which tend to threaten the viability of the same in terms of service delivery.

Again, other respondents opined that the inclusion of women in decision-making is the right step toward the observation of principles of corporate governance, in particular fairness in the treatment of all genders, envisaged by the millennium development goals number 5 and 8. Not only would the inclusion of women in key decision-making in local authorities strengthen corporate governance, but it will also in a great measure increase the general consciousness of the importance of women as equal partners in matters of development and thus reduce the gap between women and men in socioeconomic and political matters and create a more inclusive coexistence necessary toward the attainment of peaceful and tolerant societies.

Furthermore, one respondent opined that women are generally more transparent and accountable than men; hence with thus their participation would enhance these values which are necessary for public organizations and local authorities. Local authorities must be transparent and fully accountable to ratepayers. Women were also said to enhance the speed at which decisions are made since they tend to be less militant and uncompromising than men which impedes the speed at which decisions are made and taken. Thus, it was the considered view of some respondents that women tend to bring about a balance of rationality and fairness that is perceived to lack in the male chauvinistic world.

17.3.2 Factors Accounting for Poor Women Representation

Respondents were asked to rank the factors contributing to poor women representation with (1) being the most significant and (4) the least. The four factors considered were poor education, marital status, sociocultural belief, and limiting institutional framework as suggested by the OECD report of 2017. The results from respondents were averaged, and the outcome was as shown in Table 17.2.

The above-illustrated results show that respondents perceived limiting institutional framework as the major factor contributing to poor women representation in decision-making, followed by poor education, sociocultural beliefs, and lastly marital status. The need to improve institutional frameworks encompassing enabling legal framework and policy amendments were believed to be the key levers that, once attended to, substantial women participation in decision-making will be realized. Additionally, the results imply that the girl child is yet to reach the levels and quality of education enjoyed by the boy child. Substantial investment in the education of the girl child is therefore perceived as a means critical to ensure their participation in key governance issues.

17.3.3 Societal Norms and Values

From the documentary search, studies revealed that "In the differences between sexes, men are considered better and more in nature, while women are underestimated," (Philosopher Aristotle). Political participation of women is considered as a global challenge. Still, most women face enormous barriers to political participation all over the world (Khan, 2017). Patriarchal norms continue to shape women's lives in Zimbabwe. Deeply entrenched patriarchy in our African society has posed many barriers for women in political participation. It is time that the worth of a woman is counted beyond so-called "traditional" roles, to a meaningful contribution toward societal development. The burden of household chores and inequitable access to higher education also limit women's ability to enjoy the opportunities and benefits of citizenship as men on an equal footing in the political sphere. In patriarchal societies, there is always a belief that public space is not meant for women and that by nature they cannot make good leaders. These perceptions are stronger at the lower levels making it very hard for women to contest and take up leadership at these levels (Goodman & Evans, 2006). Hossain (2012) echoes that the social existing values and norms interrupt women's effective participation in local government

Table 17.2 Factors accounting for poor women representation in local authorities

Factor	Average respondents' rating of factor
Poor education	2
Marital status	4
Sociocultural beliefs	3
Limiting institutional framework	1

Key
1—most important contributing factor to poor women's representation
2—second most contributing factor to poor women's representation
3—third most contributing factor to poor women's representation
4—least contributor to poor women's representation

bodies; one example of this is that common people tease women union parishad's members as "big leaders coming" and "characterless." In Islamic communities in Africa, women going outside without "parda," free movement with another male, and going outside at night are strictly prohibited. Women are instructed to use "purdha" while they are outside their home so that they can hide from others, thus hindering women to fully participate in local authorities' activities in full confidence.

17.3.4 Limited Training and Mentoring for Women in Local Authorities

Training and mentoring programs which focus on helping women attain the knowledge, skill, and confidence to stand for postelection are barely provided for them in local government institutions in Africa, and studies have consistently identified resistance to change at a local level, with local networks often remaining closed to women Berg (2009). Training and mentorship are crucial factors in encouraging women to participate and in ensuring this participation is effective.

17.3.5 Lack of Mutual Support from Fellow Women

While it is undeniable that women bear the brunt of gender inequality because of patriarchy and other factors, it is also true that they are their detractors. One of the research findings is that the reason for low women's participation in local councils in Africa is the "pull her down syndrome," especially among Zimbabwean women. One female councilor pointed out that during campaigns, women were difficult to work with as compared with men. She indicated that women were constantly trying to outdo themselves of winning the votes. Thus, lack of mutual support among females themselves has been one of the factors affecting women's representation in local government institutions in Africa.

17.3.6 Passive Legislative and Institutional Frameworks Promoting Women's Participation in Local Authorities

The Constitution of Botswana makes no provision for quotas to ensure women's representation in publicly elected bodies on any level. Sechele (2004) states that the language of the Botswana Constitution is masculine. In Botswana, only 5% of women currently hold political positions, which is far less than the 30% goal set by the Southern African Development Community. Government statutory and institutional frameworks are an important factor in the selection of women into decision-making bodies in local government institutions.

17.3.7 Political and Domestic Violence Against Women

Interviews with female councilors highlighted the issue of political violence as a barrier both to women getting into local politics and to their ability to participate effectively once they were elected (Sachikonye, 2011). It was observed that violence against women in Zimbabwe takes mainly the following forms: physical, psychological, and forced isolation and the undermining of a woman's self-esteem, sexual violence, and economic violence, through which women may be denied access to work, income, and maintenance. Beyond the barriers to representation in office, there is a continued history of gender-based violence, including a history of violence against women during elections. The fear of domestic violence in reaction to their civic or political participation restricts women's participation. Sexual bribery is also rampant, and many women are told outright that they must have sex with party leaders if they are to advance or gain a nomination as a candidate (Bardall, 2018).

Unfortunately, the overall increase in the number of women in political and governance roles has been met with an increase in gender-based violence against female actors. This has discouraged the participation of some women in democratic and governance processes. Women have long been used by men to achieve their political goals (Maphosa et al., 2015). When the electoral environment is patriarchal and prejudiced, the marginalization of women becomes automatic (Hamandishe, 2018). They are also subjected to various forms of stigmatization and abuse by their male counterparts (Musingafi et al., 2015) including being ridiculed for their body shape or relationship status, among other factors. In this way, both their well-being and their ability to perform their duties are compromised in these local government institutions.

17.3.8 Poor Education

Empirical evidence supports the notion that formal education should be strongly associated with political participation for women and men (Duflo, 2001). "Education is the backbone of a nation" (Napoleon Bonaparte). Education can help women to obtain rights in their social, political, economic, and family lives (Sanchita & Sharma, 2016). However, Africa is still struggling to the fulfillment of the basic needs of people, and education is one of them. The educated person is knowledgeable and skilled, and they are self-confident and aware of their role in the development of the country, but the situation is remained unchanged like before in rural. They have huge ignorance about the political process, and even sometimes they don't know where to vote or whom to vote. As a result, they are losing their rights as well as their interest in political participation. Besides that, gender discrimination in education leads to lower productivity in human capital (Sanchita & Sharma, 2016). Thus, the findings gathered show that poor education among women as also contributed to limited women's participation in local government institutions. Thus, there is a need of empowering women through education for them to fully participate in local authorities. Taken together, these factors may account for the limited women's representation in local authorities in Zimbabwe.

17.3.9 Strengthening Women's Capacities in Local Government Institutions in Africa's Legislative Frameworks

The 2003 Constitution of Rwanda allowed the leaders to include progressive measures with the requirement for women not to hold less than 30% of political seats. Valji (2000) states that in 2006, the women of Rwanda captured 33.3% of district council seats nationwide and 66.6% in the capital of Kigali, while 27% nationwide in the 2001 elections. Therefore, the country's constitutional 30% quota increased the women's participation in all decision-making bodies of Rwanda from the local level to the national level. The South African constitution advocates for the participation of women in local government, but it is fraught with problems such as patriarchal mindsets and organizational structures which impede women's participation (Van Donk, 1998). The lack of economic resources is one of the biggest obstacles to women's participation in politics. Nomination fees payable for candidates are oftentimes a barrier for aspiring female candidates.

In addition to having a legal framework that values gender equality and equity in politics, Zimbabwe is a signatory to many declarations aimed at increasing women's leadership and decision-making (Hamandishe, 2018). Zimbabwe's constitution which came into effect in 2013 provides a quota of 60 seats set aside for women for proportional representation in parliament. This is an increase in the number of women in politics from 16% to 34% which is a positive development. The downside is that the quota system does not have clear provisions on how to include young women and, more importantly, it does not extend to local government.

17.3.10 Empowerment of Women

Empowerment of women involves awareness raising, building self-confidence, expanding choices, and increasing access to and control over resources. The important instruments of empowerment include information and networking activities often entailing a process through which women acquire knowledge, skills, and a willingness to critically analyze their situation and take appropriate action to change the status quo in society. Several initiatives aimed at women's empowerment have been implemented in Africa. Examples include the following:

- Development of gender policies at national and local authority levels. Some have involved incorporating laws, legislation, and quotas aimed at making local gov-

ernment institutions and structures more inclusive (The Republic of Zimbabwe National Gender Policy 2013–2017).
- Gender equality indicators and indexes at local, national, and regional levels. These are aimed at monitoring, for example, education levels, labor force participation, incomes, and percentage of council members of both women and men (Gender Equality Index, administered by the African Development Bank).
- Affirmative action includes women in decision-making processes. For example, the Southern African Development Community (SADC) governments have committed themselves to 50% of occupancy by women in political and decision-making structures by 2020.
- Other countries have established offices and departments coordinating women's issues, including the promotion of women's activities in decision-making and municipal management and women's initiatives for self-empowerment, as individuals as well as in groups. These include mutual self-help groups as well as networking and solidarity-building activities (WOZA, Women of Zimbabwe Arise was formed in 2003 by Jenni Williams).
- Women development funds and grants, for instance, the Women's Development Fund was established in 2005 in Zimbabwe.
- Special measures on women's access to justice, e.g., Zimbabwe is a signatory to the international human rights frameworks for women's rights.

17.4 Discussion of Findings

It appears apparent that respondents considered cultural factors such as norms, beliefs, and practices to have significantly improved from the past and that their influence on the ability of women to participate in the making of key governance decisions has become of little consequence. This seems to be related to the factor of marital status. So, it can be inferred that whether a woman is married or not, their participation in decision-making is inconsequential, if at all any effect. These findings are in sharp contrast with the researchers conducted by previous scholars such as Su et al., (2023), Zou et al., (2009) and Gilberts (1999) whose findings were that slowly evolving cultural factors such as those stated above were the most contributors to poor women participation in decision-making. In the said studies, it was discovered that socialization was the single most powerful reason why women's positions at work continued to be discounted while men's positions were upheld. Rutoro (2013) argues that women who make it to leadership positions outside perceived feminine roles may be accepted as unique and unrepresentative of other women in society. The World Development Report of 2018 also submits that lack of education for women is associated with the lower proclivity to altruistic behaviors and it curtails women's voice at work and in institutions regarding matters that concern them. As such, a new paradigm seems to be growing in this regard which is likely to change the trajectory of women standing in society toward a more balanced setup.

Representation of women in decision-making posts and being policy-makers is an important indicator of their social and political status. Respondents were asked to proffer as well as outline the measures already taken toward enhancing women's representation. It was noted that women are for the most part missing from the managerial positions in local councils in Zimbabwe. The respondents therefore shared recommendations on what can be done to ameliorate the status of women who are underrepresented in key decisions of governance. From the study, the researcher gathered that most women recruited as councilors tend to be treated as political pawns who have no real power, according to women councilors' responses. Women are also objectified and seen as sex objects, and their contributions are not viewed in any manner beyond that (Alpha Media Holdings, 2017).

17.5 Conclusions and Recommendations

The research findings indicated that women face problems of poor representation as well as low participation in decision- and policy-making. The factors commonly identified as barriers to women's representation are limiting institutional and legal framework, poor education, sociocultural beliefs, and marital status. Generally, women tend to be poorly represented in macro positions which are identified with power and predominate in policy-making and decision-making occupations as indicated by the findings. Therefore, women's representation should be enhanced in the two essential areas which are policy-makers and members of decision-making bodies in local government institutions.

The current local government environment in Zimbabwe does not provide a safe space for female councilors. Sexual abuse, among other forms of GBV, is frequent. Men feel threatened when women seemingly invade "their" space (and even more so if the women are academically superior) and reassert their self-imposed authority. At the same time, women who arrive in workspaces have often been socialized to defer to men and are undermined as a result of negative gender norms and a patriarchal society.

From the findings gathered, safeguarding policies for Zimbabwe's local authorities, policies are just on paper and lack the practical implementation that would create safe spaces for women in local government. Their weak implementation can be attributed to perpetrators being in charge of policy implementation, as well as weak accountability mechanisms in general.

The introduction of Zimbabwe's quota system did have the desired effect of increasing female participation in local government as well as in other spheres of government, but, because of these challenges, it has been less effective in empowering women than anticipated. The perceived and actual barriers to their participation mean that the number of active women in local government is not expected to increase.

There is a need to shift the mindset of men who possess the power to be genuine in supporting, empowering, and protecting women. They have a critical role to play, as they are best suited to challenge other men who perpetrate harassment. Those who perpetuate patriarchy should espouse a paradigm shift, letting go of traditional views and approaches, so that women can occupy their rightful space in the spirit of a national gender policy that advocates for 50–50 representation in local government institutions in Zimbabwe.

- Local authorities should also consider a more robust employment quota system that would see an equal representation between men and women in terms of employment levels.
- Councils should advance educational loans to women at the lower ranks so that they can attain the necessary skills and education to rise to influential positions.
- Councils should lobby the Ministry of Local Government and Public Works so that council representation between men and women is at par.
- Local authorities should carry out community outreach programs that are going to see more young women applying for managerial vacancies and subsequent promotion of the same.
- The gender-focal person and gender champion should be given more power and resources to carry out promotional activities as far as women's representation is concerned.
- Governments should advance more meaningful investment/entrepreneurial loans to economically empower women and thus give more independence and social leverage to be heard in a society that is skewed toward giving an ear to one who is more economically independent as compared to those of a relatively low economic ranking.

References

Ahikire, (2003). Women's engagement with political parties in contemporary Africa: Reflections on Uganda's experience. http://www.peacewomen.org/assets/file/Resources/Academic/part_womensengagementpoliticalpartiesafricauganda_ahikire_2010.pdf

Alpha Media Holdings. (2017, May 17). *Women in Zimbabwe face barriers to equal participation in politics*. Retrieved from Hivos.Org: https://hivos.org/news/women-in zimbabwe-face-barriers-to-equal-participation-in-politics/

Araujo, J. F. F. E., & Tejedo-Romero, F., (2016). Women's political representation and transparency in local governance. Available online at: https://ideas.repec.org/a/taf/flgsxx/v42y2016i6p885-906.html

Bardall, D. G. (2018). *Violence against women in elections in Zimbabwe: An IFES assessment*. International Foundation For Electoral Systems.

Berg, B., (2009). Qualitative Research Methods. 7th Edition, Allyn & Bacon, Boston

Bradley, H. (2013). Gender. John Wiley & Sons.

Brollo, F., & Troiano, U. (2016). What happens when a woman wins an election? Evidence from close races in Brazil. *Journal of Development Economics*, 122(C), 28–45.

Chapman, S. (2004). *Sociology the ultimate study guide*. Revise A2.

Donk, M. V. (1998). Local government & gender at the gender advocacy programme (GAP), Cape Town; Urban development planning at the development planning unit (DPU), London. Avaliable at: https://www.tandfonline.com/doi/citedby/10.1080/10130950.2000.9675847?scroll=top&needAccess=true&role=tab&aria-labelledby=cit

Duflo, E., (2001). Schooling and labor market consequences of school construction in indonesia: evidence from an unusual policy experiment. https://www.fsb.miamioh.edu/lij14/411_paper_school2.pdf

Duflo & Chattopadhyay (2004). Women as policy makers: Evidence from a India –wide randomized policy experiment. Working Paper 8615 http://www.nber.org/papers/w8615

Ebenstein (1973). https://academic.oup.com/psq/article-abstract/88/4/767/7144887

Gilberts, P. R., (1999). Discourses of female violence and societal gender stereotypes. 8(11), November 2002.

Goodman & Evans (2006). Step-by-step guide to critiquing research. Part 2: qualitative research. *British Journal of Nursing, 16*(12), 738–744

Hamandishe, A. (2018). *Rethinking women's political participation in Zimbabwe's elections*. South African Institute of International Affairs.

Harold, J. W., (2010). State effects and the emergence and success of female gubernatoria candidates. State Politics & Policy Quarterly published online 3 August 2011. Volume 11 Issue 4, December 2011. https://journals.sagepub.com/toc/spaa/11/4

Holman & Smith (2014). Women in Local Government: What We Know and Where We Go from Here. 49(4), December 2017. https://journals.sagepub.com/toc/slgb/49/4 https://books.google.com/books?hl=en&lr=&id=8qo0bz4QWHAC&oi=fnd&pg=PT5&dq=Booke+%26+Bradley+(2013+women++representation&ots=sm_kZLMTKl&sig=vh2V17ZplIFyZwDx9gRAPnUwUDs

Hossain, M. A. (2012). Influence of social norms and values of rural Bangladesh on women's participation in the union parishad. *Indian Journal of Gender Studies, 19*(3), 393–412.

Irwin, (2009). Gender inequality and the role of women within graphic design.

Khan, N. (2017). *Women's political participation: Where are we today?* Huff Post.

Kerr et al. (1998). https://www2.psych.ubc.ca/~schaller/528Readings/Kerr1998.pdf

Kurebwa (2014). Rural women's representation and participation in local governance in the masvingo and mashonaland central provinces of Zimbabwe. https://www.researchgate.net/publication/284486563_Rural_Women's_Representation_and_Participation_in_Local_Governance_in_the_Masvingo_and_Mashonaland_Central_Provinces_of_Zimbabwe

Maphosa, M., Tshuma, N., & Maviza, G. (2015). Participation of women in Zimbabwean politics and the mirage of gender equity. *Ubuntu: Journal of Conflict and Social Transformation, 4*(2), 127–159.

Mapuva, J. (2013). The feminist discourse and the development of a civic virtue in Zimbabwe: Case of Women of Zimbabwe Arise (WOZA). *Journal of African Studies and Development, 5*(8), 261–270.

Mays, N., & Pope, C. (2020). Quality in qualitative research. *Qualitative research in health care*, 211–233.

McDonagh, E. (2002). Political citizenship and democratization: The gender paradox. *American Political Science Review, 96*(3), 535–552.

McDowell, L., & Pringle, R. (1992). *Defining women: Social institution and gender division*. Policy Press.

McFadden P. (1997). Contemporarily: Sufficiency in a Radical African Feminist Life https://read.dukeupress.edu/meridians/article/17/2/415/136650/Contemporarity Sufficiency-in-a-Radical-African

Meier & Funk (2017). The causes and consequences of women's representation in local government. Available at: https://oaktrust.library.tamu.edu/bitstream/handle/1969.1/161594/FUNK-DISSERTATION-2017.pdf?sequence=1&isAllowed=y

Mhlophe, (2021). Are Zimbabwe's local authorities safe spaces for female councillors? By Social Healing and Accountability Research July 2021. https://www.alignplatform.org/sites/default/files/2021-08/share_report.pdf

Musingafi, M. C., Kwaedza, K. E., & Chamunuka, L. (2015). Gender, women participation and representation in local governance: The case of Chivi communal areas in Masvingo. *Journal of Law, Policy and Globalization, 38*, 39–46.

Opare, S., (2005). Engaging women in community decision-making processes in rural Ghana: Problems and prospects. Available online at: https://www.researchgate.net/publication/263334613_Engaging_women_in_community_decisionmaking_processes_in_rural_Ghana_Problems_and_prospects

Panday, P. K. (2008). Representation without participation: Quotas for women in Bangladesh. *International Political Science Review, 29*(4), 489–512.

Patton, M. (2002). Qualitative research and evaluation methods. In *Thousands oaks (CA)*. Sage Publications Ltd.

Ravitch, S. M., & Carl, N. M. (2019). *Qualitative research: Bridging the conceptual, theoretical, and methodological*. Sage Publications.

Reynolds, K., (2017). Women in business: advantages, challenges, and opportunities. https://www.hult.edu/blog/women-in-business-advantages-challenges-and-opportunities/

Reynolds, A. (1999). *Women in African legislatures and executives: The slow climb to power*. Electoral Institute of South Africa.

Rutoro, E. (2013). Gender equity dilemma and teacher education in Zimbabwe: The quest for gender justice. https://www.semanticscholar.org/paper/GENDER-EQUITY-DILEMMA-ANDTEACHER-EDUCATION-IN-THE-Rutoro-Ed./2af823c902b6169fbbc0e6574e65c2cc67cc5f79

Sachikonye, L. M. (2011). Zimbabwe's Lost Decade: Politics, Development & Society. Ukraine: Weaver Press. Available at https://books.google.com/books?id=pKnOM8irpPgC&printsec=frontcover&dq=Sachikonye+(2011),&hl=en&newbks=1&newbks_redir=1&sa=X&ved=2ahUKEwiHmP-l-vv-AhWbiFwKHWNnClQQ6AF6BAgDEAI

Sanchita, & Sharma. (2016). Determinants and indicators of women empowerment: A walk through psychological patterns and behavioural implications. *Research Journal of Business and Management, 11*(1), 15–27.

Santiago, I. M. (2015). The participation of women in the Mindanao peace process. Research paper. https://www.ecoi.net/en/file/local/1397435/1788_1490867798_women.pdf

Sechele, S. (2004). *Women representation in parliament.*

Smith, J. A. (2015). Qualitative psychology: A practical guide to research methods. Sage, London.

Sundell & Wangnerud (2012). Corruption as an obstacle to women's political representation: Evidence from local councils in 18 European countries Volume 22, Issue 3, https://journals.sagepub.com/doi/abs/10.1177/1354068814549339

Su, M. M., Wall, G., Ma, J., Notarianni, M., & Wang, S. (2023). Empowerment of women through cultural tourism: perspectives of Hui minority embroiderers in Ningxia, China. *Journal of Sustainable Tourism, 31*(2), 307–328.

Valji, N., (2000). The importance of gender parity in the UN'S efforts on international peace and security. *Journal of Diplomacy and International Relations, XX*(2), http://blogs.shu.edu/journalofdiplomacy/files/2019/08/Valji-and-Castillo-The-Importance-of-Gender-Parity-in-the-UNs-Efforts-on-International-Peace-and-Security.pdf

Women's Political Participation: Africa Barometer (2021), https://www.idea.int/sites/default/files/publications/womens-political-participation-africa-barometer-2021.pdf

Zimbabwe Gender Commission Act. (2021). (Chapter 10:31), Section 30.

Zou, X., Tam, K. P., Morris, M. W., Lee, S. L., Lau, I. Y. M., & Chiu, C. Y. (2009). Culture as common sense: perceived consensus versus personal beliefs as mechanisms of cultural influence. *Journal of personality and social psychology, 97*(4), 579.

Chapter 18
The Digital Economy, Digital Financial Inclusion, and Digital Taxation in the Industry 4.0: A South African Perspective

David Mhlanga and **Miriam Hofisi**

Abstract There is a general claim that digital financial inclusion is important for balancing gender differences and inequality and favorably influences economic development, according to existing literature. Results from all over the world support the claim that financial inclusion enables the poor and financially excluded to enhance their quality of life and sustainably grow their businesses. It offers financial products that are more affordable, accessible, and safe. Taxing the digital economy has become a hot topic around the world even before the pandemic because of the Fourth Industrial Revolution's technologies' rapid rise in the digital economy. Around the world, there has been a lot of work done on taxation proposals for the digital economy in general. To better understand the connections between the digital economy, digital taxes, and digital financial inclusion from the standpoint of South Africa, this chapter investigated such topics. This chapter discusses trust in digital financial services as well as the usage of digital financial services in the digital economy and the taxing of the digital economy. It was found in the chapter that taxing the digital economy could have detrimental effects especially on digital financial inclusion since the disadvantaged people who utilize these services might lose faith in them.

Keywords Digital financial inclusion · Digital economy · Fourth Industrial Revolution taxation

D. Mhlanga (✉)
The University of Johannesburg, College of Business and Economics, Johannesburg, South Africa

M. Hofisi
North-West University, Vaal Triangle Campus, Johannesburg South Africa

D. Mhlanga, E. Ndhlovu (eds.), *Economic Inclusion in Post-Independence Africa*, Advances in African Economic, Social and Political Development,
https://doi.org/10.1007/978-3-031-31431-5_18

18.1 Introduction

The general argument that financial inclusion plays a critical role in evening out inequality, and gender differentials, and positively contributes toward economic development is established in extant literature (Asongu et al., 2020; Demirgüç-Kunt et al., 2022; Nchofoung & Asongu, 2022; Ozili, 2021). Results across the globe attest to the assertion that financial inclusion is an enabler of the poor and financially excluded to improve quality of life as well as sustainable entrepreneurship. It provides safer, cheaper, and more accessible financial products (Morgan & Long, 2020, The South African Financial Inclusion Policy. World Bank, 2022). As such, digital financial services (DFSs) have exponentially grown in sub-Saharan Africa. Their growth was catalyzed by the COVID-19 pandemic which limited human movement in lockdowns (Kouladoum et al., 2022; Mpofu & Mhlanga, 2022). At least 33% of adults from sub-Saharan Africa had mobile money accounts, a proportion that is greater than the rest of the world in the uptake of mobile money account holders (Demirgüç-Kunt et al., 2022:3). DFSs are reputed for their plausibility to reach out to the underserved and excluded who have been alienated by the traditional brick and mortar banking systems. They have had remarkable results in narrowing the gender gap from 9% in 2018 to 6% in 2021 (Mhlanga & Dunga, 2020; Demirgüç-Kunt et al., 2022:36).

Financial inclusion dynamics in South Africa pose a unique challenge in comparison with the rest of the sub-Saharan region. While the economy of the country is comparable to the Organisation for Economic Co-operation and Development (OECD) countries, with 91% of adults financially included in the formal sector, results undertaken by Mastercard and Visa show that usage levels are low, with 61% of adults relying on cash transactions and informal channels (Mhlanga and Beneke 2021). The Gini coefficient of South Africa is 0.62, making the country the highest unequal country in the world (Bhomoi, 2020; Mhlanga, 2020). The country is marred by unequal wealth distribution, skewed along racial lines. The labor market is the largest contributor to income inequality, and women earn 30% less than men (STATS, SA). Ten percent of the South African population earns more than 50% of the household income in the country, while 40% of the poorest earn 7% of the household income (Bhomoi, 2020; Mhlanga, 2020). Further to that, the economy is highly dual, characterized by small, medium, and microenterprises (SMMEs) that rely on informal channels for capital, who hardly survive the past 3 years, and poor households who also rely on predatory loan sharks for survival. As noted by Mastercard and Visa, the challenge in South Africa is the usage of the available channels. Research carried out by these two reflects a concerning trend where SMMEs and the poor often resort to using cash and informal channels for transactions as well as borrowing. Market dictates often influence consumer behavior on the demand and supply curve (Mpofu & Mhlanga, 2022). The behavior of these poor may indicate serious underlying factors that push them to resort to unsafe transactions which can be counterintuitive to financial inclusion. These factors have been highlighted as high transactional costs that are incurred by the poor. Likewise,

Bongomin et al. (2019) expressed caution over high transactional costs brought about by banks and by tax levies against DFSs as deleterious and could reverse the inroads that have been gained by the digitalization of financial services.

The absolute lack of physical presence of digital businesses brings a refreshed focus on how they can be taxed with the existing laws (Morinobu, 2018). Traditionally, e-commerce was directly taxed when it had a permanent establishment. However, the digital economy calls for new regulatory frameworks for states to extract much-needed revenue (Lucas-Mas & Junquera-Varela, 2021). The ability to conduct business without physical presence renders challenging to tax. Milogolov and Berberov (2022) noted that nations like South Africa rank highest in the region in terms of taxation laws and level of digitalization. Economic growth is strongly determined by, among other factors, the extractive capacity of a given state (Dincecco & Katz, 2016; Fukuyama, 2013). Santoro et al. (2022) and Lucas-Mas and Junquera-Varela (2021) reiterate that DFSs are proficient in increasing efficiency in taxation, effective communication, reducing tax evasion, and corruption. While digitalization of the economy poses a golden opportunity to increase the extractive capacity in South Africa, caution needs to be exercised in doing so. Levying taxes to the DFSs can be detrimental to the poor and leads to financial exclusion of the poor (Bongomin et al., 2019; Mpofu & Mhlanga, 2022). This chapter seeks to investigate the challenges associated with the taxation of digital economy for the African economies with a particular focus on South Africa.

18.2 Conceptual Exposition of Financial Inclusion

Financial inclusion has been a topical subject in economic development for the past decade. Its relevance is tethered to contemporary developments where access to affordable credit and other financial products is viewed as key to the poor, and SMMEs. While financial inclusion is not viewed as a solution to the plight of the poor, it is considered as an enabler for the poor to move out of poverty and achieve sustainable development goals (SDGs). The World Bank (2022:1) defines financial inclusion as the degree that households and small enterprises could gain an access to financial services, such as deposits, loans, payments, remittances, and insurance. While the conceptualization of the World Bank alludes to key facets of inclusion of access to products, its focus is one-sided by looking at the demand side of financial inclusion. Although access is a critical matter, the South African financial sector shows that the majority of adults have access to bank accounts. However, the usage of these services is important. This brings us to the definition by the Consultative Group to Assist the Poor (CGAP)'s report in 2011, which defines financial inclusion as the means that formal financial services—such as deposit and savings accounts, payment services, loans, and insurance—are readily available to consumers and that they are actively and effectively using these services to meet their specific needs. It stands to reason that consumers can only become active users if they are informed of the existence of products and that usage is not formidable (Morgan & Long, 2020).

The Alliance for Financial Inclusion (AFI) (2012) drew three major facets of financial inclusion that have been fundamental in defining it holistically. First is the access dimension where the availability of formal, regulated financial services is key. In addition, these products are supposed to have physical proximity and be affordable. Results from the surveys carried out by Mastercard and Visa demonstrate that availability in South Africa narrowly refers to the actual availability of products without affordability being factored in. Secondly, usage as defined by the AFI refers to the detailed patterns of product usage which are actual usage of regulated financial services, regularity, frequency, and time used. This is critical in identifying nuanced loopholes within financial products. Financial product consumers in South Africa have been noted to rely heavily on informal channels even though they are patronized informal service products. Such consumer behavior may reflect that financial services harbor serious weaknesses that inhibit meaningful inclusion. Menyelim et al. (2021) add that inclusion should especially be conceptualized as inclusive when it serves the underserved by mitigating equality and poverty boosting capital to the poor. Thirdly, quality is the last facet which focuses on tailored products that speak to the needs of clients and appropriate segmentation to develop products for all income levels. Contrariwise, consumers of financial products in South Africa seem to be tailored without the needs of all income groups given that the poor households and SMMEs have not managed to find financial products to use them effectively (The Financial Inclusion Policy of South Africa 2022; Mhlanga and Beneke 2021).

In the same vein, the South African policy for financial inclusion recognizes the importance of adopting a multifaceted conceptualization of financial inclusion. Financial inclusion in South Africa can play a critical role in fighting poverty. The country has the highest inequality levels in the world where the richest have wealth levels that are like the OECD levels and the poorest are like the poor in sub-Saharan Africa. Furthermore, the unemployment rate of the country is more than 30%, and youth unemployment is approximately 43% (The Financial Inclusion Policy of South Africa, 2022). With these economic conditions, the United Nations prescribes self-employment as one avenue that can ameliorate unemployment. However, self-employment can only gain a foothold if capital can be tailored to aid sustainable businesses.

18.3 Digital Financial Services in the Digital Economy and the Fourth Industrial Revolution

Khera et al. (2022:13) define digital financial services as services enabled "by fintech (technological innovation in the financial sector), can help overcome the often-cited obstacles in accessing traditional financial services such as cost, geographical barriers, and information asymmetry." Malady et al. (2014) also defined DFs as financial services provided through mobile phones that include e-money and mobile money delivered. Although mobile money technologies existed for more than a decade, their relevance was catalyzed by the COVID-19 pandemic, increased access to enabling technology, access to data, and declining trust with banks, among other reasons (KPMG Australia). The World Bank (2014) acknowledges that DFSs hold an "enormous opportunity" for the financial inclusion drive in developing countries. According to KPMG Australia, financial technology (fintech) has increased in terms of financial value from US $ 100 million to US $ 19 billion in 2015 due to the increased usage. The IFC CEO, Jin-Yong Cai, during a World Bank conference remarked that DFSs are a powerful tool for employment creation, and this resonates well with the South African context where unemployment has surged after the COVID-19 pandemic. DFSs are especially efficient in providing access to finance, electronic payments, and secure financial products to SMMEs and the poor (CGAP, 2011; Gibson et al., 2015. Demirgüç-Kunt et al., 2022). Results from Kenya show that access to formal financial services by DFSs increased financial inclusion from 20% in 2006 to 80% in 2019, and at least 70% of Kenyans use MPesa, a popular fintech (Natile, 2020:75). These fintechs are renowned for increasing inclusion to the traditionally underserved by complementing the traditional financial service providers as they offer services on mobile devices. As reiterated, DFSs have increased domestic payments, savings, as well as other financial products which also protect households against poverty (Demirgüç-Kunt et al., 2022; Oji, 2015, 2021). While banks are heavily urban-centered, have products not tailored for the poor, have prohibitive fees, and require more documentation, fintech has eased these barriers (Duncombe, 2012; CGAP, Gibson, et al., 2020; World Bank, 2014). Due to their ability to operate without physical presence, fintech is ubiquitous, and a preferred avenue for accessing financial services (CGAP). The table below shows that fintech exceeds other financial institutions.

The comparison in Table 18.1 demonstrates that fintech is superior to other financial services. In comparison with the other services that banks are proud to offer, mobile connectivity and point-of-sale devices are more prevalent.

18.4 The Fourth Industrial Revolution

As Schwab (2016) puts it, "the barriers between the physical, digital, and biological domains are blurring" due to the 4IR. The Fourth Industrial Revolution (or 4IR) is a continuation of the Third Industrial Revolution's innovations. Understanding the first, second, and third industrial revolutions is crucial for getting a feel for the industrial revolution. Water and steam power were widely used to mechanize production during the First Industrial Revolution. The steam engine came to replace

Table 18.1 Estimated worldwide points of presence

Western Union	Bank branches	Post offices	ATMs	POS devices	Mobile phone connections
250,000	657,000	662,000	1,400,000	30,000,000	6,800,000,000

Source: Author's Analysis

animal power in factories during the First Industrial Revolution. While electricity was crucial to the development of mass production during the Second Industrial Revolution, the Third Industrial Revolution relied on electronics and information technology to automate manufacturing. To sum up, the 4IR is seen as the precipice of a technology revolution that is altering our daily lives, our place of employment, and our social interactions with one another (Mhlanga, 2021, 2022a). The 4IR is unlike any other revolution because of its unprecedented extent, breadth, complexity, and accompanying transformation. As a result, novel experiences are becoming available to people for the first time in history including in the financial sector (Mhlanga, 2022a). The widespread use of point-of-sale terminals for mobile phones is quickly becoming the norm. The expansion of the digital economy is prompting governments all over the world to rethink their methods of taxation, and several of these nations are currently considering the possibility of taxing the digital economy.

18.5 Taxation of the Digital Economy

Taxing the digital economy has been topical, even before the pandemic, across the globe. The OECD has been busy working on taxation recommendations for the digital economy in general. In the year 2013, it discussed the impact of digitalization on international taxation through the Base Erosion and Profit Shifting (BEPS) Action Plan. In 2015, its discussions were revolving around addressing the tax challenges of the digital economy. In it, the existence of a value creation paradigm was noted as key. In addition, the emergence of new digital business models made the topic even more relevant. As such, the G-20 Finance Ministers also observed that the lack of regulatory framework for the rapidly growing digital economy and legal uncertainty were not proficient for tax collection. Ministers were then tasked with delivering interim reports on addressing direct taxation under a G-20 Mandate on Taxing the Digital Economy. The European Union (EU) then introduced the turnover-based digital service tax. Austria, Czech Republic, France, India, Italy, Spain, Turkey, and the UK have also enacted their DST as interim measures. Turkey has also imposed a withholding tax on e-payments. India introduced the "turnover-based equalization levy on business to business" (B2B) online advertising payments made to nonresident digital service suppliers.

Meanwhile, in Africa, discussions on taxing the digital economy have been ongoing on the platforms such as the African Tax Administration Forum (ATAF). It initiated some "suggested approach to drafting digital service tax" that can be applied as a toolkit for taxing the digital economy. African countries are diverse on their bases. Although they are dominated by MNEs, there are gaps in the digital transformation level of penetration concerning the modernity and efficiency of their tax revenue authorities (Milogolov & Berberov, 2022). Despite these disparities, it is still key for the continent to find an effective channel for revenue collection through tax. The task of appropriately extracting tax from the digital business has proven to be insurmountable if tackled by domestic governments only. Critical actors who can play a key role in this matter are the international digital tax system, global tax authority including producer and consumer countries, MNCs, and the digital service sector. The 2015 Addis Ababa Action Agenda on Financing for Development stresses the importance of cooperation among national tax authorities on international tax matters in support of the achievement of SDGs in Africa. Furthermore, the World Bank Group Digital Economy for Africa (DE4A) flagship stresses the importance of achieving the All-Africa Digital Transformation vision. Together with the Addis Ababa Action Agenda is the need to ensure that digitalization drives the extraction of tax in African countries. The countries that have introduced some tax on the digital economy are Kenya, Nigeria, Tunisia, and Zimbabwe so far.

The onset of the COVID-19 pandemic also accelerated the usage of the digital economy. This has posed serious challenges to developing countries with little capacity to extract tax. However, the digital economy can ease the burden of tax extraction. Cash-strapped governments in Africa have been compelled to look to digital businesses for tax extraction, especially after the COVID-19 pandemic. Digital businesses affected the traditional business models and how they can be taxed. Their ability to conduct business without physical presence, with differentiation of value across business functions, risks, and assets, deems it a borderless business (Lucas-Mas & Junquera-Varela, 2021). Transcending of borders by traders has brought to the fore questions of how governments will be able to extract the much-needed tax to fund public priorities. Dincecco and Katz (2016) reiterate that effective states in contemporary development trajectory play a critical role in revenue collection.

Most African countries experienced diminished sources of revenue for tax extraction when businesses faced closure or had limited operations. Most of these countries rely on commodity-based taxes such as value added tax (VAT). While on the one hand states were faced with this dilemma, on the other hand, digital business was booming. Its lack of physical presence posed challenges to tax levies as governments were faced with a new challenge of how to tax digital businesses. These businesses on the contrary experienced booming revenues as the COVID-19 lockdown restricted human movement across the globe. Deloitte (2021) reports that some digital companies experienced booming business and were compelled to hire extra staff to deal with the increased demand for goods and services. Furthermore, some tech giants have modeled their businesses on a sort that can easily avoid taxation. An example of these includes Google, Apple, Facebook, and Amazon whose corporate value is in intangible assets such as patents and copyrights (Morinobu, 2018). The European Commission discovered that the tax rate of digital businesses was a mere 9.5% (Morinobu, 2018:2). The percentage is not a true reflection of the corporate value of these businesses. Tax avoidance lamentably gives international digital giants a competitive urge over tax-paying local digital businesses. It is on this basis that governments across the globe sought to impose tax levies on digital businesses. Included in these businesses are digital financial services. Digitalization of tax collection through DFSs and digital identities is efficient in identifying clients, communicating with them, and giving high-quality data on taxpayer profiles (Santoro et al., 2022). As such, it reduces compliance costs, and clients can use the same platforms to make payments, and monitoring compliance is easier. While revenue collection is undoubtedly important, taxing these services in Africa is likely to cause financial exclusion in the long run.

18.6 Digital Financial Services

The expansion of DFS usage was amplified by the COVID-19 pandemic that limited human movement across the globe. While digital services have synergistically reached out to the unbanked and underserved, it is foolhardy to overlook the potential of DF's inequitable economic development, especially in South Africa where inequality is highest. The United Nations recently warned African countries that they could risk losing revenue to the value of US $ 350 billion if they do not harness the digitization of their economies. Notwithstanding, digitalization also presents an opportunity for African governments to tap revenue from the digital economy (Mpofu & Moloi, 2022). It is an inalienable role of the state to collect taxes. The capacity of a state to influence growth is strongly tied to the ability to extract revenue. Be that as it may, caution needs to be exercised where the collection of taxes should not be counterintuitive to limiting the scope of financial inclusion (Mpofu & Moloi, 2022). Lucas-Mas and Junquera-Varela (2021) warn that it is bound to have deleterious effects on investment across borders. Karombo in concurrence also noted that "taxing e-commerce and fintech platforms in this nascent stage is working against the growth and adoption of such platforms." Literature is also dotted with examples that attest to the fact that taxation of DFSs currently has deleterious effects. In Uganda, the 1% tax levy on transaction costs imposed led to a US $ 192 million loss over 3 months (Abuka in Bongomin et al., 2019: 187).

On the contrary, South Africa broadened its existing indirect taxes on value added tax. In addition, the country is one of the few which already had direct tax recommendations for the digital economy as early as 2016 through the Davis Tax Committee (DTC). The DTC makes recommendations to the state to consider the economic circumstances in taxing the digital economy. Kenya, Nigeria, Tunisia, and Zimbabwe have already introduced direct service tax to DFSs (Mpofu & Moloi, 2022). However, taxing DFSs or heavy transaction fees is viewed as unfair given that this sector is likely to even out inequality. In addition, they cause financial exclusion in the long run (Bongomin et al., 2019; Mpofu & Moloi, 2022; World Bank, 2018). Taxation is known to affect the market equilibrium as consumers react to price increases in products (Bongomin et al., 2019). Goods such as DFS whose uptake has been phenomenal have the potential to hurt customers if the tax burden is prematurely added. GSMA (2018) further adds that the tax burden levied against DFSs is a risk to the underserved as it discourages investment in Internet coverage. Resultantly, harsh taxation compels customers to cash transactions that also evade taxation (Mastercard; Ndung'u, 2019). Taxing DFSs does not necessarily increase the tax base but may reverse the milestones reached in financial inclusion (Ndung'u,

2019). On the contrary, tax exemptions are known to increase inclusion as observed during the pandemic when MPesa in Kenya exempted transactional charges for remittances received at a certain threshold (). Furthermore, tax exemptions create employment, cushion the poor against economic shocks, increase the affordability of DFSs, and increase access to insurance, savings, and payments through mobile money (Alampay et al. 2017; GSMA, 2019; Muthiora & Raithatha, 2017; Oji, 2015; Natile, 2020). Currently, universal coverage is still a lag, and levying taxes can be inimical to financial inclusion (Bongomin et al., 2019). Therefore, governments must mitigate the tax burden on both clients and service providers.

While most African countries are faced with the daunting task of reaching high rates of financial inclusion, South Africa deals with the challenge of the usage of these services. Although account ownership stands at 91%, the poor rely on informal channels and cash transactions. The government is faced with the daunting task of increasing the usage of these services and tax evasion. The National Development Plan in 2012 implored the financial sector to achieve a 90% rate by 2030. Results indicate that those figures are reachable, but that does not translate to financial inclusion. In the same vein, Mastercard observed that reliance on cash transactions is still rampant in South Africa despite the availability of digital services. While statistics confirm that 91% of adults have accounts and 81% have bank accounts, 78% of those adults use nonbank channels, while 61% use informal channels (MasterCard). Although there are 80 million bank cards in circulation, 17 million SASSA cards, and a mobile penetration level of 157%, informal channels are still commonly used. Although statistics confirm inclusion, further studies show that the poor and SMMEs are not effectively included. Poorly designed financial products often alienate the poor from formal financial systems. Often, transaction fees drive out the poor. Mastercard () corroborates this idea by adding that most adults with bank accounts only use their accounts to receive money, which they withdraw as cash for the rest of the month. While financial inclusion is renowned for bringing financial products ranging from loans, savings, and others to the poor, consumer behavior insinuates that there is a void in the financial systems. Despite the findings from a survey carried out by Mastercard, the cost of using cash was estimated to be 0.52% of the country's GDP—23 billion per annum (Mastercard). This burden of using cash is mostly carried by low-income earners and SMMEs.

The South African economy is heavily dualized, and the country's attempt to reduce economic disparities has failed, as evidenced by the Gini coefficient, which is 6.3. This is vindicated by the typical characteristics of these consumers. A typical female-headed household is known to rely on social security, borrow from loan sharks, and only use the SASSA card to withdraw cash. Likewise, the SMMEs based in townships face stiff competition from established businesses, have a customer base of the poor, borrow from informal channels, and are survivalist in nature. According to the National Financial Inclusion Policy report, most of these people reiterate that transaction fee is prohibitive, while borrowers are often blacklisted by banks. It stands to reason that if financial products are not tailored to suit the needs of clients, account holders fall victim to the bank systems.

Although the Twin Peaks system of financial regulations stressed the government's position on financial inclusion, results indicate that inclusion is yet to gain a foothold. The National Financial Inclusion Strategy needs to be imbued with fairness. Financial products need to be tailor-made to the needs of the intended beneficiaries. In this light, financial inclusion is likely to yield results. Further to that, the United Nations in 2021 recommended self-employment as one strategy that could combat the skyrocketing unemployment in the post-COVID period. Self-employment relies heavily on equitable access to capital for the poor. Moreover, DFSs have the potential to reduce poor people's heavy reliance on the government for social security. When access to capital is available and user-friendly, poor households as well as informal businesses can chart sustainable livelihoods through their enterprises (GSMA, 2019, 2020; Mpofu & Moloi, 2022). Therefore, the government needs to be warned of its stance on the taxation of DFSs. While short-term goals in levying taxes will give the state the much-needed tax revenue, in the long run, financial inclusion will remain far-fetched (Mpofu & Moloi, 2022).

18.7 Methodology

This article is based on the review of secondary data sources and benefits from a few journals, some policy reports, as well as reports from national and international organizations. Figure 18.1 outlines the manuscripts considered in this study.

We conducted a thorough analysis of the relevant literature to shed light on the issue at hand. According to Tawfik et al. (2019), the first step toward conducting an effective systematic literature review is conducting a preliminary search to identify articles that are relevant to the topic at hand. Because of this, we can be assured that the offered idea is sound, that we won't waste time rehashing old ground, and that we'll have access to enough relevant papers when evaluating the idea. Figure 18.1 shows a synopsis of the numerous pieces of research that were considered during the screening and selection process. It is recommended that a data-checking stage be incorporated due to the likelihood of human mistakes and prejudice. In this process, evidence images are used to compare each included item with its counterpart on an extraction sheet, allowing any discrepancies to be uncovered.

18.8 Usage of Digital Financial Services in the Digital Economy

Rapid technological developments like AI, the Internet, and cloud computing, among others, have altered the financial services industry and increased both access to and use of these services (Llewellyn-Jones, 2016; Mpofu & Mhlanga, 2022). The sub-Saharan Africa financial industry collaborated with banks, governments, and

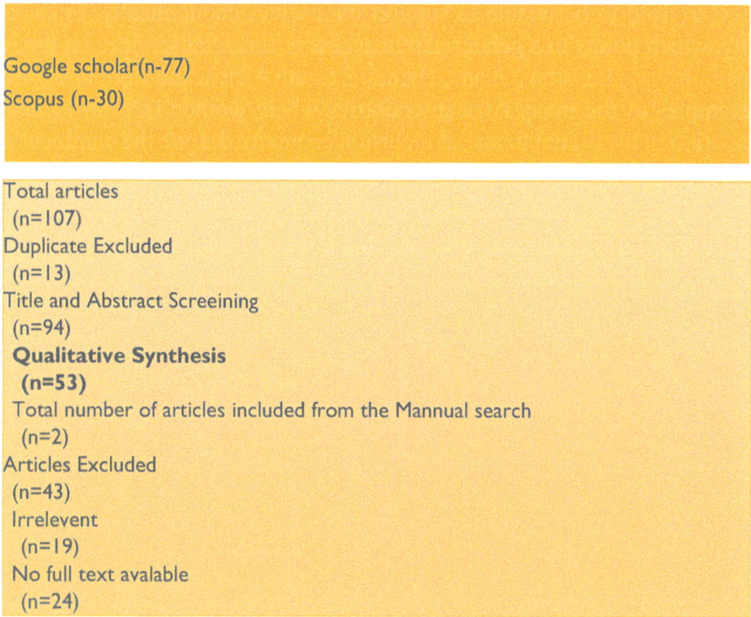

Fig. 18.1 Flow diagram of studies' screening and selection. (Source: Authors')

other organizations to develop a digital payments ecosystem as revealed by Ahmad et al. (2020). One example of success is EcoCash platform in Zimbabwe which processed transactions totaling approximately over US $ 78.4 billion in 2019 and increasing financial inclusion from as low as 32% to over 90%. As a result, there was a rise in economic and social participation (Ahmad et al., 2020). However, scholars like Demirgüç-Kunt et al. (2018), Demirgüç-Kunt and Klapper (2012), Mhlanga (2020) believe that many people, especially in rural areas and low-income nations, nevertheless lack access to financial services with cities typically having the more developed physical financial infrastructure. Sekantsi (2019) believe that there are many barriers preventing people from using formal financial services, including high banking expenses, difficulties in keeping back accounts, a lack of interoperability, and insufficient documentation. As a result of these and other considerations, Lesotho is one example of African nation that set out to implement the Lesotho Scaling Inclusion strategy, where they believe that the use of mobile money can expand access to banking services and boost financial inclusion (Mpofu & Mhlanga, 2022). Financial inclusion promotes economic growth and development in all countries by making banking services more widely available and usable by all the people from the fully banked to the barely banked to the completely unbanked (Sekantsi, 2019). Sustainable development goal 5 stresses the necessity of tackling gender inequality which can be achieved through financial inclusion. It is said that women and girls continue to face discrimination, danger, and disadvantage today (Mhlanga, 2022b).

They are said to be unable to support themselves economically, financially, or socially, which points to a gender gap in access to financial services on the African continent. Kenya, Lesotho, Ghana, Namibia, South Africa, and Zimbabwe are just a few examples of the many African countries where women face obstacles to full participation in the digital financial inclusion economy despite the continent's progress in the Fourth Industrial Revolution (Mhlanga, 2021, 2022b; Ojo, 2020; Ojo & Zondi, 2021).

Despite the belief that women face greater financial exclusion than men do, DSF has been highlighted as the solution to reducing this imbalance, via platforms like electronic and mobile money. Increasing women's access to financial resources is a top priority, and these platforms play a crucial role. Women in the informal economy of many African nations including South Africa, Kenya, and Zimbabwe who are either unbanked or underbanked have been credited with the advent of mobile money's revolutionary impact (Mhlanga, 2022c). Due to severe currency shortages in nations like Zimbabwe, mobile banking played a vital role in lowering the country's reliance on cash transactions. The nonbanked or underbanked parts of the population, who are frequently financially excluded and underserved, have access to convenient, reliable, and accessible financial services, thanks to mobile money. The price of the Internet and other digital tools was seen as a barrier to people participating in the financial system.

18.9 Taxing of the Digital Economy and Usage of Digital Financial Services

Taxes on DFS could increase the cost of social assistance while also influencing how people use money management tools. The influence on social welfare from changes in usage can be small in some cases and large in others. This is contingent upon the availability of viable alternatives to the service in issue, as well as the significance of that service to potential growth in the medium and long term. Others argue that imposing taxes on digital financial services (DFSs) will discourage people from using them, which will hurt the economy as a whole and digital financial inclusion in Africa (Munoz et al., 2022; Mpofu & Mhlanga, 2022). The United Nations has been advocating for governments to ensure that all their citizens have access to financial services, so this goes against that goal. In this context, "financial inclusion" refers to the availability and utilization of adequate, affordable, and appropriate financial services. According to Mungai and van der Linden (2021), the widespread use and acceptance of DFS in Rwanda increased after the country's central bank eliminated transaction fees for digital P2P and e-commerce transactions. Few analyses have looked at the correlation between DFS taxes and usage consequences and financial inclusion. The implications for economically vulnerable groups, such as those in the informal economy, those with low incomes, the poor, and women, may vary depending on the population under study. The tax systems of various countries can have different implications. Claiming they may have a chilling effect on people's access to credit, some argue that DFS taxes should be eliminated. These critics have also advocated for the increased use of DFS by introducing tax incentives to encourage the use of these services by businesses. If this happens, financial inclusion in low-income regions could expand. There hasn't been enough research into these claims. It is not yet clear how tax policy should be organized to encourage investments and development to increase financial inclusion. As Mungai and van der Linden (2021) point out, governments may not be able to bear the developmental consequence of taxing digital payments without rolling back the digitalization gains made during the pandemic. Because infrastructure, regulatory constraints, and Internet connectivity significantly affect the demand and supply chain of financial services, examining financial inclusion and exclusion from a tax perspective is insufficient.

Considering the ineffectiveness and abuse of tax incentives in developing countries, more research is needed into the submission of tax incentives and other incentives and their potential effects on the use of financial services and financial inclusion. The use of tax incentives for base erosion and profit shifting by multinational corporations is highlighted by Oguttu (2018) as a problem in African countries. Tax policy that targets DFS providers while exempting others that provide more conventional services will be seen as unfair and discriminatory. Since traditional financial services are often less expensive and are not subject to taxes, this would harm the expansion of digital financial inclusion (Mpofu & Mhlanga, 2022). DFS would be more expensive due to the financial impact of taxation, creating an uneven playing field for competitors. DFS companies may see less profit because of unfair competition from more established financial services. Financial inclusion might be significantly impacted if digital businesses struggled to break even. African governments should think about how to construct DFS tax policies in a way that promotes changes in the market structure that are beneficial to development, particularly regarding the interoperability of various works.

18.10 Taxing the Digital Economy, Trust, Tax Morale, and Digital Financial Inclusion

If the information on these taxes is not properly disclosed and efficiently understood, it might undermine the faith of users in the DFS. This is especially true for digital transactions, notably payments. Strong mistrust and scepticism toward government have resulted from the vagueness of tax policy, lack of consistency in policymaking procedures, and inadequate stakeholder engagement on DFS taxation in most African nations, in some cases hampering the usage of digital financial services (GSMA, 2021; Mpofu & Mhlanga, 2022). Consumers and businesses alike in Zimbabwe voiced their disapproval of the country's 2% IMTT, for instance. According to Mungai and van der Linden (2021), DFS customers in Uganda paid a total of four different taxes. Withdrawals, deposits, and all other monetary transactions were subject to taxation. Customers reacted negatively, using digital financial services less frequently because they saw this as overtaxation. Over half of all transactions between individuals stopped. The Ugandan government heard the public's concerns about the DFS tax rates and decided to lower them, levying them solely on withdrawals while abolishing the other three. Lower tax revenue could be the outcome of a decrease in trust's two potential knock-on effects: lower utilization and lower tax morale. The government's ability to impose tax rates that are consistent with the tax principle of the economy is essential to gaining the trust and acceptance of its citizens. This principle states that taxation should not result in a net negative for citizens or cause them to fall into poverty. Governments must also interact with DFS providers, the market, and consumer advocacy groups. One barrier to accurately assessing the influence of taxation on numerous economic concerns, including financial inclusion, is the lack of access to data on digital transactions by the government. African nations must work together to advance crucial tax changes and enhance DFS structures and administration. The need to draw on one another's knowledge is constant.

18.11 Conclusion and Policy Implications

In the existing body of research, the idea that digital financial inclusion plays a significant part in eradicating inequalities and redressing gender disparities, in addition to making a constructive contribution to economic growth, is becoming increasingly accepted as a point of view. The findings from various parts of the world provide credence to the idea that the provision of financial inclusion services paves the way for poor people to enhance their quality of life and engage in sustainable business endeavors. It makes financial solutions that are more secure, more affordable, and easier to access. Because of the rapid expansion of the digital economy, which is being driven by the technologies that are propelling the Fourth Industrial Revolution, taxation of the digital economy has become a salient issue all over the world, even before the epidemic. Around the world, a significant amount of effort has been put into developing taxes guidelines for the digital economy in general. Because of this, the purpose of this chapter was to examine, from the point of view of the African continent, the connections that exist between the digital economy, digital taxes, and digital financial inclusion. It was established in this chapter that taxing the digital economy might have severe and substantial repercussions for digital financial inclusion. This is because vulnerable people who utilize these services might lose trust in these services if the services are taxed.

References

Alampay, E. A., Moshi, G. C., Ghosh, I., Peralta, M. L. C., & Harshanti, J. (2017). The impact of mobile financial services in low-and lower-middle-income countries. International Development Research Centre (IDRC): Ottawa, ON, Canada.

Alliance for Financial Inclusion (AFI) (2012). Agent banking in Latin America. The AFI Discussion Paper series.

Ahmad, A. H., Green, C., & Jiang, F. (2020). Mobile money, financial inclusion and development: A review with reference to African experience. *Journal of Economic Surveys, 34*(4), 753–792.

Asongu, S. A., Biekpe, N., & Cassimon, D. (2020). Understanding the greater diffusion of mobile money innovations in Africa. *Telecommunications Policy, 44*(8), 102000.

Bongomin, G. O. C., Yourougou, P., & Munene, J. C. (2019). Digital financial innovations in the twenty-first century: Do transaction tax exemptions promote mobile money services for financial inclusion in developing countries? *Journal of Economic and Administrative Sciences, 36*(3), 185–203.

Bhomoyi, N. M. (2020). Human security and development: a case of Diepsloot, extension 12, Johannesburg (Doctoral dissertation).

Consultative Group to Assist the Poor. (2011). *Advancing financial access for the world's poor*. CGAP.

Demirgüç-Kunt, A., & Klapper, L. F. (2012). *Financial inclusion in Africa: an overview*. World Bank Policy Research Working Paper (6088).

Demirgüç-Kunt, A., Klapper, L., Singer, D., & Ansar, S. (2022). *The Global Findex Database 2021: Financial inclusion, digital payments, and resilience in the age of COVID-19.*

Demirgüç-Kunt, A., Klapper, L., Singer, D., Ansar, S., & Hess, J. (2018). Opportunities for expanding financial inclusion through digital technology. In *The Global Findex Database 2017: Measuring financial inclusion and the fintech revolution.*

Deloitte (2021)-Growth through financial inclusion. Available Online https://www2.deloitte.com/uk/en/pages/financialservices/articles/growth-through-financial-inclusion.html (Accessed 12 January 2022).

Dincecco, M., & Katz, G. (2016). State capacity and long-run economic performance. *The Economic Journal, 126*(590), 189–218.

Duncombe, R. (2012). *Understanding mobile phone impact on livelihoods in developing countries: A new research framework.*

Fukuyama, F. (2013). What is governance? *Governance, 26*(3), 347–368.

Gibson, E., Lupo-Pasini, F., & Buckley, R. P. (2015). Regulating digital financial services agents in developing countries to promote financial inclusion. *Singapore Journal of Legal Studies*, 26–45. https://search.informit.org/doi/10.3316/informit.20180720000094

GSMA (2018). State of the industry report on mobile money. Available online: https://www.gsma.com/mobilefordevelopment/wp-content/uploads/2019/02/2018-State-of-the-Industry-Report-on-Mobile-Money.pdf

GSMA (2019). 2019 Mobile Industry Report https://www.gsma.com/subsaharanafrica/resources/2019-mobile-industry-report

GSMA (2020). The causes and consequences of mobile money taxation. An examination of mobile money taxation in sub Saharan Africa. Available online: https://www.gsma.com/mobilefordevelopment/resources/the-causes-andconsequences-of-mobile-money-taxation-an-examination-of-mobile-money-transaction-taxes-in-sub-saharan-africa/ (accessed on 12 April 2022).

GSMA. (2021). *State of the industry report on mobile money 2021*. Available online: https://www.adfi.org/publications/state-industry-report-mobile-money-2021-gsma. Accessed on 12 June 2022.

Khera, P., Ng, S., Ogawa, S., & Sahay, R. (2022). Measuring digital financial inclusion in emerging market and developing economies: A new index. *Asian Economic Policy Review, 17*(2), 213–230.

Kouladoum, J. C., Wirajing, M. A. K., & Nchofoung, T. N. (2022). Digital technologies and financial inclusion in Sub-Saharan Africa. *Telecommunications Policy, 46*, 102387.

Llewellyn-Jones, L. (2016). Mobile money: Part of the African financial inclusion solution? *Economic Affairs, 36*(2), 212–216.

Lucas-Mas, C. Ó., & Junquera-Varela, R. F. (2021). Tax theory applied to the digital economy: A proposal for a digital data tax and a global internet tax agency. World Bank Publications.

Malady, L., Buckley, R. P., & Arner, D. W. (2014). Developing and implementing AML/CFT measures using a risk-based approach for new payments products and services. CIFR Paper, (028).

Menyelim, C. M., Babajide, A. A., Omankhanlen, A. E., & Ehikioya, B. I. (2021). Financial inclusion, income inequality, and sustainable economic growth in sub-Saharan African countries. *Sustainability, 13*(4), 1780.

Mhlanga, D. (2021). Artificial intelligence in the industry 4.0, and its impact on poverty, innovation, infrastructure development, and the sustainable development goals: Lessons from emerging economies. *Sustainability, 13*(11), 5788.

Mhlanga, D. (2022a). Human-centered artificial intelligence: The superlative approach to achieve sustainable development goals in the fourth industrial revolution. *Sustainability, 14*(13), 7804.

Mhlanga, D. (2022b). Selected digital financial inclusion success stories across developing economies. In *Digital Financial Inclusion* (pp. 301–322). Palgrave Macmillan.

Mhlanga, D. (2022c). Prospects and challenges of digital financial inclusion/Fintech Innovation in the Fourth Industrial Revolution. *Digital Financial Inclusion*. pp. 163–182.

Mhlanga, D., & Dunga, S. H. (2020). Measuring financial inclusion and its determinants among the smallholder farmers in Zimbabwe: An empirical study. *Eurasian Journal of Business and Management, 8*(3), 266–281.

Mhlanga, D., & Beneke, J. (2021). The fourth industrial revolution: Exploring the determinants of internet access in emerging economies. *Studia Universitatis Babes-Bolyai Oeconomica, 66*(3), 77–92.

Milogolov, N., & Berberov, A. (2022). The digital tax reform for Africa: Customised or one-size-fits-all approach? *International Review of Law, Computers & Technology, 36*(1), 28–47.

Morgan, P. J., & Long, T. Q. (2020). Financial literacy, financial inclusion, and savings behavior in Laos. *Journal of Asian Economics, 68*, 101197.

Morinobu, S. (2018). *Strategies for taxing the digital economy*. The Tokyo Foundation for Policy Research.

Mpofu, F. Y., & Mhlanga, D. (2022). Digital financial inclusion, digital financial services tax and financial inclusion in the fourth industrial revolution era in Africa. *Economies, 10*(8), 184.

Mpofu, F. Y., & Moloi, T. (2022). Direct digital services taxes in Africa and the Canons of taxation. *Laws, 11*(4), 57.

Muthiora, B., & Raithatha, R. (2017). Rethinking mobile money taxation. Available online: https://www.gsma.com/mobilefordevelopment/programme/mobile-money/rethinking-mobile-mone-taxation (accessed on 2 Jauary 2022).

Mungai, K., & van der Linden, A. (2021). *The unpopular choice: Taxing digital payments in the era of digitalisation*. Available online: https://cenfri.org/articles/taxing-digital-payments-in-the-era-of-digitalisation/. Accessed on 12 June 2022.

Munoz, L., Mascagni, G., Prichard, W., & Santoro, F. (2022). Should governments tax digital financial services? a research agenda to understand sector-specific taxes on DFS.

Natile, S. (2020). *The exclusionary politics of digital financial inclusion: Mobile money, gendered walls*. Routledge.

Nchofoung, T. N., & Asongu, S. A. (2022). ICT for sustainable development: Global comparative evidence of globalisation thresholds. *Telecommunications Policy, 46*(5), 102296.

Ndung'u, N. S. (2019). *Taxing mobile phone transactions in Africa: lessons from Kenya.* Available online: https://www.brookings.edu/research/taxing-mobile-phone-transactions-in-africa-lessons-from-kenya/

Oguttu, A. W. (2018). International tax competition, harmful tax practices and the 'race to the bottom': A special focus on unstrategic tax incentives in Africa. *Comparative and International Law Journal of Southern Africa, 51*(3), 293–319.

Oji, C. K. (2015). Promoting financial inclusion for inclusive growth in Africa. A vailable Online: https://www.africaportal.org/publications/promoting-financial-inclusion-for-inclusive-growth-in-africa/

Ojo, T. A. (2020). A study of financial inclusion and women's empowerment in South Africa: The Case of female entrepreneurs in gauteng (Doctoral dissertation, University of Pretoria).

Ojo, T. A., & Zondi, S. (2021). Impact of institutional quality and governance on financial inclusion for women in South Africa: A case of Gauteng women entrepreneurs. *The Strategic Review for Southern Africa, 43*(2), 59–82.

Ozili, P. K. (2021). Financial inclusion research around the world: A review. *Forum for Social Economics, 50*(4), 457–479. Routledge.

Santoro, F., Munoz, L., Prichard, W., & Mascagni, G. (2022). *Digital financial services and digital IDs: What potential do they have for better taxation in Africa?*

Schwab (2016). The fourth industrial revolution: what it means, how to respond. Available online: https://www.weforum.org/agenda/2016/01/the-fourth-industrial-revolution-what-it-means-and-how-to-respond/

Sekantsi, L. P. (2019). Digital financial services uptake in Africa and its role in financial inclusion of women. *Journal of Digital Banking, 4*(2), 161–174.

Tawfik, G. M., Dila, K. A. S., Mohamed, M. Y. F., Tam, D. N. H., Kien, N. D., Ahmed, A. M., & Huy, N. T. (2019). A step by step guide for conducting a systematic review and meta-analysis with simulation data. *Tropical Medicine and Health, 47*(1), 1–9.

The Financial Inclusion Policy of South Africa (2022). The financial inclusion policy of South Africa. The Financial Inclusion Policy. 2022 accessed from //efaidnbmnnnibpcajpcglclefindmkaj/https://www.treasury.gov.za/comm_media/press/2020/Financial%20Inclusion%20Policy%20-%20An%20Inclusive%20Financial%20Sector%20For%20All.pdf

World Bank (2014). World Development Report 2014: Risk and Opportunity—Managing Risk for Development. © Washington, DC. http://hdl.handle.net/10986/16092

World Bank (2018). UFA2020 Overview: Universal Financial Access by 2020. October 1 2018 ed.HEADQUARTERS The World Bank 1818 H Street, NW Washington, DC 20433 USA. https://www.gsma.com/subsaharanafrica/resources/2019-mobile-industryreport

World Bank. (2022). *Financial inclusion overview*. World Bank. http://www.worldbank.org/en/topic/financialinclusion/overview

Chapter 19
Digital Transformation in the Healthcare Sector: The Role of Artificial Intelligence for Inclusive Long-Term Care Around the World, Lessons for Africa

David Mhlanga

Abstract Future predictions indicate that the digital revolution of health services will continue to have a big impact. In the twenty-first century and the wake of the COVID crisis, it is crucial to evaluate the effects of such digital health services. Just like other services, long-term care will become more crucial for those who are 80 years old and older, as well as for older women who live longer, as the elderly population rises in tandem with their longevity. Additionally, because of longer life expectancies and an increase in the number of elderly people, the prevalence of mental health issues like dementia and Alzheimer's continues to rise, adding to the increase in demand for long-term care. In addition, when the virus hit, it disrupted the healthcare systems of several nations. In contrast, digital transformation is rapidly gaining ground in several sectors, including healthcare. Therefore, the goal of this study was to examine how the digital transformation of the healthcare industry application of artificial intelligence and machine learning has affected long-term care and how the African continent can benefit. The results of the systematic literature review technique showed that, in the post-pandemic environment, digital transformation is advantageous for the provision of long-term care because telemedicine programs can facilitate the provision of care at home. When there is a digital transformation, among other key components that can help with long-term care, issues like elder abuse and age discrimination in access to long-term services may be recorded. Therefore, it can assist long-term patient care programs around the world more, and greater focus should be given to the digital transformation of the healthcare industry.

Keywords COVID · Digital transformation · Healthcare sector · Long-term care

D. Mhlanga (✉)
The University of Johannesburg, College of Business and Economics, Johannesburg, South Africa

D. Mhlanga, E. Ndhlovu (eds.), *Economic Inclusion in Post-Independence Africa*, Advances in African Economic, Social and Political Development,
https://doi.org/10.1007/978-3-031-31431-5_19

19.1 Introduction

The healthcare industry, like many others, has changed, including the adoption of electronic systems and the replacement of on-premises servers with cloud-based ones that can be integrated with a wide range of other types of systems (Jahankhani & Kendzierskyj, 2019). The authors of this article, Raimo et al. (2022), argue that a more strategic digital transformation is required when considering the current setup and anticipated needs. There are several reasons for this, and they all strengthen and improve each other's arguments. Rapid technological progress driven by AI is leading to more precision-based medicine with enhanced patient results at the point of treatment, which benefits both medical professionals and patients by facilitating a quicker and more accurate diagnosis (Raimo et al., 2022). In recent years, businesses across all industries around the world have been adapting their operations, thanks to digital transformation and AI. Scholars I've talked to define digital transformation as an effort to enhance some aspect of a given entity by introducing novel alterations to its characteristics via the integration of various forms of computing, networking, and informational hardware and software. Simply put, digital transformation is an improvement process (Vial, 2019; Verhoef et al., 2021; Raimo et al., 2022). The pervasive features of digital technologies are changing the production, trade, and communication practices of companies of all sizes.

The digital revolution and artificial intelligence (AI) that it ushered in are major forces in the modern economy (Raimo et al., 2022). According to Holzinger et al. (2021), artificial intelligence is the primary force driving the current digital revolution and has a huge potential to benefit both people and the environment. According to the claims made by Holzinger et al. (2021), artificial intelligence has the potential to aid in the discovery of novel solutions to the most pressing problems facing our human society. These problems can range from more general ones like agriculture and forest ecosystems to more specific ones like a person's health. These innovative ideas could be used to address a variety of issues, from those affecting individual health to those affecting global ecosystems. However, it is also widely acknowledged that there is a sizable and as of now unanticipated potential for the creation of novel risks associated with the broad use of AI technology. The experts all agree on this. The authors Holzinger et al. (2021) contend that all stakeholders, including governments, policymakers, industry, and academia, must work together to develop AI with these potential threats in mind to ensure the security, traceability, transparency, explainability, validity, and verifiability of AI applications in our daily lives. This will make it possible to create AI that is comprehensible, reliable, and verifiable.

Holzinger et al. (2021) assert that as a result, it is everyone's responsibility to ensure that AI is created while keeping these potential risks in mind. Others think that it is everyone's responsibility to prevent the use of artificial intelligence technology in any way that is unethical or harmful and that it should only be put to use after it has been proven to be trustworthy and moral. We must work hard to ensure that artificial intelligence is compatible with human values, that it can pave the way for a future free from danger, and that it can assure the wellness of all people on

Earth if we are to succeed in realizing this aim. Hospitals in particular have assumed a position that is becoming more and more vital in the digital transformation that is occurring across a wide range of various enterprises in the healthcare sector. The COVID-19 pandemic was also a significant step in the hospital sector's digital revolution. The pandemic's expansion catalyzed this change. Deloitte's research indicates that since the pandemic outbreak, almost 65% of healthcare organizations have increased their use of digital technology to improve patient care and streamline administrative processes. It is widely acknowledged that one of the best solutions to the issues of relieving stakeholder demands, improving the quality of healthcare, and cutting costs is digital transformation.

The delivery of care and health services to patients may be significantly altered by the use of electronic health records, monitoring technology, telehealth, electronic communications, data analysis, and web- and cloud-based tools. This will eventually lead to a decrease in health disparities and an improvement in user well-being. Significant changes would need to be made to how patients receive healthcare and other related services to achieve this goal. In this regard, for instance, the digitization of health records, which is understood as the conversion from paper format into computerized form, has unavoidably resulted in an improvement in the general quality of healthcare delivered, in addition to leading to an increase in the provision of care and an improvement in patient safety. In this context, "digitization" refers to the process of converting something from a paper format to a digital one. A lot of work has gone into creating policies, programs, standards, and directives that streamline the process of digitalizing healthcare systems because it is believed that digital transformation is so important to the healthcare sector. The following three ideas have emerged as the most crucial ones to learn from academic research on digital transformation in healthcare companies, according to Tortorella et al. (2020). A discussion of the advantages and disadvantages of utilizing digital technologies and a list of the numerous digital technologies now in use are a few of these.

This area also covers a discussion of the advantages and disadvantages of using digital technologies. In addition, according to Massaro (2021), digital transformation may be able to help resolve issues in medical practice by introducing fresh trends in value creation. Healthcare research is a multidisciplinary area that considers the full stakeholder ecosystem. Massaro's argument was founded on the notion that by bringing new trends, digital transformation may be able to help overcome issues in medical practice. The adoption of blockchain technology, following Massaro (2021), is essential for speeding up the digital revolution now occurring in the healthcare sector. Blockchain technology, in the opinion of Massaro (2021), has the potential to quicken the digital revolution by reducing elements like data management issues. The main goal of this study is to examine how, in the context of today's rapidly evolving technology, the digital transformation of the healthcare industry is affecting long-term care.

19.2 Review of Important Literature

19.2.1 Digital Transformation in Healthcare

The process by which an organization transitions from utilizing communication tools that are not digital to utilizing those that are digital is referred to as digital transformation. However, digital transformation is more than just the technical process of moving data from paper to digital formats; it also requires a socio-technical shift in the nature and application of digital technologies. In other words, digital transformation is not just a process of moving data from paper to digital formats (Raimo et al., 2022; Mhlanga, 2022a, b). The digital transformation of healthcare processes and services is gaining pace at the local policy level as well as in the strategic decisions of worldwide healthcare companies, as Preko and Boateng (2020) have described. According to reports, digital technology has been playing an increasingly important role in healthcare institutions ever since the term "e-health" was first coined in the year 1990 (Aceto et al., 2018). The use of digital technologies in healthcare institutions has increased in recent years since these technologies have become more compact, user-friendly, and capable of processing a greater volume of data.

According to Kraus et al. (2021), the term "digital transformation" refers to an effort to improve an entity by bringing about significant changes in its properties through the integration of various forms of information, computer, communication, and networking technologies. In other words, the goal of this effort is to make the entity more digitally advanced. According to Kraus et al. (2021), the change to digital will affect a company's capacity to acquire digital resources, build digital growth strategies, adjust its internal organizational structure, and define appropriate metrics and targets. All of these aspects of a company's operations would be impacted. This phenomenon is sweeping across the business world, and it has become a hot topic of discussion in several different fields of study, including information systems, strategy, and marketing. As a result of the revolution in digital healthcare, new markets have become available, and creative business models have surfaced to address the issues that are associated with an aging population in areas such as medical practice, value generation, and others.

19.3 Empirical Literature Review

The twenty-first century has witnessed the emergence of a phenomenon known as digital disruption, which has far-reaching ramifications for a variety of aspects of both business and society. For businesses to successfully deploy digital solutions, their "working," "roles," and "business offering" structures will need to undergo significant organizational transformations. According to Massaro (2021), the research sector of the healthcare industry is an example of multidisciplinary work because it considers all of the relevant stakeholders. The emergence of fresh patterns of value creation made possible by digital transformation may help to alleviate some of the challenges that are present in clinical practice. According to Massaro (2021), blockchain technology has the potential to make this digital transformation easier by reducing the impact of elements such as data management issues. As with the worth of any other breakthrough, the value of this technology is predicated more on hope than on concrete proof; as a result, it needs to be shown. The purpose of this paper is to bridge the gap between the academic literature and real-world applications of blockchain technology in healthcare by contrasting the two perspectives on the potential of the technology. This will be done by comparing and contrasting the two perspectives on the potential of the technology.

According to Haggerty (2017), the deployment of new technology has assisted in the delivery of safe, high-quality patient care and promoted improved corporate efficiency, just as it has in the vast majority of other industries that have undergone digital transformation. According to the information provided by Haggerty, a great number of healthcare organizations have included digital services such as electronic health records (EHR), digital imaging, e-prescription services, and enterprise resource planning technologies (2017). According to Haggerty (2017), the healthcare business, along with most others, has benefited significantly from digital transformation and the effect of the fast-increasing Internet of Things. Haggerty argues that this is the case (IoT). There has never been a time in history when doctors and other medical professionals have had quicker access to digital tools and patient records than they do today. Nevertheless, the problem of ensuring network and data security has been made more challenging as a result of the complexity and volume of data that moves through the information technology networks that drive modern healthcare companies.

According to Raimo et al.'s (2022) findings, the importance of digital transformation in the healthcare industry has grown in recent years as the COVID-19 epidemic has spread over the world. According to Raimo et al. (2022)'s findings, it is possible to reduce healthcare disparities, increase the quality of healthcare that is provided, and boost the overall well-being of citizens through the utilization of digital healthcare technologies. The significance of digital transformation in healthcare is also attracting attention from the academic community, as was articulated quite well by Raimo et al. (2022). In addition, Raimo et al. (2022) claimed that there is a shortage of research into the breadth of digital transformation in healthcare and the variables that inspire healthcare companies to adopt and implement digital solutions. This was suggested in their study. In a manner analogous to this, Kraus et al. (2021) indicated that the digital revolution in the healthcare industry is becoming an increasingly relevant topic for researchers and practitioners.

Kraus et al. (2021) conducted research and analysis on the topic of determining what factors influence the adoption of digital technology in the management and operations of organizations. According to Kraus et al. (2021), the previous research on digital transformation in healthcare can be divided into the following five categories: provider operational efficiency, patient-centered approaches, organizational variables and managerial implications, workforce practices, and socioeconomic considerations. The various nodes of this model that are connected indicate how the utilization of these various technologies increased the operational efficacy of service providers. Khan and Al Amin (2021) investigated the fundamental features of healthcare digitalization and transformation in Bangladesh, to analyze the relationship between digital technology and growth factors in the current healthcare system and propose solutions to the crises that persist within the healthcare framework. To accomplish these goals, they investigated the fundamental features of healthcare digitalization and transformation in Bangladesh. According to the findings of the qualitative exploratory research, Bangladesh is currently in a transformation in both its medical and healthcare systems. Bangladesh is a developing nation that is seeing better economic viability.

In addition, Khan and Al Amin (2021) found that expanding healthcare systems all over the world are interacting with digital technology despite differences in the degree of "equality" that was achieved using digital technology. According to Burton-Jones et al. (2020), the global health business is undergoing a significant digital transition. Evaluating the success of these initiatives is essential because of the huge resources that are being invested and the far-reaching repercussions that could come from them. An article on translational research titled "Burton-Jones et al. (2020)" looked at how institutional theory could be used as a lens to make sense of the difficulties in assessing healthcare's digital changes and yield useful insights for making them better. The article was written in response to a question about how institutional theory could be used as a lens. According to Burton-Jones et al. (2020), institutional theory has the potential to explain phenomena that are observed in both the previous research and our case study. In addition, we present a demonstration of how the outcomes of assessment work might strengthen the institutional theory. With these opportunities in mind, we present a strategy for how academics and industry professionals might work together to advance the state of the art in this area of study by collaborating on research. According to Alauddin et al. (2021), the field of dentistry is one of the areas of medicine that is contributing to the digital revolution.

According to Alauddin et al., the processing of data and the production of data from digital sources have both advanced (2021). According to Alauddin et al. (2021), the Internet of Medical Things (IoMT), big data and analytical algorithms, Internet and communications technologies (ICT) including digital social media, augmented and virtual reality (AR and VR), and artificial intelligence (AI) have all played an important role in the exponential growth of digital transformation (AI). The interaction between these intricate digital aspects, as stated by Alauddin et al. (2021), is said to have considerably impacted the healthcare and biomedical industries, with a special emphasis on dentistry. According to Alauddin et al. (2021), the widespread use of these technologies will not only improve oral healthcare in many ways (such as by streamlining it, facilitating workflow, increasing oral health at a fraction of the current conventional cost, relieving dentists and dental auxiliary staff from routine and laborious tasks, and inspiring patient participation in personalized oral health care), but it will also spark these changes. Despite the implication of Binci et al. (2022) that digital transformation is a priority for the healthcare sector, very little specific information is known about the impact of digitalization, particularly of the Internet of Things (IoT), on the healthcare sector, for example, in terms of the jobs of clinicians and the experiences of patients. This is the case even though few details are known about the impact of digitalization, especially on the Internet of Things (IoT). These premises were used by Binci et al. (2022) to focus on an unexplored area of healthcare that is tied to the field of chronic heart disorders and digital transformation. Based on a socio-technical framework, Binci et al. (2022) constructed a model that included five major variables associated with medical staff and patients. These variables were related to one another. Binci et al. (2022) devised a model known as the input-process-output (IPO) model to classify variables of this kind. The cultural digital divide, structural flexibility, and a response to change all contribute to the RM outcome, which is the product of these three inputs.

According to Kruszyńska-Fischbach et al. (2021), the COVID-19 pandemic has prompted many countries to implement a wide range of preventative measures to curb the spread of the disease. These preventative measures include the development of medical teleconsultations as well as the utilization of several tools in the domain of inpatient telemedicine care. According to Kruszyńska-Fischbach et al. (2021), the introduction of digital technologies has provided an opportunity and presented a challenge for the healthcare sector. Kruszyńska-Fischbach et al. (2021) brought up the question of whether institutions are ready to utilize cutting-edge telemedicine services in the event of a COVID-19 pandemic. In a recent study conducted by Kruszyńska-Fischbach et al. (2021), the authors focused their attention on two characteristics that influence organizational e-readiness for digital transformation in Polish primary healthcare providers. The operational capabilities are the first factor, which Kruszyńska-Fischbach et al. (2021) define as "the total of valuable, limited, one-of-a-kind, and irreplaceable resources and the ability to use them." These characteristics make up the operational capabilities. The second component is made up of technological capacities, which are, in the end, what decide the extent of the dissemination of cutting-edge technology and how it is utilized. A distributed digital ledger that can withstand attacks and that is used to store data in a way that is secure, transparent, and unchangeable is what blockchain is, according to Sushma et al. (2022). Blockchain was developed to store data in a way that is secure, transparent, and unchangeable.

According to Sushma et al.'s (2022) findings, the use of this technology in the medical field has become a primary area of concentration during the past few years. The need for medical treatment is expected to continue growing, and as a result, the healthcare industry is seeking to improve how patient information is organized, shared, and protected. The reduction or removal of middlemen has increased the requirement for a trustworthy information technology infrastructure. The healthcare industry is currently struggling with several problems, including data silos, incompatible computer systems, access delays to patient records, and insufficient levels of security. According to Sushma et al. (2022), the technology behind blockchain can eradicate errors, duplicates, and inconsistencies.

19.4 Methodology

The findings of this study provide a solution to the question, "How will the digital transformation of the healthcare business affect long-term care in the Fourth Industrial Revolution?" At this point, technological advancement is ongoing and has an impact on almost every aspect of contemporary life. To provide a solution, a method that involved thoroughly reviewing the relevant literature was chosen. Tawfik et al. (2019) suggest beginning a systematic literature review with a preliminary search to discover relevant articles. This will allow the researchers to check the validity of the proposed idea, avoid repeating problems that have already been addressed, and ensure that there will be sufficient articles for conducting the analysis. Concerns such as long-term care and the digital revolution in the healthcare industry are examples of significant and crucial issues that should serve as themes for the investigation. When it comes to improving one's ability to retrieve data, Tawfik et al. (2019) suggest that it is essential to become well acquainted with the topic field by watching films and listening to presentations. If you ignore this phase, there is a possibility that the study will repeat what has already been done to save time and avoid having to deal with a problem that has been dealt with for a very long time (Lame, 2019; Mhlanga, 2022c, d).

To begin, we can use the search phrases "digital change in health, long-term care, and the industry" to search either PubMed or Google Scholar. During this examination, we looked into every possible route for reducing bias, including undertaking a manual search to recover reports that the initial computerized search may have missed. This was one of the steps that we took. We utilized a combination of five distinct approaches, including examining the references from included studies and reviews, contacting authors and experts, and making use of technologies like Scopus and Google Scholar to locate relevant papers and articles that were mentioned in other publications. These are the three methods that should be used in consecutive order to improve the outcomes of manual searching. First, we look at the works that were cited in the articles that were included; second, we perform citation tracking, which means that the reviewers keep track of all the articles that cite each of the articles that were included; this may require an electronic search of databases; and third, we keep track of all articles that are "related to" or "similar to" other articles. After having been exposed to the same title/abstract and full-text screening as those obtained from electronic databases, each of the aforementioned procedures can be carried out by a team of two or three reviewers. Additionally, any potentially relevant articles must undergo additional scrutiny against the inclusion criteria. In general, the criteria for exclusion are works that are simply abstracts, irrelevant, duplicated, or unavailable on their whole. To preserve the researcher's capacity for objectivity, certain restrictions were imposed in advance of the investigation. Articles that were published after the year 2000 and include the information that was sought after would be given priority. Figure 19.1 presents an outline of the texts that were considered for this investigation.

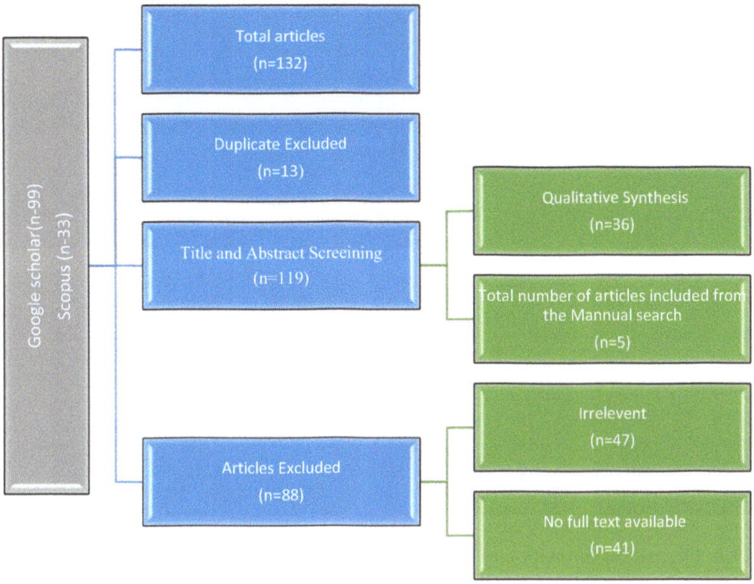

Fig. 19.1 Flow diagram of studies' screening and selection

The various researches that were considered during the screening and selection process are outlined in Fig. 19.1. Because errors and biases caused by humans are inevitable, we suggest including a data-checking stage in the process. During this step, every article that was included is checked with its counterpart in an extraction sheet by using evidence images to look for flaws in the data.

19.5 Results and Discussion

Long-term care encompasses a wide variety of services and settings, ranging from assistance with activities of daily living (ADLs) like washing, dressing, and food preparation to assistance with more complex healthcare-related services, participation in daycare programs, and institutional care. ADLs include washing, dressing, and food preparation. Most old people around the world receive care from friends, family, and neighbors in the familiar surroundings of their own homes. Most of these caregivers are women, and they volunteer their services without charge. In certain situations, it may be possible to employ an informal caregiver for a charge; however, this type of care is frequently unregulated, and its providers frequently face low compensation and few benefits. In some scenarios, it may be possible to hire an informal caregiver for a price. Several retirees either pay for their own medical and social services out of pocket, are eligible for services that are subsidized or provided free of charge by the government, or have private insurance from when they were younger. In residential facilities such as retirement homes, a far more

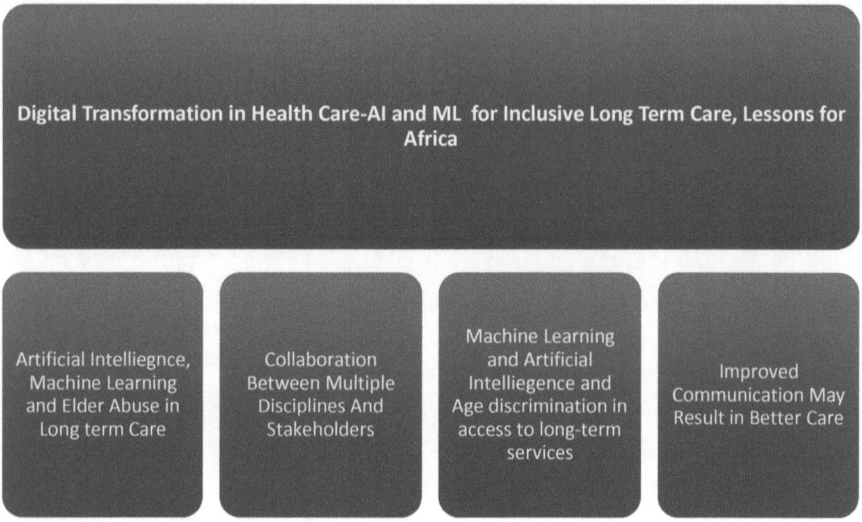

Fig. 19.2 Digital transformation in long-term care: the role of AI and machine learning

limited population receives medical care due to the nature of the setting. As a result, the following are some examples of possible uses of AI and ML in the field of long-term care.

Figure 19.2 outlines the impact of technologies like AI and machine learning that can help in addressing the challenges associated with long-term care

19.5.1 Digital Transformation, AI and ML, and Elder Abuse

According to the definition provided by Rosen et al. (2020), elder abuse occurs when a senior citizen suffers injury or is put in danger as a result of the actions or inactions of a person with whom they have a trusted connection or as a result of the senior citizen's age or a disability. Abuse can take many different forms, some more evident than others, such as physical aggression, while others, such as emotional manipulation or financial exploitation, can be more covert. Abuse of the elderly is pervasive, affecting 5–10% of old people living in the community each year; the threat is heightened for elderly people residing in nursing homes and other residential care facilities. Post et al. (2010) investigated the frequency of elder abuse committed by paid caregivers in long-term care settings and assessed the significance of a large number of risk factors for a single form of abuse as well as numerous types of elder abuse. The data were studied after the incidence and conditional incidence rates of various forms of abuse such as physical, caregiver, verbal, emotional, neglectful, and material abuse were calculated and determined. According to the findings of research carried out by Post et al. (2010), more than half of the elderly people who have been subjected to one form of abuse have also been subjected to another form of abuse. Limitations in physical functioning, limitations in the capacity to execute activities of daily life, and behavioral disorders are all significant risk factors for a wide variety of forms of abuse. Even though Yon et al. (2019) discovered that nearly one in six elderly people experienced elder abuse in the community in 2018, they also discovered that institutional abuse is likely just as common, even though there is little systematic evidence to prove the size of the problem. There was not enough research to determine the prevalence of elder abuse based on self-reported data from older residents, and total abuse estimates based on staff reports suggest 64.2% of employees acknowledged elder abuse in the past year. This is because there were not enough studies. According to the seniors, the following prevalence estimates for the various types of abuse were found: psychological abuse at 33.4%, physical abuse at 14.1%, financial abuse at 13.8%, neglect at 11.6%, and sexual abuse at 1.9%.

Yon et al. (2019) found that there is a significant frequency of elder abuse in institutions and called for international action to strengthen surveillance and monitoring of institutional elder abuse. To better inform policy action to combat elder abuse, the authors of this study found that there is a significant frequency of elder abuse in institutions. Yon et al. (2019) report that the majority of instances of elder abuse and neglect take place in care-dependent settings such as the home or an institution. All of these types of abuse, including neglect, physical and sexual abuse, as well as financial, psychological, and emotional abuse, are mentioned here. Yon et al. (2019) noted that "normal operational practice" frequently involves violations of the rights of older people. These violations include the use of restraints, locking of doors, social isolation, inappropriate use of medication, and regimented enforcement of schedules. While physical and sexual abuse is easy to identify, "normal operational practice" frequently involves violations of the rights of older people. Unfortunately, healthcare personnel rarely notice abuse or neglect of elderly patients, even though such an encounter could be a key opportunity to detect abuse and begin intervention (Rosen et al., 2020). Artificial intelligence has the potential to significantly enhance the detection of elder abuse in situations related to the provision of medical care if more sophisticated data analytics methods, such as machine learning, are developed.

19.5.2 Age Discrimination in Access to Long-Term Care Services

The implementation of digital transformation in healthcare is essential to eradicate all kinds of discrimination, in addition to removing obstacles that stand in the way of long-term care. According to Belliger and Krieger (2018), the advent of data-driven medicine has rendered ineffective the conventional model of medicine in which doctors play the role of "gods in white" and patients have no input. In this model, patients do not participate in the medical decision-making process. According to Belliger and Krieger (2018)'s theory, the advent of digital technology in the medical field has brought about several advantages for the general public in terms of connectedness, flow, transparency, and involvement. Taking into these considerations, the author of the paper contends that the unequal treatment of elderly people will be remedied as a result of the digital transformation of healthcare, which will involve the application of AI and ML, among other important technologies. According to Belliger and Krieger (2018), the Convention on the Rights of Persons with Disabilities is frequently cited as a possible source of human rights law for the elderly. Furthermore, according to Belliger and Krieger (2018), the unequal treatment of disabled older people and disabled younger people in accessing similar care services has been raised as an issue of age discrimination. Unfortuitously, in many regions of the world, the rights of disabled senior citizens are not the same as the rights of disabled children and young people. In France, if you are disabled and you are beyond the age of 60, you will not be entitled to the same benefits as a person whose ailment started before they turned 60 years old. This is cited as an example of ageism in addition to the prejudice that people with disabilities face. Recent studies conducted in Norway shed light on the disparity in the availability of caregiving resources between younger and older people. The study found that some staff members working for local authorities displayed unconscious bias against elderly individuals. According to Marchiondo et al. (2019), it has been demonstrated that feelings of age discrimination in the workplace rise with increasing age; nevertheless, there is a significant amount of heterogeneity among different age groups. There is a positive correlation between depression, self-rated health, self-reported job satisfaction, and the likelihood of continuing to work past the traditional retirement age when age discrimination is seen early on.

Marchiondo et al. (2019) suggested that older workers are more likely to experience age discrimination, which in turn predicts lower job satisfaction and self-rated health as well as increased depression symptoms but does not predict that older workers will continue to work past the age of retirement. It has been argued by Chu et al. (2021) that the COVID-19 pandemic has revealed long-standing inequalities in the long-term care sector and brought about "stringent social/physical distancing and public health quarantine guidelines that inadvertently put long-term care residents at risk for social isolation and loneliness." These guidelines were brought about as a result of the COVID-19 pandemic. However, Chu et al. (2021) found that residents of long-term care facilities often lack the technological capacity to accommodate modern technologies. This is even though virtual communication and technology have emerged as the primary means by which residents can maintain relationships with loved ones and the outside world. Based on their findings, Chu et al. (2021) concluded that there is an immediate need to replace aging technological infrastructures to enable person-centered care and to prevent potentially irreversible cognitive and psychological declines in residents by ensuring that residents can maintain important relationships with their families and friends.

19.5.3 Multidisciplinary and Multi-Stakeholders' Collaboration

Improvements in long-term care are being made possible by the widespread use of cutting-edge digital tools like artificial intelligence and machine learning. A new era of digital healthcare delivery has opened, with possibilities ranging from disease prevention and health promotion to therapeutic interventions and individual responsibility for one's health. Thus, they may help the healthcare system achieve its goals by influencing the nature of healthcare delivery. It can be difficult to generalize about the value of digital health services because their characteristics and outcomes may vary widely from one instance to the next, for instance, doctor-patient care that is perfectly coordinated, office procedures that can be automated and keep information safe, instantaneous availability of medical data, connections between a wide range of medical professionals, mutually beneficial investigational efforts, and facilitation of online scheduling. Care hacking is another key area where digital change will improve long-term care. Care hacking, as described by Belliger and Krieger (2018), is the use of digital technology, most prominently the Internet, to take charge of one's health and make innovative use of the healthcare system. Salvatore Laconesi is another famous care hacker; he used his computer skills to gain access to his brain scans and medical records and "decrypt" the medical codes they were protected with; he then published this information on the website La Cura and solicited assistance from the online community (Belliger & Krieger, 2018).

According to Belliger and Krieger (2018), Salvatore Laconesi received 500,000 responses from people all around the world. After the operation was a success, he put many of these ideas into practice, and the ripple effect of the worldwide outpouring of support should be viewed as significant in and of itself because it alters the practice of medicine. This demonstrates how digital transformation engages individuals, how it introduces a novel and previously unseen data into healthcare, and how it upends established norms and practices. This suggests the need for a healthcare industry-wide shift toward digital technologies to facilitate the kind of teamwork that improves care over the long haul. As a result of the digital revolution, citizen scientists from all walks of life can now participate in all phases of a medical study. The majority of people always have a variety of sensors of various types on them, thanks to their smartphones and other mobile gadgets. With the right software, such devices may collect crucial statistics, which can then be uploaded to the cloud or a research platform and used as part of a clinical trial or another research project.

19.5.4 Better Communications Can Lead to Better Care

It is very vital to undergo digital transformation to ensure that the tools and technology currently available for electronic medical records make it possible for care partners to share information that can be used to improve the treatment that they provide to residents. Additional information gives them the ability to adjust the care they provide or saves them time in ways that can have a significant and positively impactful influence on the health outcomes of their patients. Residents can maintain their connections with one another through digital transformation technologies such as videoconferencing technology. For example, during the COVID-19 pandemic, video calls saved the day at long-term care facilities by allowing elderly patients at risk to speak with their loved ones when visits in person were impossible (Belliger & Krieger, 2018; Mhlanga, 2022a, b, c, d). Even if there isn't an immediate danger to their health, friends and family members who wouldn't have been able to visit in person due to a lack of access to the necessary technology can now phone to check on their loved ones and see how they are doing. Because of this, the general amount of engagement that your residents get with their friends and family may rise, which in turn can benefit both their mental and physical health.

In addition, having dependable Wi-Fi connections as well as the necessary technology for video conferences might be a selling point when trying to attract new residents. As time goes on and more people acquire technological capabilities, the senior population will have an ever-increasing need for high-speed Internet. These fruits include quantified self-mobility, wellness apps, big data and data modeling, precision treatment, new forms of interaction among both physicians and patients, novel methods of utilizing health data, treatment hacking, crowd-sourced medical research, participative medicine, and shared deliberation. These fruits have their roots in network connectivity, are fed by the free flow of information, and branch off into normative expectations of participation, transparency, and authenticity. The new values and technology that are part of the digital transformation of healthcare have borne these fruits, which can be considered as developments that have emerged as a result of the change. They offer novel approaches to the generation of health-related information and knowledge, as well as to its distribution and application in ways that create value for all the relevant stakeholders. In the following, we will take a more in-depth look at some of these fruits that are now developing their full flavor in the digital health atmosphere.

19.6 Conclusion and Policy Recommendations

The objective of this chapter was to investigate how the digital transformation of the healthcare industry has affected long-term care with a particular focus on the application of artificial intelligence and machine learning. The systematic literature review supported the idea that digital transformation improves the delivery of long-term care. This is because telemedicine programs can make it easier to offer care at home using technology, especially in rural areas of developing nations where transport is a challenge. When the long-term care industry undergoes a digital revolution, it will be possible to monitor factors like elder abuse and age discrimination in access to long-term services. Long-term patient care programs around the world especially in the African continent stand to gain from the digital transformation of the healthcare sector, so the governments in Africa should devote more resources to this area more importantly collaboration among the various stakeholders.

References

Aceto, G., Persico, V., & Pescapé, A. (2018). The role of information and communication technologies in healthcare: Taxonomies, perspectives, and challenges. *Journal of Network and Computer Applications, 107*, 125–154.

Alauddin, M. S., Baharuddin, A. S., & Mohd Ghazali, M. I. (2021). The modern and digital transformation of oral health care: A mini review. In *Healthcare* (Vol. 9, No. 2, p. 118). Multidisciplinary Digital Publishing Institute.

Belliger, A., & Krieger, D. J. (2018). The digital transformation of healthcare. In *Knowledge Management in Digital Change* (pp. 311–326). Springer.

Binci, D., Palozzi, G., & Scafarto, F. (2022). Toward digital transformation in healthcare: A framework for remote monitoring adoption. *The TQM Journal, 34*(6), 1772–1799.

Burton-Jones, A., Akhlaghpour, S., Ayre, S., Barde, P., Staib, A., & Sullivan, C. (2020). Changing the conversation on evaluating digital transformation in healthcare: Insights from an institutional analysis. *Information and Organization, 30*(1), 100255.

Chu, C. H., Ronquillo, C., Khan, S., Hung, L., & Boscart, V. (2021). Technology recommendations to support person-centred care in long-term care homes during the COVID-19 pandemic and beyond. *Journal of Aging & Social Policy, 33*(4-5), 539–554.

Haggerty, E. (2017). Healthcare and digital transformation. *Network Security, 2017*(8), 7–11.

Holzinger, A., Weippl, E., Tjoa, A. M., & Kieseberg, P. (2021, August). Digital transformation for sustainable development goals (SDGs)-a security, safety and privacy perspective on AI. In *International cross-domain conference for machine learning and knowledge extraction* (pp. 1–20). Springer.

Jahankhani, H., & Kendzierskyj, S. (2019). Digital transformation of healthcare. In *Blockchain and clinical trial* (pp. 31–52). Springer.

Khan, M. M. R., & Al Amin, M. M. H. (2021). A study on digital transformation in the healthcare sector of Bangladesh: Current scenario and the future roadmap. *Journal of Governance and Accountability Studies, 1*(2), 163–176.

Kraus, S., Schiavone, F., Pluzhnikova, A., & Invernizzi, A. C. (2021). Digital transformation in healthcare: Analyzing the current state-of-research. *Journal of Business Research, 123*, 557–567.

Kruszyńska-Fischbach, A., Sysko-Romańczuk, S., Rafalik, M., Walczak, R., & Kludacz-Alessandri, M. (2021). Organizational E-readiness for the digital transformation of primary healthcare providers during the COVID-19 pandemic in Poland. *Journal of Clinical Medicine, 11*(1), 133.

Lame, G. (2019, July). Systematic literature reviews: An introduction. In *Proceedings of the design society: International conference on engineering design* (Vol. 1, No. 1, pp. 1633–1642). Cambridge University Press.

Marchiondo, L. A., Gonzales, E., & Williams, L. J. (2019). Trajectories of perceived workplace age discrimination and long-term associations with mental, self-rated, and occupational health. *The Journals of Gerontology: Series B, 74*(4), 655–663.

Massaro, M. (2021). Digital transformation in the healthcare sector through blockchain technology. Insights from academic research and business developments. *Technovation, 120*, 102386.

Mhlanga, D. (2022a). The role of artificial intelligence and machine learning amid the COVID-19 pandemic: What lessons are we learning on 4IR and the sustainable development goals. *International Journal of Environmental Research and Public Health, 19*(3), 1879.

Mhlanga, D. (2022b). Human-Centred artificial intelligence: The superlative approach to achieve sustainable development goals in the fourth industrial revolution. *Sustainability, 14*(13), 7804.

Mhlanga, D. (2022c). Stakeholder capitalism, the fourth industrial revolution (4IR), and sustainable development: Issues to be resolved. *Sustainability, 14*(7), 3902.

Mhlanga, D. (2022d). *Block Chain Technology for digital financial inclusion in the Industry 4.0, towards sustainable development?* Towards Sustainable Development. Available at SSRN: https://ssrn.com/abstract=4245904 or https://doi.org/10.2139/ssrn.4245904

Post, L., Page, C., Conner, T., Prokhorov, A., Fang, Y., & Biroscak, B. J. (2010). Elder abuse in long-term care: Types, patterns, and risk factors. *Research on Ageing, 32*(3), 323–348.

Preko, M., & Boateng, R. (2020). Assessing healthcare digitalisation in Ghana: A critical realist's approach. *Health Policy and Technology, 9*(2), 255–262.

Raimo, N., De Turi, I., Albergo, F., & Vitolla, F. (2022). The drivers of the digital transformation in the healthcare industry: An empirical analysis in Italian hospitals. *Technovation, 121*, 102558.

Rosen, T., Zhang, Y., Bao, Y., Clark, S., Elman, A., Wen, K., et al. (2020). Can artificial intelligence help identify elder abuse and neglect? *Journal of Elder Abuse & Neglect, 32*(1), 97–103.

Sushma, D. S., Jaiswal, V., & Pal, T. (2022). Digital transformation of healthcare sector by Blockchain technology. In *Transformations through Blockchain technology* (pp. 161–179). Springer.

Tawfik, G. M., Dila, K. A. S., Mohamed, M. Y. F., Tam, D. N. H., Kien, N. D., Ahmed, A. M., & Huy, N. T. (2019). A step by step guide for conducting a systematic review and meta-analysis with simulation data. *Tropical Medicine and Health, 47*(1), 1–9.

Tortorella, G. L., Fogliatto, F. S., Mac Cawley Vergara, A., Vassolo, R., & Sawhney, R. (2020). Healthcare 4.0: Trends, challenges and research directions. *Production Planning & Control, 31*(15), 1245–1260.

Verhoef, P. C., Broekhuizen, T., Bart, Y., Bhattacharya, A., Dong, J. Q., Fabian, N., & Haenlein, M. (2021). Digital transformation: A multidisciplinary reflection and research agenda. *Journal of Business Research, 122,* 889–901.

Vial, G. (2019). Understanding digital transformation: A review and a research agenda. *The Journal of Strategic Information Systems, 28*(2), 118–144.

Yon, Y., Ramiro-Gonzalez, M., Mikton, C. R., Huber, M., & Sethi, D. (2019). The prevalence of elder abuse in institutional settings: A systematic review and meta-analysis. *European Journal of Public Health, 29*(1), 58–67.

Part IV
Conclusions Economic Inclusion in Post-Independence Africa: An Inclusive Approach to Economic Development

Chapter 20
Economic and Social Inclusion in Post-independence Africa: A Conclusion

David Mhlanga and Emmanuel Ndhlovu

Abstract This chapter concludes the book *Economic and Social Inclusion in Post-independence Africa*. Drawing from published academic secondary sources as well as the contribution of this book, this chapter revisits the discourses and practices on economic and social inclusion in Africa with the view of suggesting interventions. This chapter briefly reconceptualizes these key concepts and then posits that inclusive economic and social inclusion prioritizes the inclusion of the vulnerable sections of its population.

Keywords Africa · Economic inclusion · Post-independence

20.1 Introduction

Africa is currently receiving a great deal of attention from people all over the world not just as a result of its many accomplishments and its dynamic nature but also because of its significant challenges as articulated in the introduction. This is the case not only as a result of its successes but also because of its problems. The number of people living in poverty has decreased, indicators of human development have increased, and flourishing social movements are contributing to the change of communities and bringing attention to stigmatized issues and groups of people. In addition, the number of people living in poverty in the USA has decreased by more than one million since 1990 (Das & Espinoza, 2020). The requirement of social and economic inclusion is currently at the forefront of discussion across the continent's successful implementation of new laws and programs, which has led to the expansion of technological development to previously inaccessible regions. This is since

D. Mhlanga (✉)
University of Johannesburg, College of Business and Economics, Johannesburg, South Africa

E. Ndhlovu
Vaal University of Technology, Vanderbijlpark, South Africa

D. Mhlanga, E. Ndhlovu (eds.), *Economic Inclusion in Post-Independence Africa*, Advances in African Economic, Social and Political Development,
https://doi.org/10.1007/978-3-031-31431-5_20

new laws and programs have led to the expansion of technological innovation to previously inaccessible regions.

This is happening as a direct result of the spread of technical innovation to previously inaccessible locations, which has brought about this current situation. During the last few decades, some countries located in Africa have been at the forefront of the movement toward progress. For example, throughout the past 10 years, more laws and regulations aimed at advancing gender equality have been put into action in Africa than in any other region on the entire Earth (Das & Espinoza, 2020). On the other hand, favorable gains have been dispersed unequally across Africa, just as they have been across the rest of the world, with many regions and populations falling further and further behind. This is even though Africa is one of the world's most populous continents (Söderbaum & Taylor, 2018; Anwar, 2019). There are a few different hypotheses that could explain why this is the case. As a result of the expansion of digital technology, individuals who, for instance, do not have access to mobile phones or the Internet are at risk of slipping even further behind.

20.2 Infrastructure Development, Economic Inclusion, and Sustainable Development

Investments in infrastructural development have been observed to result from better lives across societies across the world. This is particularly the case where infrastructural development is pursued in such a manner that does not pose risks, such as the possibility that the most vulnerable individuals will have their lands unreasonably taken from them or that damage will be done to the environment or to the means of subsistence that people rely on. However, these risks have been outweighed by the benefits of improved infrastructure. To put it another way, there are compromises to be made. Other groups and regions that are afflicted with state and societal instability tend to lag in a spectrum of development outcomes, whereas certain regions can experience a concentration of improvements in education and health (Ndhlovu, 2020a). This is in contrast to other regions that can experience a concentration of improvements in education and health. There is a potential for a concentration of advancements in education and health in particular places. In the most recent few years, there has been a growing international movement for enhancing and scaling up economic inclusion for the world's poorest people. This movement has been gaining momentum on a global scale. This movement is going place in every single country on the planet.

At this point, consideration is being given to the Sustainable Development Goals, often known as SDGs. To "end poverty in all its manifestations everywhere by 2030" and to "address equitable and sustainable growth" are the aims of the Sustainable Development Goals (SDGs) (SDG 8). There is currently an emphasis placed on making significant efforts (Andrews et al., 2021). It is more crucial than it has ever been to establish an economy that is both sustainable and inclusive, with the objective of "leaving no one behind," particularly on the African continent. This is because "leaving no one behind" is the goal of the United Nations Sustainable Development Goals (SDGs). As the process of developing economic inclusion initiatives for the poorest unfolds, a story of growing great hopes and enormous pessimism is taking shape. Even though transformative economic growth will ultimately be the most important factor in reducing poverty, it is essential to recognize that this kind of growth is not necessarily inclusive and does not always reach the people who have the lowest incomes. This is something that needs to be taken into consideration.

When attempting to enhance economic inclusion for those with the lowest incomes, it is necessary to recognize the existence of "poverty traps." It is also vital to highlight the reality that the removal of many barriers through the implementation of a multidimensional response is required to unleash the productive potential of individuals who are now living in poverty. It is only possible to achieve this by simultaneously removing several obstacles (Andrews et al., 2021). The limitations imposed by households, communities, economies, and institutions might have an effect that is disproportionately unfavorable on certain subgroups of the population, such as women, young people, individuals with disabilities, and people who have been uprooted from their homes. At its foundation, the social and economic exclusion is about power relations, in which societies develop sophisticated systems to perpetuate current social structures and protect the status quo. This is done to maintain the status quo. The status quo can only be preserved by preserving the social institutions that are already in place (Heleta, 2018; Thombs, 2019). One of the methods by which communities place some groups in a subservient position and others in a dominating status is by the procedures of assigning status based on attitudes, beliefs, perceptions, and behaviors. One of how communities establish the supremacy of certain groups over other groups is by using hierarchical systems. This category of behavior includes things like societal stigmas, rituals, and superstitions, to name a few examples. Under this interpretation, the word "structures and systems" might be understood to encompass not only families and communities but also judicial systems, labor markets, land markets, and knowledge systems. According to Das and Espinoza (2020), it is also very essential to emphasize how structures and processes mutually support one another and are bolstered by formal and informal institutions. This is an extremely crucial point to bring up. Due to the dominance of belief systems, superstitions, social stigmas, and other behaviors, certain groups are barred from being included in a variety of contexts all over the world. This exclusion occurs in a variety of settings (World Bank, 2017; Gumede, 2018). Fear is instilled via actions of intimidation and harassment, which prevents some groups from realizing their full potential and puts them in their place.

Fear is another technique that can be utilized to exercise social control. In addition, according to the norms of society, males and females can be delegated to perform different jobs, and some actions or physiological processes might be seen as dirty. Other practices, such as stigma and shunning, may also contribute to the invisibility of groups, such as persons who have impairments or those who have albinism. Other examples include those who have albinism. People who have albinism and people who have disabilities are two examples of members of these groups. In a similar vein, certain societies might try to hide the existence of people who have disabilities in their midst. Due to the lack of exposure, there is a possibility that these organizations will not be included in the official statistics. This is just one of the potential repercussions of this situation. This is merely one of the many scenarios that could occur. This suggests that both on the level of the family and the level of the nation, they will continue to be hidden and disregarded. Most of the time, discriminatory actions such as these are sustained because they are sanctioned by religion or by individuals who interpret the scriptures of other religions. This can be both literal and figurative (World Bank, 2017; Andrews et al., 2021).

People who have a sexual identity that does not conform are commonly criminalized and alienated from society in many different cultures. This is because of the stigma that surrounds sexual identity. It is common practice to cite various religious texts to defend the practice of criminalization and exclusion. Persons who have a sexual identity that does not conform are frequently criminalized and excluded from society in some societies. In other cultures, people who have a sexual identity that does not comply are not criminalized. Beliefs concerning cleanliness and pollution generally exclude populations, either at certain periods or at certain times of the month; taboos regarding menstruation women are prevalent in a lot of different regions all over the world. In general, these activities are examples of the types of strategies that are used to continue to sustain social control and order in their respective societies (Das & Espinoza, 2020). In addition to providing an overarching summary of the content that has been presented throughout the book, this chapter will introduce the ideas of economic and social inclusion in the context of Africa.

20.3 What Is the Meaning of Economic Inclusion?

As detailed in Chaps. 1 and 2, an encompassing market economy guarantees that all people, irrespective of their gender, national origin, family history, age, or other situational variables over which they have no control, have full and equitable access to employment, financial sectors, entrepreneurship development, and, more generally, economic opportunity. This is accomplished by ensuring that everyone has full and equal access to employment opportunities, regardless of their gender, nationality, family history, age, or other situational factors. It is essential to promote economic inclusion, also known as the expansion of economic opportunities for disadvantaged social groups, to ensure a smooth and productive transition to a market economy (Ndhlovu, 2020b). Economic inclusion refers to the expansion of economic opportunities for underprivileged social groups (Lagarde, 2014; Lawal et al., 2021). When it comes down to it, supporting a market-based system is more of a question of how effectively (human) resources are distributed than it is a matter of opinion for social policy.

As a consequence of this, openness is essential for an economic model that can be maintained over time. Therefore, economic inclusion is an important aspect of a transition because it encourages people to participate in activities that promote economic growth such as work, education, and other endeavors if they are allowed to do so. This is especially true for those who have been economically marginalized in the past (Lawal et al., 2021). The economic inclusion report, which is titled "The State of Economic Inclusion in 2021," defines economic inclusion as "the consistent integration of people and household incomes into larger overall social and economic development practices, by attempting to tackle numerous constraints or institutional obstructions encountered by the poor at various levels, including the household, such as human and physical capabilities, the neighbourhood, such as social norms, the local economy, such as direct connections to markets and segregation of labour."

Economic inclusion, from the perspective of structuralists, is more than simply taking part in global economic systems; rather, it also implies profiting from such systems. In addition, they contend that participation in the global economy may increase job levels rather than reduce them. Participation in the global economy through employment is the path to reducing poverty or developing civilization, contrary to the widespread belief that this is not the case. However, for a sizeable portion of the global labor population, the conditions of this inclusion can cause and perpetuate poverty. The most important question should not be about whether or if there are linkages to the global economy; rather, it should be on the sociological and political power dynamics that emerge because of these relationships.

20.4 Explanation of the Meaning of Social Inclusion

As stated in the book's introduction, the idea of social inclusion, which is also known as "inclusion," has been receiving more and more attention recently in the context of discussions on larger policy issues and difficulties pertinent to development. A condensed version of social inclusion is inclusion. The act of making it simpler for individuals and groups to participate in society is what's meant to be understood as "social inclusion." The phrase "making it easier for people and groups to engage in society" is what the practice of "making it easier for individuals and groups to participate in society" refers to (World Bank, 2013; Das & Espinoza, 2020). The majority of debates addressing social inclusion in Africa have taken place within the context of reducing poverty and offering aid to people who are suffering as a result of humanitarian disasters. This is because these are the primary issues at play in the continent. These conversations are being driven by the reality that, despite the significant strides that have been made toward eradicating poverty, it is estimated that more than 400 million people are still living in poverty. This is a problem that has been exacerbated by recent economic conditions. Even though social exclusion can be both a process and an outcome, the result of being excluded from society is poverty. Poverty is the result of being removed from society. The processes of exclusion can have long-term implications on the mindsets, psyches, and dignity of subordinate or excluded groups, and this exclusion, in turn,

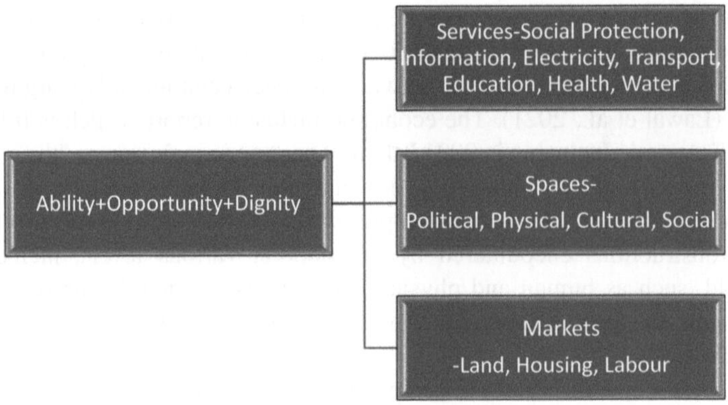

Fig. 20.1 Social inclusion framework. (Source: Authors)

undermines the ability of these groups to access the opportunities that have been made available to them (Beegle & Christiaensen, 2019). In the annals of human history, three of the most odious examples of social segregation were the practice of untouchability, the institution of slavery, and the system of apartheid in South Africa (Das & Espinoza, 2020). Figure 20.1 presents an abstract of the social inclusion framework for your viewing pleasure.

A significant component of what is meant by "social inclusion" is access to a variety of services, places, and markets. This is demonstrated in Fig. 20.1 which was provided earlier. Individuals' capacities, opportunities, and respect for their dignity are all essential components of social inclusion.

20.5 The Promotion of Economic and Social Inclusion in Africa: Who Will Be Left Behind?

Changes on the social, economic, and political levels are currently taking place across the African continent. The transitions that are described in the section are based on some overarching themes, such as changes in the population and how those changes relate to the buildup of human capital.

20.5.1 Trends in Population Distribution and the Development of Human Capital

Even though fertility rates are dropping in practically every country, the World Bank (2020) maintains that Africa is seeing the world's highest rate of demographic expansion. According to some predictions, by the year 2050, there will be 362 million young people on the continent who are between the ages of 15 and 24. At the time, fewer than 50% of the people living in this region are younger than the age of 25. The United Nations Department of Economic and Social Affairs Population Division (2017) reports that the populations of several African countries will age simultaneously. It is anticipated that by the year 2050, the population of Africans over the age of 60 will have more than quadrupled, having increased from 69 million in 2017 to 226 million. Integration of older generations of Africans is not currently a major priority because the process of integrating younger generations of Africans is currently the most pressing problem that the region needs to address. On the other hand, if the appropriate policies and opportunities are taken advantage of, Africa's rapidly expanding young population may be able to significantly accelerate economic growth and further reduce levels of poverty across the continent (Das & Espinoza, 2020).

Even while Africa has witnessed advances in health and life span, just as it has seen increases in fertility, the mortality rate for children under the age of 5 is still extremely high. The percentage of children who make it to the age of 5 is seen as an important indication of welfare, but it also has other implications. There is a correlation, for instance, between higher fertility rates and higher rates of infant and child mortality. Countries that have high rates of child mortality have a tough time investing in human capital because they are preoccupied with the most basic requirement of keeping children alive. This makes it difficult for these countries to compete internationally. According to estimations provided by the United Nations (UN), the Our World in Data project, and AfricaInData.org, the rate of child mortality has dramatically dropped between the years 1980 and 2015. This trend was observed across the continent of Africa. Between the years 1990 and 2016, the number of people living in Africa fell at a rate that was the highest among all the regions. Despite these advancements, Africa continues to have the highest infant mortality rate in the world, with 78 fatalities for every 1000 live births. This statistic pertains to children under the age of 5. To put it another way, 1 child in every 13 does not make it to their 5th birthday. In other words, the mortality rate is extremely high (Suzuki & Kashiwase 2017; Das & Espinoza, 2020). There is a wide range of variation in the rates of mortality among children under the age of 5 across countries, with unstable regimes having the highest rates overall.

20.5.2 Education Inside Africa

In addition, Africa has made substantial advancements in the field of education. However, like in other regions of the world, there are still large disparities in educational attainment depending on a variety of identifiers (Pesando, 2021; Andrews et al., 2021). The gross enrollment ratio in elementary schools across the region increased from 68% in the year 1990 to 98% in the year 2015, while the number of kids enrolled increased from 63 million to 152 million (Andrews et al., 2021). Despite the increase in the number of children attending primary school, there are still an estimated 52.3 million children of primary and lower secondary school age who are not enrolled in any type of educational program. It is believed that 45% of the world's children between the ages of 6 and 14 and 7 and 15 are not enrolled in any form of formal education. These children range in age from 6 to 14 and 7 to 15 (Bashir et al., 2018; Andrews et al., 2021). Even if reading is the most important educational goal, there are still some people who do not have the opportunity to read. In the USA, there is a significant gender gap when it comes to reading levels between men and women. The gender difference in Western Africa is the largest, while the gender gap in Southern Africa is the smallest (Das & Espinoza, 2020).

When gender is considered in conjunction with other identifiers, people are put at an additional disadvantage (Ndhlovu & Tembo, 2020). This is true not only in the educational sector but also in other areas of life. Demonstrate, with the help of census data, that female members of ethnic minorities in Senegal and Sierra Leone are at a disadvantage in terms of literacy, the completion of primary school, and graduation from high school. According to the findings of Taş et al. (2014), the likelihood of a woman in Senegal completing primary school is reduced by 10 percentage points simply because she is a woman, by 1.6 percentage points because she is a member of an ethnic minority, and by an additional 3.8 percentage points because she is a woman who is a member of an ethnic minority. As a consequence of this, the probability of a woman from a group that is considered an ethnic minority in Senegal completing primary school is approximately 15.4 percentage points lower than the probability of a man from a group that is considered an ethnic majority.

Despite the significant progress that has been accomplished in South Africa since the end of apartheid, the educational outcomes for South Africans of black and colored descent continue to be terrible. A hundred years afterward, the black population is still not at the same level of education as the white population did in 1920 when the white population had almost completed all 12 years of schooling. This ensures that the legacy of South Africa's racial conflicts in the educational system, which is still a key contributor to inequality and poverty, is not forgotten (Donohue & Bornman, 2014; World Bank, 2018). The Systematic Country Diagnostic (SCD) for Benin reaches similar conclusions, stating that native children are put at a disadvantage and leave school at an earlier age as a direct result of the lack of mother language education in elementary schools (World Bank, 2017; Das & Espinoza, 2020).

20.5.3 Transitions in the Economy, People Living in Poverty, and Opportunities for Work

Since the 1990s, there has been a considerable drop in the number of people who are regarded as being poor because of their living conditions (Das & Espinoza, 2020). On the other hand, throughout the same period, the total number of people living in poverty has increased by a substantial amount overall. This trend can be seen throughout the world. Although the percentage of the African population that lives in poverty has steadily decreased from 57% in 1990 to 41* in 2015, the total number of people who are living in poverty has increased from approximately 278 million to over 413 million. This is even though the percentage of the African population that lives in poverty has steadily decreased. This is even though the percentage of people living in poverty in Africa has been continuously declining (Das & Espinoza, 2020). There is a substantial gap in performance levels between the many countries that make up Africa, which may be attributable to a variety of different causes. The most significant of these factors is the endowment of natural resources, the fragility of the system, and the violence that exists inside it. However, there are further aspects to consider as well (Beegle et al., 2016; Das & Espinoza, 2020).

20.5.4 Technology Can Boost Social Inclusion But Leave Some Behind

The age of technology has officially begun on a worldwide scale, and we who are currently living in it are in the process of ushering it in, according to Calderon et al. (2019). However, whether these organizations have access to the knowledge and resources that apply to their situations will determine the positive effects that technology has on countries, regions, communities, and families. Even though it seems as though Africa has jumped ahead of the curve when it comes to the digital economy in many different sectors, there is still a lot of diversity among the states. For instance, the overall number of mobile cellular subscriptions is still much higher in nonfragile countries, even though the number of subscriptions has increased somewhat more quickly in fragile countries. This is because nonfragile nations have had more resources to spend on their infrastructure. This is because less susceptible nations have been able to make more investments in their infrastructure (Mhlanga, 2022a, b; Mpofu & Mhlanga, 2022).

Like this, the financial technology industry, sometimes referred to as "fintech," has experienced substantial expansion across Africa. Twenty-one percent of Africans currently have mobile money accounts, and the number of these accounts has doubled since 2014. The proportion of African residents with mobile money accounts has grown since 2014. This region makes up the biggest percentage of any on the entire planet (Mhlanga, 2020, 2022b). The M-PESA mobile money transfer system is one of the most well-known and well-established uses of financial technology in Africa. It is also one of the most well-known uses of financial technology on the continent (Mhlanga, 2022c). The results of a new World Bank study on the health of the labor market in Africa indicate that digital technology may also can spur employment growth in the region (Choi et al., 2019; Mhlanga, 2022c). Nearly 60% of the population has Internet access in this nation alone in Africa, and there is a significant correlation between this figure and the level of money the nation receives.

As one might anticipate, the amount of the population in each African country that has access to the Internet is closely related to the country's degree of affluence. This is because more developed countries have more readily available Internet connections (Das & Espinoza, 2020). According to Research Center's Spring 2017 Global Attitudes Survey, people with higher incomes and educational levels were found to be more likely to use cell phones. Das and Espinoza (2020) indicate that the findings of the survey showed that those had a higher likelihood of using cell phones, the study's findings showed that individuals were more likely to use mobile phones. People without cell phones have a far reduced range of options available to them for getting to various marketplaces, services, and sites, and these people are greatly disadvantaged (Mhlanga, 2022c).

20.6 Politics and Social Movements in Africa

When individuals or groups that feel excluded demonstrate their agency through social and political activity, progress toward social inclusion is frequently made. Many African nations have experienced an evolution in this type of participation, and the continent is observing this pattern (Ake, 2019; Mhlanga, 2022d). Voting is less likely among African youth than it is among their elders, and results from the Afrobarometer survey indicate that youth political participation has decreased over the previous 15 years. Das and Espinoza (2020) point out that recent polls show a decline in participation in formal political and civic processes, notably among young people and women in Africa. The situation is complicated by the fact that younger Africans are less likely to vote than their elders. According to research by Lekalake and Gyimah-Boadi (2016), young Africans are less likely than older Africans to engage in civic life, and young African women are even less likely to do so than young African men. Lekalake and Gyimah-Boadi (2016) also discovered that compared to their male counterparts, female respondents expressed significantly less interest in current issues and the discussions that surrounded them. This downward trend in participation in formal political processes could be due to several things, such as disenchantment or a decline in confidence in the mechanisms themselves. Additionally, it can imply that youngsters use a range of media to express their preferences, with social media's importance in this context garnering special attention.

The Internet provides a venue for groups that would not otherwise be able to express themselves through conventional forms of digital media because it is feasible to stay anonymous online. In comparison with their older counterparts of the same age, young Africans are far more active on social media and other digital platforms. Among other things, the growth of social movements shows that young people can use a variety of civic avenues to address issues that are important to them. However, general unhappiness with the state may be indicated by a prospective dissatisfaction with political processes. Social movements all over Africa are raising awareness of the value of social inclusion despite what may be a declining level of participation in formal political processes. It is well known that social and political movements have a long and distinguished history in Africa. The illustrious movements for independence and decolonization, the significant academic movements against Eurocentrism, the movements for peace and civil liberties, and the movements against various economic practices are examples of movements of this kind. The "Fees Must Fall" movement was started by students in South Africa in 2015–2016, highlighting the fact that young people are politically engaged despite not participating in formal political processes (Cini, 2019; Griffiths, 2019).

20.7 How Can Africa Accomplish Its Objective of Complete Participation in the Economic System?

The Sustainable Development Goals are possibly the most well-known global policy framework for thinking about the problem of inclusive development, according to Dörffel and Schuhmann (2022), as will be highlighted in Chap. 2 (SDGs). These objectives are designed to offer a comprehensive collection of concepts, objectives, and indicators to motivate international action in support of development that produces more equitable and long-lasting results. Dörffel and Schuhmann (2022) argue that they span a broad range, from environmental sustainability to poverty alleviation, even though concrete policy choices are yet largely unclear. One advantage of the SDGs is that they gave political priority to several development goals that had not previously gotten it. Figure 20.1 in this study illustrates a few strategies that could enhance economic inclusion in Africa.

The efforts that can help to increase economic inclusion in Africa are listed in Fig. 20.2. which can be found above. These programs promote "more and better jobs and livelihoods, increased financial literacy and better payment systems, economic inclusion as a means of strengthening women's empowerment, initiatives to strengthen financial inclusion, and gender-conscious program delivery."

Briefly stated, the book *Economic and Social Inclusion in Post-independence Africa: An Inclusive Approach to Economic Development* is made up of 20 chapters, each of which examines a different aspect of economic and social inclusion, such as financial inclusion, digital financial inclusion, and gender, among other issues. This book will be interesting to governments, development organizations, and nongovernmental organizations with a focus on development, students, and college professors.

20.8 Conclusion

Africa is currently drawing a lot of attention from people all over the world not only as a result of the numerous achievements it has accomplished and the degree of vitality it possesses but also as a result of the significant challenges that it is currently confronted with. This attention is being drawn not only because of the numerous accomplishments it has accomplished and the degree of vitality it possesses but

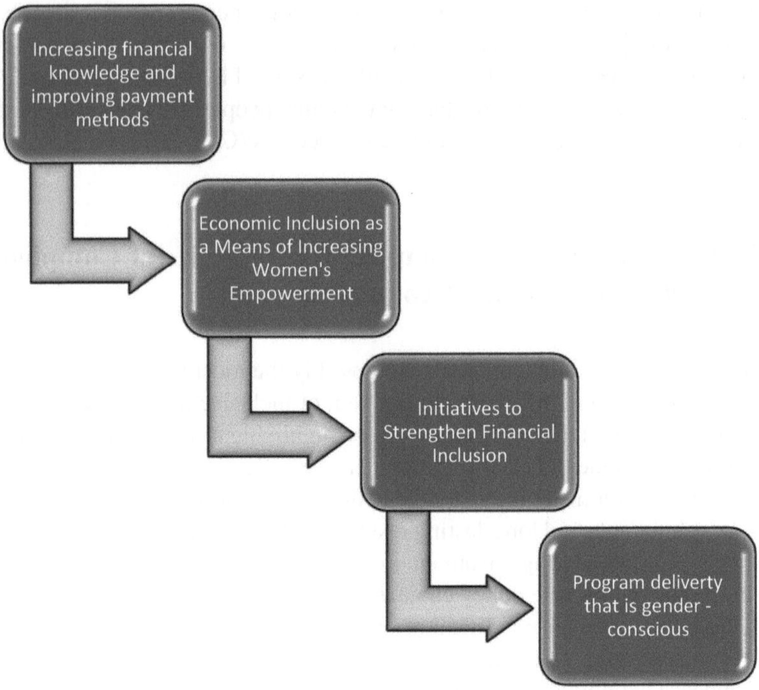

Fig. 20.2 How to make economic inclusion work in Africa (Source: Authors)

also because of the significant challenges that it is currently confronted with. The number of people who are living in poverty has gone down, human development indices have gone up, and active social movements are assisting in the transformation of communities and bringing attention to stigmatized groups of people and situations. The necessity of economic and social inclusion is currently at the forefront of discussion across the continent, thanks to the implementation of new laws and programs, which has led to the expansion of technological innovation to previously inaccessible regions. This is because new laws and programs have led to the expansion of technological innovation to previously inaccessible regions. This is because new laws and initiatives have enabled technological innovation to spread to locations that were previously inaccessible to it. This is happening as a direct result of the spread of technological innovation to previously unreachable regions, which has resulted in the current position, which has brought about this circumstance. Throughout the continent's history, only a select few of the continent's countries have been at the vanguard of the charge toward higher levels of development. The purpose of this chapter is twofold: first, to provide a conclusion to the book *Economic and Social Inclusion in Post-independence Africa*, and second, to define the path that the book will take moving forward. Reading this chapter will allow the reader to attain both goals successfully. In conclusion of this chapter, a concise summary of each of the subsequent chapters in the book was shown.

References

Ake, C. (2019). The new world order: A view from Africa. In *Whose world order?* (pp. 19–42). Routledge.

Andrews, C., de Montesquiou, A., Sánchez, I. A., Dutta, P. V., Samaranayake, S., Heisey, J., et al. (2021). *The state of economic inclusion report 2021: The potential to scale*. World Bank Publications.

Anwar, M. A. (2019). Connecting South Africa: ICTs, uneven development, and poverty debates. In *The geography of South Africa* (pp. 261–267). Springer.

Bashir, S., Lockheed, M., Ninan, E., & Tan, J-P. (2018). Facing Forward: Schooling for Learning in Africa. © Washington, DC: World Bank. http://hdl.handle.net/10986/29377

Beegle, K., Christiaensen, L., Dabalen, A., & Gaddis, I. (2016). Poverty in a rising Africa. World Bank Publications.

Beegle, K., & Christiaensen, L. (Eds.). (2019). *Accelerating poverty reduction in Africa*. World Bank Publications.

Calderon, D., Nguyen, M. L., Mezger, A., Kathiria, A., Müller, F., Nguyen, V., ... & Pritchard, J. K. (2019). Landscape of stimulation-responsive chromatin across diverse human immune cells. *Nature Genetics, 51*(10), 1494–1505.

Cini, L. (2019). Disrupting the neoliberal university in South Africa: The# FeesMustFall movement in 2015. *Current Sociology, 67*(7), 942–959.

Choi, N., Bern, M., Elias, D. O., McGinley, R. H., Rosenthal, M. F., & Hebets, E. A. (2019). A mismatch between signal transmission efficacy and mating success calls into question the function of complex signals. *Animal Behaviour, 158*, 77–88.

Das, M. B., & Espinoza, S. A. (2020). *Inclusion matters in Africa*. Available online:. https://openknowledge.worldbank.org/bitstream/handle/10986/32528/IM-Africa.pdf

Donohue, D., & Bornman, J. (2014). The challenges of realising inclusive education in South Africa. *South African Journal of Education, 34*(2).

Dörffel, C., & Schuhmann, S. (2022). What is inclusive development? Introducing the multidimensional inclusiveness index. *Social Indicators Research, 162*(3), 1117–1148.

Griffiths, D. (2019). # FeesMustFall and the decolonised university in South Africa: Tensions and opportunities in a globalising world. *International Journal of Educational Research, 94*, 143–149.

Gumede, V. (2018). Social policy for inclusive development in Africa. *Third World Quarterly, 39*(1), 122–139.

Heleta, S. (2018). Decolonizing knowledge in South Africa: Dismantling the 'pedagogy of big lies'. *Ufahamu: A Journal of African Studies, 40*(2).

Lagarde, C. (2014, May). Economic inclusion and financial integrity—An address to the conference on inclusive capitalism. In speech presented at the Conference on Inclusive Capitalism (Vol. 27).

Lawal, M. A., Shalaby, R., Chima, C., Vuong, W., Hrabok, M., Gusnowski, A., ... & Agyapong, V. I. (2021). COVID-19 pandemic: stress, anxiety, and depression levels highest amongst indigenous peoples in Alberta. *Behavioral Sciences, 11*(9), 115.

Lekalake, R., & Gyimah-Boadi, E. (2016). Does less engaged mean less empowered? Political participation lags among African youth, especially women.

Mhlanga, D. (2020). Industry 4.0 in finance: The impact of artificial intelligence (ai) on digital financial inclusion. *International Journal of Financial Studies, 8*(3), 45.

Mhlanga, D. (2022a). Prospects and challenges of digital financial inclusion/Fintech Innovation in the fourth industrial revolution. *Digital Financial Inclusion*, 163–182.

Mhlanga, D. (2022b). Financial inclusion and the fourth industrial revolution. In *Digital financial inclusion* (pp. 39–57). Palgrave Macmillan.

Mhlanga, D. (2022c). Selected digital financial inclusion success stories across developing economies. In *Digital financial inclusion. Palgrave studies in impact finance*. Palgrave Macmillan. https://doi.org/10.1007/978-3-031-16687-7_17

Mhlanga, D. (2022d). Digital financial inclusion, and the way forward for emerging markets: Towards sustainable development. In *Digital financial inclusion. Palgrave studies in impact finance*. Palgrave Macmillan. https://doi.org/10.1007/978-3-031-16687-7_18

Mpofu, F. Y., & Mhlanga, D. (2022). Digital financial inclusion, digital financial services tax and financial inclusion in the fourth industrial revolution era in Africa. *Economies, 10*(8), 184.

Ndhlovu, E. (2020a). Decolonisation of development: Samir Amin and the struggle for an alternative development approach in Africa. *The Saharan Journal, 1*(1), 87–111.

Ndhlovu, E. (2020b). The migration-livelihoods Nexus: Emerging opportunities, emerging challenges in rural Zimbabwe. *Yonsei Journal of International Studies, 12*(2), 24–40.

Ndhlovu, E., & Tembo, A. (2020). Gendered socio-economic implications of the COVID-19 pandemic in rural Zimbabwe. *BizEcons Quarterly, 12*, 21–40.

Pesando, L. M. (2021). Educational assortative mating in sub-Saharan Africa: Compositional changes and implications for household wealth inequality. *Demography, 58*(2), 571–602.

Söderbaum, F., & Taylor, I. (2018). *Regionalism and uneven development in Southern Africa: The case of the Maputo Development Corridor*. Routledge.

Suzuki & Kashiwase (2017). Despite remarkable progress, 15,000 children and 800 women still die every day mostly of preventable or treatable causes. https://blogs.worldbank.org/opendata/despite-remarkable-progress-15000-children-and-800-women-still-die-every-day-mostly

Taş, E. O., Reimão, M. E., & Orlando, M. B. (2014). Gender, ethnicity, and cumulative disadvantage in education outcomes. *World Development, 64*, 538–553.

Thombs, R. P. (2019). When democracy meets energy transitions: A typology of social power and energy system scale. *Energy Research & Social Science, 52*, 159–168.

World Bank. (2013). *Inclusion matters: The Foundation for Shared Prosperity*. World Bank. Available online: https://openknowledge.worldbank.org/handle/10986/16195

World Bank. (2017). *Social Inclusion in Africa*. Available online: https://www.worldbank.org/en/region/afr/brief/social-inclusion-in-africa

World Bank. (2018). Global Economic Prospects, January 2018: Broad-Based Upturn, but for How Long?. The World Bank.

World Bank. (2020). Global economic prospects, June 2020. The World Bank.

Index

A
Access to finance, 108, 162, 168, 170–171, 208, 226, 233, 238, 251, 263, 274, 277, 278, 333
Adoption, 13, 27, 28, 37, 40, 46, 61, 74, 94, 125, 140, 156, 158–160, 258–260, 262, 264–270, 288, 295, 305, 314, 316, 336, 348, 349, 351
Africa, 23, 46, 60, 104, 124, 150, 176, 180, 199, 232, 285, 299, 312, 361, 365
Agribusiness, 14, 229–230, 233, 261, 273–291
Agriculture, 10, 13, 60, 104–107, 109, 110, 150, 223, 226, 229, 232, 241–243, 246–249, 277–281, 283–289, 291, 302, 348
Artificial intelligence (AI), 125, 126, 168, 174, 258–270, 338, 348–361

C
Central bank digital currency, 168, 174
Challenges, 12–15, 33, 34, 36, 60, 69, 70, 72, 76, 82, 84, 85, 88, 104, 106–112, 114, 119, 124–144, 154, 155, 157, 159–161, 170, 176, 181, 199, 200, 202, 208, 215, 216, 222, 224, 225, 228–231, 233, 238–240, 245, 248, 251, 258–260, 262–270, 273, 274, 278, 282–288, 291, 302, 303, 307, 312, 319, 324, 325, 330, 331, 334, 335, 337, 351, 353, 356, 360, 365, 375, 376
Covid, 22, 27, 31, 82, 84, 85, 88, 95, 98, 99, 116, 117, 124–127, 131–133, 137, 141, 163, 180, 330, 333, 335, 336, 338, 349, 351, 353, 358, 360

D
Development, 2–4, 6, 9, 10, 13, 15, 22–24, 29, 32–36, 39, 48, 51, 60–68, 77, 82, 83, 87, 89, 92, 93, 95–97, 100, 104, 108, 111, 117, 124, 126, 128–130, 132, 133, 135, 136, 142, 143, 150–153, 159–162, 167–170, 172, 173, 175, 180, 183, 191, 198–201, 204, 207, 214, 215, 221, 223–225, 227, 229, 230, 233, 238, 241–243, 246, 248, 249, 251, 252, 261, 262, 265–270, 274, 276–281, 284–286, 289, 296–303, 306, 313, 316–323, 330, 331, 334–339, 341, 353, 360, 365–371, 375, 376
Digital economy, 8, 11, 14, 60, 81–88, 90, 92, 95, 99, 124, 128, 132, 141, 268, 330–342, 373
Digital finance, 74, 117, 127, 131, 132, 134, 135, 137, 169, 170, 172, 263, 265, 266, 268
Digital financial inclusion, 11, 12, 14, 82, 87, 88, 90, 91, 94, 96, 124–144, 163, 258, 262, 263, 330–342, 375
Digital financial literacy, 12, 124–144
Digital financial service taxes, 82–100
Digital literacy, 11, 27, 98, 126, 128–129, 134, 135, 137, 141, 142, 300
Digital transformation, 15, 87, 91, 94, 118, 125, 126, 133, 134, 137, 141, 198, 215, 216, 334, 335, 348–360
Dynamic common correlated effect (DCCE), 187–192
Dynamic seemingly unrelated regression (DSUR), 12, 188–192

D. Mhlanga, E. Ndhlovu (eds.), *Economic Inclusion in Post-Independence Africa*, Advances in African Economic, Social and Political Development, https://doi.org/10.1007/978-3-031-31431-5

E

Economic growth, 2, 24, 29, 32–34, 39, 46, 66, 68, 82, 87–91, 95, 104, 105, 112–116, 125–127, 130–136, 142, 150, 152–154, 158, 163, 169, 180, 182, 233, 248, 258, 280, 331, 339, 342, 367, 369, 371
Economic inclusion, 2–4, 10, 11, 13, 21–40, 68, 72, 150, 152, 365–369, 375, 376
Education, 2, 4, 6–8, 12, 14, 24, 25, 29, 30, 32, 33, 36, 37, 39, 48, 60, 62, 63, 65, 67, 69, 70, 73, 75, 76, 89, 98, 108, 111, 112, 131, 133, 143, 151, 155, 156, 163, 169, 198–201, 204, 209, 211, 215, 223, 226, 227, 277, 279, 280, 282, 285–286, 291, 296–309, 315, 318, 319, 321–325, 366, 369, 371–372
Excluded, 4, 6, 8, 13, 35, 37, 38, 46, 63, 64, 68, 69, 71–76, 87, 88, 105–113, 115–117, 119, 124, 126, 127, 130, 131, 136, 143, 150, 152, 153, 157, 159, 160, 169, 226–229, 231, 233, 239, 241, 243, 244, 247, 259, 260, 262–270, 330, 340, 368, 369, 374

F

Farmer, 104–112, 114, 117, 119, 158, 160, 222–233, 239, 241–251, 261, 263, 280, 282, 285–288, 290, 291
Financial inclusion, 10–13, 22, 27, 31–33, 35–38, 40, 74, 82–100, 104–119, 124–137, 139, 140, 142, 143, 150–164, 167–176, 221–233, 238–252, 258–260, 262–270, 330–333, 336–342, 375
Fintech, 8, 27, 37, 38, 87, 88, 98, 118, 119, 124–128, 132, 135–137, 142, 161, 168, 169, 171–175, 258, 262, 267, 332, 333, 336, 373
Foreign direct investment (FDI), 179–192
Fourth Industrial Revolution Taxation, 342

G

Gender, 2, 3, 6, 7, 10, 12–14, 23–27, 32, 35–37, 39, 40, 46, 50, 61, 62, 64, 65, 69, 77, 110–112, 125, 131, 133–135, 150, 153, 155, 169, 171, 174, 198, 201, 204–213, 223, 269, 273–276, 278–280, 282, 286, 296–308, 312–316, 318, 320–325, 330, 339, 340, 342, 366, 368, 372, 375
Ghana, 12, 13, 22, 55, 90, 105, 115, 130, 135, 155, 156, 161, 163, 183, 198–216, 340
Gross domestic product (GDP), 36, 51–55, 84, 95, 104, 131, 135, 151, 182–186, 189–192, 317, 337

H

Healthcare sector, 15, 348–361

I

Inclusion, 4, 13, 22–24, 26, 32, 33, 39, 46, 47, 49, 54, 55, 60, 63–65, 67–70, 73, 74, 76, 104, 106, 107, 110, 114, 116, 118, 119, 127, 128, 135, 142, 144, 198–216, 233, 243–248, 260, 270, 300, 301, 318, 331–333, 337–339, 354, 369
Inclusive development, 9, 11, 13, 35, 82–100, 131, 238–240, 242–252, 284, 375
Information communication technology (ICT), 25, 27, 46–55, 61, 74, 83, 352

L

Land recipients, 13, 222–226, 228, 229, 231–233
Land reform, 13, 221–233, 243–245, 248, 249, 274, 277, 290
Lives, 2, 7, 22–40, 48, 61–64, 67, 72, 73, 76, 99, 108, 111, 125, 131, 156, 163, 168, 170, 172, 174, 199, 200, 227, 275, 300, 307, 313, 314, 317, 319, 321, 330, 334, 342, 348, 354, 357, 359, 366, 371–374
Local authorities & women's representation, 14, 311–325
Long term care, 15, 348–360

M

Market size, 181, 184, 185, 188, 189, 191
Mobile money, 8, 11, 27, 31, 37, 38, 82, 87–89, 95, 97, 98, 106, 108, 110–112, 115, 116, 119, 124, 128, 130, 131, 133, 135, 136, 140, 152, 153, 155, 159–162, 330, 332, 337, 339, 340, 373
Mobile money taxes, 11, 82–100, 141

N

Natural resources, 7, 12, 26, 51–55, 181, 184–186, 188–192, 373

P
Peasants, 13, 238, 239, 241, 245, 247–251
Political inclusion, 11, 46–55
Political risk, 12, 180–192
Poor, 4, 12–14, 21–40, 47, 48, 88, 94, 98, 105–107, 111–113, 116, 117, 119, 125, 128, 131, 133, 135, 136, 143, 153–155, 158, 159, 161, 168–170, 172, 174, 176, 199, 200, 208, 215, 223, 224, 228, 231, 233, 238–240, 244, 245, 247–249, 263, 267, 280, 284, 288, 301, 312, 313, 318–319, 321–324, 330–333, 337, 338, 340, 342, 369, 372
Post-independence, 2–15, 24, 199, 200, 214–216, 365–376
Post-independence development, 149–164
Poverty, 1, 2, 4, 6, 7, 10, 15, 22, 24, 26, 28, 30, 31, 33–35, 37, 39, 40, 48, 60, 62–64, 67, 68, 88, 89, 96, 99, 104–106, 108–110, 113, 119, 125–136, 150–154, 157, 158, 168–170, 172, 199–201, 203, 222, 233, 238, 240, 243, 248, 250–252, 258, 263, 267, 276, 277, 280, 304, 331–333, 342, 365–367, 369, 371–373, 375, 376

S
Science, technology, engineering and mathematics (STEM), 295–309
Smallholder farmers, 11, 104–119, 223, 226, 227, 248, 261, 262, 286
Social inclusion, 2–15, 47–49, 51–54, 60–77, 142, 198, 201, 202, 204, 206–208, 210–212, 214–216, 313, 365–376
South Africa, 7, 9, 13, 14, 55, 61, 69, 86, 106, 113, 115, 117, 136, 140, 141, 182, 221–233, 269, 273–280, 283–288, 291, 330–332, 336, 337, 340, 370, 372, 375
Sustainable development, 2, 9, 11, 13, 21, 22, 25, 30, 35, 39, 60–77, 83, 88, 98, 104, 125, 142, 158, 163, 170, 238, 277, 278, 301, 305, 314, 331, 339, 366–368, 375
System generalized method of moments estimator, 11, 47

T
Transformation, 2, 5, 14, 22, 37, 49, 54, 60, 71, 126, 199, 215, 216, 230, 276, 277, 283, 287, 289, 296, 301, 304, 334, 350, 352, 376

W
Welfare, 6, 13, 39, 40, 68, 70, 93, 127, 170, 172, 176, 198, 199, 215, 216, 265, 281, 283, 284, 340, 371
Women, 2, 3, 6, 7, 9–12, 14, 22, 23, 25, 26, 30, 31, 33–40, 50, 60–62, 64, 68, 69, 72, 74, 77, 88, 93, 94, 109–112, 116, 125, 129, 130, 135, 150, 153, 156, 157, 161–163, 171, 174, 176, 207, 208, 210, 211, 214, 215, 227, 262, 263, 266, 274–291, 296–309, 312–325, 330, 339, 340, 355, 367, 368, 372, 374, 375
Women empowerment, 14, 40, 273–291

Z
Zimbabwe, 14, 55, 69, 84, 86–89, 96, 111, 130, 131, 136, 141, 154, 232, 238–252, 296–309, 312–325, 335, 336, 339–341

MIX
Papier aus verantwortungsvollen Quellen
Paper from responsible sources
FSC® C105338

If you have any concerns about our products,
you can contact us on
ProductSafety@springernature.com

In case Publisher is established outside the EU,
the EU authorized representative is:
Springer Nature Customer Service Center GmbH
Europaplatz 3, 69115 Heidelberg, Germany

Printed by Libri Plureos GmbH
in Hamburg, Germany